THE AGGADA OF THE BAVLI AND ITS CULTURAL WORLD

Program in Judaic Studies
Brown University
Box 1826
Providence, RI 02912

BROWN JUDAIC STUDIES

Number 362
THE AGGADA OF THE BAVLI
AND ITS CULTURAL WORLD

edited by
Geoffrey Herman and Jeffrey L. Rubenstein

THE AGGADA OF THE BAVLI AND ITS CULTURAL WORLD

Edited by

Geoffrey Herman
Jeffrey L. Rubenstein

Brown Judaic Studies
Providence, Rhode Island

Library of Congress Cataloging-in-Publication Data

Names: Herman, Geoffrey, editor. | Rubenstein, Jeffrey L., editor.
Title: The Aggada of the Bavli and its cultural world / edited by Geoffrey Herman and Jeffrey L. Rubenstein.
Description: Providence, RI : Brown Judaic Studies, [2018] | Series: Brown Judaic Studies ; Number 362 | Includes bibliographical references and indexes.
Identifiers: LCCN 2018023868 (print) | LCCN 2018026222 (ebook) | ISBN 9781946527103 (ebk.) | ISBN 9781946527080 (pbk. : alk. paper) | ISBN 9781946527097 (hbk. : alk. paper)
Subjects: LCSH: Aggada—History and criticism. | Talmud—Legends. | Iraq—Civilization—To 634. | Iran—Civilization—To 640. | Judaism—Relations—Christianity. | Christianity and other religions—Judaism. | Judaism—Relations—Zoroastrianism. | Zoroastrianism—Relations—Judaism.
Classification: LCC BM516.5 (ebook) | LCC BM516.5 .A464 2018 (print) | DDC 296.1/27606—dc23

Printed on acid-free paper.

Contents

III. The Syriac and Christian Context

IV. The Zoroastrian Context

Abbreviations

AB	Anchor Bible
AcOr	*Acta Orientalia*
AfO	*Archiv für Orientforschung*
AJBI	*Annual of the Japanese Biblical Institute*
AJEC	Ancient Judaism and Early Christianity
AMS	Paul Bedjan, ed., *Acta martyrum et sanctorum*, 7 vols. Paris/ Leipzig: Harrassowitz, 1890–1897.
ANRW	*Aufsteig und Niedergang der römischen Welt: Geschichte und Kultur Roms im Spiegel der neueren Forschung.* Part 2, *Principat.* Edited by Hildegard Temporini and Wolfgang Haase. Berlin: de Gruyter, 1972–
AOASH	*Acta Orientalia Academiae Scientiarum Hungaricae*
AoF	*Altorientalische Forschungen*
AS	*Aramaic Studies*
AYB	Anchor Yale Bible
AYBRL	Anchor Yale Bible Reference Library
BASOR	*Bulletin of the American Schools of Oriental Research*
BBR	*Bulletin for Biblical Research*
BETL	Bibliotheca Ephemeridum Theologicarum Lovaniensium
BJRL	*Bulletin of the John Rylands University Library of Manchester*
BJS	Brown Judaic Studies
BR	*Biblical Research*
BSOAS	*Bulletin of the School of Oriental and African Studies*
CIJ	*Corpus Inscriptionum Judaicarum.* Edited by Jean-Baptiste Frey. 2 vols. Rome: Pontifical Biblical Institute, 1936–1952.
CMC	Cologne Mani Codex
CSCO	Corpus Scriptorum Christianorum Orientalium
CurBR	*Currents in Biblical Research*
EIr	*Encyclopaedia Iranica.* Edited by Ehsan Yarshater. London: Routledge & Kegan Paul, 1982–.
ErIsr	*Eretz-Israel*
FAT	Forschungen zum Alten Testament
FF	Foundations and Facets
HBM	Hebrew Bible Monographs
HCS	Hellenistic Culture and Society
HR	*History of Religions*

HSCP	*Harvard Studies in Classical Philology*
HSS	Harvard Semitic Studies
HTR	*Harvard Theological Review*
HUCA	*Hebrew Union College Annual*
JA	*Journal Asiatique*
JAAR	*Journal of the American Academy of Religion*
JAOS	*Journal of the American Oriental Society*
JECS	*Journal of Early Christian Studies*
JESHO	*Journal of the Economic and Social History of the Orient*
JJS	*Journal of Jewish Studies*
JJTP	*Journal of Jewish Thought and Philosophy*
JNES	*Journal of Near Eastern Studies*
JQR	*Jewish Quarterly Review*
JR	*Journal of Religion*
JRAS	*Journal of the Royal Asiatic Society*
JRS	*Journal of Roman Studies*
JSIJ	*Jewish Studies, an Internet Journal*
JSJ	*Journal for the Study of Judaism in the Persian, Hellenistic, and Roman Period*
JSJSup	Journal for the Study of Judaism Supplements
JSNTSup	Journal for the Study of the New Testament: Supplement Series
JSOR	*Journal of the Society of Oriental Research*
JSOTSup	Journal for the Study of the Old Testament: Supplement Series
JSQ	*Jewish Studies Quarterly*
JSS	*Journal of Semitic Studies*
JTS	*Journal of Theological Studies*
LHBOTS	Library of Hebrew Bible/Old Testament Studies
LSTS	Library of Second Temple Studies
MGWJ	*Monatschrift für Geschichte und Wissenschaft des Judentums*
Mus	*Le Muséon: Revue d'études orientales*
NETS	*A New English Translation of the Septuagint.* Edited by Albert Pietersma and Benjamin G. Wright. New York: Oxford University Press, 2007.
NHMS	Nag Hammadi and Manichaean Studies
NPNF[2]	*Nicene and Post-Nicene Fathers,* Series 2
NTL	New Testament Library
NTS	*New Testament Studies*
OECS	Oxford Early Christian Studies
OeO	Oriens et Occidens
OIC	Oriental Institute Communications
OLA	Orientalia Lovaniensia Analecta
OrChr	*Oriens Christianus*
PAAJR	*Proceedings of the American Academy of Jewish Research*

RA	*Revue d'assyriologie et d'archéologie orientale*
REJ	*Revue des études juives*
RGRW	Religions in the Graeco-Roman World
RlA	*Reallexikon der Assyriologie.* Edited by Erich Ebeling et al. Berlin: de Gruyter, 1928–
SHR	Studies in the History of Religions
SJLA	Studies in Judaism in Late Antiquity
SNTSMS	Society for New Testament Studies Monograph Series
SPhiloA	*Studia Philonica Annual*
StBibLit	Studies in Biblical Literature (Lang)
StPB	Studia Post-biblica
StPohl	Studia Pohl
SVTP	Studia in Veteris Testamenti Pseudepigraphica
TSAJ	Texte und Studien zum antiken Judentum/Texts and Studies in Ancient Judaism
USQR	*Union Seminary Quarterly Review*
VC	*Vigiliae Christianae*
VTSup	Supplements to Vetus Testamentum
WGRW	Writings from the Greco-Roman World
WO	*Die Welt des Orients*
WUNT	Wissenschaftliche Untersuchungen zum Neuen Testament
ZA	*Zeitschrift für Assyriologie*
ZDMG	*Zeitschrift der Deutschen Morganländischen Gesellschaft*
ZNW	*Zeitschrift für die neutestamentliche Wissenschaft und die Kunde der älteren Kirche*
ZPE	*Zeitschrift für Papyrologie und Epigraphik*

Introduction

The aggada of the Bavli has received copious scholarly attention in recent years, including significant study of both exegetical and narrative traditions. The focus of interest has included such topics as literary art, the relationship to Palestinian versions and earlier sources, the role of the Bavli editors, inner-textual contextualization and the connection to halakhic material, and historical reliability.[1] An additional dimension of Bavli aggada is its relationship with the surrounding cultures.

The Babylonian Talmud, in which all is "mixed" (b. Sanh. 24a), was created in a culturally diverse region in which the remains of many ancient and more recent cultures were to be found. One thereby encounters in the Sasanian era not only the ancient Babylonian culture but the Iranian culture, the culture of the Eastern Christians, Manichaeans, Mandaeans, Jews, and also bearers of Hellenistic culture as well.[2]

1. See, for just a few examples, Shamma Friedman, "La'aggada hahistorit batalmud habavli," in *Saul Lieberman Memorial Volume*, ed. Shamma Friedman (New York: Jewish Theological Seminary, 2001), 119–64; Jeffrey L. Rubenstein, *Talmudic Stories: Narrative Art, Composition, and Culture* (Baltimore: Johns Hopkins University Press, 1999); Barry S. Wimpfheimer, *Narrating the Law: A Poetics of Talmudic Legal Stories*, Divinations (Philadelphia: University of Pennsylvania Press, 2011); and the studies collected in Jeffrey L. Rubenstein, ed., *Creation and Composition, The Contribution of the Bavli Redactors (Stammaim) to the Aggada*, TSAJ 114 (Tübingen: Mohr Siebeck, 2005). On the relationship between aggadic traditions and parallel versions in the Palestinian and Babylonian rabbinic literature, see Ofra Meir, *Rabbi Judah the Patriarch: Palestinian and Babylonian Portrait of a Leader* [Hebrew] (Tel Aviv: Hakibbutz Hameuhad, 1999); see also Ronit Nikolsky and Tal Ilan eds., *Rabbinic Traditions between Palestine and Babylonia*, Ancient Judaism and Early Christianity (Leiden: Brill, 2014). On aggada, including Bavli aggada and historical method, see, e.g., Amram D. Tropper, *Like Clay in the Hands of the Potter, Sage Stories in Rabbinic Literature* [Hebrew] (Jerusalem: The Zalman Shazar Center for Jewish History, 2011); idem, *Rewriting Ancient Jewish History: The History of the Jews in Roman Times and the New Historical Method*, Routledge Studies in Ancient History 10 (London: Routledge, 2016). For a study of method relating to biblical midrash, including the Bavli aggada, see, e.g., Joshua Levinson, *The Twice Told Tale: A Poetics of the Exegetical Narrative in Rabbinic Midrash* [Hebrew] (Jerusalem: The Hebrew University Magnes Press, 2005). Further examples will be addressed in the discussion of previous scholarship below.

2. On the impact of traditions from the eastern Roman Empire on the Bavli aggada, see Richard Kalmin, *Migrating Tales: The Talmud's Narratives and Their Historical Context* (Berkeley: University of California Press, 2014). See especially his important conclusions on 236–39.

Echoes of the conversation of this cultural multi-vocality are still evident in the Talmudic text where the embroidery of Babylonian aggadic traditions was woven from different materials drawn from diverse cultures. In this region these cultures came into contact and various of their elements mixed in a phenomenon of transculturation.

The articles in this volume offer new readings of the aggadic traditions of the Bavli that engage contemporary traditions and texts from these ambient cultures. It is hoped that, alongside the traditional approaches in the study of rabbinic aggada, the studies presented here demonstrate the importance of this intercultural conversation.

Persian Literature and Bavli Aggada

One of the earliest cultural contexts addressed in the course of the study of the Babylonian Talmud and its aggada was the broad Persian religious and cultural milieu. An interest in engaging the Persian context of the rabbinic sources, including but not limited to the Babylonian Talmud, dates back to the nineteenth century. This was part of a broader trend by scholars of rabbinics to study the Persian religious literature that also embraced various areas of research such as philology, law, theology, and more generally the history of the Sasanian empire. With regard to aggada, in particular, a number of significant parallels were identified, particularly in the realms of mythology, angelology, and demonology.[3]

Scholarship concerned with the interface of Iran and the Babylonian Talmud in more recent decades has continued to probe the Persian milieu for diverse topics including historical issues,[4] family, sexuality, and social

---

3. The important early works on philology were by Alexander Kohut, Zsigmond Telegdi, Bernard Geiger, and Wilhelm Bacher. The foremost scholar in this field more recently is Shaul Shaked. See, e.g., Shaul Shaked, "Between Iranian and Aramaic: Iranian Words Concerning Food in Jewish Babylonian Aramaic, with Some Notes on the Aramaic Heterograms in Iranian," in *Irano-Judaica V*, ed. Shaul Shaked and Amnon Netzer (Jerusalem: Ben-Zvi Institute, 2003), 120–37. Michael Sokoloff, in *A Dictionary of Jewish Babylonian Aramaic of the Talmudic and Geonic Periods* (Ramat Gan: Bar-Ilan University Press, 2002) has offered the most up-to-date summary of all the information on Persian loans. On angelology and demonology, see Alexander Kohut, *Über die jüdische Angelologie und Daemonologie in ihrer Abhängigkeit vom Parsismus* (Leipzig: Brockhaus, 1866). For a brief overview of this period, see G. Herman, "Ahasuerus, the Former Stable-Master of Belshazzar and the Wicked Alexander of Macedon: Two Parallels between the Babylonian Talmud and Persian Sources," *AJS Review* 29 (2005): 284–88.

4. See, e.g., Moshe Beer, "Notes on Three Edicts against the Jews of Babylonia in the Third Century C.E." [Hebrew], in *Irano-Judaica*, ed. Shaul Shaked (Jerusalem: Ben-Zvi Institute, 1982), 25–37 = idem, in *The Sages of the Mishna and the Talmud: Teachings, Activities and Leadership*, ed. Emmanuel Friedheim, Daniel Sperber, and Rafael Yankelevitch (Ramat Gan: Bar-Ilan University Press, 2011), 188–200; Jacob Neusner, *A History of the Jews in Babylonia*, 5 vols. (Leiden: Brill, 1965–1970); Robert Brody, "Judaism in the Sasanian Empire: A Case

mores,[5] and has been interested in legal,[6] ritual,[7] theological,[8] and cultural aspects.[9]

Study in Religious Coexistence," in *Irano-Judaica II,* ed. Shaul Shaked and Amnon Netzer (Jerusalem: Ben-Zvi Institute, 1990), 52–62; Isaiah Gafni, "Babylonian Rabbinic Culture," in *Cultures of the Jews. A New History,* ed. David Biale (New York: Schocken Books, 2002), 223–65; Richard Kalmin, "Sasanian Persecution of the Jews: A Reconsideration of the Talmudic Evidence," in *Irano-Judaica VI,* ed. Shaul Shaked and Amnon Netzer (Jerusalem: Ben-Zvi Institute, 2008), 87–125; Geoffrey Herman, *A Prince without a Kingdom: The Exilarch in the Sasanian Era,* TSAJ 150 (Tübingen: Mohr Siebeck, 2012).

5. Isaiah Gafni, "The Institution of Marriage in Rabbinic Times," in *The Jewish Family: Metaphor and Memory,* ed. David Kraemer (New York: Oxford University Press, 1989), 13–30; Eliyahu Ahdut, "The Status of the Jewish Woman in Babylonia in the Talmudic Era" (Ph.D. diss., Hebrew University of Jerusalem, 1999); Adiel Schremer, *Male and Female He Created Them: Jewish Marriage in the Late Second Temple, Mishnah and Talmud Periods* [Hebrew] (Jerusalem: The Zalman Shazar Center, 2003); Yaakov Elman, "'He in His Cloak and She in Her Cloak': Conflicting Images of Sexuality in Sasanian Mesopotamia," in *Discussing Cultural Influences: Text, Context, and Non-Text in Rabbinic Judaism,* ed. Rivka Ulmer, Studies in Judaism (Lanham, MD: University Press of America, 2007), 129–64; Shai Secunda, "The Construction, Composition and Idealization of the Female Body in Rabbinic Literature and Parallel Iranian Texts: Three Excursuses," *Nashim* 23 (2012): 60–86; Yishai Kiel, *Sexuality in the Babylonian Talmud: Christian and Sasanian Contexts in Late Antiquity* (New York: Cambridge University Press, 2016).

6. See, e.g., Maria Macuch, "Allusions to Sasanian Law in the Babylonian Talmud," in *The Talmud in Its Iranian Context,* ed. Carol Bakhos and M. Rahim Shayegan, TSAJ 135 (Tübingen: Mohr Siebeck, 2010), 100–111; Yaakov Elman, "Marriage and Marital Property in Rabbinic and Sasanian Law," in *Rabbinic Law in Its Roman and Near Eastern Context,* ed. Catherine Hezser, TSAJ 97 (Tübingen: Mohr Siebeck, 2003), 227–76; idem, "Returnable Gifts in Rabbinic and Sasanian Law," in Shaked and Netzer, *Irano-Judaica VI,* 150–95; idem, "'Up to the Ears in Horses Necks': On Sasanian Agricultural Policy and Private 'Eminent Domain,'" *JSIJ* 3 (2004): 95–149.

7. See Yishai Kiel, "Shaking Impurity: Scriptural Exegesis and Legal Innovation in the Babylonian Talmud and Pahlavi Literature," in *Encounters by the Rivers of Babylon: Scholarly Conversations between Jews, Iranians and Babylonians in Antiquity,* ed. Uri Gabbay and Shai Secunda, TSAJ 160 (Tübingen: Mohr Siebeck, 2014) 413–34; idem, "Redesigning *Tzitzit* in the Babylonian Talmud in Light of Literary Depictions of the Zoroastrian *kustīg,*" in *Shoshannat Yaakov: Jewish and Iranian Studies in Honor of Yaakov Elman,* ed. Shai Secunda and Steven Fine, Brill Reference Library of Judaism 35 (Leiden: Brill, 2012), 185–202.

8. See Yaakov Elman, "Rav Yosef in a Time of Anger" [Hebrew], *Bar Ilan Annual* 30–31 (2006): 9–20; David Brodsky "'Thought Is Akin to Action': The Importance of Thought in Zoroastrianism and the Development of a Babylonian Rabbinic Motif," in *Irano-Judaica VII,* ed. Geoffrey Herman, Julia Rubanovich, and Shaul Shaked (Jerusalem: Ben-Zvi Institute, forthcoming 2018).

9. See Yaakov Elman, "Acculturation to Elite Persian Norms and Modes of Thought in the Babylonian Jewish Community of Late Antiquity," in *Neti'ot Le-David: Jubilee Volume for David Weiss Halivni,* ed. Ephraim Bezalel Halivni, Zvi Arie Steinfeld, and Yaakov Elman (Jerusalem: Orhot Press, 2004), 31–56; Geoffrey Herman, "Table Etiquette and Persian Culture in the Babylonian Talmud" [Hebrew], *Zion* 7 (2012): 149–88; idem, "'Like a Slave before His Master': A Persian Gesture of Deference in Sasanian Jewish and Christian Sources," *Aram* 26 (2014): 93–100; Jason Sion Mokhtarian, *Rabbis, Sorcerers, Kings, and Priests: The Culture of the Talmud in Ancient Iran* (Oakland: University of California Press, 2015).

Aggadic Narratives

Among the first significant studies to mark the critical engagement of the Persian context in the study of the more extended aggadic stories found in the Babylonian Talmud was Daniel Sperber's study on the Rav Kahana episode, "On the Unfortunate Adventures of Rav Kahana: A Passage of Saboraic Polemic from Sasanian Persia," published in 1982.[10] Sperber's objectives were modest in that he sought to use the Persian motifs to date the aggada and position it within a Sasanian milieu. Nevertheless, the methodology he employed was noteworthy. He pointed to images found on Sasanian material artifacts and depicted in literary sources and to Persian loanwords featuring within the accounts.

Similarities in structure and form between aggadic stories in the Bavli and Persian sources, and sources reflective of a broader Sasanian literary heritage are the subject of some recent studies. The pertinent contemporaneous Persian sources are typically royal narratives, relating the exploits of kings and the court. Geoffrey Herman's "The Story of Rav Kahana *(BT* Bava Qamma 117a-b) in Light of Armeno-Persian Sources"[11] considered, in addition, an Armenian account.[12] Similarly, Jeffrey Rubenstein, in "King Herod in Ardashir's Court: The Rabbinic Story of Herod (b. B. Bat. 3b-4a) in Light of Persian Sources," pointed to the thematic and structural parallels between the Bavli's account of the construction of the temple by Herod, and Persian sources on the rise of the first Sasanian monarch, Ardashir, as reflected in such sources as Kār Nāmag ī Ardašīr-ī Pābagān.[13] Similarities in structure and form were also suggested by Herman in "Insurrection in the Academy: The Babylonian Talmud and the Paikuli Inscription."[14] This article compared the Bavli's account of the disposition of Rabban Gamaliel and appointment of R. Eleazar b. Azaria in his stead with elements of the narrative structure in the third century Paikuli inscription. Elsewhere Her-

10. Daniel Sperber, "On the Unfortunate Adventures of Rav Kahana: A Passage of Saboraic Polemic from Sasanian Persia," in Shaked, *Irano-Judaica*, 83–100, reprinted as "The Misfortunes of Rav Kahana: A Passage of Post-Talmudic Polemic," in Daniel Sperber, *Magic and Folklore in Rabbinic Literature* (Ramat Gan: Bar-Ilan University Press, 1994), 145–64. For the identification of an Iranian epic motif in an earlier Jewish source, the account of the two Jewish rebels from Babylonia, Anilaeus and Asinaeus, recalled by Josephus, see Geoffrey Herman, "Iranian Epic Motifs in Josephus' Antiquities (XVIII, 314–370)," *JJS* 57 (2006): 245–68.

11. Geoffrey Herman, "The Story of Rav Kahana (BT Bava Qamma 117a-b) in Light of Armeno-Persian Sources," Shaked, *Irano-Judaica VI*, 53–86.

12. One particular scene was further discussed in Geoffrey Herman, "One Day David Went Out for the Hunt of the Falconers: Persian Themes in the Babylonian Talmud," in Secunda and Fine, *Shoshannat Yaakov*, 111–36, here 130–34.

13. "King Herod in Ardashir's Court: The Rabbinic Story of Herod (B. Bava Batra 3b-4a) in Light of Persian Sources," *AJS Review* 38 (2014): 249–74.

14. Geoffrey Herman, "Insurrection in the Academy: The Babylonian Talmud and the Paikuli Inscription," *Zion* 74 (2014): 377–407.

man had pointed to parallels between the account of the rise of Ardashir and elements in the Bavli's aggadic take on the story of Purim.[15]

The broader Persian context has been seen to shape and inspire Bavli aggadot in other ways. A recent example is the proposal by Shana Schick that Beruriah's image as an educated woman, as reflected in the Bavli's account, corresponds well with educational possibilities for women in Zoroastrian religious culture.[16] Manichaean texts, particularly those recorded in Iranian languages, can also enter the picture. Herman's recent "The Talmud in Its Babylonian Context: Rava and Bar Sheshakh; Mani and Mihrshah" compares a Bavli account of a fateful meeting between Rava and a local Babylonian leader with a source framed in a similar fashion, recorded in Parthian, which describes a meeting between Mani and the ruler of Mesene, Mihrshah.[17]

Mythology

The impact of Iranian myth on Bavli aggada, recognized from the beginnings of *Wissenschaft des Judentums*, has been the focus of many recent studies. The legendary city of Luz (b. Soṭah 46b), where the Angel of Death has no permission to enter, was depicted in the Bavli under the influence of Iranian myth, inspired by the Iranian Kangdiz, where Pešyōtan was forgotten by death, according to a study by Reuven Kiperwasser.[18]

Kiperwasser and Dan Shapira, in a series of articles bringing together disparate mythical elements,[19] have argued that "rabbinic mythmakers created their own imagined world from elements of Iranian and other

15. Herman, "Ahasuerus, the Former Stable-Master," 283–97.

16. Shana Strauch Schick "A Re-examination of the Bavli's Beruriah Narratives in Light of Middle Persian Literature," *Zion* 74 (2014): 409–24.

17. Geoffrey Herman, "The Talmud in Its Babylonian Context: Rava and Bar Sheshakh; Mani and Mihrshah" [Hebrew], in *Between Babylonia and the Land of Israel: Studies in Honor of Isaiah M. Gafni*, ed. Geoffrey Herman, Meir Ben Shahar, and Aharon Oppenheimer (Jerusalem: Zalman Shazar Center, 2016), 79–96.

18. Reuven Kiperwasser, "The Misfortunes and Adventures of Elihoreph and Ahiah in the Land of Israel and in Babylonia: The Metamorphosis of a Narrative Tradition and Ways of Acculturation," in Nikolsky and Ilan, *Rabbinic Traditions between Palestine and Babylonia*, 232–49.

19. Reuven Kiperwasser and Dan D. Y. Shapira, "Irano-Talmudica I: The Three-Legged Ass and *Ridyā* in B. Ta'anith: Some Observations about Mythic Hydrology in the Babylonian Talmud and in Ancient Iran," *AJS Review* 32 (2008): 101–16; eidem, "Irano-Talmudica II: Leviathan, Behemoth and the 'Domestication' of Iranian Mythological Creatures in Eschatological Narratives of the Babylonian Talmud," in Fine and Secunda, *Shoshannat Yaakov*, 203–35; R. Kiperwasser and Dan D. Y. Shapira, "Encounters between the Iranian Myth and Rabbinic Mythmakers in the Babylonian Talmud," in Gabbay and Secunda, *Encounters by the Rivers of Babylon*, 285–304; Reuven Kiperwasser and Dan D. Y. Shapira, "Irano-Talmudica III: Giant Mythological Creatures in Transition from the Avesta to the Babylonian Talmud," in

mythologies."[20] They dealt with the tales of Rav Abba bar Bar Ḥanna. For instance, the Ridyā, of mythological proportions, featuring in b. Ta'an. 25b and described as a three-year-old heifer (עגלה תלתא), who mediates between the abysses; is compared with the giant three-legged ass (*xar ī sē-pāy*) in the midst of a sea. The latter is part of the mythological hydraulic process, as depicted in Zoroastrian mythological accounts such as the Bundehišn. The tales in b. B. Bat. 73a–75b, too, that relate a series of creatures of enormous proportions, correspond remarkably with Zoroastrian mythological sources, in particular, from Bundehišn chapter 24. Indeed, as they argue, the similarities outlined between the Bundehišn and the Bavli, and in the order of the mythical creatures presented in these sources, suggest a common prototype. Likewise, the comparison of the Divine to a lion in b. Ḥul. 59b evokes images familiar from ancient Mesopotamian iconography. Their studies highlight the complexity of the interrelationship of mythological features, with earlier Mesopotamian mythology impacting the Jewish and Zoroastrian mythological scenarios.

Studies comparing various Zoroastrian myths on figures, such as Yima and Zarathustra, with rabbinic accounts of the biblical figures Abraham, Nimrod, and Enoch, have recently been undertaken by Yishai Kiel.[21]

Dreams and Astrology

The complex relationship between rabbis and the practice of dream interpretation and its professionals is compared to the reputation of the magi for dream interpretation in Richard Kalmin's "Talmudic Attitudes toward Dream Interpreters: Preliminary Thoughts on Their Iranian Cultural Context."[22] Jeffrey Rubenstein, in "Astrology and the Head of the Academy," considers talmudic passages that display astrological influence on the rabbinic appointment process in light of the significance of astrology in Sasanian imperial ideology and ascension narratives.[23]

Orality and Textuality in the Iranian World: Patterns of Interaction across the Centuries, ed. Julia Rubanovich, Jerusalem Studies in Religion and Culture 19 (Leiden: Brill, 2015), 65–92.

20. Kiperwasser and Shapira, "Encounters," 285.

21. Yishai Kiel, "Reimagining Enoch in Sasanian Babylonia in Light of Zoroastrian and Manichaean Traditions," *AJS Review* 39 (2015): 407–32; idem, "Creation by Emission: Recreating Adam and Eve in the Babylonian Talmud in Light of Zoroastrian and Manichaean Literature," *JJS* 66 (2015): 295–316; idem, "Abraham and Nimrod in the Shadow of Zarathustra," *JR* 95 (2015): 35–50.

22. Richard Kalmin, "Talmudic Attitudes toward Dream Interpreters: Preliminary Thoughts on Their Iranian Cultural Context," in Bakhos and Shayegan, *Talmud in Its Iranian Context*, 83–99.

23. Jeffrey L. Rubenstein, "Astrology and the Head of the Academy," in Fine and Secunda, *Shoshannat Yaakov*, 301–21. See too Rubenstein, "Talmudic Astrology: *Bavli Šabbat* 156a–b," *HUCA* 88 (2007): 31–37.

Religious Polemics

A few studies have focused on aggadic sources in the Talmud that engage, explicitly or implicitly, in religious polemics with Zoroastrianism. Eliyahu Ahdut's "Jewish Zoroastrian Polemics in the Babylonian Talmud"[24] covers many examples of overt polemics. Yaakov Elman's "Who are the Kings of East and West in Ber 7a? Roman Religion, Syrian Gods and Zoroastrianism in the Babylonian Talmud"[25] deals with identifying the religious context of the talmudic account of ritual prostration of kings before the sun. Recently, Natalie Polzer proposes viewing the talmudic account of the humiliation of Haman in the Talmud in light of Zoroastrian rules of purity.[26]

Syriac Literature and Bavli Aggada

For many years Syriac literature was neglected as a resource to provide context for Bavli traditions, both aggadic and halakhic. In recent years, however, there has been an increased awareness of the potential value of Syriac material for shedding light on the Bavli. As Syriac is a dialect of Aramaic, cognate terms may therefore point to shared conceptions and ideas. More importantly, there exist copious Syriac texts from the third through seventh centuries, corresponding to the late Amoraic and redactional eras of the Bavli.

Philology

Philologists were among the first scholars to use Syriac writings to illuminate Bavli words, many of which are found in aggadic passages. Jacob Levy, Marcus Jastrow, and Michael Sokoloff occasionally turn to Syriac cognates to explain obscure words in their dictionaries.[27] The most fruitful

---

24. Eliyahu Ahdut, "Jewish-Zoroastrian Polemics in the Babylonian Talmud," in *Irano-Judaica* IV, ed. Shaul Shaked and Amnon Netzer (Jerusalem: Ben-Zvi Institute, 1999), 17–40. See too Shaul Shaked, "Zoroastrian Polemics against Jews in the Sasanian and Early Islamic Period," in Shaked and Netzer, *Irano-Judaica* II, 85–104.

25. Yaakov Elman, "Who Are the Kings of East and West in Ber 7a? Roman Religion, Syrian Gods and Zoroastrianism in the Babylonian Talmud," in *Studies in Josephus and the Varieties of Ancient Judaism: Louis H. Feldman Jubilee Volume*, ed. Shaye J. D. Cohen and Joshua Schwartz, Ancient Judaism and Early Christianity 67 (Leiden: Brill, 2007), 43–80.

26. Natalie C. Polzer, "The Fatal Chamber Pot and the Idol of Pe'or—Covert Anti-Zoroastrian Polemic in the *Bavli?*," *JJS* 62 (2016): 267–90.

27. An example from the Geonic period is found in a Geniza fragment, Cambridge CUL T-S NS 100.32. Dealing with a passage in b. Šabb. 109b that mentions a certain בר קשא, we find the explanation קס אלנצראני יסמא קשא והדא בן אלקס ("The priest of the Christians is

such study employs philology as a springboard to a deeper understanding of cultural processes. Thus, Jonas Greenfield compared the saying attributed to Rav Naḥman, "The *magus* mumbles [*ratin*] and knows not what he says; the *tanna* recites and knows not what he says" (b. Soṭah 22a), to similar mocking representations of the *magus* in Syriac writings and set the Bavli's portrayal of the Zoroastrian clergy in a wider context.[28] Moulie Vidas built on Greenfield's observation and argued that Rav Naḥman's observation in fact polemicizes against recitation of Mishna, a particular form of rabbinic religiosity, by comparing it with the mindlessness of Zoroastrian learning and seeks to promote the analytical study of rabbinic traditions. He also reflected on the parallel in the seventh-century *Life of Isho'sabran* by Isho'yahb III noted by Greenfield in which the author deprecates the methods of oral repetition of the magi, contrasting it with proper Christian learning.[29]

Shlomo Naeh, in "Freedom and Celibacy: A Talmudic Variation on Tales of Temptation and Fall in Genesis and Its Syrian Background,"[30] analyzes the story of Rav Ḥiyya b. Ashi, seduced by his own wife in b. Qidd. 81b, and argues that the passage "sheds light on the attitude of the Babylonian rabbis toward the ideal of sexual abstinence, a widespread concept in the neighboring Syrian Christian Culture."[31] Naeh focuses on the wife's declaration that she is a *ḥaruta* (אנא חרותא דהדרי מיומא), which Rashi claims is the name of a famous prostitute. In a detailed philological study, however, Naeh connects the word *ḥaruta* with the Syriac root ܚܪܪ, meaning "freedom, liberation," and the term ܡܚܪܪܘܬܐ, which "occurs in the semantic field of sexual ethics." He cites a wealth of Syriac texts where this term means freedom from one's sexual nature, hence sexual discipline or ascetic celibacy. Yet the same word, with its base meaning of freedom, also appears with the opposite meaning: freedom from regula-

called *'qasha'* and this one is the son of the priest). See Sokoloff, *Dictionary of Jewish Babylonian Aramaic*, 1048, s.v. קשא; idem, *A Syriac Lexicon: A Translation from the Latin, Correction, Expansion, and Update of C. Brockelmann's Lexicon Syriacum* (Winona Lake, IN: Eisenbrauns, 2009), 1418, s.v. *qasha*.

28. Jonas C. Greenfield, *"Raten magushe,"* in *Joshua Finkel Festschrift*, ed. Sidney Hoenig and Leon Stitskin (New York: Yeshiva University Press, 1974), 63–69.

29. Moulie Vidas, *Tradition and the Formation of the Talmud* (Princeton, NJ: Princeton University Press, 2014), 162–65. "Given the Talmud's use of the murmuring magus in a polemic within the Jewish community, it is possible that this scene is not only about a boy teaching a Zoroastrian how to be a Christian, but also about Isho'yahb teaching his Christian readers what practices are not acceptable in Christianity." The same tradition is referenced by Kiperwasser and Ruzer in the article mentioned below in n. 86.

30. Shlomo Naeh, in "Freedom and Celibacy: A Talmudic Variation on Tales of Temptation and Fall in Genesis and Its Syrian Background," in *The Book of Genesis in Jewish and Oriental Christian Interpretation: A Collection of Essays*, ed. Judith Frishman and Lucas Van Rompay, Traditio exegetica Graeca 5 (Leuven: Peeters, 1997), 73–89.

31. Ibid., 73.

tion and free exercise of impulses, hence debauchery and licentiousness. Naeh suggests that both Syriac meanings fit perfectly with the story: "The woman, unwillingly 'guarding her freedom,' masquerades as a prostitute and offers the man an opportunity for freedom, for libertine debauchery. The man, who had been vigilant in the ascetic struggle for freedom from sexual urges, all at once capitulates to the other aspect of freedom—the unleashing of passion."[32] He argues that the sexual ethic assigned to Rav Ḥiyya b. Ashi, which associates marital sex with the evil impulse, is essentially unprecedented in the Bavli, and therefore "the use of a foreign loanword as the key element in the narrative was intended specifically to point up the foreign sources of Rav Ḥiyya b. Ashi's theory of ascetic celibacy."[33] The disastrous end of the story, namely, the painful suicide of the rabbi, would seem to polemicize against such a foreign (Christian) ethic.[34]

Aphrahat, Ephrem, Narsai

The Syriac writings of the church fathers Aphrahat and Ephrem, who lived in the Persian Empire during the fourth century, were recognized early on as a potential resource for contextualizing Bavli aggada. Already scholars of the late nineteenth and early twentieth century searched for parallels between Aphrahat's *Demonstrations* (written between 337 and 345 CE) and rabbinic literature. They, however, rarely analyzed the sources in detail, nor did they single out the Bavli from other rabbinic documents. Furthermore, they did not always clarify whether the direction of the borrowing was by the rabbis from Aphrahat and Ephrem or the reverse.[35] A representative example is the following from a monograph by Frank Gavin in a subsection entitled "Concrete Instances of Aphraates' dependence upon Jewish thought, and affiliation with it": "Aphraates says in homily XII that the serpent was none other than Satan. The Devil foiled God's plan for raising man even to a still higher state, should he have obeyed God's command. In the last resort, R. Shimeon b. Laqish says all evil is traceable to a

32. Ibid., 83.

33. Ibid., 88.

34. See too Burton L. Visotsky, "Three Syriac Cruxes," *JJS* 42 (1991): 167–75.

35. For some early work, see Louis Ginzberg, "Aphraates, the Persian Sage," *Jewish Encyclopedia* (New York: Funk and Wagnalls, 1901–1906) 1:663–65; Frank Gavin, "Aphraates and the Jews," *JSOR* 7 (1923): 131–66. Gavin provides references to the earlier work of Salomon Funk, "Die Haggadischen Elemente in den Homilien des Aphraates, des persisichen Weisen" (Vienna: Knöpflmacher, 1891), and other scholars. For other references, see Jacob Neusner, *Aphrahat and Judaism: The Christian Jewish Argument in Fourth-Century Iran*, StPB 19 (Leiden: Brill, 1971), 10–11. See too Sebastian Brock, "Jewish Traditions in Syriac Sources," *JJS* 30 (1979): 225–26.

single source, for 'Satan, the evil *yeṣer*, and the angel of Death are all one,'" footnoting b. B. Bat. 97a.[36]

Jacob Neusner, in *Aphrahat and Judaism: The Christian Jewish Argument in Fourth-Century Iran*, made a more systematic attempt to uncover evidence of a rabbinic response to Aphrahat's attacks on Judaism. He categorizes Aphrahat's pronouncements on various theological topics ("rejection of Israel," "celibacy," "the practical commandments," etc.) and sets them out in parallel columns with references to the scriptures cited and possible parallels in the Bavli and in other rabbinic compilations.[37] Neusner does not offer much analysis of the particular passages and arrives at a negative conclusion: "Babylonian rabbis knew little, if anything, of Aphrahat's critique of Judaism, either in general or in any detail."[38]

Naomi Koltun-Fromm, in *Hermeneutics of Holiness: Ancient Jewish and Christian Notions of Sexuality and Religious Community*, examines many of the same parallels as Neusner but comes to the opposite conclusion. She analyzes Aphrahat's conceptions of marriage, celibacy, and holiness in relationship to biblical, Second Temple, and rabbinic sources.[39] Koltun-Fromm argues that both Aphrahat and the rabbis were a part of the "Persian-Mesopotamian context" and "shared a common Aramaic 'public' library; that is, they had access to similar compilations or collections of exegetical traditions."[40] She provides a detailed study comparing Aphrahat's view that Moses separated from his wife and became celibate following the revelation at Mount Sinai to similar rabbinic views, referring to many rabbinic sources including some Bavli passages.[41] She also argues for a shift in rabbinic ideas from "ascribed holiness" to "achieved holiness" through various types of ascetic practices, including "sexual restraint within marriage," and draws analogies to Aphrahat's discourse on sexuality as a means of authority and a path to holiness.[42]

Kolton-Fromm's second book, published in 2011, *Jewish-Christian*

36. Gavin, "Aphraates," 138–39.

37. Neusner, *Aphrahat and Judaism*, 159–95.

38. Ibid., 187.

39. Naomi Koltun-Fromm, *Hermeneutics of Holiness: Ancient Jewish and Christian Notions of Sexuality and Religious Community* (New York: Oxford University Press, 2010). Her earlier article "Sexuality and Holiness: Semitic Christian and Jewish Conceptualization of Sexual Behavior," *VC* 54 (2002): 375–95, also presents the parallel traditions of Moses's celibacy.

40. Koltun-Fromm, *Hermeneutics of Holiness*, 186.

41. Ibid., 187, 199. See too the reference to b. Ber. 21b, at 204.

42. Ibid., 211–38: "I think it not insignificant that sexuality becomes central to rabbinic discourse on authority and holiness, and that it provides a means both to actualize their own elitist ascetic agenda and a tool for achieving hegemony over the Jewish community. Aphrahat, too, looks to sexuality, and particularly to sexually related behavior that he defines as holy (celibacy), to help him create borders between competing religious communities in Mesopotamia. For these religious leaders, sexual restraint plays a pivotal role in formulating their sense of self, both individually and communally" (237–38). See too Eliezer Diamond,

Conversation in Fourth Century Persian Mesopotamia, also investigated parallel traditions in rabbinic literature and in Aphrahat's *Demonstrations.*[43] She suggested that certain Bavli (and other) rabbinic traditions could be understood as polemics directed to counter Aphrahat's explicit polemics against the Jews. Kolton-Fromm juxtaposed Bavli traditions on the election of Israel, the ingathering of exiles, and the meaning of the Passover sacrifice with corresponding passages from Aphrahat so as to reconstruct the fourth-century "conversation."[44]

Ishay Rosen-Zvi, in his work on the evil inclination/*yeṣer ha-raᶜ*, concurred with Kolton-Fromm in seeing Aphrahat, along with several other Syriac writings, as important comparanda for Bavli views on sexuality. Rosen-Zvi turns to Aphrahat to support his theory that "the *yeṣer* was placed in this sexual context only in a comparatively late, mostly post-Amoraic, period."[45] He points to "similar phrases and idioms' in the views of sexual lust in Aphrahat and in the Bavli, though neither Aphrahat nor other Syriac writings use the term *yaṣra bisha.* He therefore concludes that the "Syriac compositions thus provide us with evidence that in the third century and the first half of the fourth, sexual discourse is profound and fruitful but has not yet incorporated the *yeṣer* into its vocabulary."[46] In a recent article, Adam Becker, building in part on Rosen-Zvi's work, reviews attestations of the term *yaṣra* in Aphrahat, Ephrem, and other earlier Syriac texts, before a detailed analysis of the term in the homilies of Narsai, an important member of the school of Nisibis, who died around 500 CE.[47] Becker finds many similarities in the term as it appears in rabbinic literature, primarily the Bavli, and in Narsai, including the conception that the *yaṣra/yeṣer* is "a source of sin unconnected to the biblical narrative of creation." Yet he also stresses that there are differences, such as Narsai's view that the *yaṣra,* as the source of desire, is inherently problematic, as opposed to the Bavli's more positive evaluation of desire, and hence its view that the *yeṣer* "can be good provided it is moderated

---

Holy Men and Hunger Artists: Fasting and Asceticism in Rabbinic Culture (New York: Oxford University Press, 2003), 85.

43. Naomi Koltun-Fromm, *Jewish-Christian Conversation in Fourth Century Persian Mesopotamia: A Reconstructed Conversation,* Judaism in Context 12 (Piscataway, NJ: Gorgias Press, 2012). Parts of the book were published earlier as Naomi Koltun-Fromm, "A Jewish-Christian Conversation in Fourth-Century Persian Mesopotamia," *JJS* 47 (1996): 45–63.

44. See too Eliyahu Lizorkin, *Aphrahat's Demonstrations. A Conversation with the Jews of Mesopotamia,* CSCO 64 (Leuven: Peeters, 2012).

45. Ishay Rosen-Zvi, *Demonic Desires: 'Yetzer Hara' and the Problem of Evil in Late Antiquity,* Divinations (Philadelphia: University of Pennsylvania Press, 2011), 116.

46. Ibid., 117. Rosen-Zvi also mentions parallels between the rabbinic *yeṣer* and monastic demonology. However, he relies primarily on secondary literature and Greek texts and does not point specifically to Syriac parallels (41–43).

47. Adam Becker, "The 'Evil Inclination' of the Jews: The Syriac Yatsra in Narsai's Metrical Homilies for Lent," *JQR* 106 (2016): 179–207.

(b. Sanh. 107b; b. Soṭah 47a)."[48] Becker also points out that the concept of the *yaṣra* is largely absent from Syriac writings that postdate Narsai. Nevertheless, he concludes: "With regard to the *yeṣer/yaṣra* the Syriac sources may be most useful for better appreciating the particularities of rabbinic usage, but they may also suggest that Jews and Christians in Mesopotamia continued to affect one another in some way after the fourth century yet before the great intellectual engagement Jews, Christians, and Muslims would enjoy later in the Islamic Period."[49]

The Rabbinic Academy and the Christian Academy at Nisibis

Among the first serious attempts at comparative study of Bavli aggadic traditions and Syriac literature were studies that focused on the rabbinic academy as depicted in the Bavli and Syriac sources concerning the Christian academy at Nisibis. Rabbinic scholars accessed the Syriac sources mostly through the work of Arthur Vööbus, especially his *History of the School of Nisibis*, published in 1965, and also his two volumes on Syriac asceticism.[50]

In the early 1980s, two articles employed these Syriac sources to shed light on the traditions depicting the Babylonian rabbinic academy.[51] Shaye J. D. Cohen, in "Patriarchs and Scholarchs"[52] (1981), focused on the Pales-

48. Ibid., 204. On the evil inclination, see too Yishai Kiel, "The Wizard of Az and the Evil Inclination: The Babylonian Rabbinic *Yetzer* in Its Zoroastrian and Manichaean Context" (forthcoming).

49. Becker, "Evil Inclination," 207.

50. Arthur Vööbus, *History of the School of Nisibis*, CSCO 266 (Leuven: Peeters, 1965); idem, *History of Asceticism in the Syrian Orient: A Contribution to the History of Culture in the Near East*, 3 vols., CSCO 184, 197, 500 (Leuven: Peeters, 1958–1988), esp. vols. 1 and 2.

51. There were a handful of references to the Syriac academy before these articles by Cohen and Gafni. Jacob Neusner, in the third volume of his *A History of Jews of Babylonia* (Leiden: Brill, 1968), 195–200, devoted a few pages to general comparisons between the rabbinic academy and Christian monastery, based entirely on the work of Vööbus. He noted, for example, the use of military imagery in the literature of both communities (fight, battle, the "war of the Torah"), attitudes to women, some ascetic values, miracle stories, and so forth. But Neusner here was not elucidating Bavli aggada; rather, he was attempting to understand the social history of the rabbis. The first chapter of David M. Goodblatt's important book *Rabbinic Instruction in Sasanian Babylonia*, SJLA 9 (Leiden: Brill, 1975), opens: "According to A. Vööbus histories of the schools constituted a popular literary genre among Nestorian Syriac writers. The Babylonian Jews did not, so far as we know, follow the example of their Christian neighbors" (11). Goodblatt's study in any case was focused on sorting out the Geonic and talmudic traditions themselves—he came to the groundbreaking conclusion that the Babylonian Amoraim studied in disciple circles rather than academies—and consequently devoted scant attention to the Syriac sources themselves. He did point out a few parallels, most of them philological, such as that the talmudic term *metivta* seems to mean "session" in several passages, cognate with the Syriac *mautba* (ܡܘܬܒܐ); see, e.g., 79 n. 34, 76 n. 22.

52. Shaye J. D. Cohen, "Patriarchs and Scholarchs," *Proceedings of the American Academy for Jewish Research* 48 (1981): 57–85. Quotations in this paragraph are from 75, 80, 85.

tinian "Rabbinic academy" of the Patriarch R. Yehuda HaNasi. Cohen's analysis was largely based on the Bavli version of the patriarch's death and testament in b. Ketub. 103a–b compared with Hellenistic and Roman parallels, and he suggested that "at least to some extent, the patriarch was a scholarch and the patriarchal academy a philosophical school." The Bavli passage refers to מסורת חכמה and סדרי נשיאות, which Cohen translated as "the tradition of the office of Hakham (Sage)" and "the orders of the patriarchate." These he considered terms for the rules and regulations of the school, and he observed that the "internal procedures of the Christian school of Nisibis were governed by a written set of 'canons' [ܩܢܘܢܐ]. Syriac writers regularly refer to the 'established order' [ܛܟܣܐ = τάξις] of the school." In a footnote Cohen referenced Barhadbeshabba's *The Cause of the Foundation of the Schools* and Vööbus's citations of canons of Narsai, Rabbula, and Maruta. In the final two paragraphs of the article, however, Cohen conceded that to assume the "fundamental historicity" of his Bavli sources "is untenable," and accordingly, "Perhaps then the parallels between patriarchs and scholarchs tell us more about the Hellenization of Babylonian Jewry in the fourth and fifth centuries than about the Hellenization of Palestinian Jewry in the second." Indeed, Bavli scholarship since 1981 has demonstrated the extent to which the Bavli redactors reworked earlier, especially aggadic, sources.[53] The parallel to the Christian academy in Nisibis, located in the Sasanian, not the Roman, Empire, and founded in the fifth century, would obviously fit better with this conclusion. At all events, Cohen was among the first to delineate parallels between Syriac writings of, or about, the Christian academies of Sasanian Persia and the Bavli.

Isaiah Gafni, the following year (1982), published a much more detailed engagement with the Christian schools in the Sasanian Empire, entitled "Nestorian Literature as a Source for the History of the Babylonian *Yeshivot*."[54] Gafni, too, drew on Barhadbeshabba's *Cause of the Foundation of Schools*, on canons written at the end of the fifth and sixth centuries (mostly from Vööbus), and on a few other sources. He claimed that these sources about "daily life of the school in Nisibis"[55] could illuminate life in the rabbinic academies. Among the parallels Gafni pointed out were (1) the annual calendar of studies, in which students were dismissed twice per year when agricultural labor was required, compared with Rava's instruction to his students "please do not appear before me" (b. Ber. 35b)[56];

53. See Jeffrey L. Rubenstein, "Criteria of Stammaitic Intervention in Aggada," in Rubenstein, *Creation and Composition*, 417–40.

54. Isaiah Gafni, "Nestorian Literature as a Source for the History of the Babylonian *Yeshivot*" [Hebrew], *Tarbiṣ* 51 (1981): 567–76.

55. Ibid., 569.

56. Ibid., 571–72: במטותא מנייכו ביומי ניסן וביומי תשרי לא תתחזו קמאי כי היכי דלא תטרדו במזונייכו כולא שתא.

(2) a possible relationship between some Syriac and talmudic terms; (3) the benches (ܣܩܡܠܐ) and rows (ܣܕܪܐ) upon which students sat, mentioned in Syriac sources, and similar terms in the Bavli, such as the "first row" (דרא קמא) in the story of Rav Kahana's visit to the Land of Israel;[57] (4) affinities between the account of Narsai, arriving in Nisibis and founding a school there, and Rav, arriving in Sura and founding his school there.[58] Gafni was most interested in presenting the sources and did not make strong claims about historical influence, suggesting these are "general motifs, that could be absorbed in literature that deals with similar frameworks that operated in domains of the same society and empire."[59]

The work of Becker on the Nisibis academy and related Syriac school traditions provided additional sources and analysis to contextualize some of the Bavli's traditions about the academy and academic life. Becker published *Fear of God and the Beginning of Wisdom: The School of Nisibis and the Development of Scholastic Culture in Late Antique Mesopotamia* in 2006 (based on his 2004 dissertation) and *Sources for the Study of the School of Nisibis* in 2008,[60] including an English translation of the *Cause of the Foundation of the Schools*. In the introduction to the former work, Becker observed, "The study of the East-Syrian school movement may also help to clarify the elusive history of the development of the Rabbinic academies (*yeshivot*) and their literary correlative, the Babylonian Talmud."[61] In fact, Becker began to consider the relationships between the Syriac Christian traditions and the Bavli in an earlier article, "Bringing the Heavenly Academy Down to Earth" (2003), that analyzed the motif of a heavenly classroom or academy/study circle (*metivta de'raqi'a*) that appears in both Syriac and Bavli sources. Despite many similarities, Becker concluded that the two traditions picture the relationship between the terrestrial and celestial schools in different ways.[62] Becker subsequently provided a more detailed assessment of the Syriac and rabbinic schools in an article entitled "The Compar-

57. Ibid., 573–74.

58. Ibid., 574–75.

59. Ibid., 575. The later dating of the rise of the Babylonian rabbinic academy to the post-Amoraic or Stammaitic period, as argued by David Goodblatt and Jeffrey Rubenstein, made for a better temporal alignment of these parallels, as the Syriac sources mostly date to the fifth and sixth centuries. Gafni also pointed out parallels between Geonic traditions, such as references to persecutions and closings of the rabbinic academies in the fifth and sixth centuries, to the closing of the Nisibis academy for two years, 541–542, at the order of the king and the magi (571). The Geonic sources are beyond the purview of this volume; however, given the possibly late date of the redaction of the Bavli, there is reason to see the Bavli itself as a Geonic source, or from roughly the same period as early Geonic traditions.

60. Adam Becker, *Fear of God and the Beginning of Wisdom: The School of Nisibis and Christian Scholastic Culture in Late Antique Mesopotamia*, Divinations (Philadelphia: University of Pennsylvania Press, 2006), esp. 3, 124–25 n. 249.

61. Ibid., 18.

62. Adam Becker, "Bringing the Heavenly Academy Down to Earth," in *Heavenly Realms*

ative Study of 'Scholasticism' in Late Antique Mesopotamia: Rabbis and East Syrians."[63] As the title suggests, Becker employs the category of scholasticism to conceptualize the commonalities between the rabbinic and Christian academies, noting parallels in the use of the *shekhinah/shekhinta*, service of the heart, pious scholarship as path to holiness, angelic opposition to humans' special status, and the equation of scholarly merit with religious merit, in addition to the parallels noted by Gafni.[64] Both Jeffrey Rubenstein and Daniel Boyarin drew on Becker's work (in addition to Gafni's) to describe aspects of the scholastic culture of the late Babylonian academy.[65]

Recently Mira Balberg and Moulie Vidas published "Impure Scholasticism: The Study of Purity Laws and Rabbinic Self-Criticism in the Babylonian Talmud" (2012), which argues for an antischolastic trend within the Bavli based on aggadic sources that contrast the study of laws of "leprous and tent impurity" (*nega'im ve-ohalot*) and occasionally other purity laws with various types of inner piety.[66] While recognizing the parallels noted above, they also reference Becker's discussion of "Christian monastic authors who objected to the practices and ideas" of the Nisibis academy and other such schools.[67] Balberg and Vidas cite a number of passages from Dadisho of Bet Qatraye and Simeon d'Taybute from the seventh century

---

and Earthly Realities in Late Antique Religions, ed. Ra'anan Boustan and Annette Yoshiko Reed (Cambridge: Cambridge University Press, 2004), 174–91.

63. Adam Becker, "The Comparative Study of 'Scholasticism' in Late Antique Mesopotamia: Rabbis and East Syrians," *AJS Review* 34 (2010): 91–113.

64. See too Adam Becker, "Polishing the Mirror: Some Thoughts on Syriac Sources and Early Judaism," in *Envisioning Judaism: Studies in Honor of Peter Schäfer on the Occasion of His Seventieth Birthday*, ed. Ra'anan Boustan et al., 2 vols. (Tübingen: Mohr Siebeck, 2013), 2:897–915. Becker is generally cautious about the use of Syriac parallels to explain the Bavli: "Despite some interesting verbal parallels that may exist between the two pedagogical cultures, I do not think Syriac sources offer straightforward, comparative material for the Babylonian Talmud.... With few exceptions, there are no smoking guns, no simple parallels, no Syriac tales that serve as potential sources that clearly and definitively explain obscurities in rabbinic texts" (900–901).

65. Jeffrey L. Rubenstein, *The Culture of the Babylonian Talmud* (Baltimore: Johns Hopkins University Press, 2003); Daniel Boyarin, "Hellenism in Jewish Babylonia," in *The Cambridge Companion to the Talmud*, ed. Charlotte Elisheva Fonrobert and Martin Jaffee (Cambridge: Cambridge University Press, 2007), 349–58; Boyarin notes that "such comparisons bespeak a common intellectual, discursive, spiritual milieu between patristic Christianity and Babylonian rabbinic Judaism (349). See too Boyarin, *Socrates and the Fat Rabbis* (Chicago: University of Chicago Press, 2009), 135–40: "Another significant factor in the increased 'Hellenizing' of the Babylonian Rabbis may very well be the increased movement of Syriac Christian sages after 489 AC after the bishop of Edessa was given permission to close down the theologically suspect 'School of the Persians' in that city. Its adherents, thereupon, fled over the Persian border and founded their school at Nisibis" (138–39; see also 220).

66. Mira Balberg and Moulie Vidas, "Impure Scholasticism: The Study of Purity Laws and Rabbinic Self-Criticism in the Babylonian Talmud," *Prooftexts* 32 (2012): 312–56.

67. Ibid., 341, drawing on Becker, *Fear of God*, 188–94.

that criticize the "equation of scholarship and holiness, of academic study and devotion," analogous to the antischolastic talmudic traditions. They noted, however, that, while the Christian critique devolves from outside of the schools from a different social group, the Bavli's critique is internal, an internal tension within the rabbinic academy.

The Late Antique Holy Man

The influential work of Peter Brown on the holy man in late antiquity and on late antique religion in general offered new contexts to understand rabbinic traditions about the sages, holy men, miracles, and other pietistic practices.[68] Brown adduced sources from throughout the Mediterranean world, but he quoted often from Syriac literature from the Roman East. Typically, rabbinic scholars referenced Brown's scholarship without investigating Brown's sources themselves to shed light on various Bavli traditions.[69] Some scholars, however, especially in recent years, have carried out closer analyses of the Syriac writings themselves and their relationship to Bavli sources, especially portrayals of the rabbis (and other figures) performing miracles and adopting ascetic practices. Thus, Michal Bar-Asher Siegal, in her *Early Christian Monastic Literature and the Babylonian Talmud,* compares numerous Bavli traditions with "monastic sources from Egypt popularly circulating in the Persian Empire at the time of the composition and redaction of the Babylonian Talmud."[70] Among

68. Peter Brown, "The Rise and Function of the Holy Man in Late Antiquity," in idem, *Society and the Holy in Late Antiquity* (Berkeley: University of California Press, 1982), 103–53; see also idem, *The World of Late Antiquity, AD 150–170* (London: Harcourt Brace Jovanovich, 1971); idem, *The Making of Late Antiquity* (Cambridge: Harvard University Press, 1978).

69. See Marc Hirshman, "Moqdei qedusha mishtanim: honi unekhadav," *Tura* 1 (1989): 113–16; David Levine, "Holy Men and Rabbis in Talmudic Antiquity," in *Saints and Role Models in Judaism and Christianity,* ed. Marcel Poorthuis and Joshua Schwartz, Jewish and Christian Perspectives 7 (Leiden: Brill, 2004), 45–58; and, in the same volume, Chana Safrai and Ze'ev Safrai, "Rabbinic Holy Men," 59–78; Richard Kalmin, "Holy Men, Rabbis and Demonic Sages in the Judaism of Late Antiquity," in *Jewish Culture and Society under the Christian Roman Empire,* ed. Richard Kalmin and Seth Schwartz, Interdisciplinary Studies in Ancient Culture and Religion 3 (Leuven: Peeters, 2003), 211–49. Eliezer Diamond, in an article "Lions, Snakes and Asses: Palestinian Jewish Holy Men as Masters of the Animal Kingdom," in *Jewish Culture and Society under the Christian Roman Empire,* ed. Richard Kalmin et al. (Leuven: Peeters, 2003), 251–83, examined the motif of the holy man's control of the animal domain, discussing such accounts as R. Ḥanina unhurt by the bite of a deadly lizard (b. Ber. 33a), a venomous serpent that guarded the cloak of R. Eleazar (b. ʿErub. 54b), the roaring lions that did not harm R. Simeon b. Ḥalafta (b. Sanh. 59b), the pious donkey of R. Pinḥas b. Yair, and others. Diamond quotes numerous primary sources, though not from Syriac texts. Likewise Baruch M. Bokser, in "Wonder-Working and the Rabbinic Tradition: The Case of Hanina Ben Dosa," *JSJ* 16 (1985): 42–92, quotes a few original Greek sources.

70. Michal Bar-Asher Siegal, *Early Christian Monastic Literature and the Babylonian*

her main sources is the Apophthegmata Patrum (Sayings of the Desert Fathers), a collection of sayings, stories, and traditions of the Syrian, Palestinian, and Egyptian ascetic monks of the fourth and fifth centuries, a text extant in many versions and preserved in several languages, including Syriac.[71] Bar-Asher Siegal argues that the Syriac Christian traditions had a profound influence on some Bavli depictions of rabbis as holy men. For example, the differences between the Bavli's version of the famous story of R. Shimeon Bar Yoḥai and the cave (b. Šabb. 33b–34a), as compared with the version found in the Yerushalmi and other Palestinian midrashic compilations, can be attributed to the influence of these Christian monastic traditions: "the figure of Rashbi in the BT looks and acts very much like the early desert fathers of the fourth and fifth centuries ... the great and long-standing influence of this portrayal of Rashbi is indebted, at least in its conception, to literary connections to early Christian holy men traditions."[72] Similarly, Bar-Asher Siegal discerns monastic parallels to the stories of R. Yoḥanan and Resh Laqish in b. B. Meṣ. 84b and of the repentance of Eleazar b. Dordya in b. ʿAbod. Zar. 17a.[73]

In his "A Rabbinic Translation of Relics," Jeffrey Rubenstein notes that the account of the death and burial of R. Eleazar b. R. Shimeon in b. B. Meṣ. 84b exhibits several features unattested or extremely rare in rabbinic sources, including a conflict over the body of the dead sage and its reburial in a different location. These features, he argues, are best understood as having been influenced by accounts of the cult or relics and "translations of the relics" of Christian holy men, many of which can be found in contemporary Syriac writings.

Talmud (Cambridge: Cambridge University Press, 2013), 14. See too her article, "Shared Worlds: Rabbinic and Monastic Literature," *HTR* 105 (2012): 423–56.

71. Siegal believes that these traditions were disseminated widely: "Therefore, I claim these Syriac traditions reached the monks of the Persian Empire, and, as a result, the composers of the Talmudic traditions" (*Monastic Literature*, 11). Catherine Hezser, in an article published in 1994, "Apophthegmata Patrum and Apophthegmata of the Rabbis," in *La narrativa cristiana antica* (Rome: Institutum Patristicum Augustinianum, 1994), 453–64, had already compared stories of the desert fathers in the *Apophthegmata Patrum* with the biographical anecdotes of the rabbis. Hezser draws mostly on the Greek version, and her comparanda are exclusively Palestinian rabbinic traditions.

72. Siegal, *Monastic Literature*, 150–69; quotation from 168. Although many of the Christian sources quoted by Siegal are extant only in Greek (or quoted from Greek versions), she argues, "The similarities between the monastic and rabbinic sources indicate the familiarity of the rabbinic authors with Christian holy men traditions, a familiarity likely based on Syriac translations of the major works of the early Egyptian desert fathers that had been brought to the Persian Empire" (167).

73. Ibid., 121–27, 170–90.

Other Aspects of Theology and Culture

Various scholars have drawn on Syriac writings in more detailed studies of a particular talmudic theological concept, literary motif, or narrative element. Thus, Christine Shepardson, "Interpreting the Ninevites' Repentance: Jewish and Christian Exegetes in Late Antique Mesopotamia,"[74] observed that the Bavli, along with a long Syriac *memra* attributed to the fourth-century deacon Ephrem (but perhaps dating to the fifth or sixth century), as well as other *memre* by Ephrem, Narsai, and Jacob of Serugh, provide a very positive assessment of the repentance of the Ninevites.[75] Several of these studies drew on the Syriac martyrdoms collected in the Persian Martyr Acts. In *The Sense of Sight in Rabbinic Culture*, Rachel Neis explores "visual asceticism" in rabbinic sources, including the "lowered gaze" (as opposed to the "phallic gaze") that rabbis adopted to avoid looking at erotic sights, especially the bodies of women.[76] She observes a similar motif in the Acts of Anahid, which notes that when she was brought to the house of some notables, "the chaste girl did not raise her eyes in the slightest to look at them." Like the rabbis described in several Bavli sources, here "the modest woman preserves her honor by casting her eyes downward."[77] Other scholars have investigated whether the Babylonian rabbis or the Exilarchs were involved in tax collection on behalf of Sasanian Persia, or alternatively, were exempt from taxes, by comparing the Bavli sources with the Acts of Simeon Bar Seba'e, which thematizes the refusal of Simeon, the (putative) Catholicos, to accept a double tax levy on Christians.[78] While the focus of these scholars was the historical question, they analyzed several aggadic traditions in their quest for the historical truth, including an extended aggadic compilation at b. Ned. 62b.[79] Several talmudic stories tell of interactions between Ifra Hormiz, the mother of King Yazdgird, and the rabbis (b. B. Bat. 8a–b; 10b–11a; b. Zebaḥ. 116b; b. Nid. 20b, 24b). A few scholars have sought to illuminate these stories by analyzing a tradition found in Syriac sources, including The Martyrdom

74. Christine Shepardson, "Interpreting the Ninevites' Repentance: Jewish and Christian Exegetes in Late Antique Mesopotamia," *Hugoye* 14 (2011): 249–77.

75. Ibid., 275. However, Shephardson writes that we cannot know whether the Syriac authors knew the Bavli tradition or whether the Babylonian rabbis knew the Christian tradition (274).

76. Rachel Neis, *The Sense of Sight in Rabbinic Culture* (Cambridge: Cambridge University Press, 2013), 143–46.

77. Ibid., 144. Neis analyzes b. Pesaḥ. 113a–b. See also 38 n. 99 and 138 and the notes there.

78. Moshe Beer, "Were the Babylonian Amoraim Exempt from Taxes and Customs" [Hebrew], *Tarbiṣ* 33 (1964): 247–58; David Goodblatt, "The Poll Tax in Sasanian Babylonia: The Talmudic Evidence," *JESHO* 22 (1979): 233–95; Geoffrey Herman, *A Prince without a Kingdom: The Exilarch in the Sasanian Era*, TSAJ 150 (Tübingen: Mohr Siebeck, 2012), 176–80.

79. E.g., Goodblatt, "Poll Tax," 280–87.

of Tarbo, that the wife of Shapur was Jewish or was sympathetic to the Jews.[80]

Geoffrey Herman, in "'Bury My Coffin Deep!' Zoroastrian Exhumation in Jewish and Christian Sources," discusses several aggadic sources about burial that grapple with the difficulties caused by Zoroastrian opposition to burying corpses in the earth (due to concern for impurity).[81] Thus, R. Yose b. Qisma's deathbed instructions, quoted in the title of the article "conveys the anxiety that the Persians will exhume his tomb if he is not buried deep enough."[82] Herman quotes from numerous Syriac sources, including many of the Persian Martyr Acts, where Christians face the same difficulties in burying the body of the martyrs. In some cases the Persians post guards to prevent Christians taking the body, while in other accounts the Christians steal the body, often helped by miracles.[83] The combination of evidence from "Jewish and Christian Sources, each with their own focus on the exhumation phenomenon, when examined together, have been mutually enriching."[84]

A story of a corrupt judge who accepts bribes found in b. Šabb. 116a–b, which many scholars see as an anti-Christian polemic and a parody of Luke 12:13–21, has been further illuminated by Holger Zellentin in comparison with the Syriac Diatessaron, Peshitta, and the writings of the church father Ephrem.[85]

Reuven Kiperwasser and Serge Ruzer examined conversion narratives in rabbinic sources, including the famous stories of the proselyte who approaches Hillel and Shammai in b. Šabb. 31a, in light of *Life of Isho'sabran*, by the Catholicos Isho'yahb III, written in the mid-seventh century.[86]

---

80. *AMS* 2:254; Jacob Neusner, "Babylonian Jewry and Shapur II's Persecution of Christianity from 339 to 379," *HUCA* 43 (1972): 77–102, and the references to previous scholarship; A. F. de Jong, "Zoroastrian Religious Polemics and Their Contexts," in *Religious Polemics in Context: Papers Presented to the Second International Conference of the Leiden Institute for the Study of Religions (LISOR) Held at Leiden, 27–28 April, 2000*, ed. Theo. L. Heema and Arie van der Kooij, Studies in Theology and Religion 11 (Assen: Royal Van Gorcum, 2004), 52–54.

81. Geoffrey Herman, "'Bury My Coffin Deep!' Zoroastrian Exhumation in Jewish and Christian Sources," in *Tiferet LeYisrael: Jubilee Volume in Honor of Israel Francus*, ed. Joel Roth, Yaacov Francus, and Menahem Schmelzer (New York: Jewish Theological Seminary, 2010), 31–60.

82. Ibid., 50.

83. Ibid., 37–41.

84. Ibid., 53.

85. Holger Zellentin, "Margin of Error: Women, Law, and Christianity in Bavli Shabbat 116a–b," in *Heresy and Identity in Late Antiquity*, ed. Eduard Iricinschi and Holger Zellentin, TSAJ 119 (Tübingen: Mohr Siebeck, 2008), 356–63. Zellentin argues that the Bavli authors specifically engage the understanding of the gospel passage in the Syriac tradition. See too Burton L. Vizotsky, "Overturning the Lamp," in *Fathers of the World: Essays in Rabbinic and Patristic Literatures*, WUNT 80 (Tübingen: Mohr Siebeck, 1995), 75–85; Peter Schäfer, *Jesus in the Talmud* (Princeton, NJ: Princeton University Press, 2007), 123.

86. Reuven Kiperwasser and Serge Ruzer, "Zoroastrian Proselytes in Rabbinic and

They compare the depiction of Zoroastrians and Zoroastrian learning in the Jewish and Christian texts, arguing that it constitutes an "underlying common topos." The varying uses of this topos, they suggest, reveal that issues of orality and literacy were employed as "polemical border drawing," in that both religious minorities emphasize "the reliance on the Holy Writ vis-à-vis the dominant oral culture." Given the importance of oral tradition in rabbinic culture, however, the rabbinic sources are "less extreme" than the Syriac traditions, which exhibit "an unabashedly anti-oral stance."[87]

While the key Persian and Syriac contexts continue to remain at the foreground of the comparative study of Bavli aggada, and the pre-Sasanian Mesopotamian or early Babylonian context has, over the years, attracted a degree of sustained interest, a more recent turn has been in the Manichaean and Armenian direction, and these contexts would seem to hold potential for future exploration. Perhaps most significant, however, is the growing recognition in the advantage of engaging more than one context when dealing with Bavli aggada. Indeed, it would appear that just as the Jewish religious community of Babylonia did not flourish in cultural isolation, so too one can hardly imagine that broad cultural processes within the Sasanian milieu would have been confined to certain religious communities to the exclusion of others, and it is precisely the engagement with multiple contexts that characterizes a number of the papers in this volume.

Summary of the Papers in this Volume

The papers collected in this volume offer new studies reflecting many of the new contexts that have recently served for reading Bavli aggada. We have grouped the papers according to the primary context engaged: Mesopotamian, Sasanian, Syriac-Christian, and Zoroastrian. There is, however, a great deal of overlap, and most of the papers relate to several of these contexts.

Like many religious groups in late antique Sasanian Babylonia, the Babylonian rabbis believed that the world was filled with intermediary beings who engaged with human beings in a variety of ways. The presence and nature of the demonic in the Bavli, and in particular, the rabbinic

---

Syriac Christian Narratives: Orality-Related Markers of Cultural Identity," *HR* 51 (2012): 197–218. Cf. their reworked and expanded version of this article, "To Convert a Persian and Teach Him the Holy Scriptures: A Zoroastrian Proselyte in Rabbinic and Syriac Christian Narratives," in *Jews, Christians and Zoroastrians: Religious Dynamics in a Sasanian Context*, ed. Geoffrey Herman (Piscataway, NJ: Gorgias Press, 2014), 91–127.

87. Kiperwasser and Ruzer, "Zoroastrian Proselytes," 215–18.

construction of demons as neutral and essentially passive actors who are subjugated to religious authority belongs to the much earlier Mesopotamian literary tradition. The first paper focusing on the Mesopotomian context, "A Demonic Servant in Rav Papa's Household: Demons as Subjects in the Mesopotamian Talmud," by Sara Ronis, explores one particular rabbinic narrative found at b. Ḥul. 105b, about a demon who is a servant in Rav Papa's household, using this story as a springboard to broader questions of demonic servitude and subjecthood within the rabbinic world. She argues that the rabbis' construction of the demonic participates in the contemporary demonic discourse alongside Zoroastrians, Manichaeans, and Christians in conversation with earlier Mesopotamian religious texts. The monotheistic rabbis, however, adapted the trope of demons as neutral servants of the divine plan from an earlier Sumerian and Akkadian worldview, in contrast to the beliefs of their dualistic contemporaries.

Narratives migrating between the two major rabbinic centers of Palestine and Babylonia are frequently altered in both content and form. In "Narrative Bricolage and Cultural Hybrids in Rabbinic Babylonia: On the Narratives of Seduction and the Topos of Light," Reuven Kiperwasser seeks to reconstruct a topos of light and seduction and trace its transformation in the course of its journey from Palestine to Babylonia. The manner in which this topos is employed in Palestinian rabbinic sources contrasts with its expression in Babylonian rabbinic sources. The latter, when compared with the appearance of this topos in Eastern Syriac narrative and the Manichaean mythological account of the seduction of the archons offers an example of the shared Aramaic cultural heritage of Mesopotamia.

Mesene, the southern region of the Sasanian Empire, was considered by the rabbis to lie beyond the genealogically pure boundaries of Jewish Babylonia. The rabbis, however, would appear to have singled out Mesene for particular defamation; portraying its Jewish population as genealogically inferior: the descendants of slaves and *mamzerim*. This is somewhat surprising, since there is evidence, although extremely scant, that there was an uninterrupted presence of Jews living in that region from the sixth pre-Christian century throughout the Sasanian period and much later. Yakir Paz, in his paper "'Meishan Is Dead': On the Historical Contexts of the Bavli's Representations of the Jews in Southern Babylonia," asks why the Jews of Mesene were singled out. Was intermarriage indeed prevalent in Mesene? Were they really descendants of slaves? Rather than attempting a reconstruction of the history of the Jews in Mesene, which is hindered by the dearth of information, Paz contextualizes historically the rabbinic perception of these Mesenian Jews and their region.

Diverse religious communities inhabiting the Sasanian Empire shared an attitude that treated loyalty to the king and the kingdom as a supreme value. In "'In Honour of the House of Caesar': Attitudes to the Kingdom in the Aggada of the Babylonian Talmud and Other Sasanian Sources," Geoffrey Herman describes how Manichaeans, Sasanian Christians and Babylonian rabbis told accounts of how their spiritual leaders interacted with the rulers, enjoyed a positive relationship with them, and were broadly admired for this. In the case of the talmudic sources, the comparison of Babylonian and Palestinian rabbinic sources, and in particular, parallels, shows this as a motif, highlighted in the Bavli and often introduced by the Babylonian authors. This is particularly evident in the Bavli's portrayal of the Palestinian Amora R. Abbahu and in the Bavli narrative of R. Yehoshua and the Elders of Athens.

Iranian loanwords represent indisputable evidence of Iranian phenomena in talmudic literature. They occasionally serve to express a specific discursive mood or for narrative effect. In some aggadic cycles one encounters a larger ratio of Iranian loanwords than elsewhere, and such concentrations or clusters of loanwords are the focus of the next paper in this section. Jason Mokhtarian, in "Clusters of Iranian Loanwords in Talmudic Folkore: The Chapter of the Pious (b. Ta'anit 18b–26a) in its Sasanian Context," asks whether such clusters have a particular function within these narratives. Examining as an example the cycle of aggadot about pious men in b. Ta'an. 18b–26a, he concludes that they reflect traces of cultural resonance with the Sasanian world produced by the so-called common people.

Over the past few decades, research into Babylonian talmudic sage stories has been powered by a growing consensus that much of this material can be attributed to late, unnamed producers commonly known as Stammaim. Recent work has focused particularly on the movement of rabbinic traditions from Palestine to Babylonia, while current research is very much animated by a notion of textual transformation, now enhanced by a growing appreciation of the Bavli's Sasanian context. Shai Secunda, in "Gaze and Counter-Gaze: Textuality and Contextuality in the Anecdote of Rav Assi and the Roman (b. Baba Meṣiʿa 28b)," examines this brief Babylonian anecdote in an attempt to chart its development, elucidate its narrative devices, draw out its potential historical and cultural meanings, and ultimately speculate on the type of textuality this sort of "tale in transformation" presents. Secunda correlates the Persian position with evidence from the now lost Apēdagānestān ("Code of Lost Property") and the Roman view with developments in Roman law. However, he suggests that a straightforward historical approach does not do the story justice, as it seems to bear a complex relationship with a parallel Yerushalmi tale about Alexander of Macedon (y. B. Meṣ. 2:4, 8c). Thinking about this story might help us appreciate some of the dynamics of the Bavli tale, and also will draw attention to further factors relating to rabbinic textuality.

The third section, the Syriac-Christian context, begins with Jeffrey L. Rubenstein's "Martyrdom in the Persian Martyr Acts and in the Bavli." Rubenstein discusses the accounts of martyrdom in the Babylonian Talmud and those of the Persian Martyr Acts, a "corpus" of about seventy stories of Christian martyrs from the Sasanian Empire. Although martyr narratives are rare in the Babylonian Talmud, and martyrdom does not seem to have been central to the experience of Jews during the Sasanian era, these narratives provide one comparative axis for contextualizing rabbinic Judaism and Christianity within the Sasanian world. Martyrdom narratives in the Persian Martyr Acts and in the Bavli indeed have many motifs, themes, and ideas in common. Nevertheless, the points of contrast between the two literatures are far more prominent than the similarities. The Persian Martyr Acts consistently depict martyrdom as the goal of Christian life, an occasion for celebration and joy, and a divine gift, in a way that is foreign to the Bavli. Conversion is also a significant element in many of the Persian Martyr Acts, as the renunciation of "magianism" for Christianity, typically by an aristocrat or even a royal family member, provokes the tortures and martyrdom. Many of the Persian Martyr Acts also present a very negative view of the Persian emperor, who personally engages in dialogue with the martyr and authorizes the tortures and death. The rabbinic sources, by contrast, do not celebrate martyrdom, do not feature Persian converts to Judaism, and do not involve the Persian emperor. These differences point to a fundamental distinction between the discourses on martyrdom in the Persian Martyr Acts and in the Bavli. For the Persian Martyr Acts, martyrdom is closely connected to Christian identity and perhaps even entailed by it: the embrace of Christianity is understood as the abandonment of one's previous identity, and as a rejection of Zoroastrian practices, Persian society, and the Persian emperor. In the talmudic sources identity is not at issue and Judaism is not opposed to an alternative "religion." The stories of martyrs focus more narrowly on the issues of the proper responses to persecution and of theodicy.

While the Babylonian Talmud tells many stories about Palestinian rabbis persecuted and killed by the Roman Empire, the story of Rabba bar Naḥmani (b. B. Meṣ. 86a) is the only account in the Bavli of a Babylonian rabbi being directly persecuted to the point of death in the Sasanian Empire. Simcha Gross, in "A Persian Anti-Martyr Act: The Death of Rabba Bar Naḥmani" also examines Bavli sources in light of the Persian Martyr Acts. Like many stories in the Babylonian Talmud, the story of Rabba bar Naḥmani incorporates earlier motifs and themes from elsewhere in the Bavli. At the same time, it reworks many of these motifs in rather unusual ways, and includes features that are not paralleled elsewhere. The larger plot of the story and these unusual features, would appear to have parallels in the Persian Martyr Acts. Comparing and contrasting the Persian Martyr Acts with the story of Rabba bar Naḥmani accounts for many of these features, Gross argues, and may point to a major difference in the attitudes toward persecution and resistance as markers of identity found among these two contemporary nondominant groups in Sasanian Babylonia.

Polemical stories that involve a dialogue between a rabbi and a *min* have long drawn the interest of scholars. In the next paper, "'Fool, Look to the End of the Verse': b. Ḥullin 87a and Its Christian Background," Michal Bar-Asher Siegal examines such sources in light of contemporary Christian biblical debates. Focusing on one example, b. Ḥul. 87a and its parallel in b. Sanh. 39a, she argues that an acquaintance with the major Christian polemical debates in late antique Christian writings is crucial for understanding the questions raised by the *minim* here and in other such dialogues. The rabbis could be imagined as participating in these inner Christian debates.

The fourth section, the Zoroastrian Context, opens with Yaakov Elman's "Dualistic Elements in Babylonian Aggada." Elman surveys aspects of dualism, evil, suffering, astral determinism, free will, and fate in Greco-Roman philosophy, Christianity, Manichaeism, Zoroastrianism, and rabbinic Judaism, especially the Bavli. Elman argues that the essential characteristic of dualism is that a benevolent creator shares his power and governance of the world with other forces, and this outlook was widespread in late antiquity. In this respect rabbinic Judaism too may be considered dualistic, and many Bavli sources incorporate dualistic elements as a means of grappling with the problem of evil. While some of the Bavli's views of fate, suffering, and evil were influenced by Zoroastrian traditions, the Bavli's outlook nevertheless emerged as more flexible and nuanced than that of other contemporary religious and philosophical systems. The Bavli, along with all of these religions and philosophies, was engaged in a delicate balancing act to make sense of the human condition and to account for free will, providence, fate, evil, and suffering.

The Talmud's mythological account of Adam's first encounter with the seasonal and daily cycles of light and darkness and his sacrifice of the primordial bull are the focus of "First Man, First Bovine: Talmudic Mythology in Context," by Yishai Kiel. The notion of this mythical bull on a par with the First Man, he argues, is entrenched in the Iranian and Indic traditions. Based on textual and visual representations of a mythical scene depicting the slaying of the primordial bull in various cultures, Kiel posits that the talmudic story embeds and reflects much of the symbolism attached to this myth in the surrounding cultures. Several motifs in the talmudic story also engage and respond to a complex web of visual representations of mythical bull slaying in the rock reliefs at Persepolis, Sasanian coinage, and Mithraic depictions of the tauroctony. Imbuing this inherently rabbinic tradition with new mythical symbolism, the bull sacrificed by Adam was in turn mythologized, individualized, and reconfigured in the image and likeness of indigenous traditions.

David Brodsky, "Mourner's Kaddish, The Prequel: The Sasanian Period Backstory That Gave Birth to the Medieval Prayer for the Dead," traces the origins of the theology underpinning this immensely popular custom. The Mourner's Kaddish expresses the belief that a living person can change the fate of the dead in the afterlife. This notion, however, does not seem to derive from Tannaitic Palestinian rabbinic Judaism, which advocated that firstly, one person cannot atone for the sins of another, and secondly, that people have up until their death to atone, but not afterwards. Rather, the notion seems to derive from (Amoraic) Babylonian rabbinic Judaism, and especially from the enigmatic story of R. Akiva and the dead man, in which a dead man's young son is able to atone for his father's sins and change his fate in the afterlife. This, in turn, is compatible with the Zoroastrian context of Amoraic Babylonia, with its notion that the good and bad deeds of young children are attributed to their father's account, even after his death. With this new insight, Brodsky argues that the story of R. Akiva and the dead man was likely not originally a story about an efficacious prayer for the dead but a story about how the righteous acts of a child can change the fate of his dead parent in the afterlife.

The articles in this volume are based on papers submitted for the conference "The Aggada of the Babylonian Talmud and Its Cultural World," organized by the editors, and held at New York University June 1–2, 2015. We would like to take this opportunity, once again, to thank the organizations that contributed toward making that conference possible: The Edelman Fund of the Skirball Department of Hebrew and Judaic Studies, The Center for Ancient Studies, and the Religious Studies Program of New York University. Our thanks to David Engel, Chair of the Department of Hebrew and Judaic Studies, to Matthew Santirocco, Director of the Center for Ancient Studies, and Adam Becker, Director of the Religious Studies Program, for their support and to Peter Zilberg and Hanan Mozes of the Hebrew University for their help. We are also grateful to Ryan Grubbs and Madeleine Goico, the administrative staff who made the conference possible, to Joshua Blachorsky, Maurya Horgan, and Paul Kobelski for their meticulous editing, and to Michael Satlow, for facilitating publication in the Brown Judaic Studies Series.

Geoffrey Herman
Jeffrey L. Rubenstein
August 2017

I

The Mesopotamian Context

A Demonic Servant in Rav Papa's Household

Demons as Subjects in the Mesopotamian Talmud

SARA RONIS

The last fifteen years have seen an increasing interest in the wider cultural context of the rabbis of the Babylonian Talmud. Scholars have looked to Zoroastrian,[1] Armenian,[2] and Syriac[3] texts for evidence of broader

---

I would like to thank the conveners of the conference and the conference attendees for their many fruitful comments and suggestions. My thanks as well to Shana Zaia and Jacqueline Vayntrub, who were instrumental teachers and conversation partners about the ancient Mesopotamian materials. All errors remain my own.

1. See, e.g., Yaakov Elman, "The Other in the Mirror: Iranians and Jews View One Another: Questions of Identity, Conversion, and Exogamy in the Fifth-Century Iranian Empire. Part One," *Bulletin of the Asia Institute,* vol. 19, *Iranian and Zoroastrian Studies in Honor of Prods Oktor Skjaervo* (2005): 15–25; idem, "Middle Persian Culture and Babylonian Sages: Accommodation and Resistance in the Shaping of Rabbinic Legal Tradition," in *The Cambridge Companion to the Talmud and Rabbinic Literature,* ed. Charlotte Elisheva Fonrobert and Martin Jaffee (New York: Cambridge University Press, 2007), 165–97; idem, "Acculturation to Elite Persian Norms and Modes of Thought in the Babylonian Jewish Community of Late Antiquity," in *Neti'ot Le-David: Jubilee Volume for David Weiss Halivni,* ed. Ephraim Bezalel Halivni, Zvi Arie Steinfeld, and Yaakov Elman (Jerusalem: Orhot Press, 2004), 31–56; Shai Secunda, "Studying with a Magus/Like Giving a Tongue to a Wolf," *Bulletin of the Asia Institute* 19 (2005): 151–57; idem, "The Sasanian 'Stam': Orality and the Composition of Babylonian Rabbinic and Zoroastrian Legal Literature," in *The Talmud in Its Iranian Context,* ed. Carol Bakhos and M. Rahim Shayegan, TSAJ 135 (Tübingen: Mohr Siebeck, 2010), 140–60; Yishai Kiel, "Redesigning *Tzitzit* in the Babylonian Talmud in Light of Literary Depictions of the Zoroastrian *kustīg,*" in *Shoshannat Yaakov: Jewish and Iranian Studies in Honor of Yaakov Elman,* ed. Shai Secunda and Steven Fine, Brill Reference Library of Judaism 35 (Leiden: Brill, 2012), 185–202; idem, "Gazing through Transparent Objects in Pahlavi and Rabbinic Literature," *Bulletin of the Asia Institute* 24 (2014): 27–38; Shana Strauch Schick, "Intention in the Babylonian Talmud: An Intellectual History" (Ph.D. diss., Yeshiva University, 2011).

2. See, e.g., Richard Kalmin, *Migrating Tales: The Talmud's Narratives and Their Historical Context* (Berkeley: University of California Press, 2014).

3. Jeffrey L. Rubenstein, "Talmudic Stories and Syriac Hagiographical Literature" (Lecture, Ancient Judaism Colloquium, Yale University, New Haven, Connecticut, 2013); Michal

trends in Sasanian Babylonia, as well as for particular sites of intercultural interaction and competition. The recognition that the Babylonian rabbis did not live and work in a vacuum is welcome. One multifaceted element of this complex cultural world, however, deserves more attention—the rich traditions inherited from ancient Sumer, Akkad, Assyria, and Babylonia. In what follows, I wish to consider how these ancient Mesopotamian materials shed light on the discourse of the Babylonian Talmud by focusing on one element of the rabbinic worldview, the demonic. I first examine one particular rabbinic story which describes an event in the life of a nameless demon who is a servant in Rav Papa's household.[4] I then use this story as a springboard to explore broader questions of demonic servitude and subjecthood within the rabbinic world against the background of the much older Mesopotamian materials. I argue that this specific rabbinic narrative and the rabbinic construction of demons more broadly are part of a complex network of traditions that included earlier Mesopotamian religious texts about demons.[5]

At First I Thought . . .

The story of the demon in the household of Rav Papa is found within a larger *sugya* in b. Ḥul. 105b–106a. The unit is made up of a series of eight statements by the fourth-generation Babylonian Amora Abaye.[6] In each

Bar-Asher Siegal, "Literary Analogies in Rabbinic and Christian Monastic Sources" (Ph.D. diss., Yale University, 2010); Adam Howard Becker, "The Persian Martyr Acts: A Survey of the Sources for the Study of Babylonian Judaism," (Lecture, Annual Meeting of the Association for Jewish Studies, Baltimore, 2014).

4. I use the term *servant* as shorthand for the more complex social relationships and power dynamics signified by the demon's presence "in the household of Rav Papa."

5. This example is all the more apt as it is particularly within the sphere of the demonic that scholars have chosen to see parallels to contemporaneous Zoroastrian demonology. I do not dispute the importance of the Zoroastrian materials to understanding the Babylonian Talmud. Instead, in this paper I argue that, in the rabbis' construction of the demonic, they are part of a complex network of religious thinkers made up of contemporaneous Zoroastrians, Manichaeans, and Christians *in conversation with* earlier Mesopotamian texts about demons.

6. This *sugya* has already been examined by Shamma Friedman, who notes that the entire *sugya* is a structured grouping of eight statements by Abaye about how his teacher corrected Abaye's original assumptions ("Mivneh Sifruti Be-Sugyot Habavli," in *Sugyot Be-Heker Ha-Talmud Ha-Bavli: Mehkarim Be-Inyanei Mivneh, Herkev Ve-Nusah* [New York: Jewish Theological Society of America, 2010], 136–48, esp. 145–47). Almost all groupings of seven or more statements by the same sage in the Babylonian Talmud feature a Palestinian Amora, and Friedman suggests that these *sugyot* circulated as independent collections that made their way from Palestine to Babylonia and were included wholesale within the Babylonian rabbinic tradition. In fact, the *sugya* at b. Ḥul. 105b–106a is the only example of such a collection featuring a Babylonian Amora. Friedman argues that Abaye's presence in this list

statement, Abaye attests to his original rationale behind certain laws, and then explains that the Master, most likely Rabba b. Naḥmani, taught him a different and more correct rationale.[7] The statements refer to dangerous situations or, at the very least, situations that require caution. Abaye's original rationales are practical in nature and appear to be almost obvious. By contrast, the correct rationales taught by the Master are less intuitive and thus more elusive. In four of the cases, the correct rationale is demonic in nature.[8] The majority of Abaye's statements are then followed by an anonymous story that highlights the correctness of the Master's interpretation. It is in this context that the story of Rav Papa's demon servant appears:

b. Ḥullin 105b–106a

וא׳ אביי מריש ה״א האי דשדו מיא מפומא דחצבא משו׳ ציותא
ולא היא א׳ לי מר משום דאיכ׳ מים רעים

ההוא שידא דהוה בי רב פפא אזל לאתויי מיא מנהרא איעכב...
[כי] אתא חזה דשדו מיא מפומא דחצבא א״ל אי הוה ידענא
דעבדיתו הכי לא איתעכבי.[9]

may be explained by the fact that, of all the Babylonian Amoraim, Abaye traces the largest number of his traditions from Palestine.

7. Many of the teachings have thematic parallels to the lengthy *sugya* about demons in b. Pesaḥ. 109b–112a, including the idea of evil spirits dwelling in particular locations, removing from tables at various points during a meal, loss of sight, and magic. However, in b. Pesaḥim, these related teachings are given form and meaning through the anonymous redactor, who speaks in a collective voice of authority. In b. Ḥullin, the teachings are the statements of an individual rabbi, united by Abaye's continued learning about their rationales. For a discussion of the connection between authority and anonymity, see the recent dissertation by Joshua Even Eisen, "Stammaitic Activity versus Stammaitic Chronology; Anonymity's Impact on the Legal Narrative of the Babylonian Talmud" (Ph.D. diss., Columbia University, 2013), 99–138.

8. Yaakov Elman sees this *sugya* as evidence of a very late "counter-reaction" to a late "rationalistic tendency" in the Bavli ("The World of the 'Sabboraim': Cultural Aspects of Post-Redactional Additions to the Bavli," in *Creation and Composition: The Contribution of the Bavli Redactors [Stammaim] to the Aggada*, ed. Jeffrey L. Rubenstein, TSAJ 114 [Tübingen: Mohr Siebeck, 2005], 383–415, here 409). Elman divides the demonological discourse of this *sugya*, and of the Bavli more generally, into at least three strata: an early stratum that reflects demonological concerns; a later stratum that attempts to downplay or even ridicule earlier beliefs; and finally, an even later stratum that reacts adversely to that attempt and insists that the demonic remains both relevant and important. Elman deserves credit for being the first modern scholar to critically examine this important *sugya*. In my own research, however, I see no evidence of a late rationalistic tendency in the Bavli, so I situate this text as one in a large pool of Babylonian rabbinic texts that take the existence and activity of demons seriously.

9. Ms. Vatican 123b.

> Abaye said: At first I thought the reason why one pours off [a little water] from the mouth of the jug [before drinking] was flotsam [i.e. fibers floating on the surface of the water] but now my Master has told me: It is because there is evil water.

> A certain demon in the household of Rav Papa once went to fetch water from the river but was away a long time. When he returned he saw them pouring off [a little water] from the mouth of the jug; he exclaimed: Had I known that you were in the habit of doing this, I would not have been away so long.

In order to illustrate the existence of evil water, the anonymous redactor tells the story of a demon in the household of Rav Papa and his punctiliousness in avoiding such water. This story is presented in connection with Abaye's teaching in a matter-of-fact manner, but in fact, this brief and elliptical account raises more questions than it answers about the nature of the demonic and its function within this narrative.

Scholars have only begun to examine talmudic texts about demons. As part of a larger trend in the *Wissenschaft des Judentums*, for a long time demons in the Talmud were dismissed as a metaphor, a psychological manifestation, or a foreign corruption.[10] The early dismissal of demons as Persian superstition has led even more recent scholars to overlook the important exegetical, theological, and ritual functions that demons serve in the Babylonian rabbinic worldview.[11]

For the Babylonian rabbis, the world was filled with intermediary beings visible and invisible who acted upon and interacted with human beings. Within the parameters of this story in b. Ḥullin, the demon is real and embodied; at the end of the episode the household has jugs of water filled and carried by the demon servant. The fact that the rabbis treated the demonic with the same degree of interest, seriousness, and rigor as they do other subjects, raises particular questions about this story: What makes evil water so evil? How does Rav Papa have a servant who is a demon? And why is the demon servant so punctilious in waiting to bring his water back to the household? I will treat these questions sequentially.

---

10. See, e.g., Alexander Kohut, *Ueber die jüdische Angelologie und Daemonologie in ihrer Abhängigkeit vom Parsismus* (Leipzig: Brockhaus, 1866); Osias Heschel Schorr, "Ha-Torot," *HeḤaluṣ* 7 (1865): 1–88; idem, "Ha-Torot B," *HeḤaluṣ* 8 (1869): 1–120; Heinrich Graetz, *History of the Jews*, vol. 2, *From the Reign of Hyrcanus (135 BCE) to the Completion of the Babylonian Talmud* (Philadelphia: Jewish Publication Society of America, 1893; repr., 1967), 633; Ludwig Blau, *Das altjüdische Zauberwesen* (Strasbourg: Karl Trübner, 1898).

11. For a survey of academic and religious attitudes toward demons, see Sara Ronis, "'Do Not Go Out Alone at Night': Law and Demonic Discourse in the Babylonian Talmud" (Ph.D. diss., Yale University, 2015), 1–28.

Evil Waters

The concept of "evil water" can be found as early as the Mishna, where it has two distinct but interrelated meanings. The author of m. ʾAbot 1:11 uses the expression metaphorically to refer to a place outside of Israel or the rabbinic community.[12] ʾAbot R. Nat. A 11 explains that, in this context, evil water refers to places where the Jews will intermingle with gentiles and learn from their ways, or that this refers to places where Jews will do hard labor. Less metaphorically, m. Ḥul. 3:8 includes evil water in a list of harmful substances that, when ingested, do not invalidate the kosher status of birds. In this mishna, evil water is contrasted with the danger of a snakebite, which does invalidate a bird's kosher status.[13] While a snakebite is fatal, evil water is not. According to m. Ḥullin then, evil water is a dangerous but not fatal substance that can cause physical harm to birds and perhaps, by extrapolation, to human beings.[14]

The depiction of evil water as harmful is heightened in the Palestinian Talmud, which portrays evil water as fatal and its forced consumption as a form of indirect murder.[15] Yet none of these texts articulates what it is that makes evil water so dangerous.

To further complicate this depiction, water sources, but not evil water specifically, are associated with demons throughout Palestinian literature. In one striking story in Lev. Rab. 24:3, a certain demon who dwelled in the wellspring of the town of Ṣaytor turns to the scholar Abba Yose and asks for help in fending off the encroachment of a malevolent demon. The wellspring is associated with the demonic, but its primary resident is in fact a benevolent demon who informs the town of possible danger and aids the townspeople in exorcising the evil demon.[16] Thus, evil water might perhaps be related to demonic danger in Palestinian literature.

The text and context of the story of Rav Papa's demon servant in b. Ḥullin do not provide an immediate answer to the question of what makes evil water so evil. Scholars medieval and modern have generally taken one of two approaches. Some have interpreted b. Ḥullin in light of Pales-

---

12. "Abtalyon says: Sages, be careful with your words lest you become obligated in the obligation of exile and are exiled to a place of evil water [מים הרעים], and the students who follow you drink and die and the name of Heaven is profaned."

13. Following ms. Parma. Ms. Kaufmann reads פסולה.

14. The Mishna and the Tosefta both suggest that water that has been left uncovered overnight may be contaminated with snake venom, which can then enter the human body through the mouth or the skin. It is possible that מים מגולין, "uncovered water," is associated in some way with מים רעים, "evil water," but this possibility cannot be proven.

15. See y. Sanh. 9:2, 27a, in a discussion of liability for indirect murder.

16. See also the discussion of bathhouses in Joshua Levinson, "Enchanting Rabbis: Contest Narratives between Rabbis and Magicians in Rabbinic Literature of Late Antiquity," *Tarbiṣ* 75 (2006): 295–328.

tinian associations of demons and water, leading to the suspicion that the danger of evil water in b. Ḥullin is itself demonic.[17] Others have found the Palestinian literature a less relevant background for the story, choosing to interpret it exclusively within its Babylonian context.[18] In the Babylonian Talmud, demonic danger *is* associated with water that has been drawn and exposed overnight, but never with running water.[19] In the story in b. Ḥullin, it is clear that the source of the evil water is not the jug but the river itself; the demon's waiting a long time at the river (presumably for the evil water to pass) and the household's pouring the top of the jug out both function to remove the danger to those who would drink the water.

Thus, I would argue that though the phrase מים רעים is ambiguous, it does *not* refer to a demonic danger. The demon in the story does not live near the water; he is located within the household of Rav Papa and only goes to the river to bring water back to that household. Furthermore, in the context of this narrative, the only demon explicitly mentioned is the one who is wary of the harm and who takes steps to avoid it.[20] Thus, it seems probable that the harm of "evil water" is something other than demonic harm. Perhaps it was water that was befouled in some fashion less visible than the flotsam proposed by Abaye. Here the demon is not the source of the danger but instead acts to limit and avoid the potential harm.

Serving the Rabbis

While evil water remains obscure, the presence of a demon in a subordinate position in a rabbinic household does make sense against the backdrop of the Babylonian world in which the rabbis lived. Scholars have

17. The Palestinian association of water and demons may be seen in many medieval scholars' interpretation of evil water. Thus, in his commentary on this talmudic passage in b. Ḥullin, the tenth-to eleventh-century scholar Rabbenu Gershom interpreted the phrase to mean water upon which an evil spirit dwells. Similarly, in the same vein, the eleventh-century scholar R. Shlomo b. Yitzḥaq (Rashi) suggests that the phrase "evil water" refers to water from which a demon has drunk, though in his commentary on b. Ber. 25b, Rashi glosses מים הרעים with the word סרוחים, foul or malodorous, with no gestures toward the demonic. Notably, many early modern scholars, including R. Solomon Luria, seem to prefer the more demonic interpretation of the phrase. This interpretation has been followed by Isaiah Gafni, "Babylonian Rabbinic Culture," in *Cultures of the Jews: A New History*, ed. David Biale (New York: Schoken Books, 2002), 223–66, here 246–47, among others.

18. This interpretation was suggested by Rabbenu Nissim of Gerondi, and the interpretation is adopted by the Pnei Yehoshua on b. Šabb. 100b, Rabbenu Yehonatan on the Rif, and many other medieval sages.

19. E.g., b. Pesaḥ. 112a; b. ʿAbod. Zar. 12b; b. Ber. 51a.

20. With the exception of Lev. Rab. 24:3, discussed above, we have no evidence of demons harming other demons either intentionally or by accident in rabbinic texts from either Babylonia or Palestine.

begun to explore the rabbis as part of a Zoroastrian and/or Sasanian worldview. Yet the idea of a demon as servant to a holy man is not found in Zoroastrian, Manichaean, or Syriac Christian texts from late antiquity.[21] In these texts, demons are portrayed as the inherently evil armies of Ahreman the evil god, the forces of evil, and Satan, respectively.[22] The actions

21. In the eleventh through thirteenth centuries, however, the depiction of a "penitent" demon who serves monks or other Christian holy men becomes increasingly popular in Syriac texts. This development is outside the temporal scope of the current project. See, e.g., Liza Anderson, "Story of a Demon Who Repented and Was Accepted by God, from Mingana Syriac Manuscript 205, 159a-164b," https://www.academia.edu/2151969/Story_of_a_Demon_who_Repented_and_was_Accepted_by_God. This shift is contemporaneous with a similar shift in medieval Islamic demonology, discussed below.

22. For Zoroastrianism, see *Yašt* 11.5; 14.54–56, trans. Skjærvø apud S. K. Mendoza Forrest, *Witches, Whores, and Sorcerers: The Concept of Evil in Early Iran* (Austin: University of Texas Press, 2011), 86–87; *Ābān Yašt* 21.94-95 in Herman Lommel, *Die Yäšt's des Awesta* (Göttingen: Vandenhoeck & Ruprecht, 1927), 41. An inscription at Persepolis attributed to Xerxes I mentions the Old Persian daiva three times, in reference to deities who were previously worshiped until Xerxes established the worship of Ahura Mazdā there. Scholars debate whether daēuuas were originally Iranian gods or Indian gods who were believed to inhabit the same region as the Iranian tribes, and whether Zarathustra reformed earlier religion or represented a gradual development in Iranian religion. A survey of scholarly opinions on pre-Gāthic daēuuas can be found in Clarisse Herrenschmidt and Jean Kellens, "Daiva: Old Iranian Noun (Av. Daēuua-, Opers. Daiva-) Corresponding to the Title Devá- of the Indian Gods and Thus Reflecting the Indo-European Heritage (*Deiu̯Ó-)," in *Encyclopaedia Iranica* (2011). For Middle Persian depictions of the Other as demonic, see Dēnkard Book 7.2.9, 3.50, 4.6, 4.67 in Marijan Molé, *La Légende de Zoroastre selon les textes pehlevis*, Travaux d l'Institute d'études iraniennes de l'Université de Paris 3 (Paris: C. Klincksieck, 1967), 16–17, 38–39, 42–43, 54–55; Prods Oktor Skjærvø, *The Spirit of Zoroastrianism*, Sacred Literature Series (New Haven: Yale University Press, 2011), 145; *Bundahišn* 27.42 in Behramgore T. Anklesaria, *Zand-Ākāsīh: Iranian or Greater Bundahišn* (Bombay: Dastur Framoze A. Bode, 1956), 240–41; *Zand ī Wahman Yašt* 7.36 in Carlo G. Cereti, *Zand Ī Wahman Yašn*, Serie Orientale Roma (Rome: Istituto Italiano per il Medio ed Estremo Oriente, 1995), 165; A. V. Williams, "Dēw: Lit. 'Demon' in the Pahlavi Books," in *Encyclopaedia Iranica* (2011); Forrest, *Witches, Whores, and Sorcerers*, 42. For early Christianity, see Ephrem, *Hymns on Paradise* XII.8 in Sebastian Brock, *Ephrem the Syrian: Hymns on Paradise* (Crestwood, NY: St. Vladimir's Seminary Press, 1990), 163; Ephrem, "Hymns against Julian," 1.5-10, 4.22-24 in Kathleen E. McVey, *Ephrem the Syrian: Hymns*, Classics of Western Spirituality (New York: Paulist Press, 1989), 28–29, 256; *The History of the Heroic Deeds of Mar Qardagh* 35 in Joel Thomas Walker, *The Legend of Mar Qardagh: Narrative and Christian Heroism in Late Antique Iraq*, Transformation of the Classical Heritage 40 (Berkeley: University of California Press, 2006), 40, and esp. n. 115; *The Martyrdom of Blessed Simeon bar Ṣabbaʿe* 3, 22 in Kyle Smith, *The Martyrdom and History of Blessed Simon Bar Ṣabbaʿe*, Persian Martyr Acts in Syriac 3 (Piscataway, NJ: Gorgias Press, 2014), 58–59, 68; Sebastian P. Brock and Susan Ashbrook Harvey, *Holy Women of the Syriac Orient*, Transformation of the Classical Heritage 13 (Berkeley: University of California Press, 1987), 151–56. See also Smith, *Martyrdom*, 229, for a discussion of the biography of the martyr George of Izla, which contrasts the Magian, demonic life of the martyr before conversion with his righteous life in Christ after conversion. A dissertation by Sonja Anderson, "Idol Talk: The Discourse of Idolatry in the Early Christian World" (New Haven, CT: Yale University, 2016) examines in depth this rhetoric in early Christianity. In fact, Dale Martin has noted that, in the Greco-Roman Empire, a different historical shift was occurring. He notes a difference between Greco-Roman popular

of the demon in the household of Rav Papa make no sense if the demon is understood as evil. The portrayal of a demon as a neutral servant to an authority figure *is* found, however, in much earlier ancient Mesopotamian texts.

The civilization of Sumer arose in the southern Tigris-Euphrates Valley in the Chalcolithic period (between 5500 and 4000 BCE).[23] The earliest Sumerian writings date to the fourth millennium BCE. The third millennium BCE saw the rise of the Akkadian Empire between the Tigris and Euphrates rivers north of Sumer. Unlike the Sumerians, the Akkadians were a Semitic people. Over the course of the third and second millennia BCE, Akkadian replaced Sumerian as the spoken language in Mesopotamia.[24] In the second millennium, the influx of the Amorites and the waning of Sumer led to the emergence of new powers in the region—Assyria in the north and Babylonia in the south. With the demise of Assyria in the seventh century BCE, the Babylonians took control of the whole area between the two rivers.[25] These civilizations had a rich cultural and literary tradition, and a number of narratives about deities and demons were written on cuneiform tablets that have survived to this day in some form.

Given the incredible span of ancient Mesopotamian history, diversity and dynamism characterize any attempt to synthesize a single belief system or to trace these ancient ideas forward. Many figures and themes are specific to only one of these civilizations, or even only one city-state. However, a remarkable number of older ideas survive and are adopted and adapted by the Babylonian, and then later Persian, worlds.

Though scholars have noted earlier interrelationships, the Israelites first formally encountered Mesopotamian beliefs and culture in the Babylonian exile (586 BCE–516 BCE).[26] Mesopotamian themes are found in the

beliefs about *daimones* as capricious and ambivalent that stood in tension with the philosophical belief in *daimones* as neutral or even positively marked. Early Christian thinkers such as Origen, however, reframed *daimones* as evil beings intent on harm, who functioned largely outside the control of mortals. Thus, in the west, neutral *daimones* became evil demons, and only faith in the Christian God could protect potential victims from demonic harm. See Dale B. Martin, *Inventing Superstition: From the Hippocratics to the Christians* (Cambridge: Harvard University Press, 2004), 93–108, 160–86. By contrast, the rabbis inherited Second Temple traditions about evil demons and used the rabbinic legal system to subjugate the demonic and construct demons as neutral agents who functioned as part of the rabbinic system.

23. Tammi J. Schneider, *An Introduction to Ancient Mesopotamian Religion* (Grand Rapids: Eerdmans 2011), 18–19.

24. Ibid., 20–25.

25. Ibid., 29.

26. Stephanie Dalley, "The Influence of Mesopotamia upon Israel and the Bible," in *The Legacy of Mesopotamia*, ed. Stephanie Dalley (Oxford: Oxford University Press, 1998), 57–84, 60–79; Charles E. Carter, *The Emergence of Yehud in the Persian Period: A Social and Demographic Study*, JSOTSup 294 (Sheffield: Sheffield Academic Press, 1999), 300–316.

later strata of the Hebrew Bible,[27] and, as we will see, Babylonian traditions were an important element of rabbinic culture even into the Sasanian period.

The ancient civilizations of Mesopotamia—Sumer, Akkad, Assyria, and Babylonia—were polytheistic and had diverse but linked pantheons. The Sumerians were the first to keep written records of lists of deities. According to these lists, the total number of Sumerian gods has been estimated to be between twenty-four hundred and thirty-three hundred.[28] Sumer and Akkad recognized the god Enlil as the supreme deity; the Assyrians promoted Ashur to that same position, while the Babylonians later raised up Marduk to the head of their pantheon. Many of these gods originated as localized deities of a particular city, but as the empires' borders shifted and expanded, local gods found a broader audience, and empirewide gods took on local characteristics. Given the three thousand years of recorded Mesopotamian history, it is not surprising that the pantheon changed and adapted to new circumstances while maintaining a degree of continuity.

Mesopotamian religious texts belong to a variety of genres: law codes; disputations between animate and/or inanimate objects;[29] lists of gods, temples, temple personnel, and religious language; prayer requests and incantations; hymns; wisdom literature; inscriptions; and mythological accounts such as the Babylonian Enuma Elish. Across these genres, intermediary beings are discussed primarily in narrative texts and incantations, and not in legal texts. Within the narratives, we encounter various gods, personal protective deities, and demons. There is a great deal of narrative slippage between minor gods, intermediary beings, and monsters.[30] In Mesopotamian texts, these terms were not rigidly defined and these figures were not rigidly categorized. There is even

27. See, e.g., James B. Pritchard, ed., *Ancient Near Eastern Texts Relating to the Old Testament* (Princeton, NJ: Princeton University Press, 1950), which was seminal to scholarship on Mesopotamian parallels in the Hebrew Bible. Pritchard there describes an 1872 lecture by George Smith as the foundational moment of the study of Assyriology and the Hebrew Bible, but the field only continued to grow and expand through the twentieth century.

28. Schneider, *Introduction to Ancient Mesopotamian Religion*, 54 n. 12.

29. Such as The Debate between Bird and Fish c.5.3.5 i 92.

30. Thus, for example, in the Enuma Elish Tablets 4–5, the goddess Tiamat gives birth to the eleven creatures to fight with her against Marduk and the younger gods, and these eleven are alternately categorized as monsters, and demons, and deities themselves. While her primary partner, Qingu, was killed and humankind made from his blood, Marduk crafted statues of all eleven and placed them in the *apsû*, the primordial freshwater deep, to memorialize his victory. See W. G. Lambert, *Babylonian Creation Myths*, Mesopotamian Civilizations 16 (Winona Lake, IN: Eisenbrauns, 2013), 84–107; Stephanie Dalley, *Myths from Mesopotamia: Creation, the Flood, Gilgamesh, and Others* (Oxford: Oxford University Press, 2009), 252–61.

some evidence of slippage between evil demons and evil men in later Babylonian incantations.[31]

Though many demons in incantation texts had individual names and characteristics, some demons are grouped in general classes that had specific names such as *Alû, Lilû, Lilîtu,* and *Ardat Lilî, Gallû, Rabiṣu* (lurkers), *Aḫḫazu* (seizers), UDUG, LAMA/*Lamassu, Ilu* (deities), *Ekimmu* (ghosts), *šêdu, lamaštu,* and *labaṣu.*[32] Earlier Sumerian and Akkadian names often survived into later Babylonian culture, though the nature and meaning of a particular demon might change. Demons either were the biological offspring of particular gods and goddesses or were created by particular deities out of a variety of materials.[33] While some demons are explicitly androgynous, many demons are graphically depicted as male or female. These demons often are portrayed as hybrid human-animal beings, at times incorporating ophidian elements.[34] Other demons had additional monstrous elements; the *musmahhu* demon was depicted as a seven-headed dragonlike figure. Some demons such as the *gallû* could change their shapes at will.[35]

Many ancient Mesopotamian demonic spirits, such as the UDUG, LAMA, and *gallû,* were originally neutral intermediary beings. These classes of demons were modified by the adjectives "evil" and "good" to indicate which type of demon was being described in a particular text. Thus, certain Akkadian incantations read, "Get out, evil *rābiṣu;* come in, good *rābiṣu!*"[36] In one Old Babylonian text, the scribe requests: "May the evil UDUG and the evil galla stand aside. May the good UDUG and the

31. R. Campbell Thompson, *The Devils and Evil Spirits of Babylonia: Being Babylonian and Assyrian Incantations against the Demons, Ghouls, Vampires, Hobglobins, Ghosts, and Kindred Evil Spirits, Which Attack Mankind,* vol. 1, *Evil Spirits* (London: Luzac, 1903), 129–39.

32. Ibid., xxiv–xxv.

33. See, e.g., Enki and Ninmah, 69-71; Enuma Elish Tablet 1 in Dalley, *Myths from Mesopotamia,* 237–38.

34. Snakes were associated with demons, but evidence of beneficent snake-god cults also exists. See W. Farber, "Lamastu," *RlA* 6:442; R. Pientka-Hinz, "Schlange A. In Mesopotamien," *RlA* 12:202–18.

35. Anzu II.i [Standard Babylonian Version] in Dalley, *Myths from Mesopotamia,* 213. Some modern scholars of the ancient Near East have attempted to distinguish between demons and monsters by labeling as demonic any bipedal hybrid creature and as monstrous anything depicted as walking on all fours. See, e.g., Jeremy Black and Anthony Green, *Gods, Demons and Symbols of Ancient Mesopotamia: An Illustrated Dictionary* (London: British Museum Press, 1992), 63. This distinction is a modern one and is not reflective of a meaningful taxonomy in ancient Mesopotamia. The present study therefore examines both types of beings later classified as either demons or monsters.

36. Neo-Assyrian "Medical Text," in R. Campbell Thompson, *Assyrian Medical Texts* (Milford: Oxford University Press, 1923), pl. 101, tab. 2, r. 6, cited by Anne Marie Kitz, "Akkadian Demonology and Hebrew Theology: A Phenomenological Approach," (Lecture, Annual Meeting of the Society of Biblical Literature, San Diego, 2014).

good galla be present." A later incantation asks "May the good *sédu* and the good *lamassu* daily walk by my side."[37]

Many demons served as the messengers or functionaries of particular gods, and their manifestation as "good" or "bad" depended on the mission and character of the deity they served.[38] Demons are most prominently portrayed as servants to divine beings in ancient Mesopotamian stories such as the Sumerian accounts of Inana and Ereškigal.[39] In this narrative cycle, Inana, goddess of love and warfare, descends to the underworld to attend the funeral of her brother-in-law, who was the husband of her sister Ereškigal, goddess of the underworld. After Inana sits on Ereškigal's throne,[40] she is turned into a corpse and hanged on a hook. The gods Enlil, Nanna, and Enki eventually rescue Inana and revive her, but Ereškigal sends her demons to accompany Inana out of the underworld. Ereškigal insists that Inana cannot be free of the underworld until she has sent someone else to take her place. The demons function here as servants to the goddess Ereškigal. They obey their queen's decrees and also those of her sister Inana in deciding who should replace her in the underworld. As they pass some of Inana's courtiers, the demons offer to take them in her place, but she refuses. It is only when Inana sees her lover Dumuzi, dressed in finery and enthroned underneath an apple tree with no visible signs of having mourned her absence, that she insists that the demons take him in her stead.[41]

In one variant of the Dumuzi story, during the hunt for a victim, small demons say to the larger demons, "Demons have no mother; they have no father or mother, sister or brother, wife or children.... Demons are never kind, they do not know good from evil."[42] From the perspective of Dumuzi, demons are terrifying beings who drag him into the underworld.[43] However, the demons are only obeying the orders of the various

37. Graham Cunningham, *"Deliver Me from Evil": Mesopotamian Incantations 2500–1500*, StPohl, Series maior 17 (Rome: Pontificio Istituto Biblico, 1997), 128.

38. This construction of the demonic and its presence in the Hebrew Bible have been recently noted and explored by Kitz, "Akkadian Demonology and Hebrew Theology."

39. The narrative appears in Dumuzi and Ĝeštin-ana: c.1.4.1.1, Dumuzi and his sisters: c.1.4.1.3, and Inana's Descent to the Netherworld: c.1.4.1.

40. Possibly as an act of usurpation.

41. This story continues to be told into the later Babylonian period, where the deities are named Ištar, Ereškigal, and Tammuz.

42. Dumuzi and Ĝeštin-ana: c.1.4.1.1.

43. In fact, scholars think the annual festival of mourning for Dumuzi (Tammuz in Babylonian) to mark his entry into the underworld continued to be observed into the Sasanian period. See O. R. Gurney, "Tammuz Reconsidered: Some Recent Developments," *JSS* 7 (1962): 147-60; Thorkild Jacobsen, "Towards the Image of Tammuz," *HR* 1 (1962): 189–213; Edwin M. Yamauchi, "Additional Notes on Tammuz," *JSS* 10 (1966): 10–15; JoAnn Scurlock, "K 164 ("Ba" 2, 635): New Light on Mourning Rites for Dumuzi?," *RA* 86 (1992): 53–67; Scurlock, "Images of Tammuz: The Intersection of Death, Divinity, and Royal Authority

deities whom they serve; they do so without mercy or consideration for others. They themselves are neutral, and their actions are either good or evil depending on one's perspective on the nature of the deity they serve and the ways that they serve her. The messengers of complex, capricious gods were themselves complex and capricious.

In a world where demons are subordinated servants to a range of powerful actors, the depiction of the demon in Rav Papa's household is not so strange. Rav Papa is not a god, nor are the stakes in his demon servant's mission particularly high. However, this portrayal of Rav Papa serves to elevate the rabbi explicitly to the status of a being worthy of being served by demons. A rabbi is powerful and important enough to have demonic subordinates in his household. And, as in the Sumerian account, the demon is stringent in fulfilling the task given to him; Dumuzi is delivered to the underworld and the rabbi's household gets its needed water.

Though these ancient Mesopotamian texts were composed millennia before the rise of the rabbinic movement, we do know that early Mesopotamian cults and culture remained alive in certain places on the margins of the Achaemenid Empire and at its center well into the Parthian period (150 BCE–226 CE). The Achaemenid kings continued to celebrate Mesopotamian festivals according to the Babylonian lunar calendar.[44] Fragments of Sumerian and Akkadian cuneiform texts written on clay tablets can be dated as late as the second and early third centuries CE.[45] There is even evidence that the late Sasanian king Khusro I (531–579 CE) knew of the Babylonian epic of creation, the Enuma Elish.[46] Filtered largely through Babylonian culture, aspects of early Mesopotamian culture thus survived at least until the advent of Islam.

Scholars have begun to note the survival of ancient Mesopotamian

in Ancient Mesopotamia," in *Experiencing Power, Generating Authority: Cosmos, Politics, and the Ideology of Kingship in Ancient Egypt and Mesopotamia*, ed. Jane A. Hill, Philip Jones, and Antonio J. Morales (Philadelphia: University of Pennsylvania Museum of Archaeology and Anthropology, 2013), 151–84.

44. Dalley, "Occasions and Opportunities 2," in Dalley, *Legacy of Mesopotamia*, 35–56, here 35.

45. Joachim Oelsner, "Incantations in Southern Mesopotamia—from Clay Tablets to Magical Bowls: Thoughts on the Decline of the Babylonian Culture," in *Officina Magica: Essays on the Practice of Magic in Antiquity*, ed. Shaul Shaked, IJS Studies in Judaica 4 (Leiden: Brill, 2005), 30–51, here 36–41; Dalley, "Occasions and Opportunities 2," 41–42.

46. Dalley, "The Sassanian Period and Early Islam, c. A.D. 224–651," in Dalley *Legacy of Mesopotamia*, 163–64. Furthermore, the Zoroastrian tale of King Jamshid (Yima) notes that Jamshid ruled the entire world in peace but, on three occasions, had to expand the world due to overpopulation (*Yašt*. 19). In the earlier Babylonian Epic of Atrahasis, Atrahasis too must expand the world's borders on three occasions due to overpopulation. See ibid., 172–73, for further analysis of the parallels between these two texts.

medical traditions and specific demons in Babylonian rabbinic literature.[47] My reading of b. Ḥul. 105b–106a is situated within this larger project. Yet here it is not a specific demon but a larger discursive trend that has found its way into later rabbinic texts. However, unlike in these ancient Mesopotamian texts, in the narrative of b. Ḥullin the demon is not neutral but positive, an attendant to the rabbinic community who is punctilious in his observance. The demon's punctiliousness is best understood as part of a broader rabbinic discursive move that subjugated demons to rabbinic halakha and thus to the rabbis themselves.

Demons as Subjects in the Rabbinic World

The particular discursive move that subjugated demons to the rabbis also functioned to construct demons as legal subjects and actors within the rabbinic system. The implications of this move can be seen in the story attached to another of Abaye's statements in the same *sugya* in b. Ḥullin.

> א' אביי מריש ה"א האי דלא יתבי תותי מרזבא משו' שופכי' ולא היא א' לי מר משו' דשכיחי תותי מזיקין הנהו שקולאי דהוו קאדרי חבית' דחמרא בעו לאיתפוחי אותבוה תותי מרזבא פקע אתו לקמי' דמר בר רב אשי שמתיה אתא לקמי' א"ל היכי לעביד ההוא גבר' כי אותביה באוניא א"ל אפי' הכי בדוכת' דשכיח' רבים מי אית לן רשותא למיתבר[48] את שנית זיל שלים א"ל השת' לית לי זימנ' קבע לי ואפרע קבע לי[49] זימנא ולא אתא בזימנ' כי אתא א"ל אמאי לא אתית בזימנך א"ל כל מילי דצייר וחתים וכייל ומנו' לית לן רשותא לישקול מיניה עד דמ(סקינן)[שכחינן] דהפקירא[50]

> Abaye said: At first, I thought that the reason that we do not sit under a rain spout was because of run-off. But it is not so. The Master told me: it is because demons are common there.
>
> Certain porters were once carrying a barrel of wine. Wanting to rest, they placed the barrel under a rain spout. The barrel burst. They went before Mar b. Rav Ashi. He banned [the demon].[51] [The demon] came

47. See Mark J. Geller, "Akkadian Healing Therapies in the Babylonian Talmud," in *Max-Planck-Institut für Wissenschaftsgeschichte* Preprint (2004); idem, "An Akkadian Vademecum in the Babylonian Talmud," in *From Athens to Jerusalem: Medicine in Hellenized Jewish Lore and in Early Christian Literature*, ed. Samuel Kottek and Manfred Horstmanshoff (Rotterdam: Erasmus, 2000), 13–32; and Avigail Manekin Bamberger, "An Akkadian Demon in the Talmud: Between Šulak and Bar-Širiqa," *JSJ* 44 (2013): 282–87, respectively.

48. למיתבר. Translated here according to the reading of the other manuscripts: למיתב.

49. לי. Translated according to the reading of the other manuscripts: ליה; לי'.

50. Presented here according to MS Vatican 123b.

51. This expression, שמתיה, "he banned him," has parallels in both verb and noun forms in reference to demons in the incantation bowls: Bo. 82:6, 14:9, 106:4, 90:2, in Michael Sokoloff, *A Dictionary of Jewish Babylonian Aramaic of the Talmudic and Geonic Periods* (Ramat

> before [Mar b. Rav Ashi], and said to him: What should I have done to those men, for they placed [the barrel] on my ear?! [Mar b. Rav Ashi] said to him: Even so, in a place where people are commonplace, you did not have the right to sit [here]! You acted improperly, now go and pay [for the barrel of wine]. [The demon] said to him: I do not have the money now. Set a date on which I will pay. He set a date for him but [the demon] did not come on that day [to pay for the barrel.] When he came [at a later date], [Mar b. Rav Ashi] said to him: Why did you not come at the appointed time? [The demon] said to him: We have no right to take anything that is tied up, sealed, collected, or counted, so we can only take things that are in a state of ownerlessness [and thus it took me longer to collect the money]. (b. Ḥul. 105b)

Abaye's statement about rain spouts leads to the story of a demon who is taken to court by human beings. The demon in b. Ḥul. 105b does not want to attack unsuspecting passersby. It is only when he is personally threatened that he retaliates. Even in his retaliation, he attacks not the men who placed the barrel on top of his ear but the barrel itself. The destruction of the barrel leads to a court case to determine liability. The demon appears before the court of Mar b. Rav Ashi to defend his actions. Mar b. Rav Ashi argues that the demon was obligated to pay better attention in a location in which humans are common and finds him liable. The demon is a law-abiding citizen with all the rights and responsibilities that this status entails. The demon's later apparent disrespect of the court's deadline for repayment is explicitly resolved as a matter *not* of rabbinic authority over the demonic. Instead it is due to a logistical difficulty in collecting the funds. Demons are legally restricted in what they can collect, and they obey this restriction. This example is one of a subset of Bavli teachings in which demons participate in rabbinic court proceedings as defendants and witnesses and are bound by rabbinic definitions and decrees.[52]

The demon in this story is constructed as defensive, rather than aggressive. Demons are beings with responsibility and agency who exist *within* the halakhic system, and thus they can be controlled by it and are liable to it when they disobey rabbinic teachings. This construction of the demonic runs counter to a modern understanding of the demonic as actively and independently harmful. In the Bavli's account, demons are essentially apathetic to humans, and when given the option, will avoid harming them. It is only when they feel attacked by humans invading

---

Gan: Bar-Ilan University Press, 2003), 1163. See also Markham J. Geller, "Joshua B. Perahia and Jesus of Nazareth: Two Rabbinic Magicians" (Ph.D. diss., Brandeis University, 1974), 87. In the Babylonian Talmud, it can also refer to the ban or excommunication of a person from the rabbinic community. See, e.g., b. B. Meṣ. 108b; b. B. Qam. 15b; b. Meg. 16b; b. Ḥul. 18a; b. Qidd. 70b.

52. See also b. Mak. 6b; b. Giṭ. 66a.

their personal space that demons lash out and cause harm. And even then, they are bound to appear in rabbinic courts and pay out the rabbinically decreed penalties for the harm that they cause.

The rabbis deal with the threat of multiple malevolent intermediary beings by subjugating the demonic to the rabbinic system, a move that is similar to the way that the rabbis treat a wide range of issues in their world. Using the same language and concepts as in issues of Sabbath law and holiday observance, the rabbis signal the imbrication of the demonic in their world and the seriousness with which they approached it.

The rabbis construct and constrain demons through halakhic discourse, and in so doing, they protect themselves and their followers from demonic harm. Thus, for example, in an extended *sugya* at b. Pesaḥ. 109b–112a, the rabbis use a discussion of the ritual meal on the first night of Passover as a springboard to discussing when and why demons might be provoked into attacking human beings, and how to avoid that provocation. But in framing demonic attack as responding to human provocation, the rabbis construct demons as inherently nonaggressive and neutral, except when responding to exigent circumstances.

Serving the Rabbinic Project

In constructing the demonic as relatively neutral and passive, the rabbis situate the demonic spatially within the rabbinic world. For the Babylonian rabbis, demons are found not only in their households and courtyards (b. Pesaḥ. 109b–112a) but in their houses of study (b. Giṭ. 68a)[53] and rabbinic conclaves. One of the most well-known descriptions of demons in the Babylonian Talmud is found in b. Ber. 6a, which contains a series of statements all taught by Abba Benjamin, who, though cited as a Tanna, appears only in this one *sugya* in b. Ber. 6a:

> תניא אבא בנימן או' אלמלא נתנה רשות לעין לראות אין כל בריה יכולה לעמוד בפני המזיקין ואמ' רב יוסף[54] ואיהו נפישי מינן וקיימי [ע]לן בביסלא [לעוגיא] אמ' אביי האי דוחקא דכלא מינייהו והני כרעי (דמינפקן)[דמנקפי] מינייהו והני ברכי ד[מ]שלהי מנייהו והני מאני דרבנן דבלו מחופיא דידהו.[55]

> It was taught in a *baraita*: Abba Benjamin said: If the eye had been given permission to see [them], no creature could withstand the demons. Rav Yosef said: They are more numerous than we are, and they stand around

53. See also b. Qidd. 29b, discussed below, where the demon's location in the study house is to the detriment of the rabbis.

54. Ms. Florence II-I-7 reads אביי, though all other manuscripts agree with the reading of Rav Yosef in ms. Munich 95.

55. Ms. Munich 95.

> us like a mound to a furrow. Abaye said: The pressure at the *kallah* is from them, and the bruising of one's feet is from them, and the wearying of one's knees is from them, and the wearing out of the garments of scholars is from [the demons'] rubbing.

This text contains a series of statements that emphasize the ubiquity of demons in various parts of one's life and lays out a ritual that can be undertaken in order to make these invisible demons visible. Demons are forces found throughout the rabbinic world but are most concentrated in the places where the rabbis themselves teach and learn Torah. It is Abaye who identifies and locates these demons, the same Abaye who had to learn from his Master the true reason that some water must be skimmed from the top of water that is drawn. Rav Yosef compares demonic numbers to those of the rabbis, putting the two groups in conversation and contact. Like Rav Papa's demon servant, these demons are hardly metaphorical; their presence and proximity cause real physical effects to the rabbis with whom they share the space of the *kallah*, effects that can be read on the rabbis' clothing and bodies.[56]

Why are demons present at the *kallah* at all? Is it possible that demons appear at the *kallah* for nefarious purposes? If the demons are trying to harm the rabbis and the rabbinic movement, their efforts are rather ineffective. The rabbis certainly experience the demonic presence as uncomfortable, but it does not appear to be permanently or intentionally harmful.[57] In light of b. Ḥul. 105b–106a, another interpretation appears more likely. If demons are understood to be servants of particular rabbis, and subjects of the rabbinic movement, then it is reasonable to assume that they are also participants in the movement. And indeed, in b. Pesaḥ. 110a and b. Erub. 43a, a demon named Joseph functions as a rabbinic tradent and public teacher,[58] and b. Me'il. 17a depicts a demon working with the rabbis to

---

56. For a more extensive discussion of this passage in the context of Babylonian rabbinic spatial discourse, see Sara Ronis, "Space, Place, and the Race for Power: Rabbis, Demons, and the Construction of Babylonia," *Harvard Theological Review* 110.4 (2017): 588–603. My thanks to Natalie Polzer for originally pointing me to this passage. Some scholars have suggested that this text be read as a rabbinic parody of folk-belief in demons, rather than as a sincere rabbinic statement. Simon Dentith, *Parody* (London: Routledge, 2000), 1–54; Joanne R. Gilbert, *Performing Marginality: Humor, Gender, and Cultural Critique* (Detroit: Wayne State University Press, 2004), 1–72; Jerry Palmer, *Taking Humour Seriously* (London: Routledge, 1994), 57–92, have all argued that instances of humor and parody within communities point to exactly those communal issues that are most important and most sensitive. Leaving aside the question of whether this passage is indeed meant to be a parody, I argue that it is addressing issues of sincere importance to the rabbinic community in Sasanian Babylonia.

57. There is indeed only one example in the Babylonian Talmud of an unequivocally malevolent demon who attacks rabbis, at b. Qidd. 29b. This demon is both a significant outlier, and remarkably effective at injuring rabbis.

58. See also, possibly, b. Yebam. 122a.

oppose the harmful policies of the Roman Empire.[59] Where else would one find rabbinic teachers and supporters but at the *kallah*? Demonic presence at the *kallah* thus functions as a sign of their engagement in the rabbis' Torah and the rabbinic movement as a whole. The overcrowding they cause are an unintended side-effect.

Within a rabbinic world that constructed demons as subjects and agents of the rabbinic project, the fact that Rav Papa's household includes a subordinate demon who is punctilious in his observance of rabbinic teachings is not surprising.[60] Demons became literal subjects of the rabbis, an interpretive move that also functioned to construct and elevate the rabbis as the group best able to control these intermediary beings.[61] Having a demon servant must have functioned similarly to construct and elevate a particular rabbi over specific and/or generic intermediary beings. In light of this important function performed by demons, perhaps what is surprising is how *few* rabbis report having demons as part of their households.

Conclusions

Modern culture associates the demonic with evil. The Zoroastrians and Christians of late antiquity had the same negative association. Complementarily, these religions also associated demons with foreign gods and foreign peoples. Against this backdrop, the rabbis' construction of demons as neutral subjects of rabbinic law stands out as distinct. Rather than marking an "other," here the demon exists within the rabbinic community and adds value to the rabbinic household.

In the majority of rabbinic stories and laws about demons, demons are relatively passive and benevolent figures.[62] Demons were at worst capricious and dangerous when threatened, at best legal actors in the rabbinic system. The rabbinic construction of demons thus aligned in content with ancient Mesopotamian conceptions of the world. The traditions of ancient Sumer, Akkad, Assyria, and Babylonia evolved over thousands of

---

59. See discussion in Kalmin, *Migrating Tales*, 53–75.

60. That Rav Papa's household is the one that explicitly includes demons may be drawing a parallel to b. B. Qam. 35a, where an ox in the household of Rav Papa that had a toothache went into Rav Papa's brewery, uncovered the beer, and drank enough to act as a painkiller. In multiple talmudic passages (b. Pesaḥ. 113a, b. B. Meṣ. 65a), Rav Papa is described as a brewer, which explains why it was his ox that had access to large stores of beer. The language that introduces this story, ההוא תורא דהוה בי רב פפא parallels that in Ḥullin, ההוא שידא דהוה בי רב פפא. Rav Papa's household may thus have been known as one with a wider variety of beings with agency than most. My thanks to Beth Berkowitz for pointing out this text.

61. This point has been made by Jacob Neusner, *A History of the Jews in Babylonia V: Later Sasanian Times* (Leiden: Brill, 1970), 165, where he argues, in connection with this story in b. Ḥul. 105b–106a, that the rabbis used the demonic to enhance their own power and prestige.

62. The exception is b. Qidd. 29b, discussed above.

years, but the core nature of the demonic remained relatively unchanged. In Mesopotamian tradition, demons were extraordinarily complex figures who existed somewhere on an ever-shifting spectrum from god to human being. Though some demons were pure evil, such as Lamaštu, others were beneficent actors.[63] Most demons, however, were marked as neutral. In a world in which beneficent and malevolent deities battled each other for supremacy, those demons following the orders of the beneficent (victorious) gods were themselves characterized as good; those obeying the evil (losing) gods were understood to be evil themselves. Demons were dangerous to human beings, but the source of the danger was their function as servants of the gods and royal dynasties. Demons were an extension of a sprawling and capricious pantheon of deities, with all the complexities therein. Their hybrid and ever-changing natures were written on their bodies and depicted in art and literature. These essential features of Mesopotamian demonology had a long afterlife in the cultures and religions that emerged with the advent of the Achaemenid Empire and developed during the Parthian and Sasanian periods.[64]

The rabbinic subjugation of the demonic to halakha functioned as a response to unseen dangers in conversation with, and against, ancient Mesopotamian demonology and contemporaneous dualistic traditions. For the rabbis, demons functioned within a messy and multivalent divine system handed over to the rabbis themselves to construct and maintain. At times, demons even followed the dictates of God and the Torah as interpreted by the rabbis. As a result, demons were largely not harmful to those who also followed rabbinic teachings about demons.[65]

---

63. See, e.g., the demonic figure of Lamaštu in CT 227:6 in W. Farber, "Lamaštu," in *RlA* 6:441–46; Frans A. M. Wiggermann, "Lamaštu, Daughter of Anu: A Profile," in Marten Stol, *Birth in Babylonia and the Bible: Its Mediterranean Setting*, Cuneiform Monographs 14 (Groningen: Brill, 2000), 217–52. She appears in Sumerian texts with the name *DIM.ME*. See Francelin Tourtet, "Demons at Home," in *Dūr-Katlimmu 2008 and Beyond*, ed. Hartmut Kuhne (Wiesbaden: Harrassowitz, 2010), 143. See also the demon Pazuzu, who was often portrayed as an evil underworld demon with bulging eyes, sharp talons, and a snake-headed penis but was also a guardian against injurious west winds and functioned to protect homes, pregnant women, and infants from the evil demoness Lamaštu. For more on Pazuzu, see Frans A. M.. Wiggerman, "Pazuzu," *RlA* 10:372–81.

64. C. Mueller-Kessler, and K. Kessler, "Spätbabylonische Gottheiten in spätantiken mandäischen Texten" *ZA* 89 (1999): 65–87; James Nathan Ford, "The Ancient Mesopotamian Motif of *kidinnu*, 'Divine Protection (of Temple Cities and Their Citizens),' in Akkadian and Aramaic Magic," in *Encounters by the Rivers of Babylon, Scholarly Conversations between Jews, Iranians and Babylonians in Antiquity*, ed. Uri Gabbay and Shai Secunda, TSAJ 160 (Tübingen: Mohr Siebeck, 2014), 271–83.

65. A similar approach to the demonic can be seen in the construction of the jinn in medieval Islam. The Qur'an 6:112 identifies three categories of intermediary beings: angels, demons, and the jinn. There are "believing jinn" who function to attest to the superiority of the Qur'an for doubting humans. These jinn will be judged on the day of judgment and enter paradise if found worthy. See Jacqueline Chabbi, "Jinn," *Encyclopaedia of the Qur'an*, ed. Jane

And thus, according to the story in b. Ḥul. 105b, Rav Papa had a servant who was both a demon and even more punctilious than necessary about the dangers of evil water. This demon's place within the rabbinic household and his punctiliousness both mark him as a positive figure within the text. Moreover, in this context, the demon functioned as much to bolster rabbinic authority, rabbinic law, and rabbinic thought, as he did to fetch water for the rabbi's household.

Dammen McAuliffe (Leiden: Brill, 2003). In the medieval period, jinn become followers of Muslim laws and liable to penalties for breaking these laws. D. B. MacDonald et al. ("Djinn," *Encyclopaedia of Islam*, 2d ed., ed. P. Bearman, Th. Bianquis, C. E. Bosworth, E. van Donzel, W. P. Heinrichs [online at http://dx.doi.org/10.1163/1573-3912_islam_COM_0191]) argue that "their [the jinn's] legal status in all respects was discussed and fixed, and the possible relations between them and mankind, especially in questions of marriage and property, were examined." Jinn also begin to appear in the literature as servants to poets, saints, and religious leaders, and as students of Muslim teachers. See Amira El-Zein, *Islam, Arabs, and the Intelligent World of the Jinn*, Contemporary Issues in the Middle East (Syracuse, NY: Syracuse University Press, 2009), 2–48. The latter work, while problematic in its conflation of historical periods and writings, contains a number of primary sources from medieval Muslim thinkers that describe and discuss the jinn's subjugation to Muslim belief and law. My thanks to Sarit Kattan Gribbetz for suggesting this parallel.

Narrative Bricolage and Cultural Hybrids in Rabbinic Babylonia

On the Narratives of Seduction and the Topos of Light

REUVEN KIPERWASSER

Narratives migrating between the two major rabbinic centers of Palestine and Babylonia were frequently altered and underwent changes in their content and forms. This process may also have resulted in peculiarities and ambiguities. Sometimes, what seems odd to the reader involves an unknown topos. While this topos might be attested elsewhere, it is unrecognized by the reader. In the following study I will try to reconstruct a topos that stems from the common oriental background of Babylonian storytelling. The term *topos*, itself, is borrowed from ancient rhetoric. Its meaning has been expanded by Ernst Robert Curtius, and it has become a term for "commonplaces." These commonplace features are the product of the reworking of traditional material, particularly the descriptions of standardized settings, but can be extended to almost any literary pattern.[1] Early medieval Latin literature, for instance, inherited traces of motifs and fragments of plots from classical Greco-Roman literature and used them without being aware of their source. In this way individual texts may include elements that are not the invention of the author but belong to his or her culture. The idea of the "topos" has been criticized by scholars

---

I am happy to express my appreciation to Geoffrey Herman and Jeffrey Rubenstein, the organizers of the conference, and to the participants for their thoughtful comments on the first draft of this paper. I began working on this paper at the Frankel Institute of the University of Michigan and completed it while in Berlin as an Alexander von Humboldt fellow at the Free University of Berlin. I am thankful to both institutions for their hospitality. Different drafts of the paper were read by Yury Arzhanov, Tal Ilan, Dan Shapira, and Serge Ruzer. To them and to the readers and editors of the volume many thanks for their thought-provoking questions and comments.

1. See Ernst Robert Curtius, *European Literature and the Latin Middle Ages*, trans. Willard R. Trask (New York: Pantheon Books, 1953), 80.

who have questioned whether literary texts can really transmit their literary DNA to the following generations of texts.[2] However, the presence in modern literary tradition of these unrecognized textual remnants from the distant past has now become accepted by literary critics.

I would like to identify in the text of the Bavli remnants of what I believe to be the literary repository of the common culture of the region in which this literature was created. Here I will propose the existence of the topos of seduction, or of the manifestation of a "visual eros" consisting of the following elements: (1) the appearance of a beautiful person produces light in the eye of a spectator; and (2) the absorption of the light of beauty is physical, and its incorporation in the body of the spectator can have far-reaching consequences. These elements of the reconstructed topos are quite similar in narratives of both the Palestinian and the Babylonian rabbis. There is a difference, however, between the two corpora as to the consequences of the reaction caused by the light of beauty. According to the Babylonian understanding of the physiology of desire, the incorporation of this light energy can destroy the body (or the personality),[3] and its influence could be fatal to those who fail to resist the fire of temptation.

Light can be an ambivalent symbol. Sometimes it plays a role in the manifestation of holiness or even of the Divine Presence, and there are many well-known examples thereof.[4] Yet sometimes the appearance of light expresses desire, lust, and seduction. There is no necessary link between these two processes of metaphor production, though a connection cannot be completely ruled out.[5]

Notions of ocular desire are not unique to the rabbis. As Blake Leyerly puts it, "The Ancient Greeks had understood Eros to be a pathology of the eyes."[6] Modern science describes vision as the result of light reflecting off the surface of an object and continuing until it reaches the eye and stimulates the rods and cones of the retina. This nerve stimulation is transmitted, upside down, via the optic nerve to the brain. Here, the images from

2. See Antoine Compagnon, *Le démon de la théorie: Littérature et sens commun*, La couleur des idées (Paris: Seuil, 1998), 224.

3. These two components are the same.

4. See Umberto Eco, *Art and Beauty in the Middle Ages*, trans. Hugh Bredin (1986; repr., New Haven: Yale University Press, 2002), 47–50. See also Sverre Aalen, *Die Begriffe 'Licht' und 'Finsternis' im Alten Testament im Spaetjudentum und im Rabbinismus* (Oslo: Dybwad, 1951).

5. See Galit Hasan-Rokem, "Rabbi Meir, the Illuminated and Illuminating," in *Current Trends in the Study of Midrash*, ed. Carol Bakhos, JSJSup 106 (Leiden: Brill, 2006), 236.

6. See Blake Leyerle, "John Chrystostom on the Gaze," *JECS* 1 (1993): 160–63. An excellent summary of the topic can be found in Mark D. Stansbury-O'Donnell, "Desirability and the Body," in *A Companion to Greek and Roman Sexualities*, ed. Thomas K. Hubbard, Blackwell Companions to the Ancient World 100 (Oxford: Blackwell, 2014), 31–51. See also analyses of visual theories by Rachel Neis, *The Sense of Sight in Rabbinic Culture: Jewish Ways of Seeing in Late Antiquity*, Greek Culture in the Roman World (Cambridge: Cambridge University Press, 2013), 142.

each eye are merged and turned right-side up, creating a stereoscopic image. Greek and Roman philosophers, however, had different theories with which they described the process of vision.[7] One very near the metaphorical physiology of the rabbis is related in the *Timaeus* (45B–D) of Plato. The author articulates a theory of a visual fire. According to this theory, a ray emanates from the viewer's eye, touches a statue, and brings back an impression of the statue to the *psychē*. This theory also explains how someone could react to being stared at by another person, since the visual fire reaches out and touches him or her as well.[8] This theory shares several common features with the rabbinic one. First, they both regard vision as a tactile process, akin to touching. Second, they regard vision as something that touches the mind and soul directly. Thus, to gaze upon an object is to have it physically enter into oneself. To see something catastrophic or pestilent causes the body to react physically, since the grotesque sight is like a disease entering the body. To see something ideal and perfect is to learn and uplift the soul. To look at something beautiful is to see something that one then desires. Thus, if a man desires another person, he is inclined to consummate his desire. Ancient Greco-Roman thought was often preoccupied with situations in which a viewer sees a picture or a statue, which gives rise to desire for its subject that cannot be fulfilled by the object of the gaze.[9] An especially dangerous situation entailed seeing the body of a goddess or of a god that, as in the famous story about the mortal who fell in love with Aphrodite after gazing upon her naked sculpture, evokes such a strong desire that the lack of opportunity to consummate it brings the lover to distress, depression, and inevitable suicide.[10] To look upon mortal bodies is, for these authors, less hazardous but still produces

7. Among the earliest are Democritus and the atomists, who proposed that every object emitted a tiny replica or simulacrum of itself that traveled through the air and to the eye, and from there entered the soul (*psychē*) via the hollow channel of the optic nerve. Thus, while one is looking at an object of desire, a tiny replica of this statue enters his or her *psychē*, physically connecting with the viewer. See Stansbury-O'Donnell, "Desirability and the Body," 40–41.

8. Aristotle proposed a third theory. The air is filled with a moist medium called *pneuma* ("breath/air"), and movement in *pneuma* transmits impressions from an object to the moist eye and from there to the *psychē*. Vision is rather like sound moving through air or waves through water. See Stansbury-O'Donnell, "Desirability and the Body," 40–41.

9. See the story attributed to Lucian (*Amores* 13–15) and the analysis of Andrew Calimach, *School for Love: Gay Myths from Ancient Greece* (New Rochelle, NY: Haiduk Press, 2010), 91–92. Pliny offers a briefer version of Lucian's tale of a young man smitten by the statue: "They say that a certain man was once overcome with love for the statue and that, after he had hidden himself [in the shrine] during the night-time, he embraced it and that it thus bears a stain, an indication of his lust" (*Nat.* 36.20; see J. J. Pollitt, *The Art of Ancient Greece: Sources and Documents* [Cambridge: Cambridge University Press 1990], 84).

10. See Stansbury-O'Donnell, "Desirability and the Body," 44.

strong emotion in the viewer.[11] This idea, however, was alien to rabbis, and instead they discussed the situation of the forbidden object of desire.

According to many ancient thinkers, rabbis included, vision is capable of both arousing desire and transmitting lust. This notion lies behind many of the Jewish and Christian regulations concerning the male gaze. Moreover, the tendency of the ancients to valorize visual asceticism was shared by both Palestinians and Babylonians.[12] However, there are different nuances in how the metaphorical physiology of desire was understood in these different cultures and how they evaluated the consequences of the visual eros in the body of the seduced.

As stated by Rachel Neis, "Looking with desire was dangerous because vision, with its implicit connection to touch, was not a casual form of contact."[13] The manifestation of this danger is, according to her, that, when one is seduced by vision, he will perform acts of adultery or will visually imprint a fetus with his features—and this is true for both Babylonian and Palestinian traditions. I would nuance this observation in a number of ways. The Babylonians treated the power of visual Eros in more extreme terms and attributed to it destructive spiritual powers, as I will try to show below.

Though the main aim of this paper is to present a consistent narrative bricolage of a variety of new and old components in the Bavli, instead, I will begin from the first appearance of the nucleus of the above-mentioned topos in Palestine.

Seduced Soldiers and Charmed Customs Clerks

Genesis Rabbah 40:5[14]

[When Abram entered Egypt, the Egyptians saw that the woman was very beautiful (Gen 12:14)]. And where was Sarah? He had put her in a box and locked her up.

When he came to the customs-house, he [the customs officer] said to him, "Pay the custom dues!"

He said: "I will pay."

[ויהי כבוא אברם מצרימה] וגו' ושרה היכן היא,
נתנה בתיבה ונעל בפניה, כיון דמטה מכסה אמ'
ליה הב מכסה, אמר אנא יהיב, אמ' ליה מנין
את טעין, אמר אנא יהיב דמנין, אמ' ליה מטכ־
סין את טעין, אמר אנא יהיב דמטכסין, אמ' ליה
מרגלוון את טעין, אמר להו אנא יהב דמרגלוון,
אמ' ליה לית איפשר

11. Ibid.

12. See Neis, *Sense of Sight*, 146.

13. Ibid., 168.

14. See the analysis of the story in Joshua Levinson, *The Twice Told Tale: A Poetics of the Exegetical Narrative in Rabbinic Midrash* [Hebrew] (Jerusalem: Magnes Press, 2005), 220–23.

"Are you carrying garments?"
He said: "I will pay the dues for garments." He [officer] said: "Are you carrying silk?"
He said: "I will pay for silks!"
"Are you carrying precious stones?"
He said to them: "I will pay for precious stones!"
He said to him: "Nothing goes unless you open it and we see what is inside it!"
When he opened it the land of Egypt radiated with her luster.

עד דפתחת וחמינן מה בגווה, וכיון שפתחה הבהיקה ארץ מצרים מאורה.

In this story, Abraham, aware of his wife's beauty, hid her in a box like an expensive jewel. When, after unsuccessful attempts to persuade the customs officer not to force him to open the box, Abraham is compelled to do so, the light of his wife's beauty illuminates the entire dark country of Egypt. The consequences of the explosion of Sarah's beauty are not terribly dramatic, or, at the very least, the narrator does not indicate that they are such. Let us see, however, the more dramatic consequences in the following similar account, also from the Palestinian Talmud:

y. Sanhedrin 2:2

Shmuel the Elder taught before R. Aḥa: "And David said to his men, ['Gird every man his sword,' and they girded on every man his sword, and David also girded on his sword] (1 Sam. 25:13).
'And he railed at them' (1 Sam. 25:14) — what is the meaning of 'And he railed at them?'
He incited them with words.
'And now know and see what you shall do' (1 Sam. 25:17)
[It came about as she was riding on her donkey and coming down by the hidden part of the mountain, that

תנא שמואל הזקן קומי רבי אחא : 'ויאמר דוד לאנשיו וגו'
'ויעט בהם' מהו 'ויעט בהם'? אפחין במילין.

'ועתה דעי וראי מה תעשי ותפגוש אותם',
גילת שוקה והלכו לאורה
'ותפגוש אותם'
הוקרו כולם

behold, David and his men were coming down toward her;] 'so she met them' (1 Sam. 25:20).
She showed her thigh, and they followed on by its light.
'... she met them' — all of them had ejaculations."

Here, we have a part of an exegetical narrative about a biblical female figure, Abigail, interpreting 1 Sam. 25:17.[15] It turns out that when David and his soldiers met Abigail, who came toward them alone (as explained there, i.e., without her male guard and without any knowledge of her husband) she used an unconventional military device. Employing her beauty, she exposed her thigh. The midrashist proposes that the obscure word "hidden part" (בסתר) mentioned in the verse is not the hidden part of the mountain (וירדת בסתר ההר), rather a part of the female body that is usually kept hidden.[16] David and his men were thereby able to follow her in the darkness, and, according to the parallel version of this Palestinian tradition in b. Meg. 14a, were guided by it for two miles. In both cases,

15. The image of Abigail as a seductive woman has been noted by other scholars. See Shulamit Valler, "King David and 'His' Women: Biblical Stories and Talmudic Discussion," in *A Feminist Companion to Samuel and Kings*, ed. Athalya Brenner, Feminist Companion to the Bible 5 (Sheffield: Sheffield Academic Press, 1994), 134–35. She discusses, however, only the Babylonian version of the story and mostly its first part, which is not part of my discussion here. The Babylonian version has been analyzed for gender by Judith Baskin, "Erotic Subversion: Undermining Female Agency in *b Megillah 10b–17a*," in *A Feminist Commentary on the Babylonian Talmud*, ed. Tal Ilan et al. (Tübingen: Mohr Siebeck, 2007), 228–44. A short comparison between the Babylonian and Palestinian Abigail story versions was conducted by Daniel Bodi, "Was Abigail a Scarlet Woman? A Point of Rabbinic Exegesis in Light of Comparative Material," in *Abigail, Wife of David, and Other Ancient Oriental Women*, ed. Daniel Bodi, HBM 60 (Sheffield: Sheffield Phoenix, 2013), 66–78. According to this author, Abigail used seduction in order to divert the attention of her attackers. Bodi proposes that the use of the naked female body as a means of diverting the murderous rage of the warriors is a widespread literary motif in texts from Greco-Roman antiquity. However, the one and only Greco-Roman source that he presents is from Caesar's *Gallic War* 7.47, but there the women show their bodies in order to persuade the Roman soldiers not to kill the helpless population of the city and not in order to divert the attackers from themselves. All other stories where the nudity of women discourages the warriors are taken from Scandinavian myth and late medieval sources, which are relatively far removed from the traditions of the Palestinian Talmud.

16. These words were extensively interpreted in the Babylonian version of the story, but quite differently, as telling about the ritual impurity of the heroine; see Valler, "King David and 'His' Women," 135; and Baskin, "Erotic Subversion," 241. R. Raviv makes the unconvincing suggestion that the midrashist refers here to Isa 47:2–3 ("The Encounter between David with Abigail as a Tool for the Explanation of the Methods of Rabbinic Exegesis," *Oreshet* 4 [2013]: 107).

the seduction affects simple men: David's soldiers, or Egyptian clerks, but not the noble figures who, according to the Palestinian rabbis, exemplify ideal masculinity. The ideal masculinity of the Palestinian rabbis includes visual abstinence, which, consequently, leads the rabbinic student to holiness.[17] We do not actually know what the clerk's reaction to Sarah's light was. The narrator seems to mock the Egyptians, who have never seen good-looking women like this one from the Land of Israel.[18] As for the second story, the one and only consequence of the manifestation of the visual eros in this story is that all the males ejaculated while following the bright thighs of Abigail.[19] This is, of course, impious and it brings about the condition of ritual impurity, but the narrator seems to accept it as inevitable and not at all dangerous.[20] The soldiers' reaction, which is purely physiological, is depicted here in order to amuse the reader and no more. This is not a story of a spiritual trial aimed at shaping rabbinic concepts of danger and desire. It belongs to the genre of comic anecdotes, whereby male simpletons fall for the light of female beauty.

Unconsummated Desire in the Holy Land

y. Shabbat 14:4

In the days of R. Eleazar, a man loved a woman and he was in danger of dying. They came and asked him [R. Eleazar], "May she pass before him so that he may live?" He answered them, "Let him die but not [do] that." "May he hear her voice, so that he does not die?" He replied: "Let him die, but not do that."	חד בר נש רחם איתא ביומוי דרבי אלעזר וסכן אתון שאלון ליה מהו תיעבור קומוי וייחי אמר ימות ולא כן מהו ישמע קלה ולא ימות אמר ימות ולא כן
What was it [i.e. the details of the case]?	מה הוות

17. See Neis, *Sense of Sight*, 139–46.

18. Compare the story analyzed by Neis, *Sense of Sight*, 157.

19. For the motif of males suddenly ejaculating upon the mere mention of the femme fatale, even without her actual presence, see b. Taʿan. 5b; b. Meg 15a.

20. See Michael Satlow, "'Wasted Seed,' the History of a Rabbinic Idea," *HUCA* 65 (1994): 137–75.

R. Ya'aqov bar Idi and R. Yitsḥaq bar Naḥman: One [of them] said that she was a married woman; and the other said that she was single.	רבי יעקב בר אידי ורבי יצחק בר נחמן חד אמר אשת איש וחורנה אמר פנויה
Now so far as the opinion of the one who said that she was a married woman, [the ruling] is clear; but as to the one who said that she was single?	מאן דאמר אשת איש ניחא ומאן דאמר פנויה
Did not Bar Koḥa the carpenter love a woman in the days of R. Eleazar? And he [R. Eleazar] permitted him.	והא בר כוחא נגרא רחם איתא ביומוי דר' אלעזר ושרא ליה
In the former case [we deal] with a single woman; in the latter with a married woman....	כאן בפנויה וכאן באשת איש

This passage, slightly abridged for our purposes, appears apropos another discussion about cases in which the Sabbath laws may be suspended in order to heal a sick person whose sickness, caused by desire, is accepted as dangerous.[21] Such a person may demand an unorthodox therapy, which is completely inappropriate in a routine situation. The law is that a sick person, in this situation, cannot demand sex with a forbidden object of desire. Our passage intends to illustrate that any forbidden sexual relationship is unacceptable; hence, this passage does not, in the end, relate to the theme of Sabbath laws that may be violated for the purpose of healing. All we have here is the apposition of two different cases of unconsummated desire—a very unhealthy condition that can lead to death if the tempted man is not allowed to violate a forbidden woman. In the first case, in the days of R. Eleazar, the rabbi forbade such a man to have sex with the women so as to cure him. In the similar case, however, also in the days of R. Eleazar, the rabbi permitted sex as a cure. The nuclear form of this story did not even mention whether the women was married as the reason for her being forbidden This detail was added in the following Amoraic discussion. It seems that originally the apposition of the cases was created in order to meditate on the question of whether unconsummated desire can kill. R. Eleazar was quite skeptical of the claim that unfulfilled desire might lead to death and did not view it as a dangerous illness. Furthermore, the man had obviously survived, since the narrator would otherwise have mentioned his death.[22] R. Eleazar shared the

21. See Barry S. Wimpfheimer, *Narrating the Law: A Poetics of Talmudic Legal Stories*, Divinations (Philadelphia: University of Pennsylvania Press, 2011), 42.

22. The same passage includes two stories about rabbinic Jews cured by the name of

belief of Bar-Koḥa the carpenter[23] that this unconsummated desire would kill him and permitted him to engage in therapeutic sex.[24] Obviously we are dealing here with popular conceptions of health and desire, which were not shared by the entire rabbinic community in the Tannaitic period. With time,[25] cases of ordinary men demanding the use of women for the immediate gratification of their sexual needs, claiming that otherwise they would die, lost their relevance, as attested by the teachings of the Amoraim, and were included in the discussion of Sabbath law. Thus, we can see that the idea of the fatal power of desire was known in rabbinic Palestine but was not highly valued.

Fall of Light in Babylonia

Let us now discuss one example of this topos in the Bavli. By analyzing this topos we will be able to discover how it was employed as a metaphor of desire and as a means of coping with seduction in the cultures of both

---

Jesus or by items of pagan worship. Only in one case does the narrator state that the remedy did not work and that the person who was healed died.

23. In reading this short legal narrative I differ from Wimpfheimer, who ascribed to the name of this character a symbolic meaning, arguing as follows (*Narrating the Law*, 45–46): "One might accept as a coincidence the fact that the identical scenario of a lovesick dying patient came before R. ʾElʿāzār. It is more difficult to accept such a coincidence when the figure in the story is given the allegorical name Bar Koha Nagra [*sic*]. The name literally translates as 'the one with the strength to hollow out.' The phallic semantics of such a name are too obvious to plumb, as is the fact that the name is related to the function of the character in this narrative. R. ʾElʿāzār literally permits 'the one with the strength to hollow out' in this narrative." His proposed translation and transliteration, however, are problematic. The most common meaning of נגרא is a carpenter, i.e., *nagara*. The sense "to hollow" might only be understood as the basis for the name of the strange bird called נגר טור. In this case, however, one can assume that this is merely the result of the phonetic proximity of *nagar* and *naqar*. Thus, in Lev. Rab. 22:4 (ed. Margoliot, 507) according to MS Munich we find: חד נגר טור הוה יתיב ומנקר. Unfortunately, the original version is not reflected in the main text. See too other expressions in Michael Sokoloff, *A Dictionary of Jewish Palestinian Aramaic of the Byzantine Period*, 2nd ed. (Ramat Gan: Bar-Ilan University Press, 2002), 341 (hereafter Sokoloff, *DJPA*). The word כוחא does not mean "strength" in Aramaic. In this case Wimpfheimer would have to argue that the narrator meant the Hebrew word כח in an Aramaized form, which is doubtful. It actually means "lizard" (see Sokoloff, *DJPA* 255), and we would seem to have here a playful name. Although this is the only attestation of such a name, it could still be a real name. See Tal Ilan, *Lexicon of Jewish Names in Late Antiquity*, part 2, *Palestine 200–650*, TSAJ 126 (Tübingen: Mohr Siebeck, 2012), 358.

24. Wimpfheimer rejects any historical meaning of this story, claiming, "Rather than taking the story as a historical possibility, I presume that the redactor of this sugya needed a way to challenge the view of the unmarried amora and did so by claiming a Tannaitic contradiction with another legal narrative" (*Narrating the Law*, 46).

25. See Reuven Kiperwasser, "The Immersion of Baallei Qerain," *JSQ* 19 (2012): 311–38.

the Babylonian rabbis and Syrian Christians. We shall begin with a highly significant seduction story about ʿAmram the Pious (Ḥasida).[26]

The story is presented in the context of the discussion on the rule "If there are men in the inner chamber and women in the outer, we fear intimacy" (b. Qidd. 81a). As we will see, the story represents a situation in which men and women are in different rooms, but fear is voiced not regarding the observance of the halakhic norm of intimacy but rather regarding something much more profound and culturally significant.

b. Qiddushin 81a[27]

Certain captive women came to Nehardea. They were brought up to the house of Rav ʿAmram the Pious, and the ladder was removed from under them. As one passed by, a light fell through the opening; Rav Amram

'הנך שבייאתא דאתי לנהרדעא,
אסוקינהו לבי רב עמרם חסידא
<אשקולו דרגא מקמייהו>,[28]
בהדי דקא חלפא חדא מינייהו נפל נהורא
באיפמא[29]
שקליה רב עמרם[30] לדרגא <דלא הוו יכלין

26. See Ishay Rosen-Zvi, "The Evil Impulse, Sexuality and *Yichud*: A Chapter of Talmudic Anthropology" [Hebrew], *Theory and Criticism* 14 (1999): 55–84. This story is briefly mentioned in his book, *Demonic Desires: 'Yetzer Hara' and the Problem of Evil in Late Antiquity*, Divinations (Philadelphia: University of Pennsylvania Press, 2011), 124. See also Ido Hevroni, "'Gira be-Eyney de-Satan': Contexts and Meaning in a Talmudic Polemic Story" [Hebrew], *Jerusalem Studies in Hebrew Literature* 23 (2009): 15–51.

27. This source is discussed by Sagit Mor, "The Status of Female Captives on their return to the Jewish Community in the Talmudic Literature" [Hebrew], *Jewish Studies* 42 (2003–2004): 107–18. Mor took for her analyses the version of MS Munich 95. I prefer here the version of the old Spanish print, which seems to me more consistent. See also Laliv Clenman, "The Fire and the Flesh: Self-Destruction of the Male Rabbinic Body," in *The Body in Biblical, Christian and Jewish Texts*, ed. Joan E. Taylor, LSTS 85 (London: Bloomsbury T&T Clark, 2014), 210–25, esp. 217–18.

28. This sentence is an emendation according to the Venice printing, Hagadot Ha-Talmud and Ein Yakov.

29. I think that the version of Spanish Printing, נפל נהורא באיפמא, supported by MS Munich and others, is preferable to the reading in some of the other versions. Some authors have been charmed by the version of MS Vatican 111: נפל (ריחיא)[זיהרא] באיפומיא; see below. However, the manuscript there is difficult to decipher, and even if we accept the version of the author of the Arukh, who read זיהרא in his manuscript, we can still say that this transformation of the version could easily be explained by graphic proximity of the two letters that have been switched, ז and ס. See and compare the similar phenomenon in the Syriac text, below n. 59. I am not, therefore, convinced by the explanation proposed by Mor ("Status of Female Captives," n. 23). The opposite explanation is equally plausible, namely, that the זיהרא version was influenced by the expression found in the description of R. Yoḥanan's beauty in b. B. Meṣ. 84a: זהרורי.

30. The scribe or the printer has mistakenly copied the name ʿAmram twice here, and I have corrected it.

seized the ladder, that ten men could not raise, and he alone set it up and proceeded to ascend. When he had gone half way up the ladder, he cried out, "A fire in the house of ʿAmram! Fire in the house of ʿAmram!"

The rabbis came and told him, "We are embarrassed (by you)!"

He said to them: "It is better that you be embarrassed by me in this world than that you be embarrassed by me in the world to come." He adjured his yeṣer to depart from him, and it issued forth from him in the shape of a fiery branch of the date tree. He said to it: "Behold! You are of fire/light and I am of flesh, yet I am preferable to you."

בי עשרה למדלייא, דלייא לחודיה>[31]
אותביה וקא סליק ואזיל, כי מטא לפלגיה דדרגא
רמא קלא: 'אפשח[32] נורא בי עמרם נורא בי
עמרם'
אתו רבנן אמרו ליה כסיפתין
אמר להו מוטב תכספו מנאי בהדין עלמא
ולא תכספו מינאי לעלמא דאתי
אשבעיה ליצריה דנפקת מינאי ונפק מיניה
כי דיקלא דנורא[33] אמר ליה חזי דאת מנורא
ואנא מכשרא ואנא עדיפנא מינך

Let us fill in the details of this remarkable story. Seemingly, a troop of Persian soldiers on their way to Ctesiphon pass through Nehardea with all their war trophies and also with one of the most expensive and desirable commodities at the royal courts—beautiful captive women.[34] The circumstances require that all the troops, female captives, and male captors spend

31. This sentence is an emendation according to Hagadot Ha-Talmud. Mor preferred to see it as an addition during transmission. However, it seems to me better explained as a logical development of the exposition of the story.

32. This word appears here in the right place. In Munich 95 it appears twice—before and after the exclamation of the hero. See recently J. N. Ford, "Three Hapax Legomena in the Babylonian Talmud," *Mus* 130 (2017): 1–30, esp. 10. This repetition might signify literary enforcement of the narrator, but more probably it should be attributed to scribal error. Cf. Mor, "Status of Female Captives," n. 25.

33. According to Munich 95 'כי דיקול' דנור' and in Spanish Print: כי דיקלא דנורא. I fully agree with Mor that this version is preferable. While the expression עמודה דנורא is quite common in the Bavli (see b. Mo'ed Qat. 25a–b; b. Naz. 60b; b. Ketub. 77b), it would be interesting to explore whether on some of these occasions the manuscripts use the expression דיקלא דנורא. A branch of fire stemming from the body of the human being as evidence of the divine intervention in his body appears also in b. Taʿan. 25a—צוציתא דנורא . This expression, albeit in a completely different context, appears in b. B. Bat. 73a (I will deal with this motive in my forthcoming paper, "Facing the Omnipotence"). The term has been the subject of considerable discussion; see, e.g., Daniel Boyarin,"Lĕ-Leqsiqon Ha-Talmudi," *Tarbiṣ* 50 (1981): 164–91. Ṣuṣita is a special name for a stalk that grows from grain. In a figurative sense, this is a strand of hair growing from the head or fringes freely flowing out of clothes (ibid., 169-70). However, it would seem that behind the usage of these two terms, "the palm of fire" or "the branch of fire," lies the same metaphorical conception that divine fire in the human body produces some miraculous vegetation growing from the body in the form of branch.

34. Nothing in the story itself suggests that we are dealing here with redeemed cap-

the night in Nehardea. Therefore, precautions are taken and the female captives are housed in the attic belonging to Rav ʿAmram the Pious, and the heavy ladder providing access to the attic is removed. In the dark of night one of the women passes along the edge of her temporary residence and Rav ʿAmram the Pious notices her. The expression *nafal nehora,* "light fell," is curious. Does it mean that a woman was above while the men stood below, and the light descended through the aperture?

This would not be a literal vertical *fall* of light but rather a metaphorical spreading of light. Normally, the diffusion of physical light is expressed by the expressions *ba* ("come") or, in Aramaic, *isgi*. In a few cases, when the dispersal of light comes in connection with *nafal* in the Babylonian Talmud, it is either associated with the light of the planets and stars or with the light of seductive beauty, as is the case here. However, if the light of the stars indeed falls from on high, the metaphorical "light-fall," accompanied by the appearance of beauty, always results in the kindling of human passion.

Let us observe the results of the fall of light, or rather, as I shall interpret it, the fall of fire. The fire of beauty ignites the fire of desire in the body of Rav ʿAmram the Pious, who now brings the ladder, easily climbs up, reaching halfway and then roars out: "Fire in the house of ʿAmram!"[35] This is to say that the light of beauty has kindled fire in his body and he may perish in the flames. After all, the transformation of *nehora* (light) to *nura* (fire) is very easy both phonetically and semantically.[36] Consequently, after his colleagues find Rav ʿAmram the Pious in his pajamas, so to speak, on the steps of the ladder and are ashamed by what they see, ʿAmram has an opportunity to explain the nature of desire as a product of fire. Moreover, he can declare his human victory over the power of fire. Thus, the narrator explains the physiology of passion in the following way: beauty casts a tiny amount of light/fire, which connects with the "fire" within the body, namely, the *yeṣer*,[37] and from the destructive power of passion that comes into existence in this way the person is destroyed, like a building consumed by fire. Let us now examine a second story in which light falls.

---

tives, and that they are Jewish, as proposed by traditional commentators, and Mor, "Status of Female Captives," 114.

35. The expression רמא קולא אפשח נורא בי עמרם means that the hero shouted that the fire had spread throughout the entire metaphorical house, namely, the body of ʿAmram. The meaning of פשח, previously taken as "to break, tear," "to be torn" (see Sokoloff, *DJPA*, 942) means "to cry out" as demonstrated recently by Ford, "Three Hapax Legomena," 9–14.

36. However, I know this word pun only in this text. On the usage of *nehora* as a metaphor, see Adam Becker, "The 'Evil Inclination' of the Jews: The Syriac Yatsra in Narsai's Metrical Homilies for Lent," *JQR* 106 (2016): 179–207.

37. In other textual versions of this story, this important term of rabbinic anthropology is not mentioned but seemingly implied.

b. Ketubot 65a[38]

Ḥoma, Abbaye's wife, came to Rabba and asked him, "Grant me an allowance of board," and he granted her the allowance. "Grant me an allowance of wine."

"I know," he said to her, "that Naḥmani did not drink wine." "By the life of the Master [I swear]," she replied, "that he gave me to drink from horns like this." As she was showing it to him her arm was uncovered and a light fell upon the court. Rabba rose, went home and solicited Rav Ḥisda's daughter (his wife). "Who has been at court today?" enquired Rav Ḥisda's daughter. "Ḥoma the wife of Abbaye," he replied. Thereupon she followed her, striking her with the club of the silk weavers[39] until she chased her all the way out of Maḥoza. She said to her, "You have already killed three [men], and now you come to kill another!"

חומא דביתהו דאביי אתאי לקמיה דרבא, אמרה ליה: פסוק לי מזוני, פסק לה. פסוק לי חמרא, א"ל: ידענא ביה בנחמני דלא הוה שתי חמרא, אמרה ליה: חיי דמר, דהוי משקי ליה בשו־פרזי כי האי. בהדי דקא מחויא ליה איגלי דרעא, נפל נהורא בבי דינא. קם רבא על לביתיה, תבעה לבת רב חסדא. אמרה ליה בת רב חסדא: מאן הוי האידנא בבי דינא? אמר לה: חומא דביתהו דאביי. נפקא אבתרה, מחתא לה בקולפא דשיראי עד דאפקה לה מכולי מחוזא, אמרה לה: קטלת ליך תלתא, ואתת למיקטל אחרינא

Ḥoma, Abbaye's widow came to demand provisions from the estate of her deceased husband as well as funds for wine, which is not considered a necessity for a woman living alone. According to rabbinic law, the widow is allowed to drink wine if she was properly trained and instructed by her now deceased husband. The point of this story is that the judge, who was a close friend of the deceased Abbaye, knows that the deceased himself refrained from drinking wine, and he was therefore in a position to wonder how experienced Abbaye's wife could have been. Abbaye's spirited widow answered that the deceased used to pour her wine and briskly describes how big the glasses from which she drank were. While demonstrating the size of the cups she reveals her arm. The appearance

38. Commented upon by Shulamit Valler, *Women and Womanhood in the Talmud,* BJS 321 (Atlanta: Scholars Press, 1999), 92–94. Briefly discussed by Neis, *Sense of Sight,* 165 n. 233.

39. Here I have corrected this version according to MS St. Petersburg, because the meaning of this version seems more logical. According to the other versions Ḥoma was beaten by the straps of the chest. See Sokoloff, *DJBA,* 992.

of that part of her desirable body is so seductive that it leads to an unexpected reaction. It brings the judge to the bedroom of his spouse, leading to the *femme fatale* of our story being driven out of town.[40] However, let us concentrate on the first part of the story. The expression *nafal nehora* serves here to depict a potent and dangerous desire. Let us illustrate this with other texts:

b. Berakhot 5b[41]

R. Eleazar fell ill.
R. Yoḥanan went in to [visit] him.
[He] saw that he was lying down in a dark room. [He] bared his arm, light fell in the house.

R. Eleazar was weeping.
He said to him: "Why do you weep?
If it is because [you did not study enough] Torah, so we have learned: 'It matters not whether one does much or little, provided one's heart is directed to Heaven.' If it is because of [lack of] sustenance—one does not have the privilege of enjoying two tables. If it is because of [the lack of] children? This is the bone of my tenth son!"

ר' אלעזר חלש
עאל לגביה ר' יוחנן,
חזייה דהוה (ב)[?ג?]ני בבית אפל
גליה לדרעיה נפל נהורא בביתא

בכה ר' אלעזר
אמ' ליה אמאי קא בכית
אי משום תורה שנינו אחד המרבה ואחד
הממעיט ובלבד שיכוין את לבו לשמים אי משום
מזוני אין אדם זוכה לשני שולחנות אי משום בני
דין גרמא דעשיראה ביר

40. See Mordechai A. Friedman, "Tamar, a Symbol of Life: The 'Killer Wife' Superstition in the Bible and Jewish Tradition," *AJS Review* 15 (1990): 23–61, esp. 37–39; and see Tal Ilan, "Babatha the Killer-Wife: Literature, Folk Religion and Documentary Papyri," in *Law and Narrative in the Bible and in Neighbouring Ancient Cultures*, ed. Klaus-Peter Adam, Friedrich Avemarie, and Nili Wazana, FAT 2/54 (Tübingen: Mohr Siebeck, 2012), 263–78, here 267–68.

41. For discussion, see Louis Jacobs, "The Sugya on Sufferings in b. Ber. 5 a–b," in *Studies in Aggadah, Targum and Jewish Liturgy in Memory of Joseph Heinemann*, ed. Jakob J. Petuchowski and Ezra Fleischer (Jerusalem: Magnes Press, 1981), 32–44 (English part); David Charles Kraemer, *Responses to Suffering in Classical Rabbinic Literature* (New York: Oxford University Press), 195–98; Moshe Benovitz, *Talmud Ha-Igud: BT Berakhot Chapter 1* (Jerusalem: Society for the Interpretation of the Talmud, 2006), 201–3. The story is mentioned by Neis, *Sense of Sight*, 165 n. 233. Here the text is according to MS Oxford 366.

He replied to him: "I have seen your beauty and I weep, for this beauty will rot [in the] earth." He said to him: "On that account you may surely weep."[42]	אמ' ליה שופרך חזינא ובכינא דהאי שופרא בלי ארעא אמ' ליה על דא ודאי בכית

This last narrative in the series of stories about R. Yoḥanan as a healer and healed, tells of R. Eleazar being taken ill and visited by R. Yoḥanan, who notices that R. Eleazar is lying in a dark room. Thereupon R. Yoḥanan bares his arm and the room is filled with light.[43] Yet, seeing that R. Eleazar is weeping, R. Yoḥanan asks him why he weeps and immediately proposes solutions to all the possible reasons. If it is because R. Eleazar had not studied as much of Torah as he would have liked, we have learned in the Mishna (m. Menaḥ. 13:11), "It matters not whether one does much or little, provided one's heart is directed to Heaven." If it is because of R. Eleazar's poverty,[44] not every man has the merit of enjoying two tables (i.e., to prosper in both this world and the world to come). And if R. Eleazar weeps

42. The story concludes here in the version provided by the manuscripts. However, the Soncino printing reads: ובכו תרויהו' אדהכי והכי א"ל חביבי עליך יסורין' א"ל לא הן ולא שכרן' א"ל הב לי ידך' יהב ליה ידיה ואוקמיה, ". . . and they both wept. In the meanwhile, he said to him: Are your sufferings welcome to you? —He replied: Neither them nor their reward. He said to him: Give me your hand, and he gave him his hand and he raised him." This stereotypical ending appears in two previous stories and apparently was abbreviated here.

43. The sentence in which baring one's arm and light falling appear is impersonal. Jacobs and Kraemer understood that, according to the narrator, R. Yoḥanan is the one who bares his arm, and the radiant beauty of his limb is in accordance with the description of his beauty in b. B. Meṣ. 74a. This reading fits well with the subsequent statement by R. Eleazar, who says, at least in some textual versions, "I saw your beauty." Benovitz, however, maintains that the bare arm belongs to R. Eleazar. He sees in our story either a product of intertextual borrowing or a free compilation of motifs that was transposed from their original context. First is the motif of the sage lying on his bed of illness and his arm suddenly exposed, which leads his wife to expose her feelings, Qoh. Rab. 11:1 (Benovitz mentions this source from Qohelet Rabbah, however a more ancient version of it appears in Pesiq. Rab Kah. 11:23, 198–99) and to weep about the "holy body" of her husband who is about to die. The second motif is about the same R. Eleazar, poor and hungry, falling asleep, while radiating a branch of fire from his head; b. Ta'an. 25a (I am preparing an article about this text tentatively entitled "Facing the Omnipotence"). It is quite possible that the baring of the sage's arm is a sort of topos used here, though I have certain doubts regarding the second motif, which I will discuss in a forthcoming paper. Benovitz's commentary, however, while innovative, does not fit either the grammar of the story (both the verbs "saw" and "bared" apparently connect to R. Yoḥanan and not to R. Eleazar) or the logic of narration: the beauty of R. Yoḥanan was known to the narrator, as was the poverty of R. Eleazar. Upon gazing on the visitor who brought the light of his body into the room that had been immersed in darkness, the young man was brought to tears.

44. See b. Taʿan. 25a.

because of 'children,'[45] R. Yoḥanan observes: "This is the bone of my tenth son." However, R. Eleazar answers that he is weeping because of none of these, but over the fate of beauty that will eventually come to dust.[46] This response seems quite reasonable to the elder sage and they both weep.[47] Then, as in the previous two stories, the healer asks, "Are your sufferings dear to you?" R. Eleazar then replies, "I want neither them nor their reward." Upon hearing this R. Yoḥanan says, "Give me your hand" and raises R. Eleazar from his sickbed.

This Babylonian story,[48] at first glance, has the same elements that are evident in the previous stories. The light falls in a dim room and causes difficulties. This light is the light of the beauty of a Palestinian sage, glorified eagerly on a page of the Babylonian Talmud.[49] In this latter case, however, this beauty is not the kind of beauty that can consume the spectator,

---

45. This probably means "childlessness." Therefore, he comforts the younger sage by indicating that the things could have been much worse, while the loss of child is even more painful. See Kraemer, *Responses to Suffering,* 198.

46. Recalling the two rabbis' lament over the mortality of beauty, one could say that they reflect thinking similar to the impressive Parthian hymn Angad Rōšnān, though neither had read or heard the hymn. Angad Rōšnān Vii: "Come yet nearer, and be not fond of this beauty that perishes in all (its) varieties. / It falls and melts as snow in sunshine. There is no abiding for any fair form. / It withers and fades as [a] broken rose, that wilts in the sun, whose grace is destroyed." See Mary Boyce, *The Manichaean Hymn-Cycles in Parthian,* London Oriental Series VII (London: Oxford University Press, 1954), 10-11, 156-57. See also Werner Sundermann, *The Manichaean Hymn Cycles Huyadagman and Angad Rosnan in Parthian and Sogdian: Photo Edition Transcription and Translation of Hitherto Unpublished Texts, with Critical Remarks* (London: School of Oriental and African Studies, 1990). This hymn expresses the same feeling of beauty that inevitably passes into oblivion without any hope of return, as snow that melts in the sun. The second image of the hymn is also close to the metaphorical language of the Bavli and recalls the description of the beauty of R. Yoḥanan in b. Baba Meṣiʿa and the saying found in b. Šabb. 152a: כי אתא רב דימי אמר: ינקותא - כלילא דוורדא, סבותא - כלילא דחילפא.

47. Weeping over the sad fate of beauty was so strange for Jacobs, "Sugya on Sufferings," 44, that he proposed, albeit not without trepidation: "What else but humour can be the meaning of R. Yoḥanan's declaration that he agrees with R. Eleazar when the latter states that he weeps for R. Yoḥanan's beauty eventually coming to dust. Now that is something to cry about." It is an interesting reading, applying to the narrator a somewhat sarcastic note. It is difficult to accept, however, even if the next story, which does not belong to the chain of healing stories, does have a humorous component. Jacobs's approach has been criticized by Kraemer, *Responses to Suffering,* 199 and 245 n. 24: "There is nothing humorous about suffering or in the deliberation on it in this text. Its striking him as humorous can only be on account of the immense irony of the scepticism which it expresses." Benovitz (*BT Berakhot Chapter 1,* 211), however, embraces Jacobs's explanation.

48. This story is the last one in the chain of stories that, except for this final story, is parallel to the chain of stories in Shir Ha Shirim Rab. 2:35. Although all the Palestinian stories were altered in their Babylonian redaction, as noted by Benovitz (*BT Berakhot Chapter 1,* 210), this story is a completely new Babylonian creation in which the narrator proclaims typical Babylonian values—the respect for life and a high estimation of the body.

49. See b. B. Meṣ. 84a.

and the passion is that kind of passion that cannot be realized within the rabbinic academy. The unacceptable passion component is transformed into the tears of the two men in a scene full of melancholy, nostalgia, and reflection on the struggle between life and death, whose end is known. The story invites the audience to think about talmudic aesthetics, though this is not our goal here. Interestingly, we are again confronted with the plot of temptation, and the metaphorical expression *nafal nehora* is used as a topos to express a mechanism of temptation: first a certain amount of fire falls, which allows the viewer to use this fallen fire to light up the dark room where the beautiful sage and his suffering student discuss important matters. As noted by Neis, "Rabbinic gender and sexuality is articulated by a paradoxically prohibitive gaze or by a complicatedly seductive visibility of Jewish male and (rabbinic) eros. By constructing their own masculinity in terms of a restrained gaze, and by conceiving of themselves as erotic objects of vision, the rabbis end up confounding a straightforward account of the male gaze or of masculinity." We can see here how the *nafal nehora* topos serves the narrator by expressing the model of masculinity, shaped by a very specific conception of male beauty. Male beauty is not a factor in the game of seduction, but it is the representation of an aspect of the divine.[50]

The exposure of men to the light of desire is conceptualized in the Babylonian Talmud with more force than in the Palestinian texts. We have seen a consistent development of the usage of the *nafal nehora* topos in the Babylonian Talmud and, even though the literary trope with metaphors of light and images of desire can also be found in Palestinian literature, it lacks this dramatic coloring of the struggle between death and life, as it is presented in the Bavli. The treatment of desire by the Palestinian rabbis recalls their counterparts in Roman culture. Roman writers often compare beauty to light and desire to fire and articulate the possibility that the tempted will die from the disease of love, but these are simply figures of speech. For example, the hero of Lucian's story "Lucius or the Ass" says to the woman he desires, ". . . you've been sending your invisible fire down through my eyes into my inwards parts and roasting me, even though I've done nothing wrong. Therefore, in heaven's name, heal me yourself, with that bittersweet treatment [meaning the abilities of the girl to please her partner sexually—RK] of which you've been talking and now that I'm already slaughtered, take me and skin me in any way you yourself please."[51] Afterwards they make an appointment to have sex together and

---

50. Cf. Neis, *Sense of Sight*, 158. The divine aspect of male beauty can be seen in the passage from Pesiq. Rab Kah. 10:3 (ed. Mandelbaum, 164.) I hope to analyze this passage among the others in a future study about rabbinic masculinity.

51. See "Lucius or the Ass," in *Lucian with an English Translation,* trans. M. D. Macleod (Cambridge: Harvard University Press), 53–148, here 62–63. See too *Lucian of Samosata, True*

both go about their business. It seems that despite the dramatic image of a danger that will kill the lover if he does not fulfill his desire, the trope is rather parodic and does not mean that the fire of love can cause any real disaster. Unlike their Western contemporaries, the Eastern late antique authors truly believed in their metaphorical physiology of desire and were aware of the dangerous consequences of the descent of the light of beauty. Let us bring evidence for this claim from nonrabbinic sources.

Two Attempts to Seduce Alexander the Great

Having seen the differences between the Babylonian and Palestinian texts, let us now go outside of rabbinic literature. Here, we observe that something similar to our Babylonian phenomenon is attested in the Syriac Christian literature. It is known that, unlike the authors of the Talmud, Syriac authors translated Greek literature into their language. Let us examine briefly a Syriac version of an apothegm told by many Greek authors.[52] We begin with the original Greek source.[53]

Joannis Stobaei Anthologium

Ἀλέξανδρος προτρεπομένων τινῶν αὐτὸν ἰδεῖν τὰς Δαρείου θυγατέρας καὶ τὴν γυναῖκα διαφέρουσαν κάλλει 'αἰσχρόν' ἔφη 'τοὺς ἄνδρας νικήσαντας ὑπὸ γυναικῶν ἡττᾶσθαι.'	Alexander, when some people persuaded him to look at the daughters and the wife of Darius, calling them especially beautiful, he responded: "It is shameful for men who won a victory to be defeated by women."

When Alexander the Great was invited to gaze upon the beauty of Darius's daughters, it may be assumed that the purpose of such a rendez-

History, and Lucius or the Ass, trans. Paul Turner (Bloomington: Indiana University Press, 1958), 67.

52. See Yury Arzhanov, "Regardons comment ceux qui fussent habiles à la sagesse élevaient ses âmes…": Les traductions syriaques des textes éthico-philosophiques," *Symbol 61: Syriaca, Arabica, Iranica* (Russian: Символ 61: Syriaca – Arabica – Iranica), ed. Nikolai L. Muskhelishvili and Nikolai N. Seleznyov (in Russian; Paris/Moscow, 2012), 217–37).

53. See Joannis Stobaei, *Anthologivm* 41 (5, 360 rec. C. Wachsmuth and O. Hense, vol. 3 [1884; repr., Berolini: Weidmann, 1958]), 268. This is the earliest Greek witness of the tradition. The story appears also in *Gnomologium Baroccianum* (I. Bywater, *Gnomologium Baroccianum: Sententiae graecae 263 e codice Bodleiano inter Baroccianos 50 descriptae* [Oxford, 1878], 50) and in *Corpus Parisinum* (Denis M. Searby, *The "Corpus Parisinum": A Critical Edition of the Greek Text with Commentary and English Translation: A Medieval Anthology of Greek Texts from the Pre-Socratics to the Church Fathers, 600 B.C.–700 A.D.*, 2 vols. (Lewiston, NY: Edwin Mellen, 2007), 2:645 [No. 405]), which is probably secondary to the work of Stobeus. This story was borrowed by Bar Hebraeus almost intact; see E. A. Wallis Budge, *The Laughable Stories Collected by Mâr Gregory John Bar Hebræus: The Syriac Text Edited with an English Translation* (London: Luzac, 1897), 14–15.

vous was clear enough.[54] However, the king refused because it is inappropriate for a man, who is a victor, to be "captured" by women in captivity. So far there is little in common between this story and our rabbinic temptation stories, except the assumptions that desire is dangerous and beauty captivates the captors. The Syriac translation of the story, however, differs significantly:[55]

ܐܠܟܣܢܕܪܘܣ ܡܠܟܐ ܒܢܬܗ ܕܕܪܝܘܫ ܒܫܒܝܐ ܕܒܪ ܗܘܐ. ܫܘܦܪܐ ܕܝܢ ܕܒܬܘܠܬܐ
ܠܗܝܢ ܐܝܬ ܗܘܐ. ܘܟܕ ܥܠܝܗܝܢ ܐܬܬܐܡܪ ܠܗ. ܐܦܠܐ ܕܢܚܙܐ ܐܢܝܢ ܐܬܛܦܝܣ ܗܘܐ.
ܟܕ ܐܡܪ ܕܒܗܬܬܐ ܗܝ ܗܕܐ ܠܓܢܒܪܐ ܡܬܙܟܝܢܐ ܕܡܢ ܢܫܐ ܕܫܒܘ ܐܢܘܢ. ܐܝܟܢܐ ܓܝܪ
ܕܢܘܪܐ ܡܘܩܕܐ ܠܕܩܪܒ ܠܗ. ܗܟܢܐ ܫܘܦܪܐ ܠܚܙܝܘܗܝ، ܡܫܠܗܒ ܠܗܘܢ ܒܪܓܬܐ.

> Alexander the King took captive Darius's daughters. Their beauty was very great, and when he was informed of it, he did not even want to look at them, saying: It is shameful for warriors if they are vanquished by the women whom they captured. Just as a fire is a hearth to whoever approaches it; thus is beauty to its observers, it inflames them with passion.

Thus, we again observe the familiar model of the physiology of passion that we saw in the story of Rav ʿAmram the Pious: beauty is a power that gives birth to a fire or a light, and the falling of the light into the body of the viewer has far-reaching consequences such that the viewer becomes a victim of the fire. The wise king refrained from seeing the beautiful daughters of the king in order to guard himself from the disastrous consequences of desire. The Syriac author's retelling of the Greek anecdote paints it with vivid local color, embellishing the narrative with the fire

---

54. This story is somewhat in dialogue with the famous narrative tradition about Alexander and the Amazons, the tribe of female warriors, which was metamorphosed in the Jewish sources too. See, e.g., Pesiq. Rab Kah. 9:1 (ed. Mandelbaum, 149); Richard Stoneman, "Jewish Traditions on Alexander the Great," *SPhiloA* 6 (1994): 37–53; Admiel Kosman, "The 'Man' as 'Fool-King': Alexander the Great and the Wisdom of Women," *CCAR Journal* 59 (2012): 164–68. On the myth of Alexander and different queens and princesses, see Daniel Ogden, *Alexander the Great: Myth, Genesis and Sexuality*. (Exeter: University of Exeter Press, 2011). Yury Arzhanov suggested that the narrative stems from some independent versions of the Alexander Romance (personal communication).

55. See Arzhanov, "Regardons," 217–18. For the English translation of this text, see B. H. Cowper, *Syriac Miscellanies: Or Extracts Relating to the First and Second General Councils, and Various Other Quotations, Theological, Historical and Classical* (London: Williams & Norgate, 1861), 43–45. For an edition with a German introduction, see E. Sachau, *Inedita Syriaca: Eine Sammlung syrischer Übersetzungen von Schriften griechischer Profanliteratur; mit einem Anhang* (Vienna: K. K. Hof- und Staatsdruckerei, 1870), 76–79. For the German translation, see V. Ryssel, "Neu aufgefundene graeco-syrische Philosophensprüche über die Seele," *Rheinisches Museum für Philologie* NF 51 (1896): 529–43. It is difficult to say if this expanded version of the story was produced by this Syriac author or if it has a late Greek prototype. The *Traditionsgeschichte* of this text is not my purpose here.

symbolism of his cultural environment. Also evident in the story of Rav ʿAmram the Pious, as in the story of Alexander, is the potential coupling between captives and captors and the embodied responses to the metaphoric fire. These are probably the fundamental features of the topos in question. The prototype of this narrative presumably involved a plot of a male captor and female captives with the captives' secret weapon being their power of seduction. Alexander's story remains close to the prototype. The story of Rav ʿAmram is close as well, but it is substantially reworked: the victim of seduction is no captor, but rather a rabbi who just happened upon the battlefield and was caught in the crossfire. The other two Babylonian stories that rework the fire/beauty topos emphasize the typical rabbinic values of dealing with temptation, responses to temptation, and *memento mori,* which overshadowed the plot of the beautiful female prisoner aiming to disarm her captors.

The Seduction of the Archons

One additional witness, also from the same late antique Mesopotamian realm, relates to the topos on which I have been, until now, focusing. Our previous seduction narratives, in which mortal men were seduced by luminous female beauty, will now be compared to a seduction narrative of theological significance, namely, the narrative of the seduction of the archons, a major theme of Manichaean myth. According to the Manichaean cosmogony myth, when the two ships of the light reached the zenith, the divine Third Messenger revealed his male form as well as his female form, also known as the Virgin of Light, to the female and male archons, the dark creatures, who are consequently caught up in a burning desire for him/her. The male archons then began to release the light they contain through their sperm. The Third Messenger hides his forms and filters the "light" from the sperm, which, having fallen back down upon the archons, was rejected by them and fell down onto the earth, half of it on the wet part, and half on the dry part. At this moment, the transmigration of souls began.[56]

Here is the same myth retold by the Syriac-speaking Christian author, Theodore bar Konai:[57]

56. An abbreviated form of that myth is preserved in the Coptic Manichaean work Kephalaia. See Iain Gardner, *The Kephalaia of the Teacher: The Edited Coptic Manichaean Texts in Translation with Commentary,* NHMS 37 (Leiden: Brill, 1995), 90–91. See also E. B. Smagina, *Kefalaĭa = "Glavy": koptskiĭ manikheĭskiĭ traktat / perevod s koptskogo, issledovanie, kommentariĭ, glossariĭ i ukazatel'ka* (Moskow: Vostochnaia literatura, 1998).

57. *Liber Scholiorum (Seert Version),* ed. Addai Scher, 2 vols., CSCO 55, 69 (Paris: Typographeo Reipublicae, 1910–1912), 2:316). The translation is based on John C. Reeves's translation, for which see https://www.academia.edu/5832898/Theodore_bar_Konai_on_Mani_

> When the vessels went and reached the midst of heaven, then the Messenger revealed his male and female forms, and became visible to all the Archons, the Sons of Darkness, both male and female.

At the appearance of the Messenger, who was beautiful in his forms, all the Archons were inflamed with lust, the males for the image of the female, and the females for the image of the male. Due to their lust, they began to [advance toward?] the light that they had consumed from the *five luminous deities* (ܘܫܪܝ ܠܡܬܩܠܘ ܒܪ ܠܘܬܗ ܗܘ ܢܘܗܪܐ ܕܐܟܠܘ ܡܢ ܚܡܫܐ ܐܠܗܐ ܢܘܗܪܐ).[58] Then the sin that was in them devised a plan. It mixed itself with the light {ܢܦܫܗ ܒܗܘ ܣܗܪܐ}[59] that came forth from the Archons like a portion (of yeast) in bread dough[60] and sought to enter within. . . .[61]

This Manichaean myth is a story of seduction performed by an androgynous entity known as the Third Evocation of the Messenger. This deity promenades nude before the bound captive archons, seducing males as female and females as male. Consequently, the males ejaculate onto the earth, while the females suffer miscarriages. All the forms of vegetative life stem from the male semen, and all the animal life from the female materials and the entire process occurred due to the power of the divine light included in the semen and in the miscarried fetuses.[62]

These texts relate a mythical plot full of symbolic meaning. Nevertheless, the same metaphorical physiology of desire underlies these stories as well. Beauty is a product of the divine light, and the desire evoked by beauty is a reaction of the dark creature releasing the amount of light that is embodied in his dark features. The release of the light will inevitably bring the dark creature to his death; for without this amount of light, he cannot exist. The conception of desire here is tragic: one must desire beauty, but consuming it, even visually, is fatal.

It would seem that Mani did not create this myth of light and desire *ex nihilo* but was inspired by notions that were, so to speak, in the air—commonplaces in Aramaic cultures of Mesopotamia. The popularity of Mani's doctrine stems from the fact that the ideas were rooted in the complex of

---

and_Manichaeism and John C. Reeves, *Prolegomena to a History of Islamicate Manichaeism*, Comparative Islamic Studies (Sheffield: Equinox, 2011).

58. On the Five Vital Powers and their importance to the light realm, see Timothy Pettipiece, *Pentadic Redaction in the Manichaean Kephalaia*, NHMS 66 (Leiden: Brill, 2009), 42–44.

59. All manuscripts read ܣܗܪܐ, "moon," which has been corrected to ܢܘܗܪܐ by most commentators (see John Reeves, *Jewish Lore in Manichaean Cosmogony: Studies in the Book of Giants Traditions* [Cincinnati, OH: Hebrew Union College Press, 1992], 204 n. 48; idem, *Prolegomena*, 150 n. 94).

60. See Reeves, *Prolegomena*, 150 n. 94, following Cumont; see Franz Cumont and M. A. Kugener, *Recherches sur le Manichéisme*, 3 vols. (Bruxelles: H. Lamertin, 1908–1912), 1:31 n. 2.

61. Reeves, *Prolegomena*, 150.

62. Ibid., 14.

concepts and beliefs broadly shared by the local population. The narrators of the Babylonian Talmud and the Christian storytellers did not learn the metaphorical physiology of desire from Manichaean authors but, like them, received it from the common culture. Moreover, as we saw above, the conception of the nature of desire and its connection to death is a part of the Eastern, or Mesopotamian, culture; while its Western counterpart, partially sharing the metaphors, is far removed from the pessimistic concept of the mortal danger of desire and pitiful fate of beauty in the world.

The Bavli stories discussed above are products of a narrative bricolage: a construction of a work from a diverse range of available themes. Nevertheless, behind them lies something deeper and more important: this is the not-fully-explicable process whereby people acquire objects from across different imagined communities to create new cultural identities.

Thirty-five years ago, Ilya Gershevitch, published a short lecture with a very ambitious thesis. He sought to find the source of the Manichaean concepts of beauty and its link to light. He proposed that beauty is actually synonymous with the living soul and that this conceptual proximity stems from the ancient Avestan notion that light, "more specifically daylight, and the sun, inasmuch as it is daylight, is 'the most beautiful creature' and has 'of all shapes the most beautiful shape,' namely Light is a Beauty."[63] The author based his thesis on various etymological interpretations of Manichaean terms in various Iranian languages. The attempt to uncover the sources of Manichaeism in the Avesta, related to a broader but by now far less acceptable tendency in scholarship to seek the origins of Manichaeism in Zoroastrianism, seems to me to be less compelling. Do we need to look for the sources of Manichaeism in the Avesta? Must we seek the sources of the unique traditions of the Bavli in Iranian lore? Perhaps we should resist the desire to trace the *origins* of the traditions and try to see them, rather, as evidence of cultural interaction.[64]

This study has consisted of textual readings and has sought to better understand the talmudic sources and to see them as belonging to the Mesopotamian civilization in Babylonia during the Sasanian period, which, according to the idiom of the Talmud itself, was all-inclusive.[65]

In this paper I have attempted to locate the metamorphoses of the literary traditions and changes in cultural patterns of the different rabbinic milieus that produced them. Following the ongoing scholarly undertaking

63. See Ilya Gershevitch, "Beauty as the Living Soul in Iranian Manicheism," *Acta Antiqua Academia Scientiarum Hungaricae* 28 (1980): 281–88, esp. 287.

64. On Zoroastrian elements in Manichaean lore, see Prods Oktor Skjærvø, "Reflexes of Iranian Oral Traditions in Manichean Literature," in *Literarische Stoffe und ihre Gestaltung in mitteliranischer Zeit: Ehrencolloquium anlässlich des 70. Geburtstages von Werner Sundermann*, ed. Desmond Durkin-Meisterernst, Christiane Reck, and Dieter Weber (Wiesbaden: Reichert, 2009), 269–86.

65. See b. Sanh. 24a: מאי בבל? אמר רבי יוחנן: בלולה במקרא, בלולה במשנה, בלולה בתלמוד.

to identify differences between these two rabbinic cultures, my own contribution is to argue that some of the innovations that were incorporated by the Babylonian sages derive from the realm of myth and folklore of the shared local culture. Many cultures lived together in Babylonia and interacted with one another, as well as with the cultures that preceded them. The Babylonian rabbinic culture and the culture of Christian authors drew from common sources and shared common values. Still, we do not know all the components of the cultural backdrop of these literatures.

My working hypothesis is that remnants of Iranian and even more ancient myths and stories persistently circulated among multiple cultures and are one of the principal sources for the changes the Babylonians made to their Palestinian sources. To explain the incorporation of these elements into rabbinic culture, I use the concept of transculturation, which involves cultural elements created through appropriation from and by multiple cultures, instead of the identification of a single originating culture.[66] This model is mainly extrapolated from the processes of cultural dynamics of modern times. Yet it largely corresponds to those processes that occurred in the Mediterranean and eastern cultures of late antiquity and were identified as phenomena of ancient syncretism. Therefore, when thinking about the cultural backdrop of the aggada in the Babylonian Talmud we have to abandon the old model of cultural influence, as when trying repeatedly to determine how much Greek/Persian/Aramean or even Christian elements can be found in the Babylonian Talmud. Instead we should try to understand how cultural hybrids were produced by this culture using their inherited topoi in new literary constructions.

66. See James Lull, *Media, Communication, Culture: A Global Approach*, 2nd ed. (New York: Columbia University Press, 2000).

"Meishan Is Dead"

On the Historical Contexts of the Bavli's Representations of the Jews in Southern Mesopotamia

YAKIR PAZ

> I took a slave girl captive [وسبيت جارية] and had intercourse with her for a while until we received a letter from 'Umar, "Consider the captives of Maisan [سبايا ميسان] which you have and release them." So I sent [her] back among those who returned and I do not know whether I sent her back pregnant or not. Indeed I fear there are men and women in Maisan descended from me. (Ibn Sa'd, *Tabaqat*)[1]

Introduction

Mesene,[2] the southern region of Mesopotamia, was considered by the rabbis to lie beyond the pure lineage boundaries of Jewish Babylonia.[3] Yet the

---

In writing this article I have benefited much from the suggestions and comments of my friends and colleagues whom I wish to thank: Simcha Gross, Kyle Smith, Yishai Rosen-Zvi, Michael Ebstein, Sergey Minov, Michael Shenkar, Idan Gilo, Giacomo Corazzol, Shlomo Naeh, Daniel Boyarin, and the editors of this volume, Geoffrey Herman and Jeffrey Rubenstein.

1. Muḥammad ibn Sa'd, *Biographien Muhammeds: Seiner Gefährten und der späteren Träger des Islams, bis zum Jahre 230 der Flucht*, vol. 7/1, ed. Eduard Sachau (Leiden: Brill, 1915), 92. Translation after Michael G. Morony, *Iraq after the Muslim Conquest* (Princeton, NJ: Princeton University Press, 1984), 238.

2. The name Mesene was pronounced and spelled in various forms: Hebrew/JBA:מישא (Mēšā), מישן (Mēšān), מישון (Mēšūn); Greek: μεσ(σ)ήνη; Syriac: ܡܝܫܢ (Maišān); Arabic: ميسان (Maisān), ميشان (Maišān); Latin: Mesenes; MP/Parthian: Mēšān, Mēšūn; Armenian: Մեշուն (Mēšūn); Coptic: ⲙⲁⲓ̈ⲥⲟⲛⲟⲥ. On some of the variants of the region's name, see Monika Schuol, *Die Charakene: Ein mesopotamisches Königreich in hellenistisch-parthischer Zeit*, OeO 1 (Stuttgart: F. Steiner, 2000), 276–80.

3. On the importance of genealogy and pure lineage in the Bavli, see Adiel Schremer, *Male and Female He Created Them* [Hebrew] (Jerusalem: Zalman Shazar, 2004), 147–58; Aharon Oppenheimer, "Purity of Lineage in Talmudic Babylonia," in *Sexuality and Family in History* [Hebrew], ed. Isaiah Gafni and Israel Bartal (Jerusalem: Zalman Shazar, 1998), 71–82; Richard Kalmin, "Genealogy and Polemics in Rabbinic Literature of Late Antiquity," *HUCA* 67

Babylonian rabbis were not content with this assertion alone but seemed to have gone out of their way to defame the Jews of Mesene, claiming that they were descendants of slaves, *mamzerim*, and genealogically inferior to those of the netherworld.[4] This tendency finds its most extreme expression in the following harsh indictment attributed to Rav (b. Qidd. 71b):[5]

> א"ר פפא סבא משמיה דרב: בבל - בריאה, מישן - מיתה, מדי - חולה, עילם - גוססת.
>
> Rav Papa the Elder said in the name of Rav: Babylon is healthy; Meishan is dead; Media is sick, and Elam is dying.

Mesene, from a genealogical point of view, "is dead," its lineage irredeemable, and it ranks the lowest among all regions. Such statements not only might have prevented marriage between the Jews of Babylonia and Mesene but could also have discouraged social interaction altogether. Indeed we are told a little further on in the Bavli that the inhabitants of the upper and lower Apameas—the latter in Mesene and the former just one *parasang* farther north in healthy Babylonia—did not even lend each other fire (וקא קפדי אהדדי ואפילו נורא לא מושלי אהדדי).[6] The animosity, it should be noted, seems to have been mutual.

Such a negative approach to the Mesenean Jews is somewhat surprising, since, although extremely scant, we do have evidence of an uninterrupted presence of Jews living in that region from the sixth century BCE

(1996): 77–94; idem, *The Sage in Jewish Society in Late Antiquity* (London: Routledge, 1999), 51–60; Jeffrey L. Rubenstein, *The Culture of the Babylonian Talmud* (Baltimore: Johns Hopkins University Press, 2003), 80–101; Michael L. Satlow, *Jewish Marriage in Antiquity* (Princeton, NJ: Princeton University Press, 2001), 133–61. The last three scholars also compare the importance of lineage for the Babylonian Jews in the context of Iranian culture, where genealogy and records of ancestry played a major role. For a purely literary analysis of the discussion of genealogy in b. Qidd. 70b–71a, see Moulie Vidas, *Tradition and the Formation of the Talmud* (Princeton, NJ: Princeton University Press, 2014), 81–112. Most of these studies do not take into account the historical context of the numerous geographical locations mentioned by the Bavli. See, however, Aharon Oppenheimer and Michael Lecker, "The Genealogical Boundaries of Jewish Babylonia," in *Between Rome and Babylon: Jewish Leadership and Society*, ed. Nili Oppenheimer, TSAJ 108 (Tübingen: Mohr Siebeck, 2005), 339–55.

4. See discussion below of these sources.

5. Following MS Munich 95. Cf. MS Geneve 31: אמ' רב פפא סבא <..>מיה דרב; Oxford 248: א' רב פפא סבא משמי' דרבא; Vatican 111: אמ' רב פפא. Cf. y. Qidd. 4:1, 65c: תמן אמרין מישא מתה מדי חולה. עילם וגבבאי גוססות. In Gen. Rab. 37 (ed. Theodor-Albeck, 350), where Mesene is identified with biblical Mesha (משא, Gen. 10:30), the version is: אלעזר בן פנחס אמ' מישא מיתה מדי חולה עילם גוססת. However, the attribution to R. Eleazar b. Pinhas is clearly corrupt; see already Heinrich Graetz, *Das Königreich Mesene und seine jüdische Bevölkerung* (Breslau: Schatzky, 1879), 41 n. 1. Throughout the article rabbinic texts are cited according to the *Ma'agrim* database, http://maagarim.hebrew-academy.org.il/Pages/PMain.aspx unless stated otherwise. Translations of the Bavli are modified from Isidore Epstein, ed., *The Soncino Talmud*, 18 vols. (London: Soncino Press, 1935–1948).

6. Further on this source see below.

through the Sasanian period and much later.[7] Why, then, were the Jews of Mesene singled out? Were they really descendants of slaves? Was intermarriage indeed more prevalent in Mesene? Did they not keep genealogical records?

Most scholars have taken the Talmud's statements at face value and have posited that indeed the Jews in Mesene were intermarried. So, for example, Michael Morony states matter-of-factly: "Jews of mixed descent lived in a place called Harpania near Maysan and in Maysan itself."[8] It is possible that there was more intermarriage in that region, in which case it would be important to ascertain the causes. We should be wary, however, of accepting the picture the Bavli provides as objective, since the Bavli's genealogical discussions are clearly fraught at times with politics, prejudice, and local patriotism.

Much of what was said by the rabbis concerning Mesene was most likely based not merely on specific genealogical facts but rather also on more general expressions of prejudice, as can be seen by comparing the Bavli's following statement in b. Qidd. 49b concerning Mesene with a similar statement found in a Syriac source:

עשרה קבים עזות ירדו לעולם, תשעה נטלה מישן

Ten *qabin* of impudence descended to the world, Meishan took nine.

Aharon Oppenheimer has suggested that "[p]robably the 'impudence' ... is also related to the dubious lineage of the Meseneans."[9] This indeed

7. Laurie E. Pearce and Cornelia Wunsch, *Documents of Judean Exiles and West Semites in Babylonia in the Collection of David Sofer*, Cornell University Studies in Assyriology and Sumerology 28 (Bethesda, MD: CDL, 2014); for the first century, see Josephus, *Ant.* 20.34–35 (discussed below). According to the Epistle of Rav Sherira Gaon (see Binyamin M. Lewin, *Igeret Rav Sherira Gaon* [Hebrew] [Haifa: Association for Jewish Literature, 1921], 102), Rav Ḥiyya, a Gaon in Pumbedita at about 700, came from Mesene. In the Muslim period the cities of Basra and Waṣit were significant Jewish centers. See, e.g., Jacob Obermeyer, *Die Landschaft Babylonien im Zeitalter des Talmuds und des Gaonats: Geographie und Geschichte nach talmudischen, arabischen und andern Quellen* (Frankfurt: I. Kauffmann, 1929), 336–40; Moshe Gil, *Jews in Islamic Countries in the Middle Ages*, Études sur le Judaïsme médiéval 28 (Leiden: Brill, 2004), 498–99.

8. Morony, *Iraq*, 307. Moshe Beer, a positivist, after citing the talmudic dictum that Mesene is dead, concludes: "In Babylonia—which had Torah centers—intermarriage was rare, whereas in the provinces neighbouring it in the Persian Kingdom, which were void of Torah, the Jews were assimilated through intermarriage" (my translation) ("The Political Background of Rav's Activities in Babylonia" [Hebrew], *Zion* 50 [1985]: 168). Cf. Samuel N. C. Lieu, *Manichaeism in Mesopotamia and the Roman East*, RGRW 118 (Leiden York: Brill, 1994), 8: "The Jewish teachers in Babylonia scornfully referred to the area as 'dead Mesene' in contrast to 'healthy Babylonia'; this does not mean that there were no Jews there but rather that they were there but had not kept dependable genealogical records." Cf. Jacob Neusner, *The History of the Jews in Babylonia*, vol. 2, *The Early Sasanian Period* (Leiden: Brill 1966), 258.

9. Aharon Oppenheimer (*Babylonia Judaica in the Talmudic Period* [Wiesbaden: L.

might have some truth to it. But a close reading of the larger context in which this statement appears reveals that it deals with generalizations and stereotypes concerning regions and people (e.g., Persia, Media, Arabia, Egypt) and not Jews or genealogy. Thus, Meishan here refers most likely to all the inhabitants of Mesene.

That we are dealing here with northern chauvinism toward the south (which, like any prejudice, might contain some truth) can be highlighted by the following report of the missionary efforts of Mar Mari in Mesene in The Acts of Mar Mari the Apostle:[10]

> [H]e moved to the province of Maishan [ܥܒܪ ܠܐܬܪܐ ܕܡܝܫܢ],[11] where he endured great difficulties and hard work. Though he worked very hard through Christ, he bestowed little benefit, in that only a few people came forwards to the fear of God. For the people of this region were particularly brutal, stupid, mundane, and fanatical in worshiping idols [ܚܠ ܕܗܠܟ ܓܢܒܪ̈ܝܢ ܘܣܟܠ̈ܝܢ ܘܥܠܡܢ̈ܝܢ ܐܝܟ ܐܬܪܐ ܗܘ. ܘܗܟܢ ܚܬܝܪܝܢ ܒܦܘܠܚܢ ܦܬܟܪ̈ܐ.].

Mar Mari was purportedly active during the first century. It would seem, however, that much of the anachronistic descriptions in the Acts reflect its time of composition, around the sixth century,[12] more or less contemporaneous with the redaction of the Bavli. As is readily evident, both the author of the Acts and the Bavli share a strikingly similar stereotype concerning the people of Mesene.

The Bavli's genealogical depreciatory claims concerning the Jews of Mesene should thus be treated with caution and are most probably a product of a complex mesh of reality and imagination. Yet even if we cannot always disentangle this mesh, it is no less valuable for our understanding of rabbinic and Sasanian culture to investigate the reasons, motivations, and anxieties that might have prompted such characterizations. Thus, in

---

Reichert, 1983], 254 and n. 56) refers to b. Qidd. 70b. Similarly Graetz, *Das Königreich Mesene*, 36–37: "Frechtheit galt als Symptom unehelicher oder blutschänderischer Geburt."

10. Text and translation after Amir Harrak, *The Acts of Mār Mārī the Apostle*, WGRW 11 (Atlanta: Society of Biblical Literature, 2005), 70–71, §31. The composition was most probably composed in the monastery of Dayr Qunni close to Seleucia-Ctesiphon (see ibid., xvii–xix). See below n. 90 for a similar description in the Kephalaia of Mani's failed efforts to proclaim in Mesene. On Mesene in the Persian Martyr Acts, see further Christelle Jullien, "Contribution des actes des martyrs perses à la géographie historique et à l'administration de l'empire sassanide (I)," *Res Orientales XVI: Contributions à l'histoire et la géographie historique de l'empire sassanide* (2004): 160; eadem, "Contribution des actes des martyrs perses à la géographie historique et à l'administration de l'empire sassanide (II)," *Res Orientales XVII: Des Indo-Grecs aux Sassanides: données pour l'histoire et la géographie historique* (2007): 93.

11. According to the Arabic version, Mari "went down to Dast-i-Maisan" (وانحدر مار ماري الى دستميسان) (text and translation Harrak, *Acts of Mār Mārī*, 84; 87). On this district, see below n. 75. A little further on it is said that "he entered 'Ubulla [الابلة], and in it he built a holy church." 'Ubulla, later known as Basra, was in the center of Dast-i Maisan.

12. On the dating of the Acts, see Harrak, *Acts of Mār Mārī*, xiv–xvii.

this article, I wish to contextualize the rabbinic perceptions of the Mesenean Jews.

In the first part of the study I will outline several of the distinctive geopolitical, economic, linguistic, and religious features of Mesene and argue that these may have contributed to the negative rabbinic perception of the region. In the second part of the paper, I will study a pericope in the Bavli that portrays the Mesenean Jews as descendants of the slaves of Babylonian Jews. I shall contextualize the story and argue that it should be read as a foundational story of Babylonian Jewry, which shaped its own genealogical identity by portraying the Mesenean Jews as slaves.

Part I: Mesene in Context

Around 140 BCE, Hyspaosines, a satrap under Antiochus IV, proclaimed himself king and founded a kingdom at the head of the Persian Gulf, in the surrounding district of the city of Charax (Karka d-Meshan), which he named after himself—Charax Spasinou.[13] This kingdom, which was known as Mesene, or in some Greek and Latin sources as Characene (Χαρακηνή derived from Charax), would endure for almost four centuries. During most of its rather turbulent history, Mesene remained an independent, although at times vassal, kingdom with a local dynasty and currency, constituting a distinct geopolitical entity.[14] Mesene, due to its strategic location, was an important center for international trade between the East and the Roman Empire.

Around 57 CE the Charcenean king, Attembelos III, pushed the borders of his kingdom as far north as the city of Apamea to what would be their fullest extent.[15] This seems also to have been the northern border of

---

13. The city was founded by Alexander of Macedon under the name Alexandria on the Tigris.

14. There were, however, short intervals of Parthian control. On the history of the Characenean kingdom, see the masterful study of Sheldon A. Nodelman, "A Preliminary History of Characene," *Berytus* 13 (1960): 83–121. For a recent comprehensive monograph, see Schuol, *Die Charakene*, which includes many primary sources, numismatics, and a historical overview, along with a very extensive bibliography. Yet Schuol does not use several relevant Syriac and Mandaean sources; the Jewish material is not well treated; and she pays little attention to the religious, ethnic, and linguistic aspects of Mesene. See Karlheinz Kessler's review in *AfO* 48–49 (2001–2002): 248–50. On Mesene, see further Maximilian Streck, *Die alte Landschaft Babylonien nach die arabischen Geographen*, 2 vols. (Leiden: Brill, 1900–1901), 1:280–333; Obermeyer, *Die Landschaft Babylonien*, 90–100; Oppenheimer, *Babylonia Judaica*, 241–56; John Hansman, "Characene and Charax," *EIr*, http://www.iranicaonline.org (all references to the *Encyclopedia Iranica* are based on the online version, accessed April 29, 2018).

15. As Nodelman notes ("Preliminary History," 104; cf. 110), "Under Attembelos II Characene rose from a mere district around the city of Charax to a considerable territorial state." On Apamea in Mesene (near the Seleias), see, e.g., Pliny, *Nat.* 6.31.129: "Tigris ... circa Apamiam Mesenes oppidum." For more sources, see Oppenheimer, *Babylonia Judaica*, 30–31;

the kingdom of Mesene when it was conquered by Ardashir in 221 CE and incorporated into the newly formed Sasanian Empire as the province of Mesene.

The southern boundaries of the area of pure lineage in the Bavli were very close to the administrative boundaries of this kingdom turned province (b. Qidd. 71b):[16]

עד היכן היא בבל? ... לתחתית בדיגלת עד היכא?
אמר רב פפא בר שמואל: עד אפמייא תתאה.
תרתי אפמייא הויין, חדא עיליתא וחדא תתייתא, חדא כשירה וחדא פסולה, ובין חדא לחדא פרסה, וקא קפדי אהדדי ואפילו נורא לא מושלי אהדדי,
וסימניך: דפסולתא – הא דמישתעיא מישנית

How far does Babylon extend? ... How far on the lower reaches of the Tigris? — Said Rav Papa b. Shmuel: As far as lower Apamea.

There were two Apameas, an upper and a lower; one was fit [in respect to marriage] and the other unfit, and one *parasang* lies between them; and they [their inhabitants] are particular with one another, and do not even lend fire to one another.[17] And the sign whereby [you may recognize] the unfit is the one that speaks Mesenean.

The administrative borders, unlike the genealogical ones, were not stable. The district of Kashkar (Waṣit) would later be carved out of Mesene and become an independent province. In some sources the creation of this new province is attributed to Khusro I.[18] However, as Geoffrey Herman has noted:

Getzel M. Cohen, *The Hellenistic Settlements in the East from Armenia and Mesopotamia to Bactria and India*, HCS 54 (Berkeley: University of California Press, 2013), 125–28.

16. Oppenheimer and Lecker, "Genealogical Boundaries," 343: "[T]he border which separates the two Apameas was identical to the political and administrative borders between Babylonia and Mesene." The existence of two Apameas is indicated in several classical and Arabic sources. See, e.g., Ammianus 23.6.23: "Apamea ... Mesene cognomina"; Cf. Schuol, *Die Charakene*, 281; and see Streck, *Die alte Landschaft*, 1:305–6; Hans H. Schaeder, "*Hasan al-Baṣrī*: Studien zur Frühgeschichte des Islam," *Der Islam* 14 (1925), 1–75, here 15–16; Obermeyer, *Die Landschaft Babylonien*, 86–88; Oppenheimer, *Babylonia Judaica*, 29–35; Schuol, *Die Charakene*, 186–87, 281. For an up-to-date survey, see Cohen, *Hellenistic Settlements*, 125–28.

17. On this Oppenheimer and Lecker note: "The business of borrowing fire is somewhat strange, for a parasang is not a negligible distance. This sort of thing might have been expected between very close neighbors" ("Genealogical Boundaries," 343 n. 22). It is possible that the avoidance of borrowing fire had religious and not only social reasons.

18. Morony, *Iraq*, 156; Geoffrey Herman, *A Prince without a Kingdom: The Exilarch in the Sasanian Era*, TSAJ 150 (Tübingen: Mohr Siebeck, 2012), 26. For the later subdivisions of the province, see ibid., 25–26, and Ibn Khordadbeh, "Le livre des routes et des provinces par Ibn Khordadbeh, publié, traduit, et annoté par C. Barbier de Meynard," *Journal Asiatique*, 6ième série, 29 :(1865) 5; Joseph Marquart, ed., *Ērānšahr nach der Geographie des Ps. Moses Xoranac'i* (Berlin: Weidman, 1901), 8 (text), 16 (trans.), 40–42 (comm.). On the administrative aspect of Mesene, see further Michael G. Morony, "Continuity and Change in the Administrative

> [T]wo sources attest to Kashkar being a province before the period of Khusro I. Firstly, the Bavli mentions an *'ōstāndār* of Kashkar'[19] as appearing on a document in a discussion by late third century rabbis. Secondly, Kashkar is mentioned as a seat of a bishop—implying that it was regarded as a separate province already in the proceedings of the first synod of the Persian church held in 410.[20]

It would thus seem that by the fourth century the province of Mesene no longer included Kashkar. Evidence of this new reality may also be gleaned from the Acts of Mar Mari, where we are told that Mar Mari heads to the province of Maishan (ܐܬܪܐ ܕܡܝܫܢ),[21] after converting the province of Kashkar (ܐܬܪܐ ܕܟܫܟܪ).[22] This is clearly anachronistic concerning Mar Mari's period and rather reflects the later Sasanian administrative reality known to the author of these *Acts*. As we shall see below, despite the later administrative divisions of Mesene, the Bavli's negative view of the Jews of the entire region, including Kashkar, remained intact.[23]

The border between Upper Apamea and Lower Apamea was not only administrative and political but also linguistic, as the Bavli testifies to the existence of a dialect called *Meishanit* (Mesenean) spoken in lower Apamea in Mesene.[24]

The fact that, according to the Bavli, the Mesenean dialect was spoken even at the northernmost border of the kingdom of Mesene's full reach (lower Apamea), further highlights that the region was also a linguistic entity. We know from different sources that most of the inhabitants of Mesene were Aramaic speakers,[25] and several centuries as an independent kingdom might have indeed led to the development of a local dialect. Abandoning the precedent of three centuries of Greek on the Characenean coinage, Abinergaos II (ruled 165–180 CE) began using Aramaic legends,

---

Geography of Late Sasanian and Early Islamic al-'Irāq," *Iran* 20 (1982): 30–39; Rika Gyselen, *La géographie administrative de l'Empire Sassanide: Les témoignages sigillographiques*, Res orientales 1 (Leuven: Peeters, 1989), 76–77.

19. b. Giṭ. 80b. On the administrative division of Mesene, see further below.

20. Herman, *Prince without a Kingdom*, 26.

21. Harrak, *Acts of Mār Mārī*, 70–71, §31.

22. Ibid., 68–69, §30. On Kashkar in the Persian Martyr Acts, see further Jullien, "Contribution des actes (I)," 157; eadem, "Contribution des actes (II)," 92.

23. This is important, since most scholars seemed to have ignored talmudic sources dealing with Kashkar when discussing Mesene in the Talmud.

24. For the possible connection between Mesenean and Mandaean, see below.

25. See, e.g., Strabo, *Geogr.* 16.1.8 (Hamilton and Falconer, LCL): "The country of the Babylonians is surrounded … on the south by the Persian Gulf, and the Chaldæans as far as the Arabian Mesene [καὶ τῶν Χαλδαίων μέχρι Ἀράβων τῶν Μεσηνῶν]." Cf. Christopher Brunner, "Geographical and Administrative Divisions: Settlements and Economy," in *The Cambridge History of Iran*, vol. 3, *The Seleucid, Parthian and Sasanian Periods*, part 2, ed. Ehsan Yarshater (Cambridge: Cambridge University Press, 1983), 755.

a tradition that would continue until the fall of his kingdom.[26] These legends display a distinct Aramaic dialect and script.

The distinctiveness of Mesenean is highlighted in the following account related by Ishoʿdad of Merv (fl. ca. 850) in the introduction to his commentary on Genesis, as part of his survey of the development of the different scripts:[27]

> The Persian script was created by a Mesenean man [ܠܒܪܢܫܐ ܚܕ ܡܝܫܢܝܐ] by the name of Nabu[28] who was trained in the court of the King of Assyria in Nineveh. Having learned the Hebrew and Syriac scripts he devised the Persian script, which is the most difficult of all scripts, for they think and write in Mesenean while reading aloud in Persian [ܥܠ ܕܗܘ ܚܫܒܝܢ ܘܟܬܒܝܢ ܡܝܫܢܐܝܬ ܘܩܪܝܢ ܦܪܣܐܝܬ].[29]

The writer betrays an acquaintance with the Pahlavi and possibly also Parthian script, both of which were based on an Aramaic alphabet, and their writing system made much use of Arameograms (words written in Aramaic but read-out in their Persian equivalent). As we shall see below, the Parthian script is indeed similar to the Characenean (Mesenean) script. Setting aside the possible historical background of this fictitious account, it is important to note that it attests to the fact that, even by the ninth cen-

---

26. Nodelman, "Preliminary History," 117, who adds: "This is undoubtedly symptomatic of the general decline of Hellenism in the East during the second century, but it is perhaps also a further reaction against foreign influence and an assertion of the national character of the dynasty." See also Schuol, *Die Charakene*, 234–37.

27. Apart from Isho'dad of Merv, I am aware of only one other explicit reference to Mesenean (ܡܝܫܢܐܝܬ) in Syriac sources. In his entry on ܬܫܒܘܚܬܐ (flattery), Bar Bahalul (*Lexicon syriacum*, vol. 2,ed. Rubens Duval [Paris: Leroux, 1901], 2056) states: ܬܫܒܘܚܬܐ...ܐܪܡܐܝܬ ܕܝܢ ܠܚܢܦܘܬܐ. ܡܝܫܢܐܝܬ ܕܝܢ ܐܘܬܪܐ ܗܠܝܦܬܐ.. It is unclear to me, however, to what words Bar Bahalul is referring, and they might be corrupted as there are variations in the manuscripts. For the different versions, see Robert Payne Smith, *Thesaurus Syriacus*, 2 vols. (Oxford: Clarendon, 1879–1901), 1414.

28. As already noted by Ceslas van den Eynde, trans., *Commentaire d'Išo'dad de Merv sur l'Ancien Testament, I: Genèse* (Leuven: L. Durbecq, 1955), 7–8 n. 6, the ascription of the invention of the Persian script to Nabu is most probably based on traditions linking the god Nabu to writing. Nabu was the scribe of Marduk and, as a result, became the god of writing and the patron of scribes. See Johanna Tudeau, "Nabu (god)," Ancient Mesopotamian Gods and Goddesses, Oracc and the UK Higher Education Academy, 2013, http://oracc.museum.upenn.edu/amgg/listofdeities/nabu/).

29. For the Syriac, see Jacques M. Vosté and Ceslas van den Eynde, eds., *Commentaire d'Išo'dad de Merv sur l'Ancien Testament, I: Genèse*, 6. This text is also discussed in A. Schall, "Der nestorianische Bibelexeget Išo'dad von Merw (9. Jh. n. Chr.) in seiner Bedeutung für die orientalische Philologie," in *Hkmwt bnth byth: Studia semitica necnon iranica Rudolpho Macuch septuagenario ab amicis et discipulis dedicate*, ed. Maria Macuch, Christa Müller-Kessler, and Bert G. Fragner (Wiesbaden: Harrassowitz, 1989), 271–82 (I wish to thank Sergey Minov for these references). See now also Kevin van Bladel, "Zoroaster's Many Languages," in *Arabic Humanities, Islamic Thought: A Festschrift for Everett K. Rowson*, ed. Shawkat Toorawa and Joseph Lowry, Islamic History and Civilization 141 (Leiden: Brill, 2017), 202–4.

tury, Mesenean (ܡܝܫܢܐܝܬ) was still recognized as an independent dialect of Aramaic, with a script different from, albeit related to, both Syriac and Hebrew.

Thus, for several centuries Mesene was both politically and linguistically separated from the "north." Such a separation also created, as we shall see, distinct religious and economic features. In what follows, I wish to suggest that the attitude of the northern rabbis to the Jews of Mesene could be better understood against the backdrop of the syncretistic religious climate of Mesene, the halakhic divergences between the Jews of Mesene and Babylonia, and also Mesene's economic contacts with Palmyra.

Religious Landscape

Mesene was an exceptionally fertile religious land in late antiquity. It contained various pagan cults alongside Jews and Christians and some Zoroastrians.[30] Mesene, though, was distinct in that it was also home to the Mandaeans, several Baptist sects, and to Mani, who was born and raised in the region. To date, however, there is no comprehensive study on the religions of southern Mesopotamia in the late Parthian and Sasanian periods, and its importance for the history of religion has yet to be fully appreciated by scholars. Thus, to start with, I shall survey the evidence we have for various religious traditions of the region in the first centuries of the Common Era.

As we shall see, the diverse pagan cults of Mesene seem to have impacted the way the region was perceived by Christian authors. In a similar vein, I wish to argue that the existence of several sects in the region with distinctive Jewish elements and the possibility of (real or imagined) interactions between them and the local Jews, may have contributed to the construction of the negative rabbinic image of the Mesenean Jews.

Pagans

In the Acts of Mar Mari, as we have seen above, Mesene is regarded as a hotbed of idolatry. Such a perception of the region persisted for centuries

30. We do not have much evidence about Zoroastrianism in Mesene, and it does not seem to have played a role in the way Jews and Christians viewed the region. Kerdir in his Naqsh-i Rostam inscription (line 35) boasts at having built a fire temple in Mesene (*m[y] š[ʾn]*) among other provinces (Philippe Gignoux, *Les quatre inscriptions du mage Kirdīr: Textes et concordances* [Paris: Association pour l'Avancement des Études Iraniennes, 1991], 50). This actually seems to indicate that Zoroastrianism was not widespread in the south at the time. From the late Sasanian period we have a seal of a *mogbed* (priest) of Mesene named Bāffarak (*b'plky ZY myšwn mgwpt*), see Gyselen, *La géographie administrative*, 29, 158. For another seal of a *mogbed* of an unidentified settlement (*ʾwlbr*) in Mesene see Philippe Gignoux and Rika Gyselen, *Bulles et sceaux sassanides de diverses collections* (Paris: Association pour l'Avancement des Études Iraniennes, 1987), 27 (1.5).

in Christian writings.[31] So, for example, the Chronicle of Seert describes the efforts of Gregory of Nisibis, a native of Kashkar,[32] in Christianizing the region in the late sixth century:[33]

> And he baptized every day many people and performed signs and miracles. And the people destroyed the houses of idols [فهدم الناس بيوت الاصنام] and they shattered many idols [وكسروا اصنامًا كثيرة] in the land of Maishan and Kashkar [بارض ميشان وكشكر] and he built churches in their place.

It is impossible to determine whether southern Mesopotamia was indeed "more idolatrous" than other regions, or was just represented as such. Nonetheless, the religious landscape of the region, as a gateway between east and west, would have included the worship of, among others, Babylonian, Greek, Iranian, Palmyrene, and Arab deities, alongside local cults.[34] Though meager, we have evidence that the worship of some of these deities persisted into the late Parthian and Sasanian period. This evidence most likely reflects just a fraction of the real number of cults in the region during these periods.

The Babylonian god Nergal seems to have been the chief divinity of the Characenean dynasty, as three of its monarchs, including its last king, were named Abinergaos (= Abdi-Nergal).[35] An image of a seated Hera-

31. See Philip Wood, *The Chronicle of Seert: Christian Historical Imagination in Late Antique Iraq*, OECS (Oxford: Oxford University Press, 2013), 77, 201.

32. On Gregory of Nisibis, see ibid., 202–6.

33. Chronicle of Seert 2.2 LXXIV. 508; *Histoire nestorienne inédite (Chronique de Séert)*, ed. and trans. Addai Scher, 4 vols., Patrologia Orientalis 4.3, 1908 [1.1]; 5.2, 1910 [1.2]; 7.2, 1911 [2.1]; 13.4, 1919 [2.2]). My translation.

34. For a general overview of pagans in Sasanian Iraq, see Morony, *Iraq*, 386–428. It is also possible that there were Indian influences in the region; see Brunner, "Geographical and Administrative Divisions," 755: "Not only Iranians settled there under the Sasanians, but some of the transported Zutt. The latter were more numerous toward the swamps of Asuristan; they included the Sabaj—if not Indians, possibly Malays taken captive in Hind or recruited there as sailors. The idol of Zun seen by the invading Arabs at Ubulla may have belonged to a colony of deportees or of merchants from the Indian frontier." However, the Zutt seem to have been settled in the region only in the sixth century when Khusro captured Zabulistan. See also J. Marquart and J. J. de Groot, "Das Reich Zabul und der Gott Zun," in *Festschrift Eduard Sachau zum siebzigsten Geburtstage gewidmet von Freunden und Schülern*, ed. Gotthold Weil (Berlin: G. Reimer, 1915), 248–92; Tabari, *Tarikh*, 895 (= Jacob Barth and Theodor Nöldeke, eds., *Annales: Abu Djafar Mohammed Ibn Djarir At-Tabari*, first series, vol. 2. [Leiden: Brill 1881–1882]; *The History of Al-Tabari*, vol. 5, *The Sāsānids, the Byzantines, the Lakhmids, and Yemen*, trans. Clifford E. Bosworth, Bibliotheca Persica [Albany: State University of new York Press, 1999], 150).

35. The name itself is attested already in the second millennium BCE; see Henri Seyrig, "Héraclès-Nergal," *Syria* 24 (1944–1945): 70 n. 4. The fact that the last king of Characene was Abinergaos III (ca. 210–222 CE), "testifies," as Nodelman notes ("Preliminary History," 119), "that the dynasty still adhered to the worship of Nergal." Nergal's main cult center was Kutha, but his cult is also attested in Mashkan-Shapir, Dilbat, Isin, Larsa, Nippur, Ur, and

cles, who was identified with Nergal,[36] appears on the reverse of many Mesenean coins.[37] Furthermore, a bronze statue of a standing Heracles, originating in Mesene was discovered in Seleucia. The statue contains a Greek-Parthian bilingual inscription, according to which after the Parthian king Vologases IV defeated Mithridates the king of Mesene in 150/151 he brought the statue back with him from Mesene and dedicated it to the temple of Apollo/Tir. In the Greek version, the statue is referred to as "the bronze statue of the god Heracles" (Ἡρακλέους θεοῦ), whereas in the Parthian we have the "god Vərəθraγna" (*wrtgn 'LH'*).[38] Heracles was indeed known to have been identified in the Seleucid, Parthian, and early Sasanian era with the Iranian god of victory Vərəθraγna (later: Warahran/Bahram).[39] The identification of Heracles-Vərəθraγna-Nergal in Mesene[40] points to a Greek-Iranian-Babylonian syncretism typical of the Seleucid and Parthian era in Syria and Mesopotamia.

Nippur, located in the northern part of Mesene, was an ancient religious center, mainly of the cult of Inanna/Ishtar. Archaeological excavations have revealed that reconstruction of Inanna's temple, alongside Enlil's ziggurat, took place in Nippur as late as the second half of the first century,[41] which would indicate that their worship had persisted at least into the second century.

Uruk. See Egbert von Weiher, *Der babylonische Gott Nergal* (Kevelaer: Butzon & Bercker, 1971); Frans A. M. Wiggermann, "Nergal. A. Philologisch," *RlA* 9: 215–23; Elisabeth Stone and Paul E. Zimansky, *The Anatomy of a Mesopotamian City: Survey and Soundings at Mashkan-shapir* (Winona Lake, IN: Eisenbrauns, 2004); Yağmur Heffron, "Nergal (god)," Ancient Mesopotamian Gods and Goddesses, http://oracc.museum.upenn.edu/amgg/listofdeities/nergal/.

36. Seyrig, "Héraclès-Nergal"; D. S. Potter, "The Inscriptions on the Bronze Herakles from Mesene: Vologeses IV's War with Rome and the Date of Tacitus' 'Annales,'" *ZPE* 88 (1991): 285; for the cult of Nergal-Heracles in Hatra, see, e.g., Jonas C. Greenfield, "Nergol DHŠPT'," *Acta Iranica* 28 (1988): 135–43.

37. See Schuol, *Die Charakene*, 219–41.The importance of Heracles in Characene is by no means unique. As Albert de Jong notes ("Heracles," *EIr*), Heracles was "one of the most popular Greek gods in the Hellenistic East and by far the best-attested Greek god in the Iranian world."

38. Potter, "Inscriptions on the Bronze Herakles," 277–90; Prods Oktor Skjærvø, "Aramaic in Iran," *ARAM* 7 (1995): 292–93. On the statue and the inscription, see further Fabrizio A. Pennacchietti, "L'iscrizione bilingue greco-partica dell'Eracle di Seleucia," *Mesopotamia* 22 (1987): 139–85; and Paul Bernard, "Vicissitudes au gré de l'histoire d'une statue en bronze d'Héraclès entre Séleucie du Tigre et la Mésène," *Journal des savants* 1 (1990): 3–68, who also supplies a useful overview of the geography and history of Mesene.

39. See Gherardo Gnoli and Parivash Jamzadeh, "Bahrām (1)," *EIr*; Michael Shenkar, *Intangible Spirits and Graven Images: The Iconography of Deities in the Pre-Islamic Iranian World*, Magical and Religious Literature of Late Antiquity 4 (Leiden: Brill, 2014), 159–63.

40. It should be noted, however, that the name Vərəθraγna was inscribed by the victorious Parthians and does not necessarily reflect the divine nomenclature in Mesene (I owe this caveat to Michael Shenkar).

41. Schuol, *Die Charakene*, 203–4.

Another Babylonian deity purportedly worshiped in the region is mentioned in The History of Karka d'beth Slok, composed in northern Mesopotamia most likely during the reign of Khusro II (590–628).[42] According to the History, 'Akbaha, the bishop of Karka d'beth Slok (the capital of Beth Garmai, modern day Kirkuk), while proselytizing in his region, arrives in a city named Tish'in:[43]

> It was so named after the ninety families [ܠܬܫܥܝܢ ܒ̈ܬܝܢ] which King Shapur brought from Maishan and settled in it [= the city] [ܕܐܝܬܝ ܫܒܘܪ ܡܠܟܐ ܡܢ ܡܝܫܢ ܘܐܘܬܒ ܒܗ]. They worshipped the demon Nanai [ܘܣܓܕܝܢ ܗܘܘ ܠܫܐܕܐ ܕܢܢܝ], which they brought with them from their region.

The "demon Nanai" would seem to refer to the Babylonian goddess Nanaya,[44] and this source, if it can be trusted, indicates that she was worshipped in Mesene at least up until the fourth century. More importantly, though, this report appears in a distinctly northern Mesopotamian composition that, as Richard Payne has recently pointed out,[45] is suffused with local patriotism. Thus, whether real or fictitious, the History depicts the inhabitants of southern Mesene as demon worshipers and as a source of the religious "contamination" of the northern region of Beth Garmai.

In addition to Babylonian deities, some (rather late) sources attest to the existence of several local idolatrous cults in Mesene. In The Acts of Mar Mari, the protagonist is encouraged by those accompanying him to go to Kashkar:[46]

> And they said to him: "Convert the city of Kashkar [ܕܬܠܡܕ ܠܟܫܟܪ ܡܕܝܢܬܐ], where a demon in the likeness of an eagle [ܒܕܡܘܬܐ ܕܢܫܪܐ] is worshipped and (where) a standard stands, on which there is an idol named Nishar [ܣܐ ܕܡܬܩܪܐ ܢܫܪ ܦܬܟܪܐ]."[47]

42. Richard E. Payne, *A State of Mixture: Christians, Zoroastrians, and Iranian Political Culture in Late Antiquity*, Transformation of the Classical Heritage 56 (Oakland: University of California Press, 2015), 132.

43. Paul Bedjan, ed., *Acta martyrum et sanctorum*, 7 vols. (Paris/Leipzig: Harrassowitz, 1890–1897), 2:516 (my translation).

44. Cf. Morony, *Iraq*, 386; Lieu, *Manichaeism in Mesopotamia*, 34; Payne-Smith, *Thesaurus Syriacus*, 2387. In The History of the Holy Mar Maᶜin §39 the saint is ordered to sacrifice to several deities, including "to Nanai [ܠܢܢܝ] the great goddess of all the earth" (text and translation after Sebastian Brock, *The History of the Holy Mar Maᶜin with a Guide to the Persian Martyr Acts*, Persian Martyr Acts in Syriac: Text and Translation 1 [Piscataway, NJ: Gorgias Press, 2008], 33). Nanaya also appears in Mandaean texts such as the following lead roll (BM132947+, 168′-169′, Christa Müller-Kessler and Karlheinz Kessler, "Spätbabylonische Gottheiten in Spätantiken mandäischen Texten," *ZA* 89 [1999]: 76): עסירא נאנאי ד־בורציפ ונאנאי ד־בית גוזאייא ("Bound is Nanai of Borsippa and Nanai of Bit Guzayya").

45. Payne, *State of Mixture*, 139–44.

46. Harrak, *Acts of Mār Mārī*, 69.

47. A similar tradition is reported by Theodor bar Koni (*Liber Scholiorum*, ed. Addai

The existence of a cult of Nishar in Kashkar is further substantiated by a Mandaic magic text:[48] "Bel is turned from Babylon, Nabu is turned from Borsippa, Nishra is turned from Kashkar [עפיק נישרא מן כאשכאר]."

Close to Kashkar we learn of another local cult in the early seventh century, which the aforementioned Gregory of Nisibis encounters, having been ordered by Khusro II to return to his native Kashkar:[49]

> He [Gregory] withdrew to a place in the desert between Niffur [Nippur] and Kashkar [بين نفّر وكشكر].... In his vicinity there was a village whose people worshipped serpents [يسجد اهلها الحيّات]. And he exhorted them to acknowledge God and informed them of the horridness of their cult. They did not listen to him and they remained in their heresy [واقاموا على كفرهم]. One day their priest who was in charge of the service of the serpents went to supply them food and found them all dead.

As a result of the death of their snakes, the villagers turn to Gregory to absolve them from their sins. Gregory obliges and promptly builds a church in the village. It is unclear if this story has any historical kernel as it appears in the late Chronicle of Seert. Yet once again it points to the persistent image of the region as idolatrous.

Such pagan cults were obviously not all unique to Mesene and could be found throughout Mesopotamia.[50] However, these cults seem to have played a role in a particular syncretism of southern Mesopotamia in the late Parthian and Sasanian periods and might have contributed to the perception of the region by Christian authors as "idolatrous."[51]

Scher, 2 vols., CSCO 55, 69 [Paris: Typographeo Reipublicae, 1910–1912] 1:369–70), who was the bishop of Kashkar. However, he claims that the cult of the eagle originated with the Romans, spread to Hatra and was instated by their king in Kashkar. It is possible, however, that this cult goes back at least a millennium.

48. Text and translation (slightly modified) according to Ethel S. Drower, "A Mandæan Book of Black Magic," *JRAS* 2 (1943): 180 §27 (text), 168 (translation). Drower states, "Nisra is obviously a corruption: who was the patron god of Kaskar I know not" (149). Yet, in light of various other sources, it is clear that Nishra is the correct form, as already noted by Jonas C. Greenfield, "A Mandaic Miscellany," *JAOS* 104 (1984): 81–82, with further refrences. Cf. also the list of pagan temples in b. 'Abod. Zar. 11b, which states that Nishra is in 'Arabia. For "'Arab" as a region in northern Mesopotamia, see below n. 51.

49. Chronicle of Seert 2.2 LXXIV, 512 (my translation).

50. On Babylonian traditions in the Parthian period, see now Lucinda Dirven, "Religious Continuity and Change in Parthian Mesopotamia: A Note on the Survival of Babylonian Traditions," *Journal of Ancient Near Eastern History* 1 (2014): 1–29, who focuses mainly on Syro-Mesopotamia.

51. It is worth mentioning that many incantation bowls were found in Nippur. In one of these bowls we find the following incantation: אשבעית עליכון רוחי בבל וערב רוחי אירג ומישון רוחי פרת ודגלת נהרה ("I hereby adjure you, spirits of Babylonia and Arab, spirits of the southern lowlands and Mesene, spirits of the Euphrates and the Tigris River"; text and translation from James N. Ford, "A New Parallel to the Jewish Babylonian Aramaic Magic Bowl

Christians

According to The Acts of Mar Mari, as we have seen above, Mar Mari had tried (unsuccessfully) to proselytize pagans in Mesene already at the end of the first century CE. Such a description seems to be rather anachronistic, but we do hear of several similar efforts throughout the Sasanian period. So, the Chronicle of Seert reports that during the fourth century Mar 'Abda traveled the land of Nabat (بلد النبط), probably including Mesene, baptizing Aramaeans and reconverting Marcionites.[52] His pupil, 'Abdisho', was a native of Mesene (من بلد ميشان), from a village named Arpheluna (ارفلونا). After a period spent farther north, 'Abdisho' "withdrew to Maishan [أرض ميشان] where he Christianized Rimiun and the neighboring area [ريميون ونواحيها]."[53] As we have seen above, at the end of the sixth and beginning of seventh century, Gregory of Nisibis is said to have converted many idol worshipers in Mesene and Kashkar. All these supposedly successful conversions seem rather to indicate, as Jean-Maurice Fiey had noted, that Christianity was actually not so widespread in the region.[54]

According to The Chronicle of Arbela, Mesene had a bishop already by 224 CE.[55] This claim, however, is farfetched and does not seem to have

---

IM 76106 [Nippur 11 N 78]," *AS* 9 [2011]: 261–62). On this bowl, see Stephen A. Kaufman, "Appendix C: Alphabetic Texts," in *Excavations at Nippur, Eleventh Season,* ed. McGuire Gibson, OIC 22 (Chicago: University of Chicago Press, 1975), 151–52; Shaul Shaked, "On Jewish Literature of Magic in Muslim Countries: Comments and Specimens" [Hebrew], *Peʿamim* 15 (1983): 20; Ford, "New Parallel," 249–78 (with further references on 261, no. 48). Irag (אירג) is, as Kaufman points out ("Appendix C," 151), "the earliest known occurrence of the name "Iraq," here used in its original sense of southernmost Mesopotamia." ʿArab (ערב) "designates both a relatively small region located west of Edessa in extreme northern Mesopotamia and the entire Sasanian province of North Mesopotamia, Arbāyistān" (Ford, "New Parallel," 269). Herman (*Prince without a Kingdom,* 22 n. 6) has noted the "different, distinctly local perspective of the proximate geographical scene," displayed in this bowl. An important aspect of this bowl seems to have hitherto gone unnoticed. Not only was the bowl found in Nippur, but the text itself could make sense only in that specific geographical location. For the author of the text, Babylon and Beth Arabaye represent the north and Mesene, and Iraq the south. This would indicate that the author is located in Nippur, which lies just south of border between the province of Babylonia and Mesene, and at more or less equal distance between the Euphrates and the Tigris. Another reference to Mesene in a magical context is found in an unpublished Mandaic lead roll (BM132947+, 85-88, cited according to Kessler's review, *AfO* 48–49 [2001–2002]: 248): עסירא מלכיאת ליליתא ד־שריא בכולא אתרא ד־משאן העיא וכולהן שורבאתה ("Bound is Malkat-Lilit, who dwells in the entire land of Meshan, she and all her race").

52. Chronicle of Seert 1.2, LX, 307–8.

53. Ibid., LXII, 310–11.

54. Jean-Maurice Fiey, *Assyrie chrétienne III: Bet Garmaï, Bet Aramāyé et Maišān nestoriens* (Beirut: Imprimerie Catholique, 1968), 264: "Il ne faudrait pas cependant en conclure que tout le territoire était chrétien dès le début du IVᵉ siècle; sous Tōmarṣa (363-71), le moine 'Awdīšō', disciple de Mār 'Abda, continuera l'évangelisation, et à la fin du VIᵉ siècle encore, Grégoire, futur metropolite de Nisibe, y brisera des idoles."

55. Peter Kawerau, ed., *Die Chronik von Arbela,* 2 vols., CSCO 467–68 (Leuven: Peeters, 1985), 31.

historical value.[56] The first bishop of whom we have reliable evidence is David from Prat d'Maishan (ca. 266), who, according to the Chronicle of Seert, left his post and went to evangelize in India.[57]

The Christian community grew significantly during the third and fourth century most probably based largely on the Roman prisoners of war settled in the south, especially after the mass deportations of Shapur I and later of Shapur II (on these deportations, see below).[58] Another cause for the spread of Christianity in the south seems to have been the major trade routes that ran through Mesene, mostly controlled by Palmyrian merchants. This is clearly demonstrated by the name of the bishop of Prat d'Maishan, Bolida' (ܒܘܠܝܕܐ), who is reported to have been martyred alongside Simeon bar Ṣabba'e in the fourth century.[59] Bolida' is, as Jürgen Tubach has pointed out,[60] a Palmyrian name, which would indicate that he or his ancestors were from Palmyra and probably settled in Mesene due to the Palmyrian dominance of the caravan trade to and from the region.

The circumstances of the emergence of the Christian communities in Mesene—proselytizing, mass deportations to the south, and Palmyrian presence in the region—also impacted the southern Jewish communities, as we shall see below. While there may have been distinctive regional features to pagan cults and Christianity in Mesene, the presence of Mandaeans and Baptist sects in Mesene, as well as the fact that it was the birth-

56. See Marie-Louise Chaumont, *La christianisation de l'Empire iranien: Des origines aux grandes presécutions du IVe siècle*, CSCO 499 (Leuven: Peeters, 1988), 11, 21–22; Jürgen Tubach, "Ein Palmyrener als Bischof der Mesene," *OrChr* 77 (1993): 138.

57. Chronicle of Seert 1.1, VIII, 236 (cf. ibid., XXV, 292–93): "In the days of Shahlouba and Papa, the two Metropolitans of the East, and Stephen Pontiff of Rome, there were eminent scholars: David bishop of Basra, who left his see and travelled to India, where he made many converts; Gadhimhab, bishop of Gondishapur; Ebed-Jesus, bishop of Kaskar; John, bishop of Maishan; Andrew, bishop Deir Mahraq; Abraham, bishop of Shoushter; Milas al-Razi, bishop of Susa" (trans. Anthony Alcock, https://sucialin.files.wordpress.com/2014/08/chronicle-of-sc3a9ert-i.pdf, 14. Cf. Tubach, "Ein Palmyrener," 139–40.

58. Fiey, *Assyrie chrétienne III*, 263–82.

59. History of Blessed Simeon bar Ṣabbaʿe §§1, 25 (Kyle Smith, *The Martyrdom and History of Blessed Simeon bar Ṣabbaʿe*, Persian Martyr Acts in Syriac 3 [Piscataway, NJ: Gorgias Press, 2014], 68–69, 108–9). Yoḥanan the bishop of Karka d'Maishan is also reported to have been martyred with them alongside another three bishops from other regions. None of the five bishops is mentioned in the Martyrdom. Cf. Smith's comments on this difference (*Constantine and the Captive Christians of Persia: Martyrdom and Religious Identity in Late Antiquity*, Transformation of the Classical Heritage 57 [Oakland: University of California Press, 2016], 140–41): "By including these five among the martyrs, the *History of Simeon* expands the geographical range of Shapur's persecution, making it regional, rather than just a localized, phenomenon. The text thereby raises the prestige of Christian bishoprics other than those of Seleucia-Ctesiphon and Karka d-Ledan." In light of this it is important to highlight the fact that two of the five bishops added in the History are from Mesene, which might point to an effort by the author of the History to elevate the status of the region, possibly due to its dire reputation.

60. Tubach, "Ein Palmyrener," 137–50.

place of Mani and the origins of Manichaeism, made the region religiously exceptional.

Mandaeans and Naṣoreans

Theodor bar Koni, bishop of Kashkar in the eighth century, opens his description of the heresy of the Dustaya (ܕܘܣܬܝܐ) in his *liber scholiorum* as follows:[61]

> ܐܕܘ ܐܝܟ ܕܐܡܪܝܢ ܚܕܝܒܝܐ ܗܘܐ. ܘܐܝܟ ܚܕܘܪܐ ܐܬܐ ܥܡ ܐܢܫܘܬܗ ܠܐܬܪܐ ܕܡܝܫܢ.
>
> Ado, as they say, was from Adiabene, and he came as beggar with his family to the province of Maishan.

The Dustaya, bar Koni later informs us, were named in Mesene Mandaeans (ܡܬܩܪܝܢ ܕܝܢ ܒܡܝܫܢ ܡܢܕܝܐ). On bar Koni's report Lady Drower has already noted: "although the absurdities of the tale are self-evident, Theodore bar Koni was apparently familiar with some Mandaean literature, and Ado's journey south into Mesene may be a distortion of the Mandaean migration into Khuzestan and Lower Mesopotamia."[62]

Kevin van Bladel has recently pointed out that there is no evidence for the existence of the Mandaeans prior to the mid- to late fifth century, and in light of this he argues that only then did the Mandaeans come into being *as Mandaeans*.[63] However, since throughout their texts the Man-

---

61. Theodorus bar Kōnī, *Liber Scholiorum*, ed. Scher, 2:345. For a discussion of bar Koni's description of the Mandaeans, see D. Kruisheer, "Theodore bar Koni's *Ktābā d-'Eskolyon* as a Source for the Study of Early Mandaeism," *Jaarbericht van het Vooraziatisch-Egyptisch Genootschap "Ex Oriente Lux"* 33 (1993–1994): 151–69; Kevin T. van Bladel, *From Sasanian Mandaeans to Ṣābians of the Marshes*, Leiden Studies in Islam and Society 6 (Leiden: Brill, 2017), 18–25.

62. Ethel S. Drower, *The Haran Gawaita and the Baptism of Hibil-Ziwa: The Mandaic Text Reproduced together with Translation, Notes and Commentary* (Vatican City: Biblioteca apostolica vaticana, 1953), x. See also Kurt Rudolph, "Quellenprobleme zum Ursprung und Alter der Mandäer," in *Christianity, Judaism and Other Greco-Roman Cults: Studies for Morton Smith at Sixty*, ed. Jacob Neusner, 4 vols., SJLA 12 (Leiden: Brill, 1975), 131; Christa Müller-Kessler, "The Mandaeans and the Question of Their Origin," *ARAM* 16 (2004): 47–60.

63. Van Bladel, *From Sasanian Mandaeans*, esp. 91–92. Edmondo Lupieri, who supports the thesis of Babylonian origins, had attached much importance to the fact that the Mandaean baptism is not named after John (as would be expected if they were of Palestinian origin) but rather called "the Baptism of the great Bihram." Bihram is also, as we have seen above, the Iranian name of the divine patron of the Characenean dynasty identified with Heracles. This leads Lupieri to conclude "that the Mandaeans considered the one who established their baptism to be the protector deity of the sovereigns of Characene.... This also means that the Mandaeans must have been living in Characene in such a very ancient epoch of their history that they could chose Bihram as the eponymous deity of their baptism (Edmondo Lupieri, *The Mandaeans: The Last Gnostics*, trans. Charles Hindley, Italian Texts and Studies on Religion and Society [Grand Rapids: Eerdmans, 2002], 163–64). This reconstruction has been convincingly challenged by Jorunn J. Buckley (review of *The Mandaeans: The Last Gnostics, by*

daeans refer to Naṣoreans, it would seem that the latter group antedates the Mandaeans.[64] These Naṣoreans were most likely a Jewish-Christian Baptist sect active in Mesene, possibly as early as the third century.[65] It is possible, as van Bladel suggests, that the Mandaean religion and community was formed as a result of interactions between Naṣorean priests and pagans in the fifth century.[66] The Mandaean dialect and script (and some of their texts), however, clearly predate the fifth century and reflect a local Aramaic firmly anchored in Mesene.

Earlier scholars viewed the Nabatean or Palmyrene script as the origin of the Mandaic script.[67] In 1970, Joseph Naveh suggested that the Mandaic script was derived from the Elymaic script (Khuzestan),[68] whereas Peter W. Coxton, in the same year, suggested that it was derived from the Characenean script attested on several legends of the coins minted in Mesene by the Characenean kings.[69] More recently, Charles Häberl

---

Edmondo Lupieri, *JAAR* 71 [2003]: 220–23; and Buckley, *The Great Stem of Souls: Reconstructing Mandaean History* [Piscataway, NJ: Gorgias Press, 2005], 326–27), as well as by van Bladel, *From Sasanian Mandaeans*, 80–81, who notes that "Mandaean texts contain no reference to the Iranian divinity Vərəθraγna/Bahrām."

64. Van Bladel, *From Sasanian Mandaeans*, 92.

65. On the Naṣoreans, see ibid., 89–97. It has been suggested that the Naṣoreans are to be identified with the Elchasaites (see below). However, I believe that François de Blois is correct when he states that "there is no evidence that the Elchasaites ever actually called themselves Nazoraeans. For this reason one must consider the possibility that the Mandaeans descend from some other 'Jewish Christian' sect" ("*Naṣrānī* [Ναζωραῖος] and *ḥanīf* [ἐθνικός]: Studies on the Religious Vocabulary of Christianity and of Islam," *BSOAS* 65 [2002]: 5). On the possibility that the "seed of Abraham" mentioned in the Coptic Manicheaen Synaxeis refers to the Mandaeans, see Wolf-Peter Funk, "Mani's Account of Other Religions," in *New Light on Manichaeism: Papers from the Sixth International Congress on Manichaeism*, ed. Jason David BeDuhn, NHMS 64 (Leiden: Brill, 2009), 122–25.

66. See van Bladel, *From Sasanian Mandaeans*, 94: "My hypothesis—and it is only that—is that the Mandaean sect arose from within a Jewish Christian sect already known as Nāṣoraean when one or more teachers, or perhaps even originally pagan laypeople who observed Nāṣoraean baptisms, fostered a new esoteric form of religion requiring special initiation and having its own secret texts, but for which they retained the name Nāṣoraean." Cf. de Blois "*Naṣrānī*," 4: "[T]he surviving community of Mandaeans (alias Nazoraeans) are descendants of an ancient Jewish Christian community who, presumably in the aftermath of some catastrophe, lost most of their own religious writings and subsequently adopted those of a rival community, indeed writings that contained polemics against their own former beliefs.... [T]he surviving Mandaeo-Nazoraeans represent a synthesis of two different religious traditions: that of Nazoraean Jewish Christianity and that of the non-Christian, non-Jewish, Babylonian, semi-Iranized and quasi gnostic complex of authentic Mandaeism."

67. A summary of previous scholarship on the issue appears in Chuck G. Häberl, "Iranian Scripts for Aramaic Languages: The Origin of the Mandaic Script," *BASOR* 324 (2006): 54.

68. Joseph Naveh, "The Origin of the Mandaic Script," *BASOR* 198 (1970): 32–37; idem, *Early History of the Alphabet: An Introduction to West Semitic Epigraphy and Palaeography*, 2nd ed. (Jerusalem: Magnes Press, 1987), 133–37.

69. Peter W. Coxton, "Script Analysis and Mandaean Origins," *JSS* 15 (1970): 16–30.

argued that the similarity between the Mandaic script and the Elymaic and Characenean scripts is due to the fact that all three scripts developed from the late Parthian chancery script, in close geographical proximity.[70] It would thus seem that, as van Bladel puts it, following Naveh: "The Mandaeans did not invent a new script but ... used and standardized a cursive form of the South Mesopotamian branch of Aramaic script."[71]

In light of the Mandaeans' geographical provenance, Theodor Nöldeke had suggested that Mandaic (which belongs to the eastern Aramaic family and is very similar to Jewish Babylonian Aramaic) might have been similar to Mesenean mentioned by the Bavli.[72] Unfortunately, the only documentations of a distinct Mesenean dialect are a handful of Aramaic legends on the Characenean coins.[73] Although it might be too much of a stretch to identify Mandaic with Mesenean, it is indeed very probable that Mandaic was a dialect that first developed within the linguistic context of southern Mesopotamia.

Mesene is also explicitly mentioned several times in the Mandaean corpus,[74] and it seems to have even played a role in Mandaean eschatology.[75]

---

70. Häberl, "Iranian Scripts," 55. Häberl concludes: "It cannot be mere coincidence that both the Mandaean textual tradition and their own historical traditions situate them in the vicinity of Mesene and Elymais during the latter half of the Parthian Empire. Consequently, it seems only logical to seek the context of these three scripts within the Parthian Empire during this period." As van Bladel notes, however, "This does not indicate, as Häberl suggests, that the Mandaeans' literary tradition must have begun no later than the second century" (*From Sasanian Mandaeans*, 80).

71. Ibid.; Naveh, *Early History of the Alphabet*, 135–37.

72. Theodor Nöldeke, *Mandäische Grammatik* (Halle: Buchhandlung des Waisenhauses, 1875), xxvi.

73. Nodelman ("Preliminary History," 98) notes a striking similarity between Mesenean and Mandaean: On the Characenean coins the terminal *lamed* in the god's name Nergal was elided and written as Nerig, as in the kings' name Abi-Nerig (Greek: Abinergaos). A similar elision occurs in Mandaic, where Nergal appears as Nirag/Nirig/Narig (ניריג/נירג/נארג). For Nergal in Mandaic texts, see Kessler and Kessler, "Spätbabylonische Gottheiten," 78–80. However, the forms Nirag (נירג) or Nirig (ניריג) also appear in several Jewish Babylonian incantation bowls (Dan Levene and Gideon Bohak, "A Babylonian Jewish Aramaic Incantation Bowl with a List of Deities and Toponyms," *JSQ* 19 [2012]: 67) and once in a Syriac incantation bowl (Marco Morrigi, *A Corpus of Syriac Incantation Bowls: Syriac Magical Texts from Late-Antique Mesopotamia*, Magical and Religious Literature of Late Antiquity 3 [Leiden: Brill, 2014], 57).

74. Jorunn J. Buckley ("The Colophons in the Canonical Prayerbook of the Mandaeans," *JNES* 51 [1992]: 49), cites a colophon, in which among the scribes mentioned there appears "Shabur son of Dukt, from Maishun, which is in the land of Burka." Mesene (מישון) is also mentioned in The Book of the Zodiac (Ethel S. Drower, ed., *The Book of the Zodiac* [London: Royal Asiatic Society, 1949], 126, and 209, line 2 in the manuscript)

75. A seemingly important Mandaic tradition concerning Mesene can be found in book 18 of the right side of the Ginza Rabba, known as "The Mandaean Book of Kings," which is

A fascinating tradition is preserved in Al-Biruni's eleventh-century *Chronology of the Ancient Nations*, according to which the real Ṣabians (who are to be identified with the Mandaeans),[76] settled in the region of Waṣit (Kashkar) and farther south toward Basra, well within the historical borders of Mesene:[77]

> Again, others maintain that the Hurrānians are not the real Ṣabians (الصابئة), but those who are called in the books Heathens and Idolaters. For the Ṣabians are the remnant of the Jewish tribes who remained in Babylonia, when the other tribes left it for Jerusalem in the days of Cyrus and Artaxerxes. Those remaining tribes felt themselves attracted to the rites of the Magians, and so they inclined (فصبوا, i.e. Ṣābī) towards the religion of Nebuchadnezzar, and adopted a system mixed up of Magism and Judaism like that of the Samaritans in Syria. The greatest number of them are settled at Waṣit, in Sawād-al 'Irāk, in the districts of Ja'far, Aljnmīda, and the two Nahr-alṣila. They pretend to be the descendants of Enos the son of Seth.

to be dated to the eighth century, though it contains earlier material (Julius H. Petermann, ed., *Thesaurus sive Liber Magnus, vulgo 'Liber Adami' apellatus opus Mandaeorum summi ponderis* [Leipzig: Weigel, 1867], 1:390): "And when twenty five out of the fifty years had passed, a mountain of gold [טורא ד־דאהבא] will appear in Dašt-Misaq (בדאשת מיסאק), and seven districts and seven kings will come together on it and make an assembly, and the kings will rise and elect a king of kings [וקאימיא מאלכיא, ומשאויא מליך מאלכיא]." The unintelligible Dašt-Misaq should be read as Dašt-Misan (as suggested already by S. Orscher, "Das mandäische Königsbuch: Transskribiert, übersetzt und mit Anmerkungen versehen," *ZA* 19 [1906]: 89; cf. van Bladel, *From Sasanian Mandaeans*, 61 n. 6). Dašt-i Mayšān, known in Arabic sources as دستميسان (Dastumīsān), means in Persian "the desert of Mesene." This refers to the eastern part of Mesene, between Waṣit and Basra, which became desiccated as a result of disastrous changes in the course of the Tigris in the sixth and seventh century CE. This also caused major floods that significantly increased the Marshland in southern Iraq (see Yaqut al-Hamawi, *Muʿjam al-buldān* [Beirut: Dār Ṣāder, 1986], 2:574; Morony, *Iraq*, 156–61; idem, "Continuity and Change," 31; Oppenheimer, *Babylonia Judaica*, 255; van Bladel, *From Sasanian Mandaeans*, 61; Peter Christensen, *The Decline of Iranshahr: Irrigation and Environments in the History of the Middle East, 500 BC–AD 1500* [London: I. B. Tauris, 2016], 73–74). Dašt-i Mayšān was also, according to Al-Biruni (see below), one of the main areas in which the Mandaeans were located. The Meseneans (מישונאייא) are mentioned earlier in the same book of the Ginza (Petermann, *Thesaurus*, 385–86; Lizbrarski, *Ginzā*, 413, lines 3, 24). Interestingly, Dašt-i Mayšān is also the region in which Mani grew up, according to Ibn Nadim, as we shall see below.

76. Or with the Kentaeans, a group closely related to the Mandaeans; see van Bladel, *From Sasanian Mandaeans*, 43–44.

77. Al-Bīrūnī, *al-Āthar al-bāqiya 'an-il-qurūn al-khāliya* (Eduard Sachau, ed., *Chronologie orientalischer Völker von Albêrûnî* [Leipzig: Brockhaus, 1878; repr., 1923], 206). Translated by Edward Sachau, *The Chronology of Ancient Nations* (London: W. H. Allen, 1879), 188. See also John C. Reeves, *Heralds of That Good Realm: Syro-Mesopotamian Gnosis and Jewish Traditions*, NHMS 41 (Leiden: Brill, 1996), 151.

Although devoid of strict historical value, this extraordinary fictional account is precious evidence of a tradition that viewed the Mandaeans as descendants of the Jews who lived in Mesene.[78]

Thus, the Mandaeans spoke an Aramaic dialect similar to, yet distinct from, Jewish Babylonian Aramaic, and many settled in Kashkar (where the lower Apamea was located). In addition, the Naṣorean background of the Mandaeans would explain the many Jewish traditions underlying the Mandaic religion.[79]

The possible Jewish origin of such groups as the Naṣoreans and Mandaeans, and their supposed interaction with Jews in the region, may have further contributed to the rabbis' negative perception of the Mesenean Jews. The report in the Bavli (in the anonymous layer) about the inhabitants of the upper and lower Apameas not even lending each other fire—and that the latter spoke in the Mesenean dialect—may reflect the concrete effects of such a perception.[80]

The Naṣoreans and their successors, the Mandaeans, though, were not the only communities with possible Jewish roots in Mesene, as it was also home to other Judeo-Christian Baptist sects and to Mani, to which we now turn.

Baptists and Mani

In the section of the *Fihrist* dedicated to a survey of Manichaeism, Ibn Nadim reports that Fattiq, Mani's father, was a native of Hamadan but later moved to Ctesiphon, where he frequented an idol temple:[81]

---

78. Based on al-Biruni's account, Erik Peterson has already suggested that the sharp polemic of the Babylonian rabbis against the Jews of Mesene and the marriage prohibition should be viewed in light of the presence of the Mandaeans in the region ("Urchristentum und Mandäismus," *ZNW* 27 [1928]: 93–94; cf. Geo Widengren, "The Status of the Jews in the Sassanian Empire," *Iranica Antiqua* 117 :(1961) 1 n. 2; Neusner, *History of the Jews in Babylonia,* 2:26 n. 1; Christelle Jullien andt Florence Jullien, *Apôtres des confins: Processus missionnaires chrétiens dans l'Empire Iranien,* Res orientales 15 (Bures-sur-Yvette: Groupe pour l'étude de la civilisation du Moyen-orient, 2002), 199–200. It is interesting to note that, as in the Bavli's story to be discussed below, the exilic period serves as the backdrop for the formation of the not-quite-Jewish communities in southern Mesopotamia.

79. James F. McGrath rightly points out that the adamant anti-Jewish stance found already in the earliest strata of the Mandaean literature might actually point to their close proximity to the Jews ("Reading the Story of Miriai on Two Levels: Evidence from Mandaean Anti-Jewish Polemic about the Origins and Setting of Early Mandaeism," *ARAM* 22 [2010]: 583–92).

80. Cf. the more positivist view of Widengren ("Status of the Jews," 117 n. 2): "The Jewish inhabitants of Mesene were, however, regarded as lost to Jewry.... We are reminded of the fact that the highly syncretistic Mandaean community living in Mesene also betrays a strong Jewish influence part of which it may have carried with it from Palestine, part of which may be due to the Jewish contact in Mesene."

81. Muḥammad ibn Isḥāq Ibn Al-Nadīm, *Kitâb Al-Fihrist* (ed. G. Flügel; Leipzig: Brockhaus, 1872), 328. Translated by Reeves, *Prolegomena,* 37; cf. Iain Gardner and Samuel N. C.

> One day a voice called out to him from the sanctuary of the idol-temple saying: "O Fattiq! Eat no meat! Drink no wine! Be married to no one!" This event recurred for him a number of times over a three day period. When Fattiq recognized this, he joined a group of people near Dast-(i)-Maysān [بنواحى دستميسان] known as the Mughtasila [المغتسلة]. Remnants of them are still in the districts of al-Batā'iḥ[82] in our times. They were the sect which Fattiq was ordered to join while his wife was pregnant with Mani.

Mani was probably born in the region of Gaukhay (northeast of Mesene on the east bank of the Tigris),[83] but he was raised in east Mesene among a sect which Ibn-Nadin names *Mughtasila* (the Washers) and who are referred to in the fifth century Cologne Mani Codex (CMC) as Baptists (βαπτισταί).[84] These Baptists, who followed strict dietary and purity laws and most likely had Jewish-Christian roots,[85] regarded Alchasaios as "the founder of our Law" (Ἀλχασαῖος ὁ ἀρχηγὸς τοῦ νόμου ὑμῶν).[86] This has led most scholars to infer that they should be identified with the Elchasites.[87] Mani was a Baptist in Mesene, and his native tongue would have

---

Lieu, eds., *Manichaean Texts from the Roman Empire* [Cambridge: Cambridge University Press, 2004], 47).

82. ʿal- Batā'iḥ refers to the marshland in southern Iraq (see Reeves, *Prolegomena*, 37 n. 119). On the marshland and the desert of Mesene (Dašt-i Mayšān), see further n. 75 above.

83. See Werner Sundermann, "Mani: Childhood and Youth," *EIr*; Walter B. Henning, "Mani's Last Journey," *BSOAS* 10 (1942): 945–47; Jürgen Tubach, "Manis Jugend," *Ancient Society* 24 (1993): 119–38. On the religious climate of Gaukhay in the Sasanian period, see further van Bladel, *From Sasanian Mandaeans*, 98–117.

84. A fragment from the Coptic Synaxeis seems to indicate that this particular sect of Baptists had several monasteries, which Mani visited in his youth (Funk, "Mani's Account,"120). If this is indeed the case, these monasteries would most probably have been located in Mesene.

85. See, e.g., Kurt Rudolph, "Jüdische und christliche Täufertraditionen im Spiegeldes CMC," in *Codex Manichaicus Coloniensis: Atti del simposio internazionale (Rende-Amantea, 3–7 settembre 1984*, ed. Luigi Cirillo and Amneris Roselli, Studi e ricerche 4 (Cosenza: Marra, 1986), 69–80; Kurt Rudolph, "Antike Baptisten: Zu den Überlieferungen über frühjudische und -christliche Taufsekten," in idem, *Gnosis und spätantike Religionsgeschichte: Gesammelte Aufsätze*, NHMS 42 (Leiden: Brill, 1996), 569–606; John C. Reeves, "The 'Elchasaite Sanhedrin' of the Cologne Mani Codex in Light of Second Temple Jewish Sectarian Sources," *JJS* 42 (1991): 68–91, and the articles cited below in n. 87. For the importance of CMC to Jewish history, see J. Maier, "Il codice 'Mani' di Colonia come fonte per la storia giudaica," in *Codex Manichaicus Coloniensis. Atti del Secondo Simposio Internazionale (Cosenza 27–28 maggio 1988)*, ed. Luigi Cirillo (Cosenza: Marra Editore, 1990), 57–65. For Jewish traditions in Manichaeism, see Reeves, *Heralds of That Good Realm*.

86. CMC 94 (= Ludwig Koenen and Cornelia Römer, *Der Kölner Mani-Kodex: Über das Werden seines Leibes* [Opladen: Westdeutscher Verlag, 1988], 66). Ibn Nadim also states that the Mughtasilah were founded by al-Ḥasīḥ. See Gustav Flügel, *Mani: Seine Lehre und seine Schriften* (Leipzig: Brockhaus, 1862), 133–35.

87. Luigi Cirillo, "Elchasaiti e Battisti di Mani: I limiti di un confronto delle fonti," in Cirillo and Roselli, *Codex Manichaicus Coloniensis* (1986), 97–139; and, in the same volume, Albertus F. J. Klijn, "Alchasaios et CMC," 141–52; Albert Henrichs, "Mani and the Babylo-

been Aramaic, the dominant language of the region.[88] It is likely that the syncretistic environment of the region had a decisive impact on him.[89]

Mani would later return several times to the region, mainly on his way to and from India. Through the reports of Mani's travels in Mesene we learn about the existence of several religious communities, most nota-

nian Baptists: A Historical Confrontation," *HSCP*–77 (1973): 23-59; Albertus F. J. Klijn and Gerrit J. Reinink, "Elchasai and Mani," *VC* 28 (1974): 277–89; Reinhold Merkelbach, "Die Täufer, bei denen Mani aufwuchs," in *Manichaean Studies: Proceedings of the First International Conference on Manichaeism*, ed. Peter Bryder (Lund: Plus Ultra, 1988), 105–33; Julien Ries, "Enfance et jeunesse de Mani à la lumière des documents récents," in *L'enfant dans les civilisations orientales*, ed. Aristide Théodoridès, Paulus Naster, and Julien Ries, Acta Orientalia Belgica 2 (Leuven: Peeters, 1980), 133–43; Cornelia Römer, *Manis frühe Missionsreisen nach der Kölner Manibiographie:Textkritischer Kommentar und Erläuterungen zu 121–192 des Kölner Manibiographie* (Opladen: Westdeutscher Verlag, 1994), esp. 113–46; Werner Sundermann, "Mani," *EIr*. Gerard Luttikhuizen, on the other hand, argued that the title given to Alchasaios in the CMC means that he was a (past) leader of the sect, not its founder. See Gerard P. Luttikhuizen, *The Revelation of Elchasai: Investigations into the Evidence for a Mesopotamian Jewish Apocalypse of the Second Century and Its Reception by Judeo-Christian Propagandists*, TSAJ 8 (Tübingen: Mohr Siebeck, 1985); idem, "Elchasaites and Their Book," in *A Companion to Second-Century Christian "Heretics"*, ed. Antti Marjanen and Petri Luomanen, VCSup 76 (Leiden: Brill, 2005), 335–64, esp. 359: "While it is evident that, according to the CMC and the Fihrist, Mani spent his youth in a community of Jewish-Christian Baptists, it remains doubtful whether these Baptists were Elchasaites"); idem, "Appendix: The Baptists of Mani's Youth and the Elchasaites," in idem, *Gnostic Revisions of Genesis Stories and Early Jesus Traditions*, NHMS 58 (Leiden: Brill, 2006), 170–84. However, as Gardner and Lieu note (*Manichaean Texts*, 34), the publication by Werner Sundermann ("Iranische Lebensbeschreibungen Manis," *AcOr* 36 [1974]: 138, 149ff.) of a biographical Manichaean text in Parthian with the name *'lxs'*, strongly supports the argument that Alchasaios was not just an ordinary leader.

88. See, most recently, Nils A. Pedersen, "Syriac Texts in Manichaean Script: New Evidence," in *Mani in Dublin: Selected Papers from the Seventh International Conference of the International Association of Manichaean Studies in the Chester Beatty Library, Dublin, 8–12 September 2009*, ed. Charles Horton, Klaus Ohlhafer, and Siegfried G. Richter, NHMS 88 (Leiden: Brill, 2015), 284: "[T]he first and original language of Manichaeism was Syriac"; idem and John Møller Larsen, *Manichaean Texts in Syriac: First Editions, New Editions and Studies*, Corpus Fontium Manichaeorum, Series Syriaca 1 (Turnhout: Brepols, 2013).

89. On the basis of possible influences on Mani's thought, Samuel N. C. Lieu has suggested that, while growing up, Mani encountered Bardesanites and especially Marcionites (*Manichaeism in the Later Roman Empire and Medieval China: A Historical Survey*, 2nd ed. [Tübingen: Mohr Siebeck, 1992], 37–54). Further evidence for the continued presence of Marcionites in Mesene can be found in The Life of Mar 'Abda of Deir Qoni embedded in the Chronicle of Seert (1.2, LX, 307): "The Marcionites had spread their magic among Christians. Mar 'Abdâ reconverted them.... The Marcionites were constantly trying to kill him. But their plots were foiled by Almighty God" (trans. Alcock, 53–54). 'Abda was active in Mesene in the fourth century. See Wood, *Chronicle of Seert*, 75–77.

bly Baptists, in the region.[90] In the CMC the following account is given by Mani:[91]

> 137 …) until (… I came) into (a) village called S(…) (εἰς κώμη[ν τινὰ κα] λουμένην Σ[...]) and went (into the) assembly of the (…) (ε[ἰς τὴν συ] ναγωγὴν τῶ[ν … ..]ων), the so-(called sons(?)) of the truth. The head of the (sect of) unrigh(teousness) ([ὁ ἀρ]χηγὸς τῆς αἱρ[έσεως]) said (to me: "The) exact understanding of the teaching (of our fathers …" (ἡ] δὲ ἀκρίβε[ια τῆς διδα]σκαλίας [ἡμῶν τῶν πα]τέρων)
> *10 lines lost* … 138 He conducted a) disputation with me before the men of his faith (ἀνδρῶν τοῦ αὐ[τοῦ δόγ[ματος]). In all points he was (defeated) and (drew) laughter on himself, so that he was filled with (envy) and malice. He sat down, according to the (rituals), and practices the spells (ἐπῳδὰς) of his (…) whose (…) chanting (…) and full (…) spell (…) to (…) said: ("…) your (… *6 lines lost, apparently the leader of the group chants a spell against Patticius* 139 …) so that Patticius (…) is well." In this way he chanted (over him) conjuring (…) wickedness. And so his intention came to naught. For as much as he himself (spoke) the (magic) words, my lord frustrated (his) wickedness. […] 140 in the (village …), where (?) (Patticius?) had recovered (?), (we went (?)) to Pharat, the town near the island of the people of Mesene' (ἐις Φαρὰτ' τὴν [πό]λιν πλησίον τῆς [νήσ]ου τῶν Μαϊσα[νῶν].[92]

Unfortunately, the names of both the sect and the village have not been preserved. Yet it seems possible, as Samuel Lieu convincingly argues, to reconstruct the general location of this unknown village:[93]

> The account of the debate with this unidentified sect is therefore sandwiched between Mani's journey to Media and his eventual arrival at the

90. Cf. Kephalaia 186.6–24 (Hans-Jakob Polotsky and Alexander Böhlig, eds., *Kephalaia* [Stuttgart: W. Kohlhammer 1940]; *The Kephalaia of the Teacher: The Edited Coptic Manichaean Texts in Translation with Commentary*, trans. Iian Gardner, NHMS 37 [Leiden: Brill, 1995], 195), where Mani describes his failed efforts to preach in the city of Mesene (Karka d'Meishan): "[I] came [out] from the land of Pers[ia]. I went up [to Me]sene the city ([ⲁⲧⲙⲁ] ⲯⲍⲁⲛⲟⲥ ⲧⲡⲟⲗⲓⲥ) that […] … [… I proc]laimed this knowledge.… Yet, when they had heard the voice of the voice [of truth and life]. The [rulin]g-power and the swarm of demon […] and the race of mankind […] under wickedness and hatred, they […] [they did not] allow me, [nor] did the [permit me] to preach [the truth in [tranquil]ity.… Yet the truth that I proc[laimed] among [them] they did not accept it."

91. *CMC* 137–40, 98–99; Gardner and Lieu, *Manichaean Texts*, 71–72. For digital reproduction of the manuscript, see http://www.uni-koeln.de/phil-fak/ifa/NRWakademie/papyrologie/Manikodex/bildermani.html.

92. On the island of Mesene, see Jürgen Tubach, "Die Insel der Mesene," *WO* 24 (1993): 112–26; Römer, *Manis frühe Missionsreisen*, 105–11.

93. Lieu, *Manichaeism in Mesopotamia*, 5.

> port of Pharat in Mesene, then the gateway to India. Since the journey from the village of the debate to Pharat only lasted a few days. We may assume that the village too was situated in Mesene.

The identity of the sect (αἵρεσις) has been a matter of much dispute. According to the text, they had a synagogue; their leader bore the title of ἀρχηγός; they meticulously followed the "teaching of the fathers" and made use of magic. Ludwig Koenen and Cornelia Römer, the editors of the text, reconstructed the sect's name as "Magusaeans," though in their apparatus the alternatives "Chaldaeans" and "Jews" are given. In a note, they cite in support of their reading several sources that document the polemics between Mani and the Magi.[94] However, as Judith and Samuel Lieu have pointed out, this reconstruction is not very plausible. First, it would seem unlikely that as early as the final days of Ardashir a gathering of the Magians could be found in a village in southern Mesene, outside of the main centers of the Sasanian administration.[95] It would also be strange to refer to the Magians as a sect. Another difficulty is that the term "synagogue" (συναγωγή) is not likely to be associated with the Magians. The term best suits a Jewish community, and Mani's hostility to the Jews is well documented. Even though the Lieus concede that "the alternative, Jews, fits well both community structure and response," they reject this identification claiming that there is no other evidence in the Manichaean corpus for an encounter with a Jewish synagogue.[96] They suggest, rather, that the title of the leader of the sect (ἀρχηγός) would point to a Baptist community, as it is the title given to Alchasaios and other leaders of the sect in which Mani was raised, as we have seen above.[97] This sect, however, would not have been identical with the one in which Mani was brought up, since the latter used the term ἐκκλησία rather than συναγωγή.

However, the identification of the sect as Jewish should not be so readily dismissed. As already noted by Römer, the fact that the extant Manichaean literature does not depict an encounter of Mani with a Jewish synagogue is possibly due to the very fragmentary nature of the sources

---

94. Koenen and Römer, *Der Kölner Mani-Kodex*, 98–99 and n. 1.

95. Judith M. and Samuel N. C. Lieu, "Mani and the Magians (?)—*CMC* 137–140," in *Manichaica Selecta: Studies Presented to Professor Julien Ries on the Occasion of his Seventieth Birthday*, ed. Alois van Tongerloo and Søren Giversen, Manichaean Studies 1 (Leuven: International Association of Manichaean Studies 1991), 209; see 208: "the Zoroastrian religion under the first two Sassanian King of Kings was far from widespread and … the social position of the Magians was also far from exalted."

96. Lieu and Lieu, "Mani and the Magians," 223.

97. This title is also used in Manichaean literature to refer to Mani and to the leader of the Manichaean community (it is not attested in a Jewish context); see ibid., 217. For further arguments concerning the "teaching of the fathers" and the use of magic, see ibid., 218–19.

we have and cannot be used as a sustainable argument.[98] Furthermore, the expression "The exact understanding of the teaching of our fathers" (ἡ] δὲ ἀκρίβε[ια τῆς διδα]σκαλίας [ἡμῶν τῶν πα]τέρων) best suits a Jewish community, as the Lieus themselves have convincingly shown.[99] Josephus uses the term ἀκρίβεια to characterize Judaism in general and the sect (αἵρεσις) of the Pharisees in particular.[100] The same term is also employed by Paul in Act 22:3, when he states that he was "educated at the feet of Gamaliel, strictly according to the law of our fathers [κατὰ ἀκρίβειαν τοῦ πατρῴου νόμου]." In addition, the use of magic by the leader of the sect also fits well with Jewish magical practices, and especially with the perception of Jews as magicians.[101] Thus, it would seem quite likely that Mani depicts a polemical encounter with a Jewish sect in a village in Mesene. On what happened when Mani and Patticus returned to Pharat after the encounter with the unknown sect, the CMC contains the following report:

> [ὁπηνίκα ὁ] κ(ύριό)ς μου καὶ [Παττίκιος ὁ] οἰκοδεσπό[της εἰς Φαρὰτ]' ἐληλύθα[σιν, ὡμίλησεν] ἐν τῆι ἐκ[κλησίαι τῶν βα]πτιστῶν
>
> [When] my lord and [Patticius the] overseer of the house had come [to Pharat], [he preached] in [the assembly of] the Baptists.

Mani then holds a lengthy theological debate with one of the Baptists. The identity of these Baptists is not clear. Römer has suggested they might be related to the Baptists from Dašt-i Mayšān, where Mani was born and raised, since Forat/Pharat was in its vicinity.[102] This is indeed plausible, but, even if the places are related, we are still dealing with two separate Baptist communities, in two separate (though close) geographical locations. When this possibility is taken together with the unknown (Jewish?) sect mentioned above, we get a small glimpse into the diversity of the Judeo-Christian landscape of Mesene.[103]

After the death of Ardashir in 242, Mani reached Rew-Ardasir and, having traveled through Persis and Babylonia, arrived in Mesene,[104] where he supposedly converted Mihrshah, the ruler of Mesene.[105] Mani

98. Römer, *Manis frühe Missionsreisen*, 96.

99. Lieu and Lieu, "Mani and the Magians," 219; Römer, *Manis frühe Missionsreisen*, 100.

100. In general, see Josephus, *C. Ap.* 2.149; for Pharisees: *Vita* 191; *B.J.* 1.110, 191; 2.162.

101. This too has been noted by Lieu and Lieu, "Mani and the Magians," 220–22.

102. Römer, *Manis frühe Missionsreisen*, 119.

103. For a Baptist community that Mani encounters in Rew-Ardashir, see Werner Sundermann, "Parthisch 'BSWDG'N 'Die Taüfer,'" *Acta Antiqua Academiae Scientiarum Hungaricae* 25 (1977 [pub. 1980]): 238–40.

104. Cf. Kephalaia 15.27–31 (trans. Gardner, 21: "in the last year [that Arda]shir the king died ... I crossed from the country of the Indians to the land of the Persians. Also from the land of Persia I came [to] the land of Babylon, Mesen[e] (ⲧⲙⲁⲓ̈ⲥⲁ[ⲛⲟⲥ]) and Susiana."

105. On this episode, see below.

also established several communities in the region during his lifetime. Among the titles on the extensive list of Mani's epistles preserved by Ibn Nadim, the following were directed to communities in Mesene:[106] "Epistle to Kaskar" (رسالة كسكر; no. 6);[107] "Epistle to Karkh[108] and 'Urāb" (رسالة الكرخ والعراب; no. 45) and "Epistle to Maysān, on The Day" (رسالة ميسان في النهار; no. 33). The latter epistle is possibly similar to the one cited in a Parthian fragment (M731):[109] "from the epistle (to) Meshun about the two bodies" (*'c prwdrg myšwn 'y dw tnw'r*). In the Coptic Manichaean

106. *Kitâb Al-Fihrist,* 336; trans. Reeves, *Prolegomena,* 115–17. Cf. Michel Tardieu, "L'Arabie du Nord-Est d'après les documents manichéens," *Studia Iranica* 23 (1994): 66–68 and n. 35. The other epistles directed to cities and provinces are India (no. 3); Armenia (no. 8); Babylonia (no. 23); Ctesiphon (nos. 10 and 19); Edessa (no. 31; CMC 64–65); Hatta (no. 65 = M733); Al-Ahwzā (no. 58). The rest of the epistles are either general or directed to specific people. Judging by the number of epistles, the region of Mesene seems to have been an important center of Manichaeism during Mani's lifetime.

107. According to Hegemonius's *Acta Archelai* (first half of the fourth century), Mani sent a letter to Marcellus, an inhabitant of a town in Mesopotamia named Carchar, in the Latin manuscripts (probably derived from *Karka*), or Κάσχαρ (Kaschar) in most of the Greek witnesses, where the (fictional) debate between Mani and the bishop Archelaus takes place. For the various versions of the toponym, see Jason BeDuhn and Paul Mirecki, "Placing the Acts of Archelaus," in *Frontiers of Faith: The Christian Encounter with Manichaeism in the Acts of Archelaus,* ed. BeDuhn and Mirecki, NHMS 61 (Leiden: Brill, 2007), 10. This might refer to Kashkar, as suggested already by Konrad Kessler (*Mani: Forschungen über die manichäische Religion* [Berlin: G. Reimer, 1889], 90–94). If so, it is possible that the letter to Marcellus and its content as they appear in the *Acta* could reflect the "Letter to Kaskar" mentioned by Ibn Nadim (see Iain Gardner, "Mani's Letter to Marcellus: Fact and Fiction in the Acta Archelai Revisited," in BeDuhn and Mirecki, *Frontiers of Faith,* 35). However, identifying the town as Kashkar is problematic since according to the story the town is located on the Roman side of the border, whereas Kashkar is deep in Sasanian territory. This has led Fiey to adopt the Latin toponym of Carchar, arguing that it should be identified with the Roman city of Carrhae (*Assyrie Chrétienne III,* 152–55, followed by Lieu, *Manichaeism in Mesopotamia,* 140–43. In more detail, see Samuel N. C. Lieu and Mark Vermes, *Hegemonius, Acta Archelai,* Manichaean Studies 4 [Turnhout: Brepols, 2001], 16–23). It is still possible to credit the testimony of the Greek witnesses, but in such a case, as BeDuhn notes, "we would be forced to conclude that Hegemonius built his anachronistic debate around an authentic letter of Mani, which provided him with the place name Kashkar as well as with the name of a prominent local Christian, Marcellus (perhaps one Archelaus was also mentioned in the letter), without having any detailed knowledge of either the place or the persons involved" ("A War of Words: Intertextuality and the Struggle over the Legacy of Christ in the Acta Archelai," in BeDuhn and Mirecki, *Frontiers of Faith,* 86). BeDuhn goes on to suggest (86-87) that, if Marcellus was indeed an inhabitant of Kashkar, it is possible that he was a prominent individual among the deportees settled in the city by Shapur I. On these deportations and their impact on the south, see below.

108. Spasinou Charax. According to the *Acta Archelai,* Mani receives a letter from Marcellus while abiding in *Castellum Arabionis,* which possibly refers to Spasinou Charax (see, e.g., Kessler, *Mani,* 89–96; Vermes and Lieu, *Acta Archelai,* 16). However, BeDuhn and Mirecki ("Placing the Acts," 12) suggest that it refers to Dur 'Arabaya on the east bank of the middle Tigris.

109. Prosper Alfaric, *Les écritures manichéennes,* 2 vols. (Paris: E. Nourry, 1918–1919),

Homilies, Mesene is named as one of the regions in which the Manichaeans were persecuted.[110] Mesene was thus the home for several Baptist groups, and the soil on which Mani had developed his highly syncretistic religion, through interaction with the diverse religious groups in the region, including, most probably, Jews.

As we have seen, several Christian authors explicitly portray Mesene as dominantly pagan. In the same vein, it is possible that the concentration of a variety of religious movements with distinct Jewish elements in Mesene (Naṣoreans, Mandaeans, Elchasites, and Manichaeans) might have impacted the way the region and its Jews were *perceived* by the rabbis. The (real or imaginary) possibility that the Jews of the region interacted with such religious movements might explain in part the rabbinic anxieties concerning Mesene and might help us understand their motivation to advocate social segregation between themselves and the Mesenean Jews by highlighting the latter's genealogical inferiority.

Halakhic Divergence

Besides the possibility, not explicitly stated in the Talmud, that the Jews of Mesene were perceived as associating with "heretics," several talmudic sources seem to indicate that some of the Mesenean Jews did not conform to the halakhic hegemony of the Babylonian rabbis but rather continued to orient themselves toward the Palestinian center.[111]

The main source adduced by scholars appears in b. Šabb. 37b. In a debate whether one can place cooked food and boiling water on a heated oven during the Sabbath, the important third-century Palestinian sage R. Yoḥanan permits this practice, whereas his Babylonian contemporaries, Rav and Shmuel, forbid it. In this context, Rav 'Uqba of Meishan, the only rabbi who is explicitly linked to Mesene, is said to have addressed Rav Ashi (late fourth–early fifth century) the head of the Sura academy as follows:[112]

1:72; Jason D. BeDuhn, *The Manichaean Body: In Discipline and Ritual* (Baltimore: Johns Hopkins University Press, 2000), 135; Schuol, *Die Charakene*, 178–79.

110. Nils Arne Pedersen, ed., *Manichaean Homilies*, Corpus Fontium Manichaeorum, Series Coptica 2 (Turnhout: Brepols, 2006), 76.

111. This point has already been noted by Nodelman ("Preliminary History," 112) and was later enlarged upon by Aharon Oppenheimer in his article "Contacts between Mesene and Eretz Israel" [Hebrew], *Zion* 47 (1982): 335–41 (for a German version, see idem, "Beziehungen zwischen Messene und Palästina," in Nili Oppenheimer, *Between Rome and Babylon*, 409–16), and, in the same volume, Aharon Oppenheimer, "Contacts between Eretz Israel and Babylonia at the Turn of the Period of the *Tannaim* and the *Amoraim*," 421–24.

112. Rav 'Uqba of Meishan is also mentioned in b. Šabb. 43a–b (= b. Beṣah 36a), where he once again argues with Rav Ashi.

> אתון דמקרביתו לרב ושמואל – עבידו כרב ושמואל, אנן – נעביד כרבי יוחנן.
>
> You (pl.) who are close to Rav and Shmuel, do as Rav and Shmuel, we shall do as R. Yoḥanan.

By "we," Rav 'Uqba of Mesene refers most likely not only to himself but more generally to the Jews of Mesene, who act in accordance with R. Yoḥanan's opinion. On the other hand, "you"—that is, Rav Ashi and the rest of the Babylonian Jews—follow Rav and Shmuel. The dichotomy "we"/"you" and the remark "you *who are close to Rav and Shmuel*" suggest that, although Rav 'Uqba's statement deals with a specific halakhic issue, it would be reasonable to suppose that his statement points to a more general halakhic divergence between the Mesenean and Babylonian Jews. The former were presumably close to R. Yoḥanan and adhered to the Palestinian halakha.[113]

---

113. Oppenheimer, *Babylonia Judaica*, 254; idem, "Contacts between Eretz Israel and Babylonia," 424; idem, "Contacts between Mesene," 340–41. Oppenheimer wished to further support his argument with the following story found in the Palestinian Talmud (y. Pesaḥ. 4:1, 30d): גלו ממקו' למקום וביקשו לחזור בהן, ייבא כהדא דאמ' רבי בא: בני מישא קיבלו עליהן שלא לפרש בים הגדול. אתון שאלון לרבי, אמרין ליה: אבותינו נהגו שלא לפרש בים הגדול אנו מה אנו? אמר להן: מכיון שנהגו בהן אבותיכם באיסור אל תשנו מנהג אבותיכם נוחי נפש. ("If they migrated from one place to another and wished to return, it is like what R. Ba said: The people of Meisha took upon themselves not to sail in the great sea. They came to ask Rabbi and told him: Our ancestors used not to sail in the great sea, what about us? He told them: Since your ancestors treated this as a prohibition, do not change the custom of your ancestors, the peaceful souls"). The identity of Meisha has been much disputed. In a similarly, although not identically, structured story in b. Pesah. 50b the people of Beishan (בני בישן) approach R. Yoḥanan concerning their ancestors' custom not to travel from Tyre to Sidon on a Friday. This led Samuel Klein to locate Mesha near Tyre ("The Letter of R. Menachem the Hebronite" [Hebrew], *Yedi'ot ha-Hevrah la-hakirat Erets-Yisra'el ve-'atikoteha* 6 [1939]: 21; idem, *Sefer ha-Yishuv* [Jerusalem: Mossad Bialik, 1939] 1:106–7). However, this suggestion was rightly rejected by Saul Lieberman (*Yerushalmi ki-Pshuto* [Jerusalem: Darom, 1935], 1:434; cf. Moshe Beer, *Babylonian Amoraim: Aspects of Economic Life* [Hebrew] [Ramat Gan: Bar-Ilan University Press, 1974], 157 n. 3). Lieberman argued that Meisha is a settlement in Palestine, since immediately after the story R. Ḥanina claims that Rabbi's verdict accords with the prohibition of R. Yehuda, his teacher, not to sail in the great sea, a prohibition intended to prevent people from leaving the Land of Israel (cf. y. Mo'ed Qaṭ. 3:1, 81c). Indeed an unidentified settlement named Meisha is mentioned once in t. Šeb. 4:11 as part of the confines of the Land of Israel (תחום ארץ ישראל). However, as noted by Aharon Amit (*Makom Shenahagu: Pesahim Chapter 4, Talmud ha-Igud* [Hebrew] [Jerusalem: Reuven Mas, 2009], 61), R. Ḥanina's statement seems secondary, since Rabbi regards refraining from sailing as a custom (נהגו) whereas R. Yehuda—as a prohibition (אסור). Oppenheimer ("Contacts between Mesene," 338–39; idem, "Contacts between Eretz Israel and Babylonia," 423 and n. 15; less decisively *Babylonia Judaica*, 255), following Samuel Krauss (*Qadmoniot ha-Talmud* [Hebrew] [Odessa: Moriah, 1924], 1:116) argues that מישא is the common form for Mesene in Palestinian sources. In fact, the only other occurrence of בני מישא in Palestinian sources clearly refers to Mesene (y. Qidd. 4:1, 65c). In addition, as we have seen above, a funerary inscription from Beth Shearim, where Rabbi was buried, marks the grave of a woman from Mesene. Recently, Aharon Amit (*Makom Shenahagu*, 60–62) argued that, although Meisha is to be identified with Mesene, the people who approached Rabbi had

To the previous source I would like to add another, not yet adduced by scholars in this context, which highlights the condescending view of the rabbis as to the halakhic inferiority of the southern Jews (in this case the people of Kashkar):[114]

שלחו ליה בני בשכר ללוי: כילה מהו? כשותא בכרמא מהו?[115] מת ביום טוב מהו?
אדאזיל, נח נפשיה דלוי.
אמר שמואל לרב מנשיא: אי חכימת – שלח להו.
[א] שלח להו: כילה – חזרנו על כל צידי כילה ולא מצינו לה צד היתר.
[א1] ולישלח להו כדרמי בר יחזקאל?
- לפי שאינן בני תורה.
[ב] כשותא בכרמא – עירבובא.
[ב1] ולישלח להו כדרבי טרפון? דתניא: כישות, רבי טרפון אומר: אין כלאים בכרם, וחכמים אומרים: כלאים בכרם. וקיימא לן: כל המיקל בארץ – הלכה כמותו בחוץ לארץ?
- לפי שאינן בני תורה.
[...]
[ג] מת – שלח להו: מת לא יתעסקו ביה לא יהודאין ולא ארמאין, לא ביום טוב ראשון ולא ביום טוב שני.
[ג1] איני? והאמר רבי יהודה בר שילת אמר רבי אסי: עובדא הוה בבי כנישתא דמעון ביום טוב הסמוך לשבת, ולא ידענא אי מלפניה אי מלאחריה, ואתו לקמיה דרבי יוחנן. ואמר להו: יתעסקו ביה עממין. ואמר רבא: מת ביום טוב ראשון – יתעסקו בו עממין, ביום טוב שני – יתעסקו בו ישראל, ואפילו ביום טוב שני של ראש השנה, מה שאין כן בביצה.
- לפי שאינן בני תורה.

The people of Kashkar[116] sent [a question] to Levi: (A) What about [setting up] a canopy [on the Sabbath]; (B) what about cuscuta in a vineyard? (C) What about a dead man on a Festival?
By the time he [the messenger] arrived [at Levi's home] Levi had died.
Said Shmuel to Rav Menashya: If you are wise, send them [an answer].
[So] he sent [word] to them:

---

immigrated from Mesene and settled near Tyre (based on the Bavli's version). Such a harmonistic reconstruction seems untenable (it also does not fit well with the verb גלו, as Amit himself concedes [ibid., 61 n. 40]). Nonetheless, the identification of Meisha with Mesene seems the most plausible suggestion.

114. b. Šabb. 139a. For a discussion on the third question and answer in light of other parallels, see Geoffrey Herman, "'Bury My Coffin Deep!': Zoroastrian Exhumation in Jewish and Christian Sources," in *Tiferet LeYisrael: Jubilee Volume in Honor of Israel Francus*, ed. Joel Roth, Yaacov Francus, and Menahem Schmelzer (New York: Jewish Theological Seminary, 2010), 53–59.

115. The fact that the people of Kashkar ask a question regarding vineyards, would indicate that they cultivated grapevines in the region. On the importance of this information for the location of Harpania, see n. 128.

116. Although it is written consistently as Bashkar (בשכר), the reference is to Kashkar.

(A) "As for a canopy, we have examined it from all aspects and do not find any aspect by which it can be permitted."
(A1) But let him send them [a permissive ruling] in accordance with Rami b. Ezekiel?
Because they are not learned in the Torah.
(B) "Cuscuta in a vineyard is a [forbidden] mixture."
(B1) But let him send them [a reply] in accordance with R. Ṭarfon. For it was taught: As for cuscuta, R. Ṭarfon maintains: It is not mixed seeds in a vineyard; while the Sages rule: It is mixed seeds in a vineyard. And it is an established principle: He who is lenient in respect to Palestine, the law is according to him outside of Palestine? –
Because they are not learned in the Torah.
[...]
(C) As for a corpse – he sent [word to them]: "Neither Jews nor Aramaeans[117] may occupy themselves with a corpse, neither on the first day of a Festival nor on the second."
(C1) But that is not so? For R. Yehuda b. Shilat said in R. Assi's name: Such a case happened in the synagogue of Ma'on on a Festival near the Sabbath, though I do not know whether it preceded or followed it, and when they went before R. Yoḥanan, he said to them: Let Gentiles occupy themselves with him [the dead].
Rava too said: As for a corpse, on the first day of Festivals Gentiles should occupy themselves with him; on the second day of Festivals Israelites may occupy themselves with him, and even on the second day of New Year, which is not so in the case of an egg.
Because they are not learned in the Torah.

The people of Kashkar address three rather specific questions to Levi (b. Sisi), one of the important pupils of R. Yehuda HaNasi, after he had arrived in Nehardea.[118] It is interesting to note that the people of Kashkar prefer to turn to a Palestinian sage rather than to a Babylonian one, such as Shmuel or Shmuel's father, with whom Levi was acquainted.[119]

Beyond the possible connections between the Mesenean Jews and Palestinian sages, the editorial touches in the *sugya* under discussion also highlight a more general northern halakhic chauvinism. As a result of Levi's death, Shmuel encourages Rav Menashya to answer the people of Kashkar. Each of Rav Menashya's three rulings is followed by an anonymous interpolation (A1, B1, C1) that wonders why Rav Menashya did not choose a more lenient alternative. The conclusion of each interpolation is identical: "Because they are not learned in the Torah" (לפי שאינן בני

117. As we have seen above, the inhabitants of Mesene are referred to in Classical sources as Chaldeans and in Arabic sources as Nabateans, that is, Arameans. However, the reference here seems to be to pagans in general.

118. On Levi's arrival in Nehardea, see, e.g., b. Šabb. 59b.

119. See, e.g., b. Meg. 29a; b. Ber. 30a; b. B. Bat. 42a.

תורה);[120] that is, the people of Kashkar are ignorant of the Torah and hence must be instructed stringently. However, the actual content of the intricate and specific questions posed by the people of Kashkar, which need not detain us here, does not display any ignorance, nor do Rav Menashya's answers seem to assume such ignorance. In fact, Shmuel stresses that Rav Menashya can answer these questions only if he is wise! It would thus seem that the rather forced questions in the anonymous editorial layer (the *stam*) are intended to highlight the ignorance (and waywardness?) of the Jews of Kashkar[121] and reinforce the halakhic superiority of the Babylonian rabbis. The *stam* thus further fortifies the general prejudices toward the south, this time within a halakhic context.[122]

The evidence for contacts between Palestinian and Mesenean sages is admittedly extremely meager.[123] Yet if there were indeed such contacts, they would have been facilitated by the international (mainly Nabatean) trade route between Mesene and Palestine.[124] In addition, the rise of Baby-

---

120. The phrase שאינן בני תורה appears several times in the Bavli. R. Yoḥanan uses it against the people of Gibla (b. Yebam. 46a; b. 'Abod. Zar. 59a); R. Ḥiyya against the sages of Babylonia (b. Šabb. 145b); Rav Aḥa b. Taḥlifa against the people of Ganana (b. 'Erub. 40a); and Rava against the inhabitants of Tiberias and Nehardea (b. 'Abod. Zar. 58a).

121. This could be seen also from the continuation of the *sugya,* where the Bavli adduces several examples of sages who refrained from sowing cuscuta in a vineyard (although they agreed to have it done by proxy).

122. Such northern chauvinism was also shared by Syriac authors. As we have seen above, according to the Acts of Mar Mari, the people of Mesene "were particularly brutal, stupid, and mundane." Furthermore, there also seems to have been similar shared attitudes specifically against Kashkar. The Chronicle of Seert reports that, during the heated conflict between Elishe and Narsai in the 530s, the people of Kashkar supported the latter (2.1, XXV, 151; my translation): "It was offensive to him [= Elishe] [فغلظ ذلك عليه] and he said in the presence of the people in Seleucia: 'I defeated the rest of the countries and do the people (of Kashkar), they who are in the status of vile flies [وهم بمنزلة الذباب], suppose that they shall defeat me? And shall they say: "we shall not receive him, and we have humiliated him?"' And his words reached the Kashkarians and their anger increased [واتصل بلكشاكرة كلامه فزاد غيظهم]." It would seem that in the heat of the moment Elishe (or the author of the narrative) reverts to common abuses. In this context Philip Wood (*Chronicle of Seert*, 104 n. 39) has noted that "Kashkar, as the second city of southern Iraq, may have had a natural rivalry with Ctesiphon, which would also explain the animosity towards Elishe" (for more on the accounts of this struggle, see ibid., 100–105). Thus, despite the entirely different circumstances of the rabbinic and Christian stories, both the *stam* and Elishe (according to the Chronicle of Seert) share a common animosity and prejudices toward the people of Kashkar.

123. It is worth mentioning in this context that also concerning the province of Khuzestan (Be Ḥozai, east of Mesene) we have similar evidence to direct ties with the Palestinian rabbinic center. In two cases (b. Nid. 5b and b. Ḥul. 68b), Rav Avimi of Be Ḥozai (fourth-generation Amora) is said to have transmitted *baraitot* in the Babylonian *yeshivot*. This most probably means, as Oppenheimer has noted (*Babylonia Judaica*, 78), "that tannaic traditions unknown in Babylonia reached Be Hozai from Eretz Israel."

124. On the Nabateans and Mesene, see Schuol, *Die Charakene*, 110–12, 412–15; Oppenheimer, "Contacts between Mesene," 337–38. Cf. Pliny *Nat.* 4.145: "Deinde est oppidum quod Characenorum regi paret in Pasitigris ripa, Forat nomine, in quod a Petra convenient."

lonia as an independent center of study and legal authority rivaling Palestine took place mainly from the time of Rav and Shmuel in the mid-third century, which coincided with the establishment of the Sasanian Empire. It is possible that in Mesene—which was for centuries a separate political, linguistic, and economic entity—some of the Jews did not shift their allegiances to the Babylonian sages but rather continued to conform to the halakhic hegemony of the Land of Israel.[125]

Mesene and Palmyra

The rabbinic negative representation of the Mesenean Jews might not have been motivated only by religious factors. The Bavli explicitly mentions another important factor: the interactions between Palmyra and Mesene.

Mesene's strategic location and important harbor enabled it to play a major role for several centuries in the trade between the Roman Empire and East, as is clearly illustrated in The Hymn of the Pearl, composed most probably during the second century CE:

> I passed through the borders of Maishan [ܥܒܪܬ ܬܚܘܡ̈ܝ ܡܝܫܢ] / the meeting-place of the merchants of the East, / and I reached the land of Babel … / and I came to the great Maishan [ܘܥܠܬ ܠܡܝܫܢ ܪܒܬܐ], / to the haven of the merchants, / which sits on the shore of the sea.[126]

The main caravan routes to the north were controlled by Palmyra, whereas the Nabateans controlled the western route to Petra and, farther on, Palestine. These economic contacts most probably also involved the Mesenean Jews and might have impacted their reputation. Indeed, a talmudic source in b. Yebam. 17a suggests a detrimental contact between the Jews of Palmyra and those of Mesene:[127]

> פסולי דהר פניא – משום פסולי דמישון, ופסולי דמישון – משום פסולי דתדמור, ותדמור – מש' עבדי שלמה. והיינו דאמרי אינשי: קבה רבה וקבה זוטא מיגנדרי ואזיל לשאול, ומשאול לתדמור, ומתדמור למישון, וממישון להרפניא.

---

125. See, however, Oppenheimer, "Contacts between Eretz Israel and Babylonia," 422: "It would seem that its [Y.P.: Mesene's] contacts with Palestine took place circumventing the neighboring center in Babylonia, and they grew closer presumably as a result of the negative attitude of the Jews of Babylonia towards their Jewish neighbours in Mesene." Yet the opposite scenario is more likely. That is, part of the negative attitude of the Babylonian Jews could have been due to the Meseneans' contacts with Palestine.

126. Text: William Wright, ed., *Apocryphal Acts of the Apostles*, vol. 1, *The Syriac Texts* (London: William & Norgate, 1871), 275–77; trans. A. F. J. Klijn, *The Acts of Thomas: Introduction, Text, and Commentary*, 2nd rev. ed., NovTSup 108 (Leiden: Brill, 2003), 183–85.

127. Cited according to MS Oxford Heb. d. 20/1–25.

The unfit of Harpania[128] on account of the unfit of Meshun, and the unfit of Meshan on account of the unfit of Tadmor, and the unfit of Tadmor on account of the slaves of Solomon. Thus it is that people say, "The small kab and the big kab roll down to the nether-world,[129] from the nether-

---

128. Obermeyer (*Die Landschaft Babylonien*, 197) identifies Harpania/Neharpania with Nahr Abān, situated south of Waṣit on the Tigris, whereas Schuol (*Die Charakene*, 281, 287) identifies Harpania with Apamea without supplying evidence. On the other hand, Oppenheimer (*Babylonia Judaica*, 296), identifies it with a different Nahr Abān in the neighborhood of Kufa, that is, on the Euphrates. Though conceding that there are no linguistic objections for locating it south of Waṣit on the Tigris, Oppenheimer rejects this location for two reasons: (1) The talmudic passage that claims "The unfit of Harpania on account of the unfit of Meshan" explicitly indicated that Harpania is not in Mesene. (2) "Talmudic passages mention the fertile soil of Neharpania, frequently praising its excellent produce, and the wine in particular. Although the Waṣit region too is known for its fine soil, grapevines did not grow there" (ibid., 297). Oppenheimer supports this solely on the basis of an Arabic source from which one might adduce that there are no grapevines in Kaskar. Both objections could be challenged: (1) It is possible that the reference to Meishan in b. Yebam. 17a does not include the province of Kashkar (Waṣit), and hence if Harpania was just south of Waṣit it would not be in Mesene. It is also possible that the Bavli is singling out Harpania since it is the worst place within the province of Mesene, and since it actually marks the northeastern border of Mesene (if identified with Apamea). (2) In b. Šabb. 139a, discussed above, among the three questions the people of Kashkar send to Levi, one is concerned with grapevines (כשותא בכרמא מהו?), clearly indicating that vineyards were indeed cultivated in the region. I believe Harpania should be identified with the lower Apamea. Apamea (which appears only once in the rabbinic literature) is known in Arabic sources as Famia/Fania and hence it is possible that Har/Nehar-Pania was another local version of the Greek toponym Apameia. Perhaps one could also identify Harpania/Neharpania with the toponym Zurfania/ Zurfamia (زرفامية/زرفنية) mentioned in Arabic sources as located between Waṣit and Bagdad (see, e.g., Yaqut al-Hamawi, *Muʿjam al-buldān* [Beirut: Dār Ṣāder, 3:103 ,[1986–4). Several scholars had already identified Zurfamia with one of the two Apameas (see references in Oppenheimer, *Babylonia Judaica*, 32–33 n. 15; Cohen, *Hellenistic Settlements*, 125ff.). M. J. de Goeje ("Zur historischen Geographie Babyloniens," *ZDMG* 39 [1885]: 3) suggested that Zurfamiya is to be identified with the lower Apamea and that the prefix *zur* means "lower" (from זעיר). Streck (*Die alte Landschaft*, 1:305–6), convincingly refuted de Goeje's etymology of *zur* and argued that Zurfamiya was the northernmost of the two Apameas. Schaeder ("*Hasan al-Baṣrī*," 15–16), on sounder grounds than de Goeje, also argued that Zurfamiya is the lower Apamea in the Talmud. It would seem likely that the lower Apamea was differentiated from the northern one by adding various prefixes to its name zur/nehar/har. Identifying the location of Harpania is critical, since if, indeed, Harpania is to be located within the genealogical boundaries of Mesene, several additional sources concerning Harpania could be adduced, which would contribute to our knowledge of Mesene and its Jews. There are further ramifications. Oppenheimer's argument for locating Pum Nahara in the southwestern region of Babylonia is based solely on the identification of Neharpania with Nehar Aban in the Kufa area (*Babylonia Judaica*, 371), since we know that Pum Nahara was in the vicinity of Neharpania (see b. Yebam. 17a). It would seem, however, that Pum Nahara should also be located in the vicinity of Kashkar, as Obermeyer had already suggested (*Die Landschaft Babylonien*, 192, 194). It is possible that Pum Nahara should be identified with Fam aṣ-Ṣilḥ on the river aṣ-Ṣilḥ by the Tigris north of Waṣit.

129. The exact meaning of this folk proverb is not clear to me. The connection between

world to Tadmor, from Tadmor to Meshun, and from Meshun to Harpania."

According to the first statement, Mesene's dire genealogical status is due to Palmyra (Tadmor).[130] Indeed, the rabbis, both in Palestine and in Babylonia, display much hostility not only toward Palmyra in general but also toward its Jews, possibly due to the latter's proselytizing efforts.[131] The Bavli, however, does not supply any explanation as to why the low status of the Mesenean Jews is dependent on that of Palmyreans.[132]

Heinrich Graetz, in his short monograph *Das Königreich Mesene und seine jüdische Bevölkerung* (1873), argued that the rabbis' approach to Mesene should be understood against the backdrop of the economic ties between Palmyra and Mesene, and hence between the Jews from both regions.[133] This might not be the sole reason for the rabbis' anxiety, as Graetz presumed, but it was clearly a significant one.

Up until the third century CE the caravan trade to and from Mesene was dominated by Palmyra, as is evident from dozens of Palmyrene inscriptions that mention the caravans to Spasinou Charax.[134] Due to

---

Harpania and the netherworld (Sheol) is also mentioned just before this statement: אמר רבא: והיא עמוקה משאול, שנאמר: "מיד שאול אפדם ממות אגאלם" (הושע יג 14), ואילו פסול דידהו לית להו תקנתא.

(Rava said: It (Harpania) is deeper than Sheol, for it says: "From Sheol itself I will save them, Redeem them from very Death" (Hos. 13:14). But for unfitness of these (from Harpania) there is no remedy at all).

130. See Oppenheimer, *Babylonia Judaica*, 442–45.

131. See the discussion about whether one may accept proselytes from Palmyra a little earlier on in the Bavli (b. Yebam. 16a-b). See also y. Yebam. 1:3, 3a–b; y. Qidd. 4:1, 65c–d; b. Nid. 56b. Cf. Gedalyah Alon, *Studies in the History of the Jews in Israel at the Time of the Mishna and Talmud* [Hebrew] (Jerusalem: HaKibbutz HaMeuchad, 1961), 2:11. For an effort to undermine the sources adduced by several scholars to prove a rabbinic hostility toward Palmyra, see Alan Appelbaum, "The Rabbis and Palmyra: A Case Study on (Mis-)Reading Rabbinics for Historical Purposes," *JQR* 101 (2011): 527–44. Appelbaum, however, ignores, among others, Graetz's monograph, and artificially tries to differentiate between the rabbis' perceptions of Palmyra and of the Palmyrene Jews.

132. As Tzvi Novick has noted (cited in ibid., 536 n. 28), the reason for associating the Palmyrenes with the slaves of Solomon is most probably based on 2 Chr 8:4, which states that Solomon constructed Palmyra.

133. Graetz, *Das Königreich Mesene*, esp. 36: "Es ist kein Zweifel, dass Rabs herbes Urtheil über die mesenisch-jüdischen Gemeinden von diesem Vorurtheil beeinflusst war; sie seien sämmtlich als todt, als unebenbürtig, als untauglich und unwürdig zum Connubium zu betrachten; denn sie stammten alle von Palmyrenern, und diese seien durchweg als Abkömmlinge von Salomo-Sclaven oder als Bastarde oder mindestens als Sclaven zu behandeln, mit denen eine eheliche Verbindung unstatthaft sei."

134. For a survey of the inscriptions, see Schuol, *Die Charakene*, 47–89 and references there. On the Palmyrene trade with Mesene, see most recently Raoul McLaughlin, *Rome and the Distant East: Trade Routes to the Ancient Lands of Arabia, India and China* (London: Continuum, 2010), 100–105; Andrew M. Smith II, *Roman Palmyra: Identity, Community, and State Formation* (New York: Oxford University Press, 2013), 76–82 (with bibliography).

their importance, several Palmyrenes also received official positions in the Characene kingdom, and it seems that quite a few of them settled in Mesene, especially in Spasinou Charax.[135] Furthermore, as we have seen above, the Palmyrene name of one of the bishops of Mesene most likely indicates that Palmyrene expatriates who had settled in the region formed part of the growing Christian community there.

Jewish merchants also took part in the caravan trade. Josephus describes a Jewish merchant in Mesene during the first half of the first century:

> Now during the time when Izates resided at Charax Spasini [ἐν τῷ Σπασίνου χάρακι], a certain Jewish ['Ιουδαῖος] merchant named Ananias ['Ανανίας], visited the King's wives and taught them to worship God after the manner of the Jewish tradition [ὡς 'Ιουδαίοις πάτριον]. (*Ant.* 20.34-35 [Feldman, LCL])

It is unclear though whether the merchant is a native of Mesene or just passing through (a Palmyrene?)[136]

The Bavli, as we have seen above, indicates that marriages between the Jews of Palmyra and those of Mesene were common. This might be corroborated from the following tomb inscription, from Cave 3 in Beth Shearim, the cave in which the Palmyrene tombs are located:[137]

> Μισηνὴ/ Σάρα/ ἡ Μαξίμ[α]
>
> [From] Mesene Sara [also named] Maxima

It seems likely that Sara/Maxima was married to a Palmyrene Jew, which would explain why she was interred among the Palmyrenes.

After the establishment of the Sasanian Empire, the Palmyrene trade dropped drastically and all but ceased by the mid-third century. In 273 CE Palmyra was conquered and razed by the Romans. It is thus most likely that the Bavli's dictum, and especially the proverbial saying, both of which display a familiarity with the strong contacts between Mesene and Palmyra, were composed by, or at least reflect the reality of, the first

135. Nodelman, "Preliminary History," 113; Smith, *Roman Palmyra*, 76.

136. See Nodelman, "Preliminary History," 112; Oppenheimer, "Contacts between Mesene," 337–38; Schuol, *Die Charakene*, 119–20 (with comprehensive bibliography).

137. Moshe Schwabe and Baruch Lifshitz, *Beth She'arim*, vol. 2, *The Greek Inscriptions* (Jerusalem: Israel Exploration Society and Mossad Bialik, 1957), no. 101 [Hebrew]; *CIJ* vol. 2, no. 1124. See also Oppenheimer, *Babylonia Judaica*, 249; Binyamin Mazar, "Those Who Buried Their Dead in Beth-Shearim" [Hebrew], *ErIsr* 18 (1985): 298. Nodelman ("Preliminary History," 112), citing only b. Yebam. 17a as proof, states, "The Palmyrene colony in Mesene must have been fairly large if it were possible to assert that the considerable Jewish population had been contaminated by intermarriage with it."

half of the third century CE. Such a dating of the tradition may have some rather significant consequences, as we shall see below.

We have seen, then, that Mesene was, for centuries, a distinct political and economic entity with its own dialect and diverse, and at times unique, religious landscape. The region and its Jews were thus clearly distinguishable from the "north." The "idolatrous" image of Mesene, the presence of several sects with Jewish components, Palmyrene economic dominance and integration in Mesene, alongside the possible adherence of the Mesenean Jews to Palestinian halakha, might have constituted, separately and combined, the backdrop for the Bavli's exceptional negative representation of the "southern" Jews.

Part II: The Meseneans as Descendants of Slaves

Having outlined a broad portrait of Mesene that may have impacted rabbinic perceptions of its Jews, I will now focus on a short etiological story that appears as part of the Bavli's discussions of the pure lineage of Babylonia. This story purports to anchor the reason for the Mesenean Jews' slave status in the biblical past. I wish to demonstrate how the story both reflects the political and administrative realities of the fourth century Sasanian Empire and also functions as a foundational myth of Babylonian Jewry. In b. Qidd. 72b we find the following discussion:[138]

"[ויהי כהנבאי] ופלטיהו בן בניהו מת ואפלה על פני ואזעק קול גדול [ואומר אהה אדני ה׳
כלה אתה עשה את שארית ישראל]" (יח׳ יא 13)
רב ושמואל (רב) [חד] אמ׳ לטובה וחד אמ׳ לרעה
מאן דאמ׳ לטובה
כי הא דאיסטנדירא דמישון חתניה דנבוכד נאצר הוה
של(ו)ח ליה: מכל שיביא דא[י]ת(ית) לך לא משדרת לי(ה) דקאי קמן
בעי לשדורי ליה מישר׳
א׳ל פלטיהו בן בניהו: אנן דחשיבינן ניקו קמך ועבדין ניזלו להתם
וקא׳ נביא: מי שעשה טובה בישר׳ ימות בחצי ימיו?! [...]
תסתיים דשמו׳ דאמ׳ לרעה
דא׳ר חייא בר אבין [אמר שמואל][139]: מושכני - הריהו׳ כגולה ליוחסין.
מישון (הרי הו׳) לא חשו לא משום עבדות ולא משום ממזרות אלא כהני׳ שהיו בה לא
הקפידו על הגירוש׳.[140]

138. According to MS Vatican 111.

139. Missing in Vatican 111 though clearly a scribal error as it appears in all other MSS.

140. It is interesting to compare this to R. Yoḥanan's statement in y. Ta'an. 69b: אמר ר׳ יוחנן: שמונים אלף פירחי כהונה ברחו לתוך חיילותיו שלנבוכדנצר והלכו להן אצל הישמעאלים ("R. Yoḥanan said: 80,000 young priests fled to the armies of Nebuchadnezzar and went to the Ishmaelites"). In this context (mentioning also the source about the priests in Mesene), Shlomo D. Goitein ("Who Were Muhammad's main Teachers?" [Hebrew], *Tarbiṣ* 23 [1952]: 158) has

לעולם אימ' לך שמו' דאמ' לטובה.
שמו' לטע' דאמ' שמוא': המפקיר עבדו יצא לחירות ואין צריך גט שיחרור שנ' "כל עבד איש מקנת כסף" (שמ' יב 44). עבד איש ולא עבד אשה? אלא כל שיש לרבו רשות עליו – קרוי עבד, וכל שאין לרבו רשות עליו – אין קרוי עבד.

[A] "[And it came to pass, when I prophesied], that Pelaṭia the son of Benaia died. Then fell I down upon my face, and cried with a loud voice, [and said: Alas, Lord God! Will you bring the remnant of Israel to a complete end?]" (Ez. 11:13)
Rav and Shmuel—one said: It was to his [= Pelaṭia's] credit; the other, that it was to his discredit.
He who said that it was in his favor [explains it] as follows:
[B] For the *ōstāndār* of Mesene was Nebuchadnezzar's son-in-law.
He sent [word] to him: "Of all the captivity which you have brought for yourself, you have sent none to stand before us."
He [Nebuchadnezzar] wanted to send him of the Israelites,
[but] Pelaṭia son of Benaia said to him, "We, who are important, let us stand before you here; and let our slaves go to there."
Thus the prophet cried: "That he who did good for Israel should die in the midst of his days!"...
[C] It may be proved that it was Shmuel who interpreted it to his discredit. For Rav Ḥiyya b. Abin said in Shmuel's name: Moshchoene is as the Exile in respect to genealogy. As for Mesene, no fear was entertained for it, either on account of slavery or bastardy, but that the priests who dwelt there were not scrupulous about divorced women!
[D]—I may, indeed, tell you that it was Shmuel who explained it to his credit. Yet Shmuel is consistent with his view: for he said: If one renounces ownership of his slave, he goes free and does not require a deed of manumission, for it is said, "But every man's slave that is bought for money" (Ex 12:44): Does it imply a man's slave, but not a woman's slave? Rather, [it means]: a slave whose master has authority over him is called a slave; a slave whose master has no authority over him is not called a slave.

After Ezekiel receives a harsh prophecy concerning, among others, Pelaṭia ben Benaia (whose singular biblical appearance occurs here), the latter suddenly falls down dead. Seeing this Ezekiel cries out: "Alas, Lord God! Will you bring the remnant of Israel to a complete end?"

Is Ezekiel condoning the act or protesting against it? Was Pelaṭia seen as a positive or a negative figure? The Bavli states that Rav and Shmuel disputed this point. In order to explain the rationale of viewing Pelaṭia positively (and hence his premature death as negative) the Bavli adduces an intriguing story.

---

noted that the Muslim tradition recounts that the Nasir and Quraita, the two largest Jewish tribes of Al-Medina, were priests.

The *ōstāndār* of Mesene, who was the son-in-law of Nebuchadnezzar, asks the king why he did not send any of the captives southward. Nebuchadnezzar, in response, chooses, out of the entire captivity, the Israelites to be sent to Mesene. However, Pelaṭia convinces the king to keep the Israelites with him, since they are of a high rank, and rather send their slaves to Mesene.

This story is rather curious. It has no basis whatsoever in Scripture and could not have been derived or even merely anchored in the verses no matter how great the exegetical acrobatics.[141] Moreover, the story has no historical foundation either. The recently published documents from Al-Yahudu (fifth–sixth century BCE) clearly demonstrate that many of the exiles from Judea settled in southern Babylonia, in the region that would later become Mesene.[142] In fact, many of Ezekiel's prophetic missions are concentrated in the south among such communities. In light of this, I would like to argue that the Bavli's story reflects not the biblical past but rather the Sasanian imperial context of the fourth century. This argument is based on the title of the ruler; his kinship with the king; Pelaṭia's status; and finally, the deportation policy.

The Story in Its Sasanian Context

The Title of the Ruler

The term *ōstāndār* is a Sasanian title of a ruler of a province or crown territory (*ōstān*).[143] This is a distinctive administrative title and it is not

141. It is possible, though, that the name Pelaṭia, from the root PLṬ ("to deliver from danger"), facilitated casting him in the role of a savior.

142. Pearce and Wunsch, *Documents of Judean Exiles.* Anecdotally, in one of the earliest documents from the recently published archive from Al Yahudu (southern Babylonia), dated to 552 BCE (ibid., no. 3. rev. 8-9), we find the following name as witness: ^{lú}*mu*-GIN ^{m}*ḫa-áš-bi-a-ma*/A-<*šú šá*> ^{m}⌜*pal*⌝-*ṭi-iá-a-ma* (Witnesses: ^{m}Ḫašab-Yāma, son of ^{m}Palaṭ-Yāma). It is chronologically possible, though not very plausible, that Hašabyahu is the son of Pelaṭia son of Benaia mentioned by Ezekiel. More importantly though, such documents clearly indicate that quite a few of the Jews encountered by Ezekiel were deported directly from Jerusalem to the area of Al Yahudu.

143. On the term *ostandar*, see Mansour Shaki, "A Few Unrecognized Middle Persian Terms and Phrases," in *Middle Iranian Studies: Proceedings of the International Symposium Organized by the Katholieke Universiteit Leuven from the 17th to the 20th of May 1982*, ed. Wojciech Skalmowski and Alois Van Tongerloo, OLA 16 (Leuven: Peeters, 1984), 95–102; Herman, *Prince without a Kingdom*, 23 and notes 8–9; Gyselen, *La géographie administrative*, 38; idem, *Nouveaux matériaux pour la géographie historique de l'empire sassanide: sceaux administratifs de la collection Ahmad Saeedi*, Studia Iranica 24 (Paris: Association pour l'avancement des études iraniennes, 2002), 69–75, 117–19; eadem, "L'administration 'provinciale' du *naxwār* d'après les sources sigillographiques, avec une note additionnelle sur la graphie du mot *naxwār* par Ph. Huyse," *Studia Iranica* 33 (2004): 31–46, esp. 37–39; Phillipe Gignoux, "Aspects de la vie administrative et sociale en Iran du 7ème siècle," *Contributions à l'histoire et la géographie his-*

attested elsewhere for the ruler of Mesene. In Shapur I's *res gestae*, from Naqsh-i Rustam (ca. 260 CE), Shapur states that he has founded a fire for the soul of "our son Shapur king of Mēšān" (*šāpūr ī mēšān šāh ī amā pusar* / εἰς τὴν Σαβουρ τοῦ Μησανηνῶν βασιλέως ὑιοῦ ἡμῶν) (line 23).[144] Two further sources clearly indicate that the title *Mēšūn-šāh* persisted throughout the second half of the third century. According to a Manichaean fragment in Parthian (M4579), which probably describes events between 273 and 276, Mani arrived at the destroyed palace of the *Mēšūn-šāh* (*myšwn š'(h)*; obv. line 3),[145] likely referring to Mani's previous encounter with the ruler of Mesene.[146] Finally, the Paikuli inscription, which was inscribed around 293–296 CE and describes the victory of Narseh I over Wahram III in the succession battle of 293 CE, mentions several times a certain "Ādur-Farrabay, king of Mēšān" (MP: *myš'n MLKA*/ Parth: *myšn MLKA*) as an accessory to Wahram III.[147]

However, a Manichaean Parthian fragment (M47) states that Mihrshah, the brother of Shapur (who is otherwise unattested), was the "lord of Mesene" (*[m]yšwn xwd'y* = Mēšūn-xwadāy).[148] Such a title does not conform to that of the royal inscriptions. This, alongside the clear hagiographic elements of the conversion of Mihrshah by Mani, has lead Sundermann to conclude that the entire tale has no historical value.[149] However, other

---

torique de l'empire sassanide, Res orientales 16 (Bures-sur-Yvette: Groupe pour l'étude de la civilisation du Moyen-Orient, 2004), 40–41; Arthur Christensen, *L'Iran sous les Sassanides*, 2nd ed. (Copenhagen: Munksgaard, 1944), 138–39; Theodor Nöldeke, *Geschichte der Perser und Araber zur Zeit der Sasaniden* (Leiden: Brill, 1879), 448. For the Syriac use of the term, see Claudia A. Ciancaglini, *Iranian Loanwords in Syriac* (Wiesbaden: Reichert, 2008), 103.

144. Michael Back, *Die sassanidischen Staatsinschriften: Studien zur Orthographie und Phonologie des Mittelpersischen der Inschriften zusammen mit einem etymologischen Index des mittelpersischen Wortgutes und einem Textcorpus der behandelten Inschriften*, Acta Iranica, Textes et mémoires 8 (Teheran: Bibliothèque Pahlavi; Leiden: Brill, 1978), 333.

145. See Werner Sundermann, *Mitteliranische manichäische Texte kirchengeschichtlichen Inhalts*, Schriften zur Geschichte und Kultur des Alten Orients 11 (Berlin: Akdemie-Verlag, 1981), 70. For a digital reproduction, see http://turfan.bbaw.de/dta/m/images/m4579_recto.jpg. Cf. Schuol, *Die Charakene*, 173–74; Lieu, *Manichaeism in the Later Roman*, 108.

146. Lieu, *Manichaeism in the Later Roman*, 79; Werner Sundermann, "Studien zur kirchengeschichtlichen Literatur der iranischen Manichäer III," *AoF* 14 (1987): 63.

147. Prods Oktor Skjærvø, *The Sassanian Inscription of Paikuli*, part 3.1, *Restored Text and Translation* (Weisbaden: Reichert, 1983), 44ff. §§34ff.; cf. idem, *The Sassanian Inscription of Paikuli*, part 3.2: *Commentary* (Weisbaden: Reichert, 1983), 70; Schuol, *Die Charakene*, 161–64.

148. For an edition of the text, see Mary Boyce, *A Reader in Manichaean Middle Persian and Parthian: Texts with Notes* (Teheran: Bibliothèque Pahlavi; Leiden: Brill, 1975), 37–38. For a discussion of this text in relation to a story in the Bavli, see now Geoffrey Herman, "The Talmud in Its Babylonian Context: Rava and Bar-Sheshakh; Mani and Mihrshah" [Hebrew], in *Between Babylonia and the Land of Israel, Studies in Honor of Isaiah M. Gafni*, ed. Geoffrey Herman, Meir Ben Shahar, and Aharon Oppenheimer (Jerusalem: Zalman Shazar Center for Jewish History, 2016), 79–96.

149. Sundermann, "Studien III," 62: "Nimmt man aber zu den hier vorgetragenen Beobachtungen die Feststellungen hinzu daß gerade die Erzählung von der Bekehrung

scholars have argued that the title represents the administrative reality of Ardashir's time, and that the change of the title of the ruler of Mesene from "lord" to "king" represents the growing importance of the province.[150] Be that as it may, during the second half of third century it is clear that the official title of the ruler of Mesene was *mēšān šāh*.

On the other hand, a seal from the later Sasanian period with the legend *myš'(n) štlpy* indicates that the title of the ruler of Mesene at the time was *šahrab*.[151] What period then, if at all to be taken historically, would the title *ōstāndār* reflect?

The only other appearance of the title *ōstāndār* in the Bavli, besides the *ōstāndār* of Meishan, is in b. Giṭ. 80b, where a document containing a reference to an "*ōstāndār* of Kashkar" (איסטנדרא דכשכר) is mentioned in a discussion involving Babylonian sages of the late third to early fourth century. Geoffrey Herman convincingly argued that this most probably reflects the administrative reality of the beginning of the fourth century,

des Mēšūn-xwadāy is hohen Maße hagiographish stilisiert ist, daß sie in schlechtem Parthisch geschrieben ist und auch einer durch epigraphische Merkmale all spät oder inferior gekennzeichneten Sammelhandschrift entstammt, so legen alle diese Beobachtungen zusammengenommen den Schluß nahe, daß ein Mēšūn-xwadāy Mihršāh nicht existiert hat, daß die Erzählung von seiner wunderbaren Bekehrung eine andere Erzählung mit einem historischen Kern lediglich nachahmt und vielleicht überbietet."

150. See, e.g., Boyce, *Reader*, 37: "This event must have taken place before A.C. 262, because at that date one of Šābuhr's sons was ruling Mesene" (cf. Richard N. Frye, *The History of Ancient Iran*, Handbuch der Altertumswissenschaft 3.7 [Munich: C. H. Beck, 1984], 300). A new reading of the Coptic passages describing Mani's encounter with the King of Turan indicates that the name of the king is Shapur, likely the third son of Shapur I, who is referred to as the "king of Mesene" in Naqš-i Rostam inscription (who might also be identified with Shapur the Hargbed mentioned in the Paikuli inscription; see Skjærvø, *Sassanian Inscription of Paikuli*, 3.2:44). In light of this, BeDuhn has proposed the following ("Parallels between Coptic and Iranian Kephalaia," in *Mani at the Court of the Persian Kings: Studies on the Chester Beatty Kephalaia Codex*, ed. Iain Gardner, Jason BeDuhn and Paul Dilley, NHMS 87 [Leiden: Brill 2015], 59–60): "A reasonable scenario would have the prince Shapur transferred from Turan to Mesene at the time when the Saka realms were consolidated under the administration of the prince Narseh, now come of age. Evidently the transfer entailed an elevation of the office of Mesene from 'lord' to 'king,' reflecting either the maintenance of the rank Shapur had already enjoyed as king of Turan, or the increased importance accorded to Mesene as an international trade center, or both."

151. Gyselen, *La géographie administrative*, 144 (B312) and description of the title ibid., 28–29. On the changing administrative status of Mesene, Gyselen writes (ibid., 76): "Le Mēšān, comme d'ailleurs la plupart des regions gouvernées par un roi au IIIe siècle, s'intègrera à un certain moment dans le système general de l'administration sassanide, et son nom sera donné à un *šahr*, tandis que les autres (?) provinces issues du royaume du Mēšān vont porter des noms dans lequels le mot Mēšān a disparu." Cf. Gyselen and Gignoux, *Bulles et sceaux sassanides*, 74; Herman, *Prince without a Kingdom*, 23 n. 11; for further occurrences of *šahrab* in the seals, see Gyselen, *Nouveaux matériaux*, 74–77.

when the region of Kaskhar had been carved out of Mesene and became an *ōstān*, an independent province or even a crown territory.[152]

In light of the reduced status of Mesene, the specific use of the title "*ōstāndār* of Mesene" should be seriously considered as possible historical evidence for such a title in Sasanian Mesene.[153] I would suggest that the change from the title "king" to "*ōstāndār*" is linked to the establishment of Kashkar as an independent *ōstān*. Thus, the old province of Mesene was probably divided into two *ōstān*'s, Mesene and Kashkar, each ruled by an *ōstāndār*. This administrative change, which led to the downsizing of Mesene, was possibly the result of the failed revolt of Wahram III and his accomplice Ādur-Farrabay, king of Meshan, in 293.[154] If this suggestion is correct, the Bavli's story most probably reflects the administrative reality of the fourth century, before the title *šahrab* was introduced.

Kinship

The Bavli is very specific as to the kinship between the *ōstāndār* of Meishan and Nebuchadnezzar: the former is the son-in-law of the latter.[155] Sasanian

---

152. See also references in Geoffrey Herman, "Persia in Light of the Babylonian Talmud: Echoes of Contemporary Society and Politics: hargbed and bidaxš," in *The Talmud in Its Iranian Context*, ed. Carol Bakhos and M. Rahim Shayegan, TSAJ 135 (Tübingen: Mohr Siebeck, 2010), 62–63 n. 4. Cf. Morony, "Continuity and Change," 30. Further indirect support for the administrative changes in Mesene could possibly be gleaned from The Acts of Miles (*AMS* II, 268) dated to the end of the fourth century or the beginning of the fifth century (Sebastian P. Brock, "Saints in Syriac: A Little-Tapped Resource," *JECS* 16 [2008]: 185–86). For a later date, see Wood, *Chronicle of Seert*, 81–82). After an eventful stay at Bet-Aramaye, in particular Seleucia-Ctesiphon, Miles (dies at 341) travels to the province of Meishan (ܐܬܪܐ ܕܡܝܫܢ), to a hermit who is described as living in the desert. He is then summoned by an envoy to cure the "lord of that province" (ܡܪܗ ܕܐܬܪܐ ܗܘ). The fact that his title is not "king" but merely "lord,", might reflect the "downgrading" of the status of ruler of Mesene (which most probably no longer included Kashkar). However, cf. Jullien's conclusion ("Contribution des actes [I]," 160): "Ces éléments permettent de déduire qu'un roitelet régnait encore en Mésène dans le premier quart du IVe siècle et que le royaume vassal de la dynastie sassanide se maintenait encore."

153. Herman ("Persia in Light of the Babylonian Talmud," 63, n. 4, with previous bibliography) considers the story about the *ōstāndār* of Mesene to be "little more than a midrashic exposition of a biblical text, and hence need no longer serve as historical evidence for such a title in Sasanian Mesene". As I wish to show, however, not one element of the story is in fact a midrashic exposition of the biblical text. Rather, the story seems to reflect a concrete Sasanian context projected onto the exilic period.

154. Cf. Gyselen, *Nouveaux matériaux*, 183: "Lors de la victoire de ce dernier [of Narseh over Wahram III—Y.P.]) il est bien possible que la Mésène perde son statut privilégié et soit intégrée dans le canevas provincial de l'empire. Si on se fie aux données sigilliographiques, le Mēšān ne représente au VIe siècle qu'une partie du Mēšān du IIIe siècle." Gyselen, however, does not seem to be aware of the talmudic sources, which I believe reinforce her conclusion.

155. While most probably unrelated, it is worth mentioning that, according to a Mandaean folk story, collected by Drower (*Mandaeans*, 282–86) in the 1930s, Nebuchadnezzar's daughter learned of the religion of the Mandaeans while living in Jerusalem and later fled to

kings tended in general to install family members as rulers of the provinces. We have direct evidence that that was indeed the case with Mesene in the third century. As mentioned above, Shapur, in his *res gestae*, states that he nominated his son and namesake as *mēšān šāh*, and a Manichaean fragment from Turfan (M47), cited above, claims that Mihrshah, the ruler of Meshan, was the brother of Shapur (*Sābuhr šāhān šāh brād būd Mēšūn xwadāy*). Thus, the kinship between the *ōstāndār* of Meishan and the king in the Bavli's story agrees with the Sasanian practice in general, and in Mesene in particular.

Court Jew

According to Ezek 11, on which, purportedly, the Bavli's vignette is based, Pelaṭia b. Benaia was active only in Jerusalem, where he died prematurely. Yet, surprisingly, according to the Bavli's story Pelaṭia was apparently deported from Jerusalem to Babylonia. Moreover, he seems to have risen to a position that gave him a direct audience with Nebuchadnezzar. Pelaṭ ia is actually portrayed as wise court Jew advisor/savior. Such a depiction might be modeled on several biblical (Persian) precedents such as Mordecai and Daniel. It is also possible, however, that this intimate relation reflects a Sasanian historical, or at least literary, context. As Herman has shown, religious minorities in the Sasanian Empire tended to depict their leaders as maintaining very close relations with the king.[156] Talmudic sources describe interactions and even consultations (it is inconsequential whether these are real or literary) of the Sasanian kings (especially Shapur I and II) with the exilarch and several rabbis.[157]

Deportations

According to the Bavli's story, the *ōstāndār* of Mesene's asks his father-in-law to send some of the captivity (שיביא) to the south. This request might be understood against the backdrop of the Sasanian deportations of captives from the Roman Empire to the southern provinces.[158]

Mesopotamia and converted her father. See also Lawrence Zalcman, "Christians, Noṣerim, and Nebuchadnezzar's Daughter," *JQR* 81 (1991): 411–26, who suggests that the Talmud commentator Meiri might have known a version of this story.

156. See Geoffrey Herman's contribution to this volume.

157. On the impact of the Sasanian court culture on rabbinic literature, see now Geoffrey Herman, "Insurrection in the Academy: The Babylonian Talmud and the Paikuli Inscription" [Hebrew], *Zion* 97 (2014): 377–407. See also idem, *Prince without a Kingdom*. On the talmudic narratives depicting interaction between the rabbis and Shapur, see Gerd A. Wewers, "Israel zwischen den Mächten: Die rabbinischen Traditionen über König Schabhor," *Kairos* 22 (1980): 77–100; Jason S. Mokhtarian, "Empire and Authority in Sasanian Babylonia: The Rabbis and King Shapur in Dialogue," *JSQ* 19 (2012): 148–80.

158. The most comprehensive survey of the Sasanian deportations of Roman prisoners is Erich Kettenhofen, "Deportations: II. In the Parthian and the Sasanian periods," *EIr*. Cf. Samuel N. C. Lieu, "Captives, Refugees and Exiles. A Study of Cross-Frontier Civilian

Shapur I's three campaigns against the Romans resulted in mass deportations. In his *res gestae,* Shapur I states that on his third campaign (258–260 CE), in the area of Carrhae and Edessa, he had defeated Valerian Caesar, who had assembled an army of seventy thousand soldiers from various countries (including Judea and Syria). As a result, reports Shapur:[159]

> We made prisoner ourselves with our own hands Valerian Caesar and the others, chiefs of that army, the praetorian prefect, senators; we made all prisoners and deported them to Persis. And Syria, Cilicia and Cappadocia we burned, ruined and pillaged....[160] And men of the Roman Empire, of non-Iranians, we deported. We settled them in the Empire of Iran in Persis, Parthia, Khuzestan, in Babylonia and in other lands where there were domains of our father, grandfathers and of our ancestors.

Shapur claims to have settled the thousands of captives all over his empire. However, according to the late Christian Arabic Chronicle of Seert, many of the prisoners seemed to have been sent as a labor force and settlers to newly founded (or, at least, renamed) cities in the southern and southeastern provinces, including Mesene and Kashkar:[161]

> In the eleventh year of his reign Shapur, son of Ardashir, attacked Rome and laid waste many cities. He conquered Valerian and took him prisoner [واخده اسيرًا] to Nabatea [الى بلاد النبط]. Valerian became ill and died there.... Shapur left Roman territory, taking with him the prisoners [سبي] he later settled in Iraq and Susiane and Persia and the cities that his father had built. He himself built three cities, all named after himself. One of them, in Maishan, was called Sad Shapur [في بلد ميشان وسماها سدشابور], which is (now) Deir Mahrâq. One was in Persia, still known as Shapur. He rebuilt Gundishapur.... He built a third city on the Tigris (Digla) and called it Merv-Habor, now known as 'Akborâ, with its surroundings. He settled

Movements and Contacts between Rome and Persia from Valerian to Jovian," in *The Defence of the Roman and Byzantine East: Proceedings of a Colloquium Held at the University of Sheffield in April 1986,* ed. Philip Freeman and David Kennedy (Oxford: B.A.R, 1986), 475–505; Michael G. Morony, "Population Transfers between Sasanian Iran and the Byzantine Empire," in *La Persia e Bisanzio: Atti del Convegno Internazionale,* ed. Antonio Carile (Rome: Accademia Nazionale dei Lincei, 2004), 161–79; Jullien et Jullien, *Apôtres des confins,* 153–88; Karin Mosig-Walburg, "Deportationen römischer Christen in das Sasanidenreich durch Shapur I. und ihre Folgen—Eine Neubewertung," *Klio* 92 (2010): 117–56; Christelle Jullien, "Les chrétiens déportés dans l'empire sassanide sous Šābūr Ier: À propos d'un récent article," *Studia Iranica* 40 (2011): 285–93; Warwick Ball, *Rome in the East: The Transformation of an Empire* (London: Routledge, 2004), 113–22.

159. Translated by Frye, *History of Ancient Iran,* 372. For the Greek, Pahlavi, and Parthian text, see Back, *Die sassanidischen Staatsinschriften,* 312–26.

160. Thirty-four cities are enumerated here, including Antioch.

161. Chronicle of Seert 1.1 II, 220–21. Translated by Alcock, *Chronicle of Séert,* 1:6. On the founding of Shod-Shapur, see also Schuol, *Die Charakene,* 195–97.

> prisoners in them [واسكن فى هذا المدن قومًا من السبي] and gave them land to cultivate and houses to live in. Christians too became more numerous in Persia and they built monasteries and churches.... Shapur also built a city in Kashkar, which he called Hasar Shapur [بكشكر وسماها حسرشابور] and settled with Easterners [من اهل المشرق].[162]

Two of the main destinations of the captives were the city Shad-Shapur in Mesene,[163] and Khusro-Shapur in Kashkar.

According to the chronicle and other sources, such deportations increased the number of Christians in the Sasanian Empire, in general, and in the southern regions, in particular. Yet, as Morony has noted, scholars have tended to exaggerate the number of Christian among the captives, assuming that the majority were Christians along with a few pagans, whereas, more likely, "most of Shapur's captives in the third century would have been pagan or Jewish, with a few Christians among them."[164] And indeed many of the captured cities are known to have had a significant Jewish population (e.g. Dura Europos, Antioch, and Edessa).

---

162. The chronicle continues to describe how the city was built: "This is the story of its construction. When Shapur went to Persia, he crossed the Kashkar desert and met an old man gathering wood. The king disguised himself and went to ask him about his country and family. He also asked him if it were possible to build a city there. The old man replied: 'If I can learn to write despite my advanced age, you can build a city here.' The king ordered the old man to be entrusted to teachers to carefully instruct him in the religion of the Magi and fire worshippers until he returned from Istakhr. The old man learned (to write) and the city was built." For a similar story, see Tabari, *Tarikh*, 830–31 (cf. Bosworth, *History of Al-Tabari*, 37–38).

163. Cf. Al-Tha'alibi, *Histoire des rois des Perses*, ed. and trans. Hermann Zotenberg (Paris: Imprimerie Nationale, 1900), 494 (my translation): "Having completed the capture of Daizan and securing peace with Rome, he (Shapur) turned to constructing cities and invested in it his utmost attention ... and in Maysan he constructed Shādh Sābūr [وبنى بميسان شاذ سابور]." Similarly, we find in Tabari (*Tarikh*, 830; trans. Bosworth, *History of Al-Tabari*, 37): "It is also said Sābūr built in Maysān [بميسان] (the town of) Shādh Sābūr [شاذ سابور], which is called in Aramaic Dīmā [تسمى بالنبطية ديما]." On the name Dīmā, Bosworth remarks (ibid., n. 117): "The local nabaṭi name of Dīmā (in the Cairo text, the equally incomprehensible Rīmā), remains obscure." Nöldeke also remarks in his apparatus on this toponym: "incertum." However, one should clearly prefer the Cairo text since Rīmā is well attested in various Syriac sources (cf. Marquart, *Ērānšahr*, 41). See, e.g., The Martyrdom of Pusai (*AMS* 2:210): "In the city of Shadbur, which is called in Aramaic Rāmā" (ܒܡܕܝܢܬܐ ܫܕܒܘܪ. ܗܝ ܕܡܬܩܪܝܐ ܐܪܡܐܝܬ ܪܐܡܐ ܕܡܝܫܢ). Bar Bahalul (*Lexicon syriacum*, vol. 2, 1899) writes: "Rīmā—a place in the province of Perat d'Mayshan" (ܪܝܡܐ ܫܘܡ ܐܬܪܐ ܗܘ ܡܢ ܐܦܪܟܝܐ ܕܦܪܬ ܕܡܝܫܢ); cf. Jean-Baptiste Chabot, *Synodicon orientale ou recueil des synods nestoriens* (Paris: Impr. Nationale, 1902), 33. Finally, as we have seen above, according to the Chronicle of Seert (1.2, LXII, 311), 'Abdisho' "withdrew to Maisan where he Christanized Rimiun [ريميون]." On Rīmā, see further Fiey, *Assyrie chrétienne III*, 277, who suggests tentatively that the name might be derived from "Rūm." This is highly plausible since, as we have just seen, Shod-Shapur/Rīmā was one of the main destinations of Roman prisoners, and the name might thus reflect its demography. See Jullien, "Contribution des actes (I)," 162.

164. Morony, "Population Transfers," 167.

Under Shapur II most of the captives were transported to Khuzestan—especially to Ērān-Xwarrah-Šāpūr (Shush) and Ērānšahr-Šāpūr (Syriac: Karka d'Ladan), the royal residence founded by Shapur II.[165] So, for example, in the Martyrdom of the Captives of Beth Zabdai we find a moving description of the deportation by Shapur II of nine thousand men and women, some of whom were Christians (including a bishop, priests, and deacons), from Bet Zabdai southwards to Beth Huzai (Khuzestan).[166]

Furthermore, according to the fifth-century *History of the Armenians* attributed to Faustus of Byzantium (P'awstos Buzand), Shapur II deported tens of thousands of Jewish families (the numbers are clearly vastly inflated) from Armenia and settled them in Asoristan and Khuzestan.[167]

In addition, it would seem that there was a purposeful Sasanian policy, especially under Shapur II, to encourage intermarriage in the newly founded cities between locals and captives in order to prevent the latter from escaping. This is clearly depicted in The Martyrdom of the Illustrious Pusai:[168]

> When Shapur son of Hormizd, who instigated the persecution against the churches of the east, constructed the city of Karka d'Ledan,[169] and brought captivity [ܘܐܝܬܝ ܫܒܝܬܐ] from every province [ܡܢ ܐܬܪ ܐܬܪ] and settled (them) there, it pleased him to also bring more or less thirty families from each ethnic group in the cities of the provinces of his empire and to settle them among them [= the captives]. So that by mingling with them, the captives would be bound by their families and affection [ܬܬܐܣܪܘܢ ܒܗܝܢ ܫܒܝܬܐ ܒܫܪ̈ܒܬܗܘܢ ܘܒܚܘܒܗܘܢ] and would not diminish by gradually returning through escape to the places from which they were taken captive.

Once again, we see the need for captives to inhabit the newly founded cities. Interestingly, the author of these acts immediately notes that, although Shapur II had evil intentions, God turned this situation into a blessing,

---

165. See Kettenhofen, "Deportations," with references to the Arabic sources; Lieu, "Captives, Refugees and Exiles," 495-99.

166. For a full translation of the Martyrdom of the Captives of Beth Zabdai, see now Smith, *Constantine and the Captive Christians*, 184–90.

167. Nina G. Garsoïan *The Epic Histories Attributed to P'awstos Buzand (Buzandaran Patmut'iwnk')*, Harvard Armenian Texts and Studies 8 (Cambridge: Harvard University Press, 1989), 175–76. An interesting detail, which might be relevant to the Bavli's story, is that the captives (both Jews and Armenians) are first all taken to Shapur. It is only after he humiliates and executes P'arhanjem, the wife of King Arshak, that the captives are taken and settled elsewhere. On these deportations, see Kettenhofen, "Deportations"; Widengren, "Status of the Jews," 134–37; Aram Topchyan, "Jews in Ancient Armenia: 1st century BC–5th Century AD," *Le Muséon* 120 (2007): 435-76.

168. *AMS* 2:209 (my translation).

169. A city in Beth Huzaye in the north of Susan. See further Jullien, "Contribution des actes (I)," 157.

since this intermingling facilitated the spreading of the Christian faith.[170] It is possible that such institutionalized intermarriage played a role in the rabbis' low esteem of the Mesenean Jews' lineage.

The above-cited source is of further importance, as it testifies to another, less documented part of the Sasanian deportation policy: internal deportations within the Sasanian Empire.[171] The biography of Pusai is a case in point. His father was deported from Roman territory by Shapur I and was settled in Weh-Shapur in Fars, where he took a local Persian wife. Pusai and his entire household were later resettled (or redeported) by Shapur II in the newly founded city of Karka d'Ledan.

The Bavli's story might reflect a similar reality of inner-deportations. It would seem that when the king is asked to send some of the captives to the south, these captives had already been settled in Babylonia for some time, as is evident from Pelaṭia's status.

Finally, it is worth noting that the term used by the *ōstāndār* of Mesene to refer collectively to the captives is שיביא (*shivya*), which appears only here in the Bavli. This term is similar to the standard term in Syriac for the Roman captives deported by the Sasanians, ܫܒܝܬܐ, which is used at times alongside the same verb as in the Bavli (מכל שיביא דאייתי לך; ܘܐܝܬܝ, ܫܒܝܬܐ). Furthermore, as with the Syriac sources, the term in the Bavli refers to captives from various ethnicities, as is made clear by Nebuchadnezzar choosing the Israelites out of all the captives he brought with him. Thus, the request of the *ōstāndār* of Mesene from Nebuchadnezzar to send him captives might, at the very least, be inspired and modeled generally in light of the Sasanian deportations. It is also possible, however, that this story represents a veiled response to current deportations of *Jews* to the south.

In sum: all these four elements—the title of the ruler, the kinship between him and the king, the status of Pelaṭia, and the deportations southwards—reflect a Sasanian context. Moreover, the term *ōstāndār* of Mesene alongside the specific deportation policy seems to point to the fourth century as the most likely actual historical background. It is thus possible that Nebuchadnezzar is modeled after Shapur II.

All the above-mentioned elements are woven together in order to explain why the Jews in Mesene are actually descendants of slaves. This

170. On this work, see Lieu, "Captives, Refugees and Exiles," 484–86; Josef Wiesehöfer, *Ancient Persia from 550 BC to AD 650*, trans. Azizeh Azodi (London: I. B. Tauris, 1996), 192–93; Gernot Wiessner, *Zur Märtyrerüberlieferung aus der Christenverfolgung Schapurs II* (Göttingen: Vandenhoeck & Ruprecht, 1967) 94–104; idem, "Zum Problem der zeitlichen und örtlichen Festlegung der erhaltenen syro-persischen Märtyrerakten: Das Pusai-Martyrium," in *Paul de Lagarde und die syrische Kirchengeschichte*, ed. Paul de Lagarde and Hermann Dörries (Göttingen: Lagarde-Haus, 1968), 231–51; Alan V. Williams, "Zoroastrians and Christians in Sasanian Iran," *BJRL* 78 (1996): 46–50; Smith, *Constantine and the Captive Christians*, 143–45; Payne, *State of Mixture*, 65–66.

171. See Kettenhofen, "Deportations"; Lieu, "Captives, Refugees and Exiles," 498.

is, in fact, the most important detail of the entire story. Yet how do we account for it, besides considering it a result of Pelaṭia's ruse? What was the original context of this slave tradition?

This tradition would seem quite clearly to predate the composition of the story. A little after the story the Bavli cites in the name of Shmuel a dictum according to which the Jews of Mesene were *not* slaves or *mamzerim*; rather, some priests among them had married divorcées.[172] Shmuel's statement (if the attribution is to be trusted) clearly indicates that by his time there were already people who claimed that the Jews of Mesene *were* slaves or *mamzerim* (or both). Since the Bavli's story clearly postdates both Shmuel and the opinion he opposes, what would be the basis for viewing the Mesenean Jews as slaves in the first half of the third century?

It is possible that at first the Mesenean Jews were considered descendants of slaves due to their ties with the Palmyrene Jews, who in turn were viewed as descendants of Solomon's slaves, as we saw above. Later, after the destruction of Palmyra, another etiological story was developed in order to maintain the slave status of Mesene, this time projected onto the exilic period.

In addition, as Richard Payne has pointed out, "The genealogical thinking characteristic of Iranian elites frequently conflated land and lineage,"[173] and as a result: "To be from 'outside the land,' *anšahrīg*, was straightforwardly to be a slave, a status that was likely ascribed to Christian deportees."[174] It is thus possible that slave status was also ascribed to Jewish deportees, and that the deportations of Jews to the south during the fourth century further cemented the Jewish Meseneans' dire reputation as slaves. Yet, besides these rather concrete reasons, the portrayal of the Mesenean Jews as slaves clearly serves also as a foil for the self-definition of the rabbis as free-men and noble, and the story as a whole functions as a foundational myth of Babylonian Jewry.

A Foundational Myth

In this story, Nebuchadnezzar plays a decisive role in shaping the genealogical landscape of the Jews in Mesopotamia. However, as this story has no biblical or historical grounds, one wonders why the Babylonian king was cast for such a role. Moreover, Nebuchadnezzar is presented

---

172. One should also keep in mind that Samuel himself was a priest, a fact that might have played a role in his assessment of the priests in Mesene. See, in general, Geoffrey Herman, "The Priests in Babylonia in the Talmudic Era" [Hebrew] (MA thesis, Hebrew University of Jerusalem, 1998). However, in y. Qidd. 4:1, 65c, the saying is attributed to R. Ḥanina b. Broqa in the name of Rav Yehuda.

173. Payne, *State of Mixture*, 73.

174. Ibid.

in a rather neutral light: a prudent king who is willing to listen to the advice of his court Jew. This is quite surprising when one recalls that he had just destroyed Jerusalem and deported its inhabitants to Babylonia. Such a representation may reflect a broader genealogical discourse in the Sasanian Empire.

Richard Payne has recently shown, in detail, how through the incorporation of Mesopotamian kings (especially Sennacherib and his son) into the genealogical reports embedded in their hagiographies, Christian provincial elites wished to establish themselves as nobles (ܒܢ̈ܝ ܚܐܪ̈ܐ) vis-à-vis their Iranian peers.[175] Such a turn to ancient histories in the hagiographies, which Adam Becker has labeled "Assyrianization,"[176] should be viewed, according to Payne, as an "act of political self-definition by the ecclesiastical leaders of northern Mesopotamia."[177]

A good example of the use of Mesopotamian history can be found in The History of Karka d'beth Slok, which opens with a long history of the city, highlighting the role played by three ancient kings—Esarhaddon/Sargon the son of Sennacherib, Darius III, and Seleucus Nikator—in various aspects of the construction and evolution of the city, and especially in installing aristocratic families.[178] According to The History the city was first established by Sargon:[179]

175. For the importance of genealogy and records of ancient ancestry for the Sasanians see ibid., 144–52, and references there. See also Maria Macuch, "Zoroastrian Principles and the Structure of Kinship in Sasanian Iran," in *Religious Themes and Texts of Pre-Islamic Iran and Central Asia: Studies in Honour of Professor Gherardo Gnoli on the Occasion of His 65th Birthday, 6th December 2002*, ed. Carlo G. Cereti, Mauro Maggi, and Elio Provasi, Beiträge zur Iranistik 24 (Wiesbaden: Reichert, 2003), 231–46.

176. Adam Becker, "The Ancient Near East in the Late Antique Near East: Syriac Christian Appropriation of the Biblical East," in *Antiquity in Antiquity: Jewish and Christian Pasts in the Greco-Roman World*, ed. Gregg Gardner and Kevin Osterloh, TSAJ 123 (Tübingen: Mohr Siebeck, 2008), 394–415. See his definition of the term: "By 'Assyrianization' I mean the process whereby Syriac-speaking Christians in Mesopotamia employed the Assyrian they found in the Bible as well as in Greek sources translated into Syriac as a model for understanding themselves and their place in the world" (ibid., 5). Cf. Joel Thomas Walker, "The Legacy of Mesopotamia in Late Antique Iraq: The Christian Martyr Shrine at Melqi," *ARAM* 18–19 (2006–2007): 501; idem, *The Legend of Mar Qardagh: Narrative and Christian Heroism in Late Antique Iraq*, Transformation of the Classical Heritage 40 (Berkeley: University of California Press, 2006), 249–54.

177. Payne, *State of Mixture*, 162–63.

178. Cf. ibid., 141–42.

179. *AMS* 2:509. Cf. Payne, *State of Mixture*, 141, who adds: "Long after the Assyrian, Achaemenian, and Seleucid dynasties had disappeared, their aristocracies continued to wield power in northern Mesopotamia in the History of Karka's vision of the mythical-historical landscape of the region. Through these legendary stories, its hagiographer drew a distinction between nobles with Mesopotamian and those with Persian—in the sense of deriving from Fars—lineages, which reflected the self-conceptions of the late Sasanian houses in the city."

> He [Sargon] named Karka, which he built, after his name and he made it free [ܘܥܒܕ ܚܐܪܐ ܒܥܒܕܗ], and he gave it the entire region in which it was established, so that they [i.e., the inhabitants of the region] would be slaves to it [the city] [ܢܗܘܘܢ ܠܗ ܥܒܕܐ] ... and he transferred [ܘܐܝܬܝ] and installed in it a great family [ܫܪܒܬܐ ܪܒܬܐ] from the land of the Assyrians from among the notables of the kingdom [ܡܢ ܡܪ̈ܘܪܒܢܐ ܕܡܠܟܘܬܐ].

Sargon apparently subjugated the entire region of Beth Garmai to the political authority of the noble inhabitants of Karka, most of whom he himself settled there. Such a foundational account traces Karka's aristocracy's right to rule its hinterland all the way back to the foundation of the city by the Assyrian king.

Unlike the Christians, the rabbis do not claim to be autochthonous or descendants of Assyrian nobility. Nonetheless, similar to the Christian appropriation of Mesopotamian kings for their genealogical politics, the rabbis make use of Nebuchadnezzar in order to substantiate their claim to pure lineage.[180] By accepting Pelaṭia's claim that the Jews are "important" (אנן דחשיבינן), Nebuchadnezzar grants royal confirmation to the elevated genealogical status of the Jews in Babylonia, whom he himself installed in the region, and purges them from their baser elements by sending their slaves to Mesene.

Thus, this short account functions as a foundational story of Babylonian Jewry, which anchors its claim to genealogical superiority at the dawn of its presence in Babylonia. Such an early setting predates (in its narrated time) another foundational myth, clearly articulated by R. Elazar: "Ezra did not go up from Babylonia until he made it like pure sifted flour."[181] This myth is based on the tradition, as it appears in m. Qidd. 4:1 (based on the book of Ezra, e.g., Ezra 2), that ten genealogical classes left Babylonia with Ezra (including *mamzerim*, foundlings, and other low-ranking classes). R. Elazar claims that, as a result, Ezra left behind him a genealogically pure Jewish community.[182] Yet, according to our story, more than

---

180. Payne's argument (*State of Mixture*, 147), which he bases on Christian hagiographies, seems to be valid also to our story: "Northern Mesopotamian materials reveal how provincial aristocrats participated in the culture of genealogical politics."

181. b. Qidd. 69b (= 71b). Cf. the statement transmitted by Rav Yehuda b. Rav Shmuel b. Shilat in the name of Rav (b. Ketub. 111a) or by Rav Yehuda in the name of Shmuel (b. Qidd. 69b; 71a): כל הארצות עיסה לארץ ישראל וארץ ישראל עיסה לבבל ("All lands are dough in comparison to the Land of Israel, and the Land of Israel is dough in comparison to Babylonia").

182. Al-Biruni's report concerning the origins of the Mandaeans (cited above), represents a kind of counter-foundational myth to the one given by R. Elazar: "For the Ṣabians are the remnant of the Jewish tribes who remained in Babylonia, when the other tribes left it for Jerusalem in the days of Cyrus and Artaxerxes. Those remaining tribes felt themselves attracted to the rites of the Magians, and so they inclined towards the religion of Nebuchadnezzar, and adopted a system mixed up of Magism and Judaism like that of the Samaritans in Syria."

a century before Ezra, and even before the arrival of the Achaemenids, Nebuchadnezzar himself had already started to purify the lineage of the Babylonian Jews, and hence the latter can boast of an ancient, pre-Iranian, noble status.[183] In fact, it is through the rejection of the Mesenean Jews as slaves coupled with the myth of Ezra that the Jewish Babylonian genealogical identity is formed.

This story, therefore, which seems to be merely an expansion of a biblical narrative, turns out to constitute a foundational myth firmly anchored in Sasanian contexts and anxieties. The details (*ōstāndār*, deportation policy, kinship, court Jew) reflect in some way a reaction to Sasanian political and administrative circumstances of the fourth century, while the story as a whole partakes in the discourse of genealogical politics prevalent among provincial elites of the empire. The result is a radical rewriting of the history of the relations between Babylonian and Mesenean Jews. Unlike the traditions which seem to suggest that the low status of the Mesenean Jews is a product of gradual deterioration (bastards, mixed marriage, contact with Palmyra, priests marrying divorcées), this story goes much further and claims that the Mesenean Jews were never genealogically pure and thus were never part of the Babylonian Jewish community. The genealogical border and barrier between Mesene and Babylonia is claimed to be as old as Babylonian Jewry itself.

Slaves, Not Slaves, or Manumitted Slaves? Rav, Shmuel, and the Stam

Having analyzed the story itself, it is worth examining, in conclusion, the editorial context in which it is embedded. Directly following the story, the Bavli cites Shmuel's statement that limits the genealogical problem to priests who had married divorcées, explicitly opposing the opinion that the Mesenean Jews were slaves or bastards. In light of this statement, the

183. It is interesting to note that, from the tenth century onward, we have many reports that the grave of Ezra (Uzayr) was located in Mesene and was frequented by both Jews and Muslims. The earliest report is probably by Rav Sherira Gaon in 985 CE; see Avraham ben Ya'akov, *Holy Graves in Babylonia* [Hebrew] (Jerusalem: Mossad HaRav Kook, 1973), 38, 140; and see 138–88 for a comprehensive collection of all reports, both ancient and modern, concerning the grave. Cf. Martin Jacobs, *Reorienting the East: Jewish Travelers to the Medieval Muslim World*, Jewish Culture and Contexts (Philadelphia: University of Pennsylvania Press 2014), 121; and Gil, *Jews in Islamic Countries*, 499. According to the twelfth-century traveler Benjamin of Tudela: "1,500 Jews live near the sepulchre of Ezra, the priest, who went forth from Jerusalem to King Artaxerxes and died here. In front of his sepulchre is a large synagogue" (Marcus N. Adler, *The Itinerary of Benjamin of Tudela: Critical Text, Translation and Commentary* [London: Henry Frowde, 1907], מח-מט [text]; 53 [translation]). It is not clear how far back prior to the tenth century this tradition dates or whether it functioned in any way as a counterhistory for the Jews of Mesene.

stam implies that it is unlikely that a story depicting Pelaṭia as a savior and the Mesenean Jews as slaves would have been endorsed by Shmuel, who openly denies the slave status of the Mesenean Jews. Against the backdrop of all the negative statements concerning the Jews of Mesene, Shmuel's opinion stands out. He directly opposes the current trends by significantly minimizing the genealogical inferiority of the Mesenean Jews.

Shmuel seems to have been acquainted both with Mesenean Jews and with Mesene itself. Not only is Shmuel reported to have encouraged Rav Menashya to answer the people of Kashkar, after the death of Levi, as we saw above, but in another source he considers trade and commerce with Mesene as quite normal and discloses knowledge of the economic reality in Mesene in the first half of the third century.[184]

The harsh indictment "Meishan is dead" is attributed in most manuscripts to Rav. If this attribution is to be trusted, then it is possible that he is one of the opponents against whom Shmuel argues concerning the status of the Jews of Mesene. Such a debate in the first generation of the Babylonian Amoraim would have taken place not long after the establishment of the Sasanian Empire, in which Mesene had become a province, and before the final demise of Palmyra. At that period, for the first time in centuries, the Jews of Babylonia and Mesene shared the same political and administrative system. It is possible that, as a result of the removal of political boundaries, the rabbis in Babylonia invested in constructing a genealogical border by highlighting the Mesenean Jews' inferior status.

Yet it would seem that in later generations Rav's approach won the day. This can be clearly seen by the way the *stam* reconfigures Shmuel's statement in order to prove that he, too, could indeed endorse the story. Despite Shmuel's clear and direct rejection of the slave status of the Meseneans, the *stam* makes an exceptional effort to undermine his statement and prove that even he would agree that the Jews of Mesene are indeed descendants of (manumitted) slaves. Such a radical reinterpretation might indicate that the animosity toward the south had been further cemented over the centuries.

Conclusion

In this article I have sought to contextualize the extremely negative rabbinic representation of the Mesenean Jews. Sidestepping the question of whether the Jews of Mesene really were descendants of slaves, bastards, or intermarried, as the rabbis claim, I have focused rather on examining the historical, religious, and economic features of Mesene and its Jews that

184. See b. B. Qam. 97a–b—there in dispute with Rav concerning outdated coins. Cf. Oppenheimer, *Babylonia Judaica*, 255.

might explain some of the rabbinic motivations and anxieties regarding the region. Such an analysis, which balances facts about the region with the rabbinic prejudices, can also offer us a glimpse into the history of the Mesenean Jews, themselves, of which we have almost no sources outside of the Bavli.

In the first part, I argued that the unique religious climate of Mesene, the possible adherence of Mesenean Jews to Palestinian legal authority, and their ties with Palmyra might have constituted the backdrop for the rabbis' hostility toward the Mesenean Jews. In the second part, I contextualized a short vignette, according to which the Mesenean Jews were originally the slaves of the Babylonian Jews, sent southward by Nebuchadnezzar. I have suggested that this story actually reflects fourth-century administrative and political circumstances of the Sasanian Empire. The Sasanian mass deportations of the third–fourth century from Syria to southern Mesopotamian, which likely included Jews, might have also contributed to the slave image of the southern Jews. The story itself, I believe, should be viewed as a foundational story in which the Mesenean slave status serves as foil to the royally confirmed superior status of the Babylonian Jewish community.

The story in fact marks the culmination of the negative rabbinic portrayal of the Mesenean Jews by claiming that the geographical and genealogical border between the south and the north was set in place upon the arrival of the Jews in Babylonia. Yet the ongoing, and continually escalating, adamant anti-Mesenean rhetoric of the rabbis and their constant efforts to construct a social-genealogical border, might actually point to the porousness of that very border. Interactions between Babylonian and Mesenean Jews were possibly the norm that some of the rabbis were combating.

Besides Mesene, many other Jewish communities lived outside the boundaries of pure Babylonia. We know precious little about them, however, and the little we do know often comes only from the Bavli. It is therefore of the utmost importance to constantly remind ourselves that the Bavli is a product of a particular scholarly elite confined to a very limited geographical area. This elite had its own agenda and invested much effort in constructing genealogical boundaries and cultivating prejudices that might have had significant social and religious implications. Thus, we should use the Bavli's representation of other Jewish communities with caution. Many times such representations might actually tell us more about the rabbis themselves than about the communities they describe. Nonetheless, the effort to understand the historical, political, economic, and religious circumstances that led to the rabbinic representations of specific communities, while taking into account the various biases, might also help us reconstruct the diversity of the Jewish communities in the Sasanian Empire.

Finally, in this paper we have seen several cases where Syriac Christian authors shared with the rabbis similar negative stereotypes about the inhabitants of Mesene. This highlights the scholarly potential of *comparative prejudices* in the study of the Sasanian Empire. Previous work on Sasanian and talmudic geography has focused mainly on locating the various places and on analyses of economic and demographic aspects. However, the diverse biased geographical representations and the variety of local prejudices and stereotypes are no less important for the reconstruction and understanding of the period. Comparing how Christians, Jews, Zoroastrians, Manichaeans, Mandaeans, and other ethnic and religious groups viewed specific regions and their inhabitants will provide us with a more nuanced understanding of the intricate social dynamics of the Sasanian Empire.

II

The Sasanian Context

"In Honor of the House of Caesar"

Attitudes to the Kingdom in the Aggada of the Babylonian Talmud and other Sasanian Sources

GEOFFREY HERMAN

The history of ancient Persia as we have received it, from the Achaemenid inscriptions until the elusive *Xwadāy-nāmag* and subsequent *Šāh-nāma,* is very much an account of its kings and courts. This is especially pronounced in the contemporary sources,[1] where notions of kingship and the figure of the king (and, on rare occasions, a queen) within this society are the focus of much attention, symbolism, myth, and court ritual. This is attested in the Persian literature of the Sasanian era, and earlier in the Parthian and Achaemenid eras. The Persian court drew the attention of the foreign observers writing in Greek, Hebrew, Latin, and Arabic who furnish detailed descriptions of the palace, the royal customs, the attire, servants, and court rituals. Indeed, not only political thought but also art, literature, and religion were often viewed through a royal prism. Stories and legends willingly embrace the task of accentuating the almost mystical aura surrounding the king and the royals,[2] and the sources reflecting both Parthian and Sasanian culture treat loyalty to the king and the kingdom as a supreme value.[3] This attitude toward

1. Modern scholars acknowledge the inordinate attention devoted to the king and royalty in accounts of ancient Persia. Josef Wiesehöfer's popular textbook, *Ancient Persia: From 550 BC to 650 AD* (London: I. B. Tauris, 1996), to offer one example, organizes his accounts of the Parthians and Sasanians under three sections: (1) the testimonies; (2) the king and his subjects; and (3) the rest. The "testimonies," themselves, are mostly royal inscriptions.

2. A useful collection of material for the Sasanian era can be found in Manijeh Abka'i-Khavari, *Das Bild des Königs in der Sasanidenzeit,* Texte und Studien zur Orientalistik 13 (Hildesheim: Olms, 2000). For this theme as it is played out in the relations between Rome and Persia in the Sasanian era, see Matthew P. Canepa, *The Two Eyes of the Earth: Art and Ritual of Kingship between Rome and Sasanian Iran,* Transformation of the Classical Heritage 45 (Berkeley: University of California Press, 2009).

3. For references, see Geoffrey Herman, "Iranian Epic Motifs in Josephus' Antiquities, (XVIII, 314-370)," *JJS* 57 (2006): 252-54.

the kingdom also impacted many of the non-Persian inhabitants of the empire and is evident in the literature of the Christian, Manichaean, and Jewish minority religious communities.

In this paper, I shall briefly survey the evidence from Manichaeism and Sasanian (Syriac) Christianity before turning to the aggadot - and one aggada in particular, in the Bavli that relate to the king and the kingdom.

Manichaean Sources

Manichaeism, as a religious system, ostensibly developed in a Sasanian environment far removed from the royal court and its concerns, although some later sources would claim distinguished Arsacid lineage for its founder, Mani. The first and only time Manichaeism would, itself, acquire the trappings of a kingdom with its temporal governance and achieve the status of state religion was with the Uyghur khaganate of the eighth century CE. And yet, many of the early Manichaean texts place its leaders in close proximity with Sasanian royals, their court being central to Mani's career.

The tradition recorded in Al-Nadīm's *Fihrist*, to begin with, synchronizes the public emergence of Mani with the coronation of Shapur I, as indeed the Cologne Mani Codex links Mani's call by his *sysygos* with Ardašīr's conquest of Hatra and when "King Shapur I took the 'greatest diadem.'"[4] Indeed, Mani's composition, *Šāburagān*, was said to be dedicated to Shapur and written (or perhaps translated) in Middle Persian with this king in mind. Al-Nadīm also states that Mani had met Shapur's brother, Peroz, who had arranged his meeting with the king. It has been suggested that such depictions of Mani's appearance before the king reflect a topos well attested in Parthian and Sasanian Mesopotamia but much less so to the west of the Euphrates,[5] with the appearance of Zarathushtra at the court of King Vishtaspa as a model.[6]

Manichaean sources, furthermore, speak of letters of protection pro-

---

4. Cologne Mani Codex 18.2–8. See Cornelia Römer, "Manis Reise durch die Luft," in *Codex Manichaicus Coloniensis: Atti del Secondo Simposio Internazionale (Cosenza 27–28 maggio 1988)*, ed. Luigi Cirillo, Studi e ricerche 5 (Cosenza: Marra, 1990), 82–89; Werner Sundermann, "Studien zur kirchengeschichtlichen Literatur der iranischen Manichäer I," *AoF* 13 (1986): 49 (= W. Sundermann, *Manichaica Iranica: Ausgewählte Schriften*, 2 vols., Orientale Roma 89 [Rome: Istituto italiano per l'Africa e l'Oriente, 2001], 226).

5. Albert De Jong, "The *Cologne Mani Codex* and the Life of Zarathushtra," in *Jews, Christians and Zoroastrians: Religious Dynamics in a Sasanian Context*, ed. Geoffrey Herman, Judaism in Context 17 (Piscataway, NJ: Gorgias Press, 2014), 140; see 143–44 for the parallels for Armenia, Georgia, and Edessa with the Acts of Thomas and the Addai doctrine.

6. De Jong, "*Cologne Mani Codex*," 146; Prods Oktor Skjaervø, *Introduction to Manichaeaism*, https://www.fas.harvard.edu/~iranian/Manicheism/Manicheism_I_Intro.pdf, 26.

cured for Mani from Shapur I.[7] Mani is said in a source to have been part of the royal *komitaton*, although precisely what this might have entailed is unclear.[8] According to Alexander of Lycopolis, Mani accompanied King Shapur I in his campaign against Valerian (255–256 CE).[9]

The Manichaean sources also treat at length the challenge of converting the royals or at least convincing them of the veracity of Manichaeism. This is clearly evident from the composition of the *Šāburagān*, but we also hear in the Coptic Narrative about the Crucifixion that, upon the death of Shapur I, Mani visits and converts Hormazd, Shapur I's son and successor.[10] We also have the Parthian accounts of the conversion of the Turānšāh and Mihrshah, the brother of Shapur I, and king of Mesene.[11]

Mani's end, too, is closely involved with the court. According to Al-Birūnī it was connected to Mani's failure to heal a relative of the king.[12] The Middle Persian fragment M3 presents itself as an eyewitness report of Nūḥzādag, Mani's interpreter, of Mani's ominous appearance at the court of King Warahran II.[13] Proximity to the court and the king seems to function as a subtle polemic against other religious leaders. Thus, in the Narrative about the Crucifixion, Mani accesses the king directly, whereas his opponents, including Kerdīr and Zoroastrian priests must go through indirect channels.[14]

Such engagement with rulers continues with Mani's successors. A fragmentary account tells of a Manichaean apostle, Mār Gabryahb, going

---

7. Narrative of the Crucifixion, in Nils Arne Pedersen, ed., *Manichaean Homilies*, Corpus Fontium Manichaeorum, Series Coptica 2 (Turnhout: Brepols, 2006), 48.

8. *Kephalaia*, ed. H.-J. Polotsky and A. Böhlig, vol. 1, Hälfte [Lieferung 1–10] (Stuttgart: Kohlhammer, 1940), 15.33–34.

9. This might itself, however, be a calumny identifying Mani and his religion with the Roman Empire's archenemy at that time and thereby supporting the polemical agenda of the author. See Augustus Brinkman, *Alexandri Lycopolitani, contra Manichaei opiniones disputatio*, Bibliotheca scriptorum Graecorum et Romanorum Teubneriana (Leipzig: B. G. Teubner, 1895), 4.20. See L. J. van der Lof, "Mani as the Danger from Persia in the Roman Empire," *Augustiniana* 24 (1974): 75–84.

10. Pedersen, *Manichaean Homilies*, 42.

11. On the latter, see now Geoffrey Herman, "The Talmud in Its Babylonian Context: Rava and Bar-Sheshakh; Mani and Mihrshah," in *Between Babylonia and the Land of Israel: Studies in Honor of Isaiah M. Gafni* [Hebrew], ed. Geoffrey Herman, Meir Ben Shahar, and Aharon Oppenheimer (Jerusalem: Zalman Shazar Center, 2016), 79–96.

12. Birūnī, following Jabrā'il b. Nuḥ. See Werner Sundermann, "Studien zur kirchengeschichtlichen Literatur I, 64 = Sundermann, *Manichaica Iranica*, 241.

13. See W. B. Henning, "Mani's Last Journey," *BSOAS* 10 (1942): 949–53 [= *Acta Iranica*, 1977, II, 89–93].

14. See Pedersen, *Manichaean Homilies*, 45. This point is made by De Jong, "*Cologne Mani Codex*," 138. He rightly raises questions about the ability of such a text to inform us on the Sasanian legal procedures. A similar suspicion may be applied to the Christian martyrdom texts. Cf. Christelle Jullien, "Peines et supplices dans les *Actes des martyrs persans* et droit sassanide: nouvelles prospections," *Studia Iranica* 33 (2004): 243–69.

to the king of Revān;[15] and another relates how King Amaró of Hira interceded for the Manichaeans in the period of Narseh.[16] Mani's successor, Mar Adda was also involved in court miracles, traveling to the court of Palmyra, where Mani also turns up to help heal Nafša, the queen's sister, from an illness.[17]

Many of these sources are dated relatively early within the Manichaean corpus, appearing in Coptic, Greek, or Parthian, and they have been studied with great interest by historians. Their earlier date does not preclude the likelihood that they depict Mani's life and that of his successors with the aim of creating an impression of a close relationship between Mani and the royal court. In this sense, they are precursors to the Sasanian Christian sources that we will consider next.

Christian Sources

In Sasanian Christian sources, one finds echoes of the same tendency that is explicit in Manichaean sources. It is evident in a number of genres of Christian Syriac sources. The synod proceedings of the Sasanian church, for instance, and indeed the accounts of the supreme church leadership, the catholicos, emphasize the connections with the palace and the royal support for their leaders.[18]

Hagiographical literature often points to the close relationship between the saint and the king. In the sixth-century hagiographical Life of Mar Awgin, Mar Awgin has an audience before the king where the latter asks him to heal a child since "I know that all that you ask of your Lord, he gives you."[19] Mar Mari goes to the king of Erbil to cure the king,

---

15. See Desmond Durkin-Meisterernst, "Mār Gabryahb," in *Vom Aramäischen zum Alttürkischen: Fragen zur Übersetzung von manichäischen Texten; Vorträge des Göttinger Symposiums vom 29/30 September 2011*, ed. Jens Peter Laut and Klaus Röhrborn, Abhandlungen der Akademie der Wissenschaften zu Göttingen 29 (Berlin: de Gruyter, 2014), 31–48.

16. See Carl Schmidt and H. J. Polotsky, *Ein Mani-Fund in Ägypten: Originalschriften des Mani und seiner Schüler*, SPAW, Phil-hist. Kl, Sonderausgabe 1933.1 (Berlin: de Gruyter, 1933), 27–28 [28–29]. An Old Turkish fragment depicts the conversion of Havzā, the king of Waruzān (Peter Zieme, *Manichaeisch-turkische Texte*, Berliner Turfan Texte V [Berlin: Akademie-Verlag, 1975], 50-52).

17. Sundermann, "Studien zur kirchengeschichtlichen Literatur I," 60 (= Sundermann, *Manichaica Iranica*, 237).

18. On this, see Geoffrey Herman, *A Prince without a Kingdom: The Exilarch in the Sasanian Era*, TSAJ 150 (Tübingen: Mohr Siebeck, 2012), 152–53. See too Sebastian Brock, "Christians in the Sasanian Empire: A Case of Divided Loyalties," in idem *Syriac Perspectives on Late Antiquity* (London: Variorum Reprints, 1984), 11.

19. See British Library, Add. 12. 174 fol. 274B. This recalls Ifra Hormiz's remark concerning Rava in b. Ta'an. 24b (according to MS Yad HaRav Herzog): לא תהוי לך בי פיקאר בהדי יהודאי דכל דבעי ממריהו יהיב להו (Have no business with those Jews as all that they ask of their Lord, he grants them).

converts a military general of the king (ܪܒܚܝܠܐ ܕܝܠܗ ܕܡܠܟܐ) by the name of Zardush ܙܪܕܘܫ along with the entire court, and similar events are told for other places, each with its "king," on the itinerary of this saint.[20] In the Life of Sabrisho, the king acts contrary to the Magi in his protection of the Christians.[21]

The so-called Huzestan Chronicle, from the very end of the Sasanian era, is the pinnacle of the effort to portray a close relationship between the church and its leadership and the Sasanian kingdom, ignoring the Magi almost completely. Here, in one of the more explicit examples, the image of the catholicos is described as appearing to the Sasanian king in a dream, when he goes out to battle.[22]

The king and court enjoy a prominence in the Persian martyrdom literature. The Christian martyr is frequently a courtier or a nobleman, a friend or servant of the king and, on occasion, a member of the royal family.[23] Indeed, conversion of members of the royal family is a topos.[24] Gubarlaha and Qazo are the son and daughter of Shapur II; Dado, his relative.[25] The son of Khusro I was allegedly baptized by a martyr named Ahudemmeh.[26] The martyrs tend to interact directly with the king.[27] Mar Qardagh demonstrates his prowess before an impressed King Shapur II.[28]

---

20. Mar Mari 8-10.

21. Paul Bedjan, *Histoire de Mar-Jabalaha: De trois autres Patriarches, d'un prêtre et de deux laïques, Nestoriens* (Paris: Harrassowitz, 1895) 306.

22. For the Christian agenda mixed in with the historiographical side of this chronicle, completely neutralizing the position of the Magi (and also demoting the place of the Jews), see Geoffrey Herman, "Holy Relics in Mata Mehasya: Christians and Jews after the Muslim Conquest of Babylonia," in *Volume in Honor of Prof. Shaul Shaked*, ed. Yohanan Friedman and Etan Kohlberg (Israel Academy of Sciences and Humanities, forthcoming).

23. See Muriel Dubié, "Devenir chrétien dans l'iran sassanide: La conversion à la lumière des récits hagiographiques," in *Le problème de la christianisation du monde antique*, ed. Hervé Inglebert, Sylvain Destephen, and Bruno Dumézil, Textes, images et monuments de l'Antiquité au haut Moyen âge 10 (Nanterre: Picard, 2010), 329–58; Ph. Gignoux, "L'identité zoroastrienne et le problème de la conversion," in *De la conversion*, ed. Jean-Christophe Attias, Patrimoines (Paris: Cerf, 1997), 13–36. The martyrs of Tur Bera'in are the children of the local king. See too Jacob Intercisus (*AMS* 2:539–58), Azad (Bedjan, *AMS* 2:244).

24. Pirgushnasp is the nephew of King Shapur II (*AMS* 4:222–49).

25. *AMS* 4:141–43.

26. As recorded in the late Chronicle of Seert, ed. and trans Addai Scher, 4 vols., Patrologia Orientalis 4.3:33–36).

27. For a non-Syriac example, the Georgian History of King Vaxtang Gorgasali, a part of the historiographic compendium known as the Georgian Chronicles (K'art'lis C'xovreba), mentions an aristocrat of Persian origin named Varaz-Mihr at the court of the Georgian king Vaxtang Gorgasali, during the second half of the fifth century (*K'art'lis C'xovreba*, ed. Qauxch'ishvili, S.G., 2 vols [Tbilisi: Sabchota Sakartvelo, 1955–1959], 1:172).

28. See Joel Thomas Walker, *The Legend of Mar Qardagh: Narrative and Christian Heroism in Late Antique Iraq*, Transformation of the Classical Heritage 40 (Berkeley: University of California Press, 2006), 20–21.

The image of the king, both his approach to the martyrs and the martyrs' approach to the king, is of interest. The Persian kings, it would seem at first glance, can only be either religiously neutral and not particularly committed to Zoroastrianism, or evil and pernicious Zoroastrian zealots. In the first case, the Persian king stands in contrast with the Magi. He is portrayed as reluctant to punish the Christian martyr, while the Magi are the instigators.[29] An example can be brought, for instance, from the Syriac Martyrdom of Narseh. This is a text that both more strongly reflects a local Sasanian background and reveals greater familiarity with Zoroastrianism than many other Christian works of this genre and exhibits confidence in the Sasanian legal system.[30] When the king is approached concerning a wave of apostates to Christianity with the request, "Command me that I might return them to Magianism, which they have abandoned, from Christianity which they have taken up," the king responds with a striking sensitivity for this genre, "You are granted authority over them to convert them, *without any killing*, but only through intimidation and with some beatings."[31]

The mirror image of this is where the martyrs declare their loyalty to the king and emphasize that there is a distinction between loyalty to one's religion and loyalty to the kingdom. One of the more emphatic statements is made by Gushtazad, who features in the Simeon bar Sabae's *History and Martyrdom* cycle. In these texts, the martyrs underline their loyalty to the king, and the accounts emphasize a distinction between the person and the religion of the king.[32] Such an approach is more in line with the atmosphere of *Sasanian* Christians and reflects the kind of sentiments that *this* community would wish to express for itself.

The image of the king as a cruel persecutor can also be found. He is at one with the Magi in seeking to enforce the observance of the Zoroastrian religion upon the martyr. This depiction of the king may well be more reflective of the image of Persia that *Roman* Christian authors, writing in Syriac, would have expressed, once the Roman Empire became Christian.

---

29. See Mar Qardagh, e.g., Walker, *Legend of Mar Qardagh*, 54, 55. Here the king seeks to absolve himself from the accusations of the Magi (together with the nobles). The king is upset (56). At the end of this account, however, the image of the king changes dramatically (60–61). The martyr speaks harshly against the king, is rebuked for this, evokes the trope of obeying the divine King of Kings rather than the earthly one. In the account of Mar Simeon b. Sabae, the saint is also brazen before the king.

30. See Geoffrey Herman, "The Last Years of Yazdgird I and the Christians" in Herman, *Jews, Christians and Zoroastrians*, 78, 82.

31. Geoffrey Herman, ed. and trans., *Persian Martyr Acts under King Yazdgird I*, Persian Martyr Acts in Syriac 5 (Piscataway, NJ: Gorgias Press, 2016), 4.

32. On the Simon bar Sabae texts, see Martyrdom, #33; History, #57–58.

The Babylonian Talmud

The Jewish sources display similar concerns with regard to the king and the royal court to those of the Manichaean and Christian sources. It is well recognized that Babylonian Jews felt a strong sense of belonging in Babylonia, and specifically as a part of *Sasanian* Babylonia. This is expressed in many ways in their literature, in their local pride in a perceived superiority of Jewish lineage, for instance, which follows closely the *political* geographical borders of Sasanian Babylonia. Legally this finds potent expression in the ruling "the law of the kingdom is binding."[33] Beyond this, it is expressed in their confidence in the reigning legal system and their recognition of its reliance on due process, registers, and the records of court proceedings.[34] It is also reflected in the Babylonian Jews' relationship with the rulers and the kingdom.[35] This is not to say that such tendencies are completely absent in the Palestinian rabbinic literature, but there is nevertheless something distinctive and more pronounced in the Babylonian rabbinic literary ouvre.[36]

In a recent paper, I outlined the impact of imperial court culture on the rabbinic self-perception and depictions of their academies.[37] The palatial or imperial culture spread throughout the empire and had an impact on the Jews and rabbis of Babylonia. Living within this imperial context, they could not but be affected by it. The royal palace culture was also viewed with admiration as an ideal worthy of imitation, and the Babylonian rabbinic academy and the literature woven around it and about it may therefore be conceptualized and interpreted in light of this imperial context.

33. On the historical context of this dictum, see Herman, *Prince without a Kingdom,* 202–7. Note also the statement in b. Šebu. 35b: הא דאמר שמואל מלכותא דקטלא חד משיתא בעלמא לא מיענשא (Behold! Shmuel said; A kingdom that kills one sixth of the world is not punished) and also b. 'Arak. 6a (and other places?) in the name of Shmuel: אי אמר מלכותא עקרנא טורי עקר טורי ולא הדר ביה (If the kingdom would say: We shall uproot mountains; it would uproot mountains and not back down).

34. The sources are well known. For such confidence in the Sasanian legal system in a Syriac source, see Herman, *Persian Martyr Acts under King Yazdgird I,* xx.

35. One should distinguish between the attitude toward the kingdom and the eschatological perspective, as reflected in a number of aggadic sources, such as the beginning of b. Avodah Zarah; or b. Yoma 77a, or sources casting aspersions on the Achaemenid kings. See n. 38 below.

36. See Catherine Hezser, *The Social Structure of the Rabbinic Movement in Roman Palestine,* TSAJ 66 (Tübingen: Mohr Siebeck, 1997), 435–49, which focuses primarily on the image of the Patriarch as a client of Rome. Certainly, the foundation story of Yoḥanan b. Zakkai's interaction with Vespasian is "paradigmatic rather than historiographical" (ibid., 436), providing a model for a successful relationship between a rabbi and Rome, a relationship between patron and client.

37. Geoffrey Herman, "Insurrection in the Academy: The Babylonian Talmud and the Paikuli Inscription" [Hebrew], *Zion* 79 (2014): 377–407.

The rabbinic academy is indeed imagined and portrayed in the Talmud as a "kingdom," a mirror image and microcosm of the palace. Here, its leaders sit in a luxurious manner, they "reign," doormen guard the entrance, and certain court "rituals" are observed. In that article, I traced ways in which Babylonian rabbis employed imperial themes familiar to them from the Sasanian milieu in describing within their aggada the contemporary rabbinic academy, and when developing tales of court intrigue and usurpation narratives set in the rabbinic academy. Below I will review actual attitudes toward sovereignty expressed in the aggadic sources of the Bavli, and how the rabbis relate to the crown and imagine their rabbinic heroes interacting with it.

Rabbis and Kings

A number of talmudic stories contain interaction between Babylonian rabbis and Persian sovereigns, namely, the sources that bring Shmuel into conversation with Shapur I; Rava with Ifra Hormiz, and (also Rav Ḥama) with Shapur II, and Huna bar Natan (and other rabbis) with Yazdgird I. These stories, depicting an interesting, mostly positive, relationship between the rabbis and kings, have been much discussed by scholars.[38] The less explicit, often incidental, rabbinic reflections that concern the king, not necessarily the Sasanian monarch, are less well known. These sources tend to exude considerable respect for the crown.

According to the Bavli, it is a great honor to view the king. Rav Sheshet "went out to see the king" (b. Ber. 58a), evoking an exchange with a *min*.[39] While this notion has its Palestinian rabbinic equivalent,[40] the Bavli also introduces respect for the king in places not anticipated from the context. An example is R. Zeira's complaint about the undesirable result of his good deed, which can be found in b. Ber. 9a:

38. For recent studies, see Shai Secunda, *The Iranian Talmud: Reading the Bavli in Its Sasanian Context,* Divinations (Philadelphia: University of Pennsylvania Press, 2014), 100–106; Jason Sion Mokhtarian, "Empire and Authority in Sasanian Babylonia: The Rabbis and King Shapur in Dialogue," *JSQ* 19 (2012): 148–80. I will also not consider rabbinic attitudes to the Achaemenid kings. On this, see Jason Sion Mokhtarian, "Rabbinic Depictions of the Achaemenid King Cyrus the Great: The *Babylonian Esther Midrash* (bMeg. 10b-17a) in Its Iranian Context," in *The Talmud in Its Iranian Context,* ed. Carol Bakhos and M. Rahim Shayegan, TSAJ 135 (Tübingen: Mohr Siebeck, 2010), 112–39.

39. As Richard Kalmin notes that this whole account is something of a parable where the king stands in for God (*Jewish Babylonia between Persia and Roman Palestine* [Oxford: Oxford University Press, 2006], 100).

40. Cf. y. Ber. 3:1, 6a for priests permitted to defile themselves to see a gentile king in the name of R. Yannai, and the testimony on R. Ḥiyya bar Abba defiling himself in order to see Diocletian.

והאמ׳ ר׳ זירא: אנא סמכי ואיתזקי. אמרו ליה: במאי איתזקת? דאמטית אסא בי מלכא. אגרא יהבי למיחזי אפי מלכא. דאמ׳ ר׳ יוחנן: לעולם ישתדל אדם לקראת פני המלכים ולא לקראת פני מלכי ישראל בלבד אלא לקראת פני המלכים של אומו׳ העולם שאם יזכה יבחין בין מלכי אומות העולם למלכי ישראל.

But did R. Zeira not say: I linked [the Redemption benediction to the Prayer] and I was harmed. They said to him: How were you harmed? I brought myrtle to the palace. You were rewarded in seeing the face of the king! As R. Yoḥanan said: One should strive (to behold) the face of kings, and not merely the faces of Jewish kings alone, but Gentile kings for if one succeeds, he will distinguish between the Gentile and Jewish kings.

The Bavli requires that its heroes treat royalty with respect. While Rabba bar Naḥmani is pursued by a royal agent (פריסתקא דמלכא) he takes refuge in an inn, but the royal agent arrives at that same inn (b. B. Meṣ. 86a). The agent is magically knocked unconscious, but he cannot be left this way since he is one of the king's men (גברא דמלכא הוא). Despite being a fugitive from the crown, the rabbi takes the trouble to revive the royal agent out of respect for the king (and concern for his innkeeper).[41]

Another example is the tale of Bava ben Buta (b. B. Bat. 4a), who, despite all the harm done to the sages by Herod insists on citing from Eccl 10:20: "Do not revile the king, even in your thoughts" (גם במדעך מלך אל תקלל), arousing Herod's admiration for the rabbis' discretion (צניעותא).[42] The series of stories describing the relationship between Rabbi and Antoninus is well attested already in Palestinian sources. The Bavli, however, expands these and introduces references to respect for the kingdom or punishment for lack of respect. In a conversation between Rabbi and Antoninus (b. 'Abod. Zar. 10b) the scriptural verses that condemn the kings of Edom are toned down thus: "but the verse has there 'Edom, its kings and ministers'—'its kings' but not *all* of its kings" (... והכתי[ב] שמה 'אדום מלכיה ושריה' - מלכיה ולא כל מלכיה). Elsewhere (b. 'Abod. Zar. 10b), R. Ḥanina bar Ḥama, upon leaving the place of meeting between Rabbi and Antoninus, and finding one of the royal guards dead, deliberates on whether to inform Antoninus of the death of his servant. On the one hand, he should not be the bearer of bad news; but, on the other, just leaving would be construed as "making light of the king" (קא מזלזילנא במלכותא). On the same page of the Bavli, we learn that Rabbi would climb on Antoninus's back to mount his bed each night. Rabbi, however, is concerned since "it is not respectable to make light of the king to such a degree" (לאו ארח ארעא

41. For more on this source, see the contribution in this volume by Simcha Gross.

42. On suggestive Persian parallels to this talmudic account, see now Jeffrey Rubenstein, "King Herod in Ardashir's Court: The Rabbinic Story of Herod (B. Bava Batra 3b-4a) in Light of Persian Sources," *AJS Review* 38 (2014): 249–74.

לזלזולי במלכותא כולי האי).[43] A similar expression of this concern in the Bavli is found in the depiction of Mordechai's response to Haman conveying the royal command to honor him in b. Meg. 16a: דלא אורח ארעא לאשתמושי במאני דמלכותא (It is not respectful to make use of the royal garments). In b. Pesaḥ. 57b, Issachar, Ish Kefar Barqai, has his hands cut off for an arrogant response with the remark, זילא מלכותא עליה כולי האיי (Is the kingdom so base to you?!).[44]

The distinction ascribed to the kingdom is also reflected in stories that the Bavli tells about Palestinian rabbis. The Bavli has a tendency in revised or invented Babylonian versions of Palestinian accounts to portray rabbis as interacting with the rulers in a positive manner. In the Bavli's version of the deposition of Rabban Gamaliel, but not in the Palestinian version, the rabbinic leader must be capable of interacting with the rulers, to go to the palace (בי קיסר).[45] Another example, one of considerable historical significance, is the late third-century R. Abbahu of Caesarea. He is portrayed in the Bavli as closely associated with the palace in four separate sources. Thus:

1. b. Ketubbot 17a (= b. Sanhedrin 14a)

> ר' אבהו כי הוה אתי ממתיבתא לבי קיסר נפקן אמהתא[46] דבי קיסר לאפיה ומשרין ליה הכי רבא דעמיה ומדברנא דאומתיה בוצינא דנהורא[47] בריך מתייך לשלם.[48]
>
> When R. Abbahu would come from the academy to the House of Caesar, the royal maidens would come out before him and sing to him as follows: "master of his people and leader of his nation, lamp of light, blessed is your arrival in peace!"

---

43. For a comparison of the Palestinian and Babylonian traditions on Rabbi and Antoninus, see Ofra Meir, *Rabbi Judah the Patriarch: Palestinian and Babylonian Portrait of a Leader* [Hebrew] (Tel-Aviv: Hakibbutz Hameuchad, 1999), 263–300. For a historical assessment of these traditions, see Aharon Oppenheimer, *Rabbi Judah ha-Nasi* [Hebrew] (Jerusalem: Zalman Shazar Center, 2007), 43–50. For a broader comparison of the aggadic sources here on Rabbi and Antoninus between the Palestinian and Babylonian sources, see Alyssa M. Gray, "The Power Conferred by Distance from Power: Redaction and Meaning in b. A.Z. 10a–11a," in *Creation and Composition: The Contribution of the Bavli Redactors (Stammaim) to the Aggada*, ed. Jeffrey L. Rubenstein, TSAJ 114 (Tübingen: Mohr Siebeck, 2005), 26–72. For an examination of the Bavli's adaptation of this theme in light of anti-Zoroastrian or anti-Manichaean polemics, see now Ron Naiweld, "There Is Only One Other: The Fabrication of Antoninus in a Multilayered Talmudic Dialogue," *JQR* 104 (2014): 81–104.

44. On a reading of this account as originating in Jewish-Christian polemic, see Aaron Amit, "A Rabbinic Satire on the Last Judgment," *JBL* 129 (2010): 679–97.

45. See Herman, "Insurrection in the Academy," 377-407.

46. אמהתא. MS Yad Harav Herzog and MS Oxford Bodl. Heb. D. 45 (2674) 6-7, for the Sanhedrin parallel: מטרוניאתא

47. בוצינא דנהורה. This phrase does not appear elsewhere in the Bavli. In b. Šabb. 30a we encounter בוצינא דנורא, which, perhaps, is the basis for the phrase in our source, in the question by R. Tanḥum of Neve, apparently a Palestinian homiletic source. Cf., too, b. Ned. 66b.

48. בריך מתייך לשלם. Repeated in the Sanhedrin parallel.

2. b. Ḥagigah 14a:

שר חמשים א"ר אבהו מכאן שאין מעמידין תורגמן על הציבור פחות מחמשים ונשוא פנים זה שנושאין פנים לדורו בעבורו - למעלה, כגון ר' חנינא בן דוסא; למטה, כגון ר' אבהו בי קיסר.

"The prince of fifty" (Isaiah 3:3): R. Abbahu said: From here [we learn] that one does not set a translater over the community who is younger than 50, "and distinguished" (Isaiah, 3:3)—one whom they act well to his generation on his account, above—such as R. Ḥanina b. Dosa; below, such as R. Abbahu at the House of Caesar.

3. b. Yebamot 65b [b. Yoma 73a].

Here it is suggested that the two rabbis, Rav Assi and Rav Ami, do not express their objection to R. Abbahu's halakhic attribution outright on account of the honor due to the House of Caesar (משום כבוד/יקרא (ד)בי קיסר).

4. b. Soṭah 40a:

כל יומא הוה מלוה רבי חייא בר אבא לרבי אבהו עד אושפיזיה משום יקרא דבי קיסר.

Every day R. Ḥiyya b. Abba would accompany R. Abbahu to his host in honour of the House of Caesar.

R. Abbahu's influence with a city authority figure is also reflected in a fifth story, in b. 'Abod. Zar. 4a, concerning Rav Safra.[49] In all these traditions, the Bavli elaborates upon his reputation in ways not even suggested in the Palestinian tradition. The closest we get to his influence in court in Palestinian sources is a short remark in y. Meg. 3:2, 74a of him bribing officials in Caesarea.[50] Hence, it would appear that the image of R. Abbahu as a powerful and influential court figure under Diocletian, not merely due to his residence in the city of Roman governance but to his actual status before the Romans is the product of his reframing by the Babylonian Talmud and is without a single source of clear Palestinian provenance.[51] For the Palestinian sources his distinction is essentially confined to the rab-

49. This story has been much discussed in scholarship. A recent discussion is by Michal Bar-Asher Siegal, *Early Christian Monastic Literature and the Babylonian Talmud* (New York: Cambridge University Press, 2013), 5–6. R. Abbahu is referred to in b. 'Abod. Zar. 28a as "an important man"; this, however, could refer to his reputation in religious affairs alone.

50. On this episode, see Michal Avi-Yonah, *In the Days of Rome and Byzantium* [Hebrew] (Jerusalem: Bialik Institute, 1980), 58.

51. Cf. Lee I. Levine, "R. Abbahu of Caesarea," in *Christianity, Judaism and Other Greco-Roman Cults, Studies for Morton Smith at Sixty*, ed. Jacob Neusner, 4 vols., SJLA 12 (Leiden: Brill, 1975), 4:56–76; Kenneth Holum, "Identity and the Late Antique City: The Case of Caesaea," in *Religious and Ethnic Communities in Later Roman Palestine*, ed. Hayim Lapin,

binic world.[52] What we see here, on the other hand, is not only the Bavli's association of R. Abbahu with the crown but also that he enjoys respect by all, including other rabbis, because of this. In the first source he is portrayed unequivocally as a national leader. His association with the crown is depicted here with more than a tinge of excitement.

More familiar from Palestinian rabbinic literature is a wariness of proximity to the powers that be. One is bidden to pray for their welfare, but not out of any enthusiasm; and it is better not to be known to them at all.[53]

Alongside concern for offending the kingdom is concern for maintaining peaceful relations with the kingdom. This is expressed in a few places in the Babylonian Talmud, such as in the discussion in b. B. Bat. 10b on the need to accept a charity donation from the gentile (Persian) royal, "on account of maintaining peace with the kingdom" (משום שלום מלכות).[54]

There would appear to be a tendency for the Bavli to upgrade the position of the gentile in conversation with Tannaim. The gentile who is not a king often becomes a king in the Bavli. Sometimes the nature of the interaction between the two is also upgraded. The Bavli occasionally places R. Yehoshua b. Ḥananya in dialogue with or debate before Caesar.[55] In many of these conversations with Tannaim, there is no Palestinian parallel; with others, in the Palestinian parallel the non-Jewish interlocutor is not the king but a *matronita*, a philosopher, or a heretic (*min*).[56]

The Bavli's engagement with the topic of contact between rabbis and kings, then, suggests an overriding attitude of honor toward the crown,

---

Studies and Texts in Jewish History and Culture 5 (Bethesda: University of Maryland, 1998), 168–69.

52. For useful collections of his traditions, see G. Perlitz, "Rabbi Abbahu," *MGWJ* 36 (1887): 60–88, 119–26, 269–74, 310–20; W. Bacher, *Aggadot hatannaim veAmoraim* 2:1 (Tel Aviv, 1926), 84–135; and for a more recent study of the rabbinic scholarship institutions in Caesarea, see Hayim Lapin, "Jewish and Christian Academies in Roman Palestine: Some Preliminary Observations," in *Caesarea Maritima: A Retrospective After Two Millennia*, ed. Avner Raban and Kenneth G. Holum, Documenta et monumenta Orientis antiqui 21 (Leiden: Brill, 1996), 496–512.

53. For example, m. ʾAbot 2:3.

54. For שלום מלכות, see too b. Giṭ. 56a; 80a; 86a.

55. See, e.g., b. Ḥag. 5b. Additional Bavli conversations between this rabbi and Caesar or Caesar's daughter are in b. Ber. 56a; b. Šabb. 119a, 152a; b. Ta'an. 7a [= b. Ned. 50b]; b. Sanh. 90b (there "Romans" ask him a question); b. Ḥul. 59b, 60a. For a recent study of such dialogue involving R. Yehoshua see Mira Balberg, "The Emperor's Daughter's New Skin: Bodily Otherness and Self-Identity in the Dialogues of Rabbi Yehoshua ben Ḥanania and the Emperor's Daughter," *JSQ* 19 (2012): 181–206.

On the broad phenomenon and its historical significance, see Moshe D. Herr, "The Historical Significance of the Dialogues between Jewish Sages and Roman Dignitaries," *Scripta Hierosolymitana* 22 (1971): 123–50.

56. For example, Rabban Gamaliel with Caesar (b. Sanh. 39a); compared with 'Abot R. Nat. VIII (*matronita* and R. Yehoshua).

specifically the gentile crown, under whom they lived. Of significance here is the relative absence of religious tension in all that pertains to the relationship with the crown. The kings' Zoroastrianism is de-emphasized and often denied. The king is never associated with persecution that can only have a religious motive.[57] This is reserved for the Magi. In their imagination, the king was an institution distinct from the Zoroastrian milieu of which he was a part. They could even imagine that the king was religiously neutral. This is the case in the account in b. 'Abod. Zar. 65a of Rav Yehuda sending a gift to Ardaban on his religious festival.[58] In this source, Rav Yehuda brings him the gift since he "knows" that the king does not practice idol worship.[59]

This is in striking contrast to the perception of the king in the Zoroastrian tradition in this period. Indeed, there is a certain dichotomy between the way the rulers perceive themselves, on the one hand, and the way they are portrayed in the literature of the subordinate religious communities, on the other. The ruling Sasanian dynasty was not merely *nominally* Zoroastrian. Throughout the Sasanian era—and even afterwards in a symbolic fashion—the Sasanian royal dynasty represented something sacred, something deeply Zoroastrian, even if the way in which Zoroastrianism was understood, or interpreted, might be varied from one king to the next. In fact, in the Sasanian official propaganda from the first Sasanians to the last, the kings portrayed themselves consistently as devout propagators of the Zoroastrian faith,[60] members of non-Zoroastrian religions preferred to draw a sharp distinction between the Magi and the royals. They tended to minimize the *Zoroastrian* nature of the kingdom and of its rulers.[61]

---

57. See b. Mo'ed Qaṭ. 26a on Shapur I's response to the slaughter of Jews in Caesarea-Mazaka. King Shapur II's question about burial in b. Sanh. 46b is significantly ambiguous.

58. The name is Ardaban according to the better textual witnesses but has not hitherto been recognized as a royal name in scholarship. For the details, see Herman, "Talmud in Its Babylonian Context," 86–87.

59. The appearance of this Parthian sovereign alongside Rav Yehuda does not fit our usual chronology and calls for its own explanation.

60. See Karin Mosig-Walburg, *Die frühen sasanidischen Könige als Vertreter und Förderer der zarathustrischen Religion: Eine Untersuchung der zeitgenössischen Quellen,* Europäische Hochschulschriften 3.166 (Frankfurt am Main: Lang, 1982); Albert De Jong, "Sub Specie Maiestatis: Reflections on Sasanian Court Rituals," in *Zoroastrian Rituals in Context*, ed. Michael Stausberg, SHR 102 (Leiden: Brill, 2004), 345–49; Jamsheed K. Choksy, "Sacral Kingship in Sasanian Iran," *Bulletin of the Asia Institute* 2 (1988): 36–40. Whether this was in order to control religion, as Shaked observes, does not affect the argument. See Shaul Shaked, *Dualism in Transformation: Varieties of Religion in Sasanian Iran* (London: School of Oriental and African Studies, University of London, 1994), 99–131.

61. It bears note that one can see certain similarities between the situation described here and the declared attitude of many Hellenistic Jews toward their sovereigns.

R. Yehoshua and the Academy of Athens

In the context of discussing the attitude to the kingdom, I would like to consider the account of the capture of the members of the Academy of Athens by R. Yehoshua b. Ḥananya in the service of the Roman Caesar found in b. Bek. 8b–9a. This extensive account starts with a dialogue between Caesar and the rabbi, with the rabbi accepting the challenge of capturing the sages of Athens and bringing them to Caesar. It describes the devices employed by the rabbi to discover and entrap the Athenians; with various tests, riddles,[62] and a competition of wits along the way.[63] Here I shall consider the construction of this story from other Palestinian sources and highlight the Bavli's divergence from them,[64] finally focusing on the theme of this paper—the attitude toward the crown that is expressed therein. The source is as follows:[65]

1. אמ׳ לי׳ קיסר לר׳ יהוש׳ בן חנניה נחש לכמה מיעבר ומוליד א״ל לשב שני והא סבי דבי אתונא ארבעינהו ואולידו לתלת הנהו מיעברי הוו מעיקר ארבע והא קא משמשי שמושי אינהו נמי משמשי באדם[66] והא חכימי אינון אנן חכימן[67] מיניהו אי חכמיתו זיל זכינהו ואייתינהו ניהלי א״ל כמה הוו להו שיתין גברי א״ל עיביד לי ספינתא דאית בה שיתין בתי וכל ביתא אית בה שיתין ביסתרקי עבד לי׳.
2. כי מטא להתם על לבי טבחא אשכחי׳ לההוא גברא דקא עביד חיותא אמ׳ לי׳ רישך לזבוני א״ל אין א״ל בכמה א״ל בפלגא זוזא יהב לי׳ לסוף א״ל אנא [?א/מ?י ?כ/ס?פרת] רישך[68] דחיות׳ אמרי א״ל רישך אמרי לך ואיבעית דאשבקך סגי אחוי לי פתחא[69]

62. On riddles in rabbinic literature, briefly referring to our source, see Dina Stein, "A King, a Queen, and the Riddle Between: Riddles and Interpretation in a Late Midrashic Text," in *Untying the Knot: On Riddles and Other Enigmatic Modes*, ed. Galit Hasan-Rokem and David Shulman (New York: Oxford University Press, 1996), 125–47, esp. 129–30.

63. Traditional Talmud scholars have attempted to read deep meaning into these riddles. The catalog of the Israel National Library contains some two dozen traditional monographs devoted to this question, composed between the eighteenth and twenty-first centuries.

64. For one study on this narrative, see Louis Jacobs, *Structure and Form in the Babylonian Talmud* (Cambridge: Cambridge University Press, 1991), 76–80.

65. I have presented the text according to London – BL Add. 25717 (402), a late thirteenth- to–early fourteenth-century Ashkenazi manuscript, adding the division into sections and punctuation. Variants between this manuscript and the other manuscripts and printed editions are relatively minor, for the considerations of this paper. Some are cited below according to the following abbreviations: V: Vilna print; L: New York—JTS MS 5529.178-180 (Rab. 1914); V_1: MS Vatican 119; V_2: MS Vatican 120; M: MS Munich 95.

66. באדם. LV_1V_2 כאדם.

67. חכימן. V_1V_2 חכימינן.

68. רישך. V_1V_2L ריש.

69. פתחא. L בבא.

דסבי[70] דבי אתונא א״ל מס( )[ת]פינא דכל מחוי קטלי לי א״ל דרי כרוכא דקניא וכי מטית זיקפה דליתחזי כמאן דמיתפח

3. אזל אשכח הרבונא[71] מגואי וזר רבונאי[72] מבראי דאי חזו כרעאי דעיילה קטלי להו לבראי ודנפקא קטלי להו לגואי אפכיה לסנדלי׳ קטלונהו לכולהו אזל אשכח מלעיל ינוקי ומלתחת סבי א׳ אי יהיבנא שלמה לעילאי לתתאי קטלי לי אמרי אנן קשישינן מיניהו ואי יהיבניהו שלמה לתתאי עילאי קטלי לי אמרי אנן עדיפינן מיניהו דעילאי יהבינן א׳ להו שלמא לכולכו אמרי לי׳ מאי ע?(י)?בידתיך א״ל חכימא דיהודאי אנא בעינא למיגמר חוכמתא מיניכו אמרו ליה אי הכי ניבעי מינך מילתא א׳ להו ליחי?י/ו? אי זכיתי לי כל דבעיתו עיבידו בי ואי זכינא לכו איתו איכלו גבאי בספינתא ...

4. איתינהו כל (כ)[ח]ד וחד כי חזי שיתין סתרקי[73] א׳ כולהו חבראי להכא אתו א״ל לספינא[74] שדי[75] ספינתך בהדי דקאתי שקל עפרא מעפרייהו כי מטא לבי בליעי מלא כוזא דמיא מבי בליעי כד אתי אוקמינהו קמי קיסר חזינהו מענך[76] א״ל לאו נינהי שקל מעפרייהו ושדא עילויהו אקשו לאפי מלכא א״ל כל דבעית עיביד בהו איתו אינהו מיא דאיתי מבי בליעי שדנהו בתיגרא א׳ להו מליוה להאי ואיזילו לכו מלו ושדו ביה קמאי ובלע להו מלו עד דשמיט כתפייהו וכלו ואזול.

1. Caesar asked R. Yehoshua b. Ḥananya: How long is the period of gestation and birth of a snake? — He replied to him: Seven years. But did not the elders of the Athenian school couple [a male serpent with a female] and they gave birth in three (years)? — Those had already been pregnant for four years. But they had sexual contact! They have sexual intercourse in the same manner as humans. But are they not wise! We are wiser than they. If you are wise, go and defeat them, and bring them to me. He asked him: How many are they? Sixty men. He said to him: Make me a ship containing sixty compartments, and in each compartment there are sixty cushions. He did this for him.

2. When [R. Yehoshua] reached there, he entered a slaughter-house. He found a certain man who was dressing an animal. He asked him: Is your head for sale? The other replied: Yes. Thereupon he asked him: For how much? He answered: For a half a *zuz*. He gave him [the money]. Finally, he said to him: Did you think I (intended) the head of the animal? He said to him: I said *your* head, and If you wish me to leave you alone, go and show me the door of the school of the Athenian sages. The man replied: I am afraid, for whoever points them out, they kill him. (R. Yehoshua) said: Carry a bundle of reeds, and when you arrive set it up as if to rest.

3. He went and found guards outside and guards inside; for when they would see footprints of somebody entering, they used to kill the inside

---

70. דסבי LV_1V_2M missing.
71. הרבונא. V_1 רבאני V_2 דרבנאי.
72. וזר רבונאי. V_1 ודרבאני V_2 ודרבנאי.
73. סתרקי. V_1 ביסתרקי.
74. לספינא. V_2 MV לספונא.
75. שדי. LV_1MV שרי.
76. מענך. V_1 דהוו מעני.

guards, and of someone leaving, they killed the outside guards. He reversed [the direction] of his shoe and they killed all the guards. He proceeded and found the young men sitting high up and the elders below. He thought: If I greet those above, then those below will kill me, saying: we are more elderly than them; but if I greet those below, those above will kill me, saying we are preferable to them, being above. He said to them: Peace to you all! They asked him: What are you doing here? He replied to them: I am a sage of the Jews, I wish to learn wisdom from you. They said: If so, we will ask you questions. He answered them: Very well. If you defeat me, then whatever you wish, do unto me; but if I defeat you, come and dine with me on the ship …

4. He brought them to eat in the ship, one by one to his [separate chamber]. When they saw the sixty cushions, each one thought that all the companions would come to this [chamber]. He ordered the captain to set sail. As they were about to journey, he took some earth from their [native] soil. When they reached the straits, they filled a jug of water from the waters of the straits. When they arrived, they were presented to the Emperor. He observed that they were depressed, [being far from their native land]. He said: these are not the same [people]. He, therefore, took a piece of the earth of their country and cast it at them. Thereupon, they grew haughty towards the King. He then said to R. Yehoshua: Whatever you desire, do with them. He fetched the water which [the Athenians] had taken from the straits and poured it into a ditch. He said to them: Fill this and depart. They tried to fill it by casting therein the water, one after the other, but it was absorbed. They went on filling until [the joints] of their shoulders became dislocated and they perished.

In this account, R. Yehoshua acts in the service of the Roman emperor to defeat the Athenian sages. The latter, secretive and hostile, are gathered in an academy in a city accessible from the sea (presumably Athens). The sources of inspiration for this narrative have been sought far and wide. Scholars early on proposed a relationship between this tale and parts of the classical account of the daughters of Danaus, itself a foundation myth from Greece. The ship, with fifty oars for the fifty daughters, was adapted here for a similarly large number of Athenian elders—sixty. The whirlpool waters featuring in their punishment at the very end of the talmudic story likewise evoke the punishment the daughters received for murdering their prospective husbands according to this myth.[77] Alternatively, a subtle anti-Christian polemic has been seen to lurk behind a few of the riddles.[78] More explicit parallels are found in two Palestinian midrashic

77. See esp. Paul Rieger, "The Foundation of Rome in the Talmud: A Contribution to the Folklore of Antiquity," *JQR* 16 (1926): 227–35.

78. See Moritz Güdemann, *Religionsgeschichtliche Studien* (Leipzig: Oskar Leiner, 1876), 89, 135–38.

traditions: Genesis Rabba and Lamentations Rabba The very beginning of the Bavli narrative corresponds clearly with an anecdote in Genesis Rabba that involves a philosopher inquiring of Rabban Gamaliel concerning the gestation habits of a snake.[79] While R. Gamaliel cannot respond, R. Yehoshua b. Ḥananya provides him with the answer, demonstrating not only his superiority over R. Gamaliel but also the advantage of knowledge acquired from Scripture over the zoological experimentation practiced by the philosopher.[80] The exchange takes place in the course of a visit to Rome.

The remaining portion of the story has its counterpart in a second Palestinian source, Lamentations Rabba's gloss on the first verse of Lamentations (S. Buber edition, 46–51). This contains a cycle of anecdotes involving Athenians and Jerusalemites visiting one another's cities.[81] During these visits, the Jerusalemites consistently outsmart the Athenians.[82] The correspondence here is less direct than the first Midrash, but still, multiple topics in the Lamentations Rabba text recur in the Talmud's version in different forms.[83] It would appear, then, that the redactor of the Bavli nar-

---

79. See Binyamin Ze'ev Bacher, *Aggadot haTannaim, I,* trans. A. Z. Rabinovitz (Jerusalem/Berlin: Dvir, 1932), 122. The source itself is as follows (ed. Theodor-Albeck, 185–86): פילוסופוס אחד ביקש לידע לכמה הנחש מוליד, כיון שראה אותם מתעסקים זה בזה נטלן ונתנן בחבית והיה מספק להם מזונות עד שילדו, כיון שעלו הזקנים לרומי שאלם לכמה הנחש מוליד, נתכרכמו פני רבן גמליאל ולא יכול להשיבו. פגע בו ר' יהושע ופניו חוליינות, אמר לו מה פניך חוליינות, אמר לו שאילה נשאלתי ולא יכולתי להשיבה, ומה היא, לכמה נחש מוליד, אמר לו לז' שנים, אמר לו מן הן, אמר לו הכלב בחייה מיליד לנ' יום וכת' 'ארור אתה מכל הבהמה ומכל חית השדה' [בראשית ג: יד] כשם שהבהמה ארורה מן החיה שבעה כך נחש ארור מן הבהמה שבעה. בפתי רמשה סלק אמר ליה, התחיל מטיח ראש בכותל, אמר כל מה שעמלתי לז' שנים בא זה והושיטה לי בקנה אתמהא.

80. Incidentally, the zoological information displayed in this passage is quite inaccurate.

81. On this cycle, see Eli Yassif, "The Cycle of Tales in Rabbinic Literature," *Jerusalem Studies in Hebrew Literature* 12 (1980): 139–40. Earlier studies of relevance include W. Bacher, "Les Athéniens à Jérusalem," *REJ* 40 (1900): 83–84; Louis Ginzberg, "Athenians in Talmud and Midrash," *Jewish Encyclopedia* (1902), 2:266–67. This midrashic source has itself been treated as the source for some later oriental legends. See, e.g., W. Bacher, "Alter jüdischer Volkswitz in der muhammedanischen Literatur," *MGWJ* 19 (1870): 68–72; Siegmund Fraenkel, "Die Sharfsinnsproben," *Zeitschrift für vergleichende Literaturgeschichte und Renaissance-Literatur,* NF, 3 (1890): 220–35; Israel Lévi, "Contes Juifs: Le chameau borgne," *REJ* 11 (1885): 209–23, which focuses on the Lamentations Rabba account of the blind camel, paralleled elsewhere in the Babylonian Talmud.

82. On aspects of this source, see Galit Hasan-Rokem, *Web of Life: Folklore and Midrash in Rabbinic Literature,* trans. Batya Stein, Contraversions (Stanford: Stanford University Press, 2000), 45–56. An English translation of the entire pertinent Midrash appears there on 46–51; eadem, "An Almost Invisible Presence: Multilingual Puns in Rabbinic Liteature," in *The Cambridge Companion to the Talmud and Rabbinic Literature,* ed Charlotte Elisheva Fonrobert and Martin Jaffee (Cambridge: Cambridge University Press, 2007), 222–39.

83. See already Solomon Judah L. Rapoport, *Erech Millin, I* (Prague: M. I. Landau, 1852), 253, s.v. אתינא אתונס אתונא, who observes the parallels and suggests that the Babylonian Talmud preserves a later impression of the academic achievements of Athens. Cf. Gedaliah

rative had before him much, if not all, of the cycle of anecdotes that appear in the Lamentations Rabba text we have before us. Solomon Rapoport had already observed the similarity between the sources, pointing to parallels in the riddles that feature in both versions in slightly different form, such as the goats, chickens, eggs, and cheese.[84] The Babylonian version also borrows other thematic aspects aside from the riddles from the Lamentations Rabba version and redeploys them in constructing its own story plot. For example, the Bavli's discovery of the hideout of the Athenian sages despite the Athenians' reticence to reveal it to strangers, is probably inspired by the discovery by the Jerusalemite heir of the abode of the guardian of his fortune, despite an agreement among the Athenians not to reveal it to a foreigner, as appears in the Midrash. The manner of making the discovery is almost identical: in the Midrash the Jew, upon arrival in Athens, purchases wood (קיסין), including delivery, from a local, who carries it to the required address; in the Bavli a butcher is coerced into carrying a bundle of reeds (כרוכא דקניא), resting beside the entrance of the said address.[85] The head of the fowl symbolically served to the head of the household recalls the head of the animal ploy at the butcher's shop. The ship, too, is central to both accounts.[86] The challenge of drawing the Athenians out is mirrored in one of the anecdotes where a Jerusalemite takes upon himself the task of enticing a certain troublesome Athenian who is in the habit of mocking the Jerusalemites and bringing him to Jerusalem for exposure and chastisement. The Babylonian Talmud, then, has revised this account using all these sources, freely incorporating thematic elements from these other Palestinian *agadot*.

In this Babylonian version of the story there are also clear *Babylonian* elements, such as the use of the typological number 60 and the employment of Persian loanwords (**darbān, wistarag*).[87] The use of the "native soil trick" is a motif that is later known from Persian sources.[88]

Alon, *The Jews in Their Land in the Talmudic Age*, 2 vols. (Jerusalem: Magnes Press, Hebrew University, 1984), 2:591.

84. וכמעט נראה כמו מקור אחד לסיפורים ההם בתלמוד ובמדרש (*Erekh Milin*, 253). See too Bacher, *Aggadot haTannaim*, I:1, 125.

85. This is something of a non sequitur. The move from the butcher in his abattoir to carrying the reeds is not a smooth progression.

86. In the Midrash, the trunk of the fowl served at the table is referred to as a ship (אילפא).

87. See already Bacher, *Aggadot haTannaim*, I:1, 222 n. 5. On the Persian words, see Michael Sokoloff, *A Dictionary of Jewish Babylonian Aramaic of the Talmudic and Geonic Periods* (Ramat Gan: Bar-Ilan University Press; Baltimore: Johns Hopkins University Press, 2004), 204, 350.

88. See Geoffrey Herman, "The Story of Rav Kahana (BT Baba Qamma 117a-b) in Light of Armeno-Persian Sources," *Irano-Judaica VI*, ed. Shaul Shaked (Jerusalem: Ben Zvi Institute, 2008) 83–84.

There are also other notable changes relating more to its essence. While the Palestinian version is inclusive, speaking generally about anonymous Jerusalemites, in one instance mentioning a temple priest but generally strikingly unperturbed by questions of religious observance,[89] the Babylonian Talmud rabbinizes the story, introducing a suitable rabbi from the relevant time period: the Tanna, R. Yehoshua, who already appears in the Genesis Rabba parallel.[90]

Of particular interest here is the Roman hostility toward the elders of Athens. The emperor perceives these philosophers, accurately it transpires, as disloyal, secretive, and a threat to himself. Such attitudes are not part of the Palestinian sources we have mentioned. The Genesis Rabba parallel speaks of a philosopher, which would naturally be Greek philosophy, and places him in Rome, suggesting that philosophy sits well in Rome. Lamentations Rabba, on the other hand, focuses on the city of Athens, which, to be sure, is treated as signifying the greatest of classical wisdom, but the Midrash says nothing of Rome. The Bavli, then, has separated wisdom from Rome and introduced animosity between them. Furthermore, it has placed the Jews on the side of Rome, against the Athenians.

An appreciation of the full length to which the Babylonian Talmud has gone here can be gained by considering the context and objectives of the Palestinian "source" and its Babylonian revision. The Palestinian source offers nostalgic reminiscence of the greatness of Jerusalem against the most distinguished of cultures when it comes to wisdom prior to its destruction by Rome. Gone are both Jerusalem and the animosity toward Rome.[91] The rabbi is loyal, and Rome's ostensible allies, the Greeks, are disloyal. The Jew, in the service of Rome, subjugates them and reveals their disloyalty, while at the same time demonstrating his own obedience to Rome. The motivation for such a reversal is the power of the idea of the dignity of the kingdom in the eyes of the Babylonian storyteller.

While the Babylonian narrative can be assumed to postdate the Palestinian sources mentioned, it might be interesting to explore possible contexts from the later period of the Sasanian era that might have inspired the development of such a story which assumes this relationship between

---

89. In this respect, it reveals its universal essence, recalling the nature of the parables found in rabbinic literature. On the parables and their nonrabbinic or even non-Jewish origins, see Ze'ev Safrai, "Rabbinic Parables as an Historical Source," in Herman, Ben Shahar, and Oppenheimer *Between Babylonia and the Land of Israel*, 287–318.

90. Additional Bavli conversations between this rabbi and Caesar or Caesar's daughter are in b. Ber. 56a; Šabb. 119a; 152a; Ta'an. 7a [= Ned. 50b]; Sanh. 90b (there "Romans" ask him a question); Ḥul. 59b; 60a.

91. A Bavli parallel (b. Sanh. 104a-b) to a different part of this Lamentations Rabba cycle has also expunged Jerusalem, and, indeed, the destruction aura, transferring the source to the Galilee. See Galit Hasan-Rokem, "'Spinning Threads of Sand': Riddles as Images of Loss in the Midrash on Lamentations," in Hasan-Rokem and Shulman, *Untying the Knot*, 117.

Athens and Rome. One possibility is the famous closure of the pagan Athenian academy, dated to 529 CE, in the wake of Christian friction and persecution, even the migration of the sages to Persia in the sixth century.[92] This was the culmination of a longer period of friction as Christian Rome struggled internally with its relationship with its pagan literary legacy and against pagan adherents of this legacy.

A few Syriac sources also view Athens critically, perhaps more as a symbol of Greek philosophy than as a real place. The History of Mar Abba depicts the sixth-century Mar Abba traveling to Athens, where he disputes with Athenian sages.[93] The Syriac Martyrology of Mar Pinḥas, dated to the seventh century at the earliest, on the other hand, which relates that the martyr stemmed from Atines (ܐܬܝܢܣ), apparently Athens, where he was instructed in philosophy,[94] appears to view this connection positively. The implication of suggesting a close relationship between these developments and the Bavli's narrative, would be that the Bavli is adopting the Roman Christian agenda as its own.[95] This would seem unlikely.

However appealing such possibilities might seem, it is evident that this Babylonian author knows little of substance about the Athenian academy, apart from its hostility toward the Romans. He lacks anything tangible about this academy or its members and its depiction seems to follow various stereotypes of a local Babylonian nature. One thing is nevertheless fairly clear. The Bavli has used this story to underline the importance of respect and loyalty to the reigning king. The hostility to the Athenians is not explained by more than that they have no respect for the king and the crown. At the end their punishment is explained as the consequence of their arrogance before the king.

---

92. For the key source, see A. Cameron, "Agathias on the Sasanians," *Dumbarton Oaks Papers* 23–24 (1969–1970): 67–183. The scholarship on this episode, and more generally on the fate of the philosophers in this period, is enormous. Some important and recent studies are the following: Alan Cameron, "The Last Days of the Academy at Athens," in *Proceedings of the Cambridge Philological Society* 195 [NS 15] (1969): 7–29. See too "Atheneans will be worsted by Gallileans," from the pen of sixth-century Romanos, cited in Averil Cameron, *Christianity and the Rhetoric of Empire: The Development of Christian Discourse*, Sather Classical Lectures 65 (Berkeley: University of California Press, 1991), 190.

93. Mar Abba 7 (Jullien edition, 11 [trans.], 9 [text]).

94. *The Story of Mar Pinḥas*, ed. and trans. Adam Carter McCollum, Persian Martyr Acts in Syriac 2 (Piscataway, NJ: Gorgias Press, 2013) xv–xvi, 4–5, 20, which presents the deliberations between Athens and Tanis in Egypt. See too Basil Lourié, "Notes on Mar Pinḥas: A 'Nestorian' Foundation Legend; the Liturgy Implied; Polemics against Jewish Mysticism; an Early Christian Apology Used; Syrian Monasticism from Athens," *Scrinium* 10 (2014): 422–54; for Syrians and the Others, see 452–54; Lourié discusses the phenomenon of Syriac monasticism from Athens with additional examples.

95. For an exploration of this possibility in different form, see Moulie Vidas, "Greek Wisdom in Babylonia," in *Envisioning Judaism: Studies in Honor of Peter Schäfer on the Occasion of His Seventieth Birthday*, ed. Ra'anan S. Boustan et al., 2 vols. (Tübingen: Mohr Seibeck, 2013), 1:287–305. He does not mention the rabbinic sources discussed in this paper.

The attitude toward the king conveyed in this story is in line with the broader approach we have discussed earlier. This is explicit in the actual conversation between Caesar, R. Yehoshua, and the Athenians, but it is also intimated, implicitly, through various intertextual allusions. We find echoes here of two other gentile kings who were on excellent terms with Jews or with a rabbi: the depiction of the guards protecting the Athenian academy recalls the servants protecting the secret meetings between Yehuda I and the Roman emperor Antoninus (b. 'Abod. Zar. 10b); and the placement of the sixty sages in separate cabins in the ship recalls the account of the Septuagint translation by King Ptolemy (b. Meg. 9a) who placed the seventy-two sages in seventy-two houses (והושיבם בשבעים בתים).

Conclusion

The comparative study of the interaction between the various religious communities and the Sasanian crown naturally offers the advantage of highlighting shared themes, or, where relevant, striking differences. The similarities might lessen the uniqueness of the imagined historical "narrative" of the individual religious communities inhabiting the Sasanian Empire but, on the other hand, recognizing such distinctive features common to Jews, Manichaeans, or Christians, allows for a closer examination and appreciation of what it meant to be a religious community within the Sasanian sphere.

Clusters of Iranian Loanwords in Talmudic Folkore

The Chapter of the Pious (b. Ta'anit 18b–26a) in Its Sasanian Context

JASON MOKHTARIAN

Iranian loanwords represent indisputable evidence of Iranian phenomena in talmudic literature.[1] Although the loanwords are limited in num-

1. On Iranian loanwords in the Talmud, see Paul de Lagarde, *Gesammelte Abhandlungen* (Leipzig: F. A. Brockhaus, 1866); Joseph Perles, *Etymologische Studien zur Kunde der rabbinischen Sprache und Alterthümer* (Breslau: Schletter, 1871); Alexander Kohut, *Aruch Completum* (Vienna, 1878–1892); Zsigmond Telegdi, "Essai sur la phonétique des emprunts iraniens en araméen talmudique," *JA* 226 (1935): 177–256; Samuel Krauss, Bernhardo Geiger, Ludovico Ginzberg, Immanuele Löw, and Benjamino Murmelstein, eds., *Additamenta ad Librum Aruch Completum Alexandri Kohut* (Vienna: Alexander Kohut Memorial Foundation, 1937); Shaul Shaked, "Aramaic iii., Iranian Loanwords in Middle Aramaic," *Encyclopaedia Iranica*, online ed., 1986; Shaked, "Irano-Aramaica: On Some legal, Administrative, and Economic Terms," in *Corolla Iranica: Papers in Honour of Prof. Dr. David Neil MacKenzie on the Occasion of His 65th Birthday on April 8th, 1991*, ed. Ronald E. Emmerick and Dieter Weber (New York: Lang, 1991), 167–75; Shaked, "Iranian Elements in Middle Aramaic: Some Particles and Verbs," in *Medioiranica: Proceedings of the International Colloquium Organized by the Katholieke Universiteit Leuven from the 21st to the 23rd of May 1990*, ed. Wojciech Skalmowski and Alois van Tongerloo, OLA 48 (Leuven: Peeters and Departement Orientalistiek, 1993), 147–56; Shaked, "Items of Dress and Other Objects in Common Use: Iranian Loanwords in Jewish Babylonian Aramaic," in *Irano-Judaica III: Studies Relating to Jewish Contacts with Persian Culture throughout the Ages*, ed. Shaul Shaked and Amnon Netzer (Jerusalem: Ben-Zvi Institute, 1994), 106–17; Shaked, "Between Iranian and Aramaic: Iranian Words Concerning Food in Jewish Babylonian Aramaic, with Some Notes on the Aramaic Heterograms in Iranian," in *Irano-Judaica V: Studies Relating to Jewish Contacts with Persian Culture throughout the Ages*, ed. Shaul Shaked and Amnon Netzer (Jerusalem: Ben-Zvi Institute, 2003), 120–37; Michael Sokoloff, *A Dictionary of Jewish Babylonian Aramaic of the Talmudic and Geonic Periods* (Ramat Gan: Bar-Ilan University Press; Baltimore: Johns Hopkins University Press, 2002); Geoffrey Herman, *A Prince without a Kingdom: The Exilarch in the Sasanian Era*, TSAJ 150 (Tübingen: Mohr Siebeck, 2012), esp. 215 n. 29; Jason Sion Mokhtarian, *Rabbis, Sorcerers, Kings, and Priests: The Culture of the Talmud in Ancient Iran* (Oakland: University of California Press, 2015), 57–66; Theodore Kwasman, "Loanwords in Jewish Babylonian Aramaic: Some Preliminary Observations," in *The Archaeology and Material Culture of the Babylonian Talmud*, ed. Markham J. Geller, IJS

ber and significance—in some ways even pointing to a lack of Persian influence on the Talmud[2]—they still are valuable in helping us understand the broader Sasanian environment of Jewish society in this period. While historically the scholarship on Persian loans in the Talmud has not been without its problems, recent advances, including the 2002 *Dictionary of Jewish Babylonian Aramaic* by Michael Sokoloff, and many important essays on the loanwords by Shaul Shaked have contributed to providing a solid base for future studies.[3]

One approach for researching the aggada is by focusing on the Iranian loanwords and studying how these borrowings function in their textual or historical contexts. Similar to the use of Greek and Latin loanwords in Palestinian rabbinic literature, the Babylonian Talmud often invokes Iranian loanwords in order to express a specific discursive mood or narrative affect. More specifically, the Iranian loanwords often represent authoritative or upper-class imagery, voices, or moods, and thus appear in texts about authoritative figures such as the Romans,[4] Persians,[5] Arabs,[6] or the Exilarch.[7] Moreover, there is evidence that the Iranian loanwords were common in Jewish folklore, as we shall see in this essay, thereby indicating that everyday Jews were linguistically acculturated to their Iranian environment.

Within the Bavli, one can highlight specific aggadic cycles, including ones with ostensible folkloric elements, that contain a relatively higher

---

Studies in Judaica 16 (Leiden: Brill, 2015), 333–86. On the number of loanwords, see Mokhtarian, *Rabbis, Sorcerers* 57 and 187 n. 96, and Kwasman, "Loanwords," whose article lists over 270. Jewish Babylonian Aramaic is an umbrella term under which there are various dialects; see Matthew Morgenstern, "Linguistic Notes on Magic Bowls in the Moussaieff Collection," *BSOAS* 68 (2005): 349–67, esp. 350; Yochanan Breuer, "Aramaic in Late Antiquity," in *The Cambridge History of Judaism*, vol. 4, *The Late Roman–Rabbinic Period*, ed. Steven T. Katz (New York: Cambridge University Press, 2006), 457–91, esp. 475–76.

2. The number of Iranian loanwords in the Talmud is many fewer than the thousands of Greek and Latin words in rabbinic literature; on this, see Isaiah Gafni, "Babylonian Rabbinic Culture," in *Cultures of the Jews: A New History*, ed. David Biale (New York: Schocken, 2002), 223–66, esp. 259 n. 66. On this as a point of criticism of Irano-Talmudica, see Robert Brody, "Irano-Talmudica: The New Parallelomania?," *JQR* 106 (2016): 209–32, esp. 211.

3. Sokoloff, *Dictionary of Jewish Babylonian Aramaic* [henceforth *DJBA*]. For an overview of past contributions, see David Goodblatt, "The Babylonian Talmud," in *ANRW* 19.2: 257–337, esp. 280–81; and see Kwasman, "Loanwords," 337.

4. See Appendix 2 below.

5. See Mokhtarian, *Rabbis, Sorcerers*, 190 n. 125.

6. See, e.g., אברתא, "thyme" (cf. NP *abār*), and אגדנא, "asa foetida" (cf. NP *angudān*), in b. ʻAbod. Zar. 29a; זיהרא, "venom; anger" (cf. MP *zahr*), in b. Giṭ. 45b; סיואה or סייב, "black" (cf. Middle Parthian *syāw*), in b. Nid. 20a; and פדיבר, "servant" (cf. MIr. **padi-bar*), and ספסירא, "sword" (MP *šafšēr*), in b. Ber. 6b. See also "spear" in b. Taʻan. 22b (below). This paper uses the following abbreviations: OP (Old Persian), MP (Middle Persian), NP (New Persian).

7. See Herman, *Prince without a Kingdom*, 215 n. 29.

ratio of Iranian linguistic borrowings. Such concentrations, or clusters of loans, raise important questions about what purpose they serve and how one can read talmudic stories within their broader cultural orbit. Do they, for example, collectively point to the influence of external tales from nonrabbinic, including Middle Persian, cultures on Babylonian talmudic aggadot?

Here I will be exploring the function of a cluster of seventeen Iranian loanwords in the cycle of aggadot about pious men found in the third chapter of Bavli Ta'anit (18b–26a), which discusses the efficacy of prayers and fasts to bring about rain during a drought.

Crucially, in the case of the legend cycle to be examined, which scholars characterize as folkloric in nature (see below), the relatively high frequency of loanwords, I will argue, are traces of cultural resonances with the Sasanian world on the stories produced in the voice of the so-called common people. Talmudic folk aggada is a complex scholarly category,[8] and one can debate what materials represent the views of nonrabbinic Jews. Nevertheless, there does exist some scholarly consensus that folkloric stories exist in certain regions of the Bavli, especially in the source that I will be studying here.

Iranian Loanwords in the Chapter of the Pious

In this paper I will explore the broader context of the Iranian loanwords in the collection of legends in b. Ta'an. 18b–26a, [9] which later medieval commentators call the Chapter of the Pious.[10] Often the Iranian loanwords appear in only some of the manuscripts, and in some cases Aramaic synonyms appear in their place.[11] Typically, although not always,[12] it is the Yemenite manuscript, MS Jerusalem, Yad haRav Herzog, that preserves the Persian words due to its independent and authentic transmission,

---

8. On the history of researching rabbinic literature as folklore, see Dina Stein, "Let the 'People' Go? The 'Folk' and Their 'Lore' as Tropes in the Reconstruction of Rabbinic Culture," *Prooftexts* 29 (2009): 206–41.

9. See Eli Yassif, *The Hebrew Folktale: History, Genre, Meaning,* trans. Jacqueline S. Teitelbaum, Folklore Studies in Translation (Bloomington: Indiana University Press, 2009), 115–17; Henry Malter calls them "Oriental" (*The Treatise Ta'anit of the Babylonian Talmud: Critically Edited and Provided with a Translation, Introduction, and Notes,* Library of Jewish Classics [1928; repr., Philadelphia: Jewish Publication Society of America, 1967], xvii).

10. See Malter, *Treatise Ta'anit,* esp. xvii.

11. See other examples in Mokhtarian, *Rabbis, Sorcerers,* 55, 59, and 188 n. 104.

12. In the aggadot from b. Ta'an. 20a–25a analyzed in this paper, around half of the Iranian loanwords are fairly consistent in the manuscripts. MS Jerusalem–Yad haRav Herzog 1 contains additional loanwords, each of which has usually been replaced by an Aramaic synonym (or generic word) in the other manuscripts and printed editions.

according to studies by, among others, Michael Krupp, Shelomo Morag, and Yechiel Kara.[13] The Ashkenazi and Sephardic manuscript branches,[14] though dated earlier than the Jerusalem manuscript, at times transmit the Iranian words with imprecise orthography or do not include ones that appear in the Jerusalem manuscript. There are, however, exceptions. One instance is in the story about Ḥoni the Circlemaker falling asleep for seventy years before waking up to see "that his donkey had given birth to many herds [רמכי רמכי]." The Iranian loanword (cf. MP *ramag*) in this line appears in the prints and some manuscripts but not in others.[15] In a critical edition of this text, Malter has suggested that the sentence actually comes from some external source.[16]

---

13. On the Yemenite manuscripts, see Michael Krupp, "Manuscripts of the Babylonian Talmud," in *The Literature of the Sages,* part 1, *Oral Tora, Halakha, Mishna, Tosefta, Talmud, External Tractates,* ed. Shmuel Safrai (Philadelphia: Fortress, 1987), 346–66, esp. 349–50 and 352; Shelomo Morag and Yechiel Kara, *Babylonian Aramaic in Yemenite Tradition: The Noun* [Hebrew] (Jerusalem: Magnes Press, 2002); and Mordechai Sabato, *A Yemenite Manuscript of Tractate Sanhedrin and Its Place in the Textual Tradition* [Hebrew] (Jerusalem: Ben Zvi Institute, 1998). On this manuscript of Ta'anit, see Eliezer Diamond, "A Model for a Scientific Edition and Commentary for 'Bavli Ta'anit,' Chapter I with a Methodological Introduction" (Ph.D. diss., Jewish Theological Seminary, 1990). For a challenge to this thesis, however, see Matthew Morgenstern, *Studies in Jewish Babylonian Aramaic Based upon Early Eastern Manuscripts,* HSS 62 (Winona Lake, IN: Eisenbrauns, 2011), 32–35.

14. For more on the manuscripts, see Malter, *Treatise Ta'anit,* xviii–xxxi.

15. For example, compare MS Munich 95, where it appears, with MS Jerusalem–Yad haRav Herzog.

16. On this line, see Jeffrey L. Rubenstein, *Stories of the Babylonian Talmud* (Baltimore: Johns Hopkins University Press, 2010), 75; Malter, *Treatise Ta'anit*; Yonah Fraenkel, *Aggadic Narrative: Harmony of Form and Content* [Hebrew] (Tel Aviv: Hakibbutz Hameuchad, 2001), 187–89. Cf., too, אושפיזא, "inn," reconstructed as Old Persian **ašpinja-* and attested in Parthian; although ubiquitous in the Bavli, it appears in b. Ta'an. 21a only in MS Oxford Opp. Add. fol. 23. For a reconstruction to OP **aspinja-*, see Claudia A. Ciancaglini, *Iranian Loanwords in Syriac,* Beiträge zur Iranistik 28 (Wiesbaden: Reichert, 2008), 118–19. The word אושפיזא, which means "lodging," "inn," or "hospitality," and its derivatives (e.g., אושפיזכנא, "landlord, host") are found in at least a dozen talmudic aggadot, many of which are travel stories about someone in search of lodging (see esp. b. Ḥul. 7a–b, which includes a tale about an Arab). The ubiquity of the word in the Bavli does not prove that the passage is linguistically Iranized in the Sasanian period. In fact, the commonness of the word implies that Jewish Babylonian Aramaic's adoption of it is not unique. The Iranian word "inn" is attested in other languages of the late antique East—including but not limited to Syriac, Mandaic, Parthian, and Sogdian (see Ciancaglini, *Iranian Loanwords,* 118–19; Mary Boyce, *A Word-list of Manichaean Middle Persian and Parthian,* Acta Iranica 9a [Téhéran: Bibliothèque Pahlavi; Leiden: Brill, 1977], 22, s.v. *ispinj,* "halting-place, abiding-place"; H. W. Bailey, "Iranian Studies II," *Bulletin of the School of Oriental Studies* 7 [1933]: 69–83, esp. 74–76). The word אושפיזא was likely channeled through Official Aramaic (Ciancaglini, *Iranian Loanwords,* 37, 118–19) or some of the various Aramaic dialects that existed in the Achaemenid and Parthian periods (see Margaretha L. Folmer, *The Aramaic Language in the Achaemenid Period: A Study in Linguistic Variation,* OLA 68 [Leuven: Peeters, 1995], 16–19). Geo Widengren argues for a Parthian origin (*Iranisch-semitische Kulturbegegnung in partischer Zeit,* Arbeitsgemeinschaft

This collection of legends has one of the highest[17] concentrations of Iranian loanwords in the entire Talmud. These stories explore the merits of various poor or disabled holy men and miracle workers from both Palestine and Babylonia, including sages, but also doctors and miracle workers, from Second Temple figures through the Tannaim to the Babylonian Amoraim. These legends—in particular, the tales about Ḥanina ben Dosa's miracles that appear in b. Ta'an. 24b–25a—have received a great deal of scholarly attention.[18] Without further study it would be difficult to discern the editorial relationship between all of these materials in chapter 3, which also includes lengthy *baraitot* and halakhic discussions, as well as other aggadot not directly about pious men but probably "folkloric" nevertheless. According to an important study of Ḥanina ben Dosa by Galit Hasan-Rokem, these tales represent "a literary unit of a relatively high unity" revolving around the theme of "prayer."[19] The extent to which all

---

für Forschung des Landes Nordrhein-Westfalen, Geisteswissenschaften 70 [Cologne: Westdeutscher Verlag, 1960], 102). If an early dating for this word's entrance into Aramaic is correct, then it follows that the Babylonian rabbis are not technically invoking a Middle Iranian loanword but are instead drawing from an inherited Aramaic lexicon that had already absorbed Iranian "inn." Still, though it has pre-Sasanian origins, it is possible that the MP version of the word was reborrowed into Talmudic Aramaic in late antiquity, as Ciancaglini explains in the case of loanwords in Syriac (*Iranian Loanwords*, 58–59). As for the meaning of MP *aspinj*, late Sasanian–early Islamic works such as the *Ardā Wīrāz Nāmag* and the *Kārnāmag* praise the virtue of offering hospitality to visitors. See *Ardā Wīrāz Nāmag* ch. 22 (Fereydun Vahman, *Ardā Wīrāz Nāmag: The Iranian "Divina Commedia"* [London: Curzon Press, 1986], 201); *Ardā Wīrāz Nāmag* ch. 52 (Vahman, *Ardā*, 217); *Kārnāmag* 8:7 (Frantz Grenet, *La geste d'Ardashir fils de Pâbag: Kārnāmag ī Ardaxšēr ī Pābagān* [Die: Éditions à Die, 2003], 86-87), on the battle between Ardashir and the Kirm. Although it is notable that the semantic range of the word is similar in both MP and Jewish Babylonian Aramaic, the MP sources do not offer much by way of comparison of content to the talmudic passages.

17. Compare b. B. Meṣ. 83a–86a, which contains a greater number of Iranian loanwords in less text than b. Ta'an. 20a–25a.

18. For a list of some of the scholarship on the third chapter of Ta'anit and some of the pious men mentioned therein, see Galit Hasan-Rokem, "Were the Hazal Aware of the Term Folklore?" [Hebrew], in *Higayon L'Yona: New Aspects in the Study of Midrash, Aggadah and Piyut in Honor of Professor Yona Fraenkel*, ed. Joshua Levinson, Jacob Elbaum, Galit Hasan-Rokem (Jerusalem: Magnes Press, 2006), 199–229, which is reprinted in English as Galit Hasan-Rokem, "Did Rabbinic Culture Conceive of the Category of Folk Narrative?," *European Journal of Jewish Studies* 3 (2009): 19–55; Joseph Blenkinsopp, "Miracles: Elisha and Hanina ben Dosa," in *Miracles in Jewish and Christian Antiquity: Imagining Truth*, ed. John C. Cavadini, Notre Dame Studies in Theology 3 (Notre Dame, IN: University of Notre Dame Press, 1999), 57–81; Baruch M. Bokser, "Wonder-Working and the Rabbinic Tradition: The Case of Ḥanina ben Dosa," *JSJ* 16 (1985): 42–92; Gad Ben-Ami Zarfatti, "Pious Men, Men of Deeds, and the Early Prophets" [Hebrew], *Tarbiṣ* 26 (1957): 126–53. Other relevant scholarship is cited in the notes below. On differences between praying for rain in Palestine and Babylonia, see Raphael Patai, "The 'Control of Rain' in Ancient Palestine: A Study in Comparative Religion," *HUCA* 14 (1939): 251–86, esp. 284–86.

19. See Hasan-Rokem, "Rabbinic Culture," 51–52.

the narratives about pious men in chapter 3 conform to a similar unity is, however, questionable, since it seems to be the case that the biographies were independent compositions woven together and adapted to fit the specific context in which they appear (i.e., prayer and fasts for rain).[20] Although some rabbis make an appearance, the general message of these legends demonstrates the righteousness of the common people.[21] In the end, part of the value of researching folklore—and the Iranian elements therein—is to gain a better understanding of the diversity of Babylonian Jewry and to seek to determine the precise relationship between, in this case, Babylonian rabbis, pious men (including the legendary ones of the past), and everyday people.[22]

What does the presence of the Iranian loanwords in these folkloric stories about pious men tell us? Does the fact that it is often the common people who invoke the Iranian loanwords imply that there was a deeper level of linguistic Iranization among nonrabbinic Jews? And does this linguistic Iranization automatically imply the existence of textual borrowings from the outside, or some other form of cultural permeability to the non-Jewish cultures living in Sasanian Mesopotamia? It should be noted, admittedly, that Persian loanwords appear in the aggadot of the Bavli featuring both Babylonian and Palestinian rabbis, as well as nonrabbinic figures.

I. Rav Huna's Golden Carriage

One story in the Chapter of the Pious engages Tannaitic traditions regarding holy men who prevent dilapidated structures from collapsing. Rav Adda bar Aḥava, in b. Ta'an. 20b, records a memory by the fourth-generation Amora Rafram bar Papa about one of Rav Huna's good deeds—namely, how in his old age Rav Huna was carried around town in a "golden carriage/litter" while declaring which walls should be demolished. If the owners could not afford to rebuild the structure, Rav Huna would perform a good deed by using his own funds to do so. This two-word phrase, גוהרקא דדהבא, "golden carriage," contains an Iranian loan-

20. See ibid., 39; Yassif, *Hebrew Folktale*, 116; Tal Ilan, *Massekhet Ta'anit: Text, Translation, and Commentary*, Feminist Commentary on the Babylonian Talmud (Tübingen: Mohr Siebeck, 2008), 257.

21. Eli Yassif, in a study of Jewish folklore, describes the stories in the Chapter of the Pious as a "manifested folk reaction against the sages' outspoken belittling of the *am ha'aretz*," who despite being uneducated in Torah are "favored by the Creator Himself above those engaged in Torah" (*Hebrew Folktale*, 116).

22. There is a lengthy bibliography that engages this question about Jewish Palestine, but a smaller one on Jewish Babylonia. On the former, see Shaye J. D. Cohen, "Epigraphical Rabbis," *JQR* 72 (1981): 1–17. On the ties between the rabbis and the *Ḥasidim*, see Shmuel Safrai, "Teaching of Pietists in Mishnaic Literature," *JJS* 16 (1956): 15–33, esp. 32–33.

word, גוהרקא, "chair, litter, carriage" (cf. MIr **gāhwārak*; MP *gāhwārag*, "cot, cradle," and Armenian *gahaworak*). In this text and elsewhere in the Bavli the גוהרקא symbolizes the wealth and prestige of Jews like Rav Huna.[23] This loanword similarly crops up elsewhere in the Talmud,[24] including in a story about the Exilarch and two Iranized Babylonian Amoraim, Rav Naḥman and Rava.[25] Thus, a common function of the Iranian loanwords in talmudic aggadot is to express prestige.[26]

The use of the Aramaic adjective in b. Ta'an. 20b alongside the Iranian loanword is replicated in other talmudic phrases. Thus, we find "a leg of *a table of gold*" in b. Ta'an. 25a (see below); "*chains of gold*" (מניכא דדהבא); and "gold bread on a *gold table*" (נהמא דדהבא אפתורא דדהבא) in a story about Alexander the Great (b. Tamid 32a).[27] Similarly, b. Šabb. 119a describes a "chair" (תכתקא; from Iranian, see below) on which R. Abbahu sits as being made of ivory.[28] These images, including that of Rav Huna's golden car-

---

23. See Herman, *Prince without a Kingdom*, 216–17 and n. 41: "Carrying important women, including the wife of the Exilarch on a chair is addressed in *y. Beṣa* 1:6 (60c)."

24. See b. Giṭ. 31b; b. B. Meṣ.73b.

25. On the Iranization of these two rabbis, see Yaakov Elman, "Talmud, ii: Rabbinic Literature and Middle Persian Texts," *Encyclopaedia Iranica*, online ed., 2010: www.iranica.com/articles/talmud-ii.

26. See John Bowden, "Lexical Borrowing," in *Encyclopedia of Linguistics*, ed. Philipp Strazny (New York: Taylor and Francis, 2005), 620–22, esp. 621: "Prestige is often involved in situations where one language is thought by its speakers to have more prestige than the other."

27. This latter phrase is used in a dialogue between Alexander the Great and the sages, where the latter explains to the former that his power comes from Satan. Alexander responds harshly to the insult by dressing them in purple and putting "chains of gold around their necks" before forcing them to show him the way to Africa. He comes to a place where there are only women. At Alexander's request, the women, whom he eventually calls wise, bring him "gold bread on a gold table."

28. See b. Šabb. 119a (cf. Matt 13). This text represents an example of how linguists must be cautious in evaluating the loanwords based on the entry of the word into Aramaic. The potential loanwords in this *sugya* are תכתקא, "chair," גודנא, "garment," and שרגא, "lamps." Although the word תכתקא, "chair," is related to MP *taxtag*, "tablet, plank, board" (cf. also *taxt*, "throne"), the other potential borrowings in this passage are not as evident. The second possible Iranian loanword is גונדא, from Persian *gund*, "to dress," for גודנא, "a type of garment" (see *DJBA*, 266, with ref. to *Additamenta ad librum Aruch Completum*'s Persian explanation). This, however, is conjectural. Problematic in a different way is שרגא, "lamp," since the borrowing appears to predate the Sasanian period. It is attested in numerous Iranian and Semitic languages (see Ciancaglini, *Iranian Loanwords*, 265) and likely originates from Parthian (on which see *DJBA*'s reconstruction to Middle Parthian **širāg* [1177–78]; and Widengren, *Iranisch-semitische Kulturbegegnung*, 102). According to Boyce, *Word-list*, 31, the Parthian form is *čarāg* [cr'g], "lamp." In MP it is *čirāg* (David Neil MacKenzie, *A Concise Pahlavi Dictionary* [New York: Oxford University Press, 1971], 23). Mandaic, Jewish Babylonian Aramaic, and Syriac all begin the word with š. The fact that other languages contain this word leaves open the possibility that Jewish Babylonian Aramaic was exposed to it from an intermediary language rather than directly from Persian. Finally, in b. Šabb. 119a, the

riage, are related to the upper-class status of the Sasanian elite. As the official language of the Sasanian empire, Middle Persian was the language of high culture associated with the aristocracy, and the Talmud expresses this positive attitude toward the Persian language on several occasions.[29] The loanwords in talmudic aggadot often conform to this attitude regarding Persian's elevated standing.

The Babylonian Talmud also contains another Iranian loanword meaning "litter, carriage," דייספק (cf. MIr. **dēspak* < OP **dvai-aspaka* > Armenian *despak*). For instance, we read in b. Giṭ. 57a that "on account of the shaft of a *carriage* Bethar was destroyed."[30] This word is conspicuous in Armenian and Persian texts. In Sebeos's *Armenian History*, which dates to the late Sasanian–early Islamic period, the author describes Armenian victories over Khusro Anushirwan, and among the war spoils is "the golden carriage of great value, which was set with precious stones and pearls and was called by them the '*glorious' carriage* [*despak*]."[31]

According to this passage, the Persians *themselves* referred to the royal transport as "the glorious carriage,"[32] suggesting that this was a well-known term that entered into other languages such as Armenian and Jewish Babylonian Aramaic.[33] The motif of a Persian royal carriage

---

word "stater" is from Greek (*DJBA*, 123; and Kwasman, "Loanwords," 368) but does appear in Middle Persian as *stēr*. The motif of the ivory throne in reference to the Sasanian kings appears in Ferdowsi's *Šāhnāme*, as explained in Richard Ettinghausen, *From Byzantium to Sasanian Iran and the Islamic World: Three Modes of Artistic Influence*, L. A. Mayer Memorial Studies in Islamic Art and Archaeology 3 (Leiden: Brill, 1972), 29. In 1 Kgs 10:18–20, Solomon's throne is made of ivory.

29. See b. Soṭah 49b and b. B. Qam. 82b-83a. For more on this text, see Willem F. Smelik, *Rabbis, Language and Translation in Late Antiquity* (Cambridge: Cambridge University Press, 2013), 92–93, as well as the quotation on 102 on how educated Babylonians were "undoubtedly mastering additional languages such as Greek or Persian. Yet there is no denying that this generalization masks our ignorance of the actual linguistic versatility of Babylonian Jews, whose community is largely hidden from view through the absence of any reliable historical sources beyond the Talmud, the incantation bowls and incidental literary references in Syriac." For other texts on Persian language, see Esth. Rab. 4:12, b. Meg. 18a, and b. Šabb. 115a.

30. See too b. Ḥul. 79a: "Abba said to his servant: 'When you harness the mules to my carriage see that they are very like each other and then harness them.'"

31. See R. W. Thompson, *The Armenian History attributed to Sebeos*, 2 vols., Translated Texts for Historians 31 (Liverpool: Liverpool University Press, 1999), 1:8 and n. 51.

32. Whether this Armenian text accurately represents the original MP phrase is hard to determine in part because the MP corpus does not offer much useful information about it; see *Dēnkard* 8.38.11, for one occurrence. On royal imagery in Arabic sources, see Shaul Shaked, "From Iran to Islam: On Some Symbols of Royalty," *Jerusalem Studies in Arabic and Islam* 7 (1986): 75–91, esp. 80.

33. Another example from Armenian literature can be cited here—namely, Pseudo-Agathangelos's *History of St. Gregory and the Conversion of Armenia*, a late Sasanian or early Islamic martyrological and hagiographical work that describes the reception of Christianity

also surfaces in other literature from late antiquity and the early Islamic periods, including the sixth-century Byzantine historian Procopius,[34] the Armenian text the *History of St. Gregory and the Conversion of Armenia*, and the New Persian works the *Šāhnāme* and *Vis o Rāmin*.[35] Despite the lateness of some of these sources, there is evidence that this practice of using a royal carriage actually predates the Sasanians, perhaps originating as early as the Achaemenid period. Middle Iranian **dēspak* is a derivative of Old Persian **dvai-aspaka*, "carriage drawn by two horses."[36] Moreover, the Greek historians Herodotus and Xenophon both describe the Achaemenid kings and other members of the royal class, especially women, as being carried around in jewel-covered carriages.[37] The image of a Persian royal carriage and the Iranian word **dēspak* were, thus, ubiquitous throughout antiquity in east and west alike.

---

in Armenian territory. In this text the same image of a "golden *litter*" appears in reference to Drtad, a Christian son of King Khusro. Drtad sends the litter to pick up his love-interest, whom he eventually tortures and rapes for resisting him. This text is online at vehi. net/ istoriya/armenia/ agathangelos/en/AGATHANGELOS.html.

34. See Matthew P. Canepa, *The Two Eyes of the Earth: Art and Ritual of Kingship between Rome and Sasanian Iran*, Transformation of the Classical Heritage 45 (Berkeley: University of California Press, 2009), 170–71. He quotes Procopius on what was included in the spoils won by Belisarius, who had gone to war for Justinian against the Sasanians: "thrones of gold and carriages in which it is customary for a king's consort to ride."

35. See Oliver Wardrop, *Visramiani: The Story of the Lovers of Vis and Ramin, A Romance of Ancient Persia* (London: Royal Asiatic Society, 1914), 12: "She gave the letter to a swift messenger and sent it to Shahro. When the nurse's letter came to Vis's mother and she heard the praise of her daughter, and how she was grown up, she gave the scribe a coronet of gold and many other great possessions, and so enriched him that the wealth would suffice from generation to generation. Then Shahro sent to her daughter to Marav, with pomp, as is the custom with sovereigns, a *golden litter* adorned with jewels and pearls, many *Khodjas*, handmaidens and servants." Although this text is attested in an eleventh-century Georgian version, it likely has Parthian origins and appears to have existed in MP. See, for example, Vladimir F. Minorsky, "*Vīs u Rāmīn, a Parthian Romance*," *BSOAS* 4 (1946): 741–63, esp. 741–45. Finally, the image of a golden litter is also in the *Šāhnāme*, including in the context of sending a princess to marry the other empire's king; see, e.g., Abolqasem Ferdowsi, *Shahnameh: The Persian Book of Kings*, trans. Dick Davis, with foreword by Azar Nafisi (New York: Penguin Books, 2016), 181, 562, 583, and 892.

36. See *DJBA*, 329.

37. On the Achaemenids' use of carriages, including the *harmamaxa* for women, see Ezra M. Stratton, *The World on Wheels; Or, Carriages, with Their Historical Associations from the Earliest to the Present Time* (New York: E. M. Stratton, 1878), 110–13; and Nigel Tallis, "Transport and Warfare," in *Forgotten Empire: The World of Ancient Persia*, ed. John Curtis and Nigel Tallis (Berkeley: University of California Press, 2005), 210–35, esp. 211–12, on how, according to the Greek sources, these were "used by the king, by royal officials such as ambassadors, and by royal women, children and staff of the court." The vehicle appears to have been used to carry women; see Lloyd Llewellyn-Jones, *King and Court in Ancient Persia, 559 to 331 BCE*, Debates and Documents in Ancient History (Edinburgh: Edinburgh University Press, 2013), 104–5.

Ḥanina ben Dosa's Golden Table

With respect to the first-century sage Ḥanina ben Dosa, the Bavli is at the end of a long tradition, often clearly building on earlier Palestinian traditions about this figure.[38] Geza Vermes has explained the development this way: "The miracle stories handed down in Aramaic and collected in b. Ta'an. 24b–25a seem to be mostly secondary elaborations" whose "main interest lies in background details deriving from the primary tradition."[39] Just as scholars have rightly contextualized the Tannaitic stories about the Galilean miracle worker, Ḥanina ben Dosa, who in one episode gets bitten by a snake while in prayer, in light of the cultural milieu of Jesus and first-century miracles,[40] so too can they contextualize later Babylonian aggadot about him in a broader Sasanian milieu since there existed an autonomous stream of tradition in Amoraic Babylonia. The Bavli constructs a different persona for this figure. In a classic article on Ḥanina ben Dosa, Baruch Bokser proves that the Bavli "totally transforms Ḥanina's image, depicting him as a master who 'comes to the rescue' of a community in danger."[41] One also sees this Babylonian tradition in the Jewish Aramaic incantation bowls that scholars often characterize as reflective of popular religion, not unlike the Chapter of the Pious. Ḥanina ben Dosa appears in many bowls for healing.[42] In light of these points, it is clear that at least some of the talmudic aggadot about Ḥanina ben Dosa are Babylonian rabbinic cultural expressions that historicize the earlier Palestinian rabbinic past in order to speak to the needs of their contemporary communities. As Hasan-Rokem explains, the tales about Ḥanina ben Dosa in the Chapter of the Pious "reflect a Babylonian fantasy about the legendary past in Palestine, and do not present a realistic description."[43] The Babylonian rabbis expressed nostalgia for the earlier generations of scholars who had the capacity to perform miraculous deeds of which they themselves were not capable.[44] As we see below, the attribution of Iranian loanwords

38. On how the Bavli "routinely rabbinizes nonrabbinic figures," including Ḥanina ben Dosa and Ḥoni the Circlemaker, see the literature cited in Richard Kalmin, *Migrating Tales: The Talmud's Narratives and Their Historical Context* (Berkeley: University of California Press, 2014), xi (preface) n. 3 and the explanation on x.

39. Geza Vermes, "Ḥanina ben Dosa: A Controversial Galilean Saint from the First Century of the Christian Era," *JJS* 23 (1972): 28–50, esp. 39.

40. On this, see Hasan-Rokem, "Rabbinic Culture," 34 and 52–53; and Geza Vermes, *Jesus the Jew: A Historian's Reading of the Gospels* (Philadelphia: Fortress, 1981), 72–78.

41. Bokser, "Wonder-Working," 60.

42. See Shaul Shaked, James Nathan Ford, and Siam Bhayro, eds., with Matthew Morgenstern and Naama Vilozny, *Aramaic Bowl Spells: Jewish Babylonian Aramaic Bowls*, Magical and Religious Literature of Late Antiquity 1 (Leiden: Brill, 2013), 53–54.

43. Hasan-Rokem, "Rabbinic Culture," 43.

44. See the overview of miracles in rabbinic culture in Ephraim E. Urbach, *The Sages:*

to earlier or distant characters—whether Palestinian Tannaim, Amoraim, or earlier Second Temple figures—is a discursive technique that the Babylonian storytellers used in order to speak about the Jewish past in a style that their contemporary Babylonian audience would understand.

The main concern of the passage in b. Ta'an. 25a is how one should respond to living in misery and shame. Ḥanina ben Dosa's wife is ashamed of her poverty, and would heat an empty oven every Sabbath eve. When an evil neighbor sought to expose her, and knocked on the door, "she [Ḥanina's wife] was ashamed and went into the *inner room* [אידרונא]." She was saved by a miracle when the oven was found to be full of bread. She then tells her husband to pray so that they may receive nourishment to relieve their suffering. In response Ḥanina ben Dosa asks for mercy and receives "from the likeness of a hand" one "leg of a golden table." He then sees in a dream that the righteous will eat at a three-legged golden table while he will eat at a two-legged one, since he had already received his reward: relief in the present is at the expense of the future reward. Suffering in the material world is a positive sacrifice for a pious man. After Ḥanina ben Dosa reveals to his wife that her idea will lead them to "eat on an imperfect table" in the future, Ḥanina ben Dosa, in an ironic twist, again has to request mercy for the one golden leg to be taken back.

These stories contain two Iranian loanwords: אידרונא or אינדרונא (MP *andarōn*) and אכואנא (MP *xwān*). The first loanword is attested elsewhere in the Bavli and the Aramaic bowls. In the talmudic passage above, however, it appears in the printed editions.[45] Moreover, the second Iranian loanword, "table," surfaces in the thirteenth-century Spanish MS Oxford Opp. Add. fol. 23. The Oxford manuscript's borrowing from Iranian suggests

---

Their Concepts and Beliefs, trans. Israel Abrahams, 2nd enl. ed. (Jerusalem: Magnes Press, 1979), 97–123.

45. MS Jerusalem instead reads לביתיה. For more on manuscript differences, see Samuel Frank Thrope, "Contradictions and Vile Utterances: The Zoroastrian Critique of Judaism in the Škand Gumānīg Wizār" (Ph.D. diss., University of California, Berkeley, 2012), 101–2 n. 38. He explains there that except for MS Jerusalem "all the other extant manuscripts (though not the Vilna edition nor the Pesaro printing of 1516) make no mention of the heavenly hand descending to deliver the table leg. Instead, these versions state that it was cast down to him without specifying the means or identifying an agent." The author also identifies parallel passages in the rabbinic corpus, including b. Ber. 32a. For a discussion of the changes of this story through the process of its transmission, see Hasan-Rokem, "Rabbinic Culture," 46, evaluating Fraenkel's argument about the "the amplification of the tale in the printed version." The loanword appears elsewhere in the Talmud and the bowls and is likewise attested in Targumic Aramaic, Syriac, Mandaic, and Arabic (*DJBA*, 111). On this word, see Shaul Shaked, "Iranian Words Retrieved from Aramaic," in *Languages of Iran: Past and Present; Iranian Studies in Memoriam David Neil MacKenzie*, ed. Dieter Weber, Iranica 8 (Wiesbaden: Harrassowitz, 2005), 169–72. On the Greek *andrones* ("dining room"), see Ian Morris, "Remaining Invisible: The Archaeology of the Excluded in Classical Athens," in *Women and Slaves in Greco-Roman Culture: Differential Equations*, ed. Sandra R. Joshel and Sheila Murnaghan (New York: Routledge, 2001), 193–220, esp. 214–17.

a Middle Persian background to one performance of this aggada, which contains numerous parallels attested in ninth and tenth-century Arabic and Pāzand sources (e.g., *1,001 Nights* and the *Škand Gumānīg Wizār*) that stem from non-extant Middle Persian precursors. Although the extant versions of both *1,001 Nights* and the *Škand Gumānīg Wizār* are from around the ninth century, Middle Persian versions of both texts were in circulation in the late Sasanian period, not so long after the activity of the late Amoraim or anonymous editors. Let us now consider both of these comparisons.

There are connections between Jewish and talmudic stories and the Arabic collection of folklore called *1,001 Nights* or *Arabian Nights*. In the late nineteenth century, the Hungarian rabbi and scholar Joseph Perles, published a number of articles in the *Monatsschrift für Geschichte und Wissenschaft des Judenthums* comparing rabbinic stories with *1,001 Nights*. The Bavli's motif of a "golden table" in b. Ta'an. 25a is a similar theme to ones found in the Arabic work,[46] though there are significant differences between the motif of the "golden table" and the *1,001 Nights'* motif of a "ruby in a throne," found in rabbinic midrash on R. Shimon b. Ḥalafta.[47] It is noteworthy that MS Oxford Opp. Add. fol. 23—the only witness to have the Iranian loanword—is from Cairo, Egypt,[48] a key locale in the publication history[49] of *1,001 Night*'s travels, from what are likely Indian origins into Middle Persian[50] and then later into Arabic, its canonical language today. The Middle Persian text does not exist, but the tenth-century Arabic historians, Mas'udi and Ibn Al-Nadim both report the existence

46. See the series of articles by Josef Perles, "Rabbinische Agada's in 1001 Nacht: Ein Beitrag zur Geschichte der Wanderung orientalischer Märchen," *MGWJ* 22 (1873): 14–34, 61–85, 116–25.

47. Theodore Kwasman (personal communication).

48. See Krupp, "Manuscripts," 355: "A note gives Cairo 1557 as date of purchase."

49. Antoine Galland's French edition *Les mille et une nuits, contes Arabes traduits en français*, 12 vols. (1704–12, 1717) is based on the Syrian manuscript from the fourteenth century along with other materials. As for Egypt, alongside the mid-twelfth-century attestations (see below), there is also a late eighteenth-century version from Egypt that was published by Hermann Zotenberg (but is now lost), as well as an Arabic version published in Egypt in 1835. For a useful timeline of the publication history of *1,001 Nights*, see "Timeline of Publication History: The Arabian Nights," available at www.bridgingcultures.neh.gov/muslimjourneys/ items/show 157. For more on this book, see Dwight Reynolds, "A Thousand and One Nights: A History of the Text and Its Reception," in *The Cambridge History of Arabic Literature: Arabic Literature in the Post-Classical Period*, ed. Roger Allen and D. S. Richards (New York: Cambridge University Press, 2006), 270–91.

50. On the MP version of this work, see Duncan Black MacDonald, "The Earlier History of the Arabian Nights," *JRAS* (1924): 353–97, esp. 362–65; Nabia Abbott, "A Ninth-Century Fragment of the 'Thousand Nights': New Light on the Early History of the Arabic Nights," *JNES* 8 (1949): 129–64, esp. 145, dating a Syrian fragment to the ninth century; and Ch. Pellat, "Alf Layla Wa Layla," *Encyclopaedia Iranica* I/8, 831–35, available online at www.iranicaonline.org/articles/alf-layla-wa-layla.

of a Middle Persian version. As for the relationship between the Arabic and Middle Persian versions, Mas'udi describes the process as one of translation: "These are like the books transmitted to us and translated for us from the Pahlavi, Indian, and Greek, the origin of which was similar to these, such as 'The Book of *hazār afsāna*,' or, translated from Persian to Arabic, 'of a thousand *khurāfas*,' for *khurāfa* in Persian is called *afsāna*. The people call this book 'A Thousand Nights and a Night.'"[51] The *1,001 Nights* thus underwent multiple points of expansion and adaptation over the course of many centuries. It is a repository of traditions that includes eighth-century Arabic translations of the Middle Persian *Hazār afsāna* and subsequent additions from other sources such as al-Jahshiyārī and, in the twelfth-century, Egyptian tales.[52] The stories were widely circulated in different languages for different audiences—Persians, Arabs, and Jews. Subsequent to M. de Goeje's 1888 entry in *Encyclopedia Britannica*, numerous scholars have unearthed Jewish sources, especially those dealing with Esther and Solomon, in the compilation of *1,001 Nights*.[53] Interestingly, however, it is in the twelfth-century collection of *1,001 Nights* from Cairo where the Jewish tales get added, at least according to Perles and Victor Chauvin's early twentieth-century research on the Egyptian recension.[54]

The Jewish chapters, such as "Story of a Man of Jerusalem," were probably added by an editor who drew from the writings of Wahb ibn

51. MacDonald, "Earlier History," 362; other manuscripts read "Persian" in lieu of Pahlavi. Similarly, Ibn Al-Nadim reports in the *Fihrist* that, as MacDonald explains, "the first Arabic Nights was a straight translation of the Persian *Hazār Afsāna*, although later it fell into the hands of litterateurs and rhetoricians who took it up and variously improved and expanded it." See MacDonald, "Earlier History," 376–77.

52. "The Thousand and One Nights," *Encyclopedia Britannica*, available at www.britannica.com/topic/The-Thousand-and-One-Nights.

53. On the Jewish sources and editors of *1,001 Nights*, see Richard Gottheil and Joseph Jacobs, "Arabian Nights," in *Jewish Encyclopedia* (1901–1906), www.jewishencyclopedia.com/articles/1684-arabian-nights; Victor Bochman, "The Jews and 'The Arabian Nights,'" *Israel Review of Arts and Letters* (1996), www.forward.com/the-assimilator/127889/one-thousand-and-one-nights-too-jewish-for-somee/#ixzz44VzCmkgY; Joseph Sadan, "The *Arabian Nights* and the Jews," in *The Arabian Nights Encyclopedia*, vol. 1, ed. Ulrich Marzolph and Richard van Leeuwen, with the collaboration of Hassan Wassouf (Santa Barbara: ABC Clio, 2004), 42–46. On the possible connections of *1,001 Nights* with Testament of Solomon, see F. C. Conybeare, "The Testament of Solomon," *JQR* 11 (1898): 1–45, esp. 14. On motifs from the Epic of Gilgamesh that appear in the *1,001 Nights* through the medium of Jewish sources, see Stephanie Dalley, "Gilgamesh in the Arabian Nights," *JRAS* 1 (1991): 1–17, esp. 1–2 with n. 6 citing E. Littmann, "Alf Layla wa-Layla," *Encyclopedia of Islam*, 2nd ed. (Leiden: Brill, 1979). On de Goeje's arguments, see MacDonald, "Earlier History," 355; and esp. Pellat, "Alf Layla Wa Layla," who summarizes the author's position and reception: "M. J. de Goeje (*Encyclopaedia Britannica*, 9th ed., 1888, XVII, 316–18; cf. *EI* I, 361) in fact endeavored to prove that the frame-story of the Thousand and One Nights was related to the Book of Esther and that both are derived from the folklore of ancient Persia.... But the theory of M. J. de Goeje was not accepted." The author then cites secondary research that demonstrates the Indian origins.

54. Gottheil and Jacobs, "Arabian Nights."

Munabbih, a Jewish convert to Islam in the time of Muhammad. This important Arabic historian of the seventh and early eighth centuries from Yemen had intimate knowledge of Jewish and Syriac traditions, including from the Babylonian Talmud and Letter of Simeon, and had access to a work called the "Book of Jewish Matters"[55] alluded to above. As S. D. Goitein notes in a study of the Cairo Geniza, Jews in twelfth-century Egypt read and loaned out *1,001 Nights* as attested in a documentary record of a bookseller's list of books lent out, which includes *1,001 Nights*. Goitein explains that this is perhaps the earliest reference to the title of the collection as *1,001 Nights*:[56]

> When a Jewish bookseller lent a copy of *Thousand and One Nights* (this title, in its full form, appears, perhaps for the first time in the Geniza) to one of his customers, it stands to reason that the customer copied some or all of it for entertaining private or public audiences. The Geniza has preserved illustrations from the ancient Indian 'mirror of princes' known under its Arabic title *Kalīla wa-Dimna*, for instance, a picture of "a raven holding the tail of a rat."[57]

Since MS Oxford Opp. Add. fol. 23, from Egypt, is the only Talmud witness to contain the Iranian loanword in a motif that has parallels to *1,001 Nights*, it might be that it is recording a Middle Persian background. Babylonian talmudic folklore is part of a broader nexus of legend cycles or other types of literature that were ubiquitously circulated by and shared among different ethnic, political, and religious groups in their own languages from antiquity to late antiquity to the early Middle Ages, such as *1,001 Nights*, but also the *Alexander Romance* and others.

In addition to *1,001 Nights*, there is an undeniable parallel between b. Ta'an. 24b–25a and a passage in the *Škand Gumānīg Wizār*, a ninth-century Zoroastrian polemic against Judaism and other religions composed by Mardānfarrox ī Ohrmazddādān.[58] The original Middle Persian version of the *Škand* does not exist. The version extant today is composed in a later form of transcription called Pāzand. The Pāzand recension of the *Škand*

55. There is a lot of historical information about Wahb ibn Munabbih. For an overview, see Nabia Abbott, "Wahb B. Munabbih: A Review Article," *JNES* 36 (1977): 103–12; and Abd Al Duri, with introduction by Fred M. Donner, *The Rise of Historical Writing among the Arabs*, ed. and trans. Lawrence I. Conrad (Princeton, NJ: Princeton University Press, 1983), 122–35, including references listed on 122 n. a. On Wahb ibn Munabbih's knowledge of Talmud and Syriac, see Duri, *Rise of Historical Writing*, 125.

56. See, however, Bochman, "Jews and 'The Arabian Nights,'" who states that he has found an earlier reference.

57. Shlomo D. Goitein, *A Mediterranean Society: The Jewish Communities of the World as Portrayed in the Documents of the Cairo Geniza*, vol. 5, *The Individual* (Berkeley: University of California Press, 1988), 43. See also idem, "The Oldest Documentary Evidence for the Title *Alf Laila wa-Laila*," *JAOS* 78 (1958): 301–2.

58. See Thrope, "Contradictions," 99–100.

(as well as a Sanskrit one) was produced by the Indian scholar Neryosang Dhaval, who lived perhaps in "the first half of the 12th century,"[59] or possibly later. As a form of writing, Pāzand literature was not merely a process of transcription but also one of interpretation and the rendering of Pahlavi books into a new dialect. Pāzand studies thus need to engage the dialectical nature of the language, for example, *bahō̱t* and *šahō̱t* (MP *bawēd* and *šawēd*), attested in Judeo-Persian and early New Persian.[60] As Samuel Thrope has elucidated in a recent study of our passage translated below, this section of chapter 14's polemic against Judaism sets out to disprove that God is omniscient and omnipotent. It contains a lengthy description of God inquiring with Abraham regarding his health. As God sits down on a cushion, Abraham orders his son Isaac to "bring light and pure wine" to him,[61] which he does. Abraham invites God to drink the wine and eat the bread, but God refuses, stating: "I will not drink since it is not from Heaven nor is it pure."[62] But Abraham is then able to convince God that the wine is from heaven and pure, so God consumes it. The *Škand* in line 51 questions all this: Why would God come as a bodily human to eat and drink wine with Abraham? It is soon after this that we get the text that parallels the talmudic aggada about Ḥanina ben Dosa and his family's suffering. Here is the passage from *Škand* 14:58–74, the chapter on Judaism, as translated by Samuel Thrope:

> And it says in that place: "There was a sick man who, with his wife and children, was suffering greatly, poor and without resources. He was always diligent and active in prayer and fasting and supplication to God. One day in his prayer he requested in secret: 'Give me some happiness in my lot so that my life will be easier.'
>
> An angel descended and said to him: 'God has not apportioned in the stars a lot better than this. It is not possible to apportion a new lot. But, in recompense for your supplication and prayer, I have created for you a *four-legged jeweled throne in heaven*. If necessary, I will give you one leg of that throne.'
>
> That prophet asked the counsel of his wife. His wife said: 'It is better that we be satisfied with a poor lot and bad life in the material world than if we, among our companions, have a three-legged throne in heaven. But if you can, obtain our lot by another means.'
>
> That angel came again saying: 'Even if I destroy the firmament and create anew the heaven and earth and fashion and create anew the move-

59. See Shahpurshah Hormasji Hodivala, "The Dates of Hormazdyār Rāmyār and Neryosang Dhaval," *Journal of the K. R. Cama Oriental Institute* 8 (1926): 85–133.

60. See Thrope, "Contradictions," 20–21, on these grammatical phenomena. In some manuscript traditions, the first six chapters of the *Škand* are attested in Pahlavi; yet these Pahlavi versions are actually Pahlavi translations of the Pāzand versions.

61. Ibid., 224.

62. Ibid., 225.

ment of the stars, it is not evident from that whether your fate would be better or worse.'"

From these words it is apparent that he himself is not the dispenser of lots and destiny, their allotment is not according to his will and he cannot change fate. The revolution of the sphere, the sun, moon, and stars are not in the compass of his knowledge, will, and command. This as well, that the throne that he announces: "I will give it in heaven," is not a product of his work and creation.[63]

The passage references a "three-legged" and "four-legged jeweled throne in heaven" (*taxt-ə kəš cihār pāe əž gōhar aṇdar vahəšt*). The Persian word for "throne, chair" (*taxt*) is the same as the loanword in b. Ta'an. 25a. Both the Ḥanina ben Dosa story and this text from the *Škand* begin with the same scenario and protagonist: a pious man who prays but whose family is suffering because of a lack of resources. What each requests is identical (i.e., relief from suffering), even though the precise term they use differs: Ḥanina asks for mercy, whereas the anonymous sick man in the *Škand* requests happiness (*frōxī*). Still, each character receives the same offer—one leg of a golden or jewel-encrusted throne or chair that the family would inherit in the world to come. In each story, the wife of the protagonist decides against the proposition of receiving the throne-leg in this world. As Thrope has highlighted in his comparison of these two passages, the *Škand* downplays God's capacities, thus replacing "a disembodied hand descending from heaven"[64] with an angel. Thrope explains well the nature of Mardānfarrox's polemic against God's omniscience based on his understanding of the story about the suffering man who requests relief:

> In his critique, Mardānfarrox interprets the angel as a messenger of God; the angel's speech and actions reflect God's own power and capabilities. As he is portrayed in this passage, God cannot have the power befitting an omnipotent and omniscient deity. God is unable to change the fate of the suffering saint and his family. Moreover, even if he were to destroy the heavens and fashion them anew, he is ignorant of whether this change would result in a better or worse situation. As the wife remarks, a chair leg in this world, even a jeweled one, is cold comfort when, in eternity, one will be left with a broken throne. The wife's reference to their heavenly company points to shame as a driving force in her refusal to accept the chair leg; this theme also appears in the talmudic parallel.[65]

---

63. The translation is taken from Thrope, "Contradictions," 99–100.

64. Ibid., 104.

65. Ibid., 100–101. On 102, Thrope notes that the *Škand*'s statement "regarding the angel's inability to promise a better fate even if he makes the world anew, is found later in the same section of the Talmud in connection to a different impoverished rabbinic hero, Rabbi Elazar ben Pedat."

Lines 70–74 of the *Škand* are a polemical response to the story that appears in b. Ta'an. 25a. Mardānfarrox clearly knew this talmudic folklore in some fashion, adding to its Middle Persian connections. Although the character in the *Škand* passage above is anonymous, the reference to the man as a "prophet" or "messenger" (*pədąbar*) in line 66 is likely an allusion to Ḥanina ben Dosa or at least a pious man. As this clear parallel between b. Ta'an. 25a and *Škand* 14:58–74 illustrates, Babylonian talmudic folklore is historically situated at the crossroads of Sasanian and post-Sasanian Zoroastrian culture. The Iranian loanwords in talmudic folklore are signposts of such external postures and the Bavli is an intermediary resource of traditions.

The Story of Naḥum Ish Gamzu

Our next set of stories in b. Ta'an. 20a–25a is about a poor pious Tanna named Naḥum Ish Gamzu. In the second of these stories about Naḥum, the pious man is chosen by his fellow Jews to present a gift to the Roman Caesar. The gift, which the story does not specify, is put into a ספטא, "chest."[66] This is an Iranian loanword (cf. MIr. **sapat*) that is likewise attested in Mandaic, Syriac, and Arabic. While staying at an inn on the way, residents steal the gift from Naḥum's chest and replace it with dirt. Naḥum realizes this but is resigned ("this too is for the best") and, nevertheless delivers it. Caesar, insulted, wants to kill the Jews. Elijah, however, rescues Naḥum through the deception that the dirt that he brought to Caesar had miraculous properties that would lead the Romans to conquer another city. As a reward, "they went into *the treasury of the king* [בי גנזא דמלכא][67] and filled his chest with valuable stones and pearls."[68] Naḥum returns to that same inn with a chest full of valuables from the treasury of the king and explains to the people what transpired. Upon hearing the story, the residents of the inn tear down their building and sell their dirt to Caesar hoping they would gain riches. The residents' plan, of course, fails, and Caesar annihilates them.

This story is a case where a Middle Iranian loanword ("chest") plays a central position in the plot in a story of Babylonian provenance about the Romans. Interestingly, this story also contains another loanword from the earlier language of Old Persian: בי גנזא, "treasury," related to Old Persian **ganza.*[69] The foreign word "treasury" appears to have entered into

66. On this word, see *DJBA,* 824; Telegdi, "Essai sur la phonétique," 249. Cf. New Persian *safad*. The word is in seven talmudic texts and sometimes does not carry the connotation of high status.

67. MS Jerusalem.

68. The line "they sent him off with great honor" is not in MS Jerusalem.

69. See *DJBA,* 210, 273, and 295 (*ganjwar).* The word is also attested in Syriac and Mandaic.

the Jewish Aramaic lexicon at an early date, perhaps via Official Aramaic in the Achaemenid period, and thus may not technically be evidence of Sasanian-era Iranian linguistic penetration. Still, the placement of these early-entry words in passages with other Iranian loanwords or in reference to Persian figures[70] is conspicuous, and there may have been Middle Persian influences that we are unable to trace. Sokoloff, for instance, in his *Dictionary of Jewish Babylonian Aramaic,* traces גנזורא, "treasury-guard," in b. Ber. 56a to the Middle Persian form *ganjwar*.[71] Without a more complete record, it is hard to discern the extent to which the talmudic storytellers were cognizant of Iranian words that were already ingrained in Jewish Aramaic prior to the Talmud.

The word "chest" in b. Ta'an. 21a demonstrates another trend in the literary function of the Iranian loanwords in talmudic aggadot—namely, that the objects referred to by their Iranian terms are often a driving force in a story's narrative. In b. Ta'an. 21a, the "chest" is the locus of the entire

70. There are instances where Achaemenid or Parthian-era borrowings appear in talmudic narratives about Persians or in passages with other loanwords, a detail that perhaps suggests that the Talmud realizes that these words are from another language. This point of view may, however, be too reliant on the idea that the rabbis had a deep awareness of the etymologies of their vernacular, a question that in my view is unresolved. Moreover, such a premise that early-entry loanwords are being used by the Babylonian rabbis with knowledge of their Persian origins can sometimes lead scholars to unproductively compare sources based on the assumption that since there exists linguistic evidence of Iranization, then one can unearth cultural parallels as well. An example is the story from b. Qidd. 29b, where Rav Aḥa b. Ya'aqov encounters a demon in Abaye's school, which comes to him as a seven-headed serpent, one head of which falls off each time the rabbi bends down to pray. Abaye, who employs the Iranian loanword there, is associated with Iranian loanwords in other talmudic aggadot. This story's inclusion of Iranian אושפיזא, "hospitality," alongside the topic of demons, together perhaps invites one to make a positivistic comparative reading vis-à-vis the Iranian context. The serpent [תנינא] mentioned in the tale, for instance, surfaces in a list of creatures given in the legends about Rabba bar bar Ḥannah's sea adventure in b. B. Bat. 73a–75b and may be paralleled in later Pahlavi sources such as the *Pahlavi Rivāyat Accompanying the Dādestān ī Dēnīg*; on the Iranian context of this term and these stories, see Reuven Kiperwasser and Dan D. Y. Shapira, "Irano-Talmudica, II: Leviathan, Behemoth, and the 'Domestication' of Iranian Mythological Creatures in Eschatological Narratives of the Babylonian Talmud," in *Shoshannat Yaakov: Jewish and Iranian Studies in Honor of Yaakov Elman,* ed. Shai Secunda and Steven Fine, Brill Reference Library of Judaism 35 (Leiden: Brill, 2012), 203–25, esp. 208 and 209 n. 22, where the authors refer to past studies by H. W. Bailey (on the Arameogram TNYNA, which represents the "Aramaic word for 'monster of the sea'"); and W. B. Henning, "Two Manichaean Magical Texts with an Excursus on the Parthian ending -ēndēh," *BSOAS* 12 (1947): 39–66, esp. 42, where the author concludes: "*tnyn'* = *tannīnā*, too, is not hitherto known as a Pahlavi word; it could be either loanword or ideogram (for *aždahāg* ?)." The Avesta also describes the mythical dragon Zahhak as having seven heads, a detail matching b. Qidd. 29b. Unfortunately, these parallels do not necessarily prove Iranian-Jewish intersections since the motif of a seven-headed dragon is also attested in "Sumero-Semitic culture, art and literature," as explained in Prods Oktor Skjærvø, "Aždahāi., In Old and Middle Iranian," *Encyclopaedia Iranica* (online ed., last updated 2011). For example, Rev 12.

71. *DJBA*, 295.

story's ironic twists. This same phenomenon can be found in b. Ta'an. 21b–22a, where the Iranian loanword ביסתרקי, "mattresses," has a key role in a tale about Abba the bloodletter, a physician who refuses to accept money for helping the rabbis. At one point Abaye decides to test the physician's piety by sending rabbis to steal his mattresses. Here is a translation of b. Ta'an. 21b–22a according to MS Jerusalem:

> One day Abaye sent a pair of rabbis to test (Abba the bloodletter). (Abba the bloodletter) seated them, fed them, and gave them a drink. He spread *mattresses* [ביסתרקי] for them.[72] When they got up in the morning they took them to the marketplace to sell them and passed by (Abba the bloodletter). They said to him: How much are these mattresses worth? He said to them: Such-and-such. They said to him: Perhaps they are worth more? He said to them: This is what I paid for them. They said to them: Take them, master. He said to them: From that moment I stopped thinking about them. They said to him: What did you suspect? (He said to them): Perhaps (there was) a good deed that happened upon the rabbis.

The mattresses in this story—again described in terms of monetary value—are, like the "chest" in b. Ta'an. 21a, the object of antagonism, and are well known as a common Iranian element in the Bavli.

Conclusion

The Iranian loanwords, with all the necessary attention paid to issues of philology, offer talmudists a set of data that proves linguistic ties between Jews and Persians in late antique Babylonia. These data raise a series of questions. As with the Greco-Roman context, we must probe the role the loanwords play in the rabbinic texts. Why do the rabbis use such loanwords? What do these loanwords mean about rabbinic knowledge of and influence from Persian culture? For instance, as we have seen in this essay, it appears that in at least the one instance examined in this article, there is a cluster of loanwords in talmudic folklore produced in the voice of the so-called common people.

Moreover, some of the Iranian loanwords in the Chapter of the Pious are attested in literary motifs that were ubiquitously shared across various languages and among various peoples from antiquity to the late Middle Ages. Key examples include Rav Huna's "golden carriage," a motif that perhaps stems from the Achaemenid period and continues through Ferdowsi's *Šāhnāme* and Arabic sources; or Ḥanina ben Dosa's "golden table," which has resonances in the Arabic collection of stories *1,001 Nights,* and obvious parallels to the *Škand Gumānīg Wizār,* whose author probably

72. Neither MS Jerusalem nor MS London-BL Harl. 5508 (400) adds "at night," which appears in other witnesses.

knew a version of the specific tale. These shared features, which are manifest on the level of the single word (or loanword) or phrase (as opposed to entire sentences or passages), with these external sources suggest that the Talmud was influenced from the outside.[73] The Iranian loanwords are, in the end, glimpses and shadowy single-word traces of the Bavli's cultural situation in the heartland of Mesopotamia, between the Roman West and the Sasanian East, and chronologically between antiquity and the rise of Islam. These loanwords and their respective motifs do not necessarily imply deeper narrative influences between the non-Jewish and talmudic sources, though at the same time it is hard to deny that finding loanwords in texts that one wants to compare with the Iranian context supports the viability of discovering "influences" through such comparisons. What they do demonstrate, however, is how the cultural import of common literary motifs could be transported from one civilization to the next across time and space.[74] To be sure, other loanwords are cases of assimilated Iranian words into Jewish Babylonian Aramaic, sometimes due to the fact that they refer to an object for which there exists no Aramaic equivalent. With respect to Babylonian folklore, Jewish culture's boundaries were porous vis-à-vis the Sasanian cultural environment. The Iranian loanwords in the Chapter of the Pious can be understood as traces of this "Sasanianization" of the Babylonian Jews and their folklore.[75]

Appendix I: Iranian Loanwords in b. Ta'anit 20a–25a

[20a] גזירפטא, "court official" < *gazir*, "officer" + MIr. **pati*, "lord"[76]
[20b] גהורקא, גוהרקא, "chair, litter, carriage" < MIr. **gāhwārak*[77]

---

73. Although it is generally true, as Kalmin highlights in *Migrating Tales*, 238, that many of the above-named works, especially the Middle and New Persian ones, are "late and derivative," dating from the ninth to eleventh centuries, there is evidence that points to earlier, now-lost MP versions of those works.

74. On this, see esp. Kalmin, *Migrating Tales*.

75. The emphasis on the Babylonian context is not to deny the role of the eastern regions of the Roman Empire or Palestinian rabbinic traditions in the formation of Babylonian talmudic aggadot, including the Chapter of the Pious, since these processes—reception, transmission, adaptation, or creation—played out simultaneously. There are Palestinian sources that parallel aggadic sections of the Chapter of the Pious; see, e.g., Ilan, *Massekhet Ta'anit*, 196–98, on y. Ta'an. 3:13, 67a and b. Ta'an. 20b.

76. See *DJBA*, 274; Kwasman, "Loanwords," 357; and Mokhtarian, *Rabbis, Sorcerers*, 117–20. For the appearance of קולפא, "club, blow," in b. Ta'an. 20a ("the blows of my mother are better than the kisses of my stepmother"), with which one can compare New Persian *kūpāl*, see *DJBA*, 992, and Ilan, *Massekhet Ta'anit*, 192, on this being in the New York manuscript, citing Malter.

77. See *DJBA*, 262; Kwasman, "Loanwords," 367; and Telegdi, "Essai sur la phonétique,"

[21a] ספטא, סיפטא, "box, chest" < MIr. **sapat*[78]
[21b] ביסתרקא, "bedding, mattress" < MIr. **bistarak*[79]
[22a] זנדנקנא, "jailor" < MIr. **zēndānakān*[80]
[22a] דורדיא, "lees" < cf. NP *durdī*
[22a] דשתנא, "menstruating woman" < MP *daštān*
[22b] ניזג, "spear" < MP *nēzag*[81]
[23a] רמכא, "herd" < MIr. **ramak*[82]
[23b] היזמתא, "prickly shrub" < MIr. **hēzm*[83]
[23b] גואלקא, גוולקא, "sack" < MIr. **ǰuwālak*[84]
[23b] רוזיקא, "daily ration, provision" < MIr. **rōzīk*[85]
[24a] קוסטא, "district" < MP *kust*[86]
[24b] אמבוהא, "crowd" < MP **ambuh*[87]
[24b] פיקר, "dispute" < OP **pati-kāra* (MIr. **paykār*)[88]
[25a] אידרונא, "inner room" < MP *andāron*[89]
[25a] אכואנא, "table" < MP *xwān*[90]

Appendix II. Iranian Loanword Cluster in b. Giṭṭin 56a–58a on the Romans

Iranian loanwords appear frequently in talmudic contexts that include Romans.[91] An aggadic unit that involves the Romans in b. Giṭ. 56a–58a

236, explaining it via metathesis and disagreeing with Lagarde's emendation. See also Herman, *Prince without a Kingdom*, 217 n. 38.

78. See *DJBA*, 824; and Kwasman, "Loanwords," 371.

79. See *DJBA*, 204; and Kwasman, "Loanwords," 345.

80. This essay will not treat the loanwords in b. Ta'an. 22a; on this text, see Geoffrey Herman, "'One Day David Went Out for the Hunt of the Falconers': Persian Themes in the Babylonian Talmud," in Secunda and Fine, *Shoshannat Yaakov*, 111–26, esp. 123–25.

81. Cf. ניסכא, ניזכא < Iranian **naizaka-*, on which see *DJBA*, 752; Kwasman, "Loanwords," 347; and Jonas C. Greenfield and Shaul Shaked, "Three Iranian Words in the Targum of Job from Qumran," in *'Al Kanfei Yonah: Collected Studies of Jonas C. Greenfield on Semitic Philology*, ed. Shalom M. Paul, Michael E. Stone, and Avital Pinnick, 2 vols. (Jerusalem: Magnes Press, 2001), 344–52, esp. 347–49.

82. See *DJBA*, 1088; and Kwasman, "Loanwords," 359.

83. See *DJBA*, 375; and Kwasman, "Loanwords," 362. It is not in MS Oxford Opp. Add. fol. 23 or in MS Vatican 134. MS Jerusalem has brackets [ ].

84. See *DJBA*, 264; and Kwasman, "Loanwords," 344.

85. See *DJBA*, 1063–64; and Kwasman, "Loanwords," 351.

86. See *DJBA*, 1000; Kwasman, "Loanwords," 349; and Mokhtarian, *Rabbis, Sorcerers*, 55.

87. See *DJBA*, 137; and Kwasman, "Loanwords," 358.

88. See *DJBA*, 903; and Kwasman, "Loanwords," 371.

89. See *DJBA*, 111; and Kwasman, "Loanwords," 348.

90. See *DJBA*, 129; and Kwasman, "Loanwords," 345. The *aleph* is a prosthetic. Cf. the compound אכוונגרא, כואנגאר, "table-steward" (MP *xwāngār*), in two texts about King Yazdegird and the Exilarch, respectively (b. Ketub. 61a and b. Mo'ed Qaṭ. 12a).

91. See, e.g., זינא, "weapon" (cf. MP *zēn*), in b. B. Bat. 4a; and תגא, "crown" (cf. MP *tāg*), and מרזבנא, "prefect," in b. Meg. 6b. There are rich aggadot about Romans that contain

contains no fewer than fourteen different Iranian borrowings: גושקרא, דייספק, אושפיזא, שרגא, גושפנקא, תגא, גונדא דרומאי, סיפוסקא,[92] פריסתקא, איברא, פוסתא, אינדג, הרמנא.[93] The account of Martha the daughter of Boethius's quest for fine flour[94] includes asking for גושקרא[95] which means in New Persian, according to Francis Joseph Steingass, "coarse, unsifted flour."[96] This source creates a dramatic tension through the repetition of the wealthy Jerusalemite's desire for flour. The third out of four types of flour listed here is an Iranian loanword attested in no other Jewish Babylonian Aramaic texts.

Iranian loanwords. See, e.g., b. B. Meṣ'ia 83b with פהרגבנא, "guard," and פרוונקא, "guide, messenger." For still others, see a story in b. Meg. 26b, with the Iranian loanword אידרונא, "inner room," about Roman Jews dealing with the problem of their synagogue opening to an inner room where a corpse lay; and the tale of R. Yehoshua b. Ḥanania's encounters with the Athenian sages and the Roman Caesar (presumably Hadrian) in b. Bek. 8b–9a. In this latter text are the loanwords ביסתרקא, "bedding" (cf. MP *wistarag*), דרבנא, "guard, doorkeeper" (MP *dar-pānag*), and זגא, "hen" (MIr. **zāg*). [On this story see Herman's contribution to this volume]. This lengthy aggada is part of a legend cycle that is carried into later Arabic and Persian literature. On the common narrative in Arabic and MP traditions about sages in dialogue with monarchs, which our aggada above parallels, see Dina Stein, "A King, a Queen, and the Riddle Between: Riddles and Interpretation in a Late Midrashic Text," in *Untying the Knot: On Riddles and Other Enigmatic Modes*, ed. Galit Hasan-Rokem and David Shulman (New York: Oxford University Press, 1996), 125–47, esp. 129-30. On connections to the *Book of Ahikar*, see Yassif, *Hebrew Folktale*, 214. Although it is about the Greeks, the story is a product of Babylonia, with no known parallels in Palestinian rabbinic literature; see Louis Jacobs, *Structure and Form in the Babylonian Talmud* (New York: Cambridge University Press, 1991), 22 n. 3. Its Babylonian setting is proven by the presence of the Iranian loanwords.

92. In b. Giṭ. 56b the word סיפוסקא, "bran" is attested (see MS Vatican 140). As seen here, loanwords for foods commonly appear in medical remedies: "How did the healers remedy R. Zadok? On the first day they gave him מיא דפארי ('bran-water') to drink; on the following day מיא דסיפוסקא ('*bran*-water'); on the following day flour-water, until his stomach got wider and wider."

93. In the final passage of b. Giṭ. 56a–58a on the Romans, the Talmud adds several new loanwords into the mix—אינדג*, "a little" (printed eds.; see *DJBA*, 118; and cf. MP *andak*), and פוסתא, "a sheet"—when discussing the location of biblical prooftexts. Here is a short excerpt from b. Giṭ. 58a, based on the printed editions: "[The first one] asked: 'How far am I from that verse?' He said: 'A *small amount* [אינדג*], a *sheet* [פוסתא] and a half.' He said to him: 'If I had reached that verse, I would not have needed you.'" The first loanword is a conjectural reconstruction. See Vilna: אינגד; Soncino Print 1488: אינגר; MS St. Petersburg–RNL Evr. I 187 and MS Munich 95: אינגך; and MS Vatican 140: אינך. The second Iranian loanword is less disputed, clearly being related to MP *pōst*, "skin, hide," a fact that I believe corroborates the first word's connection to Iranian.

94. b. Giṭ. 56a.

95. Per Vilna, MS Arras 889, MS Munich 95, and MS Vatican 140. Cf. MS Munich Bayerische Staatsbibliothek, Cod. hebr. 153 (II, 1): גישקרא. Some manuscripts begin the word with כ instead of ג—e.g., MS New York JTS Rab. 1718.93-100 and MS New York JTS Rab. 1729.64-67.

96. Francis Joseph Steingass, *A Comprehensive Persian-English Dictionary* (London: Routledge, 1892), 462, s.v. *xuškār*. Steingass states that it is short for *xušk-ārd*: *xušk* means "dry, pure" and *ārd* is the MP form of "flour" (cf. MacKenzie, *Concise Pahlavi Dictionary*, 11).

R. Yoḥanan ben Zakkai's escape in a coffin from the besieged city of Jerusalem and the sage's encounter with the Roman emperor Vespasian then follows. In responding to the king's retort to his initial praise, the sage states *"in fact* [איברא] you are a king, for if you were not a king ..." using the Iranian adverb איברא, "in truth, indeed, in fact." The use of the Iranian adverb as part of the rabbi's response to Vespasian creates a higher and more formal register for the tenor of his oral dialogue. In the Talmud the word איברא appears in characters' spoken words, as seen in b. B. Bat. 168a ("He said: 'I am certain it was you.'"). In b. B. Meṣ. 8b Rav Yosef uses the same word in response to Abaye during a legal debate. These usages are consistent with the meaning of this word in MP literature, where the equivalent term *ēwar* appears as either an adverb meaning "certain(ly), assured(ly), evident."[97] The Roman messenger who announces the death of Caesar is the Iranian loan, פריסתקא, a word that appears in several other aggadot that are ripe for contextualization.[98]

Later, after Roman troops (גונדא דרומאי) thwart Jewish rebellions, they warn Caesar about the Jewish threat. The monarch then takes off "his crown," an Iranian word, and beseeches God. This passage contains several words of Iranian origins that are of relatively high frequency in the Bavli: גונדא, "troop," תגא, "crown," שרגי, "lamps," and גושפנקא, "signet ring."[99] This final term גושפנקא appears to have a range of meanings: it can mean a type of signet ring worn as jewelry, a legal sealing, or something used in medicinal contexts. In all these cases it is clearly depicted as an object of real or supernatural power.[100] The Middle Persian cognate *angustbān* is attested once, in an early Middle Persian text with some Parthian words, entitled "The Babylonian Tree" (*Draxt ī Āsūrīg*), where it is associated with the nobility.[101] In b. Giṭ. 57b, Caesar uses the ring as a way

97. For this meaning, see MacKenzie, *Concise Pahlavi Dictionary*, 31–32; Mahmood Jaafari-Dehaghi, *Dādestān ī Dēnīg*, part 1, *Transcription, Translation, and Commentary* (Paris: Association pour l'Avancement des Études Iraniennes, 1998), 44–45 (ch. 2.6), 50–51 (chs. 4.3 and 5.2), and elsewhere; Jehangir C. Tavadia, *Šāyast-nē-šāyast: A Pahlavi Text on Religious Customs* (Hamburg: de Gruyter, 1930), 30 (ch. 3.22-23). The more technical meaning of the term in a Sasanian legal context, "authentic," "valid," "trustworthy," as seen often in the *Mādayān ī Hazār Dādestān*, does not have a parallel in the Bavli.

98. See b. 'Abod. Zar. 65a; b. B. Meṣ. 86a; b. Ber. 58a. In b. 'Abod. Zar. 65a, for instance, Rava sends a gift to a non-Jew named Bar-Sheshaq, whom the sage sees "sitting up to his neck in rosewater" with naked prostitutes around him. Bar-Sheshaq asks Rava whether anything better exists in the world to come, to which Rava eventually responds to the man that he should fear the ruling authorities. After this exchange a messenger (פריסתקא) tells them that the king has requested their presence, at which point the gentile's eye bursts.

99. See *DJBA*, 273.

100. See b. Giṭ. 68a; for medicine, see b. Ber. 6a.

101. See Christopher Brunner, "The Fable of the Babylonian Tree, Part II: Translation," *JNES* 39 (1980): 291–302, esp. 292 lines 55–58: "They make belts of me which they stud with

to get his subject to accept his authority: "Caesar said to him: 'I will throw my signet ring [גושפנקאי] to you. Bend over and pick it up so that they say of you that he has accepted the authority [הרמנא, from Middle Parthian **hramān*] of the king.'"[102]

pearls. I am morocco boots for the nobles, finger-stalls for the renowned, the king's companions." For more, see also Christopher Brunner, "The Fable of the Babylonian Tree, Part I: Introduction," *JNES* 39 (1980): 191–202.

102. b. Giṭ. 57b (MS Vatican 130). See also the appearance of this loanword in b. Ḥul. 57b, where R. Shimon b. Ḥalafta tests ants as a metaphor for kingship. In a story about Rav Shila's encounters with the government in b. Ber. 58a the word is similarly used in the context of imperial authority.

Gaze and Counter-Gaze

Textuality and Contextuality in the Anecdote of Rav Assi and the Roman (b. Baba Meṣiʿa 28b)

SHAI SECUNDA

In 2003, a conference was convened by Jeffrey Rubenstein at New York University under the heading "The Contribution of the Bavli's Redactors to the Aggada."[1] The years since that gathering, leading up to another NYU workshop entitled "The Aggada of the Babylonian Talmud and Its Cultural World," for which this paper was composed, have seen the solidification of a set of philological tools, further development of cultural approaches to rabbinic literature, and the rapid growth of contextual readings of the Bavli. It is worth reflecting on how the titles of the earlier and more recent conferences signal a gradual shift in focus from (a) examining the role of the Bavli's unnamed redactors (Stammaim) in the production of Babylonian sage stories per se—an insight advanced in Rubenstein's *Talmudic Stories*[2]—to (b) considering the cultural import of Babylonian aggada, developed in works such as Daniel Boyarin's *Carnal Israel*[3] and linked specifically to Stammaitic innovation, once again by Rubenstein,[4] then (c) to appreciating the significance of the Bavli's Sasanian context, energetically undertaken by Yaakov Elman,[5] among whose students I am

1. The proceedings were later published as Jeffrey L. Rubenstein, ed., *Creation and Composition: The Contribution of the Bavli Redactors (Stammaim) to the Aggada*, TSAJ 114 (Tübingen: Mohr Siebeck, 2005).

2. Jeffrey L. Rubenstein, *Talmudic Stories: Narrative Art, Composition, and Culture* (Baltimore: Johns Hopkins University Press, 1999). About a decade later, a second volume by Rubenstein was published as *Stories of the Babylonian Talmud* (Baltimore: Johns Hopkins University Press, 2010).

3. Daniel Boyarin, *Carnal Israel: Reading Sex in Talmudic Culture*, New Historicism 25 (Berkeley: University of California Press, 1993).

4. Jeffrey L. Rubenstein, *The Culture of the Babylonian Talmud* (Baltimore: Johns Hopkins University Press, 2003).

5. Representative publications include Yaakov Elman, "Acculturation to Elite Persian

grateful to count myself. The current forum considers the cultural world of Bavli aggada or, put differently, the relationship between talmudic text, setting, and culture.

In his writing on talmudic narrative, Rubenstein has argued that the same unnamed authorities responsible for the redaction of the halakhic passages of the Bavli also produced many of the Bavli's sage stories. In this work he builds on the conclusions of his mentor, David Weiss-Halivni, who carefully distinguished between the Talmud's unattributed Aramaic legal discussions and the attributed Hebrew Amoraic dicta they frame in order to develop a theory of talmudic production.[6] Rubenstein has similarly pointed to unattributed literary activity in arguing that the Bavli's lengthy stories were actually produced by the Amoraim's successors, the Stammaim. Interestingly, many of the philological criteria he uses to make this point are in fact adapted from the work of Shamma Friedman, the other major pioneer of Talmud source criticism.[7] These criteria include both ongoing analysis of Palestinian rabbinic parallels and the delineation of the Stammaim's harvesting of themes and motifs from elsewhere in the Bavli. Thus, Rubenstein's work advanced quickly from merely arguing for the influence of the Stammaim in producing talmudic narratives as a fact, to considering the cultural import of the changes wrought by the Babylonian storytellers, which he attributed to rabbinic societal and geocultural shifts. Such an approach was receptive to the growing research into the Bavli's Sasanian context, as the latter might explain and confirm some of the distinctive features of the Bavli's reworked aggadot.[8]

Norms in the Babylonian Jewish Community of Late Antiquity," in *Neti'ot Le-David: Jubilee Volume for David Weiss Halivni,* ed. Ephraim Bezalel Halivni, Zvi Arie Steinfeld, and Yaakov Elman (Jerusalem: Orhot, 2004), 31–56; idem, "Middle Persian Culture and Babylonian Sages: Accommodation and Resistance in the Shaping of Rabbinic Legal Tradition," in *The Cambridge Companion to the Talmud and Rabbinic Literature,* ed. Charlotte Elisheva Fonrobert and Martin Jaffee (Cambridge: Cambridge University Press, 2007), 165–97; idem, "'Up to the Ears' in Horses' Necks (B.M. 108a): On Sasanian Agricultural Policy and Private 'Eminent Domain,'" *Jewish Studies – Internet Journal* 3 (2004): 95–149.

6. The research itself can be accessed in the ongoing commentarial project of David Weiss-Halivni, *Sources and Traditions,* 8 vols. (Tel Aviv: Mosad Bialik; Jerusalem: Magnes Press, 1968–). A collection and translation of the introductions to these volumes has been published as David Weiss Halivni, *The Formation of the Babylonian Talmud,* trans. Jeffrey L. Rubenstein (Oxford: Oxford University Press, 2013).

7. Many of Friedman's relevant studies have been collected in Shamma Friedman, *Talmudic Studies: Investigating the Sugya, Variant Readings and Aggada* [Hebrew] (Jerusalem: Jewish Theological Seminary of America, 2010) .

8. Note, however, that Yaakov Elman has registered some criticism of the project on this front. See Yaakov Elman, review of *The Culture of the Babylonian Talmud* , by Jeffrey L. Rubenstein, *JR* 86 (2006): 700–702. Another review relevant to the current discussion is Isaiah Gafni, "Rethinking Talmudic History: The Challenge of Literary and Redaction Criticism,"

There is a sense that the ground has again begun to shift in the study of rabbinic literature in general, with implications for Bavli research in particular. For one, the distance between text and culture has simultaneously been further driven apart yet also bridged by scholars who in one way or another treat rabbinic texts as "discourses" in the critical-theoretical sense.[9] Within such a framework, the direct historicity of talmudic literature is denied so that one cannot move unencumbered from late antique rabbinic texts to late antique rabbinic culture. In the other direction, however, the Talmud as discourse possesses considerable ideological force through which it subsequently engenders Jewish culture. Relatedly—though on more explicitly philosophical grounds—in his book *The Open Past: Subjectivity and Remembering in the Talmud*,[10] Sergey Dolgopolski has questioned Weiss-Halivni's and Friedman's reconstructions of the rabbinic authorities who redacted the Talmud. He uncovers a number of fallacies in assuming that talmudic discussions manifest the conscious and active creation of the Talmud by anonymous rabbis. Dolgopolski's critique may emerge from beyond the traditional confines of Talmud criticism, yet perhaps for this very reason it is able to locate problems of which talmudists might otherwise have remained ignorant.

Even when reconsidering a particular issue within the framework of contemporary Talmud scholarship, such as how to explain various parallel passages shared by the Bavli and Yerushalmi, it is becoming clear that not all textual variations can be easily accounted for by the available models of Stammaim "reworking" earlier Palestinian kernels, "adding" Babylonian colorings, or "including" stock phrases.[11] More recent attention to the oral production and the subsequent aural and scribal receptions of

---

Jewish History 25 (2011): 355–75. In recent years, aside from organizing the conference where the papers collected in this volume were delivered, Rubenstein has produced original Irano-Talmudic research of his own. See, e.g., Jeffrey L. Rubenstein, "King Herod in Ardashir's Court: The Rabbinic Story of Herod (B. Bava Batra 3b-4a) in Light of Persian Sources.," *AJS Review* 38 (2014): 249–74; idem, "Talmudic Astrology : Bavli Šabbat 156A-B," *HUCA* 78 (2007): 109–48.

9. The seeds for this approach were planted, once again, in Boyarin, *Carnal Israel*. See Charlotte Elisheva Fonrobert, "On 'Carnal Israel' and the Consequences: Talmudic Studies since Foucault," *JQR* 95 (2005): 462–69. Nevertheless, only in more recent years have such theoretical paradigms been applied to rabbinic literature in a more thoroughgoing manner. Recent examples include Mira Balberg, *Purity, Body, and Self in Early Rabbinic Literature* (Berkeley: University of California Press, 2014); Beth A. Berkowitz, *Defining Jewish Difference: From Antiquity to the Present* (New York: Cambridge University Press, 2012); and Ishay Rosen-Zvi, *The Mishnaic Sotah Ritual: Temple, Gender and Midrash*, JSJSup 160 (Leiden: Brill, 2012).

10. Sergey Dolgopolski, *The Open Past: Subjectivity and Remembering in the Talmud* (New York: Fordham University Press, 2013).

11. See, e.g., Moulie Vidas, *Tradition and the Formation of the Talmud* (Princeton, NJ: Princeton University Press, 2014).

the talmudic text has complicated matters even further. In some circles, the Talmud is now understood to be as much (if not more) a product of its producers as formed by its readership.[12] By grappling with the Bavli's discursivity, orality, and performativity, this recent scholarship highlights the Talmud's distinctive "textuality," all while considering its implications for posing cultural questions about the Talmud and its world.[13]

In this paper I apply some of the insights gained on the preceding topics as I read a brief talmudic anecdote and meditate on the themes of text, setting, and culture. Note that, unlike the rich and lengthy talmudic stories that Rubenstein and his colleagues have mainly treated, the talmudic story that I have chosen is by design remarkably short in length. I will first present the anecdote and then adduce and briefly discuss relevant parallels from its geopolitical context. Subsequently, I will consider the narrative's discursive context and thereby underline its textuality, though hopefully in a way that does not distance the text from the human beings who produced it, but which instead evinces the text's embodiment in the form of incessant text production and transmission in Babylonian rabbinic society. Ideally, this will enable me to say something larger about Babylonian rabbinic society as I read the textual shifts for larger geohistorical and cultural transformations.

---

12. Talmudists have been paying increasing attention to the Bavli's oral nature for some years now. See, e.g., Yaakov Elman, "Orality and the Redaction of the Babylonian Talmud," *Oral Tradition* 14 (1999): 52–99; and Yaakov Sussman, "Oral Torah in Its Literal Sense" [Hebrew], in *Mehqerei Talmud III: Talmudic Studies Dedicated to the Memory of Professor Ephraim E. Urbach*, ed. David Rosenthal and Yaakov Sussman (Jerusalem: Magnes, 2005), 209–384. A notable, recent exploration that has twinned oral approaches with literary theoretical questions of reader reception is undertaken in Zvi Septimus, "The Poetic Superstructure of the Babylonian Talmud and the Reader It Fashions" (Ph.D. diss., University of California, Berkeley, 2011).

13. I am using the term *textuality* here, against its conventional sense, to refer to the distinct qualities of *relatively* fixed linguistic expressions—that is, "texts"—be they transmitted in writing, orally or via some other means. Presenting talmudic stories as overtly textual objects emphasizes that their textual characteristics and "representedness" should come before other significations, including historical, cultural, and intellectual, in scholarly analysis. Before a more nuanced definition of talmudic textuality can be presented, talmudists like myself will have to heed the call of theorists like D. C. Greetham to cultivate a deeper awareness of the particular theories of text that underlie the work of every text scholar—including those talmudists who mistakenly assume an inherent divide between "regular" scholarship and "Theory." See D. C. Greetham, *Theories of the Text* (Oxford: Oxford University Press, 1999). For some preliminary observations in this direction, see Shai Secunda, "'This, but Also That': Historical, Methodological, and Theoretical Reflections on Irano-Talmudica," *JQR* 106 (2016): 233–41.

b. Baba Meṣᶜia 28b[14]

ר׳ אסי[15] אשכח ארנקא[16] דדינרי. חזייה ההוא[17] רומא׳[18] [והוה][19] קא מחסס.[20] אמ׳ ליה:
שקול לדעתך![21] לאו פרסאי אנן דאמרי אבדתא למלכא.

Rav Assi found a moneybag of dinars. A Roman saw him and he [i.e., Rav Assi] was apprehensive. He said to him: "Take it for yourself! We are not Persians who say 'lost property belongs to the king.'"

All but one of the main elements in this story can be correlated to a "cultural world" in the geopolitical sense: There are the characters, which include a Palestinian rabbi, a Roman interlocutor, Persian lawyers who relate the legal norm, and a Persian sovereign; there is the object of desire—the wallet of cash—at the center; and the setting is, presumably, Roman Palestine.

At the same time, there is a group of more ephemeral contextual "locations" of the text that might also be related to discursive "worlds" of their own: (1) The anecdote was composed at some point during late antiquity, though it is presently difficult to determine whether it was partially or entirely formed in Sasanian Babylonia, or if it grew mainly out of Palestinian rabbinic precursors. (2) The anecdote appears in (a) a Babylonian rabbinic *sugya* about the protocol for announcing recovered lost property "located" in (b) the talmudic chapter that discusses the rules governing lost things, found within (c) the mammoth compilation known as the Babylonian Talmud. (3) The anecdote may have been adapted or changed before, during, and/or after redaction, possibly due to interaction with parallel rabbinic texts. (4) Subsequently, the anecdote was transmitted over the centuries as part of the Bavli via different media (oral recitation,

14. The passage is transcribed from MS Hamburg, with one noted change incorporated in the text and significant variants recorded in the footnotes.

15. אסי] MSS Florence, Vatican 115, Vatican 117, and Munich; אמי] MS Hamburg and Escorial and ed. Vilna. See n. 22, below.

16. ארנקא] (also Cambridge T-S 329.638-641: רנקא[.]); אודיא Escorial and ed. Vilna (אודייא); אוריתא Florence; אודדא Vatican 115; אורדיא Vatican 117 and Munich (אורדי׳).

17. ההוא] MSS Vatican 115, Vatican 117, Munich, and printed eds.; לההוא MS Escorial and MS Florence (prior to the erasure of the ל).

18. רומא׳] All MSS (not abbreviated); בר נש ed. Vilna (based on an overzealous censor's change in ed. Basel, which influenced subsequent editions).

19. והוה קא] הוה קא MS Vatican 117; וקא MS Escorial; דהוה קא Vatican 115, Munich; דהוה MS Florence; דקא (ed. Vilna).

20. מהסס] מחסס MSS Florence and Vatican 115; מרתת MSS Escorial, Vatican 117, and ed. Vilna (מירתת).

21. שקול לדעתך] MS Vatican 115; זיל שקול לנפשך MSS Escorial, Vatican 117, printed eds.; שקול לנפשך MSS Florence, and Munich.

codex, manuscript, printing, etc.) with further changes possible throughout this time.

The diminutive narrative unfolds briskly and compactly, yet it possesses a dynamism that can be observed by measuring the short movements between its different geohistorical and discursive locations, and by monitoring their shifting perspectives. Again, Rav Assi was a third-century Babylonian-born rabbi who was remembered in rabbinic tradition as having immigrated to Palestine.[22] There, he discovers a lost moneybag and, while in view of a Roman bystander, is apprehensive about whether he should take it. Interestingly, represented in the manuscripts are two competing versions about how exactly to read the gaze and its relationship to the rabbi's apprehension: According to one tradition, the gaze is the Roman's, who sees Rav Assi hesitating for some unexplained political or halakhic reason and in light of Roman law encourages the rabbi not to be nervous and to take it.[23] A more subtle version preserved in some witnesses suggests that the rabbi *observes* the Roman *observing him* and hence hesitates, probably for political reasons, only to be assured that all is well.[24] Furthermore, the Roman perspective is contrasted with that of the Persian law governing Babylonia, which rules that lost property must go to the Sasanian sovereign. One might also recall that, although the anecdote itself describes an interchange occurring in Roman Palestine in which Sasanian Babylonia is present via quotation yet remains beyond the border and offstage, it is told and incorporated in the Babylonian Talmud—a

22. See y. Ber. 3:1, 6a-b; b. Qidd. 31b. (Note, however, that b. Moʿed Qat. 25a may refer to both Rav Ammi and Rav Assi as children in Babylonia, though the source is not entirely clear.) As noted above, there are witnesses that record the rabbi's name in the anecdote as Rav Ammi (a typical variant)—Rav Assi's regular interlocutor, about whom there is no clear tradition of immigrating to Palestine from Babylonia. On the two rabbis and their interchangeability in the manuscripts, see Chanoch Albeck, *Introduction to the Talmud Babli and Yerushalmi* [Hebrew] (Tel Aviv: Devir, 1969), 227–29. In light of the story's implication that the rabbi was unsure of the legal norm under Roman dominion and his presumed knowledge of the Persian principle, it would make the most sense if the main character was indeed a rabbi who was remembered to have emigrated from Sasanian Babylonia to Roman Palestine. It bears emphasizing, however, that one cannot definitely establish "Rav Assi" as the "correct" or "original" reading. There is no definitive stemmatic analysis of this talmudic tractate or chapter, nor, given the current state of evidence, is even such an analysis possible. Given the originally oral form of the text, it is possible that different versions, one with Rav Assi and the other with Rav Ammi, were current both prior to and following the incorporation of the anecdote into the talmudic passage.

23. This is essentially the reading of MSS Hamburg, Vatican 115, Vatican 117, Munich, and printed eds. and other manuscripts: "חזייה ההוא רומאה והוה קא מחסס, A Roman saw him and he [i.e., Rav Assi] was apprehensive."

24. MS Escorial (and MS Florence before an emendation) has a ל, indicating the Roman as a direct object, and a conjunctive ו, which sequentially links the gaze to the apprehension: "חזייה לההוא רומאה וקא מרתת, He saw the Roman and he trembled."

product of Sasanian Babylonia, where Palestine was an ever-present factor that nevertheless lay at some distance in the neighboring Roman Empire.

A Geohistorical Reading

A somewhat positivistic, contextual approach to this story would focus on its primary geohistorical elements and match them with their "cultural worlds." Accordingly, Rav Assi's actions (or hesitative lack thereof) might first be related to his status as a rabbi who presumably cares about what rabbinic law has to say about lost property. Indeed, the Pentateuch encourages finders not to shirk the responsibility of spotting stray animals and lost garments and requires finders to seek out and restore the lost property to their rightful owners (Exod 23:3 and Deut 22:1–3). As with most biblical institutions, the rabbis received this heritage as God's immutable word, yet at the same time managed to emphasize an opposing notion, namely, a principle of "finders, keepers" nicely encapsulated in the Middle Hebrew neologism *meṣiʿa* ("*found* property"), wherein unmarked lost objects are considered ownerless and may be legally taken by the finder. A related talmudic innovation maintains that anyone who discovers a lost object that does indeed have an identifying "mark" (*siman*) is obligated to officially announce its discovery so that the original owner can reclaim it, as the presence of such a mark would ensure that the owner had not relinquished hope and thus retains ownership.[25] According to the reading that Rav Assi's hesitation is halakhically motivated, it may have to do with a lack of clarity about whether the moneybag has a legally significant mark, and thus whether he can take it for himself.[26]

While the rabbinic ruling on the moneybag may be unclear, the bystander is supremely confident that, from a Roman perspective, there is no question that the object may indeed be taken. Fully aware of the chronological problems, I have recently suggested[27] how one might correlate this position with a specific "legal cultural world," namely, that reflected in discussions of treasure trove in Roman law—the closest analogue to the rabbinic code of lost property—though I stress that the legal field of treasure trove is distinct from the rabbinic rules of restoring lost

25. This idea, which is known in (Late) Middle Hebrew as יאוש ("giving up hope"), achieves its full classical rabbinic articulation only in the Bavli.

26. The Tannnaim assume that money alone is not considered to possess an identifying mark (m. B. Meṣ. 2:3; t. B. Meṣ. 2:10). However, there are "external" markings, such as money in piles (m. B. Meṣ. 2:3; t. B. Meṣ. 2:7) or money in bags (m. B. Meṣ. 2:2), that can aid in the owner's recovery. As usual, the Talmuds devote further discussion to the matter. See, e.g., b. B. Meṣ.25a–b.

27. Shai Secunda, "'Lost Property to the King!': Babylonian Rabbinic Laws of Lost Property in the Shadow of Sasanian Bureaucracy," *BAI* (forthcoming).

property.[28] The earliest recorded ruling on the subject is attributed to the emperor Hadrian (76 CE–138 CE), who ruled that if a finder discovers hidden treasure, it is to be split equally between the finder and the owner of the property where it was found. If the property was owned by the emperor, then the emperor would take half; if owned by the public or the city, then the *fiscus* would take its share.[29] Roman law on the matter underwent a number of developments that, arguably, could explain the rabbi's apprehension about how to proceed. First, Hadrian's rule was reversed in 315 CE when Constantine declared that half the treasure must go to the Roman *fiscus* no matter where it was found. A later ruling dated to January 380 again reversed the law and stated that the property owner receives a fourth, the finder claims the rest, while the *fiscus* receives nothing. Just as the Roman bystander proudly tells Rav Assi that the Romans are more magnanimous than the Persians regarding lost property, a subsequent ruling issued about a decade later similarly draws attention to the law's "benevolence":

> If any person under the inspiration of Divine Providence or the leadership of fortune should find a treasure-trove, We allow him to enjoy his find without any fear.[30]

---

28. Generally speaking, Roman law does not consider the original owners, who may or may not have a claim of restitution, but rather focuses on unclaimed treasures that were dug up and considers whether the finder, property owner, or local and imperial authorities deserve a portion. Unlike the rabbinic system, which has an elaborate system of recovery, in Roman law there is little apparent interest in locating the original owner. A related approach may be discerned in Roman law's approach to fruit fallen from a tree, which in certain respects and under certain conditions, assumes a loss of ownership. For a detailed study on the latter, see Alan Watson, *Ancient Law and Modern Understanding: At the Edges* (Athens: University of Georgia Press, 1998), 71–83.

29. *The Institutes of Justinian*, trans. J. B. Moyle (Oxford: Clarendon, 1967), II 1.39:

The Emperor Hadrian, in accordance with natural equity, allowed any treasure found by a man in his own land to belong to the finder, as also any treasure found by chance in a sacred or religious place. But treasure found without any express search, but by mere chance, in a place belonging to another, he granted half to the finder, and half to the proprietor of the soil. Consequently, if anything is found in a place belonging to the emperor, half belongs to the finder, and half to the emperor. And hence, it follows that if a man finds anything in a place belonging to the *fiscus*, the public, or a city, half ought to belong to the finder, and half to the *fiscus* or the city.

30. Theodosian Code X 18.1–3. The translation is from the *Theodosian Code and Novels and the Simondian Constitutions*, trans. Clyde Pharr (1952; repr., Union, NJ: Lawbook Exchange, 2001), 283. As a coda, it should be noted that in the year 474, Zeno reversed the rule once again and reinstated the law that awards one half of the treasure to the finder and the other half to the landowner. It was this law that was incorporated in the definitive *Corpus Iuris Civilis*. See Johannes Dillinger, *Magical Treasure Hunting in Europe and North America: A History*, Palgrave Historical Studies in Witchcraft and Magic (Houndmills: Palgrave Macmillan, 2012).

Finally, regarding the bystander's citation of Persian law,[31] I have also argued of late[32] that this may be related to the Sasanian legal approach to lost property[33] as it emerges from a précis of late antique Zoroastrian tradition found in the eighth book of the Dēnkard.[34] The Dēnkard preserves the remains of what appears to have been a rather intricate and sometimes intrusive code of lost property known as the Apēdagānestān ("Code of Lost Property").[35] Like rabbinic law and unlike Roman law, the Apēdagānestān emphasizes the significance of identification marks (*daxšag*) and has a system for proclaiming (*srūdan*) discoveries, all in order to facilitate recovery.

Particularly relevant for the current discussion is the Apēdagānestān's reference to the involvement of an official in the return of lost property:

> And about him, the keeper of lost property, informing the town leader [*deh sālār*] when stray sheep and large cattle arrive in the region, which are stray sheep and large cattle in the flock, by species, color, and "my brand" [i.e., whose the brand is].[36]

---

31. The Roman interlocutor employs citation terminology ("that they say") when contrasting his position with that of Persian law. This is similar to another citation of Persian law found in the Bavli, "But nowadays *that the Persians write* 'it [a field on a river] is acquired by you as far as the depth of the water reaching up to the horse's neck,' we certainly remove him" (b. B. Meṣ. 108a). On this law and its significance, see Elman, "'Up to the Ears.'"

32. Secunda, "'Lost Property to the King!'" Note that I also discuss other relevant Middle Persian texts and the following talmudic reference to the rule, preserved at b. Ber. 60a (according to MS Paris 671): "For example he discovered [lost property]. Although it is bad for him afterwards—for when the king hears he will take it from him and trouble him—now it is still [good]."

33. While in Roman law "religious" sources of authority are largely absent from the civil legal system, the Avesta and its interpretive tradition constituted an important source of legal authority in Sasanian law. See Maria Macuch, "Judicial and Legal Systems Iii, Sasanian Legal System," *Encyclopedia Iranica* (New York, 2011), 15:181–96, available at http://www.iranicaonline.org/articles/judicial-and-legal-systems-iii-sasanian-legal-system. There is reason, therefore, to believe that the Dēnkard's summary of the rules of lost property reflects Sasanian law.

34. The Dēnkard is a ninth- to early tenth-century Zoroastrian compilation whose eighth book presents itself as "a summary of that which is in the various *nasks* (the twenty-one divisions) of the Zoroastrian Tradition (*dēn*)." For a discussion of this work, see, e.g., Maria Macuch, "Pahlavi Literature," in *The Literature of Pre-Islamic Iran: Companion Volume I to A History of Persian Literature*, ed. R. E. Emmerick and Maria Macuch (London: I. B. Tauris, 2009), 116–90, esp. 130–36.

35. The passage was first discussed extensively by D. N. MacKenzie, "Finding's Keeping," in *Mémorial Jean de Menasce*, ed. Philippe Gignoux and Ahmed Tafazzoli (Leuven: Impr. Orientaliste Leuven, 1974), 273–80. My readings depart from MacKenzie's in some important respects.

36. Dēnkard 8.39.14 [ed. Madan 764; ed. Dresden 570–71]: *ud abar ōy kē pah ud stōr ī apēdag ka andar ō deh rasēd āgāhēnīdan ī apēdag-dār deh-sālār kē pah ud stōr ī apēdag andar ram pad sardag ud gōn ud drōš-om.*

There is some intimation here of an official Sasanian system that involved an authority known as the *deh sālār*.[37] Other sections of the Dēnkard's summary evince a sophisticated judicial approach attuned to complications that might arise while sorting out disputes between litigants each of whom claims original ownership of the lost property. The requirement to alert an official and the weighing of complex, conflicting claims suggest that the Zoroastrian code was not supposed to function as a "do-it-yourself" guide for restoring strays, but had a bureaucratic quality to it:

> About disputes concerning stray sheep: If one (of them) says "the color (is that) of the birth mother" (but) one (says) "(it is) my brand," (and) both (are) correct; or if one (of them) mentions one mark [*daxšag*] correct (and) one (mentions) many marks of which (some are) incorrect ...[38]

There are of course some difficulties with directly associating the story's three "characters" with these three different cultural worlds, especially given the fact that Rav Assi lived during the third century when, in one way or another, Roman officials would probably have had a stake in the property. One could argue that a storyteller in the late fourth century (or even later) who had some acquaintance with Roman and Sasanian legal norms crafted or reworked the anecdote in light of contemporary realities. Such an interpretation, however, still pastes over a certain geographical ambiguity about the legal norm that "lost property goes to the king," as well as textual features of the passage which complicate a relatively straightforward, historiographical reading.

A Discursive Contextual Reading

I would like to propose a further layer of interpretation, one that is somewhat "ontological" and that may strike some talmudists as initially tiresome since it seems to cover well-trodden ground in the history of scholarship on talmudic stories.[39] I begin with the painfully obvious

37. The title *deh sālār* shows up elsewhere in Pahlavi literature, where, for example, this official's piety is metaphysically tied to the prosperity of the town of which he is the head (Dēnkard 8.20.121 and 9.61.4, which perhaps derives from Pahlavi Yasna 46.1d; cf. 48.10d).

38. Dēnkard 8.39.25 (ed. Madan 765; ed. Dresden 572): *abar pahikār ī abar pah ī apēdag ka ēk gōn ī mādar-zād ēk drōš-om gōwēd harw 2 rāst ayāb ēk daxšag-ēw rāst ēk was daxšag ī az-iš nē rāst gōwēd...*

39. Skepticism about the historiographical significance of talmudic aggada was first articulated by Jonah Fraenkel and Jacob Neusner. The introduction to Rubenstein, *Talmudic Stories*, presents a useful history of the field, including this phase. See also Joshua Levinson, "Literary Approaches to Midrash," in *Current Trends in the Study of Midrash*, ed. Carol Bakhos, JSJSup 106 (Leiden: Brill, 2006), 189–226. In the present discussion I am trying to make a related yet

observation that the anecdote is first and foremost a *text*. Obviously, the text is not the event itself—the physical, apprehensive vacillating over a lost moneybag in third-century Palestine—yet it is not even a straightforward representation of that event in the way other ancient forms of literature, such as historiographical compositions, tend to be. Some of the anecdote's readily observable qualities and the way it presents itself are conspicuously "textual," and of the sort that display properties common to rabbinic texts more generally and the Babylonian Talmud in particular. Some of the most salient qualities of this textuality are the interactive and transformative ways in which the text intersects with and evolves from other surviving literary (1) contexts, (2) "co-texts," and (3) "pre-texts" in rabbinic corpora, and the ways in which these sometimes messy features are not hidden but rather unabashedly present in the fabric of the larger work, that is, the Bavli.

To begin with, there is the immediate literary context. The anecdote immediately follows a *baraita* that discusses the protocol for announcing the discovery of lost property:

> תנו רבנן: בראשונה כל מי שמוצא אבדה מכריז עליה שלשה רגלים ואחר רגל האחרון שבעת ימים כדי שילך לביתו שלשה ויחזור שלשה ויכריז יום אחד. משחרב בית המקדש התקינו שיהו מכריזין בבתי כנסיות ובבתי מדרשות. משרבו האנסין התקינו שיהא מודיע לשכניו ולמיודעיו ודיו.
>
> Our rabbis taught: In the beginning whoever would find lost property would proclaim it for the three pilgrimage festivals and after the last pilgrimage festival seven days so that he will go to his house [outside of Jerusalem] – three days – and return [to Jerusalem] – three days – and proclaim – one day. When the Temple was destroyed they enacted that they should proclaim in the synagogues and study halls. When the oppressors increased they enacted that he should inform his neighbors and acquaintances and that would suffice.[40]

This *baraita*—versions of which also appear in the Tosefta and the Yerushalmi[41]—provides a chronological and one might say lachrymose account of the Mishna's disagreement about whether one announces the

different point that has been inspired by Dolgopolski's *Open Past* and recent work on textual theory, for example, Greetham, *Theories of the Text*, 26–63 ("Ontology: Being in the Text").

40. The text is transcribed from MS Hamburg.

41. t. B. Meṣ. 2:17 (ed. Lieberman, 69); y. B. Meṣ. 2:7, 8c. Although the Bavli's version of "when the oppressors increased" is unique, as I note in the following footnote a similar form appears regarding a related matter at t. B. Meṣ. 2:16: "when the deceivers increased." Moreover, a series of Tannaitic statements describing various societal breakdowns in the form "when the X increased" appears at the end of m. Soṭah and t. Soṭah. Thus, we need not assume that the Bavli's version represents a wholly Babylonian "contamination" of the *baraita*.

discovery for a specific time (the three pilgrimage festivals) or until the word of mouth spreads.[42] Just as modern scholars have tried to determine the referent of the *baraita*'s final, tragic stage—"when the oppressors increased in the Bavli" (recorded as "from the time of danger" in the Palestinian versions)[43]—the Bavli itself asks, "What are 'the oppressors'? Those who say: 'lost property belongs to the king' (מאי אנסין? דאמרי אבדתא למלכא)." This gloss is immediately followed by the Rav Assi story.

Hence, an important stage in conceiving of the sense and sensibility of the anecdote—and for that matter, of the Babylonian interpretation of the *baraita*'s phrase "when the oppressors increased"—is to consider the symbiotic, hermeneutical relationship it holds with the talmudic gloss. The story was almost certainly not produced solely to elucidate the gloss of the phrase "when the oppressors increased." Nevertheless, its juxtaposition to the Bavli's gloss has a two-way interpretive effect that encourages read-

42. m. B. Meṣ. 2:6.

(A) Until when is he obligated to proclaim [that he found a lost object]? Until his neighbors know of it—the words of R. Meir.

(C) R. Yehuda says: [He is obligated to proclaim for the] three pilgrimage festivals, and after the last pilgrimage festival seven days, so that he may go to his house—three days—and return—three days—and proclaim—one day.

It seems possible that the *baraita*'s diachronism was artificially constructed and reflects a historicization of formulations found in m. B. Meṣi'a (the same may be argued of m. B. Meṣ. 2:7 and t. B. Meṣ. 2:16, concerning "deceivers"). Note the significant variations below in those phrases that are *not* found in the Mishna's formulations. Perhaps this indicates that the phrases were invented to round out the Tosefta's account and turn it into three separate stages.

t. B. Meṣ 2:17

(C′) In the beginning they would proclaim it for the three pilgrimage festivals and after the last pilgrimage festival seven days;

(B′) When the Temple was destroyed they enacted that they should proclaim *for thirty days* {Variants: "three(!) days"—MS Leiden of y. B. Meṣ.; "in the synagogues and study halls"—b. B. Meṣiʿa };

(A′) *And from the [time of] danger and onward* {Variant: "when the oppressors increased"—Bavli} they enacted that *he should inform his neighbors, relatives, acquaintances, and fellow townspeople* and that would suffice {Variants: "they should inform (MS Leidin: he should inform his) relatives and (MS Leiden: his) neighbors"—y. B. Meṣ. according to MS Escorial; "he should inform his neighbors and acquaintances"—b. B. Meṣ. according to MS Hamburg. Cf. further variants in other witnesses of the Bavli.

43. The phrase "time of danger," was treated by Moshe Benovitz, "Times of Danger in Eretz Israel and Babylonia," *Tarbiṣ* 74 (2005): 5–20, with references to previous scholarship. See esp. Saul Lieberman, *Tosefta Ki-Feshuṭa: A Comprehensive Commentary on the Tosefta* [Hebrew], 10 vols. (Jerusalem: Bet ha-midrash le-rabanim shebe-Amerikah, 1992–2001), 9:162, who suggests that the *baraita* is referring to Hadrianic persecutions that kept people from congregating publically. Benovitz, on the other hand, suggests that the originally Palestinian *baraita* was doctored and, even as it is currently preserved in the Tosefta, refers to a Sasanian problem. I find Benovitz's suggestion entirely unconvincing.

ing the Bavli's interpretation of the "oppression" as having something to do with life in Sasanian Babylonia—even though the phrase first appears in a *baraita* that ostensibly describes earlier persecutions in Roman Palestine! In the other direction, one approaches the rabbi and his hesitations as relating not to a newly discovered object that may be taken, but to the difficulties of announcing the discovery of lost property in order to facilitate recovery, just as in the *baraita*.[44]

A Palestinian "Pre-Text": Alexander of Macedon and the Faraway King

The significance of the above-described ambiguity regarding the context of the "lost property to the king" norm is heightened when one notices virtually the same phrase, in Galilean Aramaic, in a Yerushalmi passage: "the treasure would be brought to the king" (סימא עלת\סלקה למלכא\למלכותא). Notably, this phrase is buried within a story that contrasts the legal norm familiar to Alexander of Macedon with that of a faraway and possibly Eastern kingdom. Indeed, the story appears within a parallel Yerushalmi passage that arguably constitutes a distant Palestinian "pre-text" for the Rav Assi anecdote—that is, a generative textual precursor from which the Bavli anecdote may have emerged.

For many years traditional and academic Talmud scholars have assumed a close and possibly genealogical relationship between the two Talmuds. The overarching significance and potentialities of this relationship have been brought to new heights in the work of scholars like Shamma Yehuda Friedman.[45] Still, not all Babylonian-Palestinian parallels are created equal. Some present virtually undeniable links between the two Talmuds and relatively minor differences which easily lend themselves to more straightforward models of Babylonian "reworking," "adaptation," and "updating." Others are more tentative and more difficult to explain. In this case it appears that the relevant parallel is of the more elusive variety:

44. This is notable since the other Bavli passage that refers to government interference with lost property (b. Ber. 60a) deals with situations where the finder may keep the object.

45. See, e.g., Shamma Yehuda Friedman, "On the Historical Aggadah of the Babylonian Talmud" [Hebrew], in *Saul Lieberman Memorial Volume*, ed. Shamma Yehuda Friedman (Jerusalem: Jewish Theological Seminary of America, 1993), 119–64. A recent collection on the topic is Ṭal Ilan and Ronit Nikolsky, eds., *Rabbinic Traditions between Palestine and Babylonia*, AJEC (Leiden: Brill, 2014).

y. Baba Mesʿia 2:4, 8c[46]

אלכסנדרוס מקדון סליק גבי מלכא קצייא. חמא ליה דהב סגין כסף סגין. אמ׳ ליה: לא דהבך ולא כספך אנא צריך! לא אתית אלא מיחמי פרוכסין דידכון היך אתון יהבין *והיך אתון נסבין[47] היך אתון דיינין.
עד דו עסוק עימיה אתא בר נש חד דאין עם חבריה דזבן חדא קיקלה וחפרונה[48] ואשכחון בה סימא דדינרי. אהן דזבן הוה מר: קיקילתא זבנית סימא לא זבנית! אהן דזבין הוה מר: קיקלתא וכל דאית בה זבינית!
עד דאינון עסיקין דין עם דין אמ׳ מלכא לחד מינייהו: אית לך בר דכר? אמ׳ ליה: אין. אמ׳ לחבריה: אית לך ברת נוקבה? אמ׳ ליה: אין. אמ׳ לון: אסבון דין לדין וסימא יהוי לתרויהון! שרי גחיך. אמ׳ ליה: למה את גחיך, לא דנית טבאות? אמ׳ ליה: אילו הוה הדין דינא גבכון היך הויתון דנין? אמ׳ ליה: קטלין דין ודין וסימא עלת למלכא![49] אמ׳ ליה: כל הכי אתון רחמין דהב סוגי?! עבד ליה אריסטון. אפיק קומי קופד דדהב תרנוגלין דדהב. אמ׳ ליה: דהב אנא אכל?! אמ׳ ליה: תיפח רוחיה דההוא גברא! דהב לית אתון אכלין? ולמה אתון רחמין דהב סוגין?! אמ׳ ליה: דנחא עליכון שמשא? אמ׳ ליה: אין. נחית עליכון מיטרא? אמ׳ ליה: אין. אמ׳ ליה: דילמ׳ אית גביכון בעיר דקיק? אמ׳ ליה: אין. תיפח רוחיה דההוא גברא! לית אתון חיין אלא בזכות בעירא דקיקא! דכת׳ ״אדם ובהמה תושיע י״״.

Alexander of Macedon journeyed to the king of the ends (of the world). He (i.e., the king) showed him much gold and much silver. He (Alexander) said to him: "Neither your gold nor your silver do I need! I have come only to observe your legal praxis; how you transact [*nasbin*] and how you judge."

While he was occupied with him someone came disputing with his fellow, for he had bought a garbage heap, dug it, and found a treasure [*sima*] of dinars. The one who bought it said: "I bought a garbage heap; I did not buy a treasure!" The one who had sold it said: "I sold a garbage heap and everything in it!"

While they were occupied with one another the king said to one of them: "Do you have a male child?" He said to him: "Yes." He said to his fellow: "Do you have a female child?" He said to him: "Yes." He said to them: Let one marry [*asbon*] the other, and the treasure will be both of theirs!

He (Alexander) began to laugh. He (the king) said to him: "Why are you laughing? Have I not judged well?" He (the king then) said to him: "If this case had been before you, how would you have judged?" He said to him: "We would have killed both and the treasure would be brought in to the king!"

---

46. The text is adapted and slightly altered from the Academy of the Hebrew Language's edition of the Yerushalmi. Note that only variants deemed relevant to the current discussion are included.

47. והיך אתון נסבין*] This addition is taken from MS Escorial (which has the form ואיך).

48. קיקלה וחפרונה] MS Escorial; MS Leiden: חלקה וחספתה.

49. קטלין דין ודין וסימא עלת למלכא] MS Leiden; MS Escorial: מרים רישיה דדין ורישיה דדין וסימתה סלקה למלכותה.

> He (the king) said to him: "Do you love gold that much?!" He (the king) prepared a meal for him. He brought before him golden meat and golden fowl. He (Alexander) said to him: "Do I eat gold?" He said to him: "May that man's breath expire! Gold you do not eat?! So why do you love gold so much?!"
>
> He (the king) said to him: "Does the sun shine upon you?" He said to him: "Yes." "Does the rain come down upon you?" He said to him: "Yes." He said to him: "Perhaps there are small cattle with you?" He said to him: "Yes" (He said to him:) "May that man's breath expire! You live only through the merit of the small cattle! As it is written: "Man and cattle do you save, O God (Ps 36:7)!"

This cunning story has justifiably merited a good deal of attention.[50] Scholars have pondered the tale's moral message.[51] Some have compared the numerous parallels of a tale that, judging by its ubiquity in rabbinic literature, was evidently quite cherished by the rabbis;[52] and others considered its place within the Alexander Romance tradition[53]—a colossal, transna-

---

50. A fairly complete bibliography up until 2003 is listed in Admiel Kosman, "Rereading the Story about Alexander and His Visit in Katzya in the Midrashic Tradition" [Hebrew], *Sidra* 18 (2003): 73–102. To my knowledge, the intertextual relationship with Psalm 36 has not been sufficiently appreciated in prior research, and so I briefly note it here: The Yerushalmi tale is about an unjust rapacious conqueror, just as the psalm opens with reference to godless and wicked schemers who "will not consider doing good" (Ps 36:4). In the Yerushalmi, Alexander goes "beyond the mountains of darkness," perhaps echoing the verse "Your beneficence is like the *highest mountains*, your justice like the great deep" (36:7). There he discovers uniquely righteous people who fight *for* their opposing litigants, and an anti-Solomonic sovereign who encourages them to join in matrimony so that their offspring can inherit the disputed property, unlike Solomon's horrifying suggestion to split a disputed baby. Although he claims that he is uninterested, Alexander really just wants to consume the place's riches, just as a subsequent verse in the psalm refers to "feast on the rich fare of your house" (36:8). Again, the king's closing exclamation that Alexander's kingdom survives only because of God's grace to innocent animals is a direct quotation of the verse "Man and cattle do you save, O God!" (36:7).

51. See esp. Jonah Fraenkel, *Studies in the Spiritual World of the Aggadic Narrative* [Hebrew] (Tel Aviv: Hakibbutz Hameuchad, 1981), 144–48.

52. Aside from the Yerushalmi, the story appears in four classical rabbinic compilations: Gen. Rab. 33:1 (ed. Theodor-Albeck, 301–3); Lev. Rab. 27:1 (ed. Margulies, 618–22); Pesiq. Rab Kah. 9:1 (ed. Mandelbaum, 148–49); and Tanḥ. 6 (37a; in ed. Buber it appears at 9:44b–45a). For a synoptic translation, see Catherine Hezser, *Form, Function, and Historical Significance of the Rabbinic Story in Yerushalmi Neziqin*, TSAJ (Tübingen: Mohr, 1993), 66–77.

53. See esp. Luitpold Wallach, "Alexander the Great and the Indian Gymnosophists in Hebrew Tradition," *Proceedings of the American Academy for Jewish Research* 11 (1941): 47–83. The interested reader should begin with this. Fascinatingly, as Julia Rubanovich has noted, some of the "Hebrew" elements of our tale were later absorbed in the medieval Persian Alexander tradition. See Julia Rubanovich, "Re-Writing the Episode of Alexander and Candace in Medieval Persian Literature: Patterns, Sources, and Motif Transformation," in *Alexander the Great in the Middle Ages: Transcultural Perspectives*, ed. Markus Stock (Toronto: University of Toronto Press, 2016), 123–52. Such absorptions and adaptations are typical of the transnational Alexander romance tradition.

tional literary genre consisting of stories told about Alexander of Macedon from antiquity well into the Middle Ages and across much of the known world.[54] A connection between the Yerushalmi's version of this story and the Rav Assi anecdote has been noted, though only in passing.[55] Indeed, proposing a genetic relationship between the two tales initially seems rather far-fetched.

Upon closer analysis, however, there are some significant links between the Yerushalmi's Alexander story and the parallel Bavli passage. First is the literary context. The Yerushalmi records this story within the second chapter of Bava Meṣiʿa (which, again, concerns the rabbinic lost property laws) and immediately prior to its discussion of m. B. Meṣ. 2:6 and its quotation of the *baraita* about announcing finds during trying times.[56] The most obvious and significant link between the Bavli and Yerushalmi here is Alexander's claim that, in his society, "the treasure would be brought in to the king" (סימא עלת\סלקה למלכא\למלכותא). This is basically equivalent to the Bavli's complaint about lost property going to the sovereign (אבידתא למלכא), though here rendered in Galilean Aramaic with a lexical shift that perhaps reflects the Roman legal institution of treasure trove (*sima*). Structurally, there also is a strong correspondence between the Rav Assi anecdote and the Alexander romance. In both we have (1) a character who finds himself in a new place—Rav Assi had previously immigrated to Palestine from Babylonia while Alexander travels from his empire to a faraway land—(2) where he is confronted with a situation in which forgotten dinars[57] have been discovered, (3) and is unsure of the presiding legal norm. (4) Ultimately, the sovereign rules on the case benevolently,

54. For a wonderful introduction to the tradition, see Daniel L. Selden, "Mapping the Alexander Romance," in *The Alexander Romance in Persia and the East*, ed. Richard Stoneman, Kyle Erickson, and Ian Richard Netton, Ancient Narrative, Supplementum 15 (Groningen: Barkhuis, 2012), 19–59.

55. Lieberman, *Tosefta Ki-Feshuṭa: A Comprehensive Commentary on the Tosefta*, 9:162.

56. The Alexander tale appears at the end of an unusually long sequence of four stories in which finders who are not legally required to return lost property do so anyway. These stories describe rabbis who "supererogatorily" return lost things to gentiles so that the latter will praise the Jewish God. Relatedly, the Alexander romance has two utopian litigants actually trying to award their disputant with the property. As for the mishnaic discussion that precedes the stories, on this matter there is some variety in the manuscripts. MS Leiden places the stories following the discussion of m. B. Meṣ. 2:4, which deals with lost property discovered in a shop, along with a case in which money is discovered among purchased produce. The latter is essentially the situation described in the first two stories in the cycle preceding the Alexander tale and indeed in the treasure discovered in the garbage heap in the Alexander tale itself. MS Escorial, on the other hand, appends the story cycle to m. B. Meṣ. 2:5, which constitutes a midrashic account of Deuteronomy's injunction to return lost garments.

57. It is notable that only the Yerushalmi version of this Palestinian Alexander tale contains the full term "treasure of dinars" (the others simply have "treasure"), thereby matching the Bavli's "moneybag *of dinars*."

(5) which is contrasted with the unfair policy back home (kill both and the king gets the treasure in the case of Alexander's empire; the lost property goes to the king, as in Persian law).

While interpretive "minimalists" may wish to downplay the existence, or at least significance, of this parallel, in my view there is simply too much in common to dismiss. At the same time, the relationship between the Rav Assi and Alexander stories is complex and quite different from more typical examples of Yerushalmi-Bavli aggadic parallels, where the narrative building blocks are more or less the same while the set-pieces have been embellished in one way or another. The present parallel suggests a type and level of textual evolution that is not always acknowledged or readily explained when one considers the movement of Palestinian rabbinic traditions to Babylonia. At the same time, it is highly unlikely that the producers of the Bavli's gloss ("what are 'the oppressors' etc.") and the accompanying Rav Assi anecdote simply received and linearly reworked the Yerushalmi passage into the talmudic gloss and sage story that has come down to us.[58]

Philologists can sometimes forget that texts are not themselves autonomous subjects that move here and there, or chameleons that change color to fit the scenery. What numerous intertalmudic parallels throughout the Bavli and Yerushalmi—including collections of relevant *baraitot*, glosses on the Mishna, tangentially related stories, all juxtaposed to the same Mishna—seem to suggest is that scholastic discussions concerning the Mishna developed by Palestinian rabbis were memorized and then reperformed by rabbis who traveled to Babylonia, before undergoing further extensive textual developments as the Bavli developed into a coherent (still oral) work.[59] This understanding may not yet help explain how such an expansive Alexander tale morphed into the tightly wound Rav Assi anecdote, yet it can help us partially understand the generation of the Bavli gloss. Specifically, the association of a story mentioning a rapacious governmental policy regarding discovered property together with a

58. The relationship between Bavli-Yerushalmi parallels and their significance for understanding the relationship between these two Talmuds, have been of the most central questions posed from the founding of critical Talmud study until today. For a recent, accessible discussion of some of the possibilities and major positions, see Vidas, *Tradition and the Formation of the Talmud*, esp. 50–54.

59. My brief account here stresses orality and thus departs from Alyssa M. Gray, *A Talmud in Exile: The Influence of Yerushalmi Avodah Zarah on the Formation of Bavli Avodah Zarah*, BJS 342 (Providence, RI: Program in Judaic Studies, Brown University, 2005), which for some reason proposes a written model of transmission of the Yerushalmi tractate to Babylonia. There simply is no evidence of a specifically *written* Yerushalmi to which the Bavli's redactors had access. Note, however, that my account also does not necessarily accept the opposing hypothesis of small units of "early Talmud." The matter deserves further study, to which I hope to devote myself soon.

discussion of proclaiming finds in times of oppression may have been still more closely linked by Babylonian rabbinic performers.[60]

A Babylonian "Co-Text": Legal Authority and the Discovery of Lost Property

Regarding the relationship between the Yerushalmi and Bavli stories, it helps to consider a possible "co-text" preserved earlier in the chapter, which may explain how the Rav Assi anecdote came to be formed by talmudic storytellers and how it represents deeper cultural shifts in Babylonian rabbinic culture regarding the imperial gaze of Sasanians and Romans. This text appears within a longer talmudic discussion about whether the site where otherwise nondescript property was discovered constitutes a legally meaningful identifying mark:

> ההוא גברא דאשכח כופרא במעצרתא.[61] אתא לקמיה דרב. אמ׳ ליה: זיל שקול לנפשך! חזייה דקא מהסס. אמ׳ ליה: פלוג ליה לחייא ברי מיניה.
>
> There was a man who found pitch at a press. He came before Rav (for legal counsel). He (i.e. Rav) said to him: "Take it for yourself!" He (Rav) saw him hesitating. He (Rav) said to him: "Divide it with Ḥiyya my son!"[62]

Like the Rav Assi anecdote, in this account there is a person who discovers lost property, hesitates about what the legal norm is regarding it, and subsequently receives assurance from an authority that he may take the property for himself. Along with the structural parallel there are also linguistic similarities, though as always we also find some illuminating variances. Both become apparent in the following table, which helps map and explain both the similarities and differences.[63]

b. Baba Meṣᶜia 28b (II)	b. Baba Meṣᶜia 23b (I)
[א׳] ר׳ אסי אשכח ארנקא דדינרי	[א] ההוא גברא דאשכח כופרא במעצרתא
	[ב] אתא לקמיה דרב

60. This link was facilitated by the Bavli's version of the final stage in the *baraita*: "when the oppressors increased," as opposed to the Tosefta and Yerushalmi's "time of danger."

61. במעצרתא] MSS Florence, Vatican 115, Vatican 117, and Munich (במעצרת׳); בי מעצרתא MS Escorial and printed eds.

62. b. B. Meṣ. 23b according to MS Hamburg.

63. The text in the table is from MS Hamburg, though I have placed some potentially significant variants from other manuscripts in braces. These variants may reflect efforts to harmonize the two stories, which took place presumably once they were both transmitted as part of a single corpus.

[ג] אמ׳ ליה זיל שקול לנפשך	
[ד] חזייה דקא מהסס	[ד׳] חזייה ההוא רומאה והוה קא {\חזייה לההוא רומאה וקא} מחסס {\מרתת}
	[ג׳] אמר ליה : {זיל} שקול לדעתך {\לנפשך}
[ה] אמ׳ ליה פלוג ליה לחייא ברי מיניה	[ה׳] לאו פרסאי אנן דאמרי אבדתא למלכא

It should first be noted that the finder of pitch (I) is not identified in any way other than by his gender (א), while in the moneybag story (II) he is designated as a rabbi (א׳). This variance may help explain why only in (I) is a rabbi consulted (ב) while in (II) no rabbi is present other than the rabbinically knowledgeable finder himself. The subsequent absence of rabbinic legal discussion (ג) in (II) may then affect how we are to read the relationship between the gaze and the finder's hesitation (ד׳). In (I) the nonrabbinic finder is still nervous about picking up the object despite the legal advice he receives (ד), apparently because he does not entirely trust the rabbinic authority. Hence, the ruling rabbi has to further attempt to persuade the finder to take the property by giving some to his own son, which shows that it is not morally tainted (ה). Similarly, according to one version of (II) it is the Roman bystander who sees the finder, Rav Assi, hesitate (ד׳)—quite possibly for halakhic reasons—and hence this legally knowledgeable observer encourages the rabbi by telling him that the dominant legal system permits the finder to take the object (ה׳). On the other hand, in the alternative reading of (II) discussed above, the rabbi physically trembles due to political concerns that come to bear when he sees a legally authoritative Roman watching him back. The rapid eye movements of this second reading are especially loaded, dynamic, and thought-provoking.

Methodologically speaking, the existence of co-texts like (I) and (II) greatly complicates the writing of talmudic history, as terminologically and linguistically parallel stories of this sort suggest that still poorly understood features of talmudic textuality are at work. A related phenomenon worth considering in this regard is the "good story that deserves retelling"—so designated in a classic article of that name by Shamma Friedman.[64] The retold tale is a recurring feature of talmudic narrative in which a sage story about two different rabbis appears twice with only minor variations, often depicting rabbis who are a generation apart and connected in some way. Sometimes, the accounts appear in relatively close proximity to one another in the text. While the reasons for the *juxtaposition*

64. Shamma Yehuda Friedman, "A Good Story Deserves Retelling—The Unfolding of the Akiva Legend," *Jewish Studies: An Internet Journal* 3 (2004): 55–93.

of such stories can be easily accounted for on redactional grounds, their double existence requires other explanations.[65]

Undoubtedly, these cases reflect some sort of textual fluidity and are indebted to the compilatory character of talmudic literature and rabbinic orality. The broad interest of talmudists in orality studies[66] and the application of the modern study of folklore to rabbinics[67] have taught us that the phenomena of virtually identical retold tales and the structurally similar "fraternal literary twins" like the ones just discussed may owe their existence to a textual environment in which stories are incessantly performed and performatively adapted so that novel legal or literary themes, concepts, devices, and other features engender fresh performances and produce new literary exemplars. Subsequently, one or more of the parallel yet distinct performed tales are preserved and incorporated in semicrystalized form into specific *sugyot*, "volumes," and corpora (i.e., the particular chapter or tractate and the Bavli as a whole), which then potentially give way to transformative processes undertaken by redactors, reciters, copyists, and interpreters. The upshot of such an account for understanding rabbinic textuality is that, if closely related stories were constantly being retold in different versions yet did not survive—aside from a few performances—then it becomes difficult to speak of some anecdotes being linearly *adapted* or *reworked* from a *specific* precursor or "co-text." And again, Dolgopolski's recent critique of Weiss-Halivni's "literary-realist" and Friedman's "literary-formalist" approaches[68] further challenges our ability to deduce from such textual transformations a shadow group of redactor editors actively cutting and pasting these stories together.

Recent work on textual fluidity provides some tools for confronting the technical aspects raised by our source and its co-text and precursor. For example, in his research on the re-"writing" of early Christian literature, István Czachesz, has mined cognitive psychology for insights into the workings of human memory and toward this goal has discussed the interplay between schemata and scripts,[69] traditional vocabulary, and

---

65. In certain cases, there is evidence such as literary leftovers or the combining of two earlier sources that one story was reworked into the other. For one example, see my Shai Secunda, "Talmudic Text and Iranian Context: On the Development of Two Talmudic Narratives," *AJS Review* 33(2009): 45–69. In the present case, however, I cannot see a compelling argument in this direction.

66. See n. 12 above.

67. Galit Hasan-Rokem, *Web of Life: Folklore and Midrash in Rabbinic Literature*, Contraversions (Stanford, CA: Stanford University Press, 2000), esp. 84–86.

68. Dolgopolski, *Open Past*.

69. A foundational psychological study of schema in this sense was F. Bartlett, *Remembering: A Study in Experimental & Social Psychology* (Cambridge: Cambridge University Press, 1932). For Barlett, schemata are "an active organization of past reactions, or of past experiences, which must always be supposed to be operating in any well-adapted organic response" (201). As for critical work on scripts, see R. C. Schank and R. P. Abelson, *Scripts,*

innovation[70] in the reproduction of late ancient stories. Applied to the present inquiry, we can posit that (I) and (II) constitute survivals of a certain mini-script, with relatively conservative linguistic features, that was current in Babylonian rabbinic circles. This particular template scripts a confrontation between authoritative legal cultures and hesitant finders of lost property. Its most basic elements consist of the discovery of lost property which may potentially be taken (א, א'); hesitation on the part of the finder to take it (ד, ד'); and encouragement by an authoritative representation of a legal culture to take it (ג+ה and ג'+ה'). Presumably, numerous permutations of this script "existed" as performed stories, though only two have survived. Both surviving anecdotes generally correspond to the template, yet are each powered by different cultural forces that engender distinctive expressions. We might posit that the storyteller who told (I) was moved to explore hierarchal distinctions between confidently knowledgeable rabbis (and their children) and insecure nonrabbis. In this way, the finder is slowly persuaded by the rabbinic onlooker to accept rabbinic authority and so enjoy a found object that has an otherwise doubtful ownership status. The storyteller of (II), on the other hand, was moved by politicized power differences between "colonized" rabbinic Jews who discover lost property and, in this case, two kinds of colonizers—Roman and Sasanian.

In the present example we seem to possess a key for understanding some of the discursive and cultural factors that may have stimulated (II)'s particular articulation of the script. Specifically, this is the relatively influential rabbinic Alexander tale that, as we saw in the Yerushalmi, had been incorporated into Palestinian discussions about the laws of lost property, including Tannaitic protocols for announcing discoveries in times good and bad. Babylonian rabbis apparently encountered some oral form of this story within this discussion and saw in it a convergence of subjects personally bound by ethical and legal duties to submit the lost property to its rightful owners, and two opposing legal cultures that tried to dictate how

Plans, Goals, and Understanding: An Inquiry into Human Knowledge Structures (Hillsdale, NJ: Erlbaum, 1977). An illustration of a simple script is someone going to a restaurant to eat: (1) actor goes to restaurant; (2) actor is seated; (3) actor orders meal from waiter; (4) waiter brings meal to actor; (5) actor eats meal; (6) actor gives money to waiter; (7) actor leaves restaurant. The script is a strong structural framework within and against which texts corresponding to and departing from the script are composed and understood.

70. István Czachesz, "Rewiring and Textual Fluidiy in Antiquity: Exploring the Socio-Cultural and Psychological Context of Earliest Christian Literacy," in *Myths, Martyrs, and Modernity: Studies in the History of Religions in Honour of Jan N. Bremmer*, ed. Jitse Dijkstra, Justin Kroesen, and Yme Kuiper, SHR 127 (Leiden: Brill, 2012), 425–41. Applying methods from the study of folklore to rabbinics, Galit Hasan-Rokem has had similarly productive results. See, e.g., her *Web of Life*, 67–87.

they should act—one ostensibly benevolent and the other patently cruel; one "Eastern"[71] and the other, "Western."

The Bavli does not preserve a "Babylonianized," embellished version of the Palestinian tale, as it sometimes does but rather a profound transformation expressed via a different script. Rav Assi discovers the lost property and weighs his halakhic obligations and rights just as the two litigants discuss what to do about the discovered treasure in the Yerushalmi tale. In the Bavli, the legally authoritative voice—the Western (Roman) bystander—tries to dictate to the rabbi how to proceed, "generously" suggesting that he take it for himself and contrasting this benevolent ruling with the greedy seizure of the Eastern (= Sasanian) sovereign back from where Rav Assi emigrated. This parallels the Yerushalmi's munificent faraway king, who overrules the litigants and proposes harmonious marriage,[72] while his view is distinguished from the rapacious Western (= Macedonian) conqueror, who would kill and then pillage. Still, this explanation of the Rav Assi anecdote and its relationship to its co- and pretexts does not entirely explain *why* the proposed shifts may have occurred, nor what these shifts might signify about Babylonian rabbinic society.

To get at this matter, it is necessary to transition from charting traceable textual transformations to conceiving of the amorphous and far more treacherous terrain known as culture. In this direction, let me point out that, unlike (I), the Rav Assi anecdote underlines the geopolitical identities of its characters. Furthermore, since difference is a particularly constitutive feature of culture—a notion of "us" is constituted by being not "them"—it is legitimate to find within the differential engagements of Roman, Persian, and rabbinic discourses some deeper understanding of Babylonian rabbinic culture.

The transformation of the Alexander tale's "East" = good, West = evil calculation into the Rav Assi anecdote's Roman = good, Persian = bad equivalence follows a recognizable pattern in which positive Palestinian rabbinic reactions to Persians are reversed in the Bavli.[73] Doubtless, such reversals reflect the difference between oriental/occidental romanticizations of the "other," and the harsher realities of the lived present. Yet there is also a dark lining to the encouraging Roman "other" as he is presented in the Rav Assi anecdote, especially since the anecdote's ending is tantalizingly open about whether the Roman bystander's recommendation to

71. The association of the faraway utopia with the East is not explicit, though it is suggested by some of the sources. See, e.g., Wallach, "Alexander the Great and the Indian Gymnosophists in Hebrew Tradition."

72. The marriage (Aramaic root נסב) might be foreshadowed in Alexander's claim that he came to observe how people in the faraway land "transacted" (also Aramaic נסב). As it turned out, in the utopia potentially fractious transactions were solved via harmonious family pairings.

73. Secunda, *Iranian Talmud*, 66–70.

take the property is in fact halakhically and ethically correct. This tension is further heightened by the anecdote's subtle use (in some versions) of a furtive, counter-gaze effect, in which an authoritative, dominating Roman first gazes at the rabbi, causing the rabbi to look back at him and hesitate/tremble.

The rabbi's apprehensive counter-gaze can be productively read from a postcolonial perspective. In the late sixth century, the Sasanian king Khusro II sent a letter to his Byzantine counterpart, Maurice, that described the two powerful Sasanian and Roman Empires as "two eyes" by which "the disobedient and bellicose tribes are winnowed and man's course is continually regulated and guided."[74] These gazes can be located in the evolution of the talmudic material from an earlier stage describing "western," probably Roman, imperial practices to one apparently referring to Sasanian legal intrusion. And both Roman and Sasanian gazes are strongly present in the current form of the Rav Assi anecdote, which may reflect the Bavli's unique "doubled" character in which Palestine and Babylonia are simultaneously experienced.[75]

A final point: In the story, two imperial gazes elicit a third, furtive, colonized, and unresolved gaze from Rav Assi—we do not know whether Rav Assi indeed took the property and, if so, whether this was for himself or in order to return it to its rightful owner. There also is a fourth "gaze" present in the reading of this passage; namely, that of the audience. Unlike the rabbi, this gaze is capable of a more critical response to imperial power: The "reader"[76] encounters the tale in a discussion of the imperial destruction of the temple and the subsequent, if less violent, bureaucratic oppression of governments who intruded on the rabbinic rules of lost property. The imperial oppression is witnessed and duly noted.

74. The letter is cited by Theophylakt Simokatta (4.11.2–3) and appears here as translated in *The History of Theophylact Simocatta*, ed. Mary Whitby and Michael Whitby (Oxford: Clarendon, 1986), 152. Fittingly, this metaphor is incorporated in the title of an important study of Sasanian and Roman imperialism. See Matthew P. Canepa, *The Two Eyes of the Earth: Art and Ritual of Kingship between Rome and Sasanian Iran*, Transformation of the Classical Heritage 45 (Berkeley: University of California Press, 2009).

75. On this point, see now Daniel Boyarin, *A Traveling Homeland: The Babylonian Talmud as Diaspora*, Divinations (Philadelphia: University of Pennsylvania Press, 2015).

76. When the text was oral, this "reader" was actually a listener. Only after the Talmud was written down can we speak of literal readers.

III

The Syriac and Christian Context

Martyrdom in the Persian Martyr Acts and in the Babylonian Talmud

JEFFREY L. RUBENSTEIN

This paper discusses the accounts of martyrdom in the Babylonian Talmud and those of the Persian Martyr Acts (henceforth: PMA), a "corpus" of about sixty stories of Christian martyrs, the majority of which are from the Sasanian Empire.[1] Although martyr narratives are rare in the

1. Some of the Martyr Acts were composed in Roman provinces, and some are post-Sasanian, although scholars have not yet established the dating and provenance of each of the Acts. If some of the Acts adduced in this paper are determined to have been composed in the West (and not to have circulated in the Sasanian world), then some of the conclusions may have to be revised. All texts are quoted from Paul Bedjan, *Acta Martyrum et Sanctorum*, 7 vols. (Paris and Leipzig: Harrassowitz, 1890–1897), unless otherwise noted (henceforth *AMS*). For bibliography on the PMA, see Christelle Jullien, "Les Actes des martyrs perses: Transmettre l'histoire," in *L'hagiographie syriaque*, ed. André Binggeli, Études syriaques 9 (Paris: Geuthner, 2012), 127–40 and the bibliography there; Geoffrey Herman, "'Bury My Coffin Deep!' Zoroastrian Exhumation in Jewish and Christian Sources," in *Tiferet LeYisrael: Jubilee Volume in Honor of Israel Francus*, ed. Joel Roth, Yaacov Francus, and Menahem Schmelzer (New York: Jewish Theological Seminary, 2010), 33 n.11; Joel Thomas Walker, *The Legend of Mar Qardagh: Narrative and Christian Heroism in Late Antique Iraq*, Transformation of the Classical Heritage 40 (Berkeley: University of California Press, 2006), 19–69; Sebastian P. Brock, *The History of the Holy Mar Ma'in with a Guide to the Persian Martyr Acts*, Persian Martyr Acts in Syriac 1 (Piscataway, NJ: Gorgias Press, 2009), 77–125. And see now Richard Payne, *A State of Mixture: Christians, Zoroastrians, and Iranian Political Culture in Late Antiquity*, Transformation of the Classical Heritage 56 (Oakland: University of California Press, 2015), esp. chapter 1, "The Myth of Zoroastrian Intolerance: Violence and the Terms of Christian Inclusion." Payne argues that there were few, if any, sustained persecutions against Christians and that the historical background of most of the martyrdom acts involve small-scale actions against a few individuals, such as Christians who provocatively destroyed fire temples or upper-class elite members of the king's intimate circle who converted to Christianity. In this paper I am interested primarily in literary representations of persecution and martyrdom, not the historical reality, so Payne's revisionist reading of the PMA does not necessarily impact my conclusions. On the manuscripts and their provenance, see now Florence Jullien,

Babylonian Talmud, and martyrdom does not seem to have been central to the experience of Jews during the Sasanian era, these narratives provide one comparative axis for contextualizing rabbinic Judaism and Christianity within the Sasanian world. Study of the Persian Martyr Acts in relation to the Bavli is a particular desideratum in light of recent scholarly work on the discourse of martyrdom among Jews and Christians in late antiquity that has focused primarily on Christian writings from the Greco-Roman world.

The project of comparing martyrdom accounts is not without methodological difficulties. The PMA can be designated a genre, meant to glorify martyrs (among other purposes), whereas martyrdom accounts are but one type of story in the Bavli, a text structured as a commentary to the Mishna and containing a diverse miscellany of materials, halakhic and aggadic, of various types and genres.[2] Within the Bavli, the accounts of martyrs do not constitute an independent tractate, subsection, or genre of their own, but, as Ra'anan Boustan has noted, "are consistently made to serve the larger discursive aims of the redactional context in which they appear, whether legal, normative, historical, or hagiographical."[3] In addition, most martyrdom stories are set in Palestine or in Tannaitic times, not in Babylonia, so they do not engage directly the issue of martyrdom in the Sasanian era.[4] These concerns are not insignificant.[5] On the other

Histoire de Mār Abba, catholicos de l'Orient: Martyres de Mār Grigor, général en chef du roi Khusro Ier et de Mār Yazd-Panah, juge et gouverneur (CSCO Scriptores Syri 254; Leuven: Peeters, 2015), xii–xlvii. On manuscripts and the reception and publication history, see Adam Becker, "The Invention of the *Persian Martyr Acts*" (forthcoming).

2. On the different genres of the PMA see Gernot Wiessner, *Untersuchungen zur syrischen Literaturgeschichte*, vol. 1, *Zur Märtyrerüberlieferung aus der Christenverfolgung Schapurs II* (Göttingen: Vandenhoeck & Ruprecht, 1967), and Sebastian Brock's summary and review, *JTS* 19 (1968): 300–309.

3. See Ra'anan S. Boustan, *From Martyr to Mystic: Rabbinic Martyrology and the Making of Merkavah Mysticism*, TSAJ 112 (Tübingen: Mohr Siebeck, 2005), 55–71: "Rabbinic martyrology typically takes the form of relatively brief and independent episodes narrating the circumstances surrounding the execution of one, or at most two, rabbinic figures. Moreover, these textual units are never found within a martyrological framework. Like all other genres of the rabbinic story, rabbinic martyrologies are consistently made to serve the larger discursive aims of the redactional context in which they appear, whether legal, normative, historical, or hagiographical.... Lacking a narrative framework of its own, rabbinic martyrology was continually adapted to the immediate discursive needs of the emerging legal and exegetical corpora in which it was transmitted." See 56 n. 13 for references to martyr accounts throughout rabbinic literature.

4. The story of the death of Rabba b. Naḥmani in b. B. Meṣ. 86a, however, is set in Babylonia. This is hardly a typical martyrdom account, although it does begin "Rabba b. Naḥmani died because of persecution [*shemada*]." On this text, see Simcha Gross's essay in this volume.

5. Another potentially significant difference is that sources in the Bavli were composed and transmitted orally, whereas the PMA were written, hence all the standard distinctions between written and oral texts apply, especially length, as some of the PMA exceed fifty pages, and some have flowery introductions and lengthy prayers put in the mouths of the

hand, the Bavli is our only extant literary work from Jewish Babylonia of the Sasanian era, so we have no real alternatives.[6] In this respect, study of martyrdom is not much different than the study of many other topics, for which the relevant sources are dispersed throughout the Bavli and appear in contexts determined by various considerations. As to the Palestinian settings, and in some cases provenance, of the texts, it is known that the Bavli editors, and perhaps Amoraic tradents too, adapted and reworked aggadic texts such that they tend to reflect Babylonian conditions, even if they are set in Palestine and/or originated as Palestinian sources. Good examples of this phenomenon are, first, the Bavli's version of the story of the "Deposition of Rabban Gamaliel," which, as Geoffrey Herman has shown recently, reflects the Sasanian royal court and contains numerous Persian motifs; and, second, the story of Rav Kahana and his visit to the Palestinian academy of R. Yoḥanan, which Daniel Sperber demonstrates is a Saboraic Babylonian polemic.[7] In fact, one of the Bavli martyrdom accounts contains the question of why the rabbi did not attend the *bei abeidan*, which Shaul Shaked and Shai Secunda derive from the Iranian *bag-dan*, temple of *bag* ("god"; or perhaps even from the god "Bagdana"), which is clear evidence of the Sasanian coloring.[8] It is worth noting that the brief tradition in b. Pesaḥ. 50a that reports that when R. Yosef b. R. Yehoshua b. Levi became ill and fell into a trance, he saw a "topsy-turvy" world "and heard them saying, 'No one can stand within the compart-

---

martyrs. Some of the PMA are very brief, however, such as the Martyrdom of Jacob and Mary, *AMS* 2:307, just one page in Bedjan's edition. See too Martyrdom of Narseh and Joseph, *AMS* 2:284–86; Martyrdom of Thekla, *AMS* 2:308–13. We also know the authors of some of the PMA, and therefore the dating, such as Babai the Great, who wrote the Martyrdom of George between 621 and 628 (text in Paul Bedjan, *Histoire de Mar-Jabalaha, de trois autres patriarches, de'un prêtre et de deux laïques, Nestoriens* [Paris: Otto Harrasowitz, 1895], 416–571); see Gerrit J. Reinink, "Babai the Great's *Life of George*," in *Portraits of Spiritual Authority: Religious Power in Early Christianity, Byzantium, and the Christian Orient*, ed. Jan Willem Drijvers and John W. Watt, RGRW 137 (Leiden: Brill, 1999). Authorship and dating of rabbinic texts is of course a major problem.

6. With the possible exception of Tractate Kallah and Kallah Rab. 1–2, which David Brodsky argues are Babylonian Amoraic works (*A Bride without a Blessing: A Study in the Redaction and Content of Massekhet Kallah and Its Gemara*, TSAJ 118 [Tübingen: Mohr Siebeck, 2006], 85–86, 417–18); and see below.

7. Geoffrey Herman, "Insurrection in the Academy: The Babylonian Talmud and the Paikuli Inscription," *Zion* 97 (2014): 377–407; Daniel Sperber, "On the Unfortunate Adventures of Rav Kahana: A Passage of Saboraic Polemic from Sasanian Persia," *Irano-Judaica* (1982): 83–100.

8. Shaul Shaked, "A Persian House of Study, A King's Secretary: Irano-Aramaic Notes," *AOASH* 48 (1995): 75; Shai Secunda, *The Iranian Talmud: Reading the Bavli in Its Sasanian Context* (Philadelphia: University of Pennsylvania Press, 2013), 51–58. See now, however, Geoffrey Herman's review of Secunda in *AJS Review* 39 (2015): 171–72. Cf. the accusation against Dado in Martyrdom of Gubarlaha and Qazo (*AMS* 4:141–42) that "Dado is a Christian ... and does not enter into the fire temple [בי נורא]."

ment of those martyred by the Kingdom [הרוגי מלכות],'" lacks the reference to martyrs in the Palestinian parallel in Ruth Rab. 3:1.[9] Moreover, the decision to preserve these accounts in the Bavli shows they were of interest and meaning to Babylonian rabbis, whatever their provenance.[10] In addition, the account of the death of Rabba b. Naḥmani in b. B. Meṣ. 86a asserts that this Babylonian sage was killed on account of a persecution (*shemada)* initiated by the (Persian) King,[11] and there is other indirect evidence of Sasanian persecutions in the Bavli,[12] as well as a reference to a massacre of Jews by King Shapur preserved in the PMA.[13] Geonic sources contain explicit references to persecutions in the course of the fifth century, a time when the Talmud was still being composed and formed, so it is fair to expect that the martyrdom narratives were meaningful to the Bavli author-editors of this age.[14]

Part of the impetus for this study is Daniel Boyarin's, *Dying for God: Martyrdom and the Making of Christianity and Judaism*, a detailed and influential exploration of the discourse of martyrdom in Judaism and Christianity.[15] Boyarin sees martyrdom as a shared discourse that emerges at

9. Saul Lieberman, "The Martyrs of Caesarea," *Annuaire de l'Institut de Philologie et d'Histoire Orientales et Slaves* 1 (1939–1944): 395–46, here 437–39.

10. Paul Mandel has argued that the Bavli transformed the account of Akiva's persecution from a "political drama" to a martyrdom, which would locate the interest in martyrdom in the Babylonian, rather than Palestinian, context ("Was Rabbi Aqiva a Martyr? Palestinian and Babylonian Influences in the Development of a Legend," in *Rabbinic Traditions between Palestine and Babylonia*, ed. Ronit Nikolsky and Tal Ilan, AJEC 89 [Leiden: Brill, 2014], 319–23).

11. For detailed analysis, see the article in this volume by Simcha Gross.

12. Moshe Benovitz, "Times of Danger in Eretz Israel and Babylonia" [Hebrew], *Tarbiṣ* 74 (2005): 5–20.

13. History of Blessed Simeon bar Sabba'e ##14–15, 90–91; Martyrdom of Blessed Simeon bar Sabba'e #13, 26, in *The Martyrdom and History of Blessed Simeon Bar Ṣabba'e*, ed. Kyle Smith, Persian Martyr Acts in Syriac 3 (Piscataway, NJ: Gorgias Press, 2014). On this massacre, see Jacob Neusner, *The Age of Shapur II*, vol. 4 of *A History of the Jews in Babylonia*, 5 vols., StPB 9, 11, 12, 14, 15 (Leiden: Brill, 1965–1970), 34; Geo Widengren, "The Status of the Jews in the Sassanian Empire," *Iranica Antiqua* 1 (1961): 133; Robert Brody, "Judaism in the Sasanian Empire: A Case Study in Religious Coexistence," in *Irano-Judaica* II, ed. Shaul Shaked and Amnon Netzer (Jerusalem: Ben-Zvi, 1990), 59.

14. Persecutions in 455 CE and 470–474 CE are mentioned in *The Epistle of Rav Sherira Gaon*, ed. B. Lewin (Berlin, 1921), 94–97. On the Sasanian context for these persecutions, see Scott McDonough, "A Question of Faith? Persecution and Political Centralization in the Sasanian Empire of Yazdgrad II (438–457 CE)," in *Violence in Late Antiquity: Perceptions and Practices*, ed. Harold A. Drake (Aldershot: Ashgate, 2006), 69–81.

15. Daniel Boyarin, *Dying for God: Martyrdom and the Making of Christianity and Judaism*, Figurae (Stanford, CA: Stanford University Press, 1999); idem, "Martyrdom and the Making of Christianity and Judaism," *JECS* 6 (1988): 577–627. On martyrdom, see too Glen W. Bowersock, *Martyrdom and Rome*, The Wiles Lectures Given at the Queen's University of Belfast (Cambridge: Cambridge University Press, 1995); W. H. C. Frend, *Martyrdom and Persecution in the Early Church: A Study of a Conflict from the Maccabees to Donatus* (New York: New York University Press, 1967); Elizabeth A. Castelli, *Martyrdom and Memory: Early Christian Culture*

roughly the same time in late antique Judaism and Christianity (which, of course, is partially the result of Judaism and Christianity not being completely distinct religions at this time). He finds in the rabbinic accounts a tension between a defiant willingness to be martyred as the ultimate expression of faith and a "trickster" policy that encourages evasion of death through dissembling or flight. Both of these responses are found among Christian writers too, although "tricksterism" is less common and death more often considered the perfection of life and the ultimate goal. In the accounts of R. Akiva's martyrdom, Boyarin sees a new idea, an "erotics" of martyrdom, in which dying for God becomes a mystical and joyful experience, the fulfillment of the commandment to love God with all one's soul, as stated in the Shema. In this new model, the martyrs "died with joy, with a conviction not only that their deaths were necessary, but that they were the highest of spiritual experiences" (107). This desire for martyrdom is widely found in Christianity where the profession "I am a Christian" is the analogue to Akiva's recitation of the Shema and is also considered the ultimate act of religious devotion and *imitatio Christi*.[16]

Boyarin's work on martyrdom, like much of his other scholarship, is enormously enriching and has contributed a great deal to our understanding of martyrdom, especially his focus (which I share) on the discourse and literary representations of martyrdom, rather than its history. At the same time, his scholarship has spawned a good number of criticisms of various types.[17] One potential problem that has not been emphasized sufficiently is that almost all of Boyarin's Christian sources are from the Greco-Roman world, including church fathers who wrote in Greek and Latin (e.g., Tertullian, Eusebius, Clement of Alexandria) and with the classical martyrdom stories of Perpetua, Polycarp, and others, rather

Making, Gender, Theory, Religion (New York: Columbia University Press, 2004); Candida R. Moss, *Ancient Christian Martyrdom: Diverse Practices, Theologies, and Traditions,* AYBRL (New Haven: Yale University Press, 2012); Lieberman, "Martyrs of Caesarea," 395–446; Alyssa M. Gray, "A Contribution to the Study of Martyrdom and Identity in the Palestinian Talmud," *JJS* 54 (2003): 242–72 and the bibliography in n.1.

16. The idea of *imitatio Christi* plays a very minor role in Boyarin's book and is mentioned only once (95) as far as I can tell. This theology deserves more attention, as I think it goes a long way to explaining certain differences between martyrdom in Judaism and Christianity, as I argue below. On martyrdom and *imitatio Christi* in general, see Joseph Barber Lightfoot, *The Apostolic Fathers,* 5 vols. (London: Macmillan, 1885–1890), 1:612–15 (though he addresses the problem of historicity of martyrdom accounts given the striking parallels to the life of Jesus); Moss, *Ancient Christian Martyrdom,* 63–65 (and the index, s.v. *imitatio Christi*); eadem, *The Other Christs: Imitating Jesus in Ancient Christian Ideologies of Martyrdom* (New York: Oxford University Press, 2010).

17. See the reviews of Boyarin's *Dying for God,* by A. J. Droge, *HR* 42 (2002): 175–80; Yaron Eliav, *Hebrew Studies* 42 (2001): 385–89; Robert Goldenberg, *JQR* 92 (2002): 586–88; J. Patout Burns, *Church History* 71 (2002): 865–67; Jan Willem van Henten, *H-Judaic* (August 2000), http://www.h-net.org/reviews/showrev.php?id=4452.

than with sources from the Persian world, whereas many of Boyarin's rabbinic sources appear in the Bavli.[18] Boyarin cites but one Syriac source, a brief passage from the History of Mar Aba, but adduces this passage not for a point about martyrdom but to argue that "in the Osrehoene at least, 'Christianity' and 'Judaism' were not yet separate religions as late as the sixth century"—a dubious claim, but not my main concern here.[19] So whatever the merits of Boyarin's work vis-à-vis Palestinian Judaism and Christianity, the Eastern Christian material has not been brought into the conversation sufficiently.[20]

Joy and Enthusiasm for Martyrdom

One of the clearest differences between the Jewish and Christian martyr accounts is the motif of enthusiasm and joy. In the PMA the martyrs regularly express tremendous joy, happiness, and gratitude for the opportunity or "privilege" of being martyred, a sensibility largely absent in the Bavli martyr texts. The closest rabbinic parallel, as Boyarin forcefully argues, is the Bavli's account of R. Akiva's death, and in particular his explanation to his disciples: "He said to them: My whole life I was troubled by this verse: *With all your soul* (Deut 6:5)—even if he takes your soul. I thought, 'When will the opportunity come that I might fill it.' Now that the opportunity is here, shall I not fill it?' He drew out [the word] 'One' until his soul expired with 'One'" (b. Ber. 61b).[21] This explanation expresses an understanding of martyrdom as a fulfillment of a divine precept and an occasion to manifest faith and devotion—hence, as a positive, rather than a negative, experience. Yet the sensibility here still differs from the Christian sources in my opinion. The main point is the degree of R. Akiva's commitment to the commandments, the piety modeled by R. Akiva in accepting the commandment to love God even to the point of death ("with all your soul"); it is not that he is enthusiastic about suffering and persecution. His goal is to fulfill the commandment, and martyrdom is more a means to that end than an end in and of itself. Moreover, there is no sense of joy or

18. In "Martyrs of Caesarea," Lieberman routinely cites Bavli texts to reconstruct the Hadrianic persecutions in Palestine, but he wrote over seventy years ago.

19. History of Mar Aba in Bedjan, *Mar-Jabalaha*, 211–14, cited in Boyarin, *Dying for God*, 22–23. On p. 26 Boyarin mentions that in the "narrative of Mar Saba, Christianity is seen as only a true form of Judaism." Boyarin also quotes the Didascalia Apostolorum, a Syriac text, several times, but this text was originally written in Greek.

20. While Boyarin sees the Bavli as the product of a type of Hellenism (as emerges clearly from his *Socrates and the Fat Rabbis* [Chicago: University of Chicago Press, 2009]), the Persian context and eastern influences should not be ignored.

21. כל ימי הייתי מצטער על פסוק זה בכל נפשך - אפילו נוטל את נשמתך, אמרתי: מתי יבא לידי ואקיימנו, ועכשיו שבא לידי לא אקיימנו? היה מאריך באחד עד שיצתה נשמתו באחד. For textual variants, see Mandel, "Was Rabbi Aqiva a Martyr?," 319–23, 336–44.

happiness. Only the parallel account of R. Akiva's martyrdom in y. Ber. 9:5, 14b // y. Soṭah 5:7, 20c has anything that can be considered joyful. In this version, when the time for reciting the Shema arrived, "He began to recite it and smile [גחך; or 'laugh']," and explained to the persecutor that he had fulfilled the first elements of the commandments of Deut 6:4, to love God with all his heart and with all his money (= the understanding of מאדך, "Your muchness") but was not certain (or was not "tested"[22]) as to whether he could fulfill the precept "with all my soul" (ובכל נפשי לא הוה בדיק לי). "And now that 'with all my soul' has come and the time for reciting the Shema has come and my mind does not waver, for this reason *I recite and smile*."[23] R. Akiva does not "smile" or rejoice that he will die, that his life will end in this way, but that he has the opportunity to fulfill the commandment and can do so without fear. In addition, as Paul Mandel has argued, it is not even clear that the Yerushalmi's account is in fact a martyrdom or whether it should be considered a "political drama," as it does not end with R. Akiva's death.[24] In any case, that the Bavli omits this sentiment from its version, though found in much the same talmudic context, namely, the discussion of m. Ber. 9:5, suggests that even this expression of satisfaction was too much for the Babylonian storytellers.

In addition, whatever the embrace of martyrdom attributed to R. Akiva as a character, the storyteller is decidedly ambivalent. As their Rabbi is about to die, the disciples question "Our Master, thus far?" After R. Akiva's death, the angels protest: "This is Torah and this its reward? [He should have been] *from those who die by your hand* [Ps 17:14]"—and not tortured to death by wicked mortals. While the story ends on a relatively optimistic note—God assures the angels, and a "heavenly voice" the humans, that R. Akiva's *"portion is life"* (quoting the next clause of Ps 17:14), that is, that R. Akiva "is destined for the world to come"—the internal tensions are palpable.

Outside of this story of R. Akiva, the Bavli has few positive things to say about martyrdom. Pappos b. Yehuda, who is placed in the same jail cell with R. Akiva, exclaims, "Fortunate [אשריך, or 'happy'] are you Akiva, for you were arrested on account of Torah. Woe to you, Pappos, for you were arrested on account of void matters [דברים בטלים; b. Ber. 61b]." But I don't think we can take this as a positive evaluation of the martyr's fate. R. Akiva's martyrdom is more meaningful as it followed his defiance of the persecu-

---

22. On the meaning of בדק, see Mandel, "Was Rabbi Aqiva a Martyr?," 315 and n. 18.

23. רבי עקיבא הוה קיים מיתדון קומי טורנוסרופוס הרשע. אתת ענתה דקרית שמע. שרי קרי קרית שמע וגחך אמר ליה סבא אי חרש את אי מבעט ביסורין את. אמר ליה תיפח רוחיה דההוא גברא. לא חרש אנא ולא מבעט ביסורין אנא. אלא כל יומי קריתי פסוק זה והייתי מצטער ואומר אימתי יבואו שלשתן לידי. [דברים ו ה] ואהבת את ה׳ אלהיך בכל לבבך ובכל נפשך ובכל מאודך. רחמתיה בכל לבי ורחמתיה בכל ממוני. ובכל נפשי לא הוה בדיק לי וכדון דמטת בכל נפשי והגיעה זמן קרית שמע ולא אפלגא דעתי. לפום כן אנא קרי וגחך.

24. See Mandel, "Was Rabbi Aqiva a Martyr?," 306–54, who suggests that the story be considered a "political drama."

tion by continuing to teach Torah, whereas Pappos had apparently capitulated to the persecutor's demands to no avail—he was arrested anyway. Were martyrdom ipso facto reason to rejoice, Pappos would not lament his arrest and impending death but celebrate it, whatever its impetus.

The story of Moses visiting R. Akiva's academy in b. Menaḥ. 29b, a late text that depends on the account of R. Akiva's death in b. Ber. 61b or some similar version, lacks any ambivalence in its objection to martyrdom. Here Moses is granted a view of "them weighing his [= Akiva's] flesh in the meat market," that is, that the persecutors sold the flesh raked off his body and perhaps the mangled corpse too for animal feed. Moses thereupon voices the protest attributed to the angels in b. Ber. 61b, "This is Torah and this is its reward?" The text ends with God rebuking Moses, "Silence! Thus I have decided," a failed theodicy, which should be understood as a rabbinic protest against the apparently meaningless suffering and death of the righteous.[25] A similar trope appears in one of the versions of Elisha b. Abuya's apostasy. According to b. Qidd. 39b, his loss of faith resulted when he saw "another thing [= a pig] drag the tongue of Huzpith the Interpreter. He said, 'The mouth that uttered pearls licks dust.'" While the Talmud provides a conventional theodicy to explain Huzpith's death (the reward materializes in the world to come), there is no enthusiasm for this kind of suffering. Far from being understood as a cause to celebrate, martyrdom is a cause for despair and loss of faith.

Other accounts of martyrdom in the Bavli are no more enthusiastic.[26] The dialogue between R. Ḥanina b. Teradyon and R. Eleazar b. Perata in b. ʿAbod. Zar. 17b is particularly telling:

> When R. Eleazar b. Perata and R. Ḥanina b. Teradyon were arrested, R. Eleazar b. Perata said to R. Ḥanina b. Teradyon: "Fortunate (or 'happy') are you for you were arrested on account of one matter. Woe is me for I was arrested on account of five matters." R. Ḥanina said to him, "Fortunate are you that you were arrested on account of five matters and you will be saved. Woe to me that I was arrested on account of one matter but I will not be saved, for you busied yourself with Torah and good deeds, while I busied myself only with Torah."

The more fortunate/happy rabbi is the one with the greater chance of avoiding martyrdom. R. Eleazar b. Perata believes his colleague more easily will

---

25. See Jeffrey L. Rubenstein, *Stories of the Babylonian Talmud* (Baltimore: Johns Hopkins University Press, 2010), 182–202.

26. The account of the "Mother and her seven sons," is devoid of sentiment. At the end a heavenly voice proclaims, "[*He sets the childless woman among her household as*] *a happy mother of children*," to inform us that the mother was reunited with her martyred children in the world to come, but tells us nothing about her attitude toward the martyrdom of her children in this world (b. Giṭ. 57b).

prevail against the single charge for which he was arrested, whereas R. Ḥanina b. Teradyon, with some type of foreknowledge, reveals that R. Eleazar b. Perata, despite the fivefold case against him, will be saved.

The accounts in the Persian Martyr Acts, by contrast, depict a completely different attitude, a longing for martyrdom as the goal and culmination of life, an enthusiasm to die such that the martyr goes to his death joyous and thrilled, with gratitude to the persecutors for giving him or her the great "gift" of death. This attitude is summed up nicely by Simeon bar Ṣabba'e, who responds to King Shapur's threat of death:

> Holy Simeon responded and said, "To be killed for God is better to me than all life. It is not in fear that this is agreeable to me, but in the joy of all my heart. Blessed is the one who is deemed worthy of this, either to suffer dishonor for God, or to be oppressed in prison, or to endure torture for truth! Especially blessed is the one who is killed for God, for to him is promised eternal and everlasting life!"[27]

The potential to die, which Shapur considers a disincentive and means of intimidation, is for Simeon an incentive and desire. He almost bubbles over with excitement here at the prospect of suffering and death. In the Martyrdom of 111 Men and Women (*AMS* 2:292), the martyrs refuse to worship the sun and state, "Quickly show us our murder that we may rejoice, and bring nigh our death that we may be pleased [בעגל חוו לן קטלן דנחדא וקרבו לן מותן דנתתניח]." Qardagh baldly states, "For death on Christ's behalf will be sweeter to me than the life of this world."[28] Conversely, not to be "privileged" with a martyr's death can be extremely disheartening. Thus, of Aitalaha we read, "When they were hastening him out and leaving, he was happy and joyful because he thought that they were taking him to him [= his friend Barhadbeshabba] to kill him.... But when he learned that it was not commanded that he [Aitalaha] be killed, he lifted up his voice and wept (wondering), 'Why have I not died with him.'"[29] Similarly, John of Arbela weeps because his brethren have been martyred

---

27. *History of Blessed Simeon Bar Ṣabba'e*, ed. Smith, #46, 130. See too the narrator of the Martyrdom of Shahdost, *AMS* 2:277: "How beloved is the coming of death to he who lives spiritually. . . . Those who love God go to God, and those who love the world, remain in the world. Those for joy, and those for sorrow."

28. Joel Thomas Walker, *The Legend of Mar Qardagh: Narrative and Christian Heroism in Late Antique Iraq*, Transformation of the Classical Heritage 40 (Berkeley: University of California Press, 2006), #58, 63. See too #63, 66. On hearing of the martyrdom of Stephen, "he rejoiced greatly and his soul exulted. He was greatly encouraged and fortified, and he yearned to die on behalf of Christ, like a thirsty man coming from the road in the heat of summer wants cold water."

29. *AMS* 4:134-35. Subsequently, when given the opportunity to escape, Aitalaha and Hophsai refuse, saying: "We will not flee like bandits. Only if you openly let us go like innocent men, in order that the true God may be glorified through us, and that the sun, which

while he has been left alive due to his unworthiness. His sadness is not because his brothers have been killed but because he has not, and he expresses the hope that he will be brought together with them in death (*AMS* 4:128). Anahid prays, "Confirm the minds of my persecutors, Lord, so that they do not disregard me and I perish, having been left behind from the flock and herd."[30] Thus, Anahid yearns to be martyred with the "flock and herd" of faithful martyrs rather than to be disregarded by the persecutors such that she would "perish" by not dying, in this odd but not uncommon reversal of (eternal) life, meaning dying for Jesus, as opposed to (meaningless, unfulfilled) "life" in this world. Likewise Narseh became disheartened when it seemed that he would be spared from execution: "when he saw that the *Magus* was turning him around, became gloomy and distressed, because he thought that he was being diverted towards the prison, and his martyrdom was not to be crowned by the sword, as was his desire."[31] The Christians who had gathered to watch the martyrdom complain to the Magus that his about-face deprives Narseh of his desire to die, and guarantee that they will not interfere to save Narseh, as was the Magus's fear. Reassured, the Magus proceeds to lead Narseh to his execution, to the gratification of all!

This enthusiasm at the prospect of martyrdom is matched by an excitement and joyful embrace of the concomitant suffering and tortures. Thus, in the passage cited above, Simeon bar Ṣabba'e longingly exclaims, "To be killed for God is better to me than all life." As he is savagely beaten, Hophsai declares, "I rejoice that I endure these for the sake of God" (*AMS* 4:136). After being tortured, imprisoned, and deprived of food and water, Mihrshabur tells his persecutor that he is "not distressed [לו מטל הדא כריא לי]" by the torture because: "I inherit eternal life by means of this hardship [אולצנא]. And this hardship is great glory [שובהרא] for me" (*AMS* 2:537).

By contrast, this desire for suffering seems to be alien to the rabbinic martyrdom accounts, as discussed above with the Bavli's version of the death of R. Akiva. R. Ḥanina b. Teradyon gives the executioner permission to increase the fire and to remove the wet tufts on his chest so that his sufferings cease and he die more quickly (b. ʿAbod. Zar. 18a). In the story of the death of Rabba b. Naḥmani, the king's emissary states, "If I am killed, I will not reveal (the whereabouts of Rabba b. Naḥmani), but if

is no God, may be blasphemed through you" (*AMS* 4:136). They do not flee and soon are martyred.

30. *Holy Women of the Syriac Orient,* trans. Sebastian Brock and Susan Ashbrook Harvey, Transformation of the Classical Heritage 13 (Berkeley: University of California Press, 1998), 89.

31. "The Martyrdom of Narseh," in *Persian Martyr Acts under King Yazdgird I,* ed. and trans. Geoffrey Herman, Persian Martyr Acts in Syriac 5 (Piscataway, NJ: Gorgias Press, 2017), 18.

I am tortured, I will reveal it." Subsequently Rabba b. Naḥmani chooses to die when he believes that a "company of soldiers" (גונדא דפרשי) is upon him, saying, "Let me die and let me not be given over to the hands of the Kingdom," perhaps also on account of fear of torture (b. B. Meṣ. 86a).[32]

Finally, the act of martyrdom itself is portrayed in celebratory terms, often referred to as a wedding, banquet, or other joyous time. The descriptions of the martyrs going forth to be killed routinely portray them joyfully singing psalms and praising God. As Candida is being led to her death after gruesome tortures, the "whole city" watches in horror "with lamentation and tears. But the face of this disciple of Christ was radiant with joy, and her mouth was full of laughter and praise. She said with a loud voice, 'I am going to my wedding feast.'"[33] Martyrdom is thus depicted as a reason for exultation, not lamentation. Here and in other passages, the distress of the onlookers at witnessing the suffering and death ironically contrasts with the joy of those actually experiencing the tortures and martyrdom.[34] Likewise, when Gregory is summoned for execution, he goes forth "happy and joyful and exulting [חדא ורוז ודאץ] like one going to a wedding."[35] Similarly, in the History of Simeon bar Ṣabba'e cited above, Simeon exhorts his fellow Christians as they face the executioner: "Let us die in joy, my brothers, with Christ.... Rejoice, my brothers, in our Lord. Rejoice greatly always." Simeon's exhortations are effective: "After this, ten executioners came forth at once and each one killed ten of them with the sword. These holy ones were offered up joyfully while their mouths were filled with laughter and their tongues full of praise."[36] In the Martyrdom of Jacob Intercisus, as the hero is being dismembered digit by digit and limb by limb, we read, "And the blessed one said. 'My heart rejoices [חדי] in the Lord. My soul exults [דצת] in his salvation [1 Sam 2:1]' ... And his countenance was radiant and he laughed [גחך]" (AMS, 2:548). In the Martyrs of Tur Berain, as the executioners approach, "The saints' mouths,

32. See too the tradition in Pesiq. Rab Kah. 11:13 (Cant. Rab. 2:7) attributed to Rav Ḥiyya b. Abba: "If someone says to you, 'Give up your soul for the sanctification of God's name,' I would give it, provided that they cut off my head immediately, unlike the generation of persecution when they put fiery lead balls under their armpits and reeds under their fingernails"—though this is a Palestinian source.

33. Translation from Sebastian Brock, "A Martyr at the Sasanid Court under Vahran II: Candida," in *Syriac Perspectives on Late Antiquity*, ed. Sebastian Brock (London: Variorum Reprints 1984), 181. See too Bowersock, *Martyrdom and Rome*, 59–60, for references to enthusiasm for death in Greco-Roman sources, including examples of martyrs laughing. And see Herbert Musurillo, *Acts of the Christian Martyrs*, 2 vols., Oxford Early Christian Texts (1972; repr., Oxford: Clarendon, 2000), 145, 201, 307.

34. On the kinds of tortures described in the PMA, see Christelle Jullien, "Peines et supplices dans les *Actes des martyrs persans* et droit sassanide: nouvelles prospections," *Studia Iranica* 33 (2004): 243–69.

35. Martyrdom of Gregory; Bedjan, *Mar-Jabalaha*, 384.

36. *History of Blessed Simeon bar Ṣabba'e*, ed. Smith, ##89–90, 196; #95, 204.

however, were filled with laughter [גוחכא], and their tongues gave praises."[37] Likewise Martha, daughter of Pusai, tells the executioner,"'Do not tie me up, for I am gladly accepting immolation for the sake of my Lord.' When she saw the knife being brandished by the officer, she laughed."[38] By contrast, when R. Ḥanina and his wife go forth to be killed they quote verses justifying their fate—that it is just punishment for their sins—and are praised by the Talmud for their piety (b. ʿAbod. Zar. 17b). For the rabbis, martyrdom is understood as a *punishment*, a manifestation of divine justice governed by the standard theodicy of reward and punishment; for the PMA, martyrdom is a great *reward* and privilege, hence a reason to rejoice.

Consequently, when characters in the PMA hear of the martyrs' deaths, they are filled with joy. Simeon bar Ṣabba'e, upon learning of the martyrdom of Gushtazad, blissfully exclaims:

> He breached the fearful wall of death and made me joyful. The path of life appeared in him and made me glad. He has become the guide for my feet on the narrow path, and he has straightened my steps and set them along the way of tribulation. Why should I linger behind? Why should I wait?
>
> He left his pledge to me: "Arise!" He left behind his face for me: "Come!" While he says to me in joy, "Simeon, not again can you rebuke me. Not again will my face become sad before yours. Enter joyfully with me into the house that you prepared [762] for me and into the rest that you arranged for me."[39]

When Shabur of Niqator hears in prison that his colleague Isaac has been stoned to death, "He rejoiced and praised God that he had been crowned (= martyred)" (*AMS* 2:55). By contrast, as we have seen, when Moses and the angels hear of, or witness, Akiva's death, they protest (b. Menaḥ. 29b; b. Ber. 61b).

This embrace of death is related to another trope that appears in some of the PMA, that the martyrs encourage the persecutors and executioners to kill them, what Glen Bowersock has observed "comes very close to a desire to commit suicide—a suicide to be arranged by an external agent but with the clear complicity of the victim."[40] In the Martyrs of Tur Berain,

---

37. *AMS* 2:35; *The Martyrs of Mount Ber'ain*, ed. and trans. Sebastian P. Brock and Paul C. Dilley, Persian Martyr Acts in Syriac 4 (Piscataway, NJ: Gorgias Press, 2014), #99, 84 (paraphrasing Ps 126:2).

38. *AMS* 2:239; *Holy Women of the Syrian Orient*, trans. Brock and Harvey, 72.

39. *The Martyrdom of Blessed Simeon Bar Sabba'e*, ed. Smith #34, 46.

40. Bowersock, *Martyrdom and Rome*, 61. See too his discussion of voluntary martyrdom, 1–6; and see his comments on the difference from Judaism (71–72). Bowersock draws on G. E. M. de Ste Croix, "Why Were Early Christians Persecuted?" *Past and Present*, 26 (1963): 21–24. See too Frend, *Martyrdom and Persecution*, 151–52, 220; Moss, *Ancient Christian*

the executioner, after killing the two brothers, "did not want to kill their sister, but the glorious woman said to him, 'Finish off your full task, and do not keep me long apart from my brothers.'" When he still refuses to do the job, the maiden persuades him to kill her by promising she will cure him—"if you swear to me that you will kill me, then I will heal you of your leprosy,"—and only after having been healed does he grant her wish and chop off her head.[41] Jacob Intercisus exhorts his persecutors to continue his dismemberment: "[These tortures] increased his zeal, and he said to the executioners: 'Why do you stand idle?... Let your eyes not have pity. Because "My soul exults (דץ) in the Lord" (1 Sam 2:1)'" (*AMS* 2:554). In the Martyrdom of the Forty Martyrs, two brothers who had provided the martyrs with food and had been spared the main slaughter by the grace of God, when they learn that the martyrs had been killed, fall on the corpses and hug and kiss them. Then "they took some of the blood of all of them [= the martyrs], and sprinkled it on their bodies, and they asked some of those executioners, saying to them, 'Kill us too with them, because our death is pleasing to us [בסים] and sweeter [חלא] than wicked and bitter life'" (*AMS* 2:344). They get their wish—apparently a happy ending.[42] Boyarin suggests that the account of R. Ḥanina b. Teradyon "provocatively gathering crowds to study Torah in public" is the "Jewish analogy, therefore, to the early Christian practices of provocatively inviting martyrdom known, somewhat misleadingly, as 'voluntary martyrdom.'"[43] Yet the rabbi neither wishes to die nor relishes the experience nor asks the persecutors to kill him, as is typical of the Christian accounts.

When we compare the brief and internally conflicted account of R. Akiva's martyrdom with the martyrdom accounts of the PMA,[44] to my

---

Martyrdom, 149–55. And see Boyarin's modest efforts to collapse this distinction between voluntary and nonvoluntary martyrdom (*Dying for God,* 121).

41. *AMS* 2:37–38; *The Martyrs of Mount Ber'ain,* trans. Brock, ##103–106.

42. See too the Martyrdom of Shahdost, *AMS* 2:280. As the martyrs are taken to be executed, "They were singing and saying in one sweet voice together.... And when they arrived at that place in which they were killed, again they said, 'Blessed is God who gave us this crown which we were gazing upon and did not withhold from us this portion that we were desiring.'"

43. Boyarin, *Dying for God,* 58. In b. Ber. 61b Pappos b. Yehuda finds Akiva gathering crowds and teaching Torah, and Akiva explains his actions with the fable of the fish and the fox, namely, that he cannot abandon the Torah, the source of life, even in a time of danger. His resistance is not motivated to provoke the persecutors, and we should probably evaluate Ḥanina b. Teradyon analogously.

44. The angelic protest at Akiva's death might also be contrasted with the tortures of Gregory, which Adam Becker notes becomes a "spectacle" witnessed by humans and angels: "On that night the prison became a theater (literally, place of visions, *bet hezwane*) for angels and human beings, gathered there and standing in great wonder, seeing a mortal human being contending with death and conquering it'" (Martyrdom of Gregory; Bedjan, *Mar-Jabalaha,* 372; see Adam H. Becker, *Fear of God and the Beginning of Wisdom: The School of Nisibis and the Development of Scholastic Culture in Late Antique Mesopotamia,* Divinations [Philadel-

mind the differences between the Jewish and Christians narratives are much deeper than the ideas in common, and of course the single narrative of R. Akiva must be balanced by the more sober perspectives in the other talmudic sources.[45] Whatever the positive construal of martyrdom in the Akivan account, it pales in comparison with the enthusiastic yearning for martyrdom, the longing for suffering, and the joy at its consummation, in the PMA.[46] The idea of *imitatio Christi* surely provides part of the explanation for this dimension of the PMA, and of course that principle will be found nowhere in the Bavli.[47]

---

phia: University of Pennsylvania Press, 2006], 331–32). The angels here are impressed, not appalled. Of Gregory's glorious death we are told "how much praise and glory was heaped on his head from both holy angels and human beings" (Bedjan, *Mar-Jabalaha*, 383).

45. Thus Boyarin writes of a passage in the Sipre roughly parallel to Akiva's explanation "even when he takes your soul," "This text then certainly gives the lie to Frend's ratio that 'the Jew might accept death rather than deny the Law. The Christian gave thanks that he had been offered the chance at martyrdom,'" citing Frend, *Martyrdom and Persecution*, 77 (99 in the reprint; Grand Rapids: Baker Book House, 1980). But I think overall there is something to be said for Frend's formulation. See too Aryeh Cohen, "Toward an Erotics of Martyrdom," *JJTP* 7 (1998): 227–56.

46. See too Reinink, "Babai the Great's *Life of George*," 176: "from the moment of his baptism, George, in Babai's words, was always longing for and every day expecting his martyrdom."

47. See, e.g., Martyrdom of Pethion, Adurhormizd and Anahid, trans. Brock and Harvey, in *Holy Women of the Syriac Orient*, 89: "Let not this cup of salvation pass by me, for it is the cup that your beloved Son, our Lord Jesus Christ, drank for our sakes, and after him so did countless tens of thousands of those who believe in you, the first of whom was your friend Stephen. Confirm the minds of my persecutors, Lord, so they do not disregard me and I perish, having been left behind from the flock and herd." Similarly, in the preface to his *Martyrdom of George*, Babai the Great writes, "May the prayers of this crowned martyr be for all those who continually live in his truth and follow in the footsteps of his orthodoxy, for which he suffered and which he signed by his cross and which he confirmed by his blood like his Lord and the rest of the holy Apostles whom he *imitated* and like whom he was made perfect"; trans. Reinink, "Babai the Great's *Life of George*," 177. See also Christelle Jullien, "Martyrs en Perse dans l'hagiographie syro-orientale: Le tournant du VIe siècle," in *Juifs et chrétiens en Arabie*, ed. Joëlle Beaucamp, Françoise Briquel-Chatonnet, and Christian Julien Robin (Paris: Centre de recherche d'Histoire de Civilisation de Byzance, 2011), 285–90; H. J. W. Drijvers, "The Saint as Symbol: Conceptions of the Person in Late Antiquity and Early Christianity," in *Concepts of Person in Religion and Thought*, ed. Hans G. Kippenberg, Yme B. Kuiper, and Andy F. Sanders, Religion and Reason 37 (Berlin: de Gruyter, 1990), 137–57; Becker, *Fear of God*, 319, 331–32. Becker refers to Gregory's suffering as "Christomimetic." See too J. P. Asmussen, "Christians in Iran," in *The Cambridge History of* Iran, vol. 3, *The Seleucid, Parthian, and Sasanian Empires*, ed. Ehsan Yarshatar, part 2 (Cambridge: Cambridge University Press, 1983), 937. Asmussen lists different elements that appear scattered in the different accounts, including the persecutor as another Judas; Friday as the day of martyrdom; the sixth to ninth hour; the reaction of nature, darkness, and earthquake; and the corpse taken away in secret.

"Tricksterism" and Avoidance of Martyrdom

The enthusiasm for martyrdom in the PMA suggests that there will be an aversion to avoiding death through deception or other "trickster" techniques, and indeed I have yet to find a clear example of this tactic, even in the few accounts that do not culminate in death (technically, accounts of "confessors" rather than martyrs.) Different strategies appear in the various accounts, from temporarily renouncing Christianity to flight, but they are all rejected.

1. *Renouncing Christianity*. The Martyrdom of Pethion, Adurhormizd, and Anahid relates that the Magian Adurfrazgard tried in vain to persuade Anahid, a young maiden, to renounce Christianity and to revert to Magianism (and to marry him or his son). In so doing, he even goes so far as to have her whipped almost to the point of death. When she refuses time and again, a relative of hers proposes: "Even if you do not revert to Magianism, at least say, 'I am not a Christian,' and then I can save you and carry you off to some place where there are Christians, and you can live there in Christianity all the rest of your life."[48] She rejects this idea outright, and is then tortured—her breasts cut off and her body covered with honey, tied to stakes, and exposed. For the author, the claim "I am not a Christian" was clearly tantamount to apostasy, an outright denial of Christian faith, and would not have been considered as deception or some type of double-talk, even if it functioned as a ruse and an escape strategy. Likewise, the History of Simeon bar Ṣabba'e relates that Gushtazad, the head eunuch and friend of King Shapur, renounced his Christianity under pressure from Shapur and his colleagues.[49] When Simeon then rejects Gushtazad and expresses anger toward him, the eunuch regrets his choice, proclaims his Christianity again, and is then martyred at the order of Shapur. Here too Gushtazad capitulates and "worships the Sun God" rather than dissemble or deceive, and the rabbis equally would have rejected such action even to save his life.[50]

2. *Compromising other beliefs*. In the Martyrdom of the Forty Martyrs, a Mobed tells seven women that he will release them if they agree to get married. They refuse and are martyred (*AMS* 2:347). Likewise, the Mobed

---

48. Trans. Brock and Harvey, *Holy Women of the Syriac Orient*, 93.

49. *History of Blessed Simeon Bar Ṣabba'e*, ed. Smith, #34, 46. The parallel account in the Martyrdom of Simeon bar Ṣabba'e, #26, 38 reports more briefly, "He had been a Christian, and during this very persecution he had been put under compulsion and bowed to the sun."

50. So too Jacob Intercisus initially renounces his Christianity due to his friendship with King Yazdegerd and the gifts the king gives him. Subsequently when his wife and mother send him a letter of rebuke, he returns to his faith and is eventually martyred (*AMS* 2:540–42). However, in this case there does not seem to be a persecution that motivates him to apostatize, nor does he dissemble.

exhorting Martha to renounce her Christianity eventually tells her, "Seeing that you are set on not giving up your religion, act as you like, but do this one thing only, and you shall live and not die; you are a young girl, and a very pretty one—find a husband and get married."[51] She too refuses on the grounds that she is already betrothed to Jesus and is killed. Marriage per se is not technically a violation of Christian principles (although in such a context it would certainly signify capitulation to the persecutors). However, given the valorization of virginity and the institution of the *bnat qyama*, to acquiesce to marriage may have been tantamount to renouncing Christianity itself. Still, the choice for death over marriage evinces a disdain to pursue opportunities to escape.[52]

3. *Faking capitulation/violation*. In Martyrdom of Aqebshma, someone "as if out of pity" approaches Joseph, who is commanded to "eat blood" and offers to bring him the juice of raisins that resembles blood so that he can appear to comply and not die. Joseph is also offered pure meat to eat so that he not need eat the meat of idolatrous sacrifices or of carrion. Of course the martyr refuses these ruses (*AMS* 2:387). Rejection of this sort of misleading actions, which are technically permitted but give the appearance of capitulating, recalls the famous account of Eleazar in 2 Macc 6:21-30 and is attested in the rabbinic version of the "Mother and her seven sons" (b. Giṭ. 57b) This notion is summarily rejected in both texts.[53]

4. *Flight*. In the Martyrdom of Aitalaha and Hophsai, the protagonist tries to avoid persecution through flight but is prevented from doing so. When a persecution comes to Arbel, he tries to flee along with all the Christians who were there, but soon after he departs he is "not able to go," apparently prevented by a divine force. He returns for a few days and tries to flee again and again is prevented "as if held by some man" because "in the future the power of Jesus would be revealed through him"—that is, he would be martyred (*AMS* 4:134). Later he is arrested and put in jail, but a Mobed orders that his bonds be loosed so that can flee. He refuses, insisting, "we will not flee like robbers ... unless you free us publicly like victors" (*AMS* 4:136). Failing to take advantage of the opportunity, he is duly sentenced to death and executed. Here, then, is a straightforward way to avoid martyrdom that requires neither deception nor tricksterism, yet the protagonist opts for death, and the author reveals the same prefer-

---

51. Trans. Brock and Harvey, *Holy Women of the Syriac Orient*, 70.

52. According to the classic rabbinic formulation that one should violate the law rather than die in all cases except for idolatry, murder, and forbidden sexual relationships (b. Sanh. 74b–75a), these cases would not call for martyrdom (although the rabbis do distinguish times of formal persecution ["royal decree"]) and public versus private, so the issue is more complicated.

53. See too the continuation of the story where a woman, who refuses to throw a stone at the martyrs, is told to poke the martyr with a reed so that she will appear to do the will of the king (*AMS* 2:389–90).

ence by relating that earlier efforts to flee were frustrated. The text seems to flirt with the idea that it is better to avoid martyrdom when possible but in the end rejects this possibility.[54]

In the Life of Mar Saba, the hero also considers fleeing to avoid the approaching pagan festival lest he be forced to participate in the worship and eat of the sacrifices. His mother and nursemaid, however, instruct him neither to flee nor to fear since he will be protected. He does not flee and is imprisoned and whipped by his uncle, though he ultimately goes free. This text also contains an interesting dialogue between Mar Saba and a colleague named Kalilishou, who hear that Christians are being persecuted in a certain area. Kalilishou exhorts his brethren to travel to that place to strengthen the faithful "and if our Lord so desires, we too will approach the crown of martyrdom." Mar Saba, however, cautions that "Peace is of great benefit. Perhaps we will fall to temptation, not being able to prevail against tortures" (*AMS* 2:651–52). They proceed to argue their cases by citing biblical verses that support their positions. Then Mar Saba discerns that his colleague will die in a month's time, so he tells Kalilishou that they should wait for a month and then they will all depart together. Kalilishou dies after a month, but Mar Saba has second thoughts about his position, so asks God for a sign and receives a vision of a youth (angel?) who instructs him to go and not fear. He leaves, has various adventures, and eventually dies a natural death. This episode is not exactly about deception or tricksterism to avoid martyrdom (although there is some tricksterism involved to avoid a debate about martyrdom!), but we do see different positions voiced concerning the desirability of avoiding the situation altogether when possible. Again the text's preference (signaled by the divine vision) is to risk being persecuted rather than avoid it, though the goal here is not necessarily to die.[55]

5. *Other opportunities to avoid martyrdom.* In Martyrdom of Narseh (*AMS* 4:170–80) the protagonist tears down a fire-temple that had been built to replace a church. He is arrested but refuses two opportunities to be released. First, the Mobed offers to release him if Narseh agrees to rebuild the fire-temple; then the king offers to release him if he denies that he destroyed the fire-temple. But Narseh refuses both times and is ultimately martyred.[56]

---

54. On Greco-Roman writers and the debate over the legitimacy of flight to avoid persecution, see Moss, *Ancient Christian Martyrdom*, 155–58.

55. Anahid takes refuge in a cave/cell (כורחא) following her father's death and is thought to have fled, but she does not seem to have fled to avoid martyrdom. See Martyrdom of Pethion, Adurhormizd and Anahid (trans. Brock and Harvey, *Holy Women of the Syriac Orient*, 86–87).

56. See Richard E. Payne, *A State of Mixture: Christians, Zoroastrians, and Iranian Political Culture in Late Antiquity*, Transformation of the Classical Heritage 56 (Oakland: University of California Press, 2015), 47–48, who calls Narseh a "militant ascetic" (298). Mar Abda also

To the extent we find "tricksterism" in the PMA it is directed toward suffering martyrdom and not avoiding it. The Martyrdom of Bar Shebya relates that, as the martyrs "were going out to be killed, they were singing and praising God." At the same time a certain Magian was setting forth from that village on a journey with his wife and sons when he saw the crowds and stopped to see what was going on. Then God "opened his eyes" with a vision of "tongues of fire fixed in the shape of a cross" shining above the bodies of the martyrs. He dismounts, changes his clothes, leaves his family, approaches Bar Shebya and tells him of his vision, pleading: "Now no one knows of me that I am not one of you. Take hold of me and give me over to die like one of your disciples, because I desire it greatly that I should be killed together with you, the holy and true and faithful people. And the Blessed One (= Bar Shebya) believed him ... and they seized him by his hand and gave him over to death. And the killers did not know" (*AMS* 2:282–84). Thus, Bar Shebya is complicit in concealing the true identity of the Magian, which, had it been known, apparently would have spared him the fate of the martyrs, thus tricking the killers unknowingly into taking the Magian's life.[57]

In the Bavli, the story of R. Eleazar b. Perata mentioned above continues with the rabbi escaping death by deceptive speech, trickery, miracles, and Elijah's assistance.[58] In another account, R. Yose b. Kisma essentially criticizes R. Ḥanina b. Teradyon for openly teaching Torah in defiance of the persecution, thus bringing about his arrest and martyrdom: "I would not be surprised if they burn you and the scroll of Torah in fire" (b. ʿAbod. Zar. 18a). The implication is that a rabbi should not brazenly defy government persecutions but rather should avoid death by concealing or temporarily avoiding Jewish practices if necessary.[59]

Thus, the lack of exploration of tricksterism as an option in the PMA contrasts with the Bavli's inclusion of stories of potential martyrs avoiding death through such techniques. The PMA even discourage avoiding martyrdom by flight from a place of persecution, which would seem less

---

destroyed a fire-temple and refused to rebuild it when given the opportunity. For a different assessment of Narseh, see Geoffrey Herman, "The Last Years of Yazdgird I and the Christians," in *Jews, Christians and Zoroastrians: Religious Dynamics in a Sasanian Context*, ed. Geoffrey Herman, Judaism in Context 17 (Piscataway, NJ: Gorgias Press, 2014), 67–90.

57. See Boyarin, *Dying for God*, 51, on Polycarp using "double language" to bring about his own martyrdom.

58. Boyarin acknowledges that his ultimate escape signals "the text's approval of his tactics" (ibid., 54).

59. Likewise, R. Eliezer uses deceptive speech to avoid prosecution for "*minut*" in b. ʿAbod. Zar. 16b.

of a problem than portraying a potential martyr dodging death through double-talk or deception.[60]

Martyrdom and Conversion

One of the more significant differences between the discourse on martyrdom in the Bavli and that of the PMA is the prominence of conversion.[61] In many of the accounts of the PMA, the martyr is a Persian, often a noble or a courtier, who converts from Magianism/Zoroastrianism to Christianity; the conversion of an aristocrat, friend, or high-ranking servant angers the Persian king and precipitates persecution and torture. In many of these accounts, the conversion to Christianity is perceived as an act of bad faith and even betrayal, and the dialogue features attempts to convince the convert to revert to Zoroastrianism as an act of friendship and loyalty. According to Joel Walker, these accounts of aristocratic converts are late, dating from a time when "persecution of Christianity under Khusro I (531–579) and Khurso II (590–628) diminished to sporadic persecution of high-profile Zoroastrian apostates."[62]

Noble and even royal Persian converts include the Martyrs of Tur Berain (the children of the [local] king PWLR, a vassal of Shapur; Mahdukht, the daughter, is sought by King Shapur for his harem; *AMS* 2:19); Gubarlaha and his sister Qazo, children of Shapur (*AMS* 4:141–63);[63] Pirgushnasp (= Saba), the nephew of Shapur (*AMS* 4:222–49); Bassus and his sister Susan, children of a Mobed (*AMS* 4:471–99),[64] Mar Qardagh, the *marzban* of Nisibis;[65] George (whose grandfather was "of royal stock" and whose father "held the rank of *ostandara*"[66]); Peroz, Yazdpanah, and more. In addition, Gushtazad was a eunuch in the king's service; Azad, a servant and friend of the king; Tataq, a court official; Mar Ma'in, a general; and Jacob Intercisus, a friend and servant of the king.[67]

---

60. On the legitimacy of flight to avoid martyrdom, which Tertullian rejected but Clement of Alexandria endorsed, see Bowersock, *Martyrdom and Rome*, 54.

61. See Payne, *State of Mixture*, 48-56, 192-98.

62. Walker, *Legend of Mar Qardagh*, 228. So Jullien, "Les Actes des Martyrs," 282-83. Payne, *State of Mixture*, 48-56.

63. J.-M. Fiey, *Saints syriaques* (Princeton: Darwin Press, 2004), #178, 87.

64. Cf. ibid., #83, 52.

65. Walker, *Legend of Mar Qardagh*, #5, 22. See too 20, where Mar Qardagh's lineage on both his mother's and father's side is praised.

66. Bedjan, *Mar-Jabalaha*, 435–36.

67. Gushtazad appears in the History/Martyrdom of Simeon bar Ṣabba'e; Azad: *AMS* 2:248–54; Tataq; Jacob Intercisus: *AMS* 2:539–58; Mar Ma'in: see Sebastian P. Brock, *History of the Holy Mar Ma'in*, Persian Martyr Acts in Syriac—Text and Translation (Piscataway, NJ: Gorgias Press, 2009), 14.

There is one martyrdom of a Jewish convert to Christianity named Asher, who takes the Christian name Abda daMeshiha and is killed by his father for converting (Martyrdom of Abda-daMeshiha, *AMS* 1:189).

The closest rabbinic "martyrdom" of a convert is the story of Qetiah b. Shalom in b. ʿAbod. Zar. 10b. Qetiah councils an emperor (*keisar*) who hates the Jews and considers persecuting them against acting but is then accused of having bested the emperor in dialogue and is sentenced to die. Seized so as to be thrown into a fiery furnace, he circumcises himself—a type of aggadic conversion—and bequeaths his possessions to R. Akiva and his colleagues. One can sense here certain ideas in common with some of the PMA. Qetiah mentions the immortality of the Jewish people and its indispensability to the existence of the cosmos, that is, the divine favor and "truth" of Judaism, much as the nobles and courtiers of the Persian kings recognize the truth of the Christian God and the Christian way of life in general. Qetiah's death sentence, however, does not result from his conversion but precedes and precipitates it and is rather a punishment for defeating the emperor's arguments.[68]

This motif of conversion, whatever its historicity, devolves in part from the nature of Christianity as a missionizing religion that transcended ethnicity. That Christianity could boast of converts among the highest ranks of Persian nobility testified to its superiority and truth and signified a type of triumph over Zoroastrianism. When Qardagh experiences various miracles—"Striking his face and weeping bitterly, he said, 'Woe is me! Woe is me! Woe is me, who has harassed a man of God. Truly, great is the God of the Christians. And He is the true God who made the heaven and the earth and everything in them. And there is not God other than Him.'"[69] He then prays that he be worthy of conversion, and he soon converts. Many of these Zoroastrian converts had received the finest education, including instruction in Zoroastrian beliefs and practices, that is, "religion." For them to renounce Zoroastrianism demonstrated its shortcomings "from the inside," so to speak.[70] Thus, Yazdpanah insists that his martyrdom "was demonstrating that their fear (= religion) was deception and not truth and that their fear stood only upon [governmental] authority."[71]

Judaism, by contrast, was equally a function of ethnicity as "religion," and the Babylonian rabbis do not seem to have proselytized much and

68. See too b. Giṭ. 57a, where "Onkelos b. Qaloniqos, son of Titus's sister, wished to convert."

69. Walker, *Legend of Mar Qardagh*, #26, 34.

70. Ibid., 230; Becker, *Fear of God*, 34.

71. Martyrdom of Gregory, Bedjan, *Mar-Jabalaha*, 402. Translation from Adam Becker, "Martyrdom, Religious Difference, and 'Fear' as a Category of Piety in the Sasanian Empire: The Case of the *Martyrdom of Gregory* and the *Martyrdom of Yazdpaneh*," *Journal of Late Antiquity* 2 (2009): 310.

may even have discouraged conversion.[72] The conflict over religion and identity, then, was very much a part of the Christian experience in Sasanian Persia. This played out in narratives of martyrs who changed their identities and religions, but it was not an acute issue for the rabbis.

Thematization of the Family

Together with the issue of conversion, some of the PMA elaborate on the impact of the martyr's conversion to Christianity on his family, as Joel Walker has discussed.[73] In some cases various family members oppose the convert; in others, members of the family too embrace Christianity; in still others, both situations occur. The family dynamics often foreshadow or reprise aspects of the larger narrative. For example, violence and rejection by the convert's family foreshadow violence and ultimately martyrdom at the command of the Mobeds or the king.

The Martyrs of Tur Berain, for example, flee from their father, a vassal of Shapur, who tries to persuade them to renounce Christianity, but the children respond, "We have another Father whose fatherhood is more excellent than yours; it was He who told us '*Everyone who does not leave father and mother, and follow me, is not worthy of me.*'"[74] This trope of a spiritual father or father in heaven as opposed to the earthly father is a commonplace, as is the notion that a Christian "family" replaces the biological. Mar Qardagh thus responds to his father's pleas that he obey the king by renouncing his father:

> Our Lord Christ calls out of us in His Gospel that *Everyone who does not leave his father and mother and brothers and sisters and wife and children and follow me is not worthy of me*. And because of this I do not want to see your face.[75]

In Martyrdom of Gubarlaha and Qazo, Gubarlaha, the son of Shapur, is tortured at the command of his father. Shapur renounces him as a son,

---

72. See Moshe Lavee, "'Proselytes Are as Hard to Israel as a Scab Is to the Skin': A Babylonian Talmudic Concept," *JJS* 43 (2012): 22–48; Isaiah Gafni, "Proselytes and Proselytism in Sassanid Babylonia" [Hebrew], in *Nation and History: Studies in the History of the Jewish People*, ed. Menahem Stern (Jerusalem: Zalman Shazar Center, 1983), 208. Perhaps Constantine's conversion and the sense that the Christians had their own king in the West contributed to this difference as well, as the same could not be thought of the Jews.

73. Walker, *Legend of Mar Qardagh*, 206–45. See too Becker, *Fear of God*, 323–24.

74. The Martyrs of Tur Berain, trans. Brock, ##56–57, 53-54; the citation is based on. Matt 10:37. See too ##35–37, 40.

75. Quoted in Walker, *Legend of Mar Qardagh*, 206. The quotation conflates Matt 10:37, 19:29 and Luke 14:25-26. See too the interesting response by Martha to the Mobed's question as to whether she is the daughter of Posi: "Humanly speaking, I am his daughter, but also by faith I am the daughter of the Posi who is wise in his God and sane in the firm stand he took on behalf of the King of kings, the King of truth."

while Gubarlaha insists that Jesus, not Shapur, is his true father (*AMS* 4:144–45). The Jewish convert Abda daMeshiha is even pursued and slain by his father (*AMS* 1:187). Anahid's father, a Mobed, wants to prevent her from becoming a Christian (until he has a dream where he is beaten by the servant of a "resplendent man" who wields a scepter).[76]

In contrast to narratives of family strife, some of the narratives involving conversion to Christianity involve the conversion of family members. Soon after Gubarlaha converts to Christianity, his sister Qazo converts too. Likewise the brother and sister of Mihrnarseh, the three sibling martyrs of Tur Berain, follow their younger brother after his miraculous healing and conversion. Saba, originally named Gushnazdad, is influenced to convert when his mother gives him to a Christian nursemaid. When he decides to become a Christian, his mother converts too (though he is later tortured by another family member, an uncle; *AMS* 2:638–646).[77] A little while after George converts to Christianity his sister, who had been his wife, converts.[78] After Anahid embraces Christianity, her father Adurhormizd converts and is martyred.[79]

In the more typical accounts of native Christian martyrs, and in some of the cases of conversion of multiple family members, the narratives portray family members united by their Christian identity and fate of (or quest for) martyrdom—a motif quite opposite to that of alienation from, and abandonment of, one's family. The Martyrdom of Zebina and Her Companions tells of two brothers who are brutally tortured and killed (*AMS* 2:39–51). The martyrdom of Pusai/Posi is followed by that of his daughter, Martha, who emphasizes their shared fate: "For this confession, for which my father Posi was also crowned, I give you thanks, O lamb of God … for whose sake the bishops, our shepherds, have been sacrificed …; and slaughtered too have been the sheep—Gushtazad and Posi my father. And now it is the turn of me, the young lamb."[80] Likewise, Anahid prays to share the fate of her father: "May I not desist from the course as I accompany my father, the aged Adurhormizd; rather, just as in the past I worshipped and poured libations at evil pagan altars, so may I now, Lord, find a place along with him in your great bridal chamber."[81]

Lacking the motif of conversion, the Bavli martyr accounts do not have the same dynamics of family members either opposing the conversion or converting along with the future martyr. To the extent fam-

76. Trans. Brock and Harvey, *Holy Women of the Syriac Orient*, 85.

77. See Payne, *State of Mixture*, 51–52, for other examples of family members exposing the conversion of a relative. And see Payne, "East Syrian Bishops, Elite Households, and Iranian Law after the Muslim Conquest," *Iranian Studies* 48 (2015): 23–25.

78. Bedjan, *Mar-Jabalaha* , 445.

79. *AMS* 2:565.

80. Trans. Brock and Harvey, *Holy Women of the Syriac Orient*, 71.

81. Ibid., 88.

ily members are mentioned, they are victims of the persecution too. In this respect the rabbinic accounts are more similar to the PMA that have related family members martyred, perhaps as a narrative strategy to allow for more robust and varied development of the thematics. The story of the "Mother and Her Seven Sons" tells of the persecution and martyrdom of seven brothers and the martyrdom-suicide of their mother (b. Giṭ. 57b). The story of R. Ḥanina b. Teradyon includes the arrest and martyrdom of his wife and persecution of his daughter (who is consigned to a brothel), and the account explains the suffering of the wife and daughter by identifying their sins (b. ʿAbod. Zar. 17b).

Narrative Cycles

Related in part to the thematization of the family in the Persian Martyr Acts is the organization of some of the accounts in "story cycles," with one martyr's tale leading into that of another. The "Pethion cycle" includes the martyrdom of Yazdin (*AMS* 2:563–65), an aristocrat converted by Pethion, and then the martyrdoms of Adurhormizd (*AMS* 2:565–83), a (former) Magian and his daughter Anahid, who were also converted by Pethion, and finally that of Pethion himself (*AMS* 2:604–31). In this "cycle," then, two of the martyrs are related while two are connected through the plot. Similarly the martyrdom of Gushtazad is a subnarrative within the martyrdom of Simeon bar Ṣabba'e, which also connects to the martyrdom of Pusai, who calls out encouragement to the Christians arrested with Simeon bar Ṣabba'e and is then arrested. The account of his martyrdom is followed by that of his daughter Martha. In the Martyrdom of Barbashmin and His Comrades, Barbashmin is slandered to the king and said to be a nephew of Simeon bar Ṣabba'e, and the king accuses him of seeking the same death as Simeon (*AMS* 2:297–98).[82] The account of the "Great Slaughter" (*AMS* 2:241–48) is the background for the Martyrdom of Azad (*AMS* 2:248–54.)

In the rabbinic sources, the martyrdom of R. Ḥanina b. Teradyon is followed by that of his wife and the persecution of his daughter, as noted above (b. ʿAbod. Zar. 17b–18b). The account of the death of R. Yose b. Kisma, who advises that one not disobey the persecutors, and thereby avoids a martyr's death by lying low, is directly connected to that of R. Ḥanina b. Teradyon, as the Romans returning from R. Yose b. Kisma's funeral find R. Ḥanina b. Teradion studying Torah and gathering students (b. ʿAbod. Zar. 18a).

82. Wiessner, *Untersuchungen zur syrischen Literaturgeschichte,* identified two cycles with interrelated texts centered on Seleucia-Ktesiphon and Karka d-Ladan (the former is organized around Simeon bar Ṣabba'e); cf. Brock's review, *JTS* 19 (1968): 300–309.

This method of linking narratives together, sometimes through putative family connections, is not uncommon in the Bavli. Thus, the story of the "holy man" figure Ḥoni the Circle-Drawer is followed by those of his grandsons, Abba Hilkiah and Ḥanan Ha-Nehbeh (b. Taᶜan 23a-b). Similarly, the story of R. Yona, "a great man of Palestine" who prayed successfully for rain, is followed by stories of his son, R. Mani, whose prayers were immediately answered (b. Taᶜan 23b).

Hostile Kings and Sympathetic Queens

In many of the PMA, the Sasanian king is depicted in extremely negative light as a rabid anti-Christian who maniacally persecutes the martyr. The king is directly involved: he personally forbids the practice of Christianity, debates the martyr or Zoroastrian convert himself, and personally orders his henchmen or Mobeds to torture the Christian. In the Martyrs of Tur Abdein, when King Shapur heard of the failure to seize the martyrs, "he flew into a great rage, giving a mighty roar like that of a raving lion that has just tasted human blood,"[83] and angrily sent off his Mobeds, instructing them to arrest the martyrs and bring them to him, and if they cannot be subdued, then to kill them and burn their bodies. The king also is responsible for tortures or the order to execute the martyrs in the accounts of Martyrdom of Shapur of Niqator and Isaac of Karka d'Bet Slok (*AMS* 2:51–56), Martyrdom of John of Arbela (*AMS* 4:128–30), Martyrdom of Narseh and Joseph (*AMS* 2:284–86), Martyrdom of Barhadbeshabba of Arbela (*AMS* 2:314–16), Martyrdom of Aitalaha and Hophsai (*AMS* 4:133–37), Martyrdom of Jacob (*AMS* 2:308), Martyrdom of the Martyrs of Gilan (*AMS* 4:166–70), and others.

Of course when the stories tell of wives, children or other relations of the king who convert to Christianity, then the king is inevitably involved in the brutal attempt to win them back. Here the abandonment of Zoroastrianism is *personal*. In *Candida*, King Vartran (a corrupt name, according to Brock, who attempts to situate the story historically), when he learns that his beloved Candida is in fact a Christian, at first is kind and patient toward her. But when she refuses to embrace Zoroastrianism he has her thrown in irons, starved, stripped naked, and whipped; he then orders that her breasts be cut off and she be paraded around the city. When Gubarlaha, son (!) of Shapur, becomes a Christian, Shapur has him whipped by twelve men, commissions his Mobeds to torture him, and subsequently orders that he be thrown under the stallions of a carriage and then strung out on a rack until he dies (*AMS* 4:142–46; Gubarlaha's Christian teacher,

83. Martyrs of Tur Berain, trans. Brock, #84.

Dado, also martyred, is from the same "ethnic stock" [or even "extended family"] as Shapur [בר גנסה הוא דילה דשבור מלכא]).

The king in these accounts represents Persian society, this-worldly authority, and false beliefs (idolatry/paganism), while the martyr opposing the king stands for the rejection of Persian society, religion, and authority, or at least the recognition that such authority is merely human and political. When the Mobed of Hadyab (Adiabene) arrests Abraham the Presbyter and orders him to obey the will of the king and worship the sun, Abraham states, "I despise you and your gods; I scorn your king and his command."[84] In this way Christian identity entails the denial of Persian gods and the Persian monarch (who was considered divine.)[85] In the Martyrdom of the Forty Martyrs, the Mobed accuses the martyrs of denying the divine Shapur, and an elder responds that Shapur is not a God because he eats, drinks, and so forth (*AMS* 2:340).[86]

In yet other cases, the king is involved in the drama in some way, or ultimately authorizes the tortures or death, but it is the magi or nobles who initiate the persecution by denouncing or slandering Christians to the king.[87] In Martyrdom of Mar Qardagh, for example, the king "loved the blessed Qardagh with all his soul. But because of the will of his nobles he was forced to summon the blessed Qardagh" for interrogation about his conversion to Christianity. When Qardagh arrives, the king sends him a message in secret: "Behold, the *magi* and all the nobles of the kingdom are threatening you and want to kill you because you have abandoned Magianism and the religion of the gods and have become a Christian. Therefore, when you enter before me, do not say that you are a Christian. Then your accusers will be put to shame."[88] Qardagh predictably pro-

84. Martyrdom of Abraham the Presbyter, *AMS* 4:130.

85. However, some of the PMA do recognize the secular authority of the king. See, e.g., *History of Simeon bar Ṣabba'e* #5, ed. Smith, 78: Simeon states, "I bow to the King of Kings, and I honor his commands with all my power ... how much the more ought we to embrace our authority and pray of the king to whose kingdom God has subjected us and in the land of whose dominion he has made us dwell? Truly, our scriptures command this of us: 'let every person be subject to the governing authorities....' [Rom 13:1–2]. We too are commanded to pray for kings and princes." Nevertheless, the king is portrayed negatively in the narrative and is responsible for the deaths of the martyrs.

86. See too Anahid's dialogue with the Magian; trans. Brock and Harvey, *Holy Women of the Syriac Orient*, 91. "'The king of kings is a great warrior who has subdued both land and sea: are you saying that he cannot get the better of your feeble fianceé...' The holy woman replied, 'my fianceé ... is resident in heaven, and so his power and authority extend over both heights and depths. What can your master—or indeed all the kings on earth—do that affects him or his in any way?'"

87. On the magi as responsible for persecutions, see Becker, *Fear of God*, 325–36; Sebastian P. Brock, "Christians in the Sasanian Empire: A Case of Divided Loyalties," *Studies in Church History* 18 (1982): 1–19, here 6.

88. Trans. Walker, *Legend of Mar Qardagh*, #49, 55.

claims his Christianity, forcing the king to pretend to be angry and to state that he renounces his friendship with Qardagh, though he continues to give Qardagh opportunities to retract despite pressure from his advisors for more severe punishments (see too Martyrdom of the Martyrs of Gilan [*AMS* 4:166–70], and Martyrdom of Narseh [*AMS* 4:170–80]). Accounts of this type evoke the dynamic in Daniel 3, and especially in Daniel 6, where King Darius is manipulated and pressured to throw Daniel into the lions' den, though the king himself "set his heart on Daniel to deliver him" (Dan 6:15). Thus, in Martyrdom of Gregory (Pirangushnasp), we are told that the king loved Christians but the magians started a persecution.[89] Indeed, Lucas Von Rompay has argued that a number of the PMA are heavily influenced by the book of Daniel and borrow ideas and phrases.[90]

In a few PMA the king is portrayed somewhat sympathetically, though he cannot avoid some complicity in the persecution. In Martyrdom of Azad, for example, the protagonist is arrested and killed when the king orders that Christians be persecuted. But the king is saddened to hear that his friend Azad has been killed—he obviously did not know Azad was a Christian—and he instructs that Christians no longer be murdered en masse and only the teachers be killed (*AMS* 2:253).

In still other cases it is only Mobeds or Zoroastrian clergy who are responsible, and the king is not mentioned at all, such as Martyrdom of Abraham the Presbyter (*AMS* 4:130–31); Martyrdom of Hnanya (*AMS* 4:131–32); Martyrdom of Barshebya (*AMS* 2:281–84); Martyrdom of Daniel and Warda (*AMS* 2:290); Martyrs of Karka d'Beth Slokh (*AMS* 2:286–89). Similarly, the party responsible for the persecution may be a petty/local king (Martyrdom of Pinḥas; *AMS* 4:208–18), or a "powerful" man (Martyrdom of Miles, *AMS* 2:260–75). The image and role of the king deserve detailed study, as this taxonomy should be developed and the implications discussed. But in general there are copious hostile representations of the Persian king.

By contrast, two related Martyrdom accounts suggest that a Sasanian queen was Jewish or close to the Jews, the Martyrdom of Tarbo,[91] and the

---

89. Bedjan, *Mar-Jabalaha*, 348–49. Earlier Jesus had inspired good will in the king such that he let Gregory receive visitors in prison.

90. Lucas Van Rompay, "Impetuous Martyrs? The Situation of the Persian Christians in the Last Years of Yazdgard I (419–420)," in *Martyrium in Multidisciplinary Perspective: Memorial Louis Reekmans*, ed. Mathijs Lamberigts and Peter Van Deun, BETL 117 (Leuven: Leuven University Press, 1995), 373–75. On the influence of Daniel, see too Dilley, *Martyrs of Mount Ber'ain*, xix–xx, who identifies the three child martyrs with Shadrach, Meshach, and Abednego; and Smith, *Martyrdom and History*, xix, who see Gushtazad as a second Daniel.

91. Martyrdom of Tarbo, trans. Brock and Harvey, *Holy Women of the Syrian Orient*, 73: "At this time it so happened that the queen fell ill. Since she was *favorably inclined to the enemies of the cross* [קריב הוא רעינה ליהודיא בעלדבבוהי דזקיפא], the Jews, they told her, making

History of Simeon bar Ṣabba'e.[92] As is well known, several rabbinic stories portray the Sasanian queen-mother Ifra Hormiz, mother of Yazdegerd (?), as sympathetic to the rabbis.[93] These traditions seem to have some affinity to the favorable portrayals of these Jewish or philo-Jewish queens in the PMA, though the precise relationship is unclear and has been debated among scholars, and the rabbinic traditions have no connection to martyrdom.[94]

In rabbinic martyrdom accounts, Persian kings and queens do not figure at all, though this again is partly a function of the accounts set in Roman contexts.[95] In the account of the "Mother and her seven sons" (b. Giṭ. 57b) the king is involved, but it is difficult to read him as the Persian king. Elsewhere in the Bavli Persian kings are rather favorably portrayed.[96]

In general the negative portrayals of the king in many of the PMA sharply contrast with the overall favorable image of the Persian king in the Bavli. At stake in the conflict between king and martyr in the PMA are

---

their customary false accusation: 'The sisters of Simeon have put spells on you because their brother has been put to death.'"

92. *History of Simeon bar Sabba'e*, ed. Smith, #12, 88: "Now the Jews, who have always been the adversaries of our people—they who killed the prophets, crucified Christ, stoned the apostles, and are always thirsting for our blood—they found an opportunity to accuse us *because of the confidence that was (accorded) to them through their relationship with the queen, since she was of their way of thinking.*" See too the version of Sozomen, *Ecclesiastical History* 2:12.

93. See b. B. Bat. 8a–b (Ifra Hormiz sends a purse of money to Rav Yosef); b. B. Bat. 10b–11a (she sends money to Rav Ammi, who does not accept it, and then to Rava, who does); b. Zebaḥ. 116b (she sends an animal sacrifice to Rava); b. Nid. 20b (she sends menstrual blood stains to Rava) and b. Taʿan 24b (she cautions Shapur, who wanted to punish Rava, not to dispute with Jews because they are favored by God). According to Iranian tradition, the Sasanian king Yazdegerd I (399–420) was married to a Jewess, the daughter of the Exilarch (see *The Provincial Capitals of Iran*, #47, quoted in Jacob Neusner, "Babylonian Jewry and Shapur II's Persecution of Christianity from 339–379 A.D," *HUCA* 43 [1972]: 96). The rabbinic traditions of Ifra Hormiz are set in the time of Shapur II (309–379), and Rav Yosef and Rava (d. 327), the third–fourth generation of Amoraim. This may be a slight retrojection of the Iranian tradition. But since the rabbis designate her as the mother, not wife, of the king, it is not clear that we are dealing with a common tradition.

94. Historians have struggled to account for these traditions and their degree of historicity, most adopting a "historical kernel approach." See the review of scholarship on this question in Neusner, "Babylonian Jewry and Shapur II's Persecution of Christianity." Barring the discovery of new sources, it does not seem that this question can be resolved.

95. Unless one counts the martyrdom/persecution of Rabba b. Naḥmani, which is initiated by the king.

96. See Alyssa Gray, "The Power Conferred by Distance from Power: Redaction and Meaning in *b. ʿAbod. Zar.* 10a–11a," in *Creation and Composition: The Contribution of the Bavli Redactors (Stammaim) to the Aggada*, ed. Jeffrey L. Rubenstein, TSAJ 114 (Tübingen: Mohr Siebeck, 2005), 64–68; Secunda, *Iranian Talmud*, 100–106; Jason Mokhtarian, "Authority and Empire in Sassanian Babylonia: The Rabbis and King Shapur in Dialogue," *JSQ* 19 (2012): 148–80. Mokhtarian discusses talmudic narratives that portray "Shapur I as a generally positive figure who represents Persian imperial authority and whose Judaized words and/or deeds demonstrate or praise rabbinic thought" (150–51).

several questions that apparently were not burning issues for the rabbis. Who is the true God, the Persian king who claimed divinity or Jesus/God of the Christians? Is the identity of the Christian, and especially the recent convert, understood primarily in relation to Iranian society and its king or to the Christian community and God? Even the truth of Christianity versus that of Zoroastrianism is played out in some of these conflicts, with the king arguing the divinity of the sun and other Zoroastrian beliefs against the Christian claims that such natural phenomena are "created, not the creator." Presumably the fact that Christianity was the official religion of the Roman Empire at this time played a role in this issue: Christian were seen by Persians—and perhaps saw themselves—as "allies" or at least as friends of a hostile power, which was not the case with Jews.[97]

However, these issues come up occasionally in rabbinic sources, though not directly in the context of martyrdom. Consider these two passages from the PMA and a talmudic story from b. Ber. 32b.

Martyrdom of Qardagh, trans. Walker, 60-61	Martyrs of Tur Berain, trans. Brock, 62-64	b. Berakhot 32b–33a[98]
Qardagh's noble relatives ... wept and said to him, "... Do not revolt against the king.... Obey the King's order, and bow down just once to the fire and sun...."	The confidant [גזירה] gave them the greeting from Shabur the king, but they did not reply with a single word to him. He was greatly annoyed and said to them "O people worthy of an evil death, do you not accept the greeting [שלמא] of the great king Shabur?" Even so they did not give any reply at all. He then took a stone and threw it at them, but it turned round backwards and hit him on the forehead, smashing into it—whereupon the entire crowd exclaimed with a loud cry, "Praised be to Christ for ever and ever, amen!"	Our Rabbis taught: It is related that once when a *Hasid* was praying by the roadside, a governor [שר] came by and greeted him and he did not return his greeting [שלום]. He waited for him until he had finished his prayer. When he had finished his prayer he said to him: Fool! Is it not written in your Torah: "Only take heed to thyself and keep thy soul diligently" and it is also written, "Take ye therefore good heed unto your souls"? When I greeted you why did you not return my greeting? If I had cut off your head with my sword, who would have demanded your blood from me? He replied to him:

97. On Christians as a potential "fifth column," see Brock, "Christians in the Sasanian Empire," 1–19.

98. Although this source appears in Hebrew with the introductory terminology of *baraitot*, it is in fact a Babylonian pseudo-*baraita*, a creation of the Bavli redactors, as demonstrated by Yonatan Feintuch, "Anonymous *Hasid* Stories in Halakhic *Sugyot* in the Babylonian Talmud," *JJS* 53 (2012): 243-47 and n. 24.

But the blessed one opened his mouth and said to them, "… For which is more grievous, that I should revolt against a wretched man who today blooms and is full of pride, but for whom there is no tomorrow? Or to revolt against the heavenly King of Kings, whose kingdom does not pass away and whose divinity does not change…. But now that I have come to know Christ who is the heavenly King and the true Hope, I will not serve impious and mortal kings. And I will not fear their threats."	The confidant—whose name was Gushtazad—having had a taste of the might of the saints, bound up his head and kept silent until they completed their prayer. The saints then said to him, "We are asking you to speak the truth to us, if you are willing to do so: is God or man great?" He replied, "Without any doubt God is great." They went on: "Why then were you angry when we were speaking with God in prayer and we did not accept from you the greeting of Shabur, who is a human being, just like everyone else?" He was silent and gave them no reply.	Be patient and I will explain to you. If, [he went on], you had been standing before a mortal king and your friend had come and given you greeting, would you have returned it? No, he replied. And if you had returned his greeting, what would they have done to you? They would have cut off my head with the sword, he replied. He then said to him: We have here then an a-fortiori argument: *If [you would have behaved] in this way when standing before a mortal king, who is here today and tomorrow in the grave, how much more so I, when standing before the King of Kings, the Holy One, blessed be He, who lives and endures for ever and ever?* Forthwith the governor was appeased (accepted his explanation), and the *Hasid* departed to his home in peace.

The martyrs of Tur Berain, like the *Hasid*, are accosted while praying by a royal official who becomes angry that they do not interrupt their prayers to greet him. Both the "governor" and "confidant" remain silent while the heroes finish their prayer, and both offer a rebuke that includes the threat of death. The martyrs and the *Hasid* offer a similar explanation of the greatness of God compared to an earthly king, and both achieve their didactic purposes through a question-and-answer dialogue. Qardagh's comparison of the heavenly king to a human king evokes the same basic theological notion (or polemic) of mortal ephemerality and divine immortality (though the issue is not interrupting prayer but obedience).[99] Note that the passages from the Martyrs of Tur Berain include a number of the typical differences from the rabbinic martyrdom accounts, including a gesture at conversion (the onlookers' praise of Christ) and the miracle, the boomeranging of the stone thrown at them (see below). At all events,

99. Though it may simply reflect standard biblical ideas, such as Pss 39:4–8, 90:4, 103:15–16.

despite the similarities, we are dealing with different contexts—again the rabbinic source does not deal with martyrdom. The rabbis obviously would have agreed with the logic of the martyrs in the PMA, but the rabbinic martyrdom sources are just not engaging those issues.

Miracles and Dream Revelations

In the PMA, the martyrs routinely perform miracles that typically delay or prevent the efforts of persecutors to imprison, torture, or kill them.[100] The miracles demonstrate that the persecutors in fact have no real power over the martyrs; only when the martyrs themselves are ready to die, and by their own free will, are the persecutors able to prevail. In the Martyrdom of Narseh, after one executioner is struck down and paralyzed for three hours when he raises his sword to kill Narseh, the Magian commands another to do the deed, but he understandably balks until Narseh persuades him: "Do as you have been commanded and fear not.... This, indeed, is not your will, but that of a force that is harsher than you. Raise your right arm and strike me with the sword, for I go as is my wish, as my request of God."[101] Thus, the persecutors are in fact impotent; they cannot injure or kill the martyr until he allows them—even encourages them—to do so. In the Martyrs of Tur Berain, the sultan's servants are struck with hallucinations so they cannot find the cave where his children-martyrs are hiding; when they descend from their horses they are "bound" and cannot move; when they try to shoot arrows toward the cave they end up shooting their own colleagues, but the martyrs heal these wounded soldiers (*AMS* 2:19–23). After other such miracles, the martyrs ask to be killed, and after the executioner initially recoils, as mentioned above, their wish is finally granted (*AMS* 2:37–38). In Martyrdom of Gubarlaha and Qazo, when a Mobed tries to burn Dado, the fire retreats and will not burn the Christian. Gubarlaha then makes the sign of the cross before a fire, and it moves nine cubits away from him (*AMS* 4:143–44). (Clearly these miracles demonstrate that the God of the Christians is more powerful than the Zoroastrian sacred fires.) When various Mobeds torture Gubarlaha by driving heated metal rods into his ears, a youth appears to him in prison, removes the rods and heals him (*AMS* 4:148). Subsequently Gubarlaha prays and a cauldron full of burning sulphur and pitch freezes like snow

100. See Philippe Gignoux, "Une typologie des miracles des saints et martyrs perses," in *Miracle et Karama: Les saints et leurs miracles à travers l'hagiographie chrétienne et islamique*, ed. Denise Aigle (Turnhout: Bibliothèque de l'École pratique des hautes études, 2000), 499–523.

101. Trans. Herman, *Persian Martyr Acts under King Yazdgird I*, 22. Another example is the miraculous boomeranging of the stone in the passage quoted above.

(*AMS* 4:153).[102] In Martyrdom of Pethion, Adurhormizd and Anahid the chains put on Pethion magically fall off of him, a rope used to bind him is burned by a heavenly fire.[103] At this point the persecutor begs Pethion to come with him willingly, since he was ordered to arrest Pethion. Pethion acquiesces and even puts the chain on himself when they arrive! Subsequently in prison the chains fall off Pethion and his fellow Christians, but he instructs them to put the chains on themselves. Tied up and thrown in a river, the water splits above and below him so he does not drown (*AMS* 2:607–10).[104] Qardagh dwells in an impregnable fortress, and the attackers repeatedly fail to prevail over him, in part due to various protective miracles. Finally he responds to his father-in-law's pleas: "But go away and let there be no anxiety and grief for you. And behold, I will petition my Lord Christ to show me whether it is time for me to die for the sake of His name. If it pleases the will of his divinity, and it is time to take the crown of martyrdom in completion of this struggle on His behalf, gladly will I go out and hand myself over to the executioners."[105] Shortly thereafter Qardagh experiences a dream vision signaling that it is time for him to die, so he willingly emerges and is killed in the presence of thousands of people who have heard of his scheduled martyrdom.

In the Bavli martyrdom stories, miracles appear only in the account of R. Eleazar b. Perata, who evades martyrdom through trickery (b. ʿAbod. Zar. 17b).[106] In this story, R. Eleazar claims he is called "master" because he is the master of weavers, not of Torah. The persecutors test him with thread, and "a miracle happened for him. A male bee came and sat on the weft and a female bee on the warp." Then another miracle happens to verify his claim that he feared being trampled at the *bei abeidan*,[107] namely, that an old man is trampled that day. And other miracles occur too. If we count

102. In Martyrdom of Mihrshabur, the martyr is thrown and sealed in a dark pit for two months and ten days without food or water. When the pit is opened the persecutors find that it is full of light, and Mihrshabur is seated in prayer, so well preserved they do not realize he is dead. They are also amazed that he was not attacked by a snake that was put in the pit with him and that had attacked previous prisoners (*AMS* 2:538–39).

103. There are some that have no miracles, including Martyrdom of Sabur of Niqator and Isaac of Karak de'beit Sloq (*AMS* 2:51–56) and Martyrdom of Narseh and Joseph (*AMS* 2:284–86).

104. In Martyrdom of George, Yazdpanah is nailed to the cross upside down, but his "left arm remains free to refute the Jews" (who argued to the executioner that he had to be tied a certain way.) When a soldier first tries to shoot him with an arrow, he misses, apparently through the providence of God; Bedjan, *Mar-Jabalaha*, 561–62.

105. Trans. Walker, *Legend of Mar Qardagh*, #59, 64.

106. Miracles also occur in the story of R. Meir's efforts to free the daughter of R. Ḥanina b. Teradyon from the brothel (b. ʿAbod. Zar. 18a), but this story is not really about martyrdom.

107. See n. 8 above.

the story of Rabba b. Naḥmani in b. B. Meṣ. 86a as a martyrdom, then we have another case of miracles in the service of escaping persecution: the royal messenger seeking Rabba has his face turned backwards and then healed, the wall imprisoning Rabba falls down, and so on. Finally, Rabba dies due to his own prayers and because he has been summoned to the heavenly academy. Thus, the miracles in the Bavli help the sages avoid martyrdom, whereas we might say that the miracles in the PMA enhance the martyrdom by underscoring that it takes place because of the willingness of the persecuted, not the power of the persecutors.

One possible case of a rabbinic account that comes closer to this motif of miracles preventing martyrdom so as to underscore the lack of power of the persecutors is the version of the death of R. Ḥanina as preserved in one manuscript of Tractate Kallah 23, among the "Minor Tractates" of the Bavli, that David Brodsky considers of Babylonian Amoraic provenance:[108]

> And they said about him [Ḥanina b. Teradion] that one time his *purim* money and his charity money got mixed together. And he was sitting and wondering and saying, "Woe is me perhaps I have become guilty of the death penalty in the heaven[ly court]." While he was sitting and wondering a [Roman] executioner came by. He said to him, "Rabbi, they decreed on you to wrap you and burn you in your Torah, and also Israel your nation." And he stood and wrapped him in his Torah. And they surrounded him with bundles of sticks. And he [the executioner] lit him, and the fire [אור] cooled and went away from him. The executioner stood in shock. He said to him, "Rabbi, are you he who they decreed to burn?" He said, "Yes." He said to him, "Why does the fire go out?" He said to him, "I adjured in the name of my master [i.e. God] that no one would touch me until I knew whether they had decreed on me from heaven. Wait one hour for me and I will let you know." And the executioner sat and wondered.... He [R. Ḥanina] said to him, "Good for nothing! The decree from heaven has agreed [that I should die] and if you do not kill me God has many killers, many bears, many leopards ... but in the end God will collect my blood from your hand."[109]

Here the murderer indeed cannot harm the rabbinic martyr until he ascertains that God's will is that he die, at which point R. Ḥanina submits and even has to encourage the executioner to proceed. The fire refusing to burn R. Ḥanina bears striking similarity to the fire retreating from Dado and Gubarlaha mentioned above. However, in this source too the death of the martyr is construed as punishment, rather than privilege and "reward" as

108. Brodsky, *Bride without a Blessing*.

109. Brodsky, *Bride without a Blessing*, 435 n. 65, from MS Oxford 2257. See too 166–67, 245–46.

characteristic of the PMA. And there is some uncertainty as to the provenance and dating of Tractate Kallah.[110]

The only other miraculous elements are the heavenly voices that follow the martyrdoms of R. Akiva and "The Mother and Her Seven Children" making it known that the martyrs were invited into the world to come. A version of this motif appears in some of the PMA: following the martyrdom of Mar Qardagh, a heavenly voice (קלא) proclaims: "You have fought well and bravely conquered, glorious Qardagh. Go joyfully and take up the crown of your victory." Similarly, Gubarlaha finally dies after a heavenly voice (קלא מן שמיא) tells him that he has triumphed beautifully and to "come in peace" (*AMS* 4:159).[111]

The miracles performed by the Christian martyrs are typical of the hagiographic "holy man" literature, and typical also of the talmudic stories about the sages, such as healing, punishing opponents and troublemakers, rainmaking, and so on. But again, the rabbinic martyrs for the most part do not perform miracles themselves.

Dream visions are also common in many of the PMA. In some cases, the vision is the cause of the future martyr converting to Christianity. In other cases, the visions encourage the martyr or consist in the martyr himself appearing to others after death. In the Martyrs of Tur Berain, while the three siblings hide in the cave, two men descend from heaven encouraging them to be strong (*AMS* 2:18). (Earlier Mihrnarse, who had been injured, experienced a dream vision, where two men led him on a tour of Christ in heaven, the sufferings of hell, and Mar Abda praying for his life, which precipitates his conversion.[112]) Anahid too has a dream vision of a splendid king who encourages her to become a Christian, and a little later her father Adurhormizd has a similar dream vision, prompting his conversion.[113] In Martyrdom of John of Arbela, an angel appears as a soldier in a dream and gives John a crown, informing John he will receive the martyrdom for which he prayed (*AMS* 4:130). Similarly, in the Martyrdom of the Forty Martyrs, one of the martyrs has a dream involving Simeon bar Ṣabba'e that portends their martyrdom.[114] In the Martyrdom of Hnanya, after being tortured and left for dead, Hnanya tells the Christians who

---

110. As opposed to Brodsky, M. B. Lerner assigns Tractate Kallah to the Geonic era; "The External Tractates," in *The Literature of the Sages, Part One*, ed. Shmuel Safrai (Assen: Van Gorcum; Philadelphia: Fortress, 1987), 394–96.

111. Trans. Walker, *Legend of Mar Qardagh*, 67-68. See too Moss, *Ancient Christian Martyrdom*, 60–61, for the heavenly voice that encourages Polycarp.

112. See Dilley's introduction to *The Martyrs of Mount Ber'ain*, xxiii–xxvii, for discussion of dream visions of this type.

113. Trans. Brock and Harvey, *Holy Women of the Syriac Orient*, 84–85.

114. Shahdost too has a dream of Simeon bar Ṣabba'e that portends his martyrdom; Martyrdom of Shahdost, *AMS* 2:276.

have found his body that he had a vision of angels going up and down between the heaven and earth (and then he dies; *AMS* 4:132). The martyr Gubarlaha, after his death, appears to those who have bought his body parts and instructs them to give the body to his sister (*AMS* 4:160).[115] The Martyrdom of Qardagh makes particularly heavy use of dream visions. At the outset, the former martyr Sergius appears to Qardagh in a dream informing him that he will become a Christian and be martyred.[116] Later Qardagh has a dream of Mar Abdisho inviting him to his cave.[117] Sergius appears to Qardagh again; an angel to Mar Abdisho; "the Lord" appears to another holy man named Beri, and there are at least five other such visions, directing the characters what to do.[118]

Dream visions of deceased rabbis and other figures bearing messages are not uncommon in rabbinic sources (e.g., b. B. Meṣ. 85b), though again they do not appear in the martyr stories.[119]

Conclusion

These topics will suffice for the present, although many other points of contrast could be discussed, including (1) the connection of many of the PMA to a shrine or cult site (as foundation legends) and to the liturgical calendar;[120] (2) the imagery of martyrs as athletes and martyrdom as a contest of the arena,[121] and the general discourse of victory and triumph, including the common epithet of the martyr as the "victorious so-and-so

115. So too Asher appears to a pregnant woman instructing her to name her son after him; Martyrdom of Abda daMeshiha, *AMS* 1:196.

116. Trans. Walker, *Legend of Mar Qardagh*, 23.

117. Ibid., 35.

118. Ibid., 37, 41, 42, 46, 51, 53, 65. See too the appearance of an angel to Pirangushnasp (= Gregory) one night, though it is not clear if he is sleeping (Martyrdom of Gregory; Bedjan, *Mar-Jabalaha*, 351 and 352–53).

119. See the interesting text from Qoh. Rab. 9:10 (24b) quoted by Lieberman in "Martyrs of Caesarea," 413: "Rabbi Aha longed to see the face of Rabbi Alexandri. He appeared to him in his dream and showed him three things: There is no compartment [in heaven] beyond that of the martyrs of Lydda…" (as emended by Lieberman). Here is a dream vision about martyrs, but it is not in the Bavli.

120. As noted by Yaron Eliav in his review in *Hebrew Studies* 42 (2001): 389. See also Richard Payne, "The Emergence of Martyrs' Shrines in Late Antique Iran," in *An Age of Saints? Power, Conflict and Dissent in Early Medieval Christianity*, ed. Peter Sarris, Matthew Dal Santo, and Phil Booth, Brill Series on the Early Middle Ages 20 (Leiden: Brill, 2011), 89–113. On hagiography itself as a type of worship, see Derek Krueger, "Writing as Devotion: Hagiographical Composition and the Cult of Saints in Theodoret of Cyrrhus and Cyril of Scythopolis," *Church History* 66 (1997): 707–19.

121. Martyrdom of Aqebshma, *AMS* 2:390; Martyrdom of Simeon b. Ṣabba'e, *AMS* 2:178; History of Saba, *AMS* 4:247. See the review of Boyarin by Han Willem van Henten, *H-Judaica* (August, 2000), reviews/showrev.php?id=4452.

[נצ׳חא]"; (3) the sweet "odor of sanctity" that often follows the death of the martyr;[122] (4) the role of New Testament passages in inspiring martyrdom (related of course to the notion of *imitatio Christi*);[123] (5) the imagery of martyrs as animal sacrifices (perhaps also related to *imitatio Christi*, "the lamb of God [John 1:29])";[124](6) the martyr's deathbed "prophecy" about the fate of the persecutors;[125] (7) the motif of onlookers or even participants in the martyrdom (such as the king's soldiers) being so impressed by the miracles or death that they convert too.[126]

The PMA are a large and diverse set of texts. Although scholars have noted a standard narrative pattern of sorts,[127] there is also a vast amount

---

122. E.g., Martyrdom of Habib, *AMS* 1:172; Acts of Abda daMeshiha, *AMS* 1:175; Martyrdom of Gregory; Bedjan, *Mar-Jabalaha*, 392. See Susan Ashbrook Harvey, *Scenting Salvation: Ancient Christianity and the Olfactory Imagination*, Transformation of the Classical Heritage 42 (Berkeley: University of California Press, 2006).

123. Smith, *Martyrdom and History*, xliv; Florence Jullien, *Histoire de Mār Abba, catholicos de l'Orient: Martyres de Mār Grigor, général en chef du roi Khusro Ier et de Mār Yazd-Panah, juge et gouverneur* (CSCO Scriptores Syri 254; Leuven: Peeters, 2015), liii–lvii; Herman, *Persian Martyr Acts Under King Yazdgird I*, 22 n. 62.

124. See the quotation from Martha, above, which continues, "At your hands, Jesus, the true High Priest, may I be offered up as a pure, holy, and acceptable offering before the glorious Trinity"; Martyrdom of Jacob Intercisus, *AMS* 2:550; Martyrdom of the Forty Martyrs, *AMS* 2:343; Martyrdom of Anahid, trans. Harvey and Brock, *Holy Women of the Syrian Orient*, 88; Martyrs of Tur Berain, trans. Brock, #5, 12. However, the account of the "Mother and Her Seven Sons" (b. Giṭ. 57b) opens with Ps 44:23 "It is for Your sake that we are slain all day long, that we are regarded as sheep to be slaughtered" and ends with the mother comparing her sevenfold sacrifice to Abraham's single binding/"sacrifice," so perhaps this is a shared motif. Martha too invokes Abraham's sacrifice in a different way: "Now I can say, not like Isaac, 'Here is the fire and the wood, but where is the lamb for the burnt offering?' but rather I can say, 'Here is the lamb and the knife, but where is the wood and the fire?'" (trans. Harvey and Brock, *Holy Women of the Syrian Orient*, 72).

125. Martyrdom of Miles, *AMS* 2:273–74; Martyrs of Tur Berain, trans. Brock, #82, 70. Rabbinic sages often "prophesy" on their deathbeds, though rabbinic martyrs do not. There is, however, a vague parallel to this latter passage, namely, Mahdukht's prophesy to Gushtazad, that he will eventually be martyred "at the order of King Shabur, on account of faith in Christ" and R. Akiva's "prophecy" (though not on his deathbed) that the wife of Turnusrufus would convert and marry him (b. ʿAbod. Zar. 29a; cf. b. Ned. 50b).

126. See, e.g., Martyrs of Tur Berain, trans. Brock, #24, 28 (the siblings), ##62–67, 56–58 (soldiers and others), #94, 80 (Gushtazad and his companions): Indeed, we are told, "Who can describe the thronging crowds of people who hurried to go to the cave of the saints? … Just the report of the saints was sufficient to convert whole regions to the faith of Christ!" (67). After the miracles wrought by Yazdpaneh some of the magi begin to "turn from their fear" (= their religion) to Christianity; Life of George, in Bedjan, *Mar-Jabalaha*, 403; History of Mar Aba, ibid., 228–29. See also the anecdote from the Life of Bar Shebya (*AMS* 2:282-84) mentioned above. The executioner who kills R. Ḥanina b. Teradyon jumps into the fire and dies, though this act seems to be less a conversion than a guaranteed way of entering the world to come (since R. Ḥanina promises him as much).

127. P. Devos, "Les martyrs persans à travers leur Actes syriaques," *Atti del convegno sul tema: La Persia e il mondo Greco-Romano* (Rome: Accademia Nazionale dei Lincei, 1966), 213–25.

of biographical material unique to each individual narrative. It is therefore not surprising that we find numerous parallels to some of the biographical anecdotes among the vast corpus of biographical anecdotes in the Babylonian Talmud.[128] In this respect comparative study of the Bavli and the PMA attest to a common cultural context and can contribute to our understanding of rabbinic Judaism in the Sasanian world. Yet, when it comes to stories of martyrs specifically, the contrasts between the Bavli and the PMA are more striking than the similarities. Jonathan Z. Smith has emphasized the need for attention to differences and not only similarities when engaging in comparative study—"What is required is the development of a discourse of 'difference,' a complex term which invites negotiation, classification, and comparison, and, at the same time, avoids too easy a discourse of the 'same'"—and I believe this insight is apposite not only for the study of Christianity and Hellenistic mystery religions, which prompted Smith's stricture, but also for the present topic.[129] The PMA attest to an enthusiasm for martyrdom and a joyful embrace of death that goes far beyond what we find in the rabbinic accounts, and which probably derives ultimately from the theology of *imitatio Christi*. The prominence of narratives of conversion of high ranking Zoroastrians and the overall hostility to the king point to efforts to define or redefine Christian identity in opposition to Persian identity, a concern that does not appear in the rabbinic martyrdom accounts. This difference is partially a function of the importance of missionizing in Christianity in general and the narrative of the spread of the church into the "East."[130] At the same time, it suggests a difference in the self-conception of Christians and the Babylonian rabbis as to their place in society and relations with the majority culture in the late Sasanian era.[131]

---

128. In addition to the parallels mentioned above, we should note the repeated motif of the difficulty of collecting and burying the martyrs' bones (due to Zoroastrian opposition to burial), as elucidated in Herman, "Bury My Coffin Deep!," which has parallels in Bavli sources but not in accounts of martyrs.

129. Jonathan Z. Smith, *Drudgery Divine: On the Comparison of Early Christianities and the Religions of Later Antiquity* (Chicago: University of Chicago Press, 1990), 42. See the review of Boyarin by Shmuel Shepkaru, *Journal of Interdisciplinary History* 32 (2001): 112: "One of Boyarin's methodological frailties is his focusing on parallels, which can be attributed to general literary martyrological motifs in nonhistorical accounts, without considering the differences that these accounts and numerous unmentioned others convey."

130. And also the influence of Western martyrdom literature and the general tradition of the persecution of Christians in the Roman Empire on the "Church of the East" (I am grateful to Geoffrey Herman for this observation).

131. It should be emphasized again that the historical experience of Jews and Christians may have been very similar, and generally free of persecution, although the literary representations of martyrdom differ, assuming Richard Payne is correct in his reading of the martyrdom accounts (Payne, *State of Mixture*).

A Persian Anti-Martyr Act

The Death of Rabba bar Naḥmani in Light of the Syriac Persian Martyr Acts

SIMCHA GROSS

In recent years, scholars have begun to situate the Babylonian Talmud in its social and cultural contexts. The largest and most prolific group of scholars are part of the so-called Irano-Talmudica school, which seeks to contextualize the Bavli in its Persian and, more specifically, Zoroastrian environment.[1] Other contexts have been explored as well.[2]

1. See Shai Secunda, *The Iranian Talmud: Reading the Bavli in its Sasanian Context,* Divinations (Philadelphia: University of Pennsylvania Press, 2014), for a helpful review of the history of the scholarship to date. A representative but by no means exhaustive list includes the following: Geoffrey Herman, "Ahasuerus, the Former Stable-Master of Belshazzar, and the Wicked Alexander of Macedon: Two Parallels between the Babylonian Talmud and Persian Sources," *AJS Review* 29 (2005): 283–97; Yaakov Elman, "Middle Persian Culture and Babylonian Sages: Accommodation and Resistance in the Shaping of Rabbinic Legal Tradition," in *The Cambridge Companion to the Talmud and Rabbinic Literature,* ed. Martin Jaffee and Charlotte Elisheva Fonrobert, Cambridge Companions to Religion (Cambridge: Cambridge University Press, 2007), 165–97; Reuven Kiperwasser and Dan Shapira, "Irano-Talmudica I—The Three-legged Ass and 'Ridyā' in B. Ta'anith: Some Observations about Mythic Hydrology in the Babylonian Talmud and in Ancient Iran," *AJS Review* 32 (2008): 101–16; Jeffrey L. Rubenstein, "King Herod in Ardashir's Court: The Rabbinic Story of Herod (B. Bava Batra 3b-4a) in Light of Persian Sources," *AJS Review* 38 (2014): 249–74. For an assessment of Irano-Talmudica and other efforts to contextualize the Bavli, see Robert Brody, "Irano-Talmudica: The New Parallelomania?" *JQR* 106 (2016): 209–32; Shai Secunda, "'This, but Also That': Historical, Methodological, and Theoretical Reflections on Irano-Talmudica," *JQR* 106 (2016): 233–41; Richard Kalmin, "The Bavli, the Roman East, and Mesopotamian Christianity," *JQR* 106 (2016): 242–47; and Simcha Gross, "Irano-Talmudica and Beyond: Next Steps in the Contextualization of the Babylonian Talmud," *JQR* 106 (2016): 248–55.

2. See Richard Kalmin, *Migrating Tales: The Talmud's Narratives and Their Historical Context* (Berkeley: University of California Press, 2014) for the use of a wide array of parallels. For Hellenism, see Daniel Boyarin, *Socrates and the Fat Rabbis* (Chicago: University of Chicago Press, 2009) and Richard Kalmin, *Jewish Babylonia between Persia and Roman Palestine* (New York: Oxford University Press, 2006).

Recent scholarship of the Bavli's historical context has, to a lesser extent, also looked to Syriac Christian institutions and sources.[3] Syriac Christians and their texts offer a potentially rich set of *comparanda* for the study of the Babylonian rabbis and the Bavli. They lived at the same time and in the same place as the Babylonian rabbis and produced a large and diverse corpus of written material. As a nondominant group living in the Sasanian Empire, Syriac Christians may highlight issues that were faced and experiences that were shared by the similarly situated Babylonian Jews.[4]

This article will study one extended rabbinic narrative—the story of Rabba bar Naḥmani in b. B. Meṣ. 86a—in light of Syriac texts. Although the Babylonian Talmud contains many stories about Palestinian rabbis who were persecuted and ultimately killed by the Roman Empire, the story of Rabba bar Naḥmani is the only account in the Bavli of a Babylo-

3. For institutions, striking parallels have been noted between rabbinic and Syriac academies. see Isaiah Gafni, "Nestorian Literature as a Source for the History of the Babylonian *Yeshivot*" [Hebrew], *Tarbiṣ* 51 (1982): 567–76; Adam H. Becker, "The Comparative Study of 'Scholasticism' in Late Antique Mesopotamia: Rabbis and East Syrians," *AJS Review* 34 (2010): 91–113; idem, "Bringing the Heavenly Academy Down to Earth: Approaches to the Imagery of Divine Pedagogy in the East-Syrian Tradition," in *Heavenly Realms and Earthly Realities in Late Antique Religions*, ed. Ra'anan S. Boustan and Annette Yoshiko Reed (Cambridge: Cambridge University Press, 2004), 174–91. Scholars of the Bavli have accepted and regularly rely on this comparison; see, e.g., Jeffrey L. Rubenstein, *The Culture of the Babylonian Talmud* (Baltimore: Johns Hopkins University Press, 2007), 35–37; Kalmin, *Jewish Babylonia*, 3–4; Daniel Boyarin, "Hellenism in Jewish Babylonia," in Jaffee and Fonrobert, *Cambridge Companion to the Talmud and Rabbinic Literature*, 336–63. For a comparison of the exilarch with the catholicos, see Geoffrey Herman, *A Prince without a Kingdom: The Exilarch in the Sasanian Era*, TSAJ 150 (Tübingen: Mohr Siebeck, 2012), 19–20. For sources, see Jeffrey L. Rubenstein, "A Rabbinic Translation of Relics," in *Ambiguities, Complexities and Half-Forgotten Adversaries: Crossing Boundaries in Ancient Judaism and Early Christianity*, ed. Kimberly Stratton and Andrea Lieber (forthcoming); Yakir Paz and Tzahi Weiss, "From Encoding to Decoding: The AṬBḤ of R. Hiyya in Light of a Syriac, Greek and Coptic Cipher," *JNES* 74 (2015): 45–65; Naomi Koltun-Fromm, *Hermeneutics of Holiness: Ancient Jewish and Christian Notions of Sexuality and Religious Community* (Oxford: Oxford University Press, 2010); Reuven Kiperwasser and Serge Ruzer, "Zoroastrian Proselytes in Rabbinic and Syriac Christian Narratives: Orality-Related Markers of Cultural Identity" *HR* 51 (2011): 197–218; eidem, "To Convert a Persian and Teach Him the Holy Scriptures: A Zoroastrian Proselyte in Rabbinic and Syriac Christian Narratives," in *Jews, Christians, and Zoroastrians: Religious Dynamics in a Sasanian Context*, ed. Geoffrey Herman, Judaism in Context (Piscataway, NJ: Gorgias Press, 2014), 91–127; Michal Bar-Asher Siegal, *Early Christian Monastic Literature and the Babylonian Talmud* (New York: Cambridge University Press, 2013). For an early and influential contribution, see Shlomo Naeh, "Freedom and Celibacy: A Talmudic Variation on Tales of Temptation and Fall in Genesis and Its Syriac Background," in *The Book of Genesis in Jewish and Oriental Christian Interpretation*, ed. Judith Frishman and Lucas Van Rompay, Traditio exegetica Graeca 5 (Leuven: Peeters, 1997), 73–89.

4. See Gross, "Irano-Talmudica and Beyond." For the use of "nondominant group" rather than "minority," see Adam Becker, "Political Theology and Religious Diversity in Sasanian Iran," in Herman, *Jews, Christians, and Zoroastrians*, 24–25.

nian rabbi in a confrontation with the Sasanian Empire that ultimately leads to his death.[5]

I will argue that this text is best understood in light of the "corpus" of Syriac martyrological texts known as the Acts of the Persian Martyrs, or the Persian Martyr Acts (PMA).[6] Many of these texts describe the martyrdom of usually prominent Christian converts from Zoroastrianism. These texts were composed throughout the Sasanian and even post-Sasanian periods, but the stories are set in the Sasanian Empire, often in the same time and place in which the Babylonian rabbis flourished.[7] Despite the obvious potential for these sources to cast light on "martyrdom" narratives in the Bavli, scholars have tended to draw comparisons to the Bavli from Western Christian martyr acts, disregarding that these texts were composed in entirely different imperial contexts.[8]

5. Robert Brody, "Judaism in the Sasanian Empire: A Case Study in Religious Coexistence," in *Irano-Judaica* II, ed. Shaul Shaked and Amnon Netzer (Jerusalem: Ben-Zvi, 1990), 52–62. See also Richard Kalmin, "Sasanian Persian Persecution of the Jews: A Reconsideration of the Evidence," *Irano-Judaica* VI (2008), 87–96. Alyssa M. Gray ("A Contribution to the Study of Martyrdom and Identity in the Palestinian Talmud," *JJS* 54 [2003]: 242–72, esp. 249) argues that in Palestinian rabbinic literature there are only stories of the martyrdoms of Tannaim, not of Palestinian Amoraim.

6. For a more in-depth look at how this corpus was formed, see Adam Becker, "The Invention of the Persian Martyr Acts," in *Proceedings of the Seventh North American Syriac Symposium*, ed. Aaron M. Butts and Robin D. Young (Washington, DC: Catholic University of America Press, forthcoming). For the creation of a single Persian Martyr Act, see in the same volume Simcha Gross, "The Sources of the *History of ʿAbdā damšiḥā* and the Creation of the Persian Martyr Acts."

7. For the former, see Becker, "Invention of the Persian Martyr Acts." For the latter, see Christian Sahner, "Old Martyrs, New Martyrs, and the Coming of Islam: Writing Hagiography after the Conquests," in *Cultures in Motion: Studies in the Medieval and Early Modern Periods*, ed. Adam Izdebski and Damian Jasiński (Krakow: Jagiellonian University Press, 2014), 89–112.

8. Indeed, they also offer a crucial corrective to the widespread and problematic contextualization of the Bavli through Christian sources from the Roman Empire, which shared neither chronological nor geographic proximity with the Babylonian rabbis. See Daniel Boyarin, *Dying for God: Martyrdom and the Making of Christianity and Judaism*, Figurae (Stanford, CA: Stanford University Press, 1999); idem, *Border Lines: The Partition of Judaeo-Christianity*, Divinations (Philadelphia: University of Pennsylvania Press, 2004); Ra'anan S. Boustan, *From Martyr to Mystic: Rabbinic Martyrology and the Making of Merkavah Mysticism*, TSAJ 112 (Tübingen: Mohr Siebeck, 2005). For a critique of the uncritical use of Western sources for the study of the Bavli, see Megan H. Williams, "No More Clever Titles: Observations on Some Recent Studies of Jewish–Christian Relations in the Roman World," *JQR* 99 (2009): 37–55, esp. 53–54, and Adam Becker, "Positing a 'Cultural Relationship' between Plato and the Babylonian Talmud: Daniel Boyarin's *Socrates and the Fat Rabbis* (2009)," *JQR* 101 (2011): 255–69. Peter Schäfer (*Jesus in the Talmud* [Princeton, NJ: Princeton University Press, 2007], 115–22) points to generic features of the PMA with which, he assumes but does not prove, Jews in Babylonia may have been familiar. Exceptions include Geoffrey Herman, "'Bury My Coffin Deep! Zoroastrian Exhumation in Jewish and Christian Sources," in *Tiferet LeYisrael: Jubilee Volume in Honor of Israel Francus*, ed. Joel Roth, Yaacov Francus, and Menahem Schmelzer

The PMA are not simply stories valorizing saints or providing a historical account of events; rather, they are ideological works reacting to life in the Sasanian Empire.[9] Whereas older scholarship tended to focus on gauging the historicity of the PMA, recent scholarship, following the approach of scholars of Western Christian and Jewish martyrdoms,[10] assumes that these martyrdom accounts are largely works of literature rather than of history,[11] whose purpose was to negotiate issues of identity for Syriac Christians within the Sasanian Empire.[12] These studies high-

---

(New York: Jewish Theological Seminary, 2010), 31–59, and Jeffrey Rubenstein's contribution in this volume.

9. See the helpful schema in Adam Becker, "Martyrdom, Religious Difference, and 'Fear' as a Category of Piety in the Sasanian Empire: The Case of the *Martyrdom of Gregory* and the *Martyrdom of Yazdpaneh*," *Journal of Late Antiquity* 2 (2009): 300–336.

10. Tessa Rajak, "Dying for the Law: The Martyrs Portrait in Jewish-Greek Literature," in *Portraits: Biographical Representation in the Greek and Latin Literature of the Roman Empire*, ed. M. J. Edwards and Simon Swain (Oxford: Oxford University Press, 1997), 39–67; Elizabeth Castelli, *Martyrdom and Memory: Early Christian Culture Making*, Gender, Theory, Religion (New York: Columbia University Press, 2004); Candida R. Moss, *The Other Christs: Imitating Jesus in Ancient Christian Ideologies of Martyrdom* (New York: Oxford University Press, 2010); See also the collection *More than a Memory: The Discourse of Martyrdom and the Construction of Christian Identity in the History of Christianity*, ed. Johan Leemans, Annua nuntia Lovaniensia 51 (Leuven: Peeters, 2005). Boyarin puts the general shift in methodology pithily: "Being killed is an event. Martyrdom is a literary form, a genre" (*Dying for God*, 116).

11. Sebastian Brock famously argues that Christians in the Sasanian Empire were persecuted because they were viewed as a potential fifth column, a sentiment articulated by Sasanian shahs in a number of martyrdoms ("Christians in the Sasanian Empire: A Case of Divided Loyalties," in *Religion and National Identity: Papers Read at the Nineteenth Summer Meeting and the Twentieth Winter Meeting of the Ecclesiastical History Society*, ed. Stuart Mews, Studies in Church History 18 [Oxford: Oxford University Press, 1982], 1–19). This view is also found in Timothy D. Barnes, "Constantine and the Christians of Persia," *JRS* 75 (1985): 126–36. Kyle Smith has critiqued this perspective as a later historiographical construct rather than a reflection of the actual cause of a persecution, whatever it may have been ("Constantine and Judah the Maccabee: History and Memory in the Acts of the Persian Martyrs," *Journal of the Canadian Society for Syriac Studies* 12 [2012]: 16–33; and idem, *Constantine and the Captive Christians of Persia: Martyrdom and Religious Identity in Late Antiquity*, Transformation of the Classical Heritage 57 [Berkeley: University of California Press, 2016]). Similarly, for persecution under Yazdgird I, Lucas Van Rompay challenges the idea, derived from a few PMA and their Western parallels, that Christians were killed because some of them violently attacked magi and fire temples. See his "Impetuous Martyrs? The Situation of the Persian Christians in the Last Years of Yazdgard I (419–20)," in *Martyrium in Multidisciplinary Perspective: Memorial Louis Reekmans*, ed. Mathijs Lamberigts and Peter van Deun, BETL 117 (Leuven: Leuven University Press, 1995), 363–75. Geoffrey Herman has even argued that there may never have been a persecution under Yazdgard I at all ("The Last Years of Yazdgird I and the Christians" in Herman, *Jews, Christians, and Zoroastrians*, 67–90).

12. See Joel Thomas Walker, *The Legend of Mar Qardagh: Narrative and Christian Heroism in Late Antique Iraq*, Transformation of the Classical Heritage 40 (Berkeley: University of California Press, 2006); Becker, "Martyrdom, Religious Difference"; Richard E. Payne, *A State of Mixture: Christians, Zoroastrians, and Iranian Political Culture in Late Antiquity*, Transformation of the Classical Heritage 56 (Oakland: University of California Press, 2015); Philip Wood,

light the constructed nature of narratives of persecution. Indeed, different writers at different times may take the same events and construct them differently.[13]

The PMA, and the scholarship of martyrdom discourse more generally, both encourage us to question the historicity of our sources and allow us to ask more incisive questions about the rabbinic construction of history and memory, particularly as they relate to the Sasanian Empire. Did Babylonian Jews construct, or avoid constructing, narratives of persecution about life in the Sasanian Empire? Did they actively erase reports of persecution? What do their narratives about persecution—or the lack thereof—attempt to communicate?[14] Lastly, given that both the rabbis and Syriac Christians are living under the Sasanian Empire, do these groups construct different narratives, and if so, why? Do they show familiarity with one another's reflections on the subject?

Based on the story of Rabba bar Naḥmani in b. B. Meṣ. 86a, I argue that Babylonian rabbis show awareness of PMA material and engage with it as a means of expressing their own thoughts about their relationship with and position in relation to the Sasanian Empire. This story's composer makes use of the narrative of the most famous Persian Martyr, Simeon bar Ṣabbaʿe, as well as other PMA but reverses them in order to endorse the *avoidance* of confrontation with the Sasanian Empire and consequent martyrdom. The composer similarly invokes but reverses the martyrdom of R. Akiva as described elsewhere in the Bavli. In crafting a narrative that reverses other literary martyrdom accounts, the composer also undermines an earlier report in the Bavli about the persecution of a rabbi, in effect erasing it. The simultaneous use of and distancing from the PMA suggests that the rabbis recognized the broad structural similarity between their situation and the situation of Syriac Christians as non-dominant groups in the Sasanian Empire, with important implications for future avenues of research.

Chronicle of Seert: Christian Historical Imagination in Late Antique Iraq (Oxford: Oxford University Press, 2013), 31–65.

13. Thus, with regard to the Church of the East, Philip Wood has recently noted that, on the one hand, persecution was an important marker of identity for the "church of the Sasanian empire," while later Syriac hagiographers often selected "more neutral representations of the martyrs as ideal priests and passive victims," and did so because it "suited the agenda of later catholicoi, who wished to pursue peaceful relations with the shah and stress their own authority over their coreligionists" (Wood, *Chronicle of Seert*, 1–2 and 65, respectively).

14. For a similar set of questions concerning Jews of the medieval period, see Menahem Ben-Sasson, "Remembrance and Oblivion of Religious Persecutions: On Sanctifying the Name of God (Qiddush ha-Shem) in Christian and Islamic Countries during the Middle Ages," in *Jews, Christians, and Muslims in Medieval and Early Modern Times: A Festschrift in Honor of Mark R. Cohen*, ed. Arnold E. Franklin, Roxani Eleni Margariti, Marina Rustow, and Uriel Simonsohn, Christians and Jews in Muslim Societies 2 (Leiden: Brill, 2014), 169–94.

I. The Story of Rabba bar Naḥmani (b. Baba Meṣiʿa 86a):[15]

A. Rav Kahana[16] said: Ḥama, the son of the daughter of Ḥassa, related to me that Rabba bar Naḥmani died on account of persecution.	א׳ רב כהנא אישתעי ליה חמא בר ברתיה דחסא דרבה בר נחמני אגב שמדה נח נפשיה
B. They denounced[17] him before the government. They [the slanderers] said: There is a man among the Jews who keeps back twelve thousand[18] Jews from the payment of the royal poll tax[19] one month in summer and one in winter.[20]	אכלו ביה קורצא בי מלכא אמרו איכא חד גברא מיהודאי דקא מבטל תריסר אלפי גברא מישר׳ ירחא בקייטא וירחא בסיתוו׳ מכרגא

15. I present the text according to MS Vatican 115 because it is complete and relatively clear. Few of the differences in the manuscripts are important for my arguments; those that are relevant will be noted.

16. MS Florence has "Ravina," though Rav Kahana is far more appropriate, as will become clear below. This confusion may have been caused by the fact that the famous statement that Rav Ashi and Ravina were the "end of *hora'ah*" immediately precedes this story.

17. Michael Sokoloff, *A Dictionary of Jewish Babylonian Aramaic* (Ramat-Gan: Bar Ilan University Press; Baltimore: Johns Hopkins University Press, 2002), 1003 (hereafter *DJBA*) translates the idiom √ʾkl + *qurṣā* as "to inform on," which would seem to imply that the content of the report is true (as is the case in b. Ber. 58a). In contrast, Stephen A. Kaufman (*The Akkadian Influences on Aramaic*, Assyriological Studies 19 [Chicago: The University of Chicago Press, 1974], 63) translates the idiom as "to slander," as does Michael Sokoloff (*A Syriac Lexicon* [Winona Lake, IN: Eisenbrauns; Piscataway, NJ: Gorgias Press, 2009], 41), who defines the expression as "to accuse falsely, slander." Of course, this expression also appears in Dan 3:8, where the denunciation is indeed true. Nevertheless, the Akkadian idiom *akālu karṣī* (*Chicago Assyrian Dictionary* A1:255–56), as well as its derivatives in Aramaic, means to "denounce," regardless of whether the accusation is true. Thus, the validity of the accusation can only be determined from the context.

18. Manuscripts Florence, Munich, Vatican 117 and the "Spanish" version of Iggeret Rav Sherira Gaon have "thirteen thousand," whereas all the other manuscripts and the "French" version of the Iggeret have twelve thousand. For the Iggeret, see B. M Lewin, *The Epistle of Rav Sherira Gaon* [Hebrew] (Haifa, 1921), 86–87. For the general preference of the so called French over the Spanish version, see Robert Brody, "The Epistle of Sherira Gaon," in *Rabbinic Texts and the History of Late-Roman Palestine*, ed. Martin Goodman and Philip Alexander, Proceedings of the British Academy 165 (Oxford: Oxford University Press, 2010), 253–64.

19. Only Vilna has דמלכא. All the other manuscripts have מכרגא without the genitive qualifier.

20. Most commentators understand this to be a reference to the two study, or *kallah*, months (Adar and Elul), as already noted by Sherira Gaon, *Iggeret*, ed. Lewin, 87. He was followed by Aharon Oppenheimer, *Babylonia Judaica in the Talmudic Period*, Beihefte zum Tübinger Atlas des Vorderen Orients, Reihe B, Geisteswissenschaften 47 (Wiesbaden: Reichert, 1983), 108; and Jacob Neusner, *The Age of Shapur II*, vol. 4 of *A History of the Jews in Babylonia*, 5 vols., StPB 9, 11, 12, 14, 15 (Leiden: Brill, 1965–1970), 42. For more on these months, see Isaiah Gafni, *The Jews of Talmudic Babylonia: A Social and Cultural History* [Hebrew] (Jerusalem, 1990), 131–44; and David M. Goodblatt, *Rabbinic Instruction in Sasanian Babylonia*, SJLA 9 (Leiden: Brill, 1975), 155-70. Goodblatt attempts to problematize this identification, as nowhere in the story does it say that the students were learning Torah, or even away from their homes

They sent a royal officer [frēstaqa] after him, but did not find him. He [Rabba] fled from Pumbedita to Ṣarifa dʿayna, and from Ṣarifa dʿayna to Apadna d-shīzha, and from Apadna d-shīzha to Agama.[21]

שדרו פריסתקא דמלכא אבתריה ולא אשכחוה ערק מפומבדיתא לצריפא דעיינא ומצריפא דעיינא לאפדנא דשיזהא ומאפדנ׳ דשיזהא לאגמא

C. The frēstaqa chanced upon the same inn in which Rabba bar Naḥmani was [hiding].
They placed a tray before him [the frēstaqa], gave him two glasses, and then removed the tray from before him; [consequently] his face was turned backwards. They [the inn attendants] said to him [Rabba], "What should we do, he is a royal officer?!" [Rabba] said, "Bring him the tray again and give him another cup to drink, then remove the tray, so that he recover." They did so, and he recovered. [The frēstaqa] said "I know that the man whom I seek is here." He searched for and found him. He said, "I will depart from here; but (even) if they kill that man [i.e. me], I will not disclose [your whereabouts]; but if they torture that man, I will disclose your whereabouts]."

איקלע ההוא פריסתקא לההוא אושפיזא דהוה רבה בר נחמני קריבו ליה תכא קמיה והבו ליה תרי כסי ודלויה לתכא מיקמיה הדר פרצופיה לאחוריה אמרו ליה מאי נעביד גברא דמלכא הוא א׳ זילו קריבו לתכא מיקמיה ואשקיוה חד כסא ודליוה לתכא מקמיה דמיתסי ועבדו ליה הכי ואיתסי א׳ מידע ידענא דגברא דקא בעינא הכא הוה בחיש[22] בתריה ואשכחיה א׳ מיזל אזילנ׳ מיהו אי מקטל קטלי לההוא גברא לא מגלינא אי נגודי מנגדי ליה לההוא גברא מגלינא

("The Poll Tax in Sasanian Babylonia: The Talmudic Evidence," *Journal of the Economic and Social History of the Orient* 22 [1979]: 273). However, as this is a story, the slanderers are reporting to the palace, and a detailed account of Jewish institutional practices would not be fitting. What's more, the parallels to this section elsewhere in the Bavli that will be discussed below clearly show that the composers had a rabbinic academy in mind. Alternatively, Rashi and others following him argue that the two months are the times of major festivals in the fall in the month of Tishre and in the spring in the month of Nissan. Goodblatt himself notes that there may be corroborating evidence for the idea that taxes were collected on festivals twice a year at the spring and fall festivals.

21. For a discussion of these locations, see Jacob Obermeyer, *Die Landschaft Babylonien im Zeitalter des Talmuds und des Gaonats: Geographie und Geschichte nach talmudischen, arabischen und andern Quellen*, Schriften der Gesellschaft zur Förderung der Wissenschaft des Judentums 30 (Frankfurt am Main: Kauffmann, 1929), 236–38; and Oppenheimer, *Babylonia Judaica*, 107–9. Due to the fact that in some manuscripts Rabba begins and ends his travels in Pumbedita, Obermeyer argued that this route was circular. Oppenheimer urges some caution here due to the difficulty in identifying all of these places as well as some variation of the names in the manuscripts. In fact, the circular route only appears in the Vilna printed edition, and so is almost certainly not original to the story. In all the manuscripts, however, Rabba flees in the beginning to Agama and flees there again after he is miraculously broken out of jail, which does have a circular nature to it, and adds to the parodic effect of the story, for more on which see below.

22. Some transcriptions of Vatican 115 read כחיש, and of Vatican 117 read נחיש, but the word should read בחיש as it appears in other manuscripts.

D. They brought him [Rabba] before him [the frēstaqa], and he [the frēstaqa] led him into an inner chamber and locked the door upon him [to keep him there as a prisoner]. [Rabba] prayed, whereupon the wall collapsed, and he fled and went to Agama.

אתיוה לקמיה עייליה לאידרונא וטרקא לבבא באנפיה בעי רחמי פרק אשיתא ערק אזל לאגמא

E. There he sat upon the trunk of a [fallen] palm[23] and was studying. He heard they were disputing in the Heavenly Academy: if the bright spot preceded the white hair, he is impure; if the white hair preceded the bright spot, he is pure. If [the order is] in doubt, what [is the ruling]? The Holy One, blessed be He, ruled: he is pure, while the whole Heavenly Academy maintained: he is impure. "Who shall decide it? Rabba bar Naḥmani; for he said, 'I am pre-eminent in the laws of leprosy; I am pre-eminent in tents.'" A messenger was sent for him, but the Angel of Death could not approach him, because his mouth did not cease reciting [even for a moment]. In the meantime, a wind blew and made a noise in the reeds. He thought it was a troop of horsemen. He said, "Let that man [i.e. me] die and not be delivered into the hands of the kingdom." As he was dying, he exclaimed, "Pure, pure!!" [whereupon] a heavenly voice went out [from heaven] and said, "Happy are you, Rabba bar Naḥmani, that your body is pure and your soul has departed in purity!"

הוה יתיב איגרדא דדיקלא וקא גריס שמע דקא מיפלגי במתיבתא דרקיעא אם בהרת קדמה לשער לבן טמא אם שער לבן קדמה לבהרת טהור ספק מאי הקב"ה א' טהור וכולהו מתיב[ת]א[24] דרקיעא אמרי טמא אמרו מאן נוכח נוכח רבה בר נחמני דא' רבה בר נחמני אני יחיד בנגעים אני יחיד באהולות[25] שדר לשליח[26] בתריה לא הוה קא מצי מלאך המות למקרבא ליה מדלא הוה שתיק פומיה מגירסא אדהכי נשא זיקא ואווש[27] ביני קני סבר גונדא[28] דפרשי הוו א' תינח נפשיה ההוא גברא ולא נמסר בידא דמלכותא כי הוה קא נח נפשיה א' טהור טהור יצתה בת קול ואמרה אשריך רבה בר נחמני שגופך טהור ויצתה נשמתך בטהרה

23. The only other place "the trunk of a palm" appears is in b. Pesaḥ. 111b, the same *sugya* containing the *zugot* scene (see the appendix).

24. The manuscript reads מתיבא.

25. In Hamburg 165 and Philadelphia—University of Pennsylvania, 90, Rabba bar Naḥmani does not make this boast himself. The meaning of the word יחיד was understood by Yaakov Sussman to mean that Rabba was the only rabbi to interpret these laws in a given manner (*Sugyot bavliot lasedarim zera'im vetohorot* [PhD diss., The Hebrew University in Jerusalem, 1969], 70 n. 115). This interpretation, however, makes it difficult to explain why Rabba in particular would be called to the Heavenly Academy. Therefore, Mira Balberg and Moulie Vidas argue that in fact it means the he is "unmatched" in his knowledge of these areas of rabbinic knowledge ("Impure Scholasticism: The Study of Purity Laws and Rabbinic Self-Criticism in the Babylonian Talmud," *Prooftexts* 32 [2012]: 328).

26. The word לא appears next in the manuscript; however, this is clearly due to dittography with what follows.

27. This is a Middle Persian loanword, from *āwāz,* meaning "to make a sound." See Sokoloff, *DJBA,* 86–87.

28. From Middle Persian *gund.* See Sokoloff, DJBA, 269–70.

A missive fell from Heaven in Pumbedita of Abaye[29] [upon which was written,] "Rabba bar Naḥmani has been summoned to the Heavenly Academy."

נפל פיתקא מרקיעא בפומבדיתא דאביי רבה בר נחמני נתבקש בישיבה של מעלה

F. So Abaye and Rabba and all the scholars went forth to attend him [at his burial], but they did not know his whereabouts. They went to Agama and saw birds which were standing and providing shade.[30] They said "This proves that he is there." They bewailed him for three days and three nights. They wanted to leave, but a missive fell [from Heaven, saying], "He who leaves shall be under a ban." So they bewailed him for seven days, and [then] a [second] missive fell [from Heaven], "Return in peace to your homes."

נפקי אביי ורבא וכולהו רבנן לאיעסוקי ביה ולא הוו ידעי דוכתיה אזלו לאגמא חזי ציפורי דהוו מטללי וקיומי אמרי ש"מ התם הוא ספדוה תלתא יומי ותלתא לילוותא בעו למיפרש נפל פיתקא כל הפורש יהא בנידוי ספדוה שבעא יומי נפל פיתקא לכו לבתיכם לשלום

G. On the day that he died a storm lifted an Arab, while riding a camel, and transported him from one bank of the River Pana to the other. He said, "[On account of what] is this?" They answered him, "Rabba bar Naḥmani has died." He exclaimed before Him, "You are the sovereign of the universe, and Rabba bar Naḥmani too is yours. Why are you destroying it [the world]?" [Thereupon] the storm subsided.

ההוא יומא דנח נפשיה דלי זעפא ודלייה לההוא טייעא כי רכיב גמלא מהאי גיסא דנהר פנא ושדייה בהך גיסא א' מאי האי אמרן ליה נח נפשיה דרבה בר נחמני אמר לפניו רבונו[31] של עולם אתה ורבה בר נחמני דידך עלמא אמאי קא מחרבת ליה נח זעפא[32]

29. Most manuscripts do not have Abaye, and it is not quite clear what "the Pumbedita of Abaye" even means, though Florence II-I-8 may be correcting this by saying that the note fell "upon the head/ארישא of Abaye."

30. So Sokoloff, *DJBA*, 505.

31. Corrected from רבינו in the manuscript.

32. Boyarin treats the anecdote that follows these lines as another coda to the story of Rabba bar Naḥmani (*Socrates and the Fat Rabbis*, 228–29). However, the wording of what follows, including the introduction of entirely different characters, makes it clear that it is an entirely separate story.

This story, much like the PMA, was assumed by earlier scholars to be an accurate account of actual events.[33] These scholars tended to employ a "kernel of history" approach to the text, separating and dismissing the miraculous elements of the story from what they considered to be its core, historically reliable story line. Their evaluation of the fundamental historicity of the story was largely based on the opening report about Rabba's death (A).[34]

According to the opening report (A), a fourth-generation Amora (R. Ḥama) informs another (Rav Kahana) that a third-generation Amora (Rabba bar Naḥmani) was among the victims of an ongoing (אנג) religious persecution (שמדא/ה).[35]

Problems arise, however, when we pair this account with the story that immediately follows (B–G). Elsewhere in rabbinic texts, a *shmad* refers to a sustained period of religious persecution.[36] The story that follows, however, does not seem to describe a broad persecution but rather the

33. Heinrich Graetz, *Geschichte der Juden von den ältesten Zeiten bis auf die Gegenwart* (Leipzig, 1908), 4:323–24, translated in Bella Löwy, *History of the Jews* (London, 1891), 2:580–81; Moshe Beer, "Concerning the Deposal of Rabba bar Naḥmani from the Headship of the Academy: A Chapter in the History of the Relationship between the Sages and the Exilarchs" [Hebrew], *Tarbiṣ* 33 (1964): 349–57. Ephraim Urbach critiqued Beer in "Concerning Historical Insight into the Account of Rabba bar Naḥmani's Death," *Tarbiṣ* 34 (1965): 156–61. Beer made corrections to his earlier article and incorporated responses to some of Urbach's critiques in *The Babylonian Exilarchate* (Tel Aviv: Devir, 1970), 210–24. Neusner gives a helpful summary and adjudication of this debate (*Age of Shapur II*, 100–102). All of these scholars remove the miraculous details of the story and either essentially retell it (Graetz), or supply an elaborate (and unsubstantiated) background to explain the story (Beer). Neusner (41–42) argues that, due to the miracles and supernatural details that appear throughout the story, it "lays no claim whatever to concrete historical reliability" but continues with a "kernel of history" approach to the story. See the fuller discussion of Neusner's remarks below.

34. Scholars who have discussed this story have attempted to date it based on the initial report, which they believed was connected to the story that followed. Beer (*Babylonian Exilarchate*, 99 n. 19 and 214) tries to assign a date to the death of Rabba by looking at other sources in the Bavli (b. Mo'ed Qaṭ. 28a), as well as Sherira's *Epistle* and *Seder Olam Zuta* (= *SOZ*) and concludes that it was either in 320 or 334 CE. He was followed by Goodblatt, "Poll Tax in Sasanian Babylonia," 272. This provides the *terminus a quo* for the events described in the story. Beer (214–15) argues that the *terminus ante quem* is provided by the Kahana who transmits the story, who, he argues, cannot be either of the two sages by that name who precede Rabba, nor the student of Rabba by that name, because he would have known how his master died without having to cite Ḥama. Of course, this argument is not very convincing, and the Kahana here may indeed be Rabba's student. Goodblatt and Beer conclude that the Kahana here is either the disciple of Rava (d. 352) and teacher of Rav Ashi or the Kahana who was a contemporary of Rav Ashi (d. 424). Therefore the *terminus ante quem*, according to them, would be sometime between 350 and 425 CE.

35. It should also be noted that Rabba is said to have died at age forty in b. Roš Haš. 18a, as well as in b. Mo'ed Qaṭ. 28a, though there it seems that his early death, as well as other tragedies that befell him during life, were due to chance, not to a misdeed.

36. For a representative but not exhaustive list, see b. Sanh. 14a, b. Roš Haš. 18b, and b. Beṣah 4b.

specific efforts to apprehend a particular rabbi. Moreover, the pursuit is not the product of a *religious* persecution; Rabba is not being pursued for his beliefs, rituals, or identity but rather for having been complicit in massive tax evasion.[37] Indeed, rather than killed by the empire, Rabba dies at the hands of God, and by his own request. Thus, this is not a story of persecution, unless the word *shmad* is used differently here than elsewhere in rabbinic literature.[38]

Taken on its own, however, this opening report of Rabba's death (A) simply reports that Rabba was one casualty in a larger period of persecution. The report fits quite well in both substance and style with formulations in later geonic chronographies, in which rabbis are said to die during a period of persecution, using either Hebrew *shmad* or Aramaic *shmada*.[39]

Since the opening report in b. B. Meṣ. 86a is stylistically and substan-

---

37. Thus, Sokoloff (*DJBA*, 78 and 1155) continues to translate *shmada* as a "religious persecution," despite the fact that this translation does not accurately describe what happens in the ensuing story.

38. Indeed, the use of this word was apparently so problematic for Sherira Gaon that he felt compelled to alter it (Lewin, *Iggeret*, 87). Sherira thus changes the word in the report to a שמדא דאורייתא, a persecution against the Torah, and removes the reference to כרגא (דמלכא), or "poll tax" entirely. Through this slight emendation, Sherira Gaon makes it seem as if the persecution was directed against Rabba for hosting mass Torah study sessions twice a year. All of the manuscripts, however, explicitly mention the כרגא/poll tax. See Boyarin, who also is troubled by the mention of persecution in the introduction and the story that follows (*Socrates and the Fat Rabbis*, 226–27).

39. For example, Lewin, *Iggeret*, 90–97. Similarly, *SOZ* reports a period of persecution around the time of Rabba's death, which is directed against "the Jews" in general, and not against any individual rabbi. *SOZ* clearly uses the term to describe a broadly based persecution that may well have targeted both Jews and Jewish practices but is clearly not directed at only a single rabbinic miscreant. The persecution is dated to 318 CE ("248 years to the destruction of the Temple") according to MS de Rossi 541 as published by Solomon Schechter, "Seder Olam Suta," *MGWJ* 39 (1895): 27, but 315 CE ("245 years to the destruction of the Temple") according to MS Paris 1279 and MS Oxford Bodl. Heb. E8 in Felix Lazarus, *Die Häupter der Vertriebenen: Beiträge zu einer Geschichte der Exilsführsten in Babylonien unter den Arsakiden und Sassaniden* (Frankfurt am Main: H. L. Brönner, 1890), 164. For the latter manuscript, see also Adolf Neubauer, *Mediaeval Jewish Chronicles and Chronological Notes*, 2 vols., Anecdota oxoniensia, Semitic Series 4, 6(Oxford; Clarendon, 1895), 2:72. The difference between these two dates is simply due to a common confusion between a ח and ה. See, however, Neusner, *Age of Shapur II*, 101, who inexplicably says *SOZ* refers to 313. See Herman, *Prince without a Kingdom*, 366–69, for a discussion of the various manuscripts and editions of *SOZ*. I do not mean to suggest that the opening report is referring to the same period of persecution that appears in *SOZ*, or to suggest that *SOZ* is referring to actual events that took place. I mean only to highlight the manner in which periods of persecution are usually reported. Urbach, however, does connect the death of Rabba with the persecution reported in *SOZ* ("Concerning Historical Insight into the Account of Rabba bar Naḥmani's Death," 156). See also Geo Widengren, "The Status of the Jews in the Sassanian Empire," *Iranica Antiqua* 1 (1961): 132–38. Gafni cites another text from the Bavli that seems to be an early manifestation of geonic chronographies ("On the Talmudic Chronology in the Iggeret Rav Sherira Gaon," *Zion* 52 [1987]: 8 and n. 29).

tively unproblematic except when paired with the following story, it is likely that the story is a later elaboration or etiology added to a laconic earlier tradition about Rabba's death.[40] Moreover, the story that follows the report incorporates many features that clearly postdate the Amoraic period, such as references to large academies and the academic semester system (the two months of *kallah* in which Jews devoted themselves to study) marking it as both later than the fourth-century Amoraim named in the account and as a literary construction.[41] Lastly, the story is remarkable for the sheer number of literary elements that it borrows from other stories, making it almost little more than a pastiche of other Babylonian sources. These considerations cast considerable doubt on the general scholarly consensus that the story is contemporary with the opening account.[42] Instead, this story exhibits all of the tendencies of a later Stammaitic story (fifth to seventh centuries CE), elaborating on the preexisting opening report.[43]

Once it is recognized that the initial account and the subsequent story are not a single unit, their relationship can be better assessed. It becomes clear that the story is not intended to elaborate the opening rabbinic account of Rabba's death but rather to undermine it, by limiting the scope

---

40. This explanation differs from that offered by Boyarin (*Socrates and the Fat Rabbis*, 225) and Inbar Raveh (*Me'at meharbeh: Ma'ase hakhamim—mivnim sifruti'im utefisat olam* [Be'er Sheva: Ben Gurion University Press, 2008], 88–91), who note the tension between the introduction and the rest of the story but treat the two as part of the same story. This structure of an initial report of martyrdom to which a subsequent narrative is added is found among many of the PMA. See Sebastian Brock, review of Gernot Wiessner, *Untersuchungen zur syrischen Literaturgeschichte*, vol. 1, *Zur Märtyrerüberlieferung aus der Christenverfolgung Schapurs II* (Göttingen: Vandenhoeck & Ruprecht, 1967) *JTS* 19 (1968): 300–309.

41. See Rubenstein, *Culture of the Babylonian Talmud*, 16–23.

42. Goodblatt states explicitly that he treats the original notice, with the tradents, and the story not as earlier piece and expansion, respectively, but as part of the report by Ḥama to Kahana ("Poll Tax in Sasanian Babylonia," 272). Neusner says, "if the story is composite, however, I cannot discern its segments" (*Age of Shapur II*, 44 n. 1).

43. Shamma Friedman noted the extensive borrowing from Babylonian sources in his "Literary Development and Historicity in the Aggadic Narrative of the Babylonian Talmud: A Study Based upon *B. M.* 83b–86a," in *Community and Culture: Essays in Jewish Studies in Honor of the Ninetieth Anniversary of the Founding of Gratz College, 1895–1985*, ed. Nahum M. Waldman (Philadelphia: Gratz College, 1987), 74 n. 44; and his "The Orthography of the Names Rabba and Rava" [Hebrew], *Sinai* 110 (1992): 156 n. 2. Consequently, he also doubted the historical reliability of the story. I will discuss the extensive borrowings only when relevant to the argument at hand and include a more comprehensive discussion of the parallels in the appendix. For the style of Stammaitic stories more generally, see Jeffrey L. Rubenstein, *Talmudic Stories: Narrative Art, Composition, and Structure* (Baltimore: Johns Hopkins University Press, 1999); idem, *Culture of the Babylonian Talmud*; idem, *Stories of the Babylonian Talmud* (Baltimore: Johns Hopkins University Press, 2010); and idem, "Introduction" and "Criteria for Stammaitic Intervention in Aggada" in *Creation and Composition: The Contribution of the Bavli Redactors (Stammaim) to the Aggada*, ed. Jeffrey L. Rubenstein, TSAJ 114 (Tübingen: Mohr Siebeck, 2005), 1–22 and 417–40.

of the persecution to a single rabbi and by attributing liability to something he, in particular, did. In effect, the attached story serves to erase the period of persecution found in the opening notice. The underlying motive behind this erasure is contained in the story itself, as we will now see.

The Story

The story itself begins with the report that people slandered (אכלו ביה קורצא) Rabba to the "house of the king" or the "government" (בי מלכא), reporting that he had somehow prevented (מבטל) twelve thousand Jews from paying the poll tax. The government, in response, dispatches a *frēstaqa*, a Persian official of some sort, to the scene (פריסתקא).[44]

The premise for this story is strikingly similar to that of the martyrdom of the contemporaneous and geographically proximate catholicos Simeon bar Ṣabba'e, the most important figure in the PMA.[45]

Simeon's martyrdom is the subject of two Syriac accounts, the earlier Martyrdom of Simeon bar Ṣabbaᶜe (hereafter: Martyrdom) and the later reworked History of Simeon bar Ṣabbaᶜe (hereafter: History).[46] In the Martyrdom, Simeon refuses to collect any taxes from Christians.[47] Simeon's proposition is straightforward: the burden of Christians is spiritual and of

44. From Middle Persian frēstag [*plystk'*]. See D. N. Mackenzie, *A Concise Pahlavi Dictionary* (London: Oxford University Press, 1990), 34; Claudia A. Ciancaglini, *Iranian Loanwords in Syriac*, Beiträge zur Iranistik 28 (Wiesbaden: Reichert, 2008), 240; Desmond Durkin-Meisterernst, *Dictionary of Manichaean Middle Persian and Parthian* (Turnhout: Brepols, 2004), 159–61; Gernot Wiessner thinks it comes from MP frēštak, but the š seems unlikely (*Untersuchungen zur syrischen Literaturgeschichte*, vol. 1, *Zur Märtyrerüberlieferung aus der Christenverfolgung Schapurs II* [Göttingen: Vandenhoeck & Ruprecht, 1967], 183).

45. For a critical edition of the Syriac text with Latin translation, see Michael Kmosko, "S. Simeon bar Ṣabba'e," *Patrología Syriaca* I, ii (Paris, 1907). For a recent English translation, see Kyle Smith, *The Martyrdom and History of Blessed Simeon bar Ṣabba ᶜe*, Persian Martyr Acts in Syriac 3 (Piscataway, NJ: Gorgias Press, 2014).

46. Wiessner (*Zur Mārtyrerüberlieferung*) argues that these two works share a common source, which itself is a composite of two earlier works. However, Kyle Smith challenged this argument, preferring to see the later History as an embellishment of the earlier Martyrdom. See Smith, "Constantine and Judah the Maccabee"; idem, *Constantine and the Captive Christians of Persia*, 110–11; and especially idem, *Martyrdom and History*, xvii–l.

47. In the earlier accounts in the Martyrdom, Simeon's objection to taxation appears to be more theologically based, framed as a choice between the dominion of man and that of Christ. In the later rewriting and reframing in the History, Simeon objects not to taxes in general but rather to a double tax levied for a war effort between Persia and Rome. In this later account, his objection to taxation is therefore more political and is also due to the heavy burden the double tax poses. See discussion in Smith, *Constantine and the Captive Christians of Persia*, 115–16; and Payne, *State of Mixture*, 39–45. In Sozomen, the double tax is meant to compel Christians to renounce Christianity. The tax is embellished further in the *Chronicle of Seert* (ed. Addai Scher, *Histoire Nestorienne* [*Chronique de Séert*] I.1 [Paris: Firmin-Didot, 1908], 300). For a brief discussion of the latter, see Widengren, "Status of the Jews," 151. The

Christ, and they are therefore not to be burdened by the dictates—including the taxes—of earthly kings, an approach that has resonance with similar notions in the New Testament.[48]

> Now the glorious bishop Simeon was strengthened in his Lord and took courage in his God, and he sent word to the king and informed him as follows: "Christ liberated his church through his death, he set his people free through his blood, he relieved those who carry heavy burdens through his passion, he lightened the yoke of the subjugated through his cross [Matt 11:28-29].... Jesus is the king of kings, and we will not put the yoke of your subjugation upon our shoulders. Far be it from us now liberated people to work once more in the service of a man. Our Lord is lord of your lordship, therefore we will not assume upon our head the lordship of our fellow men. Our God is the creator of your gods, and we do not worship his creatures such as you. He commanded us, 'do not acquire gold or silver for your purses' [Matt 10:9], thus we have no gold to give you, nor money to bring to you for taxes. His apostle warned us, 'you were ransomed with a heavy price, so do not become servants of men'" [1 Cor 7:23].[49]

Beyond the similar premises, there are numerous other parallels between the two stories. Both Simeon and Rabba lived and died in the first half of the fourth century, during the reign of Shapur II.[50] Both are reported to

---

reasoning in the later History is different, for which see Smith, *Constantine and the Captive Christians of Persia*, 111–15.

48. It is interesting to compare Simeon's refusal to pay taxes and the "render unto Caesar" passages in the New Testament, specifically Mark 12:13–17, Matt 22:15–22, and Luke 20:20–26. For the range of interpretations of these passages, see Joel Marcus, *Mark: A New Translation with Introduction and Commentary*, 2 vols., AB 27, 27A (New York: Doubleday, 2000, 2009), 2:822–26. Similarly, see the injunction in Rom 13:1–8 to pay taxes. This clearly bothered the composer of the later History, who turns what seems to be a regular tax in the Martyrdom into a double tax and explicitly cites Romans 13 and other passages to support the claim that typically Christians are *commanded* to be loyal subjects and pay taxes, as discussed in n. 44 above. The History is in keeping with what we find in later Syriac sources, for instance Isho'yahb III (Michael Philip Penn, *When Christians First Met Muslims: A Sourcebook of the Earliest Syriac Writings on Islam* [Berkeley: University of California Press, 2015], 36), the catholicos following the Arab conquests, who says, "For the fools do not even discern that we are commanded to give every authority whatever we owe him: that is, to whomever [is owed] the poll tax, the poll tax; to whomever [is owed] tribute, tribute; to whomever [is owed] reverence, reverence; and to whomever [is owed] honor, honor."

49. Smith, *Martyrdom and History*, 16–22.

50. Regarding Simeon, see Smith, *Martyrdom and History*, xx–xxiv, who briefly argues that the dating we find in the Martyrdom and History is typological and not historically accurate. Many earlier articles sought to accurately date Simeon's martyrdom, though Smith's approach is persuasive. The most important articles attempting to date Simeon's martyrdom are the following: Martin J. Higgins, "Date of Martyrdom of Simeon bar Ṣabbaʿe," *Traditio* 11 (1955): 1–17; R. W. Burgess, "The Dates of the Martyrdom of Simeon bar Sabbaʿe," *Analecta Bollandiana* 117 (1999): 9–47; R. Mercier, "The Dates in the Syriac Martyr Acts," *Analecta Bol-*

have died during periods described by the typical word for "persecution" in their respective languages—ܪܕܘܦܝܐ in Syriac, שמד/א in Hebrew/Jewish Babylonian Aramaic. The similar premises, time period, geography, and circumstances of these two stories call for us to read them together.

Due to the shared premise of the two stories, some scholars have gestured to Simeon when discussing Rabba.[51] However, these earlier scholars viewed the stories as historically accurate records and therefore viewed the similarity between them as representing parallel events occurring under similar historical circumstances. By contrast, I will show that the connection between them is one of literary dependence, by which I mean that the composers of the Rabba bar Naḥmani story were aware of and made use of this—and related—PMA.

This explains shared literary features between the stories, features that do not seem to accord with the reality of the time. For example, both Rabba bar Naḥmani and Simeon bar Ṣabba'e are presented as important leaders in their respective communities. In the Bavli, Rabba is depicted as a *rosh yeshiva,* in charge of an enormous academy with thousands of students. He is therefore held responsible for the tax evasion of his students twice a year.[52] Simeon bar Ṣabbaʿe is the catholicos, or head, of the Church of the East. Both stories, therefore, retroject later roles—catholicos and *rosh yeshiva*—into an earlier period in which these titles and institutions did not yet exist as such.[53] Both Simeon and Rabba are pursued by the Sasa-

---

landiana 117 (1999): 47–66. All argue that the martyrdom of Simeon and the outbreak of the "great massacre" took place in 344 CE. See also Sacha Stern, "Near Eastern Lunar Calendars in the Syriac Martyr Acts," *Le Muséon* 117 (2004): 447–72. Regarding scholarly attempts to date the supposed martyrdom of Rabba, see n. 32 above.

51. Neusner, *Age of Shapur II,* 43–44; Goodblatt, "Poll Tax in Sasanian Babylonia," 249–50.

52. Goodblatt gives a helpful summary of previous scholarship on the question of how exactly Rabba prevented the Jews from paying taxes, a question that presupposes that the story is historically accurate or at least that the story is predicated on some kind of reality that was indeed contemporary with Rabba ("Poll Tax in Sasanian Babylonia," 272–76). Salo Baron assumes that rabbis in fact *were* exempt from taxes and so assumes that by treating them as rabbis Rabba effectively exempted them from taxes (*A Social and Religious History of the Jews,* vol. 2 [New York: Columbia University Press, 1953], 243). Beer, however, argues that the rabbis were not in fact exempt but were campaigning to be exempt (*Babylonian Exilarchate,* 223). According to him, those attending Rabba's lecture were claiming to be rabbis and thereby seeking exemption from taxes. Julius Newman suggests that taxes were collected regionally and therefore the absence of Rabba's students from the region disrupted tax collection (*The Agricultural Life of the Jews in Babylonia between the Years 200 C.E. and 500 C.E.* [London: Oxford University Press, 1932], 178). Alternatively, they caused a lower tax assessment for a region by their absence. Newman's own interpretation of the story is that Rabba was blamed despite being "innocent of any attempt to defraud the Crown."

53. On the anachronism of the title catholicos for this period, see the brief comment in Herman, *Prince without a Kingdom,* 177 n. 75; Smith, *Constantine and the Captive Christians of Persia,* 141, and references there.

nian government on account of tax evasion by their respective constituencies, which are the Christian community as a whole in the case of Simeon and thousands of students in the case of Rabba, considered to be their leaders' responsibility. It is in fact unclear whether the catholicos and *rosh yeshiva* were actually responsible for tax collection from their respective constituencies at this time.[54] Both stories therefore assume the same—possibly fictionalized—accountability to the government on the part of their respective religious leader, whether catholicos or *rosh yeshiva*.[55]

While the thematic and conceptual parallels between the story of Rabba and Simeon are striking, there are even more striking *verbal* parallels between the story of Rabba and the Martyrdom of Barbaʿshmin, one of the Persian Martyr Acts that are a spinoff of Simeon bar Ṣabba'e, and are set at roughly the same time as Rabba's purported death.[56] Barbaʿshmin is said to be the nephew of Simeon and to have become the catholicos soon after him; he was therefore the head of the Christians (ܪܫܐ ܗܘ ܕܟܪ̈ܣܛܝܢܐ). He is martyred under Shapur II after also being accused of enabling some sort of financial evasion by his people.

In the accusation scene in the story of Rabba, there are a number of words and phrases that are exceedingly rare in the Babylonian Talmud. The phrase for slander (אכלו ביה קורצא), which is an old Semitic form, appears in only three other places in the Bavli.[57] In its other appearances, the slander is preceded by a description of the action that is then the subject of the slander, but in our story there is no preceding description. As a result, the accusation against Rabba—its nature, veracity, and motivation—is unclear. Indeed, the accusation that Rabba "prevents" (מבטל) his students from paying the poll tax is strange. Sokoloff lists it as the only example of the root בטל in the C-stem (or ʾAphel), as it is entirely uncommon to "cause someone to be idle." Finally, the *frēstaqa*, a Middle Persian loanword for some sort of servant of the king, appears in a handful of places in the Bavli. In some cases, the *frēstaqa* does indeed bring someone before the king and inspires a certain amount of fear.[58] However, while

---

54. The notion that the heads of religious communities were responsible in some way for tax collection has been questioned by Goodblatt ("Poll Tax in Sasanian Babylonia") and Herman (*Prince without a Kingdom*, 177–78). If they are right, the fact that both of these stories contain this historically inaccurate premise would make them even more strikingly similar. However, given that the Sasanian Empire may very well have encouraged Christians at this time to aid the empire in tax collection (see Payne, *State of Mixture*, 40–44), it is reasonable to assume that Jews would have been subject to similar encouragements.

55. This is in line with Smith, *Constantine and the Captive Christians of Persia*, 118–19.

56. For the relationship between these texts, see the useful summary in Brock, review of G. Wiessner, *Zur Märtyrerüberlieferung*.

57. b. Giṭ. 56a; b. Ber. 58a; and b. B. Bat. 58a. The first text contains an accusation against all Jews, and the other two texts contain an accusation against a single rabbi for functioning as an independent legislator without proper authority.

58. b. Meg. 7a, b. Ketub. 62a, b. Giṭ. 56b, b. ʿAbod. Zar 65a. In b. Meg. 7a, *frēstaqa* is

some of these difficult elements appear in other stories, it is the confluence of all of them, coupled with the obscurity of the slander that suggests we lack the key that unlocks the meaning of this story.

The key may be found in the Martyrdom of Barbaʿshmin, as the verbal parallels between the opening accusation scene in both stories are striking. The Martyrdom of Barbaʿshmin begins as follows:[59]

The martyrdom of the bishop and catholicos Barbaʿshmin, and the sixteen martyrs with him.	ܣܗܕܘܬܐ ܕܒܪܒܥܫܡܝܢ ܐܦܝܣܩܘܦܐ ܘܩܬܘܠܝܩܐ܆ ܘܕܫܬܬܥܣܪ ܣܗ̈ܕܐ ܕܥܡܗ܂
In the sixth year of our persecution, they slandered/informed on Barbaʿshmin, the bishop of Seleucia-Ctesiphon, before the king.	ܒܫܢܬ ܫܬ ܕܪܕܘܦܝܢ܆ ܐܬܐܟܠܘ ܩܪ̈ܨܘܗܝ ܕܒܪܒܥܫܡܝܢ ܐܦܝܣܩܘܦܐ ܕܣܠܝܩ ܘܩܛܝܣܦܘܢ ܩܕܡ ܡܠܟܐ܂
They were saying to him: "There is an impudent man here, who stands against our teaching. And he converts many people from our religion [*deḥleta*], and makes them idle from the work of the king, and he is disdaining the sun and insulting fire and water."	ܘܐܡܪܝܢ ܠܗ܆ ܐܝܬ ܗܪܟܐ ܓܒܪܐ ܚܕ ܡܥܙܐ܆ ܕܩܐܡ ܠܘܩܒܠ ܝܘܠܦܢ܆ ܘܐܢܫܐ ܣܓܝܐܐ ܡܗܦܟ ܡܢ ܕܚܠܬܢ܆ ܘܡܒܛܠܐ ܡܢ ܥܒܕ ܡܠܟܐ ܥܒܕ ܠܗܘܢ܂ ܘܥܠ ܫܡܫܐ ܡܒܣܐ܆ ܘܢܘܪܐ ܘܡܝܐ ܡܨܥܪ܂
The king then asked: "What is the nature of this one who does these things?" They said to him: "He is the nephew of Simeon bar Ṣabbaʿe, and he is the head of the Christians in his locale."	ܫܐܠ ܕܝܢ ܡܠܟܐ܆ ܕܗܢܐ ܐܝܟܢܗ ܕܗܢܐ ܕܗܠܝܢ ܣܥܪ؟ ܐܡܪܝܢ ܠܗ܆ ܒܪ ܚܬܗ ܗܘ ܕܫܡܥܘܢ ܒܪ ܨ̈ܒܥܐ܆ ܘܒܕܘܟܬܗ ܪܫܐ ܗܘ ܕܟܪ̈ܣܛܝܢܐ܂

Barbaʿshmin is slandered before the king (ܐܬܐܟܠܘ ܩܪ̈ܨܘܗܝ...ܩܕܡ ܡܠܟܐ).[60] The slanderers report that there is a man (ܐܝܬ ܗܪܟܐ ܓܒܪܐ ܚܕ) who rejects the teaching, ostensibly of the Magi, and who converts many people from

simply a Persian messenger or official. However, in b. Giṭ. 56b the *frēstaqa* is oddly a Roman messenger. In b. ʿAbod. Zar 65a and b. Ketub. 62a there does seem to be fear associated with the *frēstaqa,* though it should be noted that some manuscripts of the latter have drīqā instead of *frēstaqa.* For a helpful discussion of the *frēstaqa,* see Geoffrey Herman, "The Talmud in Its Babylonian Context: Rava and Bar-Sheshakh; Mani and Mihrshah," in *Between Babylonia and the Land of Israel: Studies in Honor of Isaiah M. Gafni,* ed. Geoffrey Herman, Meir Ben-Shahar, and Aharon Oppenheimer (Jerusalem: Zalman Shazar Institute, 2016), 84–85 who discusses the appearance of the word in incantation bowls and a Manichaean text.

59. Paul Bedjan, *Acta Martyrum et Sanctorum,* 7 vols. (Paris and Leipzig: Harrassowitz, 1890–1897), 2:296–97 (hereafter *AMS* 2).

60. To be sure, this appears in a number of PMA openings, such as ʿAbda (Bedjan, *AMS* 4:250), and Thecla (Bedjan, *AMS* 2:308).

the "fear," or religion, of the empire.[61] As a result, he makes them all "idle" from the work of the king (ܘܒܛܝܠܐ ܡܢ ܥܒܕ ܡܠܟܐ ܥܒܕ ܠܗܘܢ). As the words in parentheses highlight, the verbal parallels here are nearly identical. Rabba is also slandered before the king (אכלו ביה קורצא בי מלכא), and the slanderers report that there is a man (איכא חד גברא) who causes thousands not to pay the poll tax (מכרגא ... מבטל). Finally, while there is no verbal parallel for the accusation that Barbaʿshmin converts people and rejects the teaching of the Magi, the context in which Rabba is accused of preventing payment of the poll tax is also decidedly a pedagogical one, namely, the two months of the year in which the *yeshiva* was well attended. Thus, as in the case of Simeon, we once again have a Christian of similarly high position, in the same time period as Rabba, who is accused, in an almost the identical manner, of the same general offense.[62] And while there is no *frēstaqa* in the stories of Barbaʿshmin or Simeon, the *frēstaqa* does appear in other PMA as a Sasanian official involved in the martyrdom.[63]

The accusation scene in the story of Rabba's death thus seems to be modeled on similar stories in the PMA. But this parallel, I submit, was crafted precisely to highlight the *difference* between the narratives in the PMA and the story of Rabba. The stories contain similar type scenes but with almost diametrically opposed outcomes, which seem to be "structured contrasts." For example, both Simeon and Barbaʿshmin, on the one hand, and Rabba, on the other, apparently have some sway over their respective constituents' payment or nonpayment of taxes, or performance of the "work of the king" in the case of Barbaʿshmin. Both apparently cause their constituents to deprive the king of taxes or labor. But whereas Simeon and Barbaʿshmin are seized, stand before the king, and aggressively flaunt their behavior and mock the king and his power and gods, Rabba does not engage in open defiance but rather flees. Whereas Simeon and Barbaʿshmin conceptualize their disobedience as a divine precept, Rabba offers no explanations and takes no stand—he simply runs away. If the Christian figures represent "fight," Rabba represents "flight."

In all three stories, the king summons the offender. Simeon effectively surrenders himself, is taken away in chains, and is brought before the king, where his defiance of the king continues. Similarly, Barbaʿshmin is seized and brought before the king. In contrast, Rabba flees arrest but then succeeds in winning over his pursuer. While this latter element of winning

---

61. For a discussion of this term, see Becker, "Martyrdom, Religious Difference."

62. The text is from Bedjan, *AMS* 2:296–303. The English translation is my own. For a similar general accusation, but which lacks the consistent verbal parallels and thematic similarities shared by the story of Rabba and that of Barbaʿshmin, see the Martyrdom of Aqebshma in Bedjan, *AMS* 2:261–62.

63. See esp. J. B. Chabot, "Histoire de Jésus-Sabran, écrite par Jésus-Yab d'Adiabène," *Archives des missions scientifiques et littéraires* 7 (1897): 532–33, where a *frēstaqa*, along with a *rad*, plan the execution of Ishoʿsabran.

over the pursuer does not have a direct parallel in Simeon or Barbaᶜshmin, it is quite similar to what we find in other PMA where the healing power of a saint leads to the support or conversion of the king's messengers or officials.[64] But once again, elements in the story of Rabba are presented in sharp contrast to similar elements in the PMA. Unlike Simeon and the other Christian martyrs, Rabba seeks to avoid death. Indeed, even the *frēstaqa* is willing to sacrifice his life on behalf of Rabba. Dying on principle—accepted by both Simeon and even the *frēstaqa* but rejected by Rabba—is clearly another significant structured contrast between the stories.

Rabba, like Simeon and Barbaᶜshmin, ends up in prison, creating the setting for yet another structured contrast. In the case of Simeon, Barbaᶜshmin, and parallel cases in other PMAs, the martyr is brought forth from prison to speak with the king, who offers him one final chance to recant, which the martyr heroically rejects.[65] Rabba, however, has no interest in such a display of defiance; instead, he prays and is miraculously freed from prison.[66]

Rabba's curious death scene combines a number of deathbed motifs from other stories in the Bavli, but in a way that is notably awkward or ill-suited. For example, although the Angel of Death hovers nearby, it is Rabba who controls the timing and circumstances of his death, asking to be killed rather than be captured by the king's minions. This seems to render the classic Angel of Death motif, found elsewhere in the Bavli, superfluous to the story.[67] Rabba's request to "die, rather than be delivered into the hands of the kingdom," is a perfect contrast to Simeon, where the martyr prays for the opportunity to be martyred by the "kingdom:"[68]

---

64. The longest version of this type scene is in the Martyrs of Mount Ber'ain, 56–60, for which see Sebastian P. Brock and Paul C. Dilley, *The Martyrs of Mount Ber'ain*, Persian Martyr Acts in Syriac 4 (Piscataway, NJ: Gorgias Press, 2014). This is also reminiscent of the story of R. Meir in the brothel at b. ᶜAbod. Zar. 18a–b.

65. In some PMAs, the martyr dies in prison. Shirin dies while in prison (see *Holy Women of the Syriac Orient*, trans. Sebastian Brock and Susan Ashbrook Harvey, Transformation of the Classical Heritage 13 [Berkeley: University of California Press, 1998], 78–82). But in most cases, the martyr is brought forth from prison for a final public confrontation with the king or other Sasanian administrator.

66. Escape from jail by means of prayer is a widespread folk motif, but for our purposes it is worth noting that it appears in Acts 12 and 16. In Mar Qardagh, Mar Abdišo also prays and is miraculously broken out of prison (Walker, *Legend of Mar Qardagh*, 33–34). Later in the story, after a verbal confrontation between Mar Qardagh and the king's representative, Mar Qardagh also prays and is broken out of prison. But instead of fleeing, Mar Qardagh remains and prays, while "the nobles and pagans" flee to the "rushes of the marsh." This too we may be a structured contrast, as in the story of Rabba's death, it is Rabba who flees to the marshes (*agama*) after being miraculously broken out of jail. I thank Professor Jeffrey Rubenstein for this suggestion.

67. As noted by Neusner, *Age of Shapur II*, 44 n. 1.

68. Smith, *Martyrdom and History*, 48.

> He arose in prayer and said this: "Give this crown to me, Our Lord. For it is evident to you that I have wanted it because I have loved you with my whole soul and my life, and so let me see you and let me be glad. Give me rest and let me no longer live in this world."

Even Barbaʿshmin, who begins by saying he is not seeking death, ultimately embraces it:[69]

> The blessed Barbaʿshmin answered and said to him: "I do not thirst for slaughter, nor am I awaiting death. But if you permit me to go on my true path, and allow me to fulfill my perfect teaching, [even then,] if you pressure me forcefully by means of your authority to follow your error, I would seek death, because it is life. And I thirst for slaughter because it is happiness. And far be it from me to turn from the true faith of one God, that was handed over to me by Mar Simeon, the one who raised me."

Indeed, Barbaʿshmin points out immediately before his death that the reward of the martyrs is in the real kingdom (ܡܠܟܘܬܐ), where the king will experience torment.[70]

The wishes of Simeon and Barbaʿshmin, on the one hand, and Rabba, on the other, are ultimately fulfilled; Simeon and Barbaʿshmin confront the king and are martyred whereas Rabba avoids any confrontation with the king and ultimately avoids the king's punishment entirely. Yet the setting in which these three figures die differs at well; Rabba dies in hiding, without clear impetus, and alone. Simeon and Barbaʿshmin die with members of their flock and admirers watching.

After Rabba's death, his most prominent students, Abaye and Rava, along with "all the rabbis," search for Rabba's body, which they locate by observing the birds "standing and providing shade" to it.[71] While this search for a corpse is strange in the context of rabbinic literature, it is quite similar to "relic hunting" scenes found at the end of many PMA, where the body of a martyr is relocated and enshrined.[72] Though the Martyrdom

---

69. Bedjan, *AMS* 2:297–98.

70. The desire to be martyred is found in other PMA. For other examples, see Brock and Harvey, *Holy Women of the Syrian Orient*, 89 and 95; Walker, *Legend of Mar Qardagh*, 63 and 66; Martyrdom of 111 Men and 9 Women, in Bedjan, *AMS* 2:292. For more, see Jeffrey Rubenstein's paper in this volume.

71. An example of the miraculously marked grave can be found in History of ʿAbdā damšiḥā, where the site of burial is marked by fire.

72. See, e.g., Mar Pinhas (Bedjan, *AMS* 4:215–16, and Syriac and English in Adam Carter McCollum, *The Story of Mar Pinḥas*, Persian Martyr Acts in Syriac 2 [Piscataway, NJ: Gorgias Press, 2013], 14–15) and Narsai the Ascetic (Bedjan, *AMS* 4:179–80). The History of ʿAbdā damšiḥā features the miraculous marking of the place (ear attached to stone), the building of a shrine on that place, and the translation of the relics westward followed by the building of a shrine in the new location. See Aaron Michael Butts and Simcha Gross, *The His-*

of Simeon bar Ṣabbaᶜe ends somewhat abruptly and without any information about Simeon's body or any shrines that may have been dedicated to him, in the later History of Simeon bar Ṣabbaᶜe much is made of a hunt for the body of Simeon and other martyrs to effect their relocation and enshrinement. In fact, the enforced exposure of the corpses of martyrs and their retrieval by Christians through guile were common themes in Syriac texts about Persian persecution, themes that also appears in the Bavli, and the exposed flesh is often left to the birds, precisely as we find in the story of Rabba.[73] Thus, for instance, in the martyrdom of Bar Šibia, the martyrs' corpses are exposed to wild animals and birds (ܘܦܓܪܝܗܘܢ ܐܟܠܬ ܚܝܘܬ ܒܪܐ ܘܦܪܚܬܐ ܕܫܡܝܐ).[74] The almost identical language is found in the Martyrdom of Miles.[75] Once again we find a structured contrast in the Bavli: the rabbis find Rabba's body, and the site of his death is indeed miraculously marked just as with some Persian Martyrs, but the rabbis simply leave Rabba's body *in situ* and exposed![76]

In the Martyrdom, the death of Simeon inspires others to martyr themselves; indeed Barbaᶜshmin is himself following in his uncle Simeon's path, as are the sixteen people martyred alongside him. In contrast, Abaye and Rava plan an abbreviated three-day mourning period for Rabba. However, a missive from on high orders the rabbis to continue mourning for a full seven days, after which they are instructed to "return

---

tory of the 'Slave of Christ': From Jewish Child to Christian Martyr, Persian Martyr Acts in Syriac 6 (Piscataway, NJ: Gorgias Press, 2016), 146–53.

73. For a partial list in the PMA, see Wiessner, *Zur Märtyrerüberlieferung*, 219–21. Hector Ricardo Francisco, "Corpse Exposure in the Acts of the Persian Martyrs and Its Literary Models," *Hugoye* 19 (2016): 193–235; Herman, "'Bury My Coffin Deep!,'" esp. 37–40; Oric Basirov, "'Proselytisation' and 'Exposure of the Dead': Two Christian Calumnies Commonly Raised against the Sasanians," in *Faszination Iran: Beiträge zur Religion, Geschichte und Kunst des Alten Iran; Gedenkschrift für Klaus Schippmann*, ed. Shervin Farridnejad, Anke Joisten-Pruschke, and Rika Gyselen. Göttinger Orientforschungen, Reihe 3, Iranica 13 (Wiesbaden: Harrassowitz, 2015), 1–19. The contrast with these relic hunting scenes is all the more striking given that on the very next page in the Bavli there is a story that Jeffrey Rubenstein has argued reflects a kind of Jewish relic hunting scene ("A Rabbinic Translation of Relics," in *Ambiguities, Complexities and Half-Forgotten Adversaries: Crossing Boundaries in Ancient Judaism and Early Christianity*, ed. Kimberly Stratton and Andrea Lieber, forthcoming). It is worth mentioning b. Sanh. 47b in this context, where Jews remove dirt from Rav's grave in order to be healed from ailments.

74. Bedjan, *AMS* 2:283.

75. Ibid., 275.

76. Interestingly, the Karaite Jacob al-Qirqisānī recounts a version of this story which adds that the missive from heaven was sent to ensure that Rabba's corpse was in fact taken and buried, which suggests that later Jews were aware of the implication of the story that the body was left in the field and thus made this addition to foreclose such an interpretation. See Leon Nemoy, "Al-Qirqisānī's Account of the Jewish Sects and Christianity," *HUCA* 7 (1930): 356.

in peace to your homes."[77] This can be contrasted with what we find in the Life of Mār Ābā, a catholicos like Simeon bar Ṣabba'e, though from the mid-sixth century, whose death is followed by a seven-day mourning period in which his clothing is torn off by venerators to serve as relics.[78] Rabba's body, by contrast, is not enshrined, his relics are not venerated and his death is not particularly commemorated beyond the most basic Jewish mourning period.[79] His death is not imitated, and there is no indication of subsequent unrest by Jews against the Sasanian Empire. Rabba dies, is minimally—even grudgingly—mourned, and everyone moves on with their lives.[80]

In the final vignette in the story, an Arab is tossed across a river by a storm as a result of Rabba's death. The Arab confronts God, saying, "You are the sovereign of the universe, and Rabba bar Naḥmani too is yours. Why are you destroying the world?" The storm that had tossed him across the river immediately subsides. It is intriguing to note that many PMA also contain miracles following the death of the martyr, and in some cases these miracles involve Arabs as well.[81] However, while in those stories the martyr's relics or sanctuary lead to some sort of miraculous healing or other beneficial result, in the case of Rabba bar Naḥmani the miracle is in fact unhelpful and leads the Arab who is subject to the miracle to beseech God to discontinue such acts on account of Rabba's death in the future. Here too, then, the story of Rabba inverts standard tropes found throughout the PMA.

The composer of the Rabba bar Naḥmani story likely intended for the reader to make these connections with the PMA. He carefully primes the reader to expect a Persian Martyr Act only to repeatedly upset these expectations.[82] For example, the composer sets the stage for a verbal confrontation and debate between Rabba and Sasanian officials or the king himself similar to those of Simeon and the heroes of other PMAs.[83] However, Rabba

77. Might this be related to the tradition in b. Šabb. 153a to the effect that Rabba was hated by his fellow Pumbeditans? So Neusner, *Age of Shapur II*, 101.

78. Paul Bedjan, *Histoire de Mar-Jabalaha, de trois autres patriarches, de'un prêtre et de deux laïques, Nestoriens* (Paris: Otto Harrasowitz, 1895), 271–72.

79. This is particularly striking because both Simeon and Rabba are strongly associated with a city in Babylonia: Simeon with Seleucia-Ctesiphon, Rabba with Pumbedita. Simeon accordingly is enshrined in Seleucia-Ctesiphon, but Rabba is not enshrined in his home.

80. Indeed, this episode is profitably compared with the death of R. Yehuda HaNasi in b. Ketub. 103b, who is mourned constantly for thirty days and then is mourned in part for twelve months. For the mourning requirements in rabbinic texts, see, e.g., y. Moʿed Qaṭ. 3:5, 82c, and b. Sanh. 108b.

81. E.g. McCollum, *Mar Pinḥas*, 14–16; and Butts and Gross, *History of the 'Slave of Christ,'* 156–62.

82. This is how type scenes function. See Robert Alter, "Biblical Type-Scenes and the Uses of Convention," *Critical Inquiry* 5 (1978): 355–68.

83. Wiessner outlines this standard feature of dialogue in the martyrdoms (*Zur Märtyrerüberlieferung*, 202–4).

repeatedly avoids the opportunity for confrontation. Unlike Simeon and Barbaᶜshmin, Rabba never acts defiantly, never appears before the king, never debates a point of principle, and never presents obedience to Judaism as being in opposition to obedience to the king or his laws. Most crucially, Rabba also deliberately avoids martyrdom at the hands of the empire. Unlike Simeon, Rabba's remains are never enshrined, and his minimal commemoration is coerced. Rabba's death does not herald a period of persecution; his death—like his persecution—is an isolated incident.

It is certainly possible that the composers of the Bavli knew of Simeon bar Ṣabba'e in particular, and of Persian martyrs more generally. Simeon was the most famous of the Persian martyrs and is already mentioned as a martyr in the earliest dated Syriac manuscript, from the year 411 (BL. Add. 12,150).[84] Simeon's story appeared in two Syriac versions. The earlier Martyrdom also traveled westward and appears in Greek in Sozomen's *Ecclesiastical History* 2.9–10.[85] Simeon was considered the paradigmatic Persian martyr.[86] As the later History says at the outset, Simeon "was the first one to excel in the land of the East as a blessed martyr of God," and as Simeon himself says in the Martyrdom, "I will be an example for all your people in the East." In both the *Martyrdom* and the *History*, Simeon's death leads to other martyrdoms, which purportedly initiated the period known as the "Great Persecution" under Shapur II.[87] Moreover,

84. Edited by F. Nau in *Patrologia Orientalis* 10.1 (1915): 7–26. See Sebastian P. Brock, *The History of the Holy Mar Ma'in with a Guide to the Persian Martyr Acts*, Persian Martyr Acts in Syriac 1 (Piscataway, NJ: Gorgias Press, 2009), 123–25 for an English translation.

85. Kyle Smith argues that the Martyrdom was composed between the *terminus post quem* of 363 CE, based on the reference to Julian's attempt to rebuild the temple, and the *terminus ante quem* of 443 CE, since that is when Sozomen, whose own report about Simeon's martyrdom is indebted to the Martyrdom, would have completed his work. By contrast, the History seems to have been completed at a later date (Smith, *Martyrdom and History*, xxx–xii). Thus, the Martyrdom was composed well within the period of the Bavli's composition and redaction. To be clear, I do not mean to suggest that the rabbis actually read the Martyrdom of Simeon bar Ṣabba'e that we have today, or that they heard it read by others. Rather, they show awareness of the story, something they could have learned from any performance or retelling of the story before its later reworking.

86. A number of later texts, such as the Martyrs of Mount Berᶜain, date themselves earlier in Shapur II's rule but explicitly refer to details from Simeon's martyrdom, showing they were composed later. There is one martyrdom that seems to have been influenced by the cycle of martyrdoms related to Simeon, but it is dated significantly earlier and does not directly allude to Simeon or his companions. See Sebastian Brock, "A Martyr at the Sasanid Court under Vahran II: Candida," in *Analecta Bollandiana* 96 (1978): 167–81, reprinted in idem, *Syriac Perspectives on Late Antiquity*, ed. Sebastian Brock (London: Variorum Reprints, 1984), IX, and Herman, *Prince without a Kingdom*, 43 n. 117. Simeon as paradigmatic martyr is not limited to the PMA but is also in Roman historians' accounts in the early and mid-fifth century CE. See, e.g., Sozomen and Faustus of Byzantium in Jacob Neusner, "Babylonian Jewry and Shapur II's Persecution of Christianity from 337 to 379 A.D," *HUCA* 43 (1972): 86–87.

87. For a recent discussion examining the historicity of the "Great Persecution," see Smith "Constantine and Judah the Maccabee."

Simeon's martyrdom generated many spinoffs, such as Barbaʿshmin, but also Pusai, Martha, Tarbo and more.[88] Many PMA are dated based on the "years of persecution," which begin with Simeon's death.[89] Simeon's martyrdom was remembered and reshaped in numerous works throughout late antiquity and the early Middle Ages.[90]

Many other PMA enjoyed similar popularity. In a short time, the texts spread and were translated into Greek, Latin, Armenian, Georgian, Arabic, and Coptic, among other languages. Indeed, the Martyrdom of Simeon was translated into Greek at an early point and survives, along with Barbaʿshmin and other related martyrdoms, in Sogdian as well.[91] Some PMA were even composed outside of the Sasanian Empire, apparently because they were popular and allowed Christians living in Rome to live (or die) vicariously through their coreligionists.[92] In short, these texts traveled far and wide and were very popular. From an early date, cult sites and martyria were set up for these martyrs, as well as specific days to commemorate them.[93] It is thus not difficult to imagine how the composers of the story of Rabba, living in Sasanian Babylonia during this period, would have been familiar with the PMA in general, and perhaps more intimately familiar with a number of particular PMA stories.

The contrast between these narratives thus highlights the overall difference in the underlying attitude toward the Sasanian Empire that they endorse. Whereas the martyrdom accounts of Simeon and Barbaʿshmin pointed to a fundamental hostility and antagonism between Christianity and empire and embraced martyrdom and persecution as exemplary expressions of that antagonism, the story of Rabba bar Naḥmani points to a rejection of hostile or open antagonism to the empire and therefore encourages the avoidance of martyrdom.[94] Similarly, whereas the PMA

88. For Pusai, see Bedjan, *AMS* 2:208–32; for Martha, Bedjan, *AMS* 2:233–41; for Tarbo, Bedjan, *AMS* 2:254–60.

89. Wiessner, *Zur Martyrenüberlieferung*, 34; Wood, *Chronicle of Seert*, 61–62, and n. 44 there.

90. Wood, *Chronicle of Seert*, 52–65.

91. Nicholas Sims-Williams, *The Christian Sogdian Manuscript C2* (Berlin: Akademie-Verlag, 1985), esp. 137–53.

92. Herman, "Last Years of Yazdgird I and the Christians," 67–90.

93. For the history and importance of martyr shrines among Christians in Sasanian Persia, see Richard Payne, "The Emergence of Martyrs' Shrines in Late Antique Iran: Conflict, Consensus, and Communal Institutions," in *An Age of Saints? Power, Conflict and Dissent in Early Medieval Christianity*, ed. Peter Sarris, Matthew Dal Santo, and Phil Booth, Brill's Series on the Early Middle Ages 20 (Leiden: Brill, 2011), 89–113; and for the development of a single martyr cult and shrine, see Walker, *Legend of Mar Qardagh*, 246–86.

94. Alyssa M. Gray argues that we find a different kind of negotiation with the idea of martyrdom in a number of Yerushalmi *sugyot*, where the editor likens intensive Torah observance and study to a kind of martyrdom (*qiddushat hashem*) ("A Contribution to the Study of Martyrdom and Identity in the Palestinian Talmud," *JJS* 54 [2003]: 242–72). Note her

often depict the Sasanian Empire as imposing unreasonable laws on Christians and pursuing persecutory and violent courses of action against them, the story of Rabba bar Naḥmani depicts Rabba as the instigator and depicts the Sasanian Empire as inquisitive but never violent. To the rabbis, it seems, the Sasanian Empire was a reasonable entity to be negotiated, not challenged through head-on confrontation.

II. Analogical Thinking: Palestinian and Persian Martyrs

The use of the PMA in the composition of the story of Rabba bar Naḥmani suggests that the composer drew an analogy between Syriac Christians and Babylonian Jews. The PMA were useful precisely because they articulated a widespread attitude toward the Sasanian Empire by a similarly situated nondominant group. To be sure, the composer of the story of Rabba offered an alternative perspective to that found in the PMA. But the very ability to invoke the PMA based on analogical thinking shows that, to the composer, these groups shared much in common.

The composer's analogical thinking is further on display in his similar incorporation and reworking of rabbinic traditions about martyrdom, in particular traditions about R. Akiva.[95] Here too, the composer invokes a similarly situated group, though this time Jews under the Roman Empire rather than Syriac Christians under the Sasanian Empire. And here too, the composer invokes but then reverses an earlier martyrdom.

Rabba is said to have twelve thousand students, a typological number that would reasonably be understood as a parallel to R. Akiva, who is also said to have twelve thousand students.[96] Rabba's death with the

---

argument on 268 that Syriac Christian martyrdom was not a "threat to rabbinic Jews in Iran" because they were another "minority" group and not in power. This claim downplays the ideological purposes these stories served and also takes for granted that Jews did not share similar circumstances to Syriac Christians, a point that is in need of serious reevaluation.

95. Paul Mandel has recently demonstrated that the version of the story in the Bavli introduces martyrological elements not found or emphasized in earlier Palestinian versions ("Was Rabbi Aqiva a Martyr? Palestinian and Babylonian Influences in the Development of a Legend," in *Rabbinic Traditions between Palestine and Babylonia*, ed. Ronit Nikolsky and Tal Ilan, AJEC 89 [Leiden: Brill, 2014], 325–75). Around this time R. Akiva becomes the Jewish martyr par excellence, as described in Boustan, *From Martyr to Mystic*. Mandel also argues that the earliest Babylonian version of the story was not, strictly speaking, a martyrdom, because "its subject is not Aqiva's martyrdom but rather his attitude to death and his standing as a teacher." However, this evaluation does not, to my mind, disqualify the classification of this text as a martyrdom.

96. b. Ketub. 62b–63a. In the parallel in b. Ned. 50a, R. Akiva has twenty-four thousand, obviously double the twelve thousand students in b. Ketub. 62b–63a, corresponding to two study periods of twelve years. See also the death of twelve thousand Jews at Caesarea-Mazaca in b. Mo'ed Qaṭ. 26a.

word "pure" on his lips and the heavenly postmortem praise of Rabba beginning with the word אשריך would similarly invoke the famous martyrdom of R. Akiva in b. Ber. 61b.[97] In that story, the "wicked government" forbids Torah study. However, this does not deter R. Akiva, who flouts the ruling by teaching Torah in public. R. Akiva famously faces death with acceptance and even joy. He explains to his incredulous students that he is finally able to truly fulfill the requirement to love God with all of his soul, invoking Deut 6:5. R. Akiva dies while reciting the *Shema* and is praised for dying with (*eḥad*) אחד on his lips. R. Akiva, then, is martyred in joy, while invoking the core monotheistic idea.[98]

The contrast between this story and that of Rabba's death could not be starker. R. Akiva dies for teaching Torah despite a decree against doing so; Rabba, for causing mass tax evasion among those studying Torah. R. Akiva has many students and they are with him at his death; Rabba flees the academy and never sees his students again. R. Akiva dies in a public spectacle; Rabba dies alone and in hiding. R. Akiva reinforces the core monotheistic ideal at the moment of his death; Rabba decides an obscure halakic rule that has no relevance in his day nor any bearing on his situation.[99] Finally, R. Akiva dies at the hand of an "evil kingdom" (מלכות הרשעה) that he does not fear, while Rabba begs God *not* to allow him to die at the hands of the "kingdom" (דמלכותא). If R. Akiva is the rabbinic martyr par excellence, in the subtle hands of our story's composer, Rabba is the anti-martyr.[100]

The composer of the story of Rabba bar Naḥmani used the PMA and stories about the earlier Palestinian rabbinic martyrs in order to contrast different attitudes and strategies to life under imperial rule. In effect, the story compels the reader to compare the Christian martyrs in the PMA

97. This can also be seen by the fact that אשריך appears in the account of R. Akiva's martyrdom (b. Ber. 61b) but not in the other Bavli martyrdoms that feature a heavenly voice inviting the martyrs to heaven (b. ʿAbod. Zar. 10b [Ketiah b. Shalom], and b. ʿAbod. Zar. 17b–18a [R. Ḥanina b. Teradyon]). In t. Ḥul. 2:22–23 = y. ʿAbod. Zar. 2:2, 40d–41a, Ben Dama's death is followed by "happy are you (אשריך), Ben Dama, for you have departed in peace from the world," but he is not praised for dying with any words on his lips. In the version of Ben Dama's death found in b. ʿAbod. Zar. 27b he is praised for dying "in purity/בטהרה."

98. In fact, the idea of dying with *eḥad* on his lips and the section of praise that follows is not found in the Palestinian parallels of his martyrdom in y. Ber. 9:5, 14b = y. Soṭah 5:7, 20c.

99. Balberg and Vidas strengthen the incongruity between Rabba's expertise and his "precarious situation" ("Impure Scholasticism," 328–29).

100. It is also possible to view the scene with the *frēstaqa* in the inn as a reworking of a common type scene in other stories in the Bavli, in which a guard or soldier of the empire aids a rabbi (at times, even converts) at great personal risk. This type scene includes the death of R. Ḥanina ben Teradion (b. ʿAbod. Zar. 18a), R. Meir in the brothel (b. ʿAbod. Zar. 18a-b), and with Onqelos on the mountaintop (b. ʿAbod. Zar. 11a). In the story of Rabba, of course, the *frēstaqa* is willing to be killed on behalf of Rabba, but Rabba himself is unwilling to submit to self-sacrifice.

with the early Palestinian rabbinic martyrs. Both groups depicted antagonism between the nondominant group and empire as positive. They therefore serve as a foil for the alternative approach outlined in the story of Rabba bar Naḥmani. At the same time, the use of the PMA alongside the invocation of R. Akiva shows that the composer understood that, at the very least, these groups shared circumstances and were fundamentally similarly situated vis-à-vis their imperial context.

III. Conclusion

I have argued that viewing persecution as a site of memory construction provides us with a better theoretical lens with which to consider the story of Rabba bar Naḥmani, and allows us to better understand the parallels between this story and the PMA. This approach differs from those previous scholars, like Neusner, who approached the text as containing a historical kernel and therefore viewed its similarities to the story of Simeon bar Ṣabbaʿe as the outcome of proximate historical events:

> What actually happened to Rabba we do not know. Afterward rabbis recalled—at the very least—that he had died on account of mass tax evasions, as had Simeon bar Ṣabbaʿe. But no persecution of the Jews followed. Sasanian government wanted taxes, not lives, except in the case of the Christians, and for special reasons. So if a rabbi was punished for lying or evading taxes, it would have been exemplary, and not universal, punishment. Since no evidence suggests any further difficulties, I should conclude that the Jewish community learned its lesson and paid its taxes.[101]

Neusner recognizes the parallel to Simeon, but assumes that both stories accurately portray historical events. Despite some skepticism, Neusner trusts the story enough to derive from it unreported background information, such as the strategies of the Sasanian government, and also to project events not described.[102] This approach to the story of Rabba is fairly representative.[103]

The alternative approach offered here focuses instead on how stories like the Bavli's account of Rabba's death and the martyrdom accounts of Simeon and Barbaʿshmin are literary units that reconstruct and memorialize life in the Sasanian Empire in order to articulate attitudes and courses

101. Neusner, *Age of Shapur II*, 43–44. Neusner's approach does not dramatically differ from Graetz's (n. 33 above), which, in many ways, also still represents the currently accepted historiographical approach to the status of the Jews in the Sasanian Empire.

102. Wiessner (*Zur Märtyrerüberlieferung*, 182–83) takes an inverse approach to Neusner and uses the story of Rabba as confirmation for the story of Simeon. But for the dangers of this approach, see Smith, *Constantine and the Captive Christians of Persia*, 118.

103. See notes 33, 34, and 52 above.

of action in the present. The Jews may or may not have paid their taxes in the wake of Rabba's death, but some of them told and composed stories that advised flight over fight, passivity over persecution. While we may not know what happened historically, we can learn a lot from the differing postures toward empire these stories reveal.

The historical circumstances that caused the composer of the Rabba bar Naḥmani story to adopt a different posture toward the Sasanian Empire from that found in the PMA cannot be ascertained from this story alone. But a number of possibilities may be tentatively suggested. Did the Jews in fact experience better conditions than the neighboring Syriac Christians, as has so often been argued, and thereby adopt an accommodationist approach to the Sasanian Empire? This may be the case, but it is difficult to prove this precisely because of texts like the story of Rabba bar Naḥmani and the PMA, which challenge any simplistic reliance on our sources as evidence for historical events. Perhaps this story indicates that there were other Jews who promoted the opposite approach to the Sasanian Empire, one that hewed closely to the PMA, and the composer was responding to them? If so, this tension among Jews would itself echo similar tensions among Syriac Christians in the Sasanian Empire, many of whom adopted more conciliatory postures toward empire. A full answer to these questions awaits further, much needed, work that reexamines the place of the Jews in the Sasanian Empire.[104]

Finally, this paper has broad implications for the use of Syriac sources for the study of the Babylonian rabbis and the Bavli. As we have seen, the story of Rabba shows awareness of the martyrdoms of Simeon bar Ṣabbaʿe and Barbaʿshmin, as well as of larger motifs in the Persian Martyr Acts. While identifying points of contact is important for establishing connections between different groups and their texts in antiquity, even more important is how these reveal an awareness by the Babylonian Jews that their situation in the Sasanian Empire was similar to that of the Syriac Christians.[105] This should afford us license to study the two groups together even when we lack signs establishing a direct textual parallel between them. Syriac Christians and their texts offer an almost ideal reference point for gauging the kinds

104. Replacing the now outdated works of Widengren, "Status of the Jews," and Robert Brody, "Judaism in the Sasanian Empire." For an important application of modern source-critical approaches to the Bavli to texts pertaining to this issue, see Kalmin, "Sasanian Persian Persecution."

105. This shows that the more mild articulation of "the Ways that Never Parted," namely, that the two groups—even once they became recognized, standalone groups—were not always hostile to each other and could indeed see themselves as, in some ways, bound by the same circumstances and sharing a similar plight. This offers an alternative to, for instance, the brief remarks of Josef Wiesehöfer, *Ancient Persia: From 550 BC to 650 AD* (London: I. B. Tauris, 1996), 215–16, who argues that in the Sasanian period, Manichaeans and Christians, on the one hand, and Jews and Christians, on the other, were hostile to each other.

of administrative, cultural, economic, identity, and other issues that would have existed for nondominant (i.e., non-Iranian) groups, such as Jews, living in Sasanian Persia.[106] Syriac Christian literature can therefore serve as a foil for the Babylonian Talmud to better study how nondominant groups could and did respond to proximate imperial and historical circumstances in the Sasanian Empire. To be sure, these groups may have responded differently from one another (and may have had different responses among themselves), as the competing messages of the Rabba and Simeon stories demonstrate. Therefore, triangulation rather than simplistic comparison is useful precisely because it allows us to study these groups together even when we do not find moments of contact between them. It allows us to move beyond the self-representation or limits of any one group and their surviving literature and material evidence, in order to create a fuller picture of each group, as well as their shared experiences.

Appendix: Bavli Parallels

The story of Rabba bar Naḥmani's death, like many others in the Bavli, was composed by borrowing and reworking elements and recycling motifs found in many other stories in the Bavli.

Section (B): This section, which follows a report about Rabba's death due to persecution (A), is parallel to the opening of a story in b. Ber. 58a (acc. to Oxford Opp. Add. fol. 23).

R. Shila[107] whipped a man who had intercourse with a gentile. He went and informed against him to the court of the king. He said to Caesar, "There is a man among the Jews who does not receive authority yet adjudicates cases." He [Caesar] said: "Bring him." When he came he [Caesar] said to him [R. Shila], "Why did you whip that man?" He said, "Because he had intercourse with an ass." He said to him, "If so he is deserving of the death penalty!" He responded, "From the day we were exiled we do not have authority to execute, but as for you, whatever you deem worthy you should do to him."

ר׳ שילא אלקייה לההוא
גברא דבעל גויה אזל אכל
קורצא בי מלכא א׳ל לקיסר
איכא גברא חד ביהודאי דלא
נסיב רשותא ודאין דינא אמ׳
אתיוה כי אתא א׳ל אמאי
אלקיתיה לההוא גברא א׳ל
דבעל חמרא א׳ל אי הכי בר
קטלא הוא א׳ל אנן מיומא
דגלינן לית לן רשותא למיקטל
אתון כל מה דבעיתו עבידו
ביה

106. See Gross, "Irano-Talmudica and Beyond;" and Adam Becker, "Polishing the Mirror: Some Thoughts on Syriac Sources and Early Judaism," in *Envisioning Judaism: Studies in Honor of Peter Schäfer on the Occasion of his Seventieth Birthday*, ed. Ra'anan Boustan et al., 2 vols. (Tübingen: Mohr Siebeck, 2013), 2:897–916.

107. In all manuscripts the name is abbreviated R' Shila, which could stand for Rabbi Shila, a fourth-generation Tanna, or any number of Amoraim named Rav Shila. Neusner, (*Age of Shapur II*, 109), following *Iggeret* of Sherira Gaon says he is a first-generation

In the nearly identical opening to both stories, a rabbi is slandered (אכל קורצא) to the "House of the king," here identified as Caesar. Interestingly however, the strongest parallel to the story of Rabba is found in the Soncino and Vilna printed editions, in which a *frēstaqa* appears, and the king of the בי מלכא is not identified as Caesar. The printed editions also have a number of other Persian loanwords, such as *harmana* instead of *rishuta,* apparently attempting to impose a Persian context on the story.[108]

The content of the slander against Rabba presupposes a number of clearly late Stammaitic motifs concerning the rise of the rabbinic academy. The typological number twelve thousand, as stated above, is found in other Babylonian stories. For instance, it is the number of R. Akiva's students (twelve thousand in b. Ketub. 62b–63a, but twenty-four thousand in the parallel in b. Ned. 50a because he goes to study for two distinct periods there, and so acquires twelve thousand students each time).[109]

Indeed, Rabba bar Naḥmani also appears in a pericope in which the introduction of academies that enabled a large number of students to study together is retrojected back onto earlier important Amoraim (b. Ketub. 106a). This source reports the number of students rabbis had in each Babylonian Amoraic generation, with the largest number in the first generation and reduced numbers in each following generation (which in fact is the opposite of what seems to have happened in reality). The source starts with the second-generation Rav, who had twelve hundred students, moves to Rabba and Rav Yosef, who were both third-generation Amoraim and later assumed to be heads of the academy at Pumbedita,[110] who have four hundred students.[111] As I argued above, b. B. Meṣ. 86a did not adopt the same

Nehardean, See Herman, *Prince without a Kingdom,* 195, who says he is "a first generation Babylonian Amora, who acquires the right to serve as a judge directly from the king of Persia." While the text in Soncino and Vilna seems to refer to a Persian king, the other manuscripts refer to a Roman ruler. Hanoch Albeck cannot identify this figure (*Mavo La'Talmudim* [Tel Aviv: Devir, 1969], 680). Leo Landman thinks this is referring to Rabbi Shila b. Avina, a student of Rav, but his position is based on a noncritical interpretation of the sources ("Rabbi Shila and the Informer," *JQR* 63 [1972]: 136–44).

108. The story in b. Ber. 58a is clearly related to b. Taᶜan. 24b, in which the same accusation of unauthorized judgment is brought against Rava before King Shapur, who is ultimately convinced by Ifra Hormiz to take no action against him. See Secunda, *Iranian Talmud,* 170 n. 51, who suggests that b. Taᶜan. 24b was influenced by the story in b. Ber. 58a.

109. The number also appears in b. Mo'ed Qaṭ. 26a, where Shapur is said to have killed twelve thousand Jews in Caesarea-Mazaca. This number also appears in Palestinian sources. See Shamma Friedman, "A Good Story Deserves Retelling: The Unfolding of the Akiva Legend," in *Creation and Composition: The Contribution of the Bavli Redactors (Stammaim) to the Aggada,* ed. Jeffrey L. Rubenstein, TSAJ 114 (Tübingen: Mohr Siebeck, 2005), 71–100.

110. They are also depicted as heads of academies in b. Ber. 64a. See Neusner, *Age of Shapur II,* 91–92.

111. See Rubenstein, *Culture of the Babylonian Talmud,* 16–23, which, *en passant,* discusses the following source from b. Ketub. 106a.

number of students attributed to Rabba in b. Ketub. 106a, but rather from the number of students attributed to R. Akiva in b. Ketub. 62b–63a.

Section (C): Rabba flees from the *frēstaqa*, but unluckily they both end up at the same inn. The *frēstaqa* was given two cups of wine, which was considered quite dangerous, as seen from the b. Pesaḥ. 110a–b, the *locus classicus* for a discussion of the dangers of *zugot* (pairs), or even numbers of food or drink. But rather than allow him to remain ill, Rabba provides the cure, which in this case involved giving him a third drink, which resulted in an odd number of drinks instead of an even number. The idea that two drinks are dangerous and that the remedy is to add a third drink is found in b. Pesaḥ. 110b (JTS Rab. 1608). Important for us is the note appended to the end:

Rav Naḥman said: Two [cups] before the meal and one during the meal combine; one before the meal and two during the meal do not combine. Rav Mesharsheya demurred: Do we then desire to effect a remedy for the meal: we desire to effect a remedy for the person, and surely the person stands remedied! Yet all agree that two during the meal and one after the meal do not combine, *in accordance with the story of Rabba bar Naḥmani.*

אמ׳ רב נחמן תרי קמי תכא
וחד אתכא מצטרפי חד קמי תכא
ותרי אתכא לא מצטרף מתקיף
לה רב משרשיא אטו אנמן לתקוני
תכא קא בעינן אנן לתקוני גברא
קא בעינן הא מתקן וקאי דכולי
עלמא תרי אתכא וחד בתר תכא
לא מיצטרפי כמעשה דרבה בר
נחמני

It seems fairly clear that this addendum is a later gloss. The manuscripts fluctuate here in their wording, though not in substance, which may be a sign of a later addition.[112] It seems this gloss was added to note the clear connection between the Rabba bar Naḥmani story and b. Pesaḥ. 110b. Thus, the story of Rabba drew from b. Pesaḥ. 110b, and then at a later point a scribe made note of that connection in b. Pesaḥ. 110b itself.

Section (E): The motif of the heavenly academy is found elsewhere in, and is exclusive to, the Bavli, as in b. B. Meṣ. 85b and b. Taʿan. 21b. In the latter, a missive is sent from heaven to a rabbi.[113] The issue debated in the heavenly academy is taken from b. Ketub. 75b, where Rabba rules "pure" on the very same matter,[114] a matter that is the subject of debate in m. Neg. 4:11.

According to Shamma Friedman, the claim in the heavenly academy

112. Vatican 109: משום מעשה שהיה; Munich 6, Munich 95, JTS, Vatican 134: משום מעשה שהיה דרבה בר נחמני. Modena—Archivio Storico Comunale 26.2: משום מעשה דאבא בר נחמני. For the argument that manuscript variation often signals a later addition, see Shamma Friedman, "*Perek Haisha Raba* in the Bavli, with a General Prolegomenon on the Study of the *Sugya*" [Hebrew], *Sources and Traditions* 1 (1978): 275–442, esp. 306.

113. For a full list and discussion of the Bavli sources on the heavenly academy, see Becker, "Bringing the Heavenly Academy Down to Earth," 174–91.

114. Also noted by Friedman, "Orthography of the Names," 157.

that Rabba said, "I am pre-eminent in the laws of leprosy; I am pre-eminent in tents," shows awareness of b. Taᶜan. 24a–b, where Rabba boasts about the breadth of his generation's studies, but this is not decisive.

The story also incorporates the motif of the Angel of Death, who is prevented from killing someone on account of that person's unceasing Torah study. This motif is also found in b. Mak. 10a and b. Šabb. 30b.[115] However, whereas in the other sources the Angel of Death produces a noise that stops the rabbi from studying and thereby gives the Angel of Death an opportunity to kill the rabbi, in this story the noise Rabba hears stops him from studying, yet the Angel of Death does not immediately strike. Instead, it is Rabba's explicit *request* that God end his life rather than allowing Rabba to die at the hands of the kingdom that leads to his death.

Finally, Rabba's death scene incorporates a number of scenes from elsewhere. He dies saying the word *pure*, which, as noted above, invokes Rabba's ruling of "pure" in b. Ketub. 75b. He is praised by a heavenly voice (בת קול) for dying while saying "pure," which is reminiscent of both b. ᶜAbod. Zar. 27b, in which R. Yishmael praises (אשריך) Ben Dama for dying in purity, by which he means not having accepted illicit healing, and b. Sanh. 68a, where R. Eliezer b. Hyrcanus dies with purity on his lips, though there he is not praised for doing so.[116] The best parallel is certainly the martyrdom of R. Akiva in b. Ber. 61b, which similarly features a heavenly voice praising (אשריך) a rabbi for dying with an actual word on his lips.[117]

Sections (E) and (F): There are three letters from heaven in these sections. Letters from heaven appear elsewhere in the Bavli (b. Yoma 69b; b. Sanh. 64a); however, the writing on these is limited to "truth/*emet*." The parallel does not extend beyond this basic shared motif.

Sections (D), (F), and (G): The prison scene (D) as well as the final two scenes (F–G) have no parallel (aside from the shared motif of the heavenly note), which is striking in light of the abundance of parallels throughout the rest of the story. The prison scene *is* parallel to similar scenes in the PMA, and this is intended to prime the reader's expectations only to then undermine them.

The keen interest in the corpse, the commemoration, and other postmortem miracles in these final sections is also without parallel with but one exception—a text found one folio later, and which also may be indebted to Syriac Christian texts.[118]

115. The idea that one must stop learning to die also appears in b. Ketub. 104a.

116. Qirqisānī already makes the connection between the death of R. Eliezer and Rabba. See Nemoy, "Al-Qirqisani's Account," 356.

117. See also Mandel, "Was Rabbi Aqiva a Martyr?" 367.

118. As recently demonstrated in Rubenstein, "Rabbinic Translation of Relics."

"Fool, Look to the End of the Verse"

b. Ḥullin 87a and Its Christian Background

MICHAL BAR-ASHER SIEGAL

What is the nature of rabbinic stories about *minim* and their interactions with rabbinic figures?[1] What is the function of stories in which a *min* asks a question of a rabbi and is rebuffed? Are these literary depictions of actual historical polemics, or are they merely Jewish rabbinic fantasies meant to ridicule the "other"? Of course, this question has fundamental ramifications for both the historical research of Jewish–Christian interactions in late antiquity and the literary study of the composition of the talmudic corpora.

A crucial element of answering these questions is identifying who these *minim* are. Scholars have proposed many different possible referents of this term: Christians—Jewish or gentile; members of one of the Greco-Roman religions; Gnostics; Samaritans; Sadducees; and supporters of Roman rule. Most scholars now, however, agree that the term *min* or *minim* in rabbinic literature cannot easily be mapped onto a specific non-

This research was supported by the Israel Science Foundation (Grant No. 1199/17). I wish to thank the participants of the "The Aggada of the Babylonian Talmud and Its Cultural World" conference for their many good questions and suggestions. I specifically wish to thank Adela Yarbro Collins, Laura Nasrallah, Elitzur Bar-Asher Siegal, Jeff Rubenstein, Geoffrey Herman, Moulie Vidas, Naphtali Meshel, Martha Himmelfarb, AnneMarie Luijendijk, and my students in the advanced talmudic seminar class at the Goldstein-Goren Department of Jewish Thought, Ben-Gurion University of the Negev, for discussing with me some of the points presented in this paper. Rabbinic sources are quoted according to the manuscript versions as found in *Ma'agarim: The Historical Dictionary Project of the Academy of the Hebrew Language* maagarim.hebrew-academy.org.il.

1. For a survey of these sources, see, e.g., R. T. Herford, *Christianity in Talmud and Midrash* (London: Williams & Norgate, 1903); Daniel Sperber, "Min," *Encyclopedia Judaica* 14:263–64 (2nd ed.; ed. Michael Berenbaum and Fred Skolnik; Detroit: Macmillan, 2007), and Alan F. Segal, *Two Powers in Heaven: Early Rabbinic Reports about Christianity and Gnosticism*, SJLA 25 (Leiden: Brill, 1977).

rabbinic group.[2] The various works of rabbinic literature reflect different uses of this term, which sometimes can be defined more specifically in light of a particular literary context, but sometimes cannot.

Recent scholarship has greatly advanced our understanding of the *minim* stories in rabbinic literature. Such studies have focused, for example, on the importance of the chronological difference of the sources: Adolph Buechler had earlier on observed changes in the term's use over time, noting that *min* in Tannaitic sources refers to a heretical Jew, whereas in talmudic literature it denotes a non-Jewish heretic.[3] While Adiel Schremer expanded on Buechler's thesis in his book on Tannaitic literature,[4] Richard Kalmin has explored the differing uses of the term in Palestinian and Babylonian sources.[5] The latter have many more *minim* stories, in almost all of which the *min* is depicted conversing with Palestinian rabbis. Kalmin takes this as yet another indication of the Babylonian rabbis' "separation from Bible-reading non-Jews," likely influenced by Zoroastrian practices.[6]

My own recent research project focuses on several of the *minim* narratives in the Babylonian Talmud, in which I believe we can more safely determine that the *min* figure is meant to be understood in light of a Christian context. I will discuss one of these sources, b. Ḥul. 87a, in greater depth below. But I wish to return first to my original question: If we read, for example, a talmudic story where Beruria is talking to a Christian *min*, or where R. Abbahu is presented as engaging in a fierce dialogue with a Christian *min*, what is the nature of these stories? Kalmin and Shai Secunda both view such stories as providing historical evidence of some sort.[7] Kalmin reads the Babylonian stories as reflecting a historical situation, not in Babylonia but rather in Palestine. Secunda agrees that the stories "partially reflect polemical realities in Roman Palestine," but he sees the abundance of *minim* stories in the Bavli as evidence of such polemical interactions in the Persian Empire itself.[8] Supporting their argument are points of correspondence between nonrabbinic and Christian sources and the questions the *minim* ask.

---

2. See, e.g., Shaye J. D. Cohen, "A Virgin Defiled: Some Rabbinic and Christian Views on the Origins of Heresy," *USQR* 36 (1980): 3. See also Stuart S. Miller, "The *Minim* of Sepphoris Reconsidered," *HTR* 86 (1993): 377–402; Steven T. Katz, "The Rabbinic Response to Christianity," in *The Cambridge History of Judaism*, vol. 4, *The Late Roman-Rabbinic Period*, ed. Steven T. Katz (Cambridge: Cambridge University Press, 2006), 287–93.

3. Adolph Büchler, *Studies in Jewish History: The Adolph Büchler Memorial Volume*, ed. I. Brodie and J. Rabbinowitz (Oxford: Oxford University Press, 1956), 245–74.

4. Adiel Schremer, *Brothers Estranged: Heresy, Christianity, and Jewish Identity in Late Antiquity* (Oxford: Oxford University Press, 2010).

5. Richard Kalmin, "Christians and Heretics in Rabbinic Literature of Late Antiquity," *HTR* 87 (1994): 155–69.

6. Richard Kalmin, *The Sage in Jewish Society in Late Antiquity* (London: Routledge, 1999).

7. Shai Secunda, "Reading the Bavli in Iran," *JQR* 100 (2010): 310–42.

8. Ibid., 334.

Other scholars have suggested that we read the *minim* in these stories not as evidence of historical interactions but rather as articulations of inner-rabbinic attitudes. Christine Hayes sees in these texts evidence of rabbinic anxiety about their own advanced methods of midrashic biblical interpretation and the extent of their authority as interpreters of the biblical text.[9] Putting these views in the mouths of non-rabbis shows the rabbis' ability to understand the critique of their work and, to some extent, to internalize it. In other words, what we read when we read dialogues between rabbinic Jews and *minim* is a fabricated story, a discursive invention through which we can glean insights into the rabbis' own mind-set.

But are these our only options? Do we need to choose between reading talmudic dialogues between Jews and Christians as literary fiction *or* historical depiction? In this article, I will attempt to suggest a middle ground, a third way of reading some of these stories that I will demonstrate through a close reading of one example. I will suggest reading a rabbinic dialogue with a *min* as an intellectual exercise on the part of the rabbis, a pretend dialogue composed to express rabbinic thoughts. In this way, I side with Hayes's nonhistorical approach to these texts, which do not, in my view, represent actual Jewish–Christian dialogues and should not be read as such. I will propose, however, that these fictional literary creations are rooted in historical realities. Here, I come closer to Secunda and Kalmin, but I will not attempt to understand the stories in light of historical Jewish–Christian polemics. Rather, I read them in the context of internal Christian debates. I will call for a reading of the stories as a rabbinic attempt to take part in the broader conversation taking place outside their doors. These stories relate to debates taking place among various Christian subgroups in the midst of the extraordinary process of the formation of Christianity in late antiquity. These Christian debates range, for instance, from beliefs and practices to Christians' relationship to Scripture, to their attitudes toward the Roman and Persian Empires. The rabbinic texts reflect, to my mind, the thought processes of the small group of rabbis looking at the debates raging in the Christian world and imagining how they might participate in the conversation.

I will try to show that the way in which the biblical verses at the center of some of these rabbi–*min* dialogues are employed can be better understood if read in light of nonrabbinic literary material. When read through the lens of Christian writings, the talmudic stories are both better comprehended and show that the actual debate is not centered on Jewish–Christian issues specifically but, in most cases, on a broader argument found in nonrabbinic sources. When we read the specific biblical text at the center of

9. Christine Hayes, "Displaced Self-Perceptions: The Deployment of 'mînîm' and Romans in b. Sanhedrin 90b–91a," in *Religious and Ethnic Communities in Later Roman Palestine*, ed. Hayim Lapin (Bethesda, MD: University Press of Maryland, 1998), 249–89.

the talmudic dialogue as it was read in widely known debates within Christianity, the talmudic story no longer needs to be read solely as a reflection of Jewish–Christian polemic. Rather, I suggest viewing the talmudic texts as intellectual exercises in which the rabbis ask: if we were to participate in this larger conversation, how would we respond? If we were to imagine ourselves as participants in this scriptural-theological debate between Christian writers, how could we respond? In other words, I want to offer a reading of these texts as historical, insofar as they represent actual debates concerning these exact biblical verses, but ahistorical, insofar as they do not reflect actual Jewish–Christian debates over these verses. These dialogues are "guided imagery" of sorts, in which the rabbis imagine playing a part in the wider discussions of the world in which they lived.

b. Ḥullin 87a

Let us take as an example the story in b. Ḥullin 87a (MS Vatican 122):

ת״ש. [ד]א״ל ההוא מ[י]נא[10] לר׳. מי שיצר הרים לא ברא רוח. מי שברא רוח לא יצר הרים. שנ׳ ״(יוצר) כי הנה יוצר הרים ובורא רוח״. א״ל. שוטה שבעולם. שפיל לסיפיה דקרא. ״י״ צבאות שמו״.[11] א״ל. שטיא קרית ליה.[12] נקוט לי זימנא תלתא יומי ומהדרנא לך תיובתא. קבע ליה זימנ׳ תלתא יומין.[13] יתיב ר׳ תלת׳ יומין בתעניתא כי היכי דלא אשכח תשובה.[14] כי הוה בעי למיברא אמרו ליה. מינא קאי אבבא. א׳. ״ויתנו בברותי רוש ולצמאי ישקו׳ חומץ״. א״ל. ר׳. בשורות טובות אני אומ׳ לך.[15] אויבך לא מצא תשובה ועלה לגג ונפל ומת.[16] א״ל. רצונך שתסעוד אצלי. א״ל. הן. לאחר שאכלו ושתו א״ל. רצונך. כוס של ברכה אתה שותה או ארבעים זהובים אתה נוטל בשכרך. א״ל. כוס של ברכה אני שותה. יצתה בת קול ואמרה. כוס של ברכה שוה ארבעי׳ זהובים. א״ר יצחק. ועדיין ישנה לאותה משפחה בין גדולי רומי[17]. וקורין לאותה משפחה בית בר לוינוס.

---

10. In the printed version: צדוקי, "a Sadducee."

11. Notice that this version of the verse differs from the masoretic version, which has יהוה אלהי צבאות שמו, "The Lord, *the God* of hosts." I thank Geoffrey Herman for this comment.

12. This sentence is missing in MS Vatican 120–121 and MS Munich, as well as in the printed editions. It is present in *Aggadot Hatalmud* and the *Yalqut Shim'oni*. See n. 20 in *Diqduqe Soferim, ad loc.*

13. This sentence is missing in MS Vatican 120–121 and MS Munich, as well as in the printed editions.

14. The words כי היכי דלא אשכח תשובה are missing in MS Vatican 120–121 and MS Munich, as well as in the printed editions.

15. MS Vatican 120-121 and the printed edition have מבשר טובות אני לך.

16. This version is found also in Aggadot Hatalmud and the Yalqut Shim'oni. MSS Munich and Vatican 120-121 have אויבך נפל מן הגג.

17. Printed versions have הארץ instead of רומי. MS Munich does not have the last three words בין גדולי רומי

> Come and hear: A certain *min* said to Rabbi, "He who formed the mountains did not create the wind; and he who created the wind did not form the mountains, as it is said: 'For, lo, He who forms the mountains and creates the wind' (Amos 4:13)." He replied, "Oh worldly fool! Look down to the end of the verse: 'The Lord of hosts, is His name.'" He said to him, "Did you call me a fool?![18] Grant me three days time, and I shall give you an answer." He set a period of three days. Rabbi spent those three days in fasting so that [the *min*] would not find an answer. Thereafter, as he was about to partake of food, he was told, "There is a *min* standing at the door." He said, "They gave me poison for food, and for my thirst they gave me vinegar to drink" (Ps 69:22). He said to him, "Rabbi, good tidings I am about to tell you; your enemy found no answer and so he went up to the roof and fell and died." He said, "Would you be willing to dine with me?" He replied, "Yes." After they had eaten and drunk, he [Rabbi] said to him, "Would you like to receive the cup of the blessing [i.e., over which Grace after Meals was recited] or would you rather have forty gold coins as your reward?" He replied, "I would rather drink the cup of the blessing." Thereupon there came forth a Heavenly Voice and said, "The cup of the blessing is worth forty gold coins." R. Yitsḥaq said, "Members of the family [of that *min*] are still to be found amongst the notables of Rome and that family is named Bar Luianus."

At the center of this dialogue stands a discussion concerning the interpretation of Amos 4:13.[19] The *min* seems to state that this verse affirms that there were two separate entities involved in the creation of the mountains and the wind. The phrasing of the question shows that he infers this conclusion from the use of two different verbs: "*formed* the mountains and *created* the wind"—"He who *formed* the mountains did not *create* the wind, and he who *created* the wind did not *form* the mountains." His statement is answered by Rabbi, who first calls him a fool, then tells him to read on to the end of the verse, and finally quotes the end of the verse, "The Lord of hosts, is His name." This quotation apparently proves the falsehood of the *min*'s claim.

This structure of *min*–rabbi dialogue, including the key phrase, "Fool, look to the end of the verse," appears in several other stories in the Babylonian Talmud.[20] In these other passages, however, the part containing this

18. The literal translation is "Did you call him a fool?" using the 3rd person pronoun instead of the 1st person pronoun, for euphemism. See Elitzur A. Bar-Asher Siegal, *Introduction to the Grammar of Jewish Babylonian Aramaic*, 2nd rev. and exp. ed. (Münster: Ugarit-Verlag, 2016), 96, for this kind of change in person, used as a euphemism in order to avoid direct reference in sensitive contexts.

19. For a survey of other uses of verses from Amos in rabbinic literature, see Samson H. Levey, "Amos in the Rabbinic Tradition," in *Tradition as Openness to the Future: Essays in Honor of Willis W. Fisher*, ed. Fred O. Francis and Raymond Paul Wallace (Lanham, MD: University Press of America, 1984), 55–69.

20. b. Ber. 10a; b. Erub. 101a; b. Sukkah 52b.

phrase marks the end of the story, while our story continues to discuss the *min*'s reaction and its aftermath. In this case, the *min* is obviously upset by being called a fool. Indeed, in the version of MS Vatican 122, he explicitly reacts to being called a fool, declaring that he will take three days to think of a rejoinder to Rabbi's answer. We are then told that Rabbi spends these three days in fasting fearing the next round of scholastic debate.

MS Vatican 122 explicitly describes Rabbi's fast as a means to prevent the *min* from finding an answer.[21] According to this version, the fast is a way to petition God for divine help and may even be viewed as some kind of sympathetic magical act by which an action is meant to affect the behavior of another individual. We find in contemporary magical texts similar "binding spells" that are "aggressive" by nature and "were intended to inflict harm on their targets, and/or 'coercive', meaning they sought to force the targets to act in a certain way, even against their will."[22]

It seems to work: Rabbi sits to break his fast after three days, relieved that the *min* has not returned; but just as he starts to eat, he is interrupted. A *min* has come. Rabbi expresses his displeasure by quoting another biblical verse, Ps 69:22: "They gave me poison for food, and for my thirst they gave me vinegar to drink." It turns out, however, that the *min* in question is another *min* altogether, who has come to deliver good news: the first *min* is dead. According to MS Vatican 122, he has (presumably) committed suicide by jumping off a roof, having found no answer to Rabbi's challenge. In the other versions of the text, the second *min* simply reports that the first *min* has fallen off the roof and died. The difference between these versions is significant: did the *min* die an accidental death, as a result of which Rabbi was saved from the continuation of the dispute by sheer luck or as a result of his fast? Or, was the *min*'s death intentional, the result of despair over his failure to come up with an answer? Did Rabbi win the argument, or was he saved from it? In other cases in rabbinic literature, the phrase "he went up a roof and fell"—עלה לגג ונפל—usually denotes suicide.[23] So, even according to the less-detailed version, the story might still convey that Rabbi's opponent has failed in his mission and taken his own life. However, the Mishna explicitly demonstrates that the expression falling off a roof can indicate either suicide or accidental death (m. Giṭ. 6:6):

---

21. The absence of this sentence in the other manuscripts might suggest a different understanding of the purpose of Rabbi's fast. These could be multiple purposes starting from the death of the min or even praying for the ability to come up with a counterargument when needed.

22. Ortal-Paz Saar, "A Study in Conceptual Parallels: Graeco-Roman Binding Spells and Babylonian Incantation Bowls," *AS* 13 (2015): 26; and see the entire article for further bibliography on this topic, 24–53. I thank Gal Sofer for this reference.

23. See, for example, a student embarrassed by a whore (b. Ber. 23a); the famous martyrdom of the woman and her seven sons (b. Giṭ. 57b; also found in earlier Second Temple sources); or the gentile selling his red heifer (Sipre Zut. 19:2).

מעשה בבריא שא׳. כתבו [גט] {ותנו} לאשת[י]. ועלה לראש הגג ונפל [ומת. אמ׳ רבן שמע׳ בן גמל׳]. אמרו חכמ׳. אם [מ]עצמו נפל הרי זה גט. ואם הרוח דח[י]יתו אינו גט.

> It once happened that a man in sound health said, "Write out a bill of divorce for my wife." He then went up to the top of the roof and fell and died. Rabban Shimeon b. Gamaliel said, "The Sages said, 'If he fell down of his own volition, then the bill of divorce is valid; but if the wind blew him down, it is not valid.'"

Thus, both options are possible here, according to the version preserved in MS Munich. And it does make a difference in the story: did Rabbi prevail due to his scholarly abilities, or was it the hand of God that spared him? If this is a scenario imagined by the talmudic author, is he imagining a victory delivered by scholarship or by chance?[24]

After he shares his news, the second *min* and Rabbi sit down together for a meal. At this point, Rabbi poses a kind of test: would the *min* prefer a cup of wine over which Grace has been recited or forty gold coins? He chooses the cup of wine, and a heavenly voice declares this story proof of the worth of the cup of the blessing. R. Yitsḥaq adds a historical statement: this *min*'s family is a well-known Roman family by the name of Bar Luianus.

Throughout this story we see strong signs of polemical language. The tension is evident from Rabbi's initial insult ("You fool!"); the *min*'s request for three days to think of a response; Rabbi's need to fast for three days to prevent such an answer and his citation of Ps 69:22, suggesting that the debate is like eating poison; the *min*'s suicide or tragic death; the language used by the second *min*, calling the first *min*'s death "good news" and referring to him as "your enemy"; and the celebratory feast which ends the story. These elements of our story led Isaac Halevy, at the end of the nineteenth century, to suggest that there is something more going on here. He argues that Rabbi would not have taken a three-day fast upon himself, nor would the *min* have asked for a three-day extension, were there not something larger at stake than a question of biblical exegesis. Halevy surmises from the details of the story that this "was not a private argument, but rather a greater, more general issue for both of them."[25] He therefore identifies the *min* as a Roman informant/collaborator (מלשין) who puts the entire Jewish community in danger. Halevy also pointed to the parallel version of this story in b. Sanh. 39a, to which I now turn.

---

24. If, however, we take into account the fast as effective (either as a petition to God or even as a magical act), and that the events that follow are a result of this fast, then we might say that either God caused the opponent not to find an answer or caused him to accidentally fall off the roof, so the difference between the readings is minor. I thank Jeffrey Rubenstein for this comment.

25. Isaac Halevy, *Dorot Harishonim* (Frankfurt am Main: Kauffmann, 1897), 1:87.

b. Sanhedrin 39a

This passage includes the *min*'s question from b. Ḥullin, but the context and trappings are entirely different. The question is one in a series of questions placed in the mouth of the emperor (קיסר), all of which cast doubt on the singularity of the creator:

> אמר ליה קיסר לרבן גמליאל. מי שברא הרים לא ברא רוח ומי שברא רוח לא ברא הרים. דכתי׳ ״כי הנה יוצר הרים וברא רוח״. אלא מעתה גבי אדם דכת׳ ״ויברא״ ״וייצר״ הכי נמי מי שברא זה לא ברא זה ומי שברא זה לא ברא זה. טפח על טפח יש בו באדם ושני נקבים יש בו באדם. מי שברא זה לא ברא זה ומי שברא זה לא ברא זה. דכת׳ ״הנוטע אזן הלא ישמע אם יוצר עין הלא יביט״. מי שברא אזן לא ברא עין. אמ׳ ליה. אין. ושעת מיתה כולם ניפוסו.
>
> The Emperor said to Rabban Gamaliel, "He who created the mountains did not create the wind, and he who created the wind did not create the mountains, as it is written, 'For lo, He who forms the mountains and creates the wind'" (Amos 4:13). According to this reasoning, when we find it written of Adam, "And He created" (Genesis 1:27), and, "And he formed" (Genesis 2:7), would you also say that He who created this did not create that and that He who created that did not create this?! [Further,] there is a part of the human body just a handbreadth square which contains two holes (= an ear and an eye). Did He who created this not create that and He who created that not create this, because it is written, "He that plants the ear, shall he not hear? He that forms the eye, shall he not see?" (Ps. 94:9) Did He that created the ear not create the eye?! He said, "Yes." At the hour of death all are brought to agree.

Halevy uses the more elaborate story in b. Ḥullin to explain the general nature of *minim* stories in rabbinic sources, and the danger they reveal from the Jewish apostates in the Roman world. I agree with his assessment that the story in b. Ḥullin, with its more detailed description, holds the key for understanding the significance of this specific biblical debate. But, unlike Halevy, I prefer to read the story in the context of Christian discussions concerning the verse cited from the book of Amos than in light of an argument with Roman interlocutors over the question of duality.

Amos 4:13

The verse at the center of these two talmudic sources is Amos 4:13. This biblical verse is one of three doxologies found in Amos, assumed by scholars to be taken from a hymn praising Yahweh,[26] whether a later addition

26. James L. Crenshaw, *Hymnic Affirmation of Divine Justice: The Doxologies of Amos and Related Texts in the Old Testament*, SBLDS 24 (Missoula, MT: Scholars Press, 1975).

or one already used by Amos himself.[27] The unique style of these doxologies is "characterised by use of participles, in some instances followed by finite verbs, which describe the actions of Yahweh in creation and control of nature. In each case they also contain the formula The Lord (God of hosts) is his name.'"[28] It expresses a "theophanic tradition" (God can turn day into night) in line with other such theophanic expressions in Amos as a whole.

The Minor Prophets, as a collection, circulated at least as early as the first decades of the second century BCE,[29] and scholars suggest that Amos was translated into Greek by the end of the second century BCE.[30] The Septuagint version of the verse differs from the Hebrew Masoretic version. Here are the two compared:

διότι ἰδοὺ ἐγὼ στερεῶν βροντὴν καὶ κτίζων πνεῦμα καὶ ἀπαγγέλλων εἰς ἀνθρώπους τὸν χριστὸν αὐτοῦ, ποιῶν ὄρθρον καὶ ὁμίχλην καὶ ἐπιβαίνων ἐπὶ τὰ ὕψη τῆς γῆς κύριος ὁ θεὸς ὁ παντοκράτωρ ὄνομα αὐτῷ.	כִּי הִנֵּה יוֹצֵר הָרִים וּבֹרֵא רוּחַ וּמַגִּיד לְאָדָם מַה שֵּׂחוֹ עֹשֵׂה שַׁחַר עֵיפָה וְדֹרֵךְ עַל בָּמֳתֵי אָרֶץ יְהוָה אֱלֹהֵי צְבָאוֹת שְׁמוֹ
For, behold, *I am* the one who *strengthens thunder* and creates wind and *proclaims to humans his anointed*, who makes daybreak and *misty* dark and treads on the high places of the earth. The Lord, the God, the Almighty One is His name.[31]	For lo, He who *forms the mountains* and creates the wind and *reveals his thoughts to man*, makes the morning darkness and treads on the high places of the earth , the Lord, the God of hosts, is His name.

27. See bibliographical references in W. Boyd Barrick, *BMH as Body Language: A Lexical and Iconographical Study of the Word BMH When Not a Reference to Cultic Phenomena in Biblical and Post-Biblical Hebrew*, LHBOTS 477 (New York: T&T Clark, 2008), 51–52.

28. Tchadvar S. Hadjiev, *The Composition and Redaction of the Book of Amos*, BZAW 393 (Berlin: de Gruyter, 2009), 127.

29. Gunnar Magnus Eidsvåg, *The Old Greek Translation of Zechariah*, VTSup 170 (Leiden: Brill, 2015), 15, based on a reference in Sirach and textual evidence from the Dead Sea Scrolls.

30. Aaron W. Park, *The Book of Amos as Composed and Read in Antiquity*, StBibLit 37 (New York: Lang, 2001), 171. See also Jennifer Mary Dines, "The Septuagint of Amos: A Study in Interpretation" (PhD diss., University of London, 1992), 311–13. On the number and identity of the translator(s) of Amos, see George E. Howard "Some Notes on the Septuagint of Amos," *VT* 20 (1970): 108–12; Takamitsu Muraoka, "Is the Septuagint Amos VIII,12–IX,10 a Separate Unit?," *VT* 20 (1970): 496–500; idem, "In Defence of the Unity of the Septuagint Minor Prophets," *Annual of the Japanese Biblical Institute* 15 (1989): 25–36.

31. Translation taken from W. Edward Glenny, Finding Meaning in the Text :Translation Technique and Theology in the Septuag*int of Amos*, VTSup 126 (Leiden: Brill, 2009), 237. The translation by George E. Howard in NETS has: "For behold, I am the one who makes the thunder strong and creates a wind and announces his anointed to humans, makes dawn and mist and treads on the heights of the earth. The Lord God the Almighty is his name" (792).

Of the five present participles, the third—ἀπαγγέλλων εἰς ἀνθρώπους τὸν χριστὸν αὐτοῦ—is naturally the most intriguing. The MT מה שחו was translated as if it read משיחו, "his anointed." Scholars have characterized this translation as the result of either mistakes in the text before the translator or a misunderstanding of the *hapax legomenon*, שח, in the Hebrew.[32] Whether this specific translation was prompted by textual difficulties alone or by a theological agenda that drove the translator toward a specific solution to these difficulties is debated by scholars. All agree, however, that the end result reflects some sort of messianic theology.[33] In any case, the theological implications of such a translation are obvious, and this change is considered one of the more crucial messianic indications (which is not suspect as a later Christian addition) in the Septuagint. The identity of this "anointed" is debated, as well, and scholars have suggested a high priest, a Davidic king figure, or a more universal eschatological figure.[34]

A few other changes are evident in the Septuagint text: the addition of the pronoun ἐγώ, "I am," missing from the Hebrew,[35] and the rendering of the Hebrew יוצר הרים, "[the one] who forms the mountains," as στερεῶν βροντήν, "the one who strengthens thunder."[36]

Amos 4:13 in Christian Writings

This verse, "a crux for the theological discussions of the day,"[37] stood at the heart of many early Christian discussions and is quoted multiple times in the writings of the church fathers. The patristic interpretation of this verse "contributed greatly to the formulation of early Christian theology."[38] In a survey of the different references to this verse, J. G. Kelly shows that they deal mostly with three issues: debates concerning the orthodox teaching on creation; God's announcement of the anointed; and the creation of the wind/Holy Spirit. There are fierce debates between early Christian writers on these issues. For example, Tertullian uses this verse

32. See Glenny, *Finding Meaning*, 141–43, and references there. Cf. A. Gelston, "Some Hebrew Misreadings in the Septuagint of Amos," *VT* 52 (2002): 493–500.

33. See, e.g., J. Lust, "Messianism and Septuagint," in *Congress Volume: Salamanca 1983*, ed. John A. Emerton, VTSup 36 (Leiden: Brill, 1985), 174–91; Karen H. Jobes and Moisés Silva, *Invitation to the Septuagint* (Grand Rapids: Baker, 2000), 297.

34. See Glenny, *Finding Meaning*, 236–40.

35. See Glenny, *Finding Meaning*, 48.

36. See Glenny, *Finding Meaning*, 177–78, for possible reasons for this change.

37. J. G. Kelly, "The Interpretation of Amos 4:13 in the Early Christian Community," in *Essays in Honor of Joseph P. Brennan*, ed. Robert F. McNamara (Rochester, NY: Saint Bernard's Seminary, 1977), 64; see 60–77 for a survey of these sources.

38. Ibid., 74.

in his writings against Praxeas and Marcion, and different groups cite it in the controversy over the exact nature and office of the Holy Spirit.[39]

The three questions for which Amos 4:13 is invoked are not unrelated: the messianic addition preserved in the Septuagint translation called attention to the verse in the early Christian context, and other discussions emerged as a result. Let us take for example a passage from Ambrose, *On the Holy Spirit* (2.6):[40]

> Nor does it escape my notice that *heretics* have been wont to object that the Holy Spirit appears to be a *creature,* because many of them use as an argument for establishing their impiety that passage of Amos, where he spoke of the blowing of the wind, as the words of the prophet made clear.[41] … Yet, that we may keep to our point, is it not evident that in what Amos said the order of the passage shows that the prophet was speaking of the creation of this world? He begins as follows: "I am the Lord that establish the thunders and create the wind [spirit]." The order of the words itself teaches us; for if he had wished to speak of the Holy Spirit, he would certainly not have put the thunders in the first place. For thunder is not more ancient than the Holy Spirit; though they be ungodly, they still dare not say that.… But if anyone thinks that the word of the prophet is to be explained with reference to the Holy Spirit, *because it is said, "Declaring unto men His Christ,"* he will explain it more easily of the Lord's Incarnation. For if it troubles you that he said Spirit, and therefore you think that this cannot well be explained of the mystery of the taking of human nature, *read on in the Scriptures* and you will find that all agrees most excellently with Christ, of Whom it is thoroughly fitting to think that He established the thunders by His coming, that is, the force and sound of the heavenly Scriptures, by the thunder, as it were, of which our minds are struck with astonishment, so that we learn to be afraid, and pay respect to the heavenly oracles.

Ambrose was bishop of Milan in the second half of the fourth century, and he wrote in Latin. His biblical interpretations were "central to the western intellectual tradition." Seeing the events of his time as evidence of the success of Christianity in the eyes of God, Ambrose fiercely objected to those he considered heretics.[42] In this text, written around the year 381 CE, he takes issue with those who read Amos 4:13 as testimony for the creation of the Holy Spirit. Ambrose insists that Amos refers to regular wind, and not the Holy Spirit. He proves it by reading contextually and focusing

---

39. Ibid.

40. Translation according to *NPNF*^{2} 10:120–21.

41. Ambrose's version of this verse is slightly different from the Septuagint. I hope to address this point elsewhere.

42. John Moorhead, *Ambrose: Church and Society in the Late Roman World,* Medieval World (London: Longman, 1999), esp. chapter 4, "Church, State, Heretics and Pagans."

on the ordering of the verse. In the latter half of this passage, Ambrose gives a second reading of the verse, this time offering a reading of the wind as the Holy Spirit, but in a way that is still theologically acceptable in his view. The reason for his willingness to consider this second reading, he says, is because this same verse introduces the anointed. This suggests to Ambrose that we might read other parts of the verse as referring not to natural elements but rather to Jesus's incarnation. This allegorical reading works well in this context, and to those who do not see it Ambrose suggests that they "read on" (*prosequere Scripturas*) in the verses.

In this passage, Ambrose cites a specific dispute with "heretics" regarding Amos 4:13. The center of the argument concerns the verb "to create" and the notion of the "creation" of the Holy Spirit stands at the heart of the argument between Ambrose and his heretics. Ambrose focuses on the context of the verse and insists that the verse must be read in its entirety, not as fragmented pieces. This call is phrased as an exhortation to the biblical reader: "read on." These elements are all found in our talmudic passage, as well. Thus, even as it is clear that we are not speaking of direct dependence of the talmudic passage on this specific text from Ambrose, there are nevertheless clear similarities between these two contemporary literary genres centering on the same Amos verse that I wanted to highlight.

The Christian Background of the Passage in b. Ḥullin

Amos 4:13

If we are not aiming to demonstrate direct textual dependency, how does this analogous Christian text help us better understand the talmudic narrative? I wish to propose that this and other passages in late-antique Christian literature dealing with similar issues related to Amos 4:13 can be useful for understanding the short and enigmatic passage in tractate Ḥullin, and its relation to the parallel text in Sanhedrin.

Most importantly, the Latin passage from Ambrose shows that a verse central to a rabbinic *min* dialogue also stood at the center of a much broader, and very crucial, Christian theological debate in Syriac and Greek writings as well. Christians were reading this verse and arguing vehemently about its meaning. My suggestion is that what we read in the Babylonian Talmud is an exercise in guided imagery. That is, the talmudic text is imagining itself participating in this larger debate and asking: if a *min* were to walk through these doors and ask this question here, how would we answer?

There is, however, a catch: if a *min* were to enter the rabbinic *bet midrash* and pose this question, he would have to use the right kind of text: the

Hebrew Masorah rather than the Septuagint. There is no Christ announcement in the text as it stood before the rabbis. So in our imaginary scenario, the discussion focuses not on this messianic declaration but rather on the nature of the entity that is the subject of the act of "creation" and "formation." When imported into the study house, the claim to be refuted shifts and particular points of the discussion are changed. The argument thus should be read in light of the focus on the two unique verbs describing the creation of the entities in the verse, chief among them, the spirit/wind. The *min* now advocates a reading of the verse that supports a form of dualism in which the focus is on the creation of the holy spirits, and the end result is the ability of Rabbi to pull the rug from underneath the wider, non-Jewish discussion.

I admit that I cannot prove that the *min*'s words in the talmudic passage *must* be read in light of the Christian preoccupation with Amos 4:13 and its crucial importance to contemporaneous theological discussions. They certainly *can* be read as a simple claim for a dualistic creator. Sure enough, this is how it was understood in the parallel in Sanhedrin. The Sanhedrin passage, however, would appear to be secondary to the Ḥullin tradition; the Talmud here groups together several verses in order to ridicule the emperor's dualistic assertion. Notice that in Sanhedrin, in all manuscripts, the question is framed as "He who *created* the mountains did not *create* the wind and he who *created* the wind did not *create* the mountains." The distinction between the two different verbs of creation, which is the entire premise of the exegetical debate in Ḥullin, is lost in this phrasing, which focuses on the bottom line: who is the creator, the question of whether there are, in fact, two creators. The Ḥullin narrative, by contrast, revolves around the distinction between these two verbs: "He who *formed* the mountains did not *create* the wind, and he who *created* the wind did not *form* the mountains." This discussion is directly connected to the two acts of creation, which was also the premise of contemporary Christian debates surrounding this verse. It is as though we are meant to read: "He who 'created' the mountains [and all the rest of the natural elements] did not 'create' the Spirit, which was 'formed' in an entirely different manner." The Spirit is fundamentally different from the rest of creation, says the *min*, and this verse proves it. Rabbi answers this claim by quoting the end of the verse, which includes God's name and dispels any notions of other godly elements.

Moreover, the Ḥullin passage can be read as refuting the Christian reading of the verse by recentering the conversation around the Hebrew Masorah text. The added pronoun ἐγώ in the Septuagint version, "*I am* the one who …," does not exist in the Hebrew text. In the Hebrew, the list of present participles is not preceded by a grammatical subject, and therefore each participle can, in theory, be understood independently. This grammatical structure underlies the *min*'s claim in the talmudic text. Rabbi's response is that the final clause, "the Lord of hosts is his name," refers back to the preceding participles. My suggestion is that we read this framing of the debate as an attempt to "bring home" these non-Jewish biblical textual discussions. This imagined discourse is the rabbis' way of saying: if we were to have this conversation about the Amos verse using *our* text, the grammatical Christian claim would be undermined and will have to be discussed differently than it is being debated in Christian circles.

Psalms 69:22

A few other clues would support situating the *min*'s question in Ḥullin in conversation with the Christian readings of Amos 4:13. The harsh tone of the debate and the dire consequences both parties seem to expect will result from it indicate, as Halevy noted, that the stakes here appear to be very high. This is understandable if we consider the importance of this verse in the wider contemporaneous discussion. This is a verse that, per early Christian writers, declares Christ and describes doctrinal truths about the Holy Spirit. In this context, staking a claim to the verse's true meaning is no small matter.

The verse quoted by Rabbi when he thinks that the *min* has returned with an answer to his initial response is also of significance. This is a humorous scene, describing a starving rabbi who is just about to break his three-day fast—the food-filled fork almost to his lips—when a visitor is announced. In frustration, he quotes Ps 69:22, "They gave me poison for food, and for my thirst they gave me vinegar to drink." This is the only citation of this verse in the entire rabbinic corpus.[43] It is central, however, in early Christian writings, used often to describe Jesus's afflictions during his passion,[44] most evidently in John 19:28–30:[45]

43. It does appear once in 1QH XII, 11: ויעצורו משקה דעת מצמאים ולצמאם ישקום חומץ, "They have denied the drink of Knowledge to the thirsty, but for their thirsty they have given them vinegar to drink" (trans. *The Dead Sea Scrolls Study Edition,* ed. Florentino García Martínez and Eibert J. C. Tigchelaar, 2 vols. [Leiden: Brill, 1997–1998], 1:169). See Stephen P. Ahearne-Kroll, *The Psalms of Lament in Mark's Passion: Jesus' Davidic Suffering,* SNTSMS (Cambridge: Cambridge University Press, 2007), 75.

44. All the gospels have a tradition involving vinegar at the crucifixion, but each has a different tradition. According to its use in antiquity, the giving of vinegar to Jesus can be viewed as offering a dying man a stimulating beverage or as taunting him with a harmful, distasteful drink. See Robert L. Brawley, "An Absent Complement and Intertextuality in John 19:28–29," *JBL* 112 (2003): 436.

45. See Raymond E. Brown, *The Gospel According to John (xiii–xxi): Introduction, Translation, and Notes,* AB 12A (Garden City, NY: Doubleday, 1970), 929; Donald. A. Carson, "John and the Johannine Epistles," in *It Is Written: Scripture Citing Scripture; Essays in Honour of Barnabas Lindars, SSF,* ed. Donald A. Carson and H. G. M. Williamson (Cambridge: Cambridge University Press, 1988), 252. Brawley, "Absent Complement," 427–43.

> After this, when Jesus realized that everything was now completed, he said (in order to fulfill the Scripture), "I'm thirsty." A jar of vinegar [ὄξος] was standing there, so they put a sponge full of the vinegar on a branch of hyssop and held it to his mouth. After Jesus had taken the vinegar, he said, "It is finished." Then he bowed his head and released his spirit.

Although the text does not explicitly quote Psalms, scholars as well as ancient writers have understood this passage as an allusion to Ps 69:22. The text in John "leaves it up to the reader to recall the psalm,"[46] and Jesus's suffering is to be understood as an allusion to the suffering in Ps 69. Jesus is therefore fulfilling the prophecies of Scripture, which foretold the words Jesus would say while on the cross.

The use of this verse, too, in the talmudic story is thus meaningful when read in light of its significance in the Christian world. This is in essence a satirical reversal: while Christians read this verse as a reference to the Jews' giving Jesus vinegar during the crucifixion, in this instance the Christian-*min* causes the Jew, Rabbi, to (metaphorically) drink vinegar. By showing up at the very last minute, right when Rabbi is about to break his fast, he causes Rabbi to liken himself to Jesus in his prolonged suffering.

Falling off a Roof

Another possible satirical element in the talmudic passage is the combination of fasting and falling off a roof, which is also found in the New Testament. In Luke 4, Jesus is tempted by the devil in the desert for forty days, during which he does not eat. The devil asks him to perform several specific miracles in order to prove that he is the son of God, one of which is to jump off the roof of the temple. Jesus refuses. We might read the *min* in the talmudic story in satirical opposition to Jesus: he *does* jump and is not saved. However, the literary motif of death by jumping or falling off a roof is found in other rabbinic stories, though only rarely.[47] As a result, I offer this New Testament connection with some hesitation.

Good tidings

Another possible Christian connection is found in the words of the second *min*. When he announces the death of the first *min*, he uses the words: בשורות טובות אני אומר לך, "good tidings I say to you."[48] MS Vatican has:

46. Brawley, "Absent Complement," 439.

47. See above for references.

48. I am grateful to my student Yonatan Shmidt for drawing my attention to the significance of this term.

מבשר טובות אני לך, "I announce good tidings to you." We find מבשר טוב in Isa 52:7 (מה נאוו על ההרים רגלי מבשר משמיע שלום מבשר טוב משמיע ישועה, "How beautiful on the mountains are the feet of those who bring good news, who proclaim peace, who bring good tidings, who proclaim salvation"). The verbal form מבשר טובות appears only here in the entire rabbinic corpus, and the nominal form בשורות טובות appears very rarely. In fact, all of the appearances of this form are connected to the הטוב והמטיב blessing mentioned in m. Ber. 9:2:

> על הגשמים ועל בשורות טובות הוא אומ׳. ב׳ הטוב והמטיב. [ו]על שמועות הרעות הוא אומ׳. ב׳ דיין האמת.
>
> For rain and good tidings he should say, "Blessed [is he], the good and the doer of good." For bad tidings he should say, "Blessed [is he], the true Judge."

Outside this single context, the nominal form "good tidings" does not appear anywhere else in the rabbinic corpus, only in our story.[49] The Greek equivalent of this term, *euangelion* (εὐαγγέλιον), however, carries special meaning in the Christian tradition. Taken from its usage in Greek, the meaning of *euangelion* as "good tidings" in the context of announcements of important events such as births or victories had, as William Horbury writes, "quickly become[s] a quintessentially Christian term."[50] The "announcer" of Isa 52:7 had already been identified with the "anointed" of Isa 61:1 in Qumran literature.[51] In Christian traditions it soon becomes used to mean the announcement of the coming of the kingdom by Christ. The word appears many times in the New Testament, especially in the Pauline corpus. The Greek term was used without translation and denotes very early on the written gospel book;[52] as such, it is even preserved in the Babylonian Talmud (b. Šabb. 116a) as referring to "books of *minim*."

Recognizing the significance of the term בשורות טובות in the Christian contemporaneous milieu and its relative rareness in rabbinic sources, its appearance in the mouth of the *min* in Ḥullin takes on a particular importance. The storytellers are again signaling to their readers the Christian

---

49. A close parallel might be the form שמועה טובה, as in b. Giṭ. 56b. In the parallel, Lam. Rab. 1:5, the Aramaic בשורתא טבתא is used. A Second Temple source worth mentioning is Megillat Ta'anit, 28 of Adar: "Good news [בשורתא טבתא/טבא] came to the Jews, that they should not depart from the law." See Vered Noam, *Megillat Ta'anit: Versions, Interpretation, History* [Hebrew] (Jerusalem: Yad Yitzhak Ben-Zvi, 2003), 128, 312–13.

50. William Horbury, "'Gospel' in Herodian Judaea," in *The Written Gospel*, ed. Markus Bockmuehl and Donald A. Hagner; (Cambridge: Cambridge University Press, 2005), 10.

51. See ibid., 26.

52. See ibid., 7–30.

background of this figure's literary portrayal. And again the use of this term is satirical: while Christians use this exact term to announce the coming of Christ, in the talmudic story the "good news" for the rabbinic Jew is that the Christian *min*, in a sense, is *not* coming. He is dead.

Three Days

If my above reading is correct, then we cannot ignore the significance of the length of Rabbi's fast. He fasts for three days, after which he is told that the first *min* is dead, and will not come. The parallel to Jesus's own coming after his crucifixion is clear: Jesus came back after his crucifixion—and, according to his own prophecy, after three days (see, e.g., Matt 12:39–40; 27:63; 28). The *min* in our story predicts his return after three days but, at the end, is declared dead and does not come.

Standing at the Gate

The pun might even be pointier, if we take into account the portrayal of the misunderstanding: while we might have thought that the *min* had come back, since he is announced as standing at the gate, in fact he has not returned at all. The New Testament refers to signs for him being near, standing at the door/gates: "Even so, when you see all these things, you know that it is near, right at the door [θύραις]" (Matt 24:33; Mark 13:29; see also Luke 12:36). In an obvious reference to Song of Songs, "Listen! My beloved is knocking: Open to me, my sister my darling, my dove, my flawless one" (5:2), we find in Rev 3:20: "Here I am! I stand at the door [θύραν] and knock. If anyone hears my voice and opens the door, I will come in and eat with that person, and they with me."[53] Here the description of his coming is even more explicit and involves a festive meal right after his arrival. The rabbinic parody therefore is yet another pointed attack: The Christian *min* is *thought* to be at the gate, but he is not. He is quite dead. And the feasting and eating indeed take place but are done without him and in the company of the righteous *min*.

Do Not Gloat When Your Enemy Falls

Regardless of the above-mentioned possible link between falling off a roof in the New Testament and in this story, the second *min*'s announcement is still significantly phrased. Notice that the *min* is using the formula אויבך

53. See Jonathan Kaplan, *My Perfect One: Typology and Early Rabbinic Interpretation of Song of Songs* (New York: Oxford University Press, 2015), 186.

לא מצא תשובה ועלה לגג ונפל ומת, "your enemy could find no answer and so he went up to the roof and fell and died." The word אויב used here is surprising since it is a biblical word and is replaced in rabbinic literature by the word שונא. Thus, for example, the biblical words והוא לא אויב לו in Num 35:23, is treated in the Sipre Numbers 160 (MS Vatican 32): ליפסול את הסונאין מלישב בדין, "to render the enemies unfit to judge."[54] Ours is one of the very few cases in rabbinic literature in which the word אויב is employed outside of a biblical quotation.[55]

It seems that the rare use of the biblical word in the talmudic story is a deliberate pun on the verse in Prov 24:17: בנפל אויבך אל תשמח ובכשלו אל יגל לבך, "Do not gloat when your enemy falls; when they stumble, do not let your heart rejoice." While Proverbs urges us not to gloat and rejoice at the metaphoric fall of our enemies, this story tells exactly of the rejoicing and celebrating of the actual fall of an enemy.[56]

Fool

I should briefly address the insult used by Rabbi toward the *min*: שוטה, "fool." This term can indicate a low evaluation of an individual's intelligence, as when "fool" appears in rabbinic literature as a legal category, often coupled with the hearing-impaired and minors. But it seems to carry specific implications when used as a derogatory term, meant to demonstrate a critical or disrespectful attitude. The latter sense of "fool" is not very common, and it appears only in relation to specific groups, such as the Galileans (b.ʿErub. 53b) and Sadducees (b. B. Bat. 115b, quoting the Scholion to Megillat Ta'anit). Jesus is also called a fool (b. Šabb. 104b), as are a small handful of others who are criticized for foolish behavior (b. ʿAbod. Zar. 51a) or foolish sayings (b. Ḥul. 85b; b. Nid. 52b).

The insult is used in the New Testament,[57] for example, when Jesus

54. See Bendaẏid, Aba, *Leshon miḳra u-leshon ḥakhamim* (Tel Aviv: Devir, 1967), 336. I am thankful to Moshe Bar-Asher for his help with this comment.

55. For the other example, see Bendaẏid, *Leshon miḳra*, 206.

56. One more comment can be made here, but I am well aware of its relatively speculative nature. This verse from Proverbs is mentioned in a strange Mishna in Avot 4:19, where Shmuel haQatan is quoted as reciting this verse but nothing else. As commentators such as Maimonides have explained, this could have been a verse that was associated with this specific sage, his favorite verse, so to speak. This very same sage, Shmuel haQatan is the named sage that in later talmudic sources is credited with the composition of the benediction against *minim* in the *Amida* prayer. Could there be a connection here between these two traditions: on the one hand, a story about a *min* who falls to his death and the sage rejoices in his death, and, on the other, the sage who often quotes the verse against rejoicing at the fall of enemies and composes the benediction calling for the fall of the *minim*? (I am thankful to Naphtali Meshel for this great insight).

57. I am grateful to Laura Nasrallah for the Matthew reference.

calls the Pharisees μωροὶ καὶ τυφλοί ("blind fools"; Matt 23:17) or when Paul rails against the Galatians: Ὦ ἀνόητοι Γαλάται ("You foolish Galatians"; Gal 3:1). Robert H. Gundry has noted that in Matthew (7:26; 23:17; 25:2, 3, 8) the term is used specifically to signal "those who do not belong to the kingdom of heaven."[58] In the Sermon on the Mount (Matt 5:22), Jesus addresses the sin of insulting others:

> Everyone who is angry with his brother is liable to judgment. Whoever says to his brother, "Raka" [Ῥακά], is liable to the council [συνεδρίῳ].[59] Whoever says, "Fool!" [Μωρέ], is liable to the hell of fire.

Here, the Greek transcription of the Aramaic word ריקא/רקא and the Greek Μωρέ are elaborations on the prohibition against becoming angry. Scholars have tried to discern the exact difference between the two terms used by Jesus, probably stemming from the kind of "code-switch" common to bilingual communities.[60] But reading this passage in the context of the other uses of the insult "fool" in the New Testament, Gundry suggests that we should understand it as "expressing a negative judgment, private and premature, against a brother's membership in the kingdom."[61] Taking this stance even further, Don Garlington proposed that "'fool' is a shot aimed not at one's intelligence but at one's salvific condition or state of soul. That is to say, the fool has no part in the (eschatological) kingdom of God."[62] It seems, therefore, that the use of the insult "fool" carried particular content when used in this environment. It is meant to signal a certain type of opponent, who is understood in a specific theological context. This does not, therefore, contradict Jesus's use of this slur against the Pharisees. It indicates unbelievers.[63] To call someone a "fool" meant, according to Garlington, to condemn him. According to Jesus, such a condemnation is grounds for being brought before the council on a charge of murder.

---

58. Robert H. Gundry, *Matthew: A Commentary on His Handbook for a Mixed Church under Persecution*, 2nd ed. (Grand Rapids: Eerdmans, 1994), 84–85.

59. On the translation of this word as "the Sanhedrin," see survey and references in Robert A. Guelich, "Mt 5:22: Its Meaning and Integrity," *ZNW* 64 (1973): 42–44.

60. Jonathan M. Watt, "Some Implications of Bilingualism for New Testament Exegesis," in *The Language of the New Testament: Context, History, and Development*, ed. Stanley E. Porter and Andrew W. Pitts, Linguistic Biblical Studies 6 (Leiden: Brill 2013), 9–27: "Code-switching between the region's native language (Aramaic), its historic and sometimes current language of religious discourse (Hebrew—which may have been the medium when a young Jesus impressed his seniors at the temple, Luke 2:46–47), and even its tertiary language of wider communication (Greek), would have been comfortable communicative behavior. Multilingual speakers draw effortlessly from their repertoire, as Jesus and the Gospel writer seem to have done" (27).

61. Gundry, *Matthew*, 85.

62. Don Garlington, "'You Fool!': Matthew 5:22," *BBR* 20 (2010): 68.

63. See Garlington, "'You Fool!,'" 61–84

Elsewhere, I have tried to illuminate the Matthian use of *raka* and "fool" in light of other rabbinic and Second Temple sources.[64] I have suggested that Jesus's proscription is referring neither to harmless insults nor only to a general term for people who do not belong to the kingdom of heaven. I think these specific terms, Ῥακά and Μωρέ, can be better understood in light of the connotation of the words ריק (*req*), "empty," and "fool" in their Second Temple and rabbinic uses. When Jesus says that one who unjustly calls a brother *raka*, "empty one," or "fool" should suffer severe consequences, he specifically refers to an insult that suggests a misunderstanding of Torah laws. The correct interpretation of the law stood at the center of arguments between different groups at the time of Jesus and probably later, as well. The insults "empty" and "fool" are connected to this polemical environment, and it is within this setting that the Sermon on the Mount should be understood.

Thus, finding the insult "fool" in Ḥullin and the other talmudic stories that use this formulaic sentence, "Fool, look to the end of the verse," is not surprising. It is worth considering that the rabbinic stories imply a context similar to the one found in these other sources. Even if we do not turn to my suggestion that this insult has theological ramifications, recent scholarship has urged us to consider the more general function of such insults in the culture of the ancient world. Offenses such as "fool" should be seen not as harmless words but rather as "genuine social weapons intended to cause serious injury."[65] When uttered by influential persons, the use of such negative labeling can exact actual damage. Even without casting doubt on one's eschatological future, it defines someone as an outsider to the social order and as "permanently deviant."[66] Indeed, according to Jesus, using such an insult deserves punishment from the Sanhedrin. In the words of Jerome H. Neyrey, "In an honor-shame culture, there is no such thing as a harmless insult."[67]

These talmudic stories should be understood in light of this cultural background, in which insults were used as social weapons. Given the relatively rare occurrence of this insult in the general rabbinic corpus, the talmudic use of the term here is suggestive. Both figures in the stories are labeled *minim*, a term used to place them in opposition to the rabbinic figures they encounter. The *min* in question, however, is not only labeled a *min* but also labeled a fool. Compare the second *min*, who can still come to

---

64. Michal Bar-Asher Siegal, "Matthew 5:22: The Insult 'Fool' and the Interpretation of the Law in Christian and Rabbinic Sources," *Revue de l'Histoire des Religions* 234.1 (2017): 5–23.

65. Jerome H. Neyrey, *Honor and Shame in the Gospel of Matthew* (Louisville: Westminster John Knox, 1998), 192.

66. See Bruce J. Malina and Jerome H. Neyrey, *Calling Jesus Names: The Social Value of Labels in Matthew*, FF: Social Facets (Sonoma, CA: Polebridge, 1988), 35–42, "Introduction to Labelling Theory."

67. Neyrey, *Honor and Shame*, 193.

bear good tidings to Rabbi and stays to celebrate the death of a fellow *min*. He even passes some kind of a test over the wine. The first *min*, in comparison, is doubly labeled: Not only is he a *min*, but he is a fool who cannot understand how to read Scripture. The method is seemingly an easy one—read on in the verses—and yet the inability to read correctly earns this first *min* the serious insult of being called a fool. He is thus firmly cast aside in a manner that is culturally punitive. Moreover, if I am correct in my suggestion, the use of the term "fool" specifically in relation to the first *min* is intentional: he, like the *minim* in the other stories, is misinterpreting the verses, which merits the same insult that is used in other sources. A fool is the one who misinterprets Scripture.

Cup of Blessing

In the final section of the story, Rabbi celebrates the "good news" of the first *min*'s death with the second *min*. This character is identified as the "good *min*," who is on Rabbi's side, so to speak, in the debate with the other *min*. The celebration takes place in the form of a celebratory meal. The very fact that a rabbinic sage is sitting down to a meal together with a *min* is surprising. The interactions over a meal between different groups in late antiquity stood famously at the center of many of the discussions concerning identity markers of each group. In rabbinic literature the mere "commensality between Jews and non-Jews is understood as potentially 'idolatrous'" and therefore eating with non-Jews is prohibited regardless of the kashrut of the food products.[68] In the Christian literature we find a lot of discussion of the social interactions of Christians with non-Christians, for example, around the issue of participation in pagan temple banquets, as I shall discuss below. Later on, church canons famously stress the prohibitions against partaking of meals with Jews on their day of festival,[69] as well as the famous rebukes of John Chrysostom in his *Adversus Iudaeos*. The Tosefta in the second chapter of tractate Ḥullin (2:20-21) indicates the strict prohibitions around dealing with food products of *minim*, and in the rabbinic corpus I am not familiar with another case of such a meal between

---

68. Jordan D. Rosenblum, *Food and Identity in Early Rabbinic Judaism* (Cambridge: Cambridge University Press, 2010), 36.

69. See, e.g., the Apostolic Canons (fourth century), Canon LXX: "If any bishop, presbyter, or deacon, or any one of the list of clergy, keeps fast or festival with the Jews, or receives from them any of the gifts of their feasts, as unleavened bread, any such things, let him be deposed. If he be a layman, let him be excommunicated." Synod of Laodicea (fourth Century) Canon 37: "It is not lawful to receive portions sent from the feasts of Jews or heretics, nor to feast together with them." Canon 38: "It is not lawful to receive unleavened bread from the Jews, nor to be partakers of their impiety." Synod of Elvira (306 CE) Canon 50: "If any cleric or layperson eats with Jews, he or she shall be kept from communion as a way of correction."

rabbinic sages and *minim*. But in this talmudic story the *min* and Rabbi sit for a meal together. Surprisingly, this *min*, at the end of the shared meal, prefers a cup of benediction to money, but he is still identified as a *min* and is even recognized as part of a great Roman family in the tradition attributed to R. Yitsḥaq. His Roman affiliation is, however, mentioned only in a separate, later tradition and is not an integral part of the story.

What kind of a *min* is the second *min*? I suggest that this character represents a different kind of paradigm of Jewish–Christian relations than the usual *min*–rabbi stories. He obviously rejoices in the passing of the first *min*, identifying in this way with Rabbi; but he is nonetheless labeled a *min*. Relying on this *min*'s affinity with Rabbi's position and their joint celebration over the death of the first *min* might indicate the second *min*'s theological position regarding the Amos verse and the creation of the holy spirit. He could very well be of the same position as Ambrose, and in agreement with the rabbinic reading of this verse. But he is also presented as being put to some kind of a test: will he prefer to receive money or take a "cup of blessing"? His choice of the cup of blessing is presented as the right choice, identifying him with the rabbinic understanding of the importance of this "cup of blessing."

The term "cup of blessing" usually refers to the recitation of the Grace after Meals over a cup of wine, as is the case here. The exact term appears only in the Babylonian Talmud (e.g., b. Pesaḥ. 107a), but there are references to the practice of blessing over wine, either during the meal or after, already in the Mishna (e.g., m. Ber. 7:5). This "cup of blessing" seems to play a central role in the Babylonian Talmud, as demonstrated by the traditions preserved in b. Ber. 51a (MS Oxford 336):

> וא׳ר זירא א׳ר אבהו ואמרי לה במתנית׳ תאנא. עשרה דברים נאמרו בכוס של ברכה. טעון הדח׳ ושטיפה. חי ומלא עיטור עיטוף. מקבלו בשתי ידיו ומחזירו בימין. ומגביהו מן הקרקע טפח. ונותן עיניו בו. ויש אומ׳. אף משגרו לאנשי ביתו במתנה.

> R. Zeira said in the name of R. Abbahu, and some say it was taught in a *baraita*: Ten things have been said in connection with the cup used for Grace after Meals: it must be rinsed and washed; [it must be] undiluted and full; [it requires] crowning and wrapping; [it must be] taken up with both hands and placed in the right hand; [it must be] raised a handbreadth from the ground; and [he who says the blessing must] fix his eyes on it. Some say: he must send it around to the members of his household as a gift.

In the continuation of this passage, the rabbis stress the importance of this practice by attesting to the grand reward that accompanies it:

> וא׳ר יוחנן. כל המברך על כוס של ברכה כשהוא מלא נותנין לו נחלה בלא מצרים. שנא׳ "ומלא ברכת יי׳ ים ודרום ירשה". ר׳ יוסי בר חנינא אמ׳ זוכה ונוטל שני עולמים. שנא׳ "ים: ודרום ירשה."

> R. Yoḥanan says: Whoever says the blessing over a full cup is given an inheritance without bounds, as it says, "And full with the blessing of the Lord; possess the sea and the south" (Deut 33:23). R. Yose son of R. Ḥanina says: He is privileged to inherit two worlds, as it says, "possess the sea and the south."

And even the punishment of those who refuse to perform it (b. Ber. 55a):

> אמ׳ רב יהודה אמ׳ רב. שלשה מקצרין שנותיו של אדם. ואלו הן. מי שנותני׳ לו ספר תורה לקרות ואינו קורא. וכוס של ברכה ואינו מברך. והמנהיג עצמו ברבנות.

> Rav Yehuda says in the name of Rav: Three things shorten a person's years, and these are: one who is given a Torah scroll to read from and does not read; [one who is given] a cup of benediction and does not bless; and one who assume airs of [rabbinic] authority.

Wine is also used in Christian meals,[70] and this very same "cup of blessing" is mentioned in the New Testament, as it becomes part of the Christian Eucharist.[71] In 1 Cor 11:23–25 Paul gives "the earliest attestation of the way Jesus instituted the Eucharist":[72]

> For I received from the Lord what I passed on to you, that the Lord Jesus, on the night he was handed over took bread, and having given thanks, broke it, and said, "This is my body, which is for you. Do this in remem-

---

70. On wine as part of food and drink in early Christian meals, see Andrew Brian McGowan, *Ascetic Eucharists: Food and Drink in Early Christian Ritual Meals*, OECS (Oxford: Oxford University Press, 1999), 91–95. I am grateful to Adela Yarbro Collins for this reference and to Michael Satlow and Laura Nasrallah for suggesting the possibility of a connection between the Christian "cup of blessing" and the talmudic one.

71. There has been a great deal of research on connections between early Jewish and Christian meals. See, e.g., K. G. Kuhn, "The Lord's Supper and the Communal Meal at Qumran," in *The Scrolls and the New Testament*, ed. Krister Stendahl (New York: Harper & Bros., 1957), 65–93, 259–65; H.-W. Kuhn, "The Qumran Meal and the Lord's Supper in Paul in the Context of the Graeco-Roman World," in *Paul, Luke and the Graeco-Roman World: Essays in Honour of Alexander J. M. Wedderburn*, ed. Alf Christophersen et al., JSNTSup 217 (Sheffield: Sheffield Academic Press, 2002), 221–48; Joachim Jeremias, *The Eucharistic Words of Jesus*, NTL (Philadelphia: Fortress, 1966), 26–88; R. H. Fuller, "The Double Origin of the Eucharist," *BR* 8 (1963): 60–72. Scholars have suggested a connection to the cup mentioned in the Passover meal and have debated to which of the cups of the Passover meal the different Gospel traditions refer. On this, see Dan Cohn Sherbok, "A Jewish Note on *to poterion tes eulogias*," *NTS* 27 (1981): 704–9; Phillip Sigal, "Another Note to 1 Corinthians 10.16," *NTS* 29 (1983): 134–39; idem, "Early Christian and Rabbinical Liturgical Affinities," *NTS* 30 (1984): 63–90. I agree, however, with Enrico Mazza (*The Origins of the Eucharistic Prayer*, trans. Ronald E. Lane [Collegeville, MN: Liturgical Press, 1995], 66–98) and David Instone-Brewer (*Traditions of the Rabbis from the Era of the New Testament*, 2 vols. [Grand Rapids: Eerdmans, 2004–2011], 1:83) that the "cup of blessing" should first be understood as the cup of blessing of the Grace after any meal, which was used also in the Passover meal in the last supper.

72. Joseph A. Fitzmyer, *First Corinthians: A New Translation with Introduction and Commentary*, AYB 32 (New Haven: Yale University Press, 2008), 431.

> brance of me." In the same way, the cup too, after the supper, saying, "This cup is the new covenant in my blood. Do this, whenever you drink it, in remembrance of me."

Here there is a mention of the "cup after the meal." This cup is "the new covenant," constituting the central part of the symbolic meal ceremony, alongside the bread. In 1 Cor 10, Paul describes the proper Christian attitude to idolatry, using the term "cup of blessing" when referring to the cup after the meal in the Lord's Supper. It is a passage that "reveals how important the reverent celebration of the Lord's Supper is for the life of the Christian community at any time and for the common ethical conduct of life in that community"[73]

> Therefore, my dear friends, flee from the worship of idols. I speak as to sensible people; judge for yourselves what I say. The cup of blessing that we bless, is it not a sharing in the blood of Christ? The bread that we break, is it not a sharing in the body of Christ? Because there is one bread, we who are many are one body, for we all partake of the one bread. Consider the people of Israel; are not those who eat the sacrifices partners in the altar? What do I imply then? That food sacrificed to idols is anything, or that an idol is anything? No, I imply that what pagans sacrifice, they sacrifice to demons and not to God. I do not want you to be partners with demons. You cannot drink the cup of the Lord and the cup of demons. You cannot partake of the table of the Lord and the table of demons. Or are we provoking the Lord to jealousy? Are we stronger than he? (1 Cor 10:14–22)

Paul stresses that the social interactions of Christians with non-Christians, particularly taking part in pagan temple banquets, does not go hand in hand with partaking in the Lord's Supper. Drinking the cup of blessing as part of the Eucharist should ultimately serve as a separating marker between Christians and the participants in Greco-Roman temple meals.

If the *min* is indeed understood as a Christian, the talmudic story is in fact preserving a tradition that testifies to a religious praxis common to Jews and Christians. They share a meal together in celebration of the "good news," that is, the death of the first *min*. And both have in common the understanding of the importance of the "cup of blessing" for the Grace after the Meal. The cup of blessing is a separating marker between idol worshipers and Christians, but not between Jews and Christians.

This is not to say that Rabbi and the *min* were performing some kind of a Eucharist together, rather, both Jewish and Christian traditions have a high place for the "cup of blessing" in the ritual of Grace after Meals. This is evidenced in the talmudic sayings quoted above and in the central

73. Ibid., 380.

place the cup holds in the creation of the Lord's Supper. This ritual is thus a common element for Jews and Christians, and in the narrative it would be a symbolic place for a "good *min*" and a rabbi to meet.

This tradition might then show the talmudic author's acquaintance with the Eucharist tradition. This would not be surprising considering the centrality of this ritual in Christian practice. More importantly, this story is a narrative portrayal of a complex relationship between Christian *minim* and rabbinic figures, with its heroes and villains. There are those who threaten through their scriptural challenges, and their demise is cause for celebration; and there are those who celebrate with us and agree with our theological position regarding the correct reading of Amos and the holy spirit, and at the same time, use a ritualistic meeting point.

Let Their Table Be a Trap for Them

Ruhama Weiss, in a recent book, has observed a literary model of meals in the rabbinic literature, in which rabbinic figures share a meal together and during the meal there is a test of some kind, usually based on a halakic challenge.[74] In the stories she analyzes, sometimes the challenge is presented for a general discussion and on other occasions it is directed as a test to one of the meal's participants. Weiss stresses that the test is the focus of the meal and the story ends when the halakic test has ended. Weiss then devotes a portion of this book to the subject of meals with "outsiders" such as women and nonrabbinic figures.[75] She notices that these other meal stories offer an altogether different model of meal story, in which the challenging tests are no longer used and the usual meal etiquette is present. These stories present an inclusive attitude and tolerance toward those who are not used to the challenges of the scholastic rabbinic ways.

According to this literary model delineated by Weiss, our *min*–rabbi story, fits not the expected "others meal" model but rather the very rabbinic model of meal tests. The *min* in the story is presented with a test and the story ends with him making the correct choice and a halakic conclusion regarding the worth of the cup of blessing. This festive meal is a natural development of the story after Rabbi's fast, but it can also be viewed as situating this second *min* within a rabbinic literary frame. He is a model of a *min* that has common ground with rabbi—a halakhic common ground and the ability to "play" within the rabbinic literary meal challenges.

The meal can even be seen as a midrashic narrative stemming from the continuation of the verse quoted by Rabbi. As discussed above, Rabbi

74. Ruhama Weiss, *Meal Tests: The Meal in the World of the Sages* [Hebrew] (Tel Aviv: Hakibbutz haMeuchad 2010).

75. Ibid., 203–24.

quotes Ps 69:22: ויתנו בברותי ראש ולצמאי ישקוני חמץ, "They gave me poison for food, and for my thirst they gave me vinegar to drink." But the next verse in Psalms (69:23), interestingly reads: יהי שלחנם לפניהם לפח ולשלומים למוקש, "Let their table be a trap for them, a snare for their allies."[76] The verse describes a table, and by implication a meal, which serves as a trap. In one talmudic passage this verse is used to describe the trap Queen Esther laid for Haman when inviting him to the meal with the king (b. Meg. 15b). This verse was read by early Christian writers as describing the trap into which the Jews fell when they failed to realize the fulfillment of the verses from Psalms in the suffering of Jesus (see Augustine, *City of God* 18.46). I suggest that the talmudic passage in Ḥullin continues the reading of the passage from Psalms by incorporating the meal described in Ps 69:23 into the story but using this narrative element in reference to the rabbinic protagonist rather than to Christians. Rabbi is the one being served the (metaphorical) vinegar, and he is the one setting the trap in the meal: he tests the second *min* while sitting at the table.

Conclusions

I have tried to read one example of the literary genre of talmudic *minim* stories (b. Ḥul. 87a), to demonstrate the importance of drawing on external knowledge in order to better understand the narrative's content and context. As I and others have repeatedly claimed, we, as scholars of the Babylonian Talmud, can no longer be satisfied with learning the Talmud from within the rabbinic sources. In some cases, we should be armed with contemporary Christian and other non-Jewish sources in order better to understand the rabbinic text.

In this case, an acquaintance with the major Christian polemical debates surrounding Amos 4:13, debates central to contemporaneous, late-antique Christian writings, is crucial to understanding the debate between Rabbi and the first *min* in the story. The Christian debates illuminate the short interaction between the two over the biblical verse and explain the apparent urgency of both their reactions to this encounter as well as the dire consequences that result from it. This reading sheds light on the possible Christian references in this passage and highlights elements of irony and satire that would otherwise go unnoticed.

If my intertextual reading is correct, it also offers us a number of insights beyond the local passage in Ḥullin. For example, as explained above, it might establish this passage's primacy over the parallel Sanhedrin passage's secondary use of this tradition. Most importantly, it adds

76. I am thankful to my student Rephael Kauders for suggesting that the table in Psalms 69:23 might bear some importance to the story.

one more piece to the historical puzzle scholars have been trying to solve: how much Christianity in the Bavli? What can we learn about the rabbinic composers of these traditions and their knowledge of, and familiarity with, the Christian world around them? The talmudic narrative does not make our lives easy here. The *minim* stories in the Talmud are almost always very short, and they are suggestive at best. The conclusions I offer here are in need of much further evidence and cannot stand on their own. But I think scholars have realized by now that this task of answering the historical question surrounding the Babylonian Talmud will have to be taken one small step at a time. And we get closer to the answer with each and every example we study. My current project, which involves several of these talmudic *minim* stories, bears out this conclusion. In all of the other examples I analyze, I can show that the *minim*'s questions are related in one way or another to broader, contemporaneous Christian biblical debates.

These examples in turn build on my previous attempts to read a number of talmudic narratives in light of Christian monastic stories. All of these cases, taken together with recent studies by other scholars, suggest that the talmudic authors had some familiarity with the Christian world around them. In contrast to my previous work on parallel monastic traditions, in which I sought to demonstrate familiarity and analogous reception of Christian traditions in the Babylonian Talmud, in this case we are dealing with a different literary genre. First and foremost, dialogue is construed to display a polemical debate. The rabbinic figure opposes a *min*, a word that literarily means heretic. I understand the polemical nature of the talmudic portrayal of these discussions, the offensive nicknames and the atmosphere highly charged with risk, as a clear signal to the reader that here exists a point of Jewish–Christian friction. I do not think that these stories should be read as historical depictions of such an argument; rather, the narrative is imagining such a scene. In my monastic analogies, there were no explicit indications in the stories themselves of such a point of contact. On the contrary, the talmudic passages bore no signs of overt literary connection to Christianity. These connections were revealed only after a parallel reading of Jewish and Christian sources. Here, the contact is made apparent; the text calls our attention to it.

Further, these rabbinic sources, the "monastic" sources in the Babylonian Talmud, showed no overt signs of polemic against the content of the Christian material from which they drew, but rather a sort of appropriation of this material. In the *minim* stories, by contrast, we see a very clear dispute with an intra-Christian argument over the reading of biblical verses. I think that these are two sides of the same coin: the talmudic authors place arguments with Christianity in clear daylight, while the incorporation of Christian literary motifs and narratives is more subtly interwoven into the rabbinic text.

Despite these differences, both talmudic *minim* stories and appropriations of monastic material impart to scholars two crucial lessons: first, that scholars must be familiar with the outside Christian sources in order to fully understand the talmudic sources; second, that the talmudic material in fact presents a complex picture of familiarity with Christian traditions.

If we read our Ḥullin story as an intellectual exercise in which the rabbis imagined themselves as part of the broader argument within Christianity over the interpretation of Amos 4:13, we must assume that they had enough knowledge of contemporaneous Christianity to interact with that debate. In this case, we are dealing with one of the only verses in the Septuagint in which early Christians saw a clear foreshadowing of the coming of Christ. It was an important verse, as is evident from its history of interpretation, and it deals with central dogmatic issues. Of course, we should not assume a simple transfer of information from written Christian material to the talmudic authors, nor need we imagine *ḥavruta* sessions between rabbis and Christian scholars. But regardless of the mode of transmission, it appears that the talmudic authors were familiar with this particular Christian tradition and used it in an exercise in "guided imagery," the Rabbi–*min* dialogue.

In sum, our knowledge of the bigger picture, of the debates and issues that occupied the non-Jews outside the doors of our talmudic authors, seems to be essential for a better understanding of the talmudic authors and their literary creation.

IV

The Zoroastrian Context

Dualistic Elements in Babylonian Aggada

YAAKOV ELMAN

Quiet desperation is another name for the human condition.
—Wallace Stegner, *Angle of Repose*

Precisely because death, disability, and disease are the common features of the human condition, our religions and philosophies, if they are to be successful in attracting adherents, must convey an optimistic message, a fact that, studies have shown, not only serves as a comfort but helps extend our lives and buttresses our health.[1] God or the gods are ultimately benevolent; providence is an essential element of their governance of the universe. And even when this is not ostensibly the case, as in Manichaeism, where the principle of evil is coeval with good, the message is consolatory: in the end good will prevail and death and evil will be destroyed. Even the various gods of the underworld do not represent evil as embodied in death, but rather they are in charge of the place to which the dead are consigned. This essential purpose of religion is one reason it has endured over the millennia.[2]

---

1. As a recent popular book on psychology has it, "So an optimistic way of seeing the world, even if it is not entirely accurate, pays dividends, helping us to succeed on the job, on the playing field, and in school. But there is one other area where it can also work wonders: our health. Research has shown that positive illusions, even if they are unrealistic, can directly sustain and enhance our health. As a general matter, optimistic people are healthier. They have lower blood pressure, better immune function, and recover better from heart surgery" (Joseph T. Hallinan, *Kidding Ourselves: The Hidden Power of Self-Deception* [New York: Crown, 2014], 190). See in particular the work of G. E. Vaillant, who directed the Harvard Study for many years and published a number of summary volumes: G. E. Vaillant, *Triumph of Experience: The Men of the Harvard Grant Study* (Cambridge: Belknap Press of Harvard University Press, 2014).

2. See, e.g., Sam Harris, *The End of Faith: Religion, Terror, and the Future of Reason* (New York: Norton, 2004), 66–67: "It appears that even the Holocaust did not lead most Jews to doubt the existence of an omnipotent and benevolent God. If having half of your people systematically delivered to the furnace does not count as evidence against the notion that an

On the other hand, again, precisely because death, disability, and disease are the common lot of humanity, those features of human life and their relation to the gods must also be explained. It is one thing to write, as pious Babylonians were wont to do, *ana ṣili ša ilī šulum anāku*, "with the help [lit., 'in the shadow'] of the gods I am well" in their letters when things went well, but how to explain reverses? The "heavenly writing" was written by the gods.[3] And even the ancient Semitic gods of death and the underworld were in charge of the dead but not independent purveyors of it.

As Jeffrey Burton Russell noted in his history of the devil, Zoroastrian dualism may be considered an advance in human thought in that it isolated two forces and "wrench[ed] from the unity of the God a portion of his power in order to preserve his perfect goodness."[4] He noted that good and evil are often personified: on one side is God the benevolent Creator, on the other, the Devil, Satan, Ahriman, and so on. With this view, we can easily understand why fifteen years later Shaul Shaked argued that dualism is defined by "the idea that there are two cosmic powers that are separate from an early stage in the existence of the universe"[5] and is "typologically" monotheistic. He suggested, like Russell, that "dualism can hardly be considered a separate category of religion." In the Zoroastrian dualism of late antiquity, however, the evil spirit Ahriman is no longer the equal of Ohrmazd, in contrast to Manichaean dualism, where the two principles of light and darkness, good and evil, are equally balanced.[6] Moreover, Ahriman can act independently of Ohrmazd, but his Jewish or Christian cognates, Satan or the Devil, cannot.

I would therefore suggest that we may redefine the category of dualism so as to make it a more powerful analytical tool in understanding the religions of late antiquity: that is, the essential characteristic of dualism is the belief of "two powers in heaven," in which a benevolent creator shares his governance of the world with an impersonal power, that of Fate or astral determinism (which are not the same). These may also be considered dualistic in the sense that I propose, and in that respect, some

all-powerful God is looking out for your interests, it seems reasonable to assume that nothing could." But neither Harris nor Daniel C. Dennett nor the others really come to grips with why people are acting so "irrationally."

3. See Francesca Rochberg, *The Heavenly Writing: Divination, Horoscopy, and Astronomy in Mesopotamian Culture* (Cambridge: Cambridge University Press, 2004), 1–2.

4. Jeffrey Burton Russell, *The Devil: Perceptions of Evil from Antiquity to Primitive Christianity* (Ithaca, NY: Cornell University Press, 1977), 99.

5. Shaul Shaked, *Dualism in Transformation: Varieties of Religion in Sasanian Iran*, Jordan Lectures in Comparative Religion 16 (London: School of Oriental and African Studies, University of London, 1994), 21.

6. He also argues (ibid., 20) that Zurvanism was not a "Zoroastrian heresy."

versions of rabbinic Judaism may be considered dualistic, as are Zoroastrianism, Manichaeism and Roman and ancient Babylonian polytheism. Of course, one consequence of this view is that there are limits on the creator's powers, as Russell noted, a consequence that the Zoroastrian theologians faced squarely. The rabbinic system of which I speak had another "out": prayer could overcome astrology; however, as we shall see, Babylonian aggada considered an alternate possibility. And Augustine, who, as a Christian, rejected astrology and fate, placed the locus of evil in humans and the struggle against it at the center of human existence.[7]

This form of dualism arose because evil constituted a problem even for polytheists, since the gods were considered wise and benevolent, at least in the final analysis, and even ancient Mesopotamian polytheists felt the need to devise a theodicy, as demonstrated by the "Poem of the Righteous Sufferer" (*ludlul bēl nēmēqi*).[8] Note that Mesha, king of Moab, in his famous inscription, attributes the oppression of the Moabites by the Israelites to Kemosh's anger with his people.[9] Thus, some ancient and late antique religions shared a structural similarity by shifting the locus of evil beyond a benevolent power, whether personal, as in Zoroastrianism, or impersonal, as in Manichaeism. Moreover, while the planets may have been seen as evil in themselves, as in Zoroastrianism and Manichaeism, astrology could also have been seen as *neutral* in its effects, that is, providing long or short life spans without regard to the moral standing of the mortal concerned. Finally, that structural similarity extended beyond Mesopotamia both geographically and theologically, that is, beyond the Sasanian Empire and beyond monotheistic or dualistic religions. Roman polytheists also struggled with such questions; after all, our providence is derived from Latin *providentia*, and fate from *fatum*. This is not an inconsequential philological note: the very concepts of providence and fate are Hellenistic. While the problem of theodicy dates back to biblical times, the more abstract formulation of the problem, with providence and fate as competing concepts, is the fruit of Greek philosophical analysis, where providence is *pronoia* and fate is *moirai*.[10] In Sasanian Babylonia, the rabbis

---

7. See G. R. Evans, *Augustine on Evil* (Cambridge: Cambridge University Press, 1984), 92–93.

8. W. G. Lambert, *Babylonian Wisdom Literature* (Oxford: Clarendon, 1960), 63–91. See also "A Babylonian Theodicy," ibid., 21–62.

9. See James P. Pritchard, ed., *The Ancient Near East: An Anthology of Texts and Pictures* (Princeton, NJ: Princeton University Press, 1958), 209.

10. Thus, Akkadian *šimtu* refers more to a person's individual fate, that is, his mortality, than Fate with a capital F, so to speak, and the so-called "tablet of destiny" is a warrant for its possessor to rule the universe. In Homer, fate is the will of Zeus (see James Duffy, "Homer's Conception of Fate," *Classical Journal* 42 [1947]: 477–85), though even here there is a tension between Fate and Zeus's powers, though in the end he prevails). Similarly, the Babylonians

had to employ *mazzal*, while the *dastwars* had *baxt* ("allotment," parallel to *moirai*) and *brēh* ("decree") or, more precisely for the latter, *bago-baxt* ("divine decree"), as we shall see.

Unfortunately, we cannot trace the evolution of these concepts in Roman religion; as J. A. North notes in his introduction to Roman religion, "the extant evidence generally reflects not the experience of the mass of individual Romans, but the religious activity that affects the state and its activities, above all the doings of magistrates and priests. The Roman religion we know is based on this limited body of material."[11] Or, as Jörg Rüpke notes, "If we are interested in finding out about the gods of the ordinary man, of the ordinary inhabitant of Rome, male or female, neither philosophically educated nor interested in philosophy, we cannot expect to find answers by trying to systematize a theology that is at best merely implicit. We can only do so by describing practice and tackling its explicit and implicit assumptions, its problems and contradictions."[12] Nevertheless, I suggest that we may infer a good deal from those who were both officials of the state *and* philosophically inclined.

As that imperial Stoic Marcus Aurelius put it in his *Meditations*,

> So in each case you need to say: "This is due to God." Or: "This is due to the interweavings of fate, to coincidence or chance." Or: "This is due to a human being…."[13]
>
> This policy is a consequence of the principle enunciated somewhat earlier: What is divine is full of Providence. Even chance is not divorced from nature, from the inweaving and enfolding of things governed by Providence. Everything proceeds from it. And then there is necessity and the needs of the whole world, of which you are a part.[14]

The Stoic view is that the world order is reasonable, and evil does not really exist. In this regard, as in others, Manichaeism may be seen as Stoicism's converse. As Iain Gardner and Samuel Lieu put it:

---

speak of the *gods* writing on the heavens or even a sheep's liver; astral determinism was thus not an independent force.

11. J. A. North, *Roman Religion*, Greece & Rome 30 (Oxford: Oxford University Press for the Classical Association, 2000), 8.

12. Jörg Rüpke, *Religion of the Romans*, trans. Richard Gordon (Cambridge: Polity Press, 2007), 67.

13. *Meditations of Marcus Aurelius: A New Translation*, trans. Gregory Hays (New York: Modern Library, 2003), 32–33. For the Greek text, see *The Communings with Himself of Marcus Aurelius Antoninus, Emperor of Rome, Together with His Speeches and Sayings*, trans. C. R. Haines, LCL (1916; repr., Cambridge: Harvard University Press, 1953), 3.11, p. 60.

14. *Meditations of Marcus Aurelius*, 18; for the Greek text, see LCL, 28 (2.3). On this issue, see also Cicero, *De Senectute, De Amicitia, De Divinatione*, trans. William Armistead Falconer, LCL (Cambridge: Harvard University Press, 2001), 95, 97.

> Mani's teaching was summarized by the catchphrase, that "of the two principles and the three times (or moments)." The two principles are those of light and darkness: whose realms in the *beginning* are separate, the dark unknowing of the light; then during the *middle* are in part mingled, the reality of this present universe; but at the end will be the triumph and eternal victory of light over death. We should note that Manichaean dualism was absolute, *there was no need to account for the origin of evil.*[15]

We can see the attraction of such a religion to Augustine, whose overriding question was *unde malum*. And so he was a Manichaean, at least for a decade, but then, as many Romans did, he turned to Christianity. But we must remember that for a time as many Romans were Manichaeans as Christians, so that even by the end of the fourth century, when Christianity had already been the state religion for seventy-five years, Manichaeism still held its own. In the end, Cicero ends as a Stoic, denying evil;[16] as John Sellars puts it:

> For the Stoics there is no such thing as evil in the modern sense of the word.... All the seemingly unpleasant events that befall people are, according to the Stoics, strictly speaking value neutral and so are classified as "indifferents" (*adiaphora*). They are, moreover, the product of providence (*pronoia*)..... The Stoics follow Socrates in arguing that such vice is always the product of ignorance; there are no genuinely evil intentions.[17]

Augustine would have none of it, of course. As G. R. Evans puts it in her *Augustine on Evil*,

> The Stoic takes the view that the fates govern human existence, and they cannot be moved by prayer. In any case, he does not allow himself to think that things might be better in case he should be discomforted by the desire that they should not be so. The Stoic is a happy man in a cage, a man who dare not look up, in case he sees a possibility of happiness

15. Iain Gardner and Samuel N. C. Lieu, *Manichaean Texts from the Roman Empire* (Cambridge: Cambridge University Press, 2004), 11. The emphasis is my own.

16. For our purposes, the extent to which this sentiment reflects Cicero's feelings after his daughter's death is irrelevant, for at some point or other the human condition—mortality—has to be faced; our interest is simply in assessing the range of attitudes to that mortality among those for whom Roman religion was still a matter for discussion and consideration. In any case, however, see the detailed discussion in Carl Koch, "Roman State Religion in the Mirror of Augustan and Late Republican Apologetics," in *Roman Religion*, ed. Clifford Ando, Edinburgh Readings on the Ancient World (Edinburgh: Edinburgh University Press, 2003), 296–329, esp. 311–23.

17. John Sellars, "The Stoics on Evil," in *The History of Evil in Antiquity, 2000 BCE to 450 CE*, ed. Tom Angier, Chad Meister, and Charles Taliaferro (New York: Routledge-Taylor & Francis, 2016), 1.

beyond his present imagining. Augustine and the Christians look for a higher happiness.[18]

In the following remarks, I will try to trace late antique notions of good, evil, and something in between. This last notion may be called Fate or be associated with astral determinism. Still, the sources of evil are multiple and varied: hordes of demons, some with names, some without, in some cases directed by a supreme evil power (Ahriman, Satan/Lucifer, the King of Darkness, the angel of death), sometimes acting independently, and sometimes in conjunction with astral determinism, which brings stars and planets into the picture, usually with evil planets. In part this multiplicity is defensible, since humans are heir to many ailments and reverses, and each may be seen to have its own cause. However, inasmuch as all "evil" has one common denominator—its deleterious effect on the human condition (which is itself a phrase that calls those detriments to mind—one never refers to the human condition as one of bliss), they are then subsumed under one overarching power. Thus, dualism, whether theistic or not, mirrors humans' propensity to project their concerns onto the world they inhabit.

The problem then becomes how to organize these multifarious elements into a comprehensive system. The one that felt most comfortable for late antique cultures as for their predecessors was one that was hierarchically arranged, since that paralleled their own experience of the world; as Rav Sheshet puts it, "the earthly world is like the heavenly world" (b. Ber. 58a).

Nevertheless, though I will examine such elements in several of the religions of late antiquity, my focus will remain on the Bavli. This is because it offers us a fascinating glimpse of a monotheistic religion incorporating dualistic elements within itself in order to come to grips with the problem that all religions face, the problem of evil. Evil is a problem that exists not only in the world but also in the human psyche, where we all somehow think that the world ought to be ordered in a way more to our satisfaction and convenience. This incorporation of dualistic elements produced a system more flexible and nuanced than that of either major Iranian religion and, arguably, more than that sophisticated church father Augustine and others who were concerned with placing the onus squarely on Adam's frail shoulders. To take but one example, while demons are by definition evil in most religions of late antiquity, in the Bavli they may be harnessed and forced to do errands for Rav Papa (b. Ḥul. 105a), or provide information—not only about the spirit world but also halakic information—for the rabbis, as Yosef Sheda did for Rav Ḥisda, Rav Yosef, and Rava (b. 'Erub. 43a, b. Pesaḥ. 110a). Moreover, as we shall see, Zoroastrian meditations on

18. Evans, *Augustine on Evil*, 151.

the human condition assigned fate a role that encompassed both "good" and "evil" ends and further allowed it to be modified by means of human actions, a doctrine that seems to have been accepted in at least one important passage in the Bavli. This view of fate lacks the ominous connotations of either the Latin *fatum* or its descendants in Western languages.

However, once even dualistic religions such as Zoroastrianism and Manichaeism attempted to incorporate the idea of fate or astral determinism into their systems, the question of how to integrate this factor/force into the already existing theological structures posed a problem, to the point that Augustine denied the existence of both. This basic question manifested itself in at least two urgent ways: First, how to retain free will and human responsibility as factors in a world in which fate played a significant role, and, second, how to reconfigure the powers of the primary divine figure in a world in which fate also had a role to play. We will begin with the first and then move on to the second.

In the end, then, I suggest that, despite Jeffrey Rubenstein's wonderful analysis of b. Šabb. 156a–b, (1) the opinion that Jews are indeed under the influence of astral determinism is widespread in the Bavli, both in the opinions attributed to specific Amoraim and in stories told about them; (2) this opinion appears in Palestinian sources as well; (3) this is so despite its serious theological consequences for our view of divine omnipotence and providence, and for free will as well; (4) this view thus appears in rabbinic, Zoroastrian, Manichaean, and Roman sources. In addition, (5) this view may be aligned with the role assigned to an opposing force/factor/opponent of the creator(s) in Christianity, Zoroastrianism, Manichaeism, and Roman paganism, so that dualism, the idea that there are "two powers in heaven," was indeed widespread in late antiquity, but (6) there was a tendency over time, at least in Zoroastrianism, to identify fate with Ohrmazd's will and decree, in a Jungian-style integration. And finally, (7) I wish to suggest, very tentatively, that this is so because of widespread experience of what has come to be called the "human condition," which runs counter to our intuition that our survival and successful functioning often depend on our belief in the essential reasonableness of the universe and the benevolence of God or the gods. But underlying all this is the essential problem of the relation of providence and fate. And in limning the borders of these two forces we find thinkers spread across the Greco-Roman and Sasanian worlds: from Chryssipus, Cicero, Seneca, and Marcus Aureilius in Greece and Italy; and Augustine in North Africa; to Rav Naḥman, Rava, and the anonymous redactors of aggadot in the Bavli and Genesis Rabba; to the redactors of the Pahlavi Widēwdād, the Zand ī Fragard Jud-dēv-dād, the Spirit of Wisdom text, and perhaps the Zoroastrian high priest Ādurbād ī Mahrspandān, a contemporary of Rava's, to Mani. All these are joined in an effort to define and delimit these "two powers in heaven."

I

The problem, as Rubenstein recognizes, is that acknowledging the power of astrology involves placing limits on human free will and on the creator's omnipotence.

> For some Zoroastrians, however, astral determinism probably posed a theological difficulty akin to that faced by the Rabbis. Many strands of Zoroastrian theology assume free will and encourage human beings to carry out good and pious deeds so as to assist Ahura Mazda in the battle against Ahriman and evil, such that one's "fate" depended on action and could be altered at any time by Ahura Mazda's intervention. Yet certain streams of Zoroastrianism such as those associated with Zurvanism that embraced astral fatalism and determinism presumably posed a challenge to those who championed free will.[19]

But, as Rubenstein also recognized, free will and reward and punishment are two sides of the same coin, and thus the question also must involve the creator's omnipotence. He goes on to note, quoting David Pingree:

> The *Pahlavi Widēwdād* 5.9 says succinctly: "Material things are by fate, immaterial things by action."… The *Ayādgār ī Wuzurgmihr* 105–9 (*Pahlavi Texts,* 94) considers this point at further length. "Wuzurgmihr" removes determination to the background of human existence, in effect identifying it with the force of necessity which energizes all processes in the cosmos, when he says, "Fate is the reason [for whatever befalls a person]; action is the cause (*čim* and *wahanag* respectively)."[20]

This text, however, may be interpreted somewhat differently; here is the Wuzurgmihr text he referred to, with my thanks to Mahnaz Moazami:

> *tis ī ō mardōmān rasēd pad baxt bawēd ayāb pad kunišn*
> *baxt ud kunišn āgenēn ōwōn homānāg hēnd čiyōn tan ud gyān*
> *čē tan jud az gyān kālbōd ast ī a-kār ud gyān jud az tan wād-ēw ast ī agriftār ud ka āgenēn gumēxt ēstēd ōzōmand ud wazurg sūdōmand*
> *čē baxt ud čē kunišn baxt-iz čim* <*ud*> *kunišn wihānag tis ī ō mardōmān rasēd*
>
> Do things that (come) to humans come by fate or by works?
> Fate and works are so like together as body and soul,
> For the body without the soul is a useless shape, (while) the soul without the body is an intangible wind, (but) when they are mixed together (they are) powerful and great and useful,

19. Jeffrey L. Rubenstein, "Talmudic Astrology: *Bavli Šabbat* 156a–b," *HUCA* 78 (2007): 140–41.

20. Quoted from David Pingree, "Astrology and Astronomy," *Encyclopedia Iranica* 2:864–65, in Rubenstein, "Talmudic Astrology," 141–42.

> (For) which fate and which works (are such that) fate is also the reason <and> works the (precipitating) cause of things which come to humans.

Thus, fate is hardly consigned to the background. However, when Pingree deals with the theological problem posed by the need to ascertain the place of astrological influence within the larger scheme of Zoroastrian theology, and, in particular, its relation to Ohrmazd's benevolence, I think he is on the mark. For our purposes, the essential point is the following:

> Astrology offered support for the idea of the god Ohrmazd's total goodness. He could be said to have commanded the equitable distribution of material (as well as immaterial) goods through the sun, moon, and twelve zodiacal signs (*Mēnōg ī Xrad* 12); but the intrusion of the demonic planets brought injustice into the world. Belief in the twelve signs and seven planets as the proximate "determiners and arrangers of the world" (ibid., 8) required, however, one modification from classical theory. If the planetary bodies were to be regarded as evil, the sun and moon could not be included among them. The canonical "seven" was preserved by substituting the head and tail of Gōčihr.... But some confusion occurred, and Bundahišn, chap. 27.52, 188.3-5 counts a total of ten planetary bodies.[21]

This integration of astrology into Ohrmazd's benevolent ordering of the world is reflected in some Pahlavi sources, though not in all. Thus, as Pingree notes, astrology accounted for the motions of astral bodies that were, after all, Ohrmazd's creations. The details of the various Zoroastrian systems need not detain us, since we are mostly concerned with the essential structure of those systems and their relation to those suggested by the rabbis, who were divided on the issue as well. However, Zoroastrianism's division of Ohrmazd's creation into material (*gētīy*) and spiritual (*mēnōy*) worlds allows for assigning (or consigning) astrology to the realm of material reality, while spiritual matters are determined by religious actions, thus in some measure removing astral determinism from the spiritual realm. Since that spiritual realm includes Zoroastrianism's ethical triad—good thought, good speech, and good deeds—it also concerns reward and punishment, and so astral determinism inevitably has a religious dimension. In theological terms, as Pingree noted above, fate and works stand in a tension, even though fate and astrology can easily be equated. This point is of particular importance for us, since it is this division that characterizes the approach of some rabbinic sources as well.

The *locus classicus* for the discussion is of course b. Šabb 156a–b, the focus of Rubenstein's article in *HUCA*, which promulgates the view that denies the relevance of astral determinism to Jews. But, as I noted a

21. Ibid.

decade ago, an alternate arrangement, which assigns to astrology or heavenly decree the essentials of a good life, appears in the Bavli in the names of three members of one prominent rabbinic family—Rav, his son in law Rav Ḥannan b. Rava, and his great grandson-in-law Rava—and is closely paralleled by several Pahlavi texts. The simplest of these is the *Pahlavi Widēwdād* (hereafter: PW) 5.9, which, with minor changes, and following Mahnaz Moazami's recent edition (with a few minor changes in the translation on my part) reads:

> (G) *gētīy pad baxt mēnōy pad kunišn.* (H) *ast kē ēdōn gōwēd zan frazand ud xwāstag ud xwadāyīh ud zīndagīh pad baxt abārīg pad kunišn.* (I) *mard ān nēkīh ī-š nē brēhēnīd estēd ā-š hagriz abar nē rasēd az ān gyāg paydāg gairi maso aŋhō aētahē* (J) *ān-iš abar brēhēnīd estēd ā-š pad tuxšāgīh pēš be rasēd* aniiō ərəduuō zəŋgō xvarənō (K) *u-š pad wināhkārīh bawēd ka-š appār bawēd āaṯ xvarənō frapairiieiti* (L) *u-š anāgīh ī abar brēhēnīd estēd pad frārōn tuxšāgīh spōxtan tuwān* pouru xvarənaŋhō ašauua zaraθuštra (M) *u-š wināhkārīh nōg nōg awiš ōh brēhēnēd* aēšąmča narąm (N) *mard-ē ka-š pad dast ī mard-ē abāyēd murdan* (O) *bē ka pad dast ī ōy mīrēd tā nē šāyēd bē ōy tuwān kardan kū pad ōzadan ī ōy a-wināh ē pahikār-radīh xūb abāg be kunēd.*
>
> (G) [This-]worldly matters are due to fate; others are due to work. (H) There is one who thus says: Wife, offspring, property, authority, and life(-span) are by fate; other things are by action. (I) (The fact that) man will never reach that which is not destined for him is known from the passage: *gairi masō aŋhō aētahē.*[22] (J) That which is destined for him comes to him earlier by diligence: *aniiō ərəduuō zəŋgō xvarənō.*[23] (K) It is by his sinfulness when (what is destined for him) is taken away from him: *āaṯ xvarənō frapairiieiti*.[24] (L) By righteous diligence he can avoid the evil that is destined for him: *pouru xvarənaŋhō ašauua zaraθuštra.*[25] (M) Numerous acts of sinfulness are destined for him aēšąmča narąm.[26] (N) When a man must die by the hands of another man, (O) it is not possible, unless he dies at the hands of that man; (but) in case of killing an innocent person, it is proper to engage in a judicial dispute.[27]

---

22. The passage refers to the significance of fate, predestination, and how doing good deeds can change one's destiny. "What is not destined for man will never come to him. This is evident from 'The (transgression) the height of a mountain shall be his.'"

23. "What is destined for a man will come before him through diligent work: 'The other (obtains) the Fortune standing on his erect legs.'" On ərəduuō zəŋgō, see Ilya Gershevitch, *The Avestan Hymn to Mithra,* University of Cambridge Oriental Publications 4 (Cambridge: Cambridge University Press, 1967), 15:61; James Darmesteter, *Le Zend-Avesta,* 3 vols., Annales du Musée Guimet 21, 22, 24 (Paris: Maisonneuve, 1960), 2:458 and n. 100.

24. "It is because of the sins that one has committed when goodness is taken from him 'Then the Fortune vanished.'"

25. "The evil that has been destined for a person can be moved away by diligently working good deeds: 'Of the one full of Fortune, O the righteous Zarathushtra.'"

26. "And as for the sinner, the ill fortune is decreed for him: 'and of these men.'"

27. Mahnaz Moazami, *Wrestling with the Demons of the Pahlavi Widēwdād: Transcription,*

G presents the general rule, and H represents its application by which PW provides an "escape clause," whereby the influence of astral determinism can be circumvented by diligent righteousness, thus preserving free will. It is important to note that, according to L, fate can be circumvented by good deeds and hastened by evil ones; the implication then is that fate is not neutral but, as in Latin, carries a negative connotation. Conversely, according to I–J, one's good fate may be hastened. As we shall see, this dual view of fate or astral determinism appears in the Bavli as well. Indeed, we may see this bifurcation of the influence of fate and works as providing a solution to the problem debated by the Stoics and the Epicureans on the interplay of the two factors. There is a tension, even an incoherence, in the Stoic position: the Stoic universe is deterministic, on the one hand, but there is providence, on the other. One solution was that attributed to Chryssipus, who draws a distinction between

> two types of fated things: simple fated things and conjoined fated things. For Chryssipus, a simple fated thing is necessary and a product of the essence of a thing.... A woman giving birth to a baby cannot be fated to do so regardless of whether she has slept with a man; rather, the two events will be "conjoined" and co-fated (Cicero, Fat. [= *De Fato* (On Fate)] 30).
>
> Chrysippus uses this distinction between simple fated and conjoined fated things to argue that human action can in fact make a contribution to the outcome of events in a deterministic cosmos. It *will* make a difference whether we call a doctor or not, but the final outcome will nevertheless be completely determined, shaped by a range of both internal and external causes."[28]

In the end, then, the most logical solution is to apply the lawyerly technique of "statutory construction," assigning each factor its own arena in which it operates.

PW H–O is thus structurally equivalent to *Mēnōy ī Xrad* (hereafter: MX) 24 and 27, which, as Pingree noted, introduces another term, *bagobaxt*, "divinely bestowed gifts for merit," in contrast to *baxt*, the portion astrologically allotted to a person at birth. Here is the text of MX 22–24, as originally presented by Robert Zaehner, and updated by Oktor Skjærvø at my request, though I have made a few minor changes.

Translation, and Commentary, Iran Studies 9 (Leiden: Brill, 2014), 130–31. See also R. C. Zaehner, *Zurvan: A Zoroastrian Dilemma* (1955; repr., New York: Biblio & Tannen, 1972), 405-6, taken from a useful article on the subject published by Jehangir C. Tavadia, "Pahlavī Passages on Fate and Free Will," *Zeitschrift für Indologie und Iranistik* 8/1 (1931): 119–32, here 127.

28. John Sellars, *Stoicism*, Ancient Philosophies 1 (Berkeley: University of California Press, 2006), 103–4.

pursīd dānāg ō mēnōy ī xrad kū pad tuxšāgīh xīr ud xwāstag ī gētīy ō xwēš šāyēd kardan ayāb nē?
mēnōy ī xrad passox kard kū pad tuxšāgīh ān nēkīh ī nē brēhēnīd ēstēd ō xwēš kardan nē šāyēd; bē ān ī brēhēnīd ēstēd tuxšāgīh rāy hamē bē rasēd.
bē tuxšāgīh ka-š zamān nē abāg pad gētīy abē-bar bē pas-iz pad mēnōy ō frayād rasēd ud pad tarāzūg abzāyēd.

The wise man asked the Spirit of Wisdom: Can one appropriate worldly wealth and riches by one's effort or not?

The Spirit of Wisdom made answer (and said): One cannot appropriate by effort such good things as have not been fated (for one); but such as have been fated always come when an effort is made. But effort, if it is not favored by time, is fruitless on earth, but later, in the other world, it comes to our aid and increases in the balance.

pursīd dānāg ō mēnōy ī xrad kū pad xrad ud dānāgīh abāg brēh kōxšīdan šāyēd ayāb nē?
mēnōy ī xrad passox kard kū abāg-iz tagīgīh ud zōrōmandīh ī xrad ud dānāgīh pas-iz abāg brēh kōxšīdan nē šāyēd; čē ka brēhēnišn pad nēkīh ayāb pad juttarīh frāz rasēd, dānāg pad kār wiyābān bawēd ud dušāgāh [pad] kār āgāh [bawēd], ud wad-dil dilīgtar [bawēd] ud dilīgtar wad-dil [bawēd], ud tuxšāg ašgāhān [bawēd ud ašgāhān] tuxšāg bawēd: ēdōn čiyōn pad ān čiš ī brēhēnīd ēstēd bihānāg pad-iš andar āyēd ud abārīg ud har(w) čiš bē spōzēd.

The wise man asked the spirit of wisdom: Is it possible to strive against fate with wisdom and knowledge or not?

The spirit of wisdom answered (and said): Though (one be armed) with valor and strength of wisdom and knowledge, yet it is not possible to strive against fate. For once a thing is fated, whether for good or the reverse, the wise man goes astray in his work, and the man of wrong knowledge becomes clever in his work; the coward becomes brave and the brave cowardly; the energetic man becomes a sluggard, and the sluggard energetic: For everything that has been fated a fit occasion arises which pushes back all other things.

pursīd dānāg ō mēnōy ī xrad kū āyift-xwāstārīh ud kirbag-warzīdārīh ud arzānīgīh rāy yazdān ō mardōmān did-iz čiš baxšēnd ayāb nē?
mēnōy ī xrad passox kard kū baxšēnd
čē ēdōn čiyōn gōwēnd kū baxt ud bayō-baxt kū baxt ān bawēd ī az fradomīh baxt ēstēd ud bayō-baxt ān ī did-iz baxšēnd.
bē yazdān ān baxšišn ēd rāy kem kunēnd ud pad mēnōg (kem) paydāg<ēn>ēnd čē Ahriman-iz ī druwand ān bihānag pad nērōg ī 7 abāxtar xwāstag ud abārīg-iz harw nēkīh ī gētīg az wehān ud arzānīgān appurēd ud ō wattarān ud anarzānīgān abērtar baxšēd.

The wise man asked the Spirit of Wisdom: Do the gods allot anything else to men because they have sought rewards and practiced good deeds and are worthy, or not?

The Spirit of Wisdom answered: They do.

For it is just as they say: fate and *divine fate. Fate is that which was allotted from the beginning, and divine fate is that which they allot afterwards.

But they make this allotment rarely and manifest it rarely in the other world, because the accursed Ahriman too makes this a pretext to rob the good and worthy of wealth and all other material prosperity through the power of the seven planets, and to bestow it chiefly on the evil and unworthy.

Two important aspects of this text are the introduction of Ahriman and free will into the theological equation, the latter represented by the new term *bayō-baxt*, which is equivalent to PW's expanded explanation at I–O; MX thus represents a conceptual advance over PW in that it provides a handy term for what PW expresses inexactly as *kunišn*, "works, good deeds." A much more detailed text presented below, which represents a different development, is attributed to the famous Zoroastrian high priest of Shapur II's reign, *Ādurbād ī Mahraspandān*. Of course parts of it may well include folk sayings and statements taken from other sources, especially from oral tradition that were only later attributed to this famous figure.

gōwēnd kū hufraward Ādurbād ī Mahraspandān xīr ī gētīy pad 25 dar nihād būd, 5 pad brēh ud 5 pad kunišn ud 5 pad hōg ud 5 pad gōhr ud 5 pad abarmānd. zīwandagīh ud zan ud frazand ud xwadāyīh ud xwāstag abērtar pad brēh. āhlawīh ud druwandīh <ud> āhrōnīh ud artēštārīh ud wastrayōšīh abērtar pad brēh. xwardan ud raftan ud ō zanān šudan ud bušāsp kardan ud kar wizārdan abērtar pad hōg. xēm ud mihr ud wēhīh <ud> radīh ud rāstīh abērtar pad gōhr. huš ud wīr ud tan ud brāh ud dīdan abērtar pad abarmīnd.

They say that the blessed *Ādurbād, son of Mahraspandān,* divided the things of the material world into twenty-five parts: five (he assigned) to fate,[29] five to action, five to habit, five to substance, and five to heredity. Life, wife, children, authority, and wealth are mostly through fate. Righteousness and wickedness and being a priest, warrior, and husbandmen are mostly through action. Eating, walking, sex (lit., "going to one's wife"), sleeping, and satisfying one's natural needs are mostly through habit. Worthiness, friendship, goodness, generosity, and truthfulness are mostly though substance. Intelligence, understanding, body, stature,[30] and appearance[31] are chiefly through heredity.[32]

---

29. Or: "(divine) decree," see below.

30. Shaked: "luminosity."

31. Shaked: "luminosity (?)."

32. D. M. Madan, *The Complete Text of the Pahlavi Dinkart*, 2 vols (Bombay, 1911), 1:568, lines 3–12. The text and translation follow that of Shaked in his edition of the Denkard; see Ēmētān Aturpāt-i and Shaul Shaked, *The Wisdom of the Sasanian Sages (Dēnkard VI)*, Persian Heritage Series 34 (Boulder, CO: Westview Press, 1979), 174–75; and see both Zaehner, *Zurvan*, 407–8 and Shaked's notes for parallel texts. The text was apparently quite popular, and Rava's extract even more so.

Though chronologically speaking *Ādurbād ī Mahraspandān* is perhaps a contemporary of Rava's, there is, as noted, no assurance that all of this passage dates back to him, nor can we determine its chronological relationship to PW 5.9, which should probably be dated to the late fifth century,[33] though clearly PW's "other things" refers to spiritual gifts. One might assume that his list of "worthiness, friendship, goodness, generosity, and truthfulness" should also be reckoned as spiritual matters. Also noteworthy is the absence of MX's *bayō-baxt*. The Iranian fondness for lists of five (as in both Zoroastrianism and Manichaeism) seems to have induced the list maker to relate these five character traits to something other than "action." *Ādurbād* also details the results of merit, which include the attainment of social distinction, deemed to correspond to one's spiritual status as manifested in *kunišn*, "action, good deeds." However, he lists only the three higher estates, which allows him to fill out the number of five elements while also including righteousness and wickedness. While the system of four estates dates back to Avestan times ("the *āsrōnīh*, the estate of the priests [*āsrōns*]; *artēštārīh*, the estate of the warriors [*artēštār*]; *wāstaryōšīh*, the estate of the husbandmen [*wāstaryōš*]; and *hutuxšīh*, the estate of the artisans [*hutuxš*...]," in Sasanian times "the three higher estates were first put under the patronage of the three most powerful fires of the realm, symbolizing the creation of the fires by Ohrmazd for the protection of the world (*Bundahišn*, TD_2, 124, trans. Anklesaria, chap. 18.8, 158-59), as well as the prosperity of Iranian society through the functioning of the estates." And these estates are, in theory, "enshrined in a system of exclusive classes backed by doctrinal justification: 'Everything may be changed but the good and evil substance [*gōhr*] (of man)' (*Mēnōg ī xrad*, ed. Anklesaria, 9.7; trans. West, chap. 10.7, 37; *Dēnkard*, ed. Madan, 547; ed. Dresden, 400; trans. Shaked, A6b, 132--33). It is this latter view that Adurbad expresses."[34]

There is another variation in the *Ādurbād* text that is worthy of note: the use of *brēh* in place of PW's *baxt*. D. N. MacKenzie renders the latter as "fortune, fate,"[35] and the former as "fate, destiny,"[36] which overlap to a considerable extent. But *baxt* is derived from *baxtan*, "to apportion, distribute," while *brēh* derives from *brēhenīdan*, which means "to create, fashion," or "to decree." The latter verb appears in PW I, J and L and thus, like MX's *bayō-baxt*, serves to introduce a theological element in what may

33. See Alberto Cantera, *Studien zur Pahlavi-Übersetzung des Avesta*, Iranica 7 (Wiesbaden: Harrassowitz, 2004), 201–7.

34. *Encyclopedia Iranica*, vol. 5, fasc. 6, 652–58; see also Ahmad Tafazzoli, *Sasanian Society*, vol. 1, *Warriors*; vol. 2, *Scribes*; vol. 3, *Dehqāns*, Ehsan Yarshater Distinguished Lectures in Iranian Studiies 1 (New York: Bibliotheca Persica Press, 2000).

35. D. N. MacKenzie, *A Concise Pahlavi Dictionary* (London: Oxford University Press, 1990), 17.

36. Ibid., 19.

have originated as a folk saying on the inevitability of fate. As we shall see, and as both Rubenstein and I noted a decade ago, PW 5.9H is paralleled by several Babylonian rabbinic texts, which suggests that this folk saying existed in both Middle Persian and Babylonian Aramaic and was theologically modified in both religious literatures. Still, the result of this theological twist was a structural incongruity: What need is there to posit two forces that would act, or potentially act, in a malignant manner? If Ahriman accounted for the existence of evil in Ohrmazd's benevolent creation, why posit yet another force, that of astrology, that would accomplish the same purpose, theologically speaking? And why would the creator tolerate such limitations on his omnipotence?

One advantage of astral determinism is that, though it impairs the operation of free will, it is not unreservedly negative: as Rava notes, *mazzal* can result in poverty for one righteous man but wealth for another, something that Ahriman would not do. This flexibility would certainly make astral determinism a more useful theological factor than the evil spirit in accounting for the human condition. *Mazzal* is then equivalent to Fortune or Fate in that it is a neutral factor, but it does in some sense account for the world's injustice. Reward and punishment operate in a different manner, one that is accounted for in a dictum attributed to Rava or to Rav Ḥisda, his father-in-law, in b. Ber. 5a: "When a man sees sufferings [*yissurim*] coming upon him, let him examine his deeds,... and if he examined [them], and found nothing, let him attribute [the suffering] to the neglect of the study of Torah; and if he [tried to] attribute [them to that] but did not find [that sin], it is certain [*be-yadu'a*] that they are 'sufferings of love' [meant to improve him]." Then there are reverses that are due to one's membership in the community of Israel, as is reported of Rava in b. Ḥag. 5a–b.

For Zoroastrianism and Manichaeism, however, this explanation of suffering was not needed or not available. For Zoroastrianism, suffering as atonement was reserved for after death in hell or at the eschaton; in this world atonement required the direction of one's spiritual master, one's *rad*, to be efficacious. Here, for example, is a confession for one's self (*patēt ī xwad*), which, though late in form, appears to represent an early tradition, according to Mary Boyce.

> This penance I have performed to atone for sin and to obtain my share for reward for good deeds done, and for love of my soul; to bar the way to hell and open the way to heaven.... As to atone for sins that I have not been able to expiate, I am readily prepared to atone for them during the three nights after death. Should I chance to depart this life without having done penance, if one of my close relatives does penance for me, I assent to this.[37]

37. Mary Boyce, ed. and trans., *Textual Sources for the Study of Zoroastrianism* (Chicago:

And, indeed, one may seek in vain for the role of *yissurim* as atonement in Zoroastrian texts and in introductions to Zoroastrian thought. Penance, punishment, and confession are attested, but the idea that this-worldly suffering offers the sufferer atonement for sin is not. This does raise an interesting point: what constitutes *yissurim*? How much suffering, of what nature and duration and intensity? This question is addressed by a passage in b. 'Arak. 16b–17a as another expression of Middle Persian attitudes, but with a Jewish admixture. In this case, inconvenience is considered to be "suffering" and thus provides atonement; the former is Zoroastrian in inspiration, the latter biblical.

> עד היכן תכלית יסורין? אמר רבי אלעזר: כל שארגו לו בגד ללבוש ואין מתקבל עליו.
> מתקיף לה רבא זעירא, ואיתימא רבי שמואל בר נחמני, גדולה מזו אמרו: אפילו נתכוונו למזוג בחמין ומזגו לו בצונן, בצונן ומזגו לו בחמין, ואת אמרת כולי האי!
> מר בריה דרבינא אמר: אפילו נהפך לו חלוקו.
> רבא, ואיתימא רב חסדא, ואיתימא רבי יצחק, ואמרי לה במתניתא תנא: אפילו הושיט ידו לכיס ליטול שלש ועלו בידו שתים. דווקא שלש ועלו בידו שתים, אבל שתים ועלו בידו שלש לא, דליכא טירחא למישדייהו. וכל כך למה? דתניא דבי רבי ישמעאל: כל שעברו עליו ארבעים יום בלא יסורין - קיבל עולמו.
> במערבא [יז ע"א] אמרי פורענות מזדמנת לו

> What is the minimum degree of sufferings?
> Said R. Eleazar: If someone had a garment made to wear and it does not fit properly.
> Rava the Younger—according to others: R. Shmuel b. Naḥmani objected: More than this did they say: Even if it had been intended to serve him a hot [drink], and it was served to him cold, or it was intended to serve him cold, and it was served hot, [it is still acounted as "sufferings"]—and you say [only] that much [i.e., if his custom-made clothes do not fit!].
> Mar son of Ravina said: Even if his shirt gets turned inside out.
> Rava (or, as others say, Rav Ḥisda, or again, as some say. R. Yitsḥaq, or as it was said, it was taught in a *baraita*): Even if he puts the hand into his pocket to take out three [coins] and he takes out but two. Now this is only in the case [where he intended to take out] three, and [took out] two, but not if [he meant to take] two and three came into his hand, because it is no trouble to throw it back. But why all this [information]?—Because the School of R. Yishmael taught: Anyone upon whom forty days have passed without [divine] visitation, had received his world. In the West [17a] they say: Retribution is prepared for him.

"Rava the Younger"—Rava Ze'era—does not appear anywhere else in the Talmud, while in b. B. Bat. 31b a question is attributed either to Rava or R. Ze'era; the reading here could easily have begun as: "Rava, or some

---

University of Chicago Press, 1984), 60–61. The text is taken from *Pazend Texts*, ed. E. K. Antia (Bombay, 1909), 146–52.

say: R. Ze'era," with רבי or 'רב having been misread as רבא. In addition, Rava himself is quoted as using the rare word *takhlit* ("minimum degree" in b. Ber. 17a).[38] As to the alternatives Rava or Rav Ḥisda or R. Yitsḥaq, or a *baraita*, aside from its support in all the manuscripts, it should be noted that Rav Ḥisda is not only Rava's father-in-law, but the same variant appears in Rava's statement regarding "sufferings of love" in b. Ber. 5a, and R. Yitsḥaq (Nappaḥa) is known to have spent time in Maḥoza and was held in high esteem by Rava.[39]

Aside from that, nearly everyone quoted here is either a Babylonian or of Babylonian origin, with the exception of R. Shmuel b. Naḥmani and R. Yitsḥaq, who spent time there. I suggest, therefore, that this equation of inconvenience with "sufferings" is a Babylonian innovation under Zoroastrian influence.[40]

Comfort and convenience are hallmarks of Ohrmazd's creation, as he himself states at the very opening of PW (1.1–1.2), where he tells Zoroaster that he has created "a place producing peace, where [hitherto] no comfort was produced," a statement that is glossed as follows: "a place … more beautiful and more comfortable" (*nēktar ud āsāntar*).[41]

Let us now examine the rabbinic texts parallel to PW 5.9, beginning with a statement attributed to Rava, in b. Mo'ed Qat. 28a:

> אמר רבא: חיי, בני ומזוני, לא בזכותא תליא מילתא, אלא במזלא תליא מילתא. דהא רבה ורב חסדא תרוייהו רבנן צדיקי הוו, מר מצלי ואתי מיטרא, ומר מצלי ואתי מיטרא. רב חסדא חיה תשעין ותרתין שנין - רבה חיה ארבעין, בי רב חסדא - שיתין הלולי, בי רבה - שיתין תיכלי. בי רב חסדא - סמידא לכלבי ולא מתבעי, בי רבה - נהמא דשערי לאינשי, ולא משתכח. ואמר רבא: הני תלת מילי בעאי קמי שמיא, תרתי יהבו לי, חדא לא יהבו לי; חוכמתיה דרב הונא ועותריה דרב חסדא - ויהבו לי, ענותנותיה דרבה בר רב הונא - לא יהבו לי.

> Rava said: [Length of] life, children, and sustenance depend not on merit but [rather on] *mazzal*.
>
> For take [the cases of] Rabba and Rav Ḥisda: Both were absolutely righteous rabbis; [the proof of this righteousness is that] each master prayed for rain and it came.

38. And, indeed, the manuscripts (Oxford Opp. 726[370], Vatican 119 and 120, Munich 95, and British Library ADD 25717[402]) all read: "R. Ze'era, and, if you want, R. Shmuel b. Naḥmani."

39. See his entry in Hanokh Albeck, *Mavo la-Talmudim* (Tel Aviv: Devir, 1969), 252–53.

40. The statement of Mar b. R. Ravina, a fourth-generation Babylonian sage, does not appear in MS Vatican 119, and appears in reverse order in MS BL Add 25717(402) and in the Venice edition of 1522, while MS Vatican 120 has the variant Mar b. Rav. As to R. Eleazer b. Pedat, who was of Babylonian origin, MSS Vatican 120 and Munich 95 omit the attribution to him, while MS Oxford has the common scribal error of "R. Eliezer" for "R. Eleazar." In short, these variants do not impeach the essentially Babylonian cast of this passage.

41. See the edition Mahnaz Moazami of PW 1.1, *Wrestling with the Demons*, 28–29.

> [Despite this,] Rav Ḥisda lived to the age of ninety two; Rabba only lived to the age of forty. In Rav Ḥisda's household: sixty marriage feasts; in Rabba's household: sixty bereavements. At Rav Ḥisda's house there was purest wheat bread for dogs, and it went to waste; at Rabba's household there was barley bread for humans—and that could not be found.
> This too Rava said: I requested these three things of Heaven; two were given me, but the third was not: the scholarship of Rav Huna and the wealth of Rav Ḥisda were given me, but the modesty of Rabba b. Rav Huna was not given me.

Rava presents the theological problem posed by the human condition in all its starkness; despite all the biblical promises, righteousness is no guarantor of worldly happiness. And while Rava mentions only three of the five elements enumerated in PW, all five appear somewhere in the Bavli. In good Semitic fashion, Rava has listed three of them, where PW, in good Iranian fashion, lists five. Again, the use of the number sixty to represent "many" is a heritage of the ancient Babylonian use of the sexagismal numbering system. Beyond that, however, we must note that Rava based his theological principle on observation and more or less direct experience; although he, like other rabbis, was not loath to quote popular wisdom ("as people say") and even seek a scriptural warrant for it (e.g., b. B. Qam. 92a–b, where twenty-one proverbs are mentioned, and eight more are mentioned elsewhere in the Bavli[42]). Nor does he cite Scripture, for the most authoritative Scripture itself, the Torah, states the reverse, as in Deut 11:11–15, which was incorporated into the Shema. It is thus not surprising that Rava quoted no verse or midrash to support his statement, and all the rabbis he mentioned were members of the generation before his. Moreover, he goes against all but one of the authorities mentioned in the *locus classicus* of Babylonian discussions of astrology, b. Šabb. 156a–b. This suggests that Rava was quite aware that this observation of his goes counter to standard rabbinic teaching on this important matter. It also suggests that if he knew this as a proverb, he may well have been aware of its Zoroastrian source and therefore chose not to label it as a proverb; moreover, we may note as well that his reliance on observation rather than either biblical or rabbinic sources (or popular wisdom) is quite in consonance with Hellenistic thought.

Note that the passage's redactor (or Rava himself?), evidently responding to the same tensions that PW's redactor felt, moderated the influence of astrology by reporting that Rava had prayed for wealth, wisdom, and humility, though only the first two had been granted. Thus, for the rabbis prayer can undo the consequences of fate or astrology, as good deeds will

42. b. Šabb. 62b; b. Ta'an. 23a; b. Ḥag. 5a, 10a; b. Yebam. 63b; b. B. Bat. 16b.

do so in PW 5.9. This contrasts with Chryssipus's prudential man who calls in the physician when warranted.

Likewise, Rav's statement in b. Soṭah 2a parallels two other elements in PW 5.9, *zan* and *xwāstag* (wife and property).

> א"ר שמואל בר רב יצחק: כי הוה פתח ריש לקיש בסוטה, אמר הכי: אין מזווגין לו לאדם אשה אלא לפי מעשיו, שנא': 'כי לא ינוח שבט הרשע על גורל הצדיקים' (תהלים קכה, ג).
> אמר רבה בר בר חנה אמר ר' יוחנן: וקשין לזווגן כקריעת ים סוף, שנאמר: 'אלהים מושיב יחידים ביתה מוציא אסירים בכושרות' (תהלים סח, ז). איני?
> והא אמר רב יהודה אמר רב: ארבעים יום קודם יצירת הולד, בת קול יוצאת ואומרת: בת פלוני לפלוני בית פלוני לפלוני שדה פלוני לפלוני!
> לא קשיא: הא בזוג ראשון, הא בזוג שני.

> R. Shmuel b. R. Yitsḥaq said: When Resh Lakish began to expound [the subject of] Soṭah, he spoke thus: They only pair a woman with a man according to his deeds; as it is said: "For the scepter of wickedness shall not rest upon the lot of the righteous" (Ps 125:3).
> Rabba b. Bar Ḥana said in the name of R. Yoḥanan: It is as difficult to pair them as was the division of the Red Sea; as it is said: God sets the solitary in families: He brings out the prisoners into prosperity (Ps 68:7)!
> But it is not so; for Rav Yehuda has said in the name of Rav: Forty days before the fashioning of the embryo, a heavenly echo (*bat qol*) issues forth and proclaims: the daughter of so-and-so is for so-and-so; the house of so-and-so is for so-and-so; the field of so-and-so is for so-and-so!
> There is no contradiction, the latter dictum referring to a first marriage and the former to a second marriage [and so since the marriage is ordained even before birth, it cannot be dependent upon a man's conduct].

And finally, there is a statement transmitted in the name of Rav Ḥanan b. Rava, Rav's son-in-law and Rava's wife's grandfather, which accounts for the fifth element in PW 5.9, *xwadāyīh*, "authority," which appears in b. Ber. 58a.

> אמר רב חנן בר רבא אמר רבי יוחנן: אפילו ריש גרגיתא מן שמיא מנו ליה.

> Said Rav Ḥannan b. Rava in the name of R. Yoḥanan: Even an irrigation canal inspector is appointed by Heaven.

Rava assigns "children, [length of] life, and sustenance" to astral determinism, Rav has a wife ordained even before the embryo is formed, and therefore holds to the Pahlavi texts' "fate," even though Rav Yehuda, who was a traditionalist, reports it as a *bat qol*, and Rav's son-in-law, Rav Ḥanan b. Rava, assigns "authority" to an anodyne person who "is appointed by heaven." The common denominator, however, is that the influence of merit on the assignment is *denied*. Still, it is only Rava who explicitly assigns astrology a place in his scheme, while the others—Rav and his son-in-law—refer instead to some heavenly intervention that allows for the redactor of the "astrology *sugya*" in b. Šabb. 156a–b to include Rav among those who denied the influence of astral determinism on Jews. We have come a long way from the simple biblical doctrine of reward and punishment!

Nevertheless, we must attend to the differences as well as the basic similarity, in particular number and order. As noted above, in Iranian texts items are grouped in fives, while the rabbinic texts group them in sets of three. This is particularly noticeable in the case of Rav, who divides "wife" and "property" into three parts: wife, house, and field. On the other hand, Rava's list of *banei, hayyei, u-mezonei* follows the ordering principle noted by Shamma Friedman, where items are listed in order of word length.[43] This is true of the PW text as well: *zan, frazand, xwāstag, xwadāyīh, zīndagīh,* one syllable, two syllables, and three, in addition to the association, both aural and conceptual, of "wife" and "offspring."

While these texts originate within the same cultural orbit, each individual culture appropriated the basic approach in its own way. This goes beyond number and order. For while PW (and related texts, as we shall present them below), counterpose material and spiritual matters, further specified as matters determined by fate versus those determined by action, which may perhaps be more precisely defined as "deeds," that is, actions with a moral valence, Rava contrasts matters that are determined by astrological considerations—*mazzal,* and those determined by merit. Unlike PW, however, Rava does not enumerate those matters determined by merit. Indeed, as the redactor(s) go on to quote him, he goes on to relate three items that he prayed for—wealth, wisdom, and humility, only one of which appears in the Middle Persian parallels. Indeed, he is even more specific: he asked for the wealth of Rav Ḥisda (which he obtained by marrying his daughter), the wisdom of Rav Huna (who held a particular place in the estimation of both Rava and his teacher, Rav Naḥman), and the *humility* of Rav Huna's son, Rabba b. Rav Huna, a spiritual quality that the Zoroastrian magi would have assigned to deeds, and not heavenly intervention.

Thus, the issue for Rava was not fate versus works, nor was it even monotheism versus dualism, but rather fate or astral determinism versus *zekhut,* whereby the latter certainly overlapped with works, perhaps even included it entirely, but also involved God's grace, which could overcome both fate *and* works.

Rava therefore eschews the generalities of the Pahlavi text; there is no general juxtaposition of material and spiritual matters, nor the assignment

43. See Shamma Y. Friedman, "Kol ha-Qaṣar Qodem," *Leshonenu* 35 (1971): 117–29, 192–206.

of religious and social standing to action. Among other things, this avoids any invidious evaluations of the wives of these rabbis, one of which would have been his own mother-in-law. Still, Rava would certainly agree with PW on the necessity of *kunišn*, "action," to acquire either righteousness or wickedness, and thus the existence of free will despite astral influences, but grace would overcome both. In its classic discussion of astrology (b. Šabb. 156a), the Bavli goes even further: though one born under the sign of Mars will be a shedder of blood, the nature of that blood-shedding, either destructive or palliative is up to the individual.

> האי מאן דבמאדים יהי גבר אשיד דמא. אמר רבי אשי: אי אומנא, אי גנבא, אי טבחא, אי מוהלא.
> אמר רבה: אנא במאדים הואי! - אמר אביי מר נמי עניש וקטיל.

> "He who is born under Mars will be a shedder of blood."
> Rav Ashi observed: Either a surgeon, a thief, a slaughterer, or a circumciser. Rabba said: I was born under Mars. Abaye retorted: You too inflict punishment and kill [by putting people under the ban].

Although there is little doubt that the Middle Persian saying in PW 5.9G, perhaps in its Babylonian Jewish Aramaic form, served as the genesis of these statements by Rav and his successors, several important differences must be noted: first, there is no direct Hebrew/Aramaic equivalent to the MP *baxt*, "fate, allotment," and even astrology is not mentioned explicitly until Rava introduces it by employing the word *mazzal*—not the classical referent *itztaganinut* in b. Šabb. 156a or the *astrologos* of Gen. Rab. 44:12.[44] Rav referred to a "heavenly echo" that presumably announced the decision of Heaven, and Rav Ḥannan b. Rava referred directly to Heaven, which appoints even a canal inspector. Still, the idea that a person's mate and occupation are determined at his or her birth is implicit in their statements.

The variants *baxt*/*brēh* in the MP saying may illustrate the move from the notion of a fate as independent of Ohrmazd or the gods, *baxt*, and thus also of human free will, to a notion of *brēh*, related to *brēhēnīdan*, "to decree," which brings Ohrmazd and the gods back into the equation and also human free will. For this let us look at another iteration of this teaching from the ninth- to tenth-century Dēnkard, one that explicitly joins *brēh* and free will. It is also noteworthy that all the attestations of variant *brēh* come from this ninth- to tenth-century text, though the Spirit of Wisdom text does use the verb and may represent an intermediate stage. With all due hesitation, I suggest that *brēh* is equivalent to *bayō-baxt*, which is dis-

44. See Gen. Rab. 1:1 (ed. Theodor-Albeck, 433).

tinct from *baxt* alone. Indeed, the very fact that the author of the Spirit of Wisdom text felt the need to add a reference to the divine to the unadorned *baxt* is itself proof that he felt that *baxt* alone as insufficiently theologically oriented. Here is the text:

> *ēd gētīy rāyēnišn abērdar pad brēh, ud mēnōy rāyēnišn abērtar pad kunišn. az ēd mardōmān mēnōy bōzišn mādagwarīhā pad xwēš tuxšišn xwāst*
> *ān ī xwāhēd, pad-iš tuxšēd, ēwārīg ayābēd.*
> *gētīy mādayān pad yazdān frāz hištan ān ī yazdān abar gētīy xwāhišn.*
> *čē ruwān-wizāyišnīg [ī] pahrēz: pad ān ruwān-sāzišnīg tuxšāg mardōm gētīy-iz xīr, čiyōn pad-iš sūdōmandtar, handōxt; az wēh-dēn nigēz pōryōtkēšān čāštāg.*
>
> This world is controlled more by (divine) fate, and the other world more by action. Hence the salvation of man in the other world must be sought principally by his own efforts.
> That which he seeks and makes an effort (to get) he will certainly obtain.
> This world should essentially be left to the gods. (??) That of the gods should be sought above this world. (??)
> For abstention (from action) is injurious to the soul; (yet) to the man who cultivates (??) the soul and makes an effort (on its behalf) riches are accumulated in this world, for they are very useful to him—from the teaching of the Good Religion as taught by the ancient sages.[45]

The same contrast can be found in the following passage, which Mahnaz Moazami kindly brought to my attention.

> *abar ān ī hambastag mardōm az bun abarmānd az nigēz ī weh-dēn*
> *hād hambastag mardōm az bun abarmānd ēk dō ī ast baxtīg ud *bayo-baxtīg.*
> *baxtīg xwadīh ud wimand ī ōstīgān a-wardišnīg.*
> **bayo-baxtīg čiyōn-aš wardišnīg ō kārān wadišn hēnd.*
> **bayo-baxtīg winārišn abar ōstīgān baxtīg ud ōstīgān baxtīg kārīgīh ud sūd az wardišn hēnd.*
> **bayo-baxtīg ōh-iz mardōm xwadīh abar dō wimand ēk mēnōgīg ud ēk gētīgīg.*
>
> Regarding that which people are comprised from: the original inheritance, according to the exposition of the good religion:
> Indeed, people form from two (kinds of characters) from their root: *baxtīg*, their fate and **bayo-baxtīg*, the addition to their fate.
> *baxtīg* in its essence is what is constant and immutable.
> **bayo-baxtīg* is mutable—mutable according to the actions.
> The establishment of the **bayo-baxtīg* is set on a firm/strong *baxtīg*; and the activity and the profit/advantage of a firm *baxtīg* are mutable.

45. Madan, *Dinkart*, 284, 13–20; and see Zaehner, *Zurvan*, 406–7. As noted, however, the text and translation are those of Oktor Skjærvø.

> Thus the essence of the **bayo-baxtīg* of people comprises two frontiers: one is spiritual and the other material.[46]

In sum, the human condition is the product of forces in binary opposition in both Iranian and rabbinic cultures. On the Iranian side, there is *baxt* as opposed to *bayō-baxt*, or possibly *brēh*; on the rabbinic side, only Rava's statement is clear on opposing *mazzal* and *zekhut*; for Rav Yehuda in b. Soṭah 2a *mazzal* is expressed as a *bat qol*, for Rav Ḥannan b. Rava it is "Heaven." For Rav Naḥman in b. Šabb. 53a the opposition is between a change in creation and a miracle that is apparently even greater: the provision of food. For the *sugya* in b. Šabb. 156a–b the binary opposition is that of Israel and the nations: the latter are governed by *mazzal*, the former not. Presumably Israel is governed by *zekhut*. And though for Marcus Aurelius, it would seem that there are the gods and providence, in the end, for him all are conjoined: fate or "What is divine is full of Providence. Even chance is not divorced from nature, from the inweaving and enfolding of things governed by Providence. Everything proceeds from it. And then there is necessity and the needs of the whole world, of which you are a part." Like Wuzurgmihr, Marcus Aurelius wants to have it both ways, fate and works, or Fortune, Nature, Providence, and Necessity are somehow conflated. He seeks philosophical detachment, which means denying real evil (with Christianity, of course, evil got a new lease on life). On the other hand, in contrast, Augustine, who had dabbled in astrology before he became a Christian, rejected it afterwards, on the grounds that fate and astrology were irreconcilable with providence.[47]

There is another approach to the problem offered by Babylonian rabbinic sources in a Babylonian reworking of a Palestinian motif in b. Ned. 32a, where God overcomes astral determinism by main force. But before examining that aggada, and its Palestinian parallels, we must look at the second problem I mentioned at the outset: the integration of astral determinism with God's omnipotence. Why would God yield his powers over the staples of human existence—and especially children, to *mazzal*? And how are we to understand the rabbinic view of providence, especially when it relates to *mezonei*, which Rav Yehuda and Rav Naḥman, each in his own way, consider a special problem even for God? But that then raises a serious problem: what then of God's omnipotence, as Epicurus had noted centuries before?

46. *Dēnkard* book 3; Madan, *Dinkart*, 229. For French translation, see J. P. de Menasce, *Une encyclopédie mazdéenne, le Dēnkart* (Paris: Presses universitaires de France, 1958), 219.

47. Evans, *Augustine on Evil*, 92.

II

What then of the challenge to the creator's omnipotence, which both the magi and the rabbis had to deal with? To sharpen our appreciation of the challenge, let us look at an authoritative description of the Manichaean view of the question, as Werner Sundermann, the preeminent expert on it in our time, put it in a summary for the *Encyclopedia Iranica*:

> More than any other religion, even more than Zoroastrianism, his [=Mani—Y.E.] doctrine drew radical consequences from its dualistic premises. Not only did it deny god's omnipotence, it even proclaimed a deity inferior to the demonic world in the beginning and imperfect in the end, a suffering god, and a god in need of human help. These concessions to the constantly experienced evil under the sun made the question of god's responsibility for the deplorable state of the world meaningless, but provoked all the more the other question of whether god was able to render man help and protection against earthly and spiritual mischief or at least to lighten and compensate his suffering.
>
> This dilemma, to uncompromisingly uphold the dualistic dogma of god's exoneration from evil and at the same time to encourage trust and hope in god's helpfulness, was to a certain degree solved by the grandiose myth of a god developing in history, of a historical god.[48]

The decisive influence of astrology in matters of the human condition is expressed in a Babylonian aggada narrated in b. Ta'an. 25a. The story is a genuine Babylonian aggada whose essential point is not found in Palestinian sources, though some of its associated themes are, even though it concerns a Palestinian sage, R. Eleazar b. Pedat. The relevant part of this story is as follows:

> רבי אלעזר בן פדת דחיקא ליה מילתא טובא. עבד מלתא ולא הוה ליה מידי למטעם. שקל ברא דתומא ושדייה בפומיה, חלש לביה ונים. אזול לשיולי ביה, חזיוהו דקא בכי וחייך, ונפק צוציתא דנורא מאפותיה. כי אתער אמרו ליה: מאי טעמא קבכית וחייכת? - אמר להו: דהוה יתיב עמי הקדוש ברוך הוא ואמרי ליה: עד מתי אצטער בהאי עלמא? ואמר לי: אלעזר בני, ניחא לך דאפכיה לעלמא מרישא? אפשר דמתילדת בשעתא דמזוני. אמרי לקמיה: כולי האי, ואפשר?

> R. Eleazar b. Pedat was in very great want. Once after being bled he had nothing to eat. He took the peel of garlic and put it into his mouth; he became faint and he fell asleep. The Rabbis coming to see him noticed that he was crying and laughing, and that a ray of light was radiating from his forehead. When he awoke they asked him: Why did you cry and laugh? He replied: Because the Holy One, Blessed be He, was sitting

48. See his entry in the *Encyclopedia Iranica*, s.v. "Manichaeism: General Survey: The Manichaean identity," http://www.iranicaonline.org/articles/manicheism-1-general-survey.

> with me and I said to Him, How long will I suffer in this world? And He replied: Eleazar, my son, would you rather that I should turn back the world to its very beginnings? Perhaps you might then be born in an hour of sustenance? I replied: All this, and then only *perhaps*?

The text is that of the standard Vilna edition; though we have a plethora of manuscript material, its contribution to our understanding of this passage is minimal. Indeed, aside from orthographic variants, the major contribution of all the manuscripts (in contrast to the printed versions of Pesaro, Venice, and Vilna) is the expansion of "would you rather that I should turn back the world to its very beginnings?" to "would you rather that I destroy the world and rebuild it?"[49]

That this refers to R. Eleazar's astrological sign is clear from the following, "Perhaps you might then be born in an hour of sustenance?" The need to destroy and recreate the world in order to change R. Eleazar's astrological sign is somewhat puzzling, since in a similar instance regarding Abraham in b. Šabb. 156a–b, God counters Abraham's objection by offering to reposition Jupiter. Why then does the aggada in b. Ta'an. 25a deny this power to God and thus give R. Eleazar the right to refuse?

> אמר לפניו: רבונו של עולם, נסתכלתי באיצטגנינות שלי ואיני ראוי להוליד בן. אמר ליה: צא מאיצטגנינות שלך, שאין מזל לישראל. מאי דעתיך דקאי צדק במערב, מהדרנא ומוקמינא ליה במזרח.

> [Abraham] said before him: "Master of the Universe. I have seen my astrological sign, and I am unfit to have a son!"
> [God] said to him: "Go out from your astrology! What is your concern? That Jupiter is standing in the West? I will move it and make it stand in the East."

Clearly, these two aggadot reflect two disparate ways that Babylonian rabbis viewed the relationship of God and astral determinism. It is interesting to note that a Zoroastrian seems aware of the first story regarding R. Eleazar b. Pedat. *Škand Gumānig Vičār* (SGV), a ninth-century polemic, in a section devoted to a critique of Judaism, seems to refer to this aggada.

Here is the text (14.58–63):

> (58) *ud ān gyāg gōwēd kū būd ek az wēmār ka abāg xwēs zan ud frazand āzārag ud dryōš abē-bahr būd*
> (59) *ham-wār pad namāz ud rozāg ud parparistišn ī yazd abēr tuxšāg ud kardār būd*
> (60) *u-š ek rōz andar namāz ayāft xwāst kū man farrōxīh-ēw ī pad rōzig (rōzīh?) dah*

49. So MSS Gottingen 3, Yad Harav Herzog 1, BL Harl. 5508(400), Munich 95 and 140, Oxford Opp. Add fol. 23, Vat 134 and the aforementioned Vat 487.9.

(61) *u-m zīwistan asān-tar bād*
(62) *u-š frestag-ēw abar frōd (ā)mad guft kū-t rōzīg az ēn wēš pad axtar yazd nē baxt estēd. az nōg baxtan nē šāyēd.*
(63) *az nōg baxtan nē šāyēd*

58. And there they speak of one who was among the sick, with his wife and children suffering
greatly, poor and without resources.
59. At all times he was efficient and active in prayer, fasting, and the services of God.
60. One day in prayer, he made one request: Give me pleasure in my daily lot.
61. that my life may be more comfortable.
62. Then one angel, descending, said: God has not allowed to you by the stars a daily measure greater than this.
63. A new distribution is impossible.

This echoes the story regarding R. Eleazar b. Pedat, as we have just seen, though in the Zoroastrian report it is an angel who makes the offer. The angel suggests,

> if I destroy this sphere, and make anew the heaven and earth, and arrange and set the movement of the stars anew, still it is not clear whether your destiny will fall out good or bad. Thus it is clear from this answer that he himself is not the dispenser of daily portion and lot, and the division is not by his will, and he cannot change fate, and the movements of the sphere, and the sun, moon, and stars are not under his agency or knowledge, or will, or command. (SGV, 70–73)

What is particularly remarkable is that SGV itself admits the same limitation of Ohrmazd's powers, but with a justification that works in a dualistic context but not in a monotheistic one.

čiyōn tuwān sāmānomand ōwōn-iz az-iš kām
če frazānag ud kām ī frazānag harw ō ān ī šayēd būdan
u-š kām ō ān ī nē šāyēd nē widerēd
čē har ān kāmēd ī šāyēd sazēd būdan

In the same way that what is possible is circumscribed, so too is (his wish to do it),
For (god) is wise, and the wish of the wise is entirely toward that which *can* be.
And no wish toward that which can *not* occurs to him,
for he wishes all that which *can* be (and) which it is proper that it should be.[50]

50. See Prods Oktor Skjaervo, "*Tahādī*: Gifts, Debts, and Counter-Gifts in the Ancient Zoroastrian Ritual," in *Classical Arabic Humanities in Their Own Terms: Festschrift for Wolfhart*

SGV can allow itself this seeming inconsistency, because these lines appear in chapter 3, which is devoted to the question of why Ohrmazd did not crush the evil spirit, Ahriman, in his initial foray into Ohrmazd's creation ("Why Ohrmazd did not use his omnipotence to repel Ahriman?"). SGV holds it to be impossible for Ahriman to become good; but Ohrmazd's power over astral determinism is not at issue.

As far as the aggada regarding Abraham is concerned, however, its narrative is tied to the biblical account, in which Isaac must be born and so Abraham is given no right of refusal. Such constraints do not apply to R. Eleazar's situation. Still, it is important to note that the point of the Babylonian aggada is clearly to *emphasize* the difficulty of providing adequate sustenance to R. Eleazar. His refusal points up the connection between his poverty and creation as a whole: though the phrase is not employed, it is the order of creation that is at stake in this dialogue. In other words, while this aggada does not grant R. Eleazar b. Pedat the sustenance that the anonymous father of b. Šabb. 53a was given, they share the apparently Babylonian view that an individual's poverty is woven into the very fabric of creation. We might point to a popular saying quoted in b. B. Qam. 92a, that "poverty follows the poor." Indeed, Alyssa Gray has pointed to a similar Babylonian attitude in her important study, "The Formerly Wealthy Poor: From Empathy to Ambivalence in Rabbinic Literature of Late Antiquity."[51] If anything, Zoroastrianism was more concerned with ethical behavior and protection of the poor than was Roman paganism.[52]

In contrast, the parallel in b. Ned. 32a and in Gen. Rab. 44:12 merely have God reproving Abraham for using astrology.

> אמר לפניו: רבש"ע, הסתכלתי במזל שלי (ואין לי אלא בן אחד): [ואיני ראוי להוליד בן]!
> אמר לו: צא מאיצטגנינות שלך, אין מזל לישראל
>
> He said before Him: Lord of the World! I have examined my *mazzal* (and I [am to have] only one son): [and I am not worthy of engendering a son].
> He said to him: Leave your astrology, there is no *mazzal* for Israel.

In order to properly appreciate its place in Babylonian Jewish thought and to separate its Babylonian and Palestinian themes, let us first examine

Heinrichs on His 65th Birthday Presented by His Students and Colleagues, ed. Beatrice Gruendler and Michael Cooperson (Leiden: Brill, 2008), 493–520, following Pierre J. de Menasce, *Škand-gumānīk-vičār: La solution décisive des doutes* (Fribourg: Libraire de l'Université, 1945), 38–39.

51. Alyssa Gray, "The Formerly Wealthy Poor: From Empathy to Ambivalence in Rabbinic Literature of Late Antiquity," *AJS Review* 33 (2009): 101–33, esp. 130–32.

52. One official of the Sasanian regime was the driyōšān jādag-gōw ud dādwar, the "intercessor and judge of the poor." See *Encyclopedia Iranica, s.v. "driyōšān jādag-gōw ud dādwar,"* http://www.iranicaonline.org/articles/driyōšān-jādag-gōw-ud-dādwar.

its Palestinian precursor, and then that precursor's parallel in the Bavli, that is, Gen. Rab. 20:9.[53]

> בעצבון תאכלנה אמר ר׳ איסי קשה היא פרנסה כפלים כלידה, בלידה כת׳ בעצב תלדי בנים, בפרנסה כת׳ בעצבון תאכלנה, ר׳ אלעזר ור׳ שמואל בר נחמן ר׳ אלעזר אומר הקיש גאולה לפרנסה ופרנסה לגאולה מה גאולה פלאים אף פרנסה פלאים, מה פרנסה בכל יום אף גאולה בכל יום, ר׳ שמואל בר נחמן וגדולה מן הגאולה שהגאולה על ידי מלאך ופרנסה על ידי הקדוש ברוך הוא, גאולה על ידי מלאך ׳המלאך הגואל אותי מכל רע׳ (בראשית מח, טז), פרנסה על ידי הקדוש ברוך הוא ׳פותח את ידך ומשביע לכל חי רצון׳ (תהלים קמה, טז), ר׳ יהושע בן לוי א׳ מקריעת ים סוף ׳לגוזר ים סוף לגזרים׳ וגו׳ (תהלים קלו, יג) ׳נותן לחם לכל בשר׳ וגו׳ (תהלים קל״ו, כה).

> With pain shall you eat it. Said R. Issi: Sustenance is twice as difficult as giving birth; regarding birth it is written: "With pain [*etzev*] shall you give birth to children." Regarding sustenance it is written, "with pain [*itzavon*] shall you eat it." R. Eleazar and R. Shmuel b. Naḥman. R. Eleazar says: [The verse] compared the Redemption to sustenance and sustenance to the Redemption; just as the Redemption is wondrous, so sustenance is wondrous. Just as sustenance is daily, so redemption is daily. R. Shmuel b. Naḥman: And it is greater than the Redemption, for the Redemption is by means of an angel; the Redemption is by means of an angel, as it is written: "The angel that redeems me from every evil" (Gen 48:16), sustenance is by the Holy One, blessed be He, "You open Your hand, and satisfy every being its desire" (Ps 145:16). R. Yehoshua b. Levi: [Sustenance is more difficult] than the splitting of the Reed Sea, "To the One who splits the Reed Sea to pieces" (Ps 136:13) [while] "He gives bread to all flesh" (ibid.).

> [׳המלאך הגואל אותי מכל רע׳] וגומ׳ אמ׳ ר׳ יוסי בר חלפתא קשה היא הפרנסה כפלים בלידה, בלידה כתיב ׳בעצב תלדי בנים׳ (בראשית ג טז), בפרנסה כתיב בעצבון תאכלנה כל ימי חייך (בראשית ג יז).
> רבי אלעזר ורבי שמואל בר נחמן, רבי אלעזר אמ׳ הקיש גאולה לפרנסה ופרנסה לגאולה, מה גאולה כפלים אף פרנסה כפלים, מה פרנסה בכל יום אף גאולה בכל יום, ורבי שמואל בר נחמן אמ׳ וגדולה מן הגאולה, שהגאולה על ידי מלאך, ופרנסה על ידו של הקדוש ברוך הוא, גאולה על ידי מלאך ׳המלאך הגואל אותי׳, ופרנסה על ידי הקדוש ברוך הוא ׳פותח את ידיך ומשביע לכל חי׳ (תהלים קמה טז).
> ר׳ יהושע בן לוי אמר קשין מזונותיו של אדם כקריעת ים סוף ׳לגוזר ים סוף לגזרים׳ (תהלים קלו יג), וכתיב תמן ׳נותן לחם לכל בשר׳ (תהלים קל״ו, כה).

> ["The angel that saved me from every evil"], etc. Said R. Isi/R. Yose b. Ḥalafta: Sustenance is doubly more difficult than giving birth: regarding birth it is written: "You shall give birth to children with pain [*etzev*]" (Gen

53. Ed. Theodor-Albeck, 192, lines 6ff. = 98:16 (MS Vatican, Ebr. 30), 1245 (= ed. Vilna 97:3); and b. Pesaḥ. 118a.

3:16), regarding sustenance it is written: "You shall eat it with pain [*itzavon*] all the days of your life" (Gen 3:17).
R. Eleazar and R. Shmuel b. Naḥman. R. Eleazar said: He compares redemption to sustenance, and sustenance to redemption: just as redemption is twice [as difficult as giving birth], so too sustenance; just as sustenance is [needed] every day, so redemption is [needed] every day. R. Shmuel b. Naḥman said: And [sustenance is] greater than the Redemption, for the Redemption is by means of an angel, while sustenance is by the hand of the Holy One, blessed be He. Redemption is by an angel [as it is written]: "The angel who redeems me," and sustenance is by the hand of the Holy One, blessed be He: "He opens His hands, and satisfies every living creature" (Ps 145:16).
R. Yehoshua b. Levi said: Providing sustenance for everyone [*mezonotav shel adam*] is as (difficult) as the splitting of the Reed Sea, [as it is written:] "To the One who divided the Reed Sea into pieces" (Ps 136:13), and it is written there: "He gives bread to all flesh" (Ps 136:28).

R. Yose b. Halafta has produced a typical piece of rabbinic midrash: Eve's punishment, decreed in Gen 3, is that she bear children in pain, *etzev*, but Adam's is that he must produce his food with *itzavon*, which is considered a more intense form of *etzev*. Moreover, R. Eleazar [b. Pedath], expounding Gen 48, compares sustenance to the redemption for which Jacob gave thanks, and concludes that the everyday work needed for the former is more difficult than the latter.

R. Shmuel b. Naḥman building on the foregoing produces an amazing theological paradox. First, he identifies the "redemption" of Gen 48:16 with "*the* Redemption." The result is that the Redemption, which is not an everyday affair, is to be produced by an angel, while God is in charge of providing sustenance à la Pss 145 and 136. A + B = C: providing sustenance is as difficult as splitting the Reed Sea, which is an example of a particularly noteworthy miracle.

But, we may ask, what was R. Shmuel b. Naḥman's view of divine omnipotence if an everyday task that Scripture associates with God is considered to be more difficult than this great miracle? We are then faced with Lactantius's epitome of Epicurus, except, of course, that God does accomplish this tremendous task of producing sustenance. Indeed, it reminds us of Marcus's "interweavings and intertwinings of fate, to coincidence or chance" and his "inweaving and enfolding of things governed by Providence," from which "everything proceeds.... And then there is necessity and the needs of the whole world, of which you are a part"—both mentioned above. It also brings to mind Cicero's lost fifth book of *De Natura Deorum*, where, it is supposed, we must extend the comments Cotta makes in book 3, calling attention to the fact that, even if most misfortune is human-made, the gods do not protect us from it either, we must presume, because they are unaware or because they are uncaring, a denial of the argument from design (combined with a precursor of Anselm's ontological argument) of the Stoic Villeius in *De Natura Deorum* 2.30, who asserts that "I therefore declare that the world and all its parts were set in order at the very beginning and have been governed for all time by divine providence."[54]

I am not suggesting an acquaintance with Cicero on the part of R. Shmuel b. Naḥman but rather that Cicero's concerns mirror those of everyone, then as now, and that understanding the workings of Providence were of concern to everyone and had to be addressed. R. Shmuel does not explain the difficulty of providing sustenance to all. Perhaps the difficulty was moral, that is, not everyone deserves it, and doing so would violate the principles of divine justice; but one must assume that his understanding of the limitations of divine Providence did not include lack of concern or awareness.

And now its Babylonian parallel in b. Pesah. 118a:

אמר רבי יוחנן: קשין מזונותיו של אדם כפליים כיולדה. דאילו ביולדה כתיב (בראשית ג, טז) בעצב, ובמזונות כתיב ׳בעצבון׳. (אמר רבי): [ואמר רבי] יוחנן: קשין מזונותיו של אדם יותר מן הגאולה. דאילו בגאולה כתיב ׳המלאך הגאל אתי מכל רע׳ (בראשית מח טז) - מלאך בעלמא, ואילו במזונות כתיב האלהים ׳הרעה אתי׳ (בראשית מח טו).
אמר רבי יהושע בן לוי: בשעה שאמר הקדוש ברוך הוא לאדם ׳וקוץ ודרדר תצמיח לך׳ (בראשית ג, טז), זלגו עיניו דמעות, אמר לפניו: רבונו של עולם, אני וחמורי נאכל באבוס אחד? כיון שאמר לו ׳בזעת אפך תאכל לחם׳ (בראשית ג, יז)-- נתקררה דעתו.
אמר רבי שמעון בן לקיש: אשרינו אם עמדנו בראשונה, אמר אביי[55] ועדיין לא פלטינן מינה, דקא אכלינן עיסבי דדברא.

R. Yoḥanan said: Man's sustenance involves twice as much suffering as [that of] a woman in childbirth. For of a woman in childbirth it is written, "in pain" [*be-'etzev*—thou shalt bring forth children] (Gen 3:16), whereas of sustenance it is written, "in toil" [*be-'itzavon*—shalt thou eat] (Gen 3:17). R. Yoḥanan also said: Man's sustenance is more difficult [to come by] than the Redemption, for of the Redemption it is written, "the angel who hath redeemed me from all evil" (Gen 48:16) thus a mere angel [sufficed], whereas of sustenance it is written, the God "who has fed [lit., 'shepherded'] me" (Gen 48:15).
R. Yehoshua b. Levi said: When the Holy One, blessed be He, said to Adam, "Thorns also and thistles shall it bring forth to you" (Gen 3:18), tears flowed from his eyes, and he pleaded before Him, "Sovereign of the Universe! Shall I and my ass eat out of the same crib!" But as soon as He said to him, "In the sweat of your face shall you eat bread" (Gen 3:19), his mind was set at rest.

54. Cicero, *De Natura Deodorum; Academica*, trans. H. Rackham, LCL (Cambridge: Harvard University Press, 1951), 195, 197.

55. Reading with *Diqduqei Soferim*, b. Pesaḥ. 118a, n. *bet*.

> R. Simeon b. Lakish said: Happy are we that we did not remain subject to the first [and we need not eat thorns and thistles]!
> Abaye observed: Yet we have still not [altogether] escaped from it, for we eat herbs of the field.

Here, as is typical for the Bavli, a Western tradition is attributed to R. Yoḥanan, but Abaye puts a particularly Babylonian twist on it, as R. Ḥisda advises one who can afford meat, not to bother with vegetables (b. Šabb. 140b).

Here, as in. b. Ta'an. 25a, the issue of the difficulty of God's providing sustenance to His creation is accepted, but more than that, it is considered more difficult for Him than bringing the Redemption! In this regard both sources are parallel to a Zoroastrian doctrine regarding limitations of Ohrmazd's powers. Indeed, in one case, a Zoroastrian text even states that the difficulties in setting up the world order were greater than that of bringing the Frašegird, the Zoroastrian equivalent of the Redemption, which follows the destruction of evil and precedes the Resurrection. In addition, I will present three statements of the doctrine, two post-Sasanian and one that dates to the late sixth century, that is, a generation before the end of Sasanian rule. The earliest is from Zand ī Fragard ī Jud-dēv-dād, a late sixth-century super-commentary on a late fifth-century text (henceforth ZFJ),[56] the Pahlavī Widēwdād, which is itself a translation/commentary on a Young Avestan text more than a millennium earlier; the next is from a ninth-century polemic against Judaism, Christianity, and Manichaeism, the SGV; and, finally, a tenth-century account of the beginnings of the creation, the Bundahišn.

In the *Pahlavi Rivāyat Accompanying the Dādestān ī Dēnīg* we have the following:

> 52.1 *ohrmazd dwāzdah tis duš-xwārtar būd kardan kū frašegird ud tan ī pasēn fradom asmān winārd dudīgar zamīg winārd sidīgar xwaršēd pad rawišn dād tasum māh pad ham-rawišn dād panjom star pad ham-rawišn dād šašom ka jōrdā hošāg andar zamīg bē rust haftom andar urwarīhā gōnag bōy ud mizag tōm tōm dād haštom andar urwar ātaxš bē dād ud bē nē sōzēd nohom andar aškamb ī mādarān pus winārd dahom murw pad wād dād yāzdahom āb pad rawišn dād dwāzdahom abr (dād) kē-š tan mēnōg ān ī gētīg āb barēd*

> 52.1 For Ohrmazd twelve things were more difficult to do than Frašegird and the Future Body; first he established the sky, second he established the earth, third he created the sun in motion, fourth he created the moon in similar motion, fifth he created the stars in similar motion, sixth when he grew the ear of corn in the earth, seventh he created colours, smells and tastes in plants by species by species, eighth he created fire in the

56. This work has not been published. Mahnaz Moazami and I are preparing the text for publication.

plants and it did not burn (them), ninth he established the child in the mother's womb, tenth he created birds in the wind, eleventh he created water in motion, twelfth (he created) the cloud whose immaterial form carries the water for the material world.[57]

The list appears in the Greater Bundahišn 34 as well, but there Ohrmazd explains to Zoroaster why the Resurrection is not more difficult than the Creation, and from this we may infer the reason for the difficulty of creating these twelve things. Ohrmazd says:

dād padiš duškardar būd ku rist-āxāznišnīh čē-m andar rist-āxēz aXiyārīh ī čīyōn awēšān hast ī kay-am kard bawēd nē būd abar nikīr ku kay ān ī nē būd ayak-am bē kard ān ī būd čim abaz nē šāyēd kardan čē pad ān hangām az mēnōy ī zamīg ast āb xōn az urwar mōy ud az wād jān čīyōn-šān pad bundahišn padgrift xwāhom.

I created these one by one, it was more difficult than the Resurrection, in that in the Resurrection I have the help of such as, when I made them, were not. Consider that, when I made what was not, why can I not make again what has been, since at that time I shall ask from the *mēnōy* of the earth bones, from water blood, from plants hair, from wind the Jan, as they received them in the primal creation.[58]

Likewise in the Anthologies of Zādspram 34.6:

ōhrmazd guft ku awēšān dāmān kay nē būd hand am brēhēnīdan tuwān būd ud nūn kay būd wišuft abāz passāxtan hukardar

Ohrmazd said: I was able to create those creations when they were not, and now that they have existed and are broken up, it is easier to restore them.[59]

As we have seen, the theme that sustenance is more difficult than the Redemption is found in Genesis Rabba and in the Bavli. In a groundbreaking paper presented at the Irano-Judaica conference in Jerusalem in November 2010, and soon to be published, David Brodsky has pointed to the penetration of a Zoroastrian-inspired theme—that the Zoroastrian idea that sinful thoughts constitute a sin in themselves, even without an action—which is enunciated by Rav and Rava, among others in the Bavli, also appears in Genesis Rabba in the name of a Rabbi Abba, presumably Rava. Thus, it is not all that surprising that another Zoroastrian theme—

57. Allan V. Williams ed., *Pahlavi Rivāyat Accompanying the Dādestān ī Dēnīg* 52.1 (2 vols., Copenhagen: Munksgaard, 1990), 1:195, 2:90.

58. See H. W. Bailey, *Zoroastrian Problems in the Ninth-Century Books* (Oxford: Clarendon, 1943), 94, with slight changes on my part.

59. Ibid., 95.

the difficulty of various acts of Ohrmazd as being more difficult than the Zoroastrian Redemption, the Frašegird, also appears in Genesis Rabba and in the Bavli.

Still, in light of our opening discussion of providence and fate in the Roman world, this question is not as serious as originally considered, since on this issue at least, the Palestinian rabbis might have been as open to questions of regarding divine omnipotence as not absolute as it was considered later. However, the question of the history of the concept of omnipotence in late antiquity and beyond lies beyond the scope of this paper and must be deferred for now.

Nevertheless, the question of the place of the Splitting of the Reed Sea must be addressed, since, if the idea of limited omnipotence comes from the Middle Persian culture, why not adopt Creation as an example of a particularly difficult task, rather than the Splitting of the Reed Sea, especially as the argument can be made (and in fact was made by H. W. Bailey)[60] that *brēhēnīdan* can denote *creatio ex nihilo*?

First, we must distinguish the two tropes of limitation of Ohrmazd's powers and *creatio ex nihilo*. The latter was a Christian concept that first appeared in the late first century and was still disputed in the second.[61] As we see from b. Ḥag. 16a, however, the contrary opinion was attributed to two third-century Palestinian Amoraim, R. Yoḥanan and Resh Laqish; the doctrine had not yet been accepted into rabbinic Judaism.

כל המסתכל בארבעה דברים ראוי לו שלא בא לעולם כו׳. בשלמא מה למעלה מה למטה מה לאחור - לחיי, אלא לפנים - מה דהוה הוה! רבי יוחנן ורבי אלעזר דאמרי תרוייהו: משל למלך בשר ודם שאמר לעבדיו: בנו לי פלטירין גדולין על האשפה, הלכו ובנו לו. אין רצונו של מלך להזכיר שם אשפה.

Whoever speculates upon four things, it were a mercy if he had not come into the world, etc. Granted as regards what is above, what is beneath, what [will be] after, that is well. But as regards what was before—what happened, happened [so why not speculate and reveal it]!—Both R. Yoḥanan and Resh Lakish say: It is like a human king who said to his servants: Build for me a great palace upon the dunghill [which represents primordial chaos, while the palace represents ordered creation]. They went and built it for him. It is not the king's wish [thenceforth] to have the name of the dunghill mentioned.

Still, if not *creatio ex nihilo*, why not creation non-*ex nihilo*? Perhaps for the same reason Ohrmazd gives in the Greater Bundahišn: having created/

60. Ibid., 96, though he offers an alternate possibility as well.

61. See Jonathan Goldstein, "The Origins of the Doctrine of Creation *Ex Nihilo*," *JJS* 35 (1984): 127-35, and his "Creation *ex nihilo*: Recantations and Restatements," *JJS* 38 (1987): 187–94; and see Alister E. McGrath, *Theology: The Basics* (Malden, MA: Blackwell, 2004), 38–39.

ordered the world, why should God not have the power to dis-order it by miraculous intervention? Some lesser form of intervention would thus be required as an example.

It may be then wondered why some other miraculous event was not chosen as an example of a particularly difficult task. It may be that the Flood, or the destruction of Sodom and Gomorrah, or the Ten Plagues were not chosen because of their destructive nature; but why not the provision of manna in the wilderness? That may well be because of the similarity between providing sustenance for us and providing sustenance for the Israelites in the wilderness: why should one be more difficult than the other? An answer that one was only for a limited time and a certain number of people could be seen as insufficient. But we are clutching at straws. The Splitting of the Reed Sea may have been chosen for no other reason than its association with redemption and the weight of the phrase: *qeri'at Yam Suf* in place of *ma'aseh Bereishit*! The act of splitting the sea was not as intimately connected with death and destruction as the plagues or the Flood, and of the remaining miracles, while manna was an absolute good, it still lacked a certain linguistic flair.

Whatever the reason, however, the idea that omnipotence has its limits was widespread in late antiquity, and a rather extended meditation on that subject has just come to light. The passage occurs in ZFJ. Though ZFJ is one of the most interesting MP texts from a rabbinic point of view, its main interest for us now is a passage which combines ritual analysis and theological speculation, the latter of which touches directly on the question of Ohrmazd's powers and the way he chooses to employ them, or not. Providentially, as we might say, Shai Secunda and his associates have just published an edition and treatment of this passage, and I shall quote several units from that passage.[62] The essential problem is this: since one of the cardinal sins in Zoroastrianism is polluting sacred elements like fire and water, how is it that Ohrmazd brings rain on all kinds of impurities and thus allows the rain to become polluted? Can he not allow the rain to fructify the earth without having it polluted? Here is the relevant portion of Secunda et al.'s edition:

(1) [TD2 448:15–449:9] *ēn wārān kē pad hixr ud nasāy ud xrafstar ud daštān abārīg rēmanīh. hamē wārēd ka abar gīrēnd pad gyāg ī tan tōhmag dārēnd šāyēd ayāb nē nē nē nē čē rāy ēd rāy čē ohrmazd pad meh-dādestānīh (ī) xwarišn ud (ud) xwārišn ī mardōmān gōspand ī hudāg rāy wārēnēd kū-š zīyišn ud parwarišn ī mardōmān gōspand aziš bawēd andar petyāragōmandīh-ēw ēdōn šāyēd wārēnīdan ka pad hamāg gyāg bē wārēnēd meh-sūdīh ī mard ī ahlaw ud wāstar ud xwarišn ī gōspandān rāy*

62. Domenico Agostini, Eva Kiesele, and Shai Secunda, "Ohrmazd's Better Judgement (*Meh-Dādestānīh*): A Middle Persian Legal and Theological Discourse," *Studia Iranica* 43 (2014): 177–202.

This rain which is raining onto bodily refuse [*hixr*], dead matter [*nasāy*], Ahrimenic creatures, menstruation, and other forms of impurity, when they collect it (lit., "take it up"—i.e., the rain) (and) keep it in the place of the (purifying) sap [*tan tōhmag*], is it permitted or not? No, no, no! Why? Because Ohrmazd, through the principle of Better Judgment [*meh-dādestānīh*], makes it rain for the food and drink of humans (and) the beneficent cattle—so that the livelihood and the nourishment of humans (and) cattle comes from it. In a (situation of) adversity it is (equally) allowed [*šāyēd*] to make it rain in such a way that he makes it rain in every place for the Greater Benefit [*meh-sūdīh*] of the righteous man, pasture and the food of cattle.

(6) [TD2 451:5–10] *pas dādār ī ohrmazd nē tuwānīg kē wināh ī ēdōn garān ī pad nasāy ō āb ud ātaxš burd guft estēd pad and čārakkarīh abāz nē tuwān dāštan kē ān meh-sūdīh ī xwarišn ud xwārišn ī mardōmān ud gōspandān jud az ēn kardan nē tuwān bawēd.*

Then is the Creator Ohrmazd "not capable"? He who is not able to restrain such a grave sin as is said (regarding) carrying dead matter to water and fire—despite that much ability? He who is not able to perform that Greater Benefit of food and drink for people and cattle without this (i.e., bringing rain on corpses)?

(7) [TD2 451:10–12] *az ān ī ka petyārag ō dām mad andar gētīg ēč tis ī abēzag būdan kardan nē šāyēd bē kerbag ān bawēd kē-š meh-sūdīh rāy*

Since the adversary came to the creation, it is not possible [*šāyēd*] for anything in the *gētīg* to be pure (or) to make (pure). Rather, a good deed [*kerbag*] is that on account of which there is Greater Benefit.

(8) [TD2 451:12–452:2] *kerbag az wināh wēš ayāb kerbag az kerbag meh ayāb wināh az wināh keh wināh ān ō 36 bun kē wināh az kerbag meh ayāb wināh az wināh meh u-š dādestān ēdōn čārag 37 bē ōzadan rāy tis-ēw ēdōn abd čiyōn rāyēnišn ī kahas kē-š ābādānīh ī gēhān aziš bē (nē) 38 kardan nē rāyēnīdan čāšt*

Is a *kerbag* from a sin better? Or is a *kerbag* from a *kerbag* greater? Or a sin from a sin lesser? A sin is that (which goes) to the account; which (as) a sin from a *kerbag* is great, or (as) a sin from a sin is great. And the decision is such: The remedy for killing is any one thing as wonderful as the preparation [*rāyēnišn*] of an irrigation channel whence the cultivation of the world—it has been taught "making" (the irrigation channel), not "preparing."

Our section of ZFJ builds on this ancient approach, yet presents it in a new light. It describes Ohrmazd's response as a utilitarianism which is an integral part of his Better Judgment (*meh-dādestānīh*). Although the rain will inevitably fall on impurities, this is deemed acceptable since it is necessary for the Greater Benefit (*meh-sūdīh*) accomplished by sustaining the world. This perspective engenders a relative scale in which a relative good outweighs minor evils. Notably, while in the Videvdad it was sufficient for Ohrmazd to merely affirm Zarduxšt's observation, ZFJ turns this affirmation into a theological principle that guides the entire passage. The ZFJ passage is interested both in legal and theological aspects of the inevitable mixing of good and evil (*gumēzišn*). In this way, it develops the Videvdad's juxtaposition of moral, theological, proscriptive, and mythological perspectives on *gumēzišn*. ZFJ actualizes a theme that is only latent in the Videvdad, namely, the implicit likening of the human and divine realms regarding the mixing. According to ZFJ, both realms should operate in line with the utilitarian principle of the Greater Benefit (*meh-sūdīh*). When humans adopt a utilitarian approach to evil in this world they are imitating the divine. What appears at first to be a leniency is in fact *imitatio dei*. The pragmatism of human law is actually a reflection of the divine design. This notion frames, organizes, and gives meaning to the Zoroastrian ritual-legal system. Crucially, this "foundational story" ensures that Zoroastrian religious law will not be seen as merely arbitrary.[63]

The limitations on Ohrmazd's powers are a direct consequence of the eruption of Ahriman into Ohrmazd's creation, and his unwillingness to destroy Ahriman at that point. Instead, they made an agreement to continue their dispute for nine thousand years. Ahriman is of course unaware that the deck is stacked against him, so to speak, and that in the end he and all his minions will be destroyed. And so, during this time of "mixture," when good and evil will coexist, Ohrmazd's powers are limited, since he has undertaken not to destroy evil during this period. And in this respect the Christian Devil is not so different; even if his powers are more restricted than Ahriman's, God seems unable or unwilling to destroy this fallen angel.[64]

Having done this, however, there is yet another consequence, as the two post-Sasanian compilations mentioned above, SGV and the Bundahišn, state: Ohrmazd does not even consider the possibility of doing that which is in effect impossible for him to do. Thus, the Bundahišn at 1.57 states:

> *ohrmazd ān tis nē menēd i-š kardan nē tuwān*
> *ganāg mēnoy ān ī-š nē tuwān kardan menēd ud padist-iz abar barēd*

> Ohrmazd does not think of that which he is not able to do,
> (while) the Foul Spirit thinks what he is not able to do and even insists on doing it.

63. Ibid., 180-83.

64. See the discussion of Augustine's view of Satan and its difficulties in John Burton Russell, *Satan: The Early Christian Tradition* (Ithaca, NY: Cornell University Press, 1981), 210–23.

And similarly in the ninth-century *Škand-gumānīg-wizār*

> *če frazānag ud kām ī frazānag harw ō ān ī šayēd būdan*
> *čiyōn tuwān sāmānomand ōwōn-iz az-iš kām*
> *u-š kām ō ān ī nē šāyēd nē widerēd*
> *čē har ān kāmēd ī šāyēd sazēd būdan*

> In the same way that what is possible is circumscribed, so too is (his wish to do it),
> For (god) is wise, and the wish of the wise is entirely toward that which *can* be.
> And no wish toward that which can *not* occurs to him,
> for he wishes all that which *can* be (and) which it is proper that it should be.[65]

From our perspective Bundahišn 1.57 seems self-contradictory: In regard to Ohrmazd we can understand that he is wise in not wishing to go beyond his powers, but how can Ahriman be faulted for thinking of what he cannot do when in the end he does it?[66] Rather, we must assume that while he insists on attempting that which is impossible (for him?), in the end he cannot accomplish the task he insists on doing. Ohrmazd is wise in not attempting the impossible; Ahriman is impetuous, arrogant and foolish for insisting on the attempt.

There may be even more to this. In his description of Stoic physics, John Sellars makes the following point:

> Both judgement and assent … are central topics in Stoic epistemology.… At the macroscopic level it will involve an understanding of the order of causes in the cosmos as a whole, knowing what would and would not be a realistic outcome of events to desire. *This sort of physical analysis, involving the Stoic theory of fate, will tell us that, for instance, we should only desire events that are in fact possible outcomes given the order of causes currently at play.* In other words, if one were to ask what the practical implications of the study of Stoic physics might be, the answer would most likely be that a greater understanding of the way in which Nature works at both the individual and cosmic levels should have consequences for what we consider realistic objects of desire and aversion.[67]

65. Both texts are taken from Skjaervo, "*Tahādī*: Gifts, Debts, and Counter-Gifts," 493–520; the second text follows Menasce, *Škand-gumānīk-vičār*, 38–39.

66. Behramgore Tahmuras Anklesaria (*Ākāsīh of Greater Iranian Bundahišn, transliterated and translated in English* [Bombay, 1956], 16) reads *satiz-iz* instead of *padist-iz* and translates as follows: "Ohrmazd does not contemplate that thing which he cannot execute; and the Evil Spirit contemplates what he cannot perform, and also leads for quarrel." However, Skjærvø's reading and interpretation seem more in keeping with the sense of the passage, which contrasts Ohrmazd's wise restraint to Ahriman's foolish impetuousness. My thanks to Mahnaz Moazami for calling my attention to this reading.

67. Sellars, *Stoicism*, 51; emphasis added.

Thus, Ohrmazd may be construed a Stoic sage, as would the rabbinic God of b. Ta'an. 25a, who would have to overturn the world and then only *perhaps* have R. Eleazar b. Pedat be born under a star which betokened sustenance. And thus Ahriman, who insists on doing what cannot be done, is not only a fool but is uncultivated, "impious, foolish and mad," as Plutarch would have put it.[68] Is this criticism of Ahriman somehow connected with Stoic thought, or, perhaps, does it reflect a similar train of thought? It is clearly premature to consider either possibility without a good deal more work. Still, the importance of the *rad* in Zoroastrianism, that is, the sage with whom one must consult and to whom one must confess in order to receive advice on penance and absolution is undoubted.[69] Here is Shaked on the concept of the "perfect man" in Zoroastrianism (and, we might add, one must consider also the nature and role of the Elect in Manichaeism).

> The importance of the notions "Good People" or "the Righteous" in the practical life of Zoroastrians is seen in the requirement to practise the act of consultation with the wise or with the good as often as one can. "Consultation" is an act of piety in which a Zoroastrian imitates the precedent of the prophet Zoroaster, who conferred with Ohrmazd. The Avesta and Zoroastrianism as a whole are the outcome of these sessions.
>
> A symbol of the presence of Ohrmazd in the material and visible world is the Righteous Man, a quasi-mythological figure that represents the acme of human perfection. The identity between Ohrmazd and this figure is such that "anyone who has caused pleasure or affliction to the Righteous Man, has caused pleasure or affliction to Ohrmazd." A fully elaborate doctrine of the Righteous Man is presented in the first three chapters of *Dādestān ī dēnīg*. The three supreme representatives of this mythical conception are the Primal Man, Gayomard; the Prophet Zoroaster; and the ultimate Renovator of the world, the Sōšyāns. There is thus a personalized Righteous Man figure for each of the three moments of the universe, "its origin, its middle and its end," as the text puts it. The conception of man in Sasanian writings displays the same dualism that exists in the cosmos by the fact that humanity is divided into those who are good and those who are bad; it is also part of the dualistic system in that every individual human being is a playground for the good and the evil powers. At the same time man is a structure that recalls the divine world: it has a central power at the top, assisted by a number of powers, sometimes said to be six in number, like the Amahraspands, to complete the picture of the entourage of Ohrmazd. Beyond the dualistic scheme there is a strong presence in Sasanian Iran of the idea that man is an

68. Plutarch, *De stoicorum repugnantiis* (On the self-contradictions of the Stoics), 1048e; see Sellars, *Stoicism*, 37.

69. See Yishai Kiel, "Confessing Incest to a Rabbi," *HTR* 107 (2014): 401–24, and esp. 412–16; and Philip G. Kreyenbroek, "On the Concept of Spiritual Authority in Zoroastrianism," *Jerusalem Studies in Arabic and Islam* 17 (1994): 1–15.

> image of the universal structure, an idea well familiar from the Greek world, and possibly influenced by it. On the other hand, and well within the Zoroastrian tradition, it seems, is the idea of the Righteous Man, a figure of mythological dimensions, that represents the essence of human goodness and power, and is akin to Ohrmazd's presence in the world. The overwhelming figure of Gayomard, the mythological prototype of humanity, may have foreshadowed this Sasanian conception.[70]

We have thus seen that dualistic views are alive and well in the Bavli. As a final note, I would like to call attention to the understanding of the *yetzer ha-ra'* as a demonic, antinomian force that attacks a person from the outside, which Ishay Rosen-Zvi has identified with the midrashim of R. Yishmael (and not those attributed to the school of R. Akiva), but has been taken up in the Bavli in particular.[71] The reason for this reception in Babylonian rabbinic literature is to be found in Sasanian thought, specifically in the *andarz* literature collected in Dēnkard VI, as edited by Shaul Shaked over thirty years ago. We will present just one example; the interested reader may consult Shaked's edition for others.

> *pōryōtkēšān ī dānāgān pēšēnīgān ōwōn dāšt ku mardomān andar ox menišn-ē(w), ast yazd-ē(w) gāh dārēd ud ast druz-ē(w) rāh dārēd. ud andar menišn gōwišn-ē(w), ast yazd-ē(w) gāh dārēd ud ast druz-ē(w) rāh dārēd. ud andar gōwišn kunišn-(ē), ast yazd-ē(w) gāh dārēd ud ast druz-ē(w) rāh dārēd.*

> The *pōryōtkēš*, that is, the ancient sages, held thus: In men's mind there is thought, sometimes a god holds a throne (in it), sometime a demon holds up the way. In thought there is speech, sometimes a god holds a throne (in it), sometimes a demon holds up the way. In speech there is deed, sometimes a god holds a throne (in it), sometimes a demon holds up the way.[72]

---

70. Shaked, *Dualism in Transformation*, 71.

71. See Ishay Rosen-Zvi, *Demonic Desires:* Yetzer Hara *and the Problem of Evil in Late Antiquity*, Divinations (Philadelphia: University of Pennsylvania Press, 2011), 65–86.

72. See Ēmētān and Shaked, *Wisdom of the Sasanian Sages*, 2–3.

First Man, First Bovine

Talmudic Mythology in Context

YISHAI KIEL

In connection with the Roman festivals of Calends and Saturnalia mentioned in m. ʿAbod. Zar. 1:3, the Palestinian and Babylonian Talmuds record a fascinating tradition that projects the inauguration of these festivals back to Adam.[1] The attribution of these festivals to Adam seems to underscore an appreciation of the universal nature of the celebrations surrounding the winter solstice.[2] According to the talmudic tradition, as

---

1. y. ʿAbod. Zar. 1:2, 39c:

רב אמר קלנדס אדם הראשון התקינו כיון דחמא ליליא אריך אמר אי לי שמא שכתוב בו הוא ישופך ראש ואתה תשופנו עקב שמא יבוא לנשכיני ואומר אך חושך ישופיני כיון דחמא אימּמא ארך אמר קלנדס קלון דיאו

Rav said: the First Man inaugurated Calends. When he saw that the night was becoming longer he said: Woe is me! Perhaps the one about whom it is written "he will strike at your head and you shall strike at his heel" (Gen 3:15) will come to bite me. "If I say: surely darkness will conceal me (the night around me will become light)" (Ps 139:11). Once he saw that the day was becoming longer he said "calends!" – "'God is good!' (καλὸν θεό[ς])."

And compare b. ʿAbod. Zar. 8a:

ת"ר כיון שראה אדם הראשון יום שמתמעט והולך אמ׳ אוי לי שמא בשביל שסרחתי עולם חשך בעדי וחוזר לתהו ובהו וזו היא מיתה שנקנסה עלי ישב שמונה ימים בתענית כיון שנפלה תקופת טבת וראה היום שמארי׳ והולך אמ׳ מנהגו של עולם הוא עמד ועשה שמונה ימים טובים לשנה אחרת עשאן לאלו ואלו ימים טובים

Our Rabbis taught: When the First Man saw that the day was becoming shorter, he said: "Woe is me! Perhaps because I have sinned the world is being darkened on my account and returning to its state of chaos and confusion; and this is the death to which I was sentenced." So, he fasted for eight days. Once the winter solstice had elapsed and he saw that the day was becoming longer, he exclaimed: "This is the world's course!" He then inaugurated eight days of festivity. In the following year, he designated both (sets of eight days) as festivals.

2. In the Babylonian Talmud, the redactors append an apologetic clarification: "He [Adam] fixed them for the sake of Heaven, but they [the heathens] fixed them for the sake of idolatry" (הוא קבען לשם שמים והם קבעום לשום ע"ז). On the web of connections between var-

the days were becoming shorter and the nights longer,[3] Adam feared that darkness was inflicted on the world as a punishment for his primordial sin. Following the winter solstice, however, he realized that the days were becoming longer again and therefore inaugurated a festival to express his joy and thanksgiving.[4]

Immediately following this tradition, the Babylonian Talmud records another tradition that is completely absent from the Palestinian Talmud. As the sun was setting on Adam and Eve for the first time, they feared that darkness was inflicted on the world as a punishment for their primordial sin. They wept in penitence[5] until the sun rose again the next morning,

---

ious festivals associated with the winter solstice, see, e.g., Eduard Meyer, *Ursprung und Anfänge des Christentums,* 3 vols. (Stuttgart: J. G. Cotta, 1921–1923), 2:209–10; Julius Wellhausen, *Israelitische und jüdische Geschichte* (1894; repr., Berlin: de Gruyter, 1958), 244–45; Julian Morgenstern, "The Chanukkah Festival and the Calendar of Ancient Israel," *HUCA* 20 (1947): 40–75; Emmanuel Friedheim, *Rabbinisme et paganisme en Palestine romaine: Étude historique des Realia talmudiques (Ier–IVème siècles),* RGRW 157 (Leiden: Brill, 2006), 332–37; Moshe Benovitz, "'Until the Feet of the Tarmoda'i Are Gone': The Hanukkah Light in Palestine during the Tannaitic and Amoraic Periods," in *Torah Lishma: Essays in Jewish Studies in Honor of Professor Shamma Friedman* [Hebrew], ed. David Golinkin et al. (Jerusalem: Schechter Institute and Bar-Ilan University Press, 2007), 20–24.

3. Both Talmuds note that the reality reflected in the story accords with the position according to which the world was created in the month of Tishrei and not in the month of Nisan.

4. There are important differences between the Palestinian and Babylonian versions of the story. The Palestinian Talmud emphasizes the role of the serpent, which is completely absent in the Babylonian Talmud. By contrast, there are several elements in the Babylonian version of the story that are absent from the Palestinian version: the Babylonian Talmud maintains that Adam initially inaugurated eight days of fasting, which were eventually converted into eight days of festivity. The notion that Adam fasted in the aftermath of his primordial sin is recorded in several rabbinic, Christian, and Iranian sources. See Yishai Kiel, "Creation by Emission: Recreating Adam and Eve in the Babylonian Talmud in Light of Zoroastrian and Manichean Literature," *JJS* 66 (2015): 295–316; Gary A. Anderson, "The Penitence Narrative in the Life of Adam and Eve," in *Literature on Adam and Eve: Collected Essays,* ed. Gary A. Anderson, Michael E. Stone, and Johannes Tromp, SVTP 15 (Leiden: Brill, 2000), 3–42. The emphasis on eight days in particular may be connected with the prominent place of Hanukkah in the Babylonian Talmud as opposed to Palestinian rabbinic sources. On this point, see Geoffrey Herman, "Religious Transformation between East and West: Hanukkah in the Babylonian Talmud and Zoroastrianism, in *Religions and Trade: Religious Formation, Transformation and Cross-Cultural Exchange between East and West,* ed. Peter Wick and Volker Rabens, Dynamics in the History of Religions 5 (Leiden: Brill, 2012), 158–70. Another difference, which will be addressed below in detail, is the mention of Adam's realization that the relative length of the day and night is part of the natural order (מנהגו של עולם), a point explicitly noted only in the Babylonian rabbinic version, but not in the Palestinian parallel.

5. The motif in this story of Adam's weeping is perhaps connected with a broader midrashic theme concerning Adam's tears of repentance. Genesis 3:19 reads, "In the sweat of your brow you shall eat bread" (בזעת אפך תאכל לחם), referring to the sweat resulting from Adam's labor. According to a rabbinic and early Christian interpretation, however, the sweat is connected either with tears or the trembling of the body (זעזוע), which were perceived as a sign of remorse and repentance. See, e.g., Gen. Rab. 20:10 (ed. Theodor-Albeck, 194); b. Pesaḥ.

at which point they realized that darkness was simply part of the natural order. Adam then sacrificed a bull, which is identified as the primordial bull fashioned in its mature form by God. The source is as follows:[6]

> תנו רבנן (?יום?) [כ]שנברא (בו) אדם הראשון כיון ששקעה החמה אמ׳ אוי לי בשביל שסרחתי עולם חשך בעדי ועולם חוזר לתהו ובהו וזו [היא] מיתה שנקנסה עליו והיה יושב ובוכה כל הלילה וחוה בוכה כנגדו כיון שעלה עמוד השחר אמ׳ מנהגו של עולם הוא עמד והקריב שור שקרניו קודמות לפרסותיו שנ׳ ותיטב ליי משור פר מקרין מפריס ברישא מקרין והדר מפריס אמ׳ רב יהוד׳ אמ׳ רב שור שהקׂריב אדם הראשון קרן אחת היתה לו במצחו שנ׳ ותיטב ליי משור פר מקרין מפריס מקרין תרתי משמע אמ׳ רב נחמן מקרן כתי׳.

> Our Rabbis taught: (on the day) [when] the First Man was created, as the sun was setting, he said: "Woe is me! Perhaps because I have sinned the world is being darkened on my account and returning to its state of chaos and confusion and this is the death to which he (= I) was sentenced." He was sitting up all night weeping and Eve was weeping beside him.[7] When dawn broke, he said: "This is the natural course of the world!" He then arose and sacrificed a bull whose horns were (made) before its hoofs, as it is said, "This will please the Lord more than an ox or a bull that is horned and hoofed" (Ps 69:32). First "horned" and only then "hoofed." Rav Yehuda said in the name of Shmuel: The bull which Adam sacrificed had only one horn on its forehead, as it is said, "This will please the Lord more than an ox or a bull that is horned and hoofed" (Ps 69:32). But the word "horned" (*maqrin*) implies two?—Rav Naḥman b. Yitsḥaq said: it is written *maqrn* (i.e. defective, indicating a single horn).

Unlike the partial Palestinian parallels to this tradition,[8] the Babylo-

---

118a; ᾿Abot R. Nat. A:1 (ed. Schechter, 7); Life of Adam and Eve 4:1–3; Anderson, "Penitence Narrative," 16–17; James L. Kugel, *Traditions of the Bible: A Guide to the Bible as It Was at the Start of the Common Era* (Cambridge: Harvard University Press, 1998), 142–43.

6. b. ʿAbod. Zar. 8a (according to MS New York JTS Rab. 15).

7. כנגדו; this might be an allusion to Gen 2:18, 20.

8. Apart from Adam's encounter with the seasonal cycle recorded in the Palestinian Talmud, another Palestinian rabbinic tradition narrating Adam and Eve's first encounter with darkness is recorded in Gen. Rab. 11:2 (ed. Theodor-Albeck, 89):

> ר׳ לוי בשם בר נזירה ל״ו שעות שימשה אותה האורה י״ב שלערב שבת וי״ב שללילי שבת וי״ב שלשבת, כיון ששקעה החמה במוצאי שבת התחיל החשך ממשמש ובא, נתיירא אדם הראשון אך חשך ישופני אתמהא תאמר אותו (שכת׳ בו) הוא ישופך ראש וגו׳ בא להזדווג לי אתמהא, מה עשה לו הקב״ה זימן לו שני רעפים והקישן זה לזה ויצאת האור ובירך עליה הה״ד ולילה אור בעדני. כדשמואל דאמר שמואל מפני מה מברכים על הנר במוצאי שבת מפני שהיא תחלת ברייתו.

> R. Levi in the name of bar Nezira: that light (on the day that Adam was created) served for thirty-six hours; twelve on the day of Sabbath eve (Friday), twelve on the night of Sabbath eve (Friday night), and twelve on the Sabbath day (Saturday). As the sun was setting on Sabbath evening and darkness was approaching, the First Man feared (saying): "darkness will conceal me" (Ps 139:11). Perhaps the one about whom it is said: "he will strike at your head (and you shall strike at his heel)" (Gen 3:15) is coming to have sexual intercourse with me. What did the

nian Talmud distinctively connects Adam's encounter with darkness to his sacrifice of the primordial bull. While the notion of a sacrifice of a bovine ostensibly performed by Adam predates the Babylonian Talmud (see below), it is only in this context that this sacrificial act is linked to the story of Adam's encounter with the cycle of light and darkness, and it is only here that the sacrificial victim assumes individual mythical dimensions.[9]

In the present article, I seek to illuminate the Babylonian rabbinic version of this story by examining it in its broader mythical context. Based on textual and visual representations of a mythical scene depicting the slaying of the primordial bull in several adjacent cultures, I posit that the talmudic story embeds and reflects much of the symbolism attached to this myth in the surrounding cultures. At the same time, however, the mythical heritage pertaining to the slaying of the primordial bull is repackaged by the Babylonian storytellers and redactors and adapted to rabbinic terminology and its theological presumptions.

The anomalous and misplaced theme of an individual primordial bull equivalent to the figure of the First Man, a motif that is nearly absent from Palestinian rabbinic sources, is entrenched in the Iranian and Indic traditions. While in some Indic and Iranian versions of the myth, the primordial bull is sacrificed by the First Man, the Zoroastrian tradition recorded in the ninth- and tenth-century Pahlavi works subverts the sacrificial version of the myth, by attributing the slaying of the primordial bull to the Evil Spirit. While there is some evidence to suggest that the Zoroas-

---

Holy One, Blessed Be He, do? He prepared for him two stones, (Adam) struck them together, fire emerged, and he said a blessing on it. As it is said "(If I say, surely darkness will conceal me) the night around me will become light" (Ps 139:11). This is in accordance with Shmuel, for Shmuel said: "Why is the blessing on the candle recited on the Sabbath night (מוצאי שבת), because it is the beginning of its creation."

The differences between this version and the one recorded in the Babylonian Talmud are considerable. Unlike the talmudic story, Genesis Rabba provides an etiology explaining the reason for the blessing made on fire at the conclusion of the Sabbath. It does not mention the sacrifice of a bull, the focus of the talmudic narrative, and is closely related to the story of Adam's encounter with the winter solstice recorded in the Palestinian Talmud, as can be gleaned from the quoted verses (Gen 3:15; Ps 139:11) and the accentuated presence of the serpent. Interestingly, however, unlike the Palestinian Talmud, which records Adam's fear that the serpent might bite him, Genesis Rabba records his fear that the serpent might come to have sexual intercourse with him. Compare Gen. Rab. 18:6 (ed. Theodor-Albeck, 168); Daniel Boyarin, *Carnal Israel: Reading Sex in Talmudic Culture*, New Historicism 25 (Berkeley: University of California Press, 1993), 83.

9. While a similar story is preserved in ᾽Abot R. Nat. A: 1 (ed. Schechter, 7), it seems to be dependent on the Babylonian Talmud. It is not unusual for version A of ᾽Abot de-Rabbi Nathan to have incorporated Babylonian rabbinic material. See, e.g., the summary of scholarship in Anat Reizel, *Introduction to the Midrashic Literature* [Hebrew] (Alon Shvut: Tevunot, 2011), 321–22.

trian version of the myth was familiar to and engaged by certain Jews or Judeo-Christians in Sasanian Babylonia, the Babylonian Talmud appears to have incorporated a "sacrificial" version of this myth as attested in other Indic and Iranian traditions, which was adapted in turn to an existing rabbinic narrative thread concerning Adam's primal sacrifice.

I further posit that several motifs and themes in the talmudic story—namely, the connection between Adam's sacrifice of the primordial bull and his encounter with the cycle of light and darkness as well as the notion of a single-horned bull—engage and respond to a complex web of visual representations of mythical bull-slaying.

The Babylonian rabbis did not simply weave together textual and visual depictions of the mythical slaying of the (single-horned) primordial bull but adapted this complex web of myths to an existing rabbinic tradition inherited from Palestine concerning a sacrifice ostensibly performed by Adam. Imbuing this inherently rabbinic tradition with new mythical symbolism, the bull sacrificed by Adam was in turn individualized and reconfigured in the image and likeness of indigenous mythical traditions.

The talmudic story, therefore, is not necessarily modeled on a specific version of the mythical slaying of the primordial bull found in one of the surrounding cultures but is rather informed by a panoramic view of the extant textual and visual representations of this myth that pervaded the Sasanian world. The very anomaly of a rabbinic tradition depicting the mythical slaying of a distinctive and individual primordial bull, a theme that seems completely misplaced in the context of ancient Jewish and Christian exegesis, compels us to explore the broader Sasanian connections reflected in the talmudic story.

The Rabbinic Context of Adam's Sacrifice

The notion that Adam sacrificed to God—either in the Garden of Eden, after his expulsion, or on the altar of the Temple (projected back to the antediluvian period)—is rooted in Second Temple traditions concerning Adam's "priesthood." Palestinian rabbinic sources, moreover, explicitly link Adam to Ps 69:32 ("this will please the Lord more than an ox or a bull that is horned and hoofed"), insinuating that it was particularly a bovine creature that Adam had sacrificed.

The Babylonian rabbinic tradition, while continuous with and dependent on earlier rabbinic and nonrabbinic accounts of Adam's sacrifice, further imbued the sacrifice with individual mythical dimensions, which are absent from earlier Jewish reports. Thus, in the Babylonian Talmud it is not simply any bovine that Adam sacrificed but rather *the* uniquely created primordial bull fashioned by God himself. The individual mythical characteristics ascribed to Adam's bull in the Babylonian rabbinic tradition include the notion that its horns preceded its hoofs (i.e., it was created in its mature form), the idea that it was a unicorn, and the contextualization of this primeval sacrificial act with Adam's first encounter with the cycle of light and darkness.

As the Bible is completely silent about a sacrificial act ostensibly performed by Adam, and since Ps 69:32 seems to have little, if anything, to do with Adam, there appears to be no compelling reason to posit an exegetical stimulus for the emergence of this talmudic legend. Now certain exegetes have assumed that Adam sacrificed to God—either because he was perceived as a "high priest" who was placed in Eden לעבדה ולשמרה (Gen 2:15), in the sense understood as performing the sacrificial cult therein;[10] or because the world is believed to be sustained by the sacrificial cult, so it was unimaginable that the First Man did not sacrifice. Yet there is no hermeneutical imperative that it was a bovine that Adam sacrificed, let alone *the* uniquely created mythical bull fashioned by God.[11]

One of the articulations of the idea that Adam sacrificed to God appears in Genesis Rabba, interpreting the verse "and the Lord God took the man and put him in the Garden of Eden to till it and keep it" (Gen 2:15):

'לעובדה ולשמרה' – אילו הקורבנות. 'תעבדון את האלהים', 'תשמרו להקריב לי'.

> "To till it and keep it" – These are the sacrifices, (as it says) "You shall worship (תעבדון) God (on this mountain)" (Exod 3:12); "You shall take care (תשמרו) to offer to me (at its appointed time)" (Num 28:2).[12]

While the notion that Adam must have sacrificed to God can be traced back to Second Temple literature, the rabbis drew a distinctive connection between Adam and Ps 69:32, indicating that of all creatures, Adam chose to sacrifice a bovine. The rabbis took this verse to mean that the praise of God (supposedly pronounced by David) was more pleasing to the Lord

10. For the motif of Eden as a temple, see, e.g., Jub. 3:8–14, 4:23–26, 8:19; 4Q265; Gen. Rab. 16:5 (ed. Theodor-Albeck, 149); Joseph M. Baumgarten, "Purification and the Garden in 4Q265 and Jubilees," in *New Qumran Texts and Studies: Proceedings of the First Meeting of the International Organization for Qumran Studies, Paris, 1992*, ed. George J. Brooke with Florentino García Martínez, STDJ 15 (Leiden: Brill, 1994), 3–10; Jacques T. A. G. M. van Ruiten, "Eden and the Temple: The Rewriting of Genesis 2:4–3:24 in the Book of Jubilees," in *Paradise Interpreted: Representations of Biblical Paradise in Judaism and Christianity*, ed. Gerard P. Luttikhuizen, Themes in Biblical Literature 2 (Leiden: Brill, 1999), 63–94; Kugel, *Traditions of the Bible*, 108–10. According to Jubilees, however, the sacrifice took place only after the banishment from Eden, probably since the author felt uncomfortable with the possibility that Adam performed sacrificial worship while he was still naked (Kugel, *Traditions of the Bible*, 110).

11. One does not get the impression from the verses in Genesis that God created only a single pair of each animal species, as he had done with humanity.

12. Gen. Rab. 16:5 (ed. Theodor-Albeck, 149).

than the bovine sacrificed by Adam.[13] Thus, Genesis Rabba quotes this verse in particular to support the notion that both Noah and Adam sacrificed on the "great altar" in Jerusalem. Commenting on the verse "(Then Noah built an altar to the Lord, and took of every clean animal and of every clean bird) and offered burnt offerings on the altar" (Gen 8:20), we find the following:

> ר׳ אליעזר בן יעקב א׳ על מזבח הגדול שבירושלם ששם הקריב אדם הראשון. "ותיטב לײ משור פר מקרין מפריס".
>
> R. Eliezer b. Yaʿaqov said: on the great altar in Jerusalem, on which the First Man sacrificed, (as it says): "This will please the Lord more than an ox or a bull that is horned and hoofed" (Ps 69:32).[14]

While the sacrifice of a bovine by Adam is mentioned already in Palestinian rabbinic works, the Babylonian Talmud reflects a fundamental shift from the earlier tradition, as it suggests that the animal sacrificed by Adam was not merely of the bovine species but rather was *the* prototypical primordial bull, the animal equivalent of the First Man, who was fashioned by God himself. The mythical traits of the primordial bull sacrificed by Adam are further discussed in b. Šabb. 28b:[15]

> מאי הוי עלה דתחש? א"ר אלעאי אמ׳ ריש לקיש אומ׳ היה ר׳ מאיר תחש שהיה בימי משה בריה בפני עצמה היה ולא הכירו בו חכמים אי מין חיה הוא אי מין בהמה הוא וקרן אחת היתה לו במצחו ולפי שעה נזדמן לו למשה ועשה ממנו משכן ונגנז. מדקאמ׳ קרן אחת היתה לו במצחו ש׳מ טהור היה דאמ׳ רב יהודה אמ׳ רב שור שהקריב אדם הראשון קרן אחת היתה לו במצחו שנא׳ "ותיטב לײ משור פר מקרן מפריס". מקרין תרתי משמע. אמ׳ רב נחמן בר יצחק מקרן כתי׳. וליפשוט מינה דמין בהמה הוא. כיון דאיכא קרש דמין חיה הוא ולית ליה אלא חדא קרן, איכא למימר מין חיה הוא ואיכ׳ למימר מין בהמה הוא.
>
> What is our conclusion with respect to the *taḥaš* which existed during the time of Moses? — R. ʾIlʿai said in the name of Resh Laqish: R. Meir used to say that the *taḥaš* that existed during the time of Moses was of a distinct species, and the sages could not decide whether it belonged to the genus of wild animals or domestic animals; and it had one horn on its forehead, and it appeared to Moses on a single occasion, and he made from it (= from its skin) the (covering of the) Tabernacle, and then it was hidden. Now, since it is said that it had one horn on its forehead, it follows that it was a pure animal. For Rav Yehuda said in the name of Rav: the bull which the First Man sacrificed had one horn on its forehead, as it is said

---

13. On the midrashic connection between the figures of Adam and David, see also b. B. Bat. 14b.

14. Gen. Rab. 34:9 (ed. Theodor-Albeck, 317). See also Gen. Rab. 22:8 (ed. Theodor Albeck, 214–15); Lev. Rab. 2:7 (ed. Margulies, 45); Lev. Rab. 2:10 (ed. Margulies, 50).

15. b. Šabb. 28b, cited here according to MS Oxford 366.

"This will please the Lord more than an ox or a bull that is horned and hoofed" (Ps 69:32). But the word "horned" (*maqrin*) implies two? — R. Naḥman b. Yitsḥaq said: it is written *maqrn* (i.e. defective, indicating a single horn). Then, let us conclude that the *taḥaš* belonged to a genus of domestic animals? — Since there is also the *qereš*, which belonged to a genus of wild animals, and it has only one horn, one can say that the *taḥaš* was a kind of wild animal (like the *qereš*) and one can say that it was a kind of domestic animal (like Adam's bull).

This passage is concerned with the *taḥaš*, a biblical animal from whose skin the cover of the tabernacle was made.[16] According to a widely attested rabbinic tradition, the *taḥaš* was, in fact, a mythical creature: it is portrayed as a unicorn and is said to have been revealed on a single occasion, and only to Moses.[17] The rabbis are primarily interested here in the legal classification of the *taḥaš* as either a domestic animal (בהמה) or a wild animal (חיה), the implications of which bear on the question of its permissibility for the sacrificial cult and the obligation to cover its blood.

While the *taḥaš* and *qereš* are depicted as mythical unicorn creatures already in Palestinian rabbinic works,[18] the Babylonian Talmud attempts to draw a connection between, or perhaps even converge, the *taḥaš* and the mythical bull ostensibly sacrificed by Adam. The proposed connection between the two beasts is based on the tradition attributed to the third-century Babylonian rabbi Rav Yehuda, according to whom the bull sacrificed by Adam, like the *taḥaš*, had a single horn on its forehead. This identification, to be sure, is completely absent from Palestinian rabbinic sources, as there is nothing there to suggest that Adam's victim was anything more than an ordinary bovine.

Another talmudic passage concerning the primordial bull sacrificed by Adam appears in b. Ḥul. 60a as follows:

ואמ׳ רב יהודה שור שהקריב אדם הראשון קרניו קודמות לפרסותיו שנ׳ מקרין ומפריס מקרין ברישא והדר מפריס.

Rav Yehuda also said: The bull which Adam sacrificed had horns before it had hoofs, as it is said: ("And it shall please the Lord more than an ox or a bull that is) horned and hoofed" (Ps 69:32) – first "horned" and then "hoofed."[19]

This statement, which appears immediately following a verbatim parallel of the tradition attributed to Rav Yehuda in the name of Rav discussed

16. See Exod 25:5, 26:14, Num 4:10-14, Ezek 16:10.

17. On the *taḥaš* and *qereš*, see the useful (although uncritical) volume of Nathan Slifkin, *The Sacred Monsters: Mysterious and Mythical Creatures of Scripture, Talmud and Midrash* (Brooklyn, NY: Zoo Torah, 2007), 55–68.

18. See, e.g., y. Šabb. 2:3, 4d.

19. b. Ḥul. 60a (cited according to MS Hamburg 169).

above in the context of our discussion of b. Šabb. 28b and b. ʿAbod. Zar. 8a, holds that the horns of the primordial bull came before its hoofs, suggesting that the primordial bull was created in its mature form (as a bull and not as a calf) and that its horn(s) was(were) created before its hoofs.[20] The use of the plural form (קרניו) seems to contradict the notion that the primordial bull was a unicorn conveyed in the first statement. The use of the defective form (קרנו) in MS Munich 95, interpreted as the singular, may thus represent a scribal attempt to solve this contradiction or, alternatively, be a more original form of the text. Rav Yehuda's statement is paralleled in the following source from t. Ḥul. 3:20, but, as we shall see, there is reason to suspect the authenticity of this clause in the Tosefta:

> אילו הן סימני בהמה: לכל הבהמה אשר היא מפרסת פרסה ושוסעת שסע פרסות מעלת גרה בבהמה אותה תאכלו. כל מעלת גרה – אין לה שינים מלמעלה. אי זה הוא שור שקדמו קרניו לטלפיו זה פרו של אדם הראשון שנ׳ ותיטב לייי משור פר מקרין מפריס אילו הן סימני חיה: כל שיש לה קרניים וטלפיים. ר׳ דוסה אומ׳: יש לה קרניים – אי אתה צריך לשאל על הטלפים, ואע״פ שאין ראיה לדבר זכר לדבר ותיטב לייי משור פר מקרין ומפריס.[21]

> These are the signs (indicating the purity) of domestic animals: "Any animal that has divided hoofs and is cloven-footed and chews the cud—such you may eat (Lev 11:3)." Every domestic animal that chews the cud—does not have upper teeth. *Which is the bull, whose horns came before its hoofs? This is the bull of the First Man, as it is said: "And it shall please the Lord more than an ox or a bull that is horned and hoofed"* (Ps 69:32). These are the signs (indicating the purity) of a wild animal: every animal that has horns and hoofs. R. Dosa says: If it has horns you do not have to inquire about its hoofs, and although there is no (scriptural) proof for this there is a hint of this (as it says) "And it shall please the Lord more than an ox or a bull that is horned and hoofed" (Ps 69: 32).

The clause concerning Adam's bull appears to be altogether misplaced, as it should have appeared after the discussion of the purity signs of the wild animal (חיה). The Tosefta states that there are two signs of purity for wild animals—horns and hoofs. R. Dosa argues in this regard that checking for the animal's horns suffices, since an animal that has horns is necessarily hoofed as well. R. Dosa's rule is then supported by Ps 69:32, "and it shall please the Lord more than an ox or a bull that is horned and hoofed," which mentions the horns before the hoofs. At this point, one would expect the Tosefta to inquire: "But which is the bull whose horns came

20. It is further argued by the anonymous redactors that this tradition supports the position of R. Yehoshua b. Levi, according to whom the first creatures were created in their mature and full-fledged forms.

21. t. Ḥul. 3:20 (MS Vienna). No significant variants appear in MS London and the first print.

before its hoofs (and thus the horns can serve as sufficient indication of its permissibility despite the fact that it does not have hoofs)? This is the bull of the First Man, etc." In its current location, however, the clause concerning Adam's bull comes after the signs of a domestic animal (בהמה) with no apparent connection to the subject matter.

The internal displacement of the clause concerning Adam's bull suggests that it is a later interpolation into the Tosefta, that was intended to clarify R. Dosa's position and the biblical prooftext he provides. Since animals are born with hoofs but without horns, which appear at a later stage in life, one might wonder in which circumstances can the horns suffice to indicate purity in the absence of hoofs? To that end, we are informed that the horns of the primordial bull were created before its hoofs and therefore the horns alone can indicate its purity. The secondary nature of this clause, however, and its textual displacement suggest that the clause was interpolated into the text at a later stage in order to explain a textual difficulty. It remains unclear, however, whether the tradition originated in Palestine and was later attributed to Rav Yehuda, a Babylonian rabbi, by the redactors of the Babylonian Talmud, or, what I believe to be more likely, that a Babylonian rabbinic tradition found its way into the Tosefta versions we possess.[22] Either way, Adam's bull in the Tosefta does not reach the mythical dimensions attributed to the primordial bull in the Babylonian Talmud.

The Primordial Bull in Its Iranian and Indic Contexts

Several cultures have preserved a memory of a mythical slaying of the primordial bull that was located at some point in the unfolding of the cosmogonic narrative.[23] Although the nuances of this mythical episode vary

22. While this version is found in all extant textual witnesses of Tosefta Ḥullin (Vienna, London, and the first print), we are missing the independent version of MS Erfurt, since this manuscript runs only until tractate Zebaḥim. For other examples of Babylonian rabbinic interpolations into MS Vienna of the Tosefta, see Adiel Schremer, "The Text-Tradition of the Tosefta: A Preliminary Study in the Footsteps of Saul Lieberman," *Jewish Studies Internet Journal* 1 (2002): 11–43.

23. See, in general, Stith Thompson, *Motif-Index of Folk-Literature: A Classification of Narrative Elements in Folktales, Ballads, Myths, Fables, Medieval Romances, Exempla, Fabliaux, Jest-Books, and Local Legends*, 6 vols. (Bloomington: Indiana University Press, 1993), A1716.1, A1791, B871.1.1. The slaying of the primordial bull was classified by Bruce Lincoln as an Indo-European myth, since independent Indic, Iranian, Germanic, Greek, and Roman versions of this scene have survived. See Bruce Lincoln, *Priests, Warriors, and Cattle: A Study in the Ecology of Religions*, Hermeneutics 10 (Berkeley: University of California Press, 1981), 69–93. Compare, however, the Mesopotamian Epic of Gilgamesh, according to which Enkidu is said to have "seized the Bull of Heaven by its horns … spun round to the Bull of Heaven, and seized it by its thick tail. Then, Gilgamesh, like a butcher heroic, plunged his sword in

significantly from one culture to another, there seems to be a common thread that warrants, at the very least, a comparative-contrastive analysis.[24] Notwithstanding the existence of broader strands of the myth of the slaying of the primordial bull, this fact does not exempt us from tracing particular channels of cultural diffusion in the Sasanian world.[25]

Bruce Lincoln has discussed the distinctive features of a common Indo-European myth, particularly (although not exclusively) discernible in the Indo-Iranian branch, according to which both the First Man and the primordial bull were slain in the course of the cosmogonic narrative. While the primordial bull is explicitly recorded only in the Iranian and Norse accounts of this myth,[26] the Indic legends of the First Man puruṣa seem to contain traces of this figure as well.[27] Lincoln further speculates

---

between the base of the horns and the neck tendons. When they had struck down the Bull of Heaven they pulled out its innards, set them before Shamash, backed away and prostrated themselves before Shamash."See Stephanie Dalley, *Myths from Mesopotamia: Creation, the Flood, Gilgamesh, and Others* (Oxford: Oxford University Press, 1989), 81–82 (Tablet 6, lines 591–610); Alf Hiltebeitel, "Rama and Gilgamesh: The Sacrifices of the Water Buffalo and the Bull of Heaven," *HR* 19 (1980): 187–223. Another version of the slaying of the primordial bull comes from the cult of Mithras, known primarily from the visual representations of the tauroctony. See Roger Beck, *The Religion of the Mithras Cult in the Roman Empire: Mysteries of the Unconquered Sun* (Oxford: Oxford University Press, 2006), 190–239, and the discussion below.

24. The significance of the primordial bull in the cosmogonic narrative should be viewed also in the light of the economic and cultic prominence of the bovine in numerous cultures. It is possible, therefore, that differences in agricultural production and consumption had at least some impact on certain divergences, variations, and nuances in the recasting of the primordial bull in different mythological systems. Along these lines, one can explain, for example, the economic underpinnings of the shift from a mythical scene focused on a hunted animal in the Late Paleolithic period to a scene of slaughtering of a domesticated bovine in Indo-European cultures or the related buffalo in certain Southeast Asian cultures. See the important remarks in Michael Witzel, *The Origins of the World's Mythologies* (Oxford: Oxford University Press, 2012), 121.

25. Students of comparative mythology often attempt to classify and explain the existence of cross-cultural affinities between distinctive mythic traditions either in terms of synchronic or diachronic "diffusion" or in terms of archetypal universal dispositions and the common psychic of human experience (Witzel, *Origins of the World's Mythologies*, 8–15). For the purpose of the present investigation, it is perhaps useful to employ a methodology commonly used in the study of folklore, namely, that of "ecotypification," the idea of local adaptations of a common motif. See, e.g., Daniel Boyarin, "Virgins in Brothels: Gender and Religious Ecotypification," *Estudios de Literatura Oral* 5 (1999): 195–217.

26. See Lincoln (*Priests, Warriors, and Cattle*, 72–74), who quotes as his prime examples sections from the Pahlavi Bundahišn (quoted below) and the Norse Gylfaginning (6–8).

27. Lincoln (*Priests, Warriors, and Cattle*, 70–75) argues that the name puruṣa can be understood as a compound combining the words for man (*pu*) and bull (*ruṣ-a* standing for *vṛṣ-a-*). He writes, "Thus, behind the figure of puruṣa, the primordial being, lies an older notion of two primordial beings, a man and a bull together. This sort of transformation is only to be expected, for as time went on each group became more distant from its proto-Indo-European origins and underwent its own idiosyncratic course of development" (ibid.,

that, while divine or demonic entities play the role of sacrificer of the primordial bull in some versions of the drama, the original Indo-Iranian myth likely reserved this role for the First Man. Thus, he concludes, what was originally a human sacrifice of the primordial bull was either deified or demonized in later versions of the myth, so as to fit the attitudes of the particular culture toward bovine sacrifice.[28]

According to the Pahlavi tradition, Ohrmazd (Av. Ahura Mazdā) created the "uniquely created bovine" (*gāw ī ēw-dād*, also known as *ēwagdād*), as the prototype of all animals and plants and the counterpart of Gayōmard (Av. Gaya Marətan), the Zoroastrian First Man.[29] While the name of the primordial bovine appears already in two Avestan litanies (*gav- aēvō.dātā-*; Nīāyišn 3.2; Sīh Rōzag 2.12) together with *måŋha- gaociθra-* "the moon containing the seed of cattle" and *gaw-pouru.sarəδā* "the bovine of many species," the only systematic information concerning this figure is contained in the Pahlavi works.[30] The attack of the Evil Spirit on the primordial bull is described as a mirror image of his attack on Gayōmard. According to the Pahlavi Rivāyat 46:15:

> *u-š gāw az dast ī dašn bē brēhēnīd u-š andar ērān-wēz frāz dād...*
> *ud ka-š Ahrimen abar mad pad gyāg bē murd*
> *u-š šusr pad gyāg bē ō zamīg mad*
> *hamāg sardag ī gōspandān ohrmazd az ān šusr bē kard*

> Then he fashioned the bull from his right hand and placed it in the Aryan Expanse.... When Ahriman attacked, it died right away, but its semen fell on the ground, and Ohrmazd made all the animal species from that semen.[31]

---

70). The etymology is based on the suggestion of Jan Otrębski, "Aind, púruṣaḥ, púmān und Verwandtes," *Zeitschrift für vergleichende Sprachforschung* 82 (1968): 251–58. Phyllis Granoff (private communication) informs me that, while the proposed etymology is not very likely, traces of the primordial bull combined in the figure of puruṣa are found in the Bṛhadāraṇyaka Upaniṣad 1.4.4, in which the figure of puruṣa turns into a bull, which ultimately produces the animal kingdom. See *Upaniṣads*, trans. Patrick Olivelle (Oxford: Oxford University Press, 1996), 13–14.

28. Lincoln, *Priests, Warriors, and Cattle*, 80.

29. See Shaul Shaked, "First Man, First King: Notes on Semitic-Iranian Syncretism and Iranian Mythological Transformations," in *Gilgul: Essays on Transformation, Revolution, and Permanence in the History of Religions, Dedicated to R. J. Zwi Werblowsky*, ed. Shaul Shaked, David Shulman, and Gedalyahu A. G. Stroumsa, SHR 50 (Leiden: Brill, 1987), 238–56.

30. See Marijan Molé, *Culte, mythe et cosmologie dans l'Iran ancien: Le problème zoroastrien et la tradition mazdéenne, Annales du Musée Guimet: Biblithèque d'études 69* (Paris: Presses universitaires de France, 1963), 193–202; William W. Malandra, "Gāw ī ēw-dād," *EIr* 10:340; idem, "Gōšurun," *EIr* 11:176–77.

31. The text is based on Alan V. Williams, *The Pahlavi Rivāyat Accompanying the Dādestān ī Dēnīg*, Historisk-filosofiske meddelelser 20:1–60:2 (Copenhagen: Munksgaard, 1990), 1:164–65. The translation is based on Prods Oktor Skjærvø, *The Spirit of Zoroastrianism*, Sacred Lit-

We see here that, while the Pahlavi tradition may have shifted the role of the slayer of the primordial bull from the First Man to the Evil Spirit—perhaps on account of the Zoroastrian equivocal attitude to bovine sacrifice (see below)—the death of the primordial bull resulted in a positive outcome, namely, the growth of animals and plants. This would seem more compatible with a sacrificial version of the myth. Along these lines, Lincoln observes:

> Rather than being completely lost, this myth (i.e. the "sacrificial" account of the death of the primordial bull) managed to reemerge in texts composed after Zarathustra's death, somewhat transformed in accordance with the dualistic theology of the time but fully recognizable nonetheless ... the slaying of Gayōmard and his ox is attributed to Ahriman, but, in a very sophisticated way, the act of killing is itself condemned, while the beneficial results of the killing are embraced.[32]

The Pahlavi tradition preserves an additional scene, in which the soul of the primordial bull, following its death by the Evil Spirit, laments before Ohrmazd and finally agrees to resume its physical form and be consumed by humans. Thus, Bundahišn 4a1–6 (ed. Anklesaria, 52–54) and the Pahlavi Rivāyat 14.1–6 (ed. Williams, 1:78–79, 2:26–27) report that the soul of the primordial bull, Gōšurūn, came out of his body after the Ahrimanic attack and submitted a complaint before Ohrmazd. Eventually, the soul of the primordial bull agreed to reenter the material world in the shape of beneficent animals and to be consumed by humans for the benefit of Ohrmazd.[33] This scene echoes, in some sense, an alternative scenario to the slaying of the primordial bull by the Evil Spirit, suggesting, instead, a "sacrificial" model for the bull's death, in which the willingness of the bull to be consumed by humans for the benefit of Ohrmazd functions as a form of sacrifice.

---

erature Series (New Haven: Yale University Press, 2011), 82. Cf. trans. Williams, 2:74 and compare Bundahišn 4.19–21.

32. Lincoln, *Priests, Warriors, and Cattle*, 83.

33. On the complex issue of animal consumption/sacrifice in Zoroastrianism, see, e.g., Maria Macuch, "On the Treatment of Animals in Zoroastrian Law," in *Iranica Selecta: Studies in Honour of Professor Wojciech Skalmowski on the Occasion of His Seventieth Birthday*, ed. Alois van Tongerloo, Silk Road Studies 8 (Turnhout: Brepols, 2003), 109–29; Albert de Jong, "Animal Sacrifice in Ancient Zoroastrianism," in *Sacrifice in Religious Experience*, ed. Albert I. Baumgarten, SHR 93 (Leiden: Brill, 2002), 127–48. On the moral responsibility of animals, see Shaul Shaked, "The Moral Responsibility of Animals: Some Zoroastrian and Jewish Views on the Relation of Humans and Animals," in *Kontinuitäten und Brüche in der Religionsgeschichte: Festschrift für Anders Hultgård zu seinem 65. Geburtstag am 23.13.2001*, ed. Michael Stausberg, Ergänzungsbände zum Reallexikon der germanischen Altertumskunde 31 (Berlin: de Gruyter, 2001), 578–95. For primary sources see, e.g., Dēnkard 3.199, 3.200, 3.287, 3.288, 5.23.23; Selections of Zādspram 34.38–40; Bundahišn 34.2–3.

In line with the essential symmetry that exists between the cosmogonic and eschatological narratives in Zoroastrianism, it is indeed likely that the sacrifice of the eschatological bull (known as the Ox Hadayōš or Srisōg) in the end of days was mirrored, at some point, by a parallel sacrifice of the primordial bull. While the "sacrifice" of Gōšurūn enabled the consumption of meat by humans, the sacrifice of Ox Hadayōš is said to provide the beverage of immortality in the end of days (Bundahišn 24.22).

Thus, the "sacrificial" version of the slaying of the primordial bull attested in the Babylonian Talmud does not merely resurrect (and appropriate) an early version of the Indo-Iranian myth, which was ostensibly rejected by the Pahlavi account of the slaying of the bull by the Evil Spirit, but in fact negotiates an important strand within the Pahlavi tradition itself, which assumes a "sacrificial" alternative for the death of the primordial bull by the Evil Spirit.

The integration of an Iranian myth concerning the primordial bull into an existing rabbinic tradition concerning the sacrifice of Adam did not emerge, of course, in complete cultural isolation. The Babylonian rabbinic construction of Adam's bovine counterpart and its connections with the *gāw ī ēw-dād*, the bovine counterpart of Gayōmard, appear to have been facilitated by a prior and more fundamental association of Adam with Gayōmard.

While the identification of Adam and Gayōmard is known primarily from Islamic authors,[34] who sought to interweave the biblical and Iranian accounts of the "sacred history," it has been convincingly argued that these tendencies date back to the Sasanian period.[35] The convergence of Adam and Gayōmard, to be sure, can already be discerned in third-century Manichaean works written in Iranian languages.[36] The

34. The association of Adam and Gayōmard is explicitly made by Masʿūdī, for which see Arthur Christensen, *Les types du premier homme et le premier roi dans l'histoire légendaire des Iraniens*, 2 vols. in 1 (Stockholm: P. A. Norstedt, 1917–1934), 194. And see also al-Ṭabarī, *Taʾrīkh al-rusul wa-l-mulūk* [154], in *The History of al-Tabari*, vol. 1, trans. Franz Rosenthal (Albany: State University of New York Press, 1989), 325: "The Persians who say that Jayūmart is Adam ..."

35. Shaked, "First Man, First King," 245: "It seems, however, possible to assume that they [the Iranians] had already made it earlier, at the time of the Sasanians, in order to harmonize their traditions with those of their Semitic neighbors. The process of syncretistic adaptation of Iranian materials to the surrounding Semitic world may have begun long before the advent of Islam." See also Alexander Kohut, "Die talmudisch-midraschische Adamssage in ihrer Rückbeziehung auf die persische Yima und Meshiasage," *ZDMG* 25 (1871): 59–94.

36. See Prods Oktor Skjærvø, "Iranian Epic and the Manichean *Book of Giants*: Irano-Manichaica III," *Acta Orientalia Academiae Scientiarum Hungaricae* 48: *Zsigismond Telegdi Memorial Volume*, ed. Eva Jeremias (Budapest: Akad Kiadó, 1995 [1997]), 192; idem, "Counter-Manichean Elements in Kerdīr's Inscriptions: Irano-Manichaica II," in *Atti del terzo con-*

identification displayed in these texts constitutes the cultural backdrop against which I propose to examine the intimate parallels between the Babylonian rabbinic traditions of Adam's bovine sacrifice and the Iranian traditions of the primordial bull. The syncretic atmosphere that pervaded the Sasanian culture and informed the identification of Adam and Gayōmard thus facilitated, and perhaps reinforced, the refiguring of Adam's bull in the Babylonian Talmud in the image and likeness of his Iranian counterpart.

The talmudic "appropriation" of the primordial bull is also compatible with other mythical bovine creatures discussed in the Babylonian Talmud, which seem to have been appropriated from Iranian mythology and adapted to the rabbinic tradition. In a series of articles, Reuven Kiperwasser and Dan Shapira have examined Babylonian rabbinic traditions concerning mythical bovines in the light of Iranian material. In one article, they speculate that the talmudic *ridyā* reported by Rabba b. bar Ḥannah in b. Taʿan. 25b—a bovine creature with three legs that is said to have a prominent role in the regulation of the hydrological cycle—is an adaptation of the *xar ī sē pāy*, the righteous three-legged ass in the Iranian tradition (Bundahišn 24), which lives in the middle of a mythical sea.[37] Elsewhere, they examine the Babylonian version of the eschatological feast (b. B. Bat. 74b–75a) and the role of Leviathan and Behemoth (= *šor ha-bar*, the Wild Ox) in this feast in light of Iranian traditions pertaining to the eschatological bull, the Ox Hadayōš.[38] It would not be surprising, therefore, to find

gresso internazionale di studi 'Manicheismo e Oriente cristiano antico,' Arcavacata di Rende-Amantea 31 agosto–5 settembre 1993, ed. Luigi Cirillo and Alois van Tongerloo, Manichean Studies 3 (Leuven: Brepols, 1997), 336–40. Rather than identifying Adam and Eve with Mašī and Mašyānī (the first human couple and the descendants of Gayōmard), Mani seems to have identified Gayōmard (Manichaean Middle Persian, Gēhmurd) with Adam and, leaving out Mašī, identified Mašyānī (Manichaean Middle Persian, Murdiyānag) with Eve. The use of Zoroastrian mythology in the Iranian Manichaean works reflects the attempt of Mani and his followers to package the Manichaean message in a manner that would be more agreeable and familiar to local adherents to Zoroastrianism. See, in general, Prods Oktor Skjærvø, "Iranian Elements in Manicheism: A Comparative Contrastive Approach: Irano-Manichaica I," in *Au carrefour des religions: Mélanges offerts* à Philippe Gignoux; *Textes réunis*, ed. Rika Gyselen, Res Orientales 7 (Bures-sur-Yvette: Groupe pour l'étude de la civilisation du Moyen-Orient, 1995), 263–84. For talmudic engagement of Zoroastrian and Manichaean First Man traditions see Kiel, "Creation by Emission."

37. Reuven Kiperwasser and Dan Shapira, "Irano-Talmudica I: The Three-Legged Ass and Ridya in B. Ta'anit: Some Observations about Mythic Hydrology in the Babylonian Talmud and in Ancient Iran," *AJS Review* 32 (2008): 101–16.

38. Reuven Kiperwasser and Dan Shapira, "Irano-Talmudica II: Leviathan, Behemoth, and the 'Domestication' of Iranian Mythological Creatures in Eschatological Narratives of the Babylonian Talmud," in *Shoshannat Yaakov: Jewish and Iranian Studies in Honor of Yaakov Elman*, ed. Shai Secunda and Steven Fine, Brill Reference Library of Judaism 35 (Leiden: Brill, 2012), 203–35.

yet another mythical bovine creature in the Babylonian Talmud that was adapted from the Iranian tradition.

The Primordial Bull in the Magic Bowls

The primordial bull makes an appearance not only in the Babylonian Talmud but also in the Mesopotamian corpus of magic bowls. Thus, a bowl from the Moussaieff collection written in Jewish Babylonian Aramaic (M 163)[39] provides further evidence that the Iranian myth of the slaying of the primordial bull was incorporated, in one form or another, into the mythical repertoire of Jews (or, perhaps, Judeo-Christians)[40] in Sasanian Babylonia. This is a curse bowl, commissioned by two brothers named Mihlad and Baran, sons of Mirdukh, directed against a certain Isha, the son of Ifra-Hurmiz.

Dan Levene, who first published this bowl, pointed out the two main literary devices it employs: (1) the abundant use of verbs, nouns (lines 1, 28 and 30), angel names (line 14), and magical names (line 10) derived from

---

39. The bowl was published in Dan Levene, "'... and by the name of Jesus ...': An Unpublished Magic Bowl in Jewish Aramaic," *JSQ* 6 (1999): 283–308; idem, *A Corpus of Magic Bowls: Incantation Texts in Jewish Aramaic from Late Antiquity*, Kegan Paul Library of Jewish Studies (London: Kegan Paul, 2003), 120–38.

40. The text of the bowl ends with a reference to Jesus and his exalted father: "By the name of I-am-that-I-am, YHWH Sabaoth, and by the name of Jesus, who conquered the height and the depth with his cross, and by the name of his exalted father, and by the name of the holy spirits(!) forever and eternity, Amen, amen, selah. This press is true and established" (בשמיה דאהיה אשר אהיה, יהוה צבאות, ובשמיה דאישו, דכבש רומ(א) ועומ(ק)א בזקיפיה ובשו(ם) אבוי רמא ובשום רוחי קדישתא לעלם עלמין. אמן אמן סלה. שריר וקים הדין כיבשא). Based on this text, several scholars have assumed that the practitioner was, at the very least, nominally Christian. Although the allusion to the Trinity is doubtful—as the supposed reference to the Holy Spirit appears in the plural form—the text is underwritten by a clear binitarian theology and the belief in Jesus as the Son of God. Shaul Shaked assumed that, despite the bowl's reference to Jesus, the practitioner was, in all likelihood, a Jew ("Jesus in the Magic Bowls: Apropos Dan Levene's '... and by the name of Jesus ...'," *JSQ* 6 [1999]: 309–19, esp. 313–16). The language of the bowl is Jewish Babylonian Aramaic rather than Syriac; there are several Hebraisms throughout; and there appear to be some references to talmudic traditions. It is possible that the practitioner used Christian invocations, since Isha son of Ifra Hurmiz, against whom the curses are directed, might have been a convert to Christianity (despite the Iranian name of his mother). Even as a Jew, the practitioner might have been comfortable with employing the name of Jesus in a syncretic magical context. Considering the recent conclusions of Peter Schäfer and Daniel Boyarin regarding the spread of binitarian theology among Jews (even rabbinic Jews), this would not be surprising. See Daniel Boyarin, "Beyond Judaisms: Metatron and the Divine Polymorphy of Ancient Judaism," *JSJ* 41 (2010): 323–65; Peter Schäfer, *The Jewish Jesus: How Judaism and Christianity Shaped Each Other* (Princeton, NJ: Princeton University Press, 2012), 103–49. Although it is possible, I do not insist with Shaked on the "Jewish" affiliation of the practitioner, as it is also possible that s/he was a member of a Judeo-Christian sect.

the root כבש ("to press, subdue, conquer, oppress"); and (2) the use of the formula "just as X was oppressed [איתכביש], so may Isha son of Ifra Hormiz be oppressed," which is known also from Greek magical literature and referred to as the *similia similibus* formula. The similes for oppression in our text consist of a collection of references to mythical events taken from a wide range of cultures. The relevant lines from the bowl read as follows:

> והיכדין דאיתכביש רימון תורא קדמאה, הכדין ניתכביש הדין אישה בר איפרא הורמיז...
> [והיכ]דין דאיתכביש אמור גברא רבה דלסוף, הכדין ניתכביש הדין אישה בר איפרא הורמיז...
> והיכדין דאיתכביש א(מ)וס גברא קדמאה... הכדין ניתכביש וניתדריך הדין אישה בא איפרא הורמיז...

> And just as Rimon, the primordial bull, was oppressed—so may this Isha son of Ifra Hurmiz be oppressed …
> And just as Amur, the great man of the end, was oppressed—so may this Isha son of Ifra Hurmiz be oppressed …
> And just as Amus, the First Man, was oppressed … —so may this Isha son of Ifra Hurmiz be oppressed and trod under.[41]

The Zoroastrian backdrop of these lines was noted by Shaul Shaked, who asserts as follows:

> It is difficult not to see in some of these references an analogy to the Zoroastrian cosmological story. The underlying hint in three of the cryptic references is probably to some traumatic event that happened to the Bull, the Primal Man, and the Man of the End, the eschatological figure. This traumatic occurrence would presumably justify saying that they were "suppressed." Such a traumatic episode is indeed found at the core of the Zoroastrian story of creation. There, the Bull and the Primordial Man (Gayōmard) are both killed by the onslaught of Ahriman.… The allusion could be perfect, but for the presence of the two names that are entirely unfamiliar from any source known to me: Rimon and Amos,[42] for the Bull and the Man."[43]

---

41. Transcribed and translated in Levene, *Corpus of Magic Bowls*, 123 (transcription), 126 (translation).

42. Yakir Paz suggested to me that the term Rimon (רימון) used here for the primordial bull alludes to the Re᾿em (ראם) mentioned in Deut 33:17: "A firstborn bull, majesty is his! His horns are the horns of a wild ox [ראם], with them he gores the peoples, driving them to the ends of the earth." The Aramaic term for Re᾿em, which appears in some of the Aramaic translations of this verse is רימנא\רימנה (Pseudo-Jonathan, Neofiti, etc.). Compare, too, Midrash Tannaim to Deut 33:17, according to which "this wild ox [הרימן הזה] is beautiful in its horns." The term אמוס for the First Man may simply be a corruption of אנוש.

43. Shaked, "Jesus in the Magic Bowls," 312. Shaked further connects the oppression of חרום אחרום (line 23), who is said to have claimed that he was God and was subsequently punished by angelic beatings, with the Zoroastrian legend of Yima. On this issue, see of late Yishai Kiel, "Reimagining Enoch in Sasanian Babylonia in Light of Zoroastrian and Man-

While this bowl seems to echo the Pahlavi version of the myth of the slaying of the primordial bull, according to which the bull was attacked and killed by the Evil Spirit, the Babylonian Talmud appears to reflect a different version of the myth. This version may have been the "original" Indo-Iranian version but also resonates in the later Pahlavi traditions, according to which the primordial bull was sacrificed by the First Man. What the magic bowl and the Babylonian Talmud seem to have in common is their shared attempt to adapt, appropriate, or otherwise "Judaize" (or "Christianize") the Iranian myth of the primordial bull. Just as the practitioner of the curse attempts to appropriate the Iranian myth by adapting it to his purposes and changing the names of the heroes, so too the talmudic depiction of Adam's sacrifice of the primordial bull should be viewed as an attempt to adapt the Zoroastrian account to an existing rabbinic tradition.

The Unicorn at Persepolis and Mithras's Tauroctony

We have thus far attempted to explain, in rather broad terms, the innovative and peculiar notion of Adam's sacrifice of the primordial bull in the Babylonian Talmud by alluding to the Iranian backdrop of the myth. In what follows, I hope to make a case for a more intimate talmudic engagement of indigenous traditions by accounting for several anomalous details in the rabbinic narrative of b. ʿAbod. Zar. 8a. In this context, I shall illuminate the cryptic identification of the primordial bull sacrificed by Adam as a single-horned creature as well as the unexplained (yet clearly intrinsic) connection between Adam's sacrifice of the primordial bull and his encounter with the cycle of light and darkness. We will see that the Babylonian rabbinic storytellers engaged and responded to a complex web of

ichaean Traditions," *AJS Review* 39 (2015): 407–32. Another reference in this bowl (line 6) to the "white rooster" (תרנ[ג]ולא חיורא) may be an allusion to the rooster associated with Sraoša (Pahlavi Srōš), who is said to have been created to oppose the demons. For references, see Phillip G. Kreyenbroek, *Sraoša in the Zoroastrian Tradition*, Orientalia Rheno-traiectina 28 (Leiden: Brill, 1985), 118; Michael Shenkar, *Intangible Spirits and Graven Images: The Iconography of Deities in the Pre-Islamic Iranian World*, Magical and Religious Literature of Late Antiquity 4 (Leiden: Brill, 2014), 144–48; William W. Malandra, "Sraoša," *EIr* (published online August 29, 2014). For the impact of the "cosmic rooster" in Islamic literature, see Maria Subtelny, "Zoroastrian Elements in the Islamic Ascension Narrative: The Case of the Cosmic Cock," in *Medieval and Modern Iranian Studies: Proceedings of the 6th European Conference on Iranian Studies (Vienna, 2007)*, ed. Maria Szuppe, Anna Krasnowolska, and Claus V. Pedersen (Paris: Association pour l'Avancement des Études Iraniennes, 2011), 193–212. But cf. the reconstruction of the rooster's role in our bowl in Shaked, "Jesus in the Magic Bowls," 310, and Levene, *Corpus of Magic Bowls*, 129–30. As for the oppression of the "great man of the end" (גברא רבה דלסוף), I am inclined to connect this to the death and suffering of the Messiah son of Joseph as recorded in b. Sukkah 52a and Sefer Zerubbabel.

visual representations of bull-slaying on rock reliefs and coins, as well as Mithraic depictions of the tauroctony (which extended to Roman Syria, as evidenced by the Mithraeum excavated at Dura Europos), which in turn were translated by the talmudic storytellers and adapted to the particular talmudic narrative.

Multiple rock reliefs at Persepolis (see, e.g., fig. 1) depict a *single-horned* bull attacked by a lion.[44] The image of a single-horned bull under attack recalls the talmudic description of the primordial bull, which also, according to Rav Yehuda had "a single horn on its forehead." The lion–bull iconography, which was prevalent in the ancient Near East, has generated several theories concerning its astronomical,[45] zoological,[46] and ritual[47] significance. The regnant interpretation, however, contends that the lion and the bull represent either a seasonal shift associated with the winter solstice (also connected with astronomical events) or the day and night cycle,[48] as the lion is typically associated with the sun,[49] while the bull represents the moon.[50] The subsequent discovery of a seal from Sardis, with the sun

44. Rina Talgam (private communication) assures me that the images at Persepolis clearly depict a single-horned bull. Interestingly, while the primordial bull is not explicitly depicted as a unicorn in the Pahlavi texts, one of the features of the mythical *xar ī sē pāy* (the three-legged Ass) according to Bundahišn 24.10–15 is its description as a single-horned creature. Aside from the fact that the ass is classified in Pahlavi zoology as part of the bovine genus (Bundahišn 13.10), it has also been suggested that the particular mythic figure of the three-legged Ass in the Iranian tradition was reconfigured in the Babylonian Talmud (b. Taʿan. 25b) as a bovine (עגלא תלתא). See Kiperwasser and Shapira, "Irano-Talmudica I."

45. See, e.g., Willy Hartner, "The Earliest History of the Constellations in the Near East and the Motif of the Lion–Bull Combat," *JNES* 24 (1965): 1–16; idem, "Old Iranian Calendars," in *The Cambridge History of Iran,* vol. 2, *The Median and Achaemenian Periods,* ed. Ilya Gershevitch (Cambridge: Cambridge University Press, 1985), 725–38. Hartner suggests an astrological explanation for the lion–bull iconography according to which, at the winter solstice, when agricultural activities begin once more, while Leo culminates at twilight, the Bull (Taurus and Pleiades) disappears and remains invisible for a period of forty days. He thus interprets the lion–bull combat as a symbol of that important astronomical event.

46. See, e.g., Vijay Sathe, "The Lion-Bull Motifs of Persepolis: The Zoogeographic Context," *Iranian Journal of Archaeological Studies* 2 (2012): 75–85.

47. See, e.g., A. D. H. Bivar, *The Personalities of Mithra in Archaeology and Literature* (New York: Bibliotheca Persica Press, 1998), 36, who suggests that this icon represents a signpost delimiting an inner sanctum or a no-trespass zone.

48. See, e.g., Abolala Soudavar, *The Aura of Kings: Legitimacy and Divine Sanction in Iranian Kingship,* Bibliotheca Iranica: Intellectual Traditions Series 11 (Costa Mesa, CA: Mazda, 2003), 116–20.

49. Notably, a Sasanian seal depicts the upper part of the body of a figure (most likely Mithra-Helios, the sun god) emerging from a four-wheeled chariot decorated with a lion's head. See Shenkar, *Intangible Spirits and Graven Images,* 103 (description), 280 (image).

50. Notably, a Sasanian seal from the Staatliche Münzsammlung in Munich depicts a symbolic representation of Māh, the Iranian moon god, riding a chariot drawn by two bulls. The crescent moon rises like horns behind the rider's shoulders. The motif of the bull-chariot was probably borrowed from the Greco-Roman iconography of the moon goddess Selene. As late as the tenth century, al-Bīrūnī mentions a moon chariot harnessed to a fabulous bull,

Figure 1: Relief of lion attacking a single-horned bull, the Apadana, Persepolis, Iran (completed 486 BCE).

Figure 2: Cult relief of Mithras slaying the bull. Mithraeum at Dura Europos (ca. 168 AD), Syria. Yale University Art Gallery. Public domain.

and the moon depicted over an intermingling lion and bull iconography appears to validate this interpretation.[51]

Interestingly, Mithraic iconography of the tauroctony (fig. 2) found throughout the Roman East and West Syria depicts the slaying of a bull (although, to be sure, not a unicorn) by Mithras (cf. Vedic Mitra, Avestan Mithra, Pahlavi Mihr) an image that similarly represents the seasonal and/ or daily cycles of light and darkness, as Mithras, the sun God, overcomes the moon represented by a bull.[52] In the words of Roger Beck, "If Mithras in the tauroctony means the sun and the bull means the moon, then the encounter of Mithras and the bull means the conjunction of sun and moon ... and the victory of the bull-killing Mithras signifies, whatever its ulterior meaning, the sun's triumph over the moon."[53] Regardless of whether the roots of the Roman cult of Mithras should be sought in the Iranian worship of Mithra that pervaded Mesopotamia and Eastern Iran,[54] it is noteworthy that Mithras's slaying of the bull was seen by certain scholars as a competing version to the Pahlavi doctrine, which attributed the slaying of the bull to the Evil Spirit.[55]

This background, I would argue, significantly informs the talmudic attempt to associate Adam's sacrifice of the single-horned primordial bull with his primeval encounter with the cycle of light and darkness. When Adam realizes that darkness was not a punishment for his sin but rather is part of the natural order, he does not simply offer a thanksgiving offering (as often assumed) but sacrifices the primordial bull, which is depicted in the likeness of the Persepolis iconography, an act which symbolizes the overcoming of darkness by light. The prevailing imagery of the mythical slaying of the bull, representing the overcoming of the moon by the sun,

---

while discussing a Persian festival. The connection between the moon and the bull is attested also in Eastern Iran. See Shenkar, *Intangible Spirits and Graven Images*, 98–102 (discussion), 274 (images), and the bibliography listed there.

51. Elspeth R. M. Dusinberre, *Aspects of Empire in Achaemenid Sardis* (Cambridge: Cambridge University Press, 2003), 278.

52. See the up-to-date discussion of the symbolism of the tauroctony in Roger Beck, *The Religion of the Mithras Cult in the Roman Empire: Mysteries of the Unconquered Sun* (Oxford: Oxford University Press, 2006), 190–239.

53. Ibid., 199. See also (198) his quotation of Porphyry, *Antr. nymph.* 18: "The moon is a bull and the exaltation of the moon is Taurus."

54. For the question of the Iranian and Indic roots of the Roman cult of Mithras, see the summary of scholarship in Roger Beck, "Mithraism," *EIr* (published online July 20, 2002); Hans-Peter Schmidt, "Mithra, i. Mitra in Old Indian and Mithra in Old Iranian," *EIr* (published online on August 15, 2006). For the iconography of Mithra in Iran and central Asia see Franz Grenet, "Mithra, ii. Iconography in Iran and Central Asia," *EIr* (published online on August 15, 2006); Shenkar, *Intangible Spirits and Graven Images*, 102–14.

55. See, e.g., Ugo Bianchi, "Again on the Slaying of the Primordial Bull," in *Sir J. J. Zarthoshti Madressa Centenary Volume* (Bombay: Kanga, 1967), 19–25. Cf. Ilya Gershevitch, *The Avestan Hymn to Mithra*, University of Cambridge Oriental Publications 4 (Cambridge: Cambridge University Press, 1959), 64.

was thus translated by the talmudic storytellers and adapted to a narrative thread, which combined an early rabbinic tradition concerning Adam's sacrifice with the Iranian myth of the slaying of the primordial bull.

The Pahlavi tradition, to be sure, similarly connects the slaying of the primordial bull with Gayōmard's encounter with darkness. According to Bundahišn 4.19–26, immediately after the Evil Spirit strikes the primordial bull, Ohrmazd brings sleep upon Gayōmard so that he not suffer at the hands of Ahriman. At that point, "when Gayōmard came out of his slumber, he saw that the entire world of the living was dark as night" (Bundahišn 4.23).[56] In the Pahlavi tradition, Gayōmard's encounter with darkness (representing the domain of evil) naturally follows the Ahrimanic attack on the good creation and the death of the primordial bull at his hands, as darkness only emerges in the aftermath of the evil attack. In the Babylonian Talmud, by contrast, the sacrifice of the primordial bull takes place after Adam's encounter with darkness and the subsequent realization that both night and day are intrinsic parts of the same cosmic order.

In conclusion, I would like to posit that the antipodal recasting of the myth in the Bundahišn and the Babylonian Talmud echoes a significant theological shift. In contrast to the Zoroastrian version, which bespeaks a dualistic worldview in which darkness is perceived as a reflection of the domain of evil, the Babylonian rabbinic narrative reflects a monistic theology that refutes (consciously or not) the dualistic assumptions of the Zoroastrian account. Thus, Adam's initial presupposition that darkness reflects the prevailing of evil is ultimately replaced by his firm realization that both light and darkness are part of the same cosmic order and, therefore, attributable to the same divine force. Adam's subsequent sacrifice of the primordial bull, therefore, engages the Iranian myth, not merely by resurrecting a "sacrificial" version of the myth but also by suggesting a monistic alternative to the dualistic theology embedded in the Zoroastrian account of the death of the primordial bull.

---

56. The translation is based on Skjærvø, *Spirit of Zoroastrianism*, 98.

Mourner's Kaddish, The Prequel

The Sassanian-Period Backstory That Gave Birth to the Medieval Prayer for the Dead

DAVID BRODSKY

While the custom of saying Kaddish for the dead is widespread among secular and religious Jews today, its origins are shrouded in mystery. The practice became suddenly popular beginning in Medieval Ashkenaz, but where did it come from? How did it develop? Most of earlier scholarship on the Kaddish's history has focused on its twelfth- and thirteenth-century European context.[1] The origins of the beliefs that underlie

I would like to thank Daniel Frim, Mahnaz Moazami, Andrew Nagel, Patricia Tovah Stevens, and Katja Vehlow for their kind help on this article.

1. Much of the scholarship on the subject has focused on this development in Medieval Ashkenaz, which was quite pronounced. See Israel Lévi, "La commémoration des ames dans le judaïsme," *REJ* 29 (1894): 43–60; Zvi Karl, "Ha-qaddish," *Ha-shiloah* 35 (1918): 36–49, 426–30, 521–27; B. Heller, "Le conte hébreu sur l'effet des prières pour les morts," *REJ* 82 (1926): 308–12; A. Z. Idelsohn, *Jewish Liturgy and Its Development* (New York: Henry Holt, 1932), 307–8; Joseph Heinemann, "Prayers of Beth Midrash Origins," *JSS* 5 (1960): 264–80; David de Sola Pool, *The Kaddish* (New York: Union of Sephardic Congregations, 1964), 101–6; Baruch Graubard, "The Kaddish Prayer," in *The Lord's Prayer and Jewish Liturgy*, ed. Jakob J. Petuchowski and Michael Brocke (New York: Seabury, 1978), 59–72; Lawrence A. Hoffman, *The Canonization of the Synagogue Service*, University of Notre Dame Center for the Study of Judaism and Christianity in Antiquity 4 (Notre Dame, IN: University of Notre Dame Press, 1979), 56–65; Israel Ta-Shma, "Qetzat 'inyanei qaddish yatom u-minhagav," *Tarbiṣ* 53 (1984): 559–68; reprinted (and slightly revised) in *Minhag 'ashkenaz ha-qadmon* (Jerusalem: Magnes, 1999), 299–310; Myron B. Lerner, "Ma'aseh ha-tanna ve-ha-met: Gilgulav ha-sifrutiim ve-ha-halakhtiim," *Asufot: Sefer shanah le-mada'ei ha-yahadut* 2 (1987): 29–70; Ismar Elbogen, *Jewish Liturgy: A Comprehensive History*, trans. Raymond P. Scheindlin (Philadelphia: Jewish Publication Society, 1993), 81–84; Yaakov Gartner, "Ha-me'aneh ba-qaddish yeheh shmeih rabba mevorakh," *Sidra* 11 (1996): 39–53; Rella Kushelevsky, "Ha-tanna ve-ha-met ha-noded: Ha-'omnam 'aggadah lo yehudit?" *Biqqoret u-farshanut* 30 (1994): 41–63; eadem, "Ha-tanna ve-ha-met ha-noded," *Encyclopedia shel ha-sippur ha-yehudi* 1 (2004): 281–96; eadem, *Sigufim u-fituyim: Ha-sippur ha-'ivri be-'ashkenaz* (Jerusalem: Magnes, 2010), 253–71; David Blumenthal, "Observations and Reflections on the History and Meanings of the Kaddish," *Judaism* 50 (2001): 35–51; Michael Weitzman, "The Origins of the Qaddish," in *Hebrew Scholarship and the Medieval World*, ed. Nicholas de Lange (Cambridge: Cambridge University Press, 2001),

this practice, however, have not been fully explored. That is, what is the backstory that allowed for the creation of a Mourner's Kaddish, and how did it develop into the practice as we know it?

From its earliest appearance in twelfth-century Europe, the practice of saying the Kaddish for the dead has been connected with the enigmatic story of a rabbi (usually R. Akiva) who encountered a dead man being tortured in hell. The rabbi finds the man's pregnant wife, circumcises the son when he is born, teaches him Torah, and, in later versions, has him recite the Kaddish (or, alternatively, the *barkhu*) in the synagogue. When the rabbi next encounters the dead man, the rabbi is assured that the dead man's situation has improved. After recounting this story, the Maḥzor Vitry §144 states:

ועל כן נהגו לעבור לפני התיבה במוצאי שבת אדם שאין לו אב או אם לומר ברכו או קדיש.

> Therefore, the custom was for a person who did not have a father or mother to go before the ark on Saturday night to say the *barkhu* or Kaddish.[2]

R. Isaac b. Moses of Vienna (c. 1180–1250), the author of the *Or Zarua,* also connects the custom to this story (*Or Zarua, hilkhot shabbat* §50), as does Rabbeinu Baḥya b. Asher of Spain (1255–1340; in his commentary to Deut 21:8).[3] While this etiology of the practice need not be correct, the

---

131–37; Andreas Lehnardt, *Qaddish: Untersuchungen zur Entstehung und Rezeption eines rabbinischen Gebetes,* TSAJ 87 (Tübingen: Mohr Siebeck, 2002), 277–96; Edward Ullendorff, "Some Notes on the Relationship of the Paternoster to the Kaddish," *JJS* 54 (2003): 122–24; David Brodsky, *A Bride without a Blessing: A Study in the Redaction and Content of Massekhet Kallah and Its Gemara,* TSAJ 118 (Tübingen: Mohr Siebeck, 2006), 231–38; Barry Freundel, *Why We Pray What We Pray: The Remarkable History of Jewish Prayer* (Jerusalem: Urim, 2010), 239–313; David Shyovitz, "'You Have Saved Me from the Judgment of Gehenna': The Origins of the Mourner's Kaddish in Medieval Ashkenaz," *AJS Review* 39 (2015): 49–73. In this paper, I will focus primarily on the theological groundwork that made this medieval development possible.

2. *Maḥzor Vitry,* ed. Simon Hurwitz (Nürnberg: J. Bulka, 1923), 1:113; ed. Ernest Goldschmidt (Jerusalem: Makhon Otzar Haposqim, 2004), 1:224. Shyowitz ("'You Have Saved Me from the Judgment of Gehenna,'" 55 n. 27) has noted that this is only found in one manuscript of Maḥzor Vitry (MS London, used by Hurwitz for his edition), and that it may be an addition by either R. Avraham b. Natan ha-Yarḥi (1155–1215) or by R. Isaac b. Dorbelo (twelfth century). While Shyowitz argues for the latter (see also Kushelevsky, *Sigufim,* 253 [esp. n. 1], who also considers R. Isaac b. Dorbelo to be the author of this passage), I would point out that ha-Yarḥi wrote the only extant medieval commentary on Kallah Rab. 1–2 (in addition to a commentary on the Kaddish), and while we are missing the section of his commentary on Kallah Rab. 2:9 (which is our earliest record of the story of R. Akiva and the dead man), he almost assuredly knew the story, and he may even have acted along with others as its conduit to medieval Europe (though this is, of course, hypothetical). See also Israel Levi, "Commémoration des ames," 46 n.4.

3. See also Ta-Shma, "Qetzat 'inyanei qaddish yatom," 307; Kushelevsky, "Ha-'omnam 'aggadah," 52–53; eadem, *Sigufim,* 260.

claim is made soon after the custom first appeared, increasing the likelihood that the story either is closely connected with the origin of the practice, or, at a minimum, played an important role in its development.[4] The story itself, however, long preceded the practice, though its transmission seems intricately bound up with the development of the custom. As we shall see, the story has its origins in Amoraic Babylonia, although in that earlier version, there is no reference to the Kaddish or any other expiatory prayer. Rather, that story is consistent with its larger Sassanian (Zoroastrian) cultural context in considering the son to act as an extension of his father (while the son is still a minor), and therefore his good and bad deeds still to contribute to his father's ledger even though his father has already passed away.

Long-standing within Judaism is the notion that one must repent to achieve one's place in the World to Come. When and how did Judaism come to believe that, in the absence of that repentance, someone else's repentance, or even someone else saying a prayer could alleviate the deceased's condition in the afterlife? As we shall see, Palestinian rabbinic Judaism tended toward the belief that, while people may repent up until the very last moment of life, once dead, nothing further can be done. While some Palestinian sources may have conceded, in a limited number of cases, that the prayers of others had interceded, these cases will be shown below not to undermine my basic premise. Babylonian rabbinic texts, on the other hand, reflected a belief that the son is both able and obligated to help his father's case in heaven through the former's deeds. I will show that this Babylonian rabbinic theology is consistent with its Zoroastrian Persian cultural context. Curiously, though their theology was Babylonian, these Babylonian rabbinic sources designated their position as of Palestinian origin. As with most of the cases I have uncovered in which Babylonian rabbinic Judaism was faithful to its Babylonian cultural context, it conspicuously attributed its Babylonian theology to Palestinian sources, though actual Palestinian sources belie this attribution.

The theological question that Palestinian and Babylonian Jews and Zoroastrians are all trying to answer is, until when do people have to repent? And if they did not repent before they died, what, if anything, can be done for them? That is, may we donate our repentance or good deeds for the benefit of others? In order to demonstrate that the belief that the living can change the fate of the dead is unique in rabbinic Judaism to Amoraic and post-Amoraic Babylonia, we must first demonstrate its absence in late Second Temple, Tannaitic, and Amoraic rabbinic Palestine, which is what we turn to next. The first half of this paper, then,

---

4. Andreas Lehnardt argues that the practice preceded the connection with the story (*Qaddish*, 277–96), but he has few if any sources to base this on. See also Kushelevsky, *Sigufim*, 260.

will demonstrate the almost complete lack of this theology in Judea/Palestine, followed by the second half of the paper, which will look first at the theology in rabbinic Babylonia (the Babylonian Talmud and the first two chapters of Kallah Rabbati), followed finally by the Persian/Zoroastrian sources that give us a window into the larger cultural context in which the Babylonian rabbinic sources were composed.

The Second Temple Period

In 2 Maccabees (12:39-45), Judah offers a prayer and sacrifice as expiation for his fallen comrades in battle, which, at first glance, appears to be posthumous repentance. Nevertheless, 2 Maccabees is not a rabbinic (nor proto-rabbinic) text, nor necessarily Judean. My argument is not that no Jews had yet to consider that the living could atone for the sins of the dead but that *Judean/Palestinian rabbinic* Jews did not advocate such a position in the Tannaitic and Amoraic periods. Moreover, the text is not clear whether the transgressions the soldiers engaged in (taking and wearing their foes' pagan tokens) were done knowingly or whether they simply plundered the fallen enemy soldiers and innocently wore some of their clothing (along with the "sacred things from the idols" [ἱερώματα τῶν ... εἰδώλων]) in the next battle, but it proved their downfall. We may, therefore, be dealing with an unintentional sin rather than an intentional one. This is quite relevant, at least following later rabbinic theology, for intentional sins require the repentance of the sinner, while unintentional sins merely require a sin offering (with no need for repentance).[5] Judah, then, may not have been atoning for the sins of the dead in their stead but merely offering the sin offering that was required during their lifetime, which they themselves were unable to offer since the (unintended) sin was not made apparent until after their death.[6]

Tannaitic and Amoraic Palestine

A number of Palestinian rabbinic sources from the Tosefta to the Yerushalmi, Ecclesiastes Rabba, Ruth Rabba, and Avot of Rabbi Nathan declare that a person has until his or her last dying breath to repent.[7] Many

5. m. Ker 2:6; t. Šabb. 1:3 and 2:15. We should read m. Yoma 8:8 in this context: the sin offering does not require repentance to be efficacious because it is not atoning for an intentional sin.

6. Already against this notion, see Levi, "Commémoration des ames," 48–50, 56–57; Heller, "Le Conte hébreu," 308.

7. t. Qidd. 1:15–16; y. Ber. 9:1, 13b; Qoh. Rab. 1:15, 7:15; and Ruth Rab. 1:17. t. Qidd. 1:15–16 reads:

of these same Palestinian sources are equally clear that, once the person has died, the person's fate is sealed and nothing further can be done. Yerushalmi Berakhot 9:1, 13b (= Qoh. Rab. 7:15) states this quite succinctly:

> R. Yoḥanan said, "... All one's life there is surety, for so long as a person is alive he has hope, but, once he has died, his hope is lost." What is the basis? "With the death of a wicked person, hope will be lost" (Prov. 11:7).[8]

Avot of Rabbi Nathan helps clarify why a person's hope is lost after they have died, stating about the wicked that "so long as they are alive in this world they can repent, but once they die, they can no longer repent" ('Abot R. Nat. B 27); and "Just as a person cannot share the reward with his fellow in this world, so a person cannot share the reward with his fellow in the World to Come" ('Abot R. Nat. A 12); or, just as Abraham could not save Ishmael nor Isaac save Esau, so no one can repent for and save anyone else ('Abot R. Nat. B 27):

ר׳ שמעון אומ׳ היה אדם צדיק כל ימיו ובאחרונה מרד איבד את הכל שנ׳ צדקת הצדיק לא תצילנו ביום רשעו .היה אדם רשע כל ימיו ועשה תשובה באחרונה המקום מקבלו שנ׳ ורשעת הרשע לא יכשל בה ביום שובו מרשעו וגו׳

R. Shimeon says: If a person was righteous all his days, but in the end he rebelled, he lost it all, as it is said, "The righteousness of the righteous will not save him on the day of his wickedness" (Ezek 33:12). If a person was wicked all his days but repented in the end, God receives him, as it is said, "And the wickedness of the wicked, he will not be weakened by it on the day that he returns from his wickedness" (ibid.).

Even Qoh. Rab. 4:1, which states that children who died innocent may save their parents from hell, still only allows this to happen before the parents have died. Once the parents have died, their children can no longer save them (cf. Dov Weiss, "Between Values and Theology: The Case of Salvation through Children in Rabbinic Thought," in *Milin Havivin: Beloved Words* 3 [2007]: 10–13). We should note also that these are dead children, not living children who can save them, making it still far from an understanding that could allow for living children to save their dead parents from hell.

8. MS Leiden:

אמר רבי יוחנן ... כל החיים יש בטחון שכל זמן שאדם חי יש לו תקוה מת אבדה תקוותו מה טעמ׳ במות אדם רשע תאבד תקוה

Qoh. Rab. 7:15 reads:

שאלו את שמואל הקטן ... אמר להם ... כל זמן שאדם חי הקב״ה מצפה לו לתשובה, מת אבדה תקותו שנאמר (משלי יא:יז) במות אדם רשע תאבד תקוה.

They asked Shmuel ha-Qatan ... He said to them, "... So long as a person is alive, the Holy One Blessed Be He awaits his repentance, but once he has died, his hope is lost, as it is said, 'with the death of a wicked person, hope will be lost' (Prov 11:7)."

As Reuven Kiperwasser has recently noted, material in Qoh. Rab. can originate in Amoraic Palestine or Babylonia (Reuven Kiperwasser, "Early and Late in Kohelet Rabba: A Study in Redaction-criticism," *Iggud–Selected Essays in Jewish Studies* [Hebrew], ed. Baruch Schwartz, Abraham Melamed, and Aharon Shemesh, 3 vols. [Jerusalem: World Union of Jewish Studies, 2008], 1:291–312, esp. 295 n. 8). In this case, the direct parallel with the Yerushalmi, the Palestinian attributions, and the lack of a parallel in the Bavli, all speak to the Palestinian origins of this saying and its theology.

> "If I am not for myself, who will be for me?"—If I did not merit for myself in this world, who will merit for me for life in the World to Come? I do not have a father. I do not have a mother. [I do not have a brother]. Abraham our forefather could not redeem Ishmael. Isaac our forefather could not redeem Esau. . . . And thus it says, "For a live dog is better than a dead lion" (Eccl 9:4). Who is the live dog? These are the wicked, for so long as they are alive in this world they can repent, but once they die, they can no longer repent.[9]

That is, after death, hope is lost for two reasons: (1) the dead can no longer repent for themselves, and (2) no one else can repent for them.

Similarly, 4 Ezra, believed to be composed by a Jew (though not necessarily a Rabbinic Jew) in first century CE Judea, states that the dead "cannot repent and do good deeds by which they may live."[10] Moreover, in answer to the question

> if on the day of judgment, the righteous will be able to petition for the wicked or to make a request for them from the High One, or parents on behalf of their children, children on behalf of their parents, siblings on behalf of their siblings, relatives on behalf of their relatives, or friends on behalf of their friends,

the angel responds,

> The day of judgment has been decreed, and it shows all the seal of truth, for just as now a father cannot send his son, a son his father, a master his servant, or a friend the one dear to him, to be sick or sleep or eat or to be

---

9. 'Abot R. Nat. B 27:
אם אין אני לי מי לי אם [לא] זכיתי [אני] לעצמי בעולם הזה מי יזכה לי לחיי העולם הבא. אבא אין לי אימא אין לי [אח אין לי]. אברהם אבינו אינו יכול לפדות את ישמעאל. אבינו יצחק אינו יכול לפדות את עשו...וכן הוא אומר כי לכלב חי הוא טוב מן האריה המת (קהלת ט׳ ד׳) איזהו כלב חי אלו הרשעים שכל זמן שהן קיימין בעולם הזה הן יכולין לעשות תשובה. מתו אינם יכולין לעשות תשובה.
'Abot R. Nat. A 12 reads:
כשם שאין אדם חולק שכר חבירו בעולם הזה כך אין [אדם] חולק שכר חבירו לעוה"ב שנאמר והנה דמעת העשוקים ואין להם מנחם ומיד עושקיהם כח ואין להם מנחם (קהלת ד׳ א׳)... הוא היה אומר אם אין אני לי מי לי אם אני לא אזכה (בחיי) מי יזכה בי: וכשאני לעצמי מה אני. אם אני לא זוכה בעצמי מי יזכה בי בעצמי: אם לא עכשיו אימתי. אם אני לא זוכה בחיי מי יזכה בי לאחר מיתתי.
Just as a person cannot share the reward with his fellow in this world, so a person cannot share the reward with his fellow in the World to Come, as it says, "And behold the tear of the oppressed, but they have no comfort; and from the hand of their oppressors is power, yet they have no comfort" (Eccl. 4:1). . . . He used to say, "If I am not for myself, who will be for me?"—If I do not merit (during my lifetime), who will merit for me? "And when I am for myself, what am I?"—If I do not merit for myself, who will merit for me for myself? "And if not now, when?"—If I do not merit in my lifetime, who will merit for me after my death?
Cf. Sipre Deut. §329 and Ephraim Urbach, *Ḥazal: Emunot ve-de'ot* (Jerusalem: Magnes, 1969), 444.

10. 4 Ezra 7:82. ܕܠܐ ܡ̈ܨܝܢ ܕܢܬܬܘܒܘܢ ܘܢܥܒܕܘܢ ܛ̈ܒܬܐ ܕܢܚܘܢ ܒܗܝܢ

healed in his place, so too then a person will not be able to petition on behalf of another on that day, neither will one person make difficult for another. For each person then will bear his own righteousness or iniquity.[11]

In other words, these Palestinian Jewish texts of the Tannaitic and Amoraic periods directly negate any notion that there is anything that can be done to change the status of the dead in the afterlife either by the dead person him/herself or by anyone else, including the dead person's own children.[12] Not all of the Palestinian sources, however, are quite this clear or simple. Before moving on to address the theodicy of Amoraic Babylonia, then, we must consider several more complicated Palestinian texts which may evince aspects of the notion that one can atone for the sins of the dead, though we shall see that those aspects are limited to the extent that they exist at all. I shall endeavor to show that, while many of these passages were later reinterpreted as evincing this idea, and while they were therefore integral to the development of the Mourner's Kaddish in these later periods, they did not yet themselves espouse such a conception.

The printed edition and some manuscripts of Sipre Deut §210 (on Deut 21:8) read:

> The priests say, "Atone for your people Israel" (Deut 21:8). When it says, "whom you, O Lord, redeemed" (ibid.), it teaches that this atonement atones for those who went out from Egypt. "Atone for your people"—these are the living—"whom you redeemed"—these are the dead. This teaches that the dead need atonement.[13]

11. 4 Ezra 7:102–5.
ܕܐܢ ܒܝܘܡܐ ܕܕܝܢܐ ܡܫܟܚܝܢ ܙܕܝܩܐ ܕܢܫܐܠܘܢ ܐܢܘܢ ܠܪ̈ܫܝܥܐ. ܐܘ ܕܢܒܥܘܢ ܚܠܦܝܗܘܢ ܡܢ
ܡܪܝܡܐ. ܐܘ ܐܒܗ̈ܐ ܚܠܦ ܒܢ̈ܝܗܘܢ. ܐܘ ܒܢ̈ܝܐ ܚܠܦ ܐܒܗ̈ܝܗܘܢ. ܐܘ ܐܚ̈ܐ ܚܠܦ ܐܚ̈ܝܗܘܢ. ܐܘ
ܐܢܫܝܐ ܚܠܦ ܐܢܫܝܗܘܢ. ܐܘ ܪ̈ܚܡܐ ܚܠܦ ܪ̈ܚܡܝܗܘܢ ... ܘܐܡܪ ܠܝ. ܝܘܡܐ ܕܕܝܢܐ. ܝܘܡܐ ܗܘ ܦܣܝܩܐ. ܘܠܟܠ
ܡܫܘܐ ܚܬܡܐ ܕܫܪܪܐ. ܐܝܟܢܐ ܓܝܪ ܕܗܫܐ ܠܐ ܡܫܕܪ ܐܒܐ ܠܒܪܗ. ܐܘ ܒܪܐ ܠܐܒܘܗܝ. ܐܘ ܡܪܐ
ܠܥܒܕܗ. ܐܘ ܪܚܡܐ ܠܡܪܚܡܢܗ. ܕܢܬܟܫܦ ܚܠܦܘܗܝ. ܐܘ ܕܢܕܡܟ ܐܘ ܕܢܐܟܘܠ ܐܘ ܕܢܬܐܣܐ ܀ ܗܟܢܐ
ܐܦ ܗܝܕܝܢ ܠܐ ܡܫܟܚ ܐܢܫ ܕܢܒܥܐ. ܥܠ ܐܦܝ ܐܢܫ ܒܗܘ ܝܘܡܐ. ܐܦܠܐ ܕܢܥܣܩ ܐܢܫ ܥܠ ܐܢܫ. ܟܠܗܘܢ
ܓܝܪ ܗܝܕܝܢ ܢܛܥܢܘܢ ܐܢܫ ܐܢܫ ܙܕܝܩܘܬܗ ܐܘ ܚܘܒܗ.

12. This Palestinian Jewish position directly counters the fundamental Christian tenet that one person can atone for the sins of another, namely, that Christ atoned for our sins. This conflict may not have escaped the notice of an editor or copyist of the Vulgate, as that edition lacks the section of 4 Ezra (7:36–105) that posits that one person cannot atone for the sins of another (although the folio may have simply fallen out by accident). Interestingly, only in Amoraic Babylonia, farther away from the origins of Christianity, could Jews freely entertain the notion of atoning for the sins of others, as we shall presently see.

13. MS Oxford:
הכהנים אומ׳ כפר לעמך ישרא׳ כשהוא אומר אשר פדית ייי מלמד שכפרה זו מכפרת על יוצאי מצרים
כפר לעמך אלו החיים אשר פדית אילו המתים מלמד שהמתים צריכין כפרה

The *editio princeps* and MS London are nearly identical; MS Vatican has the pericope in a different order, and MS Berlin is missing the important second half of the above section

The midrash is here interpreting Deut 21:1–9, which discusses the case of a slain man whose murderer is unknown. Rather than atoning for their own sin, the townspeople are asking for atonement for a sin which they did not commit, as they proclaim outright, "Our hands did not spill this blood" (Deut 21:7; indeed, if the killer becomes known, the sacrifice is not offered—Sipre Deut. §205). Precisely because this is not an atonement for one's sins, I would argue, the midrashist asks whether only the living need atonement, or whether this atonement is for the dead as well. The midrash is not clear which dead are meant. Presumably, they are the dead former inhabitants of this town, perhaps even those who died in the interim between the murder and the sacrifice. Their souls too would need this atonement, though it could be for all people who have ever found themselves in such a situation from time immemorial. In any case, since this sacrifice is not for a sin and therefore does not require repentance to be efficacious, there is no reason why it should be any less applicable to the dead than the living. More importantly, it has nothing to do with our topic of whether one person can atone for another person's sins after the latter's death. Granted, Maḥzor Vitry, one of our earliest sources for the Mourner's Kaddish, would later read this midrash in conjunction with Pesiqta Rabbati as evidence that the Ashkenazi practices of saying prayers for the dead indeed do help them:

> "And they dispense public charity for the living and for the dead"—Only on this day (Yom Kippur) do they dispense charity for the dead, in all the land of Germany. Addition:[14] And they dispense charity on Yom Kippur for the dead because it is the day for atonement, pardon, and forgiveness, and it is an atonement for them. For thus we taught in the Pesiqta: "Lest a person should say that since a person died, charity can no longer help him, the Torah states, 'atone for your people Israel' (Deut 21:8). Since they request mercy for him, they throw him out from Hell to heaven like an arrow from a bow" (Pesiq. Rab. 20).[15] And we taught in

---

entirely, indicating the possibility that it may not be original to the Sipre. On Sipre Deut. §210, see Lévi, "Commémoration des ames," 52; Urbach, *Ḥazal*, 451–52.

14. That is, this is an addition to Maḥzor Vitry by one of the later editors (probably either R. Avraham b. Natan ha-Yarḥi or R. Isaac b. Dorbelo) found only in MS London.

15. Pesiqta Rabbati 20 (MS Parma) reads:

ואחריו מה אתה בורא? מאזנים, כיון שמין ודשין שוקלין במאזנים. ואחריו מה בורא? עקרב, כיון ששוקלין אותו ויש בו עונות מורידים אותו לגיהנם. ואחריו מה אתה בורא? הקשת, שמא תאמר כיון שירד לגהינם אין לו תעלה, כיון שמבקשים עליו רחמים זורקין אותו מגהינם כחץ מן הקשת.

And after that, what do you [God] create? The [astrological sign of] Balance [Libra], since [those things that are] estimated and threshed they weigh out on a balance [MS JTS and ed. pr.: For his deeds are weighed in the balance]. And after that, what do you create? The Scorpion [Scorpio], for they weigh him and [if] he has sins in him they take him down to Hell. And after that, what do you create? The Bow [Sagittarius], lest you say that since he went down to Hell, he has no

the Sipre, "'Atone for your people Israel' (Deut 21:8), this teaches that the dead require atonement" (Sipre Deut §210).[16]

Yet, we must understand Maḥzor Vitry as reading back into Sipre Deuteronomy the very notions that we shall show developed only later in Amoraic Babylonia. If the atonement were offered for the forefathers because the sin had spread from the murderer to his forefathers (as Ephraim Urbach interpreted the midrash, for example),[17] then we would have all the more reason to offer the sacrifice when and if we discovered the identity of the murderer, yet Sipre Deut (§205) makes explicit that the opposite is the case. Only a post-Bavli scholar would think to read this midrash out of its context of Deut 21:1–9 and instead as proclaiming the need for atonement *of sins* for the dead *in general*. Those two italicized additions are not implicit in the original midrash. Nevertheless, Maḥzor Vitry attests to the important role that Sipre Deut §210 played in the development of Medieval Ashkenazi traditions in which the living atoned for the sins of the dead.[18]

In y. Ber. 9:2, 13d, we find another statement (attributed by a couple of Palestinian Amoraim to R. Shimeon bar Yoḥai) that has been (mis)

---

coming up. Since they request mercy for him, they shoot him out of Hell like an arrow from a bow.

While this text evinces the notion that the fate of the dead can be affected by the actions of the living, this section of Pesiqta Rabbati has been dated to the Geonic period (Rivka Ulmer, *Pesiqta Rabbati: A Synoptic Edition of Pesiqta Rabbati Based upon All Extant Manuscripts and the Editio Princeps*, 3 vols. [Atlanta: Scholars Press, 1997–2002] 1:xvi, xvii, and xx n.64; cf. Leopold Zunz, *Ha-derashot be-yisrael ve-hishtalshalutan ha-historit* [Jerusalem: Mosad Bialik, 1931], 120, 389 n. 59). On its relationship to the later development of this idea, see Lévi, "Commémoration des ames," 54–55; Heller, "Le conte hébreu," 309; Urbach, *Ḥazal*, 453.

16. Maḥzor Vitry §353 (ed. Hurwitz, 1:392; ed. Goldschmidt, 3:785):

ופוסקין צדקה ברבים על החיים ועל המתים: אין פוסקין צדקה למתים בכל ארץ אשכנז רק היום לבדו:
ת׳: ומה שפוסקין צדקה ביום הכיפורים על המתים לפי שהוא יום כפרה וסליחה ומחילה וכפרה היא
להם: שכך שנינו בפסיקתא שמא יאמר אדם כיון שמת אדם אין לו תקנה בצדקה. ת״ל כפר לעמך ישר׳.
כיון שמבקשין עליו רחמים זורקין אותו מגהינם לגן עדן כחץ מן הקשת. ושנינו בסיפרי. כפר לעמך ישר׳.
מלמד שהמתים צריכין כפרה:

Similarly, the Vilna Gaon would later claim this midrash to be the basis for the custom of saying *yizkor* (the commemoration of the dead) on certain Sabbaths (see his note on Shulḥan Arukh, O.H. 284:7).

17. Urbach states, "The sin of murder also makes its abode with the fathers and forefathers of the murderer, and [therefore] the atonement for the living is also atonement for the dead" (*Ḥazal*, 452).

18. We shall see that the Bavli played an important role in reinterpreting earlier Palestinian rabbinic sources in line with the Babylonian belief that the living can indeed atone for the sins of the dead and change their fate in hell. That reinterpretation would facilitate later sources like Maḥzor Vitry to further reinterpret other Palestinian rabbinic sources like this one as they developed the Medieval Ashkenazi atonement rituals for the dead. These rituals included dispensing charity on Yom Kippur on behalf of the dead and the Mourner's Kaddish that began as a ritual on Saturday night to ease the souls of the dead as their punishments were reinstated after the Sabbath reprieve.

interpreted as evincing the notion that the living can save the dead from judgment in hell:

> R. Ḥizqiyah said in the name of R. Yirmiyah, "Thus said R. Shimeon b. Yoḥai, 'Let Abraham bring near [to the World to Come] from his [time] until mine,[19] and I will bring near from mine until the end of the generations, and if not, let Aḥiyyah the Shilonite[20] join me, and I[21] would bring the whole nation.'"[22]

While this is evidence of the notion of one person meriting the World to Come for another, R. Shimeon b. Yoḥai specifies those in his lifetime and after as those whom he is able to save, not those who already died before he was born. For this reason, he needs an earlier Jewish figure (Abraham) to save those who precede him, at which point R. Shimeon b. Yoḥai can take over and save everyone from his own day onwards. Thus, if Abraham will not join him, he still needs another ancient figure (Aḥiyya the Shilonite) to help him with those who preceded him. In the hands of the Bavli, this statement will become a declaration of the living changing the fate of the dead, as we shall presently see, but it is not yet an expression of that idea.

Of course, the parallel to this passage in Genesis Rabba (another Palestinian source) seems to have R. Shimeon bar Yoḥai claim that he and Aḥiyya can save people who preceded them as well as those who postdate them. Urbach saw this as evidence that Palestinian rabbinic Jews believed that the living could atone for the dead.[23] The passage reads:

> R. Ḥizqiyah said in the name of R. Yirmiyah, "Thus said R. Shimeon b. Yoḥai, 'If Abraham wishes, he can bring near from him and until me, and I will bring near from me until the King Messiah; and if he does not wish, let Aḥiyyah the Shilonite join with me, and we will bring from Abraham until the King Messiah.'"[24]

---

19. MS Vatican (ebr. 133) reads "until his," though this is probably an error.

20. Prophet during the reigns of Solomon and Jeroboam.

21. "We" in the Vatican MS (ebr. 133) and in the parallel in Gen. Rab. 35:2 (see below). The plural makes more sense here.

22. MS Leiden:

רבי חזקיה בשם ר׳ ירמיה: כך היה ר׳ שמעון בן יוחי או׳: יקרב אברהם מן גביה ועד גביי, ואנא מיקרב מן גביי ועד סוף כל דרי. ואין לא, יצרף אחיה השילוני עמי, ואנא מקרב כל עמא.

On this saying, see Lévi, "Commémoration des ames," 51; Heller, "Le conte hébreu," 308. From *Talmud Yerushalmi: According to Ms. Or. 4720 (Scal. 3) of the Leiden University Library with Restorations and Corrections*, ed. Yaacov Sussmann (Jerusalem: Academy of the Hebrew Language, 2001). Unless otherwise noted, all passages of the Yerushalmi are taken from this edition.

23. Urbach, *Ḥazal*, 454.

24. Gen. Rab. 35:2 (ed. Theodor-Albeck, 329–30)

ר׳ חזקיה בשם ר׳ ירמיה: כך אמר ר׳ שמעון בן יוחי: אין בעי אברהם מקרבה מגביה ועד גבי, ואנא מקרב מגבי עד מלכא משיחה, ואין לא בעי, יצטרף אחייה השילוני עימי, ואנן מקרבין מן אברהם עד מלכא משיחא.

Yet the fact that R. Shimeon b. Yoḥai needs a biblical figure to join with him would suggest that the author intends for this person to be saving those who preceded R. Shimeon b. Yoḥai, since the latter cannot. I would suggest that our version of the Yerushalmi here preserves the Amoraic Palestinian version more faithfully than does our version of Genesis Rabba, and the words "from Abraham" in that last sentence of Genesis Rabba quoted above may be a mistake and should probably read "from Aḥiyyah until the King Messiah." It is not that hard to conceive of how מן אח' (a scribal abbreviation for "from Aḥiyyah") could become מן אב' (a scribal abbreviation for "from Abraham"), with merely the tilt of a letter.[25] The error would likely have occurred because the scribe would have presumed that R. Shimeon b. Yoḥai would want to claim that the entire Jewish/Israelite people are saved from its inception (à la Abraham) all the way to the Messiah. Claiming to save the Jews/Israelites only from the time of Aḥiyya does leave a glaring gap of Israelites who remain unsaved, but for the author of this passage, I would argue, it was presumably enough that the saving stretched far back into the ancient past.

Another passage from the Yerushalmi that has been read as advocating that the living can change the status of the dead in the afterlife is y. Sanh. 10:3, 29c:

> It is taught: R. Yehuda b. Beteira says, "From the fact that it says, 'I erred like a lost sheep whom your servant sought' (Ps 119:176), just as the lost object there is ultimately sought [back], so the lost object here [the congregation of Koraḥ] will ultimately be sought [back]."
> Who prayed for them?
> R. Shmuel bar Naḥman said, "Moses prayed for them: Let Reuben live and not die (Deut 33:6)."
> R. Yehoshua b. Levi said, "Hanna prayed for them." This is according to the opinion of R. Yehoshua b. Levi, for R. Yehoshua b. Levi said, "Thus the congregation of Koraḥ was continuously sinking [in Hell] until Hanna arose and prayed for them and said, 'The Lord causes [people] to die and to live, he sends [people] down to Sheol and raises them up'" (1 Sam 2:6).[26]

Essentially, this passage is reworking and explaining the position of R. Eliezer in the Mishna (Sanh. 10:3), on which it is situated, who states:

---

25. Though unfortunately to my knowledge no manuscript of Genesis Rabba preserves such a variant attesting to my hypothesized original. Nevertheless, the parallel in the Yerushalmi does point to such a likelihood.

26. MS Leiden:

תני: רבי יהודה בן בתירה או׳: ממשמע שנ׳ ״תעיתי כשה אבד בקש עבדך״. מה אבידה האמורה להלן סופה להתבקש, אף אבידה האמורה כאן עתידה להתבקש. מי נתפלל עליהן? ר׳ שמואל בר נחמן אמ׳: משה נתפלל עליהן. ״יחי ראובן ואל ימות״. ר׳ יהושע בן לוי אמ׳: חנה נתפללה עליהן. היא דר׳ יהושע בן לוי. דאמ׳ ר׳ יהושע בן לוי: כך היתה עדתו שלקרח שוקעת ויורדת עד שעמדה חנה ונתפללה עליהן ואמרה ״יי ממית ומחיה מוריד שאול ויעל״.

Cf. Gen. Rab. 98:2.

> R. Eliezer says, "Regarding them [i.e., the congregation of Koraḥ] it says, 'The Lord causes [people] to die and to live, he sends [people] down to Sheol and raises them up'" (1 Sam 2:6).[27]

R. Yehoshua b. Levi is simply using R. Eliezer's prooftext (1 Sam 2:6) to prove that the congregation of Koraḥ was indeed ultimately saved from hell.

By connecting the "lost sheep" of Ps 119:176 to the congregation of Koraḥ being "lost," R. Yehuda b. Beteira is able to argue that just as lost sheep are wanted back by the shepherd, so the congregation of Koraḥ would one day be wanted back again by God (and, therefore, they did not permanently lose their place in the World to Come). The question that this statement begs, however, is who or what, then, would ultimately change God's mind to want them back. R. Shmuel bar Naḥman attributed it to the prayer of Moses for the descendants of Reuben, and R. Yehoshua b. Levi attributed it to Hannah, who reminded God that God "causes to die *and to live,* he sends [people] to Sheol *and brings them up*" (1 Sam 2:6). In fact, 1 Sam 2:6 is the very verse that the Tosefta (Sanh. 13:4) uses as the prooftext that God will not leave Jews (except the completely wicked) permanently in hell. The Yerushalmi's reference to this verse, then, is a reference to the very fact of the impermanence of hell for all but the utterly wicked. In other words, I would read this not so much as Hannah atoning for their sins, or even her saying a prayer that atones for their sins, but rather as Hannah's prayer reminding God of his latter role: that he not only causes people to die but brings them back to life; that he not only takes them down to hell but brings them back up again. Granted Hannah intercedes, but she ultimately does not change what was always already fated to be. Indeed, 1 Sam 2:6 is the very verse used in the corresponding section to this Mishna in the Tosefta (Sanh. 13:3) as proof for the impermanence of hell for all but the completely wicked:

> Those who weigh out in between them [i.e., neither utterly righteous nor utterly wicked] go down to *gehinnom* [i.e., hell/purgatory] and are purged and go up from it and are healed.... Regarding them Hannah said, "The Lord causes to die and to live, he sends [people] down to Hell [*Sheol*] and brings them up" (1 Sam 2:6).

Here we are told that only Jews who are *completely* wicked will permanently go to hell. Jews who are neither completely righteous nor completely wicked will go down to hell for a limited period of time so that

---

27. עדת קרח אינה עתידה לעלות, שנאמר "ותכס עליהם הארץ" בעולם הזה, "ויאבדו מתוך הקהל" לעולם הבא, דברי רבי עקיבא. רבי אליעזר אומר: עליהם הוא אומר "ה׳ ממית ומחיה מוריד שאול ויעל."
On this passage, see also 'Abot R. Nat. A 36.

they can purge themselves of their sins and go back up for eternal life. In m. Sanh. 10:3, R. Eliezer is of the opinion that the congregation of Koraḥ are among those who were not completely wicked and, therefore, will ultimately be raised back up from hell, using Hannah's prayer as evidence that God not only sends people to hell but raises them back up again. In the statement attributed to R. Yehoshua b. Levi in the Yerushalmi, Hannah is reminding God of this point and challenging whether the children of Koraḥ were indeed completely wicked. Nonetheless, we should not miss the fact that in this Palestinian rabbinic text, we have the notion that a prayer can remind God of this role and therefore can intercede in the fate of the dead in hell. It seems to be the exception to the rule: *once* upon a time, the great Hannah reminded God of his role and it affected the treatment of *one* group of people. This is not yet a prescription for a regular prayer for the dead, though it may have helped to set some of the groundwork for the later medieval practice.[28]

Another passage in the Yerushalmi that has been read as evincing a notion that the living can affect the fate of the dead is y. Ḥag. 2:1, 77c, in which R. Meir seems to succeed in altering the fate of his teacher, Elisha b. Abuya, after the latter's death. Nevertheless, the story seems to work because it finds a brief moment after death but before judgment when R. Meir can still act. The soul has not yet departed from this world. Thus, R. Meir quotes Ruth 3:13 to say that Elisha should tarry the night in this world before going. Moreover, the passage seems to assume the difficulty of such an act, which is what makes this story all the more poignant. It takes a R. Meir to be able to force God's hand against the natural order, and, even then, only by using the Bible against God. This is hardly the basis for a future regular prayer for the dead. Nevertheless, it shows that to the extent that a living person can change the fate of the dead, it is through prayer. While this attitude toward prayer is not present in the earliest version of the story about R. Akiva and the dead man that seems to be at the root of the development of the Mourner's Kaddish, it may have predisposed Medieval Askenazic Jews to read and retell that story with the thought in mind that prayer could affect the fate of the dead.

Another text that has been incorrectly read, in my opinion, as substantiating the practice of the Mourner's Kaddish in late antique or early

28. On this passage, see Lévi, "Commémoration des ames," 51–52. David Shyovitz argues that the Christian development of the notion of purgatory in the twelfth century is what led to the Mourner's Kaddish (Shyovitz, "You Have Saved Me from the Judgment of Gehenna," 66–68, 71), but, as we see, the notion of purgatory (that is, the notion that the dead could be sent to hell for a temporary period of time) was hardly new to Judaism. See also Kushelevsky, *Sigufim*, 268.

medieval Palestine is Targum Pseudo-Jonathan on Isa 29:23.[29] Isaiah 29:23 reads:

> כִּי בִרְאֹתוֹ יְלָדָיו מַעֲשֵׂה יָדַי בְּקִרְבּוֹ יַקְדִּישׁוּ שְׁמִי וְהִקְדִּישׁוּ אֶת־קְדוֹשׁ יַעֲקֹב וְאֶת־אֱלֹהֵי יִשְׂרָאֵל יַעֲרִיצוּ׃
>
> For in his seeing his children, the work of my hands, in his midst, they will sanctify my name, and they will sanctify the Holy [One] of Jacob, and the God of Israel they will reverence.

The targum translates:

> אְרֵי בְּמִחזוֹהִי גְבוּרָן דְאַעבֵיד[30] לִבנוֹהִי טָבְוָת אַברָהָם לְזַרעֵיה בָתְרוֹהִי עַל אְרַעהוֹן בֵינֵיהוֹן יְקַדְשוּן שְׁמִי וְיֵימְרוּן קַדִיש קַדִישָׁא דְיַעְקֹב וְעַל אְלָהָא דְיִשרָאֵל יֵימְרוּן תַקִיף׃
>
> For in his seeing the wonders that I shall do[31] for his children, the goodness of Abraham, for his seed after him on their land, amongst themselves, they will sanctify my name, and they will declare "holy is the Holy [One] of Jacob," and, regarding the God of Israel, they will declare "[He is] Strong."

Translated as I have above, the targum has nothing to do with the Kaddish. Rather, the targum is simply attempting to explain what Isaiah means when he declares "they will sanctify the Holy one of Jacob," and what that adds to the declaration that "they will reverence the God of Israel." For the author of the targum, it results in two separate declarations about God that the children of Israel will make: the first is that they will declare, "Holy is the Holy [One] of Israel," while the second is that they will declare God "Strong." Nevertheless, reference to the Mourner's Kaddish has been read into this targumic passage based on a sixteenth-century printed edition, in which the word על ("on") is found between the words קדיש and קדישא (ויימרון קדיש על קדישא דיעקוב), rendering something like, "and they will declare 'Holy' on/regarding the Holy [One] of Jacob." Even if this version is accurate, it would seem to work with the end of the verse to imply that the children of Israel will declare God both "holy" and "strong."[32] Nevertheless, the word "holy," literally, is the word *kaddish*, and it has been read to mean that they will recite the Kaddish on the Holy [One] of Jacob. I would argue, however, that this one precarious bit of evidence is not enough to date the practice of the Mourner's Kaddish prior to

29. For a discussion of the possible origins of this targum, see Ze'ev Safrai, "The Targum as Part of Rabbinic Literature," in *The Literature of the Sages*, part 1, *Midrash and Targum, Liturgy, Poetry, Mysticism, Contracts, Inscriptions, Ancient Science, and the Languages of Rabbinic Literature*, ed. Shmuel Safrai et al. (Amsterdam: Van Gorcum; Philadelphia: Fortress, 2006), 271.

30. Some MSS: דְאִתעְבֵיד.

31. Some MSS: "that were done."

32. See Lehnardt, *Qaddish*, 288–90.

the story of R. Akiva and the dead man. Rather, the various medieval versions and readings of that story seem to have been intricately connected with the development of the practice, as we shall presently see.

To conclude this section, Tannaitic and Amoraic Palestinian sources primarily maintain that, once someone is dead, nothing more can be done for her/him. Granted, one or two exceptions to this rule (Hannah for the congregation of Koraḥ and R. Meir for Elisha b. Abuya) may perhaps be found in the Yerushalmi, but what makes those passages so powerful is just how aberrant those cases are. In this sense, then, they serve not to establish a ritual prayer for the dead but, if anything, to undermine such a notion. They are the proverbial exception that proves the rule. According to Palestinian rabbinic sources, unless we are R. Meir interceding for his beloved teacher or Hannah reminding God that even the congregation of Koraḥ belongs in the general category of those who are neither completely righteous nor completely wicked, the rest of us can do little if anything to change the fate of the dead.

Amoraic Babylonia

On the one hand, Babylonian rabbinic Judaism continues to echo some of these Palestinian notions. On the other hand, Babylonian sources consistently adjust this Palestinian material to fit a Babylonian theodicy that allows the living to help the dead in certain circumstances, especially for children to give merit to their parents. Thus, whereas the Yerushalmi (Ber. 9:2, 13d, quoted above) was careful to record Ḥizqiyah quoting R. Yirmiyah quoting R. Shimeon b. Yoḥai as only claiming that he could save those from his own generation onward, when the Bavli retells this statement, the time frame is confused, and R. Shimeon b. Yoḥai is quoted as claiming that he can save those who lived both before and after him:

> R. Ḥizqiyah said in the name of R. Yirmiya in the name of R. Shimeon ben Yoḥai, "I can redeem the entire world from judgment from the day I was created [i.e., born] until now; and if only my son, Eliezer, were with me, from the day the world was created until now; and if only Yotam b. Uziyyahu were with us, from the day that the world was created until its end."[33]

Here, R. Shimeon b. Yoḥai begins as he does in the Yerushalmi only claiming to save people who had not died before the merit of his life had begun and thereby began to offset their sins. In the second half of his state-

---

33. b. Sukkah 45b (MS London):
א׳ ר׳ חזקיה א׳ ר׳ ירמיה משו׳ ר׳ שמע׳ בן יוחי: יכול אני לפטור את כל העול׳ כולו מן הדין מיום שנבראתי עד עכשיו, אילו אלעזר בני עמי מיום שנברא העול׳ עד עכשיו, ואילו יותם בן עוזיהו עמנו מיום שנברא העול׳ ועד סופו.

ment, however, the Bavli's version veers from the notion expressed in the Yerushalmi, claiming in its stead that he can save everyone "from the day the world was created until now." This latter sentiment is uniquely Babylonian, which we shall see better fits the Bavli's Sassanian cultural context than that of R. Shimeon b. Yoḥai himself.[34]

Similarly, whereas Avot of Rabbi Nathan (Version B, 27, quoted above) merely offers Abraham not being able to redeem Ishmael and Isaac not being able to redeem Esau as its example of the general claim that people cannot redeem others, the Bavli (Sanh. 104a) uses these same examples to limit this point to say that *parents* cannot redeem their children, but *children* can redeem their parents (ברא מזכי אבא, אבא לא מזכי ברא): "The son makes the father meritorious; the father does not make the son meritorious, as it is written, 'There is none who saves from my hand' (Deut 32:39). Abraham could not save Ishmael and Isaac could not save Esau."[35] The parallel is rather striking, and the Bavli would seem to be reinterpreting this earlier Palestinian tradition (whether or not the Bavli is reworking Avot of Rabbi Nathan itself).[36] Indeed, both the Bavli and Avot of Rabbi Nathan seem to be reworking a passage in Sipre Deuteronomy, which is adumbrated by the Bavli's use of Deut 32:39. When we turn to Sipre Deuteronomy on that verse, we find the following parallel:

> "There is no one who saves from my hand" (Deut 32:39). Parents cannot save their children. Abraham could not save Ishmael, and Isaac could not save Esau. [So far] I only learn that parents cannot save children. From

34. Contra Urbach, who reads the Bavli's notion that R. Shimeon b. Yoḥai claimed also to save those who preceded him back into the parallel in Genesis Rabba (Urbach, *Ḥazal*, 454).

35. MS Yad Harav Herzog:

ברא מזכי אבא. אבא לא מזכי ברא. דכת': ואין מידי מציל (דברים לב:לט). לא אברהם מציל את ישמעאל, ולא יצחק מציל את עשו.

Note that MS Florence lacks the word לא in אבא לא מזכה ברא, though this is most likely just a scribal error. MSS Karslruhe and Munich agree with MS Yad Harav Herzog. On the relevance of b. Sanh. 104a for the development of the Mourner's Kaddish, see de Sola Pool, *Kaddish*, 103; Kushelevsky, "Ha-'omnam 'aggadah," 47 and 50; eadem, *Sigufim*, 261–62. On this passage, see also Urbach, *Ḥazal*, 452.

36. Unfortunately, the dating of Avot of Rabbi Nathan version A and its relationship to the Bavli are far from certain, complicating this analysis (though since the passage has a parallel in Sipre Deuteronomy, this will not matter tremendously for our analysis). See Judah Goldin, *The Fathers according to Rabbi Nathan*, Yale Judaica Series 10 (New Haven: Yale University Press, 1955), xxi; M. B. Lerner, "The External Tractates," in *Compendia Rerum Iudaicarum ad Novum Testamentum, II: Literature of the Jewish People in the Period of the Second Temple and the Talmud*, vol. 3, *The Literature of the Sages*, part 1, *Oral Tora, Halakha, Mishnah, Tosefta, Talmud, External Tractates*, ed. Shmuel Safrai (Assen: Van Gorcum; Philadelphia: Fortress, 1987), 378; Menaḥem Kister, *ʿIyyunim be-'avot de-R. Natan: Nusaḥ, ʿarikhah u-farshanut* (Jerusalem: Hebrew University of Jerusalem and Yad Izhak Ben Zvi, 1998), 117–22, esp. 217–22. Indeed, most of the above scholars consider Avot of Rabbi Nathan version B to be the earlier of the two versions, with some even believing that it predates the Bavli.

> where do I learn that siblings cannot save siblings? The Bible states, "A man cannot save [his] brother" (Ps 49:8). Neither can Isaac save Ishmael nor can Jacob save Esau. Even if a person gives him all the money in the world, [the latter person] cannot give him his atonement, as it is said, "A man cannot save [his] brother … for the redemption of their soul is dear" (Ps 49:8–9). The soul in a person is precious, if he sins with it, it has no payment of indemnity [i.e., no way to redeem it, presumably after death].[37]

The Bavli would seem to be playing with and reworking this earlier tradition. Whereas Avot of Rabbi Nathan and Sipre Deuteronomy are offering blanket statements that no one can save anyone else, not *even* Abraham could save Ishmael or Isaac Esau. In the hands of the Bavli, these two examples are taken for what they have in common: *fathers* cannot save their *sons*.[38] By implication, then, sons could perhaps save their fathers! We should note that the Bavli quotes the first part of the *baraita* regarding fathers not being able to redeem their children but then fails to quote the second part about souls not having redemption, concluding, to the contrary, that children can save the souls of the parents. Through this selectivity, the Bavli is reading this earlier Palestinian tradition against the grain of its original meaning to bring it in line with Sassanian Babylonian theology (as we shall see below).[39]

Similarly, the Bavli (e.g., Qidd. 40b) quotes statements like t. Qidd. 1:15–16 that "even a person who was wicked his entire life but repented at the last moment, no wickedness is counted,"[40] but nowhere adds the

---

37. Sipre Deut. §329 (MS Berlin):

"ואין מידי מציל", אין מצילין אבות את הבנים, לא אברהם מציל את ישמעאל ולא יצחק מציל את עשו. אין לי אלא אבות ( )[ש]אין מצילים את הבנים, אחין את האחין מנין? ת"ל: "אח לא פדה יפדה (יפדה) איש", לא יצחק מציל את ישמעאל ולא יעקב מציל את עשו. ואפי' נותן אדם לו כל ממון שבעולם אין נותנין לו כפרה, שנא': "אח לא פדה יפדה איש...ויקר פדיון נפשם" יקרה היא נפש שבאדם חוטא בו אין בו תשלומין.

On this passage, see Urbach, *Ḥazal*, 444.

38. But note b. Soṭah 10b, where the power of David's outpouring of tears for his son Absalom is said to have raised him one by one up through and out of the seven layers of hell. On this passage, see Urbach, *Ḥazal*, 453.

39. Andreas Lehnardt, unfortunately, read this Tannaitic midrash through the eyes of the Bavli and therefore read the notion of children saving their parents (found exclusively in the Bavli) back into Sipre Deuteronomy and the Tannaitic period thereby. See Lehnardt, *Qaddish*, 288 n.54 (Lehnardt mistakenly cites the midrash there as §331 instead of §329, though he correctly cites it by page and line number in the Finkelstein edition, showing that this is indeed the midrash to which he intends to refer.)

40. The full text (quoted here and in the body above from b. Qidd. 40b [MS Vatican]) reads:

> ר' שמע' בן יוחי או': אפי' צדיק גמו?ר? כל ימיו ומרד באחרונה, איבד את הראש', שנ': צדקת הצדיק לא תצילינו ביום רשעו; ואפילו רשע כל ימיו ועשה תשובה באחרונה, אין מזכיר' לו שום רשע, שנ': רשעת רשע לא יכשל בה וגו'.
>
> R. Shimeon b. Yoḥai says, "Even a person who was completely righteous his entire life but rebelled at the end has lost [what he had at] the beginning, as it says, 'the

further Palestinian rabbinic point that once the person has died there is no hope for her/him. To the contrary, Babylonian sources explicitly state that there is hope after death. B. Qidd. 31b states:

> Our rabbis taught [i.e., in a *baraita*]: (A) He should honor him [i.e., his father] in his lifetime, and he should honor him in his death. (B) In his lifetime, how? If one is heard of in a place regarding a matter having to do with his father, he should not say, "Send me for myself," "Hasten me for myself," "Release me for myself," but rath[er], "Send me for father," "Release me for father." (C) In his death, how? If a person repeats a saying he heard from his [father's] mouth, he should not say, "Thus said father," but rather, "Thus said father, my lord, may I be an atonement for his rest."
>
> And this applies only within the twelve months [after his father died], from here on out, [he should say], "May his memory be for life in the World to Come."[41]

In part C of the (supposed) *baraita*, we are told that for twelve months after death (the maximum that a person can be in hell—see m. 'Ed. 2:10 and t. Sanh. 13),[42] a person's son is to act as an atonement for him/her. Presumably, afterwards, the author assumes that the parent has made it to the World to Come and therefore is no longer in need of atonement. Notably, this statement is quoted as a *baraita*, though it lacks a Palestinian parallel.[43]

---

righteousness of the righteous you shall not save in the day of his wickedness (Ezek 33:12); and even a person who was wicked his entire life but repented at the end, no wickedness is counted, as it says, 'the wickedness of the wicked he shall not stumble in it [in the day of his repentance from his wickedness].'"

This is nearly identical to t. Qidd. 1:15–16.

41. MS Oxford – Bodl. heb. b. 1 (2673) 8–9:

תנו רבנן: מכבדו בחייו מכבדו במותו; בחייו כאיצד? הנשמע בדבר אביו למקום, לא יאמר שלחוני בשביל עצמי, פטרוני בשביל עצמי, אל[א] שלחוני בשביל אבא, פטרוני בשביל אבא. במותו כאיצד? היה או' דבר שמועה מפיו, לא יאמר: כך א' אבא, אלא כך א' אבא מרי, הריני כפרת משכבו. והני מילי תוך שנים עשר חודש מיכן ואילך זכרונו לחיי העולם הבא.

See Lévi, "Commémoration des ames," 51 n.2; Urbach, *Ḥazal*, 452–53.

42. Granted, the Mishna seems to envisage this purgatorial period taking place at the end of the world, rather than immediately after the person dies as the Bavli here does, but that is a topic for a different paper.

43. This same idea can be found in Mishnat R. Eliezer 5 (ed. H. G. Enelow, 91). While this text, too, attributes this notion to Palestinian Tannaim, the text itself is of uncertain origin, with many scholars believing that it dates to the Geonic period (our earliest citation of it is found in the works of Saadia Gaon; for the dating of Mishnat R. Eliezer, see J. N. Epstein, "Le-mishnat R. Eliezer beno shel R. Yossi ha-gelili," *Tarbiṣ* 4 [1933]: 343–53 [repr. in *Meḥqarim be-sifrut ha-talmud u-be-leshonot shemiyot* 2:221–32]; Moshe Zucker, "Le-pitaron ba'ayat 32 middot u-mishnat R. Eliezer," *PAAJR* 32 [1954]: 1–39; Menaḥem Moreshet, "Li-leshonah shel '*Mishnat R. Eliezer*,'" *Bar Ilan Annual* 11 [1973]: 220; Ta-Shma, "Qetzat 'inyyanei qaddish yatom," 300–301). Whatever the precise date, what is clear is that its author is post-talmudic and made use of the Bavli (J. N. Epstein, "Mishnat R. Eliezer" *HUCA* 23 [1950]: 13 [Hebrew section; repr. in *Meḥqarim be-sifrut ha-talmud u-be-leshonot shemiyot* 2:245]). So, its manifesta-

Kallah Rabbati 2:9 presents this same idea in the form of a famous story about R. Akiva's encounter with a tortured man in hell. Though the story is recorded in Babylonian Aramaic, the author of this passage, by having R. Akiva be the protagonist, would also seem to be attempting to give an aura of Tannaitic Palestinian authority to a notion that we find exclusively in Amoraic Babylonian sources.

M. B. Lerner offered a detailed comparison of the various extant versions of the story known to him, in which he claimed to show that Kallah Rabbati's version had to be later than many of the post-talmudic versions, though he argued that the story ultimately derived from Tannaitic Palestine.[44] Israel Ta-Shma questioned Lerner's conclusions,[45] and Rella Kushelevsky also challenged Lerner's complex system of relating each of the versions to one another. She argued that the story is likely from the Amoraic period at the earliest.[46] I already provided a thorough refutation of Lerner's arguments in my book *A Bride without a Blessing*.[47] For the details, I would refer the reader to that work, but suffice it to say here that his basis for dating the version in Kallah Rab. 2:9 to the post-talmudic period is unfounded. Rather, I have shown in my book that the first two chapters of Kallah Rabbati are from Amoraic Babylonia, and, as we shall see, the story of R. Akiva and the dead man fits that context perfectly.

In a seminal article from 1994, Kushelevsky lists all forty-two versions of the story known to her at the time, analyzing them based in part on the dating of the texts in which they are found. In an updated version of the article in 2004, she addressed the seventy versions known to her at that time, offering a detailed theory of the development of the story across the different versions.[48] She placed Kallah Rabbati's version as the

---

tion of these ideas is most likely a product of Sassanian Babylonian culture, whether directly or indirectly through the Bavli. In an otherwise excellent article, Dov Weiss posits that Mishnat R. Eliezer "preserve[s] (as in our case) precious older Tannaitic material that has no analogues in the rest of the rabbinic corpus" (Weiss, "Between Values and Theology," 4 n. 20). I would argue, however, that we should be cautious about allowing the Tannaitic attributions in these texts to convince us to date these passages and this concept to Tannaitic Palestine when no definitively Tannaitic Palestinian texts manifest such a theology. Rather, I would argue that we should use the dating of the texts in which the passages are found to help us date the origins of the theology, and, here, we find that the notion dates back to the Bavli and Kallah Rab. 1–2 (both from Amoraic Babylonia) but no earlier. This theology became particularly pronounced in Medieval Ashkenaz, and it can be found in Sefer Hasidim §1171 and a host of texts that collected the story of the tanna and the dead man (found in Kallah Rab. 2:9 and parallels) which we shall presently discuss in detail.

44. M. B. Lerner, "Ma'aseh ha-tanna ve-ha-met: gilgulav ha-sifruti'im ve-ha-hilkhati'im," *Asufot* 2 (1988): 29–68.

45. Ta-Shma, "Qetzat 'inyyanei qaddish yatom," 299 n. 1.

46. Rella Kushelevsky, "Ha-'omnam 'aggadah," 62; eadem, "Ha-tanna ve-ha-met," 282.

47. Brodsky, *Bride without a Blessing*, 231–38.

48. Kushelevsky, "Ha-'omnam 'aggadah," esp. 42–45; eadem, "Ha-tanna ve-ha-met," 282–90.

third oldest out of the seventy, but still later than two witnesses from the Geonic period.[49] In my book, which was published after both of these articles by Kushelevsky, I show that both prior theories were partially correct and partially incorrect. I demonstrate that Kallah Rabbati is not a singular text, dating the first two chapters of Kallah Rabbati to ca. fourth-century Babylonia and chapters 3 through 9 of Kallah Rabbati to the later, Geonic period.[50] This is important for our purposes because, if correct, it

49. Kushelevsky favored these two sources as the earliest on the basis that they had recorded the Tannaitic hero as Rabban Yoḥanan b. Zakkai rather than R. Akiva as in Kallah Rabbati and the other sixty-seven versions, considering the story initially to have been about Rabban Yoḥanan b. Zakkai and only later changed to be about R. Akiva. I would argue that this basis for dating the relationship between these three versions is a mistake for several reasons. First, having multiple, alternative rabbinic protagonists of the same story is fairly commonplace in rabbinic literature (cf. the story of R. Akiva in Rome, discussed by Peter Schäfer, "Rabbi Akiva and Bar Kochba" in *Approaches to Ancient Judaism*, ed. William S. Green, BJS 9 [Chico, CA: Scholars Press, 1980], 2:115–16). These alternative versions can be found in contemporaneous texts and need not be indicative of one being earlier than the other. Second, Kushelevsky misses the important development of the story from its earlier theme that the righteous lifestyle of the son is what atones for the prior wicked lifestyle of his father to a focus on a prayer (first *barkhu* and later the Kaddish) that effects atonement. Significantly, Kallah Rabbati is the only version that lacks an efficacious prayer with the focus being on the conglomeration of proper behaviors, among them "praying [*le-varokhei*] in the congregation," a phrase that can easily be misinterpreted as a reference to the *barkhu*. Yet both of the versions that Kushelevesky deemed earlier than Kallah Rabbati's version consider the son saying the *barkhu* to be the act that saves the father from punishment in hell, making these versions likely later than that of Kallah Rabbati. Third, and most significant, Kushelevesky misdates Kallah Rabbati based on the incorrect dating of the text at the time she wrote these first two articles, causing her to miss the fact that Kallah Rab. 2:9 is our earliest extant textual witness. At the time, Kallah Rabbati was alternatively being dated to the third and eighth centuries. Kushelevsky decided to go with the later dating (Kushelevsky, "Ha-'omnam 'aggadah," 41 n.5, 61).

50. Brodsky, *Bride without a Blessing*. I treat this in great detail in chapter 6 of the book, but a much abbreviated summary is in order. Kallah Rabbati was rediscovered by Naḥman Coronel and published for the first time from a single manuscript in 1865. It is a gemara-like commentary on Massekhet Kallah, several chapters of Derekh Eretz, and the sixth chapter of Avot (which itself is a later addition to that text). Its name is recent, and there is no evidence that it was known as a single text prior to the last few centuries. On the contrary, many data point to the fact that these constituent parts were originally separate works that were put together only in later years. These data include manuscript evidence (i.e., half the manuscripts end with the conclusion of the first two chapters on Massekhet Kallah, marking it as "The End of Massekhet Kallah, Mishna and Gemara"), evidence from medieval sages, the very different relationships that the various sections of Kallah Rabbati have with the Babylonian Talmud, and linguistic evidence. The latter is decisive, proving that the first two chapters are linguistically distinct from the latter seven chapters, and that the first two chapters are linguistically Amoraic while the latter chapters are post-Amoraic and likely post-talmudic. To do this linguistic analysis, I took the Aramaic technical phrases in chapters 1–2 and chapters 3–9, searching to see which of them could be found in the Bavli quoted in statements attributed to Amoraic rabbis and which could be found only in the anonymous layer of the Talmud. The result was that 96 percent of these phrases in chapters 1–2 were

identifies the version of this story in Kallah Rab. 2:9 as appearing in our earliest extant text, making it, therefore, likely our earliest extant version. Apart from Kallah Rab. 2:9, the story does not appear in any other text that dates to the Tannaitic or Amoraic periods. Instead, it is known primarily from medieval sources with significant variants one from another, and it is central to the development of the Kaddish as a mourner's prayer. While I do not claim Kallah Rabbati's version to be the "original" story from which the others all developed, it is emblematic of the way this story was being told in this earlier period before it underwent certain significant changes that would lead to the development of the Mourner's Kaddish in the medieval period.

The story, as found in Kallah Rab. 2:9, reads:

> It was asked of them, "[Can children] atone for their parents' sins, or not?"
> Come hear:
> R. Akiva went out to that place. He found a certain man who was carrying a burden on his shoulders, and he could not manage it, and was crying out and sighing.
> [R. Akiva] said to him, "What was your deed [that you merited this punishment]?"
> He said to him, "I did not leave a single sin that I did not commit in that world, and now there are guards on us, and they do not let me rest."
> R. Akiva said to him, "Did you leave behind a son?" He said to him, "On your life, don't ask me [questions]! For I am afraid of the angels who lash me with fiery lashes, for they say to me, 'Why don't you hurry up?!"
> [R. Akiva] said to him, "Tell me what [next generation] you have passed on."
> He said to him, "I left a pregnant woman."
> R. Akiva entered that city. He said to [the people of the town], "Where is the son of So-and-So?"
> They said to him, "May the memory of that one whose bones should be crushed be obliterated!"
> He said to them, "Why?"
> They said to him, "That bandit eats people and brings strife to creatures,

found in Amoraic statements in the Bavli, while only 60 percent of the phrases in the other chapters could be found in Amoraic statements, with the other 40 percent found exclusively in the *stam*. When a Chi-Square analysis was performed to determine if this result was statistically significant, it yielded a P-value several decimal points below the minimum 0.05 needed to determine that the result was statistically significant and not the result of random variation. Put in laymen's terms, what all that means is that chapters 1–2 are linguistically distinct from chapters 3–9, and therefore Kallah Rabbati is not a single text. Moreover, it shows that chapters 1–2 of Kallah Rabbati are of Amoraic Babylonian origin, making them (and Massekhet Kallah on which they form a gemara) our only known Babylonian rabbinic texts edited during the Amoraic period, which in turn makes them invaluable to our study of talmudic Babylonia—though the import of that find is a topic for future articles.

and not only that, but he had sex with a betrothed maiden on the Day of Atonement!"
[R. Akiva] went to [the man's] house. He found [the man's] wife pregnant. He watched over her until she had given birth. He went and circumcised [the baby]. When [the baby] had grown up [into a child, R. Akiva] set him up in the synagogue to bless [*le-varokhei*] in the congregation.
After a few days, R. Akiva went [back] to that place [i.e., Hell].
[The man] appeared to [R. Akiva]. He said to him, "May your mind rest, for you have rested mine."[51]

The story seems to be a visit to hell in the genre of book 11 of Homer's *Odyssey*; book 6 of Virgil's *Aeneid*; 1 Enoch, the Acts of Thomas 55–57; the Apocalypses of Zephaniah (10), Peter, Paul (31–42), Mary, Baruch, Ezra, and Gorgorios; b. Giṭ. 56b–57a; the inscription of Kirdīr 24–34; Dēnkard 7.4.83–86; and the Ardā Wīrāz-nāmag, among others, which, like Dante's famous *Divine Comedy* some centuries later, are generally stories about a protagonist's travels through heaven/hell (or of some kind of communication with the dead) with descriptions of the punishments of the wicked in hell.[52] Interestingly, the punishments with which the dead man is being tortured in Kallah Rab. 2:9's version better fit the Zoroastrian context of the Ardā Wīrāz-nāmag than that found in the later versions of the story. In Kallah Rab. 2:9, the punishments are carrying a heavy burden and being lashed, both of which Claudia Leurini has shown are almost exclusively

51. Ed. Coronel (4b–5a):

איבעיא להוא: מכפרין עון אבות או לא? ת״ש: דר׳ עקיבא נפק לההוא אתרא, אשכחיה לההוא גברא דהוה דרי טונא אכתפיה, ולא הוה מצי לסגויי ביה, והוה צוח ומתאנח. א״ל: מאי עובידתיך? א״ל: לא שבקנא איסורא דלא עבידנא בההיא עלמא, ועכשיו איכא נטורין עילוון, ולא שבקין ליח דאינוח. א״ל ר׳ עקיבא: שבקת בראִ? א״ל: בחייך דלא תשלין, דדחילנא ממלאכי דמחו לי בפולסי דנורא, ואמ׳ לי׳ אמאי לא תיתי בפריע?! אל: אימ׳ ליה דקא ניחותך. א״ל: שבקית אתתא מעברתא. אזל ר׳ עקיבא עאל לההיא מדינתא. אמר להו: בריה דפלוני היכא ליה? אמרו ליה: יעקר זכרו דההוא שחיק עצמות! א״ל: אמאי? אמרו ליה: ההוא ליסטים אכל אינשי ומצער ברייתא, ולא עוד אלא שבא על נערה המאורסה ביום הכפורים! אזל לביתיה אשכח אתתיה מעוברתא, נטרה עד דילדא, אזל מהליה. לכי גדל אוקמיה בבי כנשתא לברוכי בקהלא. לימים אזל ר׳ עקיבא לההוא אתרא, איתחזי ליה, א״ל: תנוח דעתך שהנחת את דעתי.

Note: Coronel's edition is based on MS JTS 10484, this section of which has since been lost. MS Parma, which is the other outstanding manuscript of Kallah Rabbati, is also missing the pages to this section of Kallah Rabbati. The other manuscripts are much later, and Higger's edition contains numerous methodological problems. Together, this makes Coronel's edition the best extant version to use (see my *Bride without a Blessing*, 226–28).

52. For the larger genre, see Martha Himmelfarb, *Tours of Hell: An Apocalyptic Form in Jewish and Christian Literature* (Philadelphia: University of Pennsylvania Press, 1983); and eadem, *The Apocalypse: A Brief History* (Malden, MA: Wiley-Blackwell, 2010). See also Valts Apinis, "Zoroastrian Influence upon Jewish Afterlife: Hell Punishments in *Arda Wiraz* and Medieval Visionary Midrashim" (PhD diss., Latvijas Universitāte, 2010). Apinis's dissertation is insightful in general, though he does not address the midrash in Kallah Rab. 2:9 or the development of the Mourner's Kaddish, the topic at hand for this paper.

administered to men in the Ardā Wīrāz-nāmag, whereas the punishment of being burned, which is found in the other versions of the story, is exclusively reserved for women in the Ardā Wīrāz-nāmag. When it comes to this detail, then, those later versions no longer preserve the nuances of the Babylonian context in which the story originally developed.[53]

Likewise, we should note that, while the protagonist of the story is R. Akiva, presumably setting the story in Tannaitic Palestine, that context does not fit the authorship of the story, with its subtle but significant Babylonian cultural nuances. Indeed, the story directly contradicts Palestinian rabbinic theology, teaching that there is hope after death: children can atone for their parents' sins. While the story itself is a bit ambiguous, leaving somewhat unclear what precisely was efficacious (this ambiguity, I would argue, is precisely what led to the later variation among the versions that ultimately led to the development of the Mourner's Kaddish, as we shall presently see), the question introducing the story (in Kallah Rab. 2:9) clarifies that the main point of the story is that the child was able to atone for his father.[54] By leading a righteous life, the child is able to do what the father should have done in his lifetime. The essence of repentance in rabbinic Judaism is to desist from committing sins and to fulfill the commandments, and, here, the son is able to make up for his father's failing. In the story, circumcision and praying in the synagogue represent the basics of that righteous lifestyle.[55] The son seems to be seen as something of an extension of his father, and through his righteous acts the father's fate in the afterlife is altered as the repentance that he needed to have performed before death is performed posthumously for him.[56]

In post-talmudic versions of this story, this *le-varokhei be-qehala*, "to bless in the congregation," is replaced by the saying of the *barkhu*, one of the key communal blessings in the service.[57] Some versions have the

---

53. See Claudia Leurini, "Hell or Hells in Zoroastrian Afterlife: The Case of Ardā Wīrāz Nāmag," *Cahiers de Studia Iranica* 25 (2002): 218.

54. This very format of question and answer is itself quite Babylonian, common to both the Babylonian Talmud and to Zoroastrian literature (which often opens with a question [*pursišn*], followed by the answer [*passox*]).

55. Indeed, according to Genesis Rabba 26, part of the stress of being a parent is the concern that one's child is not going to synagogue.

56. On the topic of repentance in rabbinic Judaism and Zoroastrianism, especially as both developed in the post-talmudic period, see Yishai Kiel, "The Systematization of Penitence in Zoroastrianism in Light of Rabbinic and Islamic Literature," *Bulletin of the Asia Institute* 22 (2008): 119–35.

57. E.g., Moses Gaster, *The Exempla of the Rabbis: Being a Collection of Exempla, Apologues and Tales Culled from Hebrew Manuscripts and Rare Hebrew Books* (New York: Ktav, 1968), 92–93; Israel Ibn Al-Nakawa, *Menorat ha-ma'or*, ed. H. G. Enelow (New York: Bloch, 1932) 4:127; *Beit ha-midrash* 6 vols., ed. Adolph Jellinek (Jerusalem: Wahrmann Books, 1967), 1:80–81; Isaac Aboab, *Menorat ha-ma'or*, ed. Yehudah Horav and Mosheh Katzenelenbogen (Jerusalem: Mossad Harav Kook, 1961), 50–51; *Pirqei derekh eretz* 2 in *Nispaḥim le-seder Eliyahu*

Kaddish either in addition to or instead of the *barkhu*.[58] Over time, it would be the prayer rather than the pious lifestyle that would be understood as the efficacious element, even though many of the versions retain elements of that pious lifestyle, such as the example of circumcision in this version. Kallah Rab. 1–2 remained fairly obscure and little studied throughout history, and so even if its version is the *Urtext* of all later versions (and that is far from decisive), the story would not have been known to too many sages from Kallah Rab. 2:9 itself.[59] Rather, it would primarily (though not exclusively) have been transmitted orally, and for this reason the versions differ so much in their details one from another.

For our purposes, the important shift is that from *le-varokhei* to the *barkhu* to the Kaddish. This developed quite organically. The meaning of R. Akiva setting the child up in the synagogue *le-varokhei be-qehala*, "to bless in the congregation," is unclear. Presumably this was simply to make public blessings in the synagogue (part of the behaviors of a righteous Jew that his father failed to do in his lifetime), but it is not hard to imagine how later transmitters of this story might conceive of this blessing as the *barkhu*, an important blessing and also a word that in its written form (ברכו) looks nearly identical to the verb (*le-*)*varokhei* (ברוכי). Indeed, as Kushelevsky notes, the *barkhu* (along with the Kaddish) is the quintessential blessing that requires a "congregation," that is, a quorum (of ten or more) to be said.[60] This shift, therefore, can be understood quite easily whether it originally occurred in written or oral transmission. Since previous scholars had not recognized the primacy of the version of the story in Kallah Rab. 2:9, they missed that the story was not originally focused on an expiatory prayer, and that it only later morphed into the *barkhu* and then the Kaddish.[61] Once the story was divorced from the question

---

zuta, ed. Meir Friedmann (Vienna: n.p., 1904; repr., Jerusalem: n.p., 1960), 22–23; Louis Ginzberg, *Ginzei Schechter* (New York: Jewish Theological Seminary of America, 1928–29; repr., Piscataway, NJ: Gorgias Press, 2003), 1:238–40.

58. E.g., Solomon b. Samson of Worms, *Siddur Rabbeinu Shelomo*, ed. Moshe Hershler (Jerusalem: Ḥemed, 1972), 75; MS Parma 2295 (De Rossi 563; published in Kushelevsky, *Sigufim*, 254–55).

59. Though Rabbeinu Bachya (in his commentary on Deut 21:8) cites "*massekhet kallah*" (presumably, Kallah Rab. 1–2) when he references the story in connection with this practice, and, as mentioned in n. 2 above, R. Avraham b. Natan ha-Yarḥi wrote a commentary on Kallah Rabbati 1-2, and he may have been the person who added the reference to the practice of the Mourner's Kaddish to Maḥzor Vitry.

60. Kushelevsky, *Sigufim*, 258. As Kushelevsky notes, that the *barkhu* needs to be said in public (i.e., in a group of ten or more) can already be found in Sipre Deut §306.

61. Since Lerner claimed the primacy of the geniza fragment in his 1987 article ("Ma'aseh ha-tanna ve-ha-met"), scholars have generally recognized the primacy of the *barkhu* over that of the Kaddish (thus, Kushelevsky, "Ha-'omnam 'aggadah," 52–54; eadem, "Ha-tanna ve-ha-met," 282–86; eadem, *Sigufim*, 257–61; Shyowitz, "You Have Saved Me from the Judgment of Gehenna," 55–56). David de Sola Pool considered the focus of the story to

of atonement with which Kallah Rabbati introduced it, it was no longer clear whether the pious lifestyle or the prayer was what was efficacious. Once the prayer instead of the lifestyle was understood as the efficacious element, it was natural for the prayer to shift from the *barkhu* to the Kaddish, since the Kaddish already had a talmudic tradition regarding its ability to effect atonement. Thus, in b. Šabb. 119b, R. Yehoshua b. Levi is quoted as saying:

> Anyone who answers "Amen, may his great name be blessed [*amen yehei shemeih rabba mevorakh*]" with all his strength, they tear up his sentence of seventy years from bad to good, as it is said, "in tearing up the punishments in Israel [with the nation donating, bless the Lord]" (Judg 5:2)—tearing up the punishments because they blessed the Lord.[62]

Whether this statement of God's greatness (*amen yehei shemeih rabba mevorakh*) originally referred to the Kaddish or whether it was not yet associated exclusively with that prayer is uncertain, but once it was linked with the Kaddish, it seems to have affected medieval versions of our story to cause what was perceived as the efficacious prayer of the story to shift from the *barkhu* to the Kaddish. In fact, Maḥzor Vitry and MS Parma 2295 initially proclaim that the dead man will be saved from his punishment if he "has a son who stands up in the congregation and says, 'Bless the blessed Lord [*barkhu et adonai ha-mevorakh*],' and they respond, 'May His name be great [*yehei shemei rabba*],'"[63] connecting the Bavli's notion of the efficaciousness of the *yehei shemeih rabba* with Kallah Rab. 2:9's *le-varokhei* now understood as the *barkhu*.[64] These two witnesses are particularly interesting because they form a real transition between the two forms. On the one hand, when the efficacious event is proffered at the beginning of the

---

be the expiatory aspect of this response: "The value is attached to the praise of the response alone, no longer to the implied meaning of it, and this perversion of the importance attached to the response is completed in the oft occurring late legend of Akiva teaching the son of a man who was suffering in Gehinnom to say Kaddish or ברכו, thereby procuring relief from punishment for the boy's father" (de Sola Pool, *Kaddish*, 102).

62. Thus, MS Oxford:

א׳ר יהושע בן לוי: כל העונה ״אמן יהא שמיה רבא מברך״ בבל כחו, קורעין לו גזר דינו של שבעים שנה מרעה לטוב, שנא׳: בפרוע פרעות בישראל וגו׳. בפרוע פרעות משום ברכו יי״.

I am here translating the verse in line with its midrashic interpretation, as opposed to whatever its original context in the Song of Deborah might have been. On the relevance of this passage for the development of the Mourner's Kaddish, see de Sola Pool, *Kaddish*, 102. See also Urbach, *Ḥazal*, 453 n. 80. Cf. b. Soṭah 49a, which states that the world survives in part because of the declaration of the *yehei shemeih rabba* ("may his name be great").

63. For the text of the Parma MS, see Kushelevsky, *Sigufim*, 254.

64. On the conflation of the Kaddish and the *barkhu*, see Ta-Shma, *Minhag 'ashkenaz ha-qadmon*, 304–6. While Ta-Shma may be correct, I am here suggesting an alternative hypothesis for how and why these versions of this story came to conflate the Kaddish and the *barkhu*, not that these hypotheses are mutually exclusive.

story, the response of the *yehei shemei[h] rabba* to the *barkhu* is prescribed. On the other hand, when the event actually occurs at the end of the story (when the son actually gets up in the congregation and says the *barkhu*), the congregation responds as we would normally imagine, by stating "Blessed is the blessed Lord for ever and ever [*barukh adonai ha-mevorakh le-'olam va'ed*]."[65] This latter response was already fixed as the proper response to the *barkhu* at least as far back as the Tannaitic period, as stated in Sipre Deut. §306.[66] Maḥzor Vitry and the Parma manuscript are an incomplete hybridization of Kallah Rab. 2:9 with b. Šabb. 119b. They still preserve the *barkhu*, which likely derived from *le-varokhei*, and although they have now incorporated the *yehei shemeih rabba* response of b. Šabb. 119b, they have made the change in only one of the two places in which it is mentioned in the story, forgetting to change it in the other, leaving an important clue behind regarding how this version of the story evolved![67]

65. See Kushelevsky, *Sigufim*, 255. Similarly, in Gaster's *Ma'aseh Book* (to be distinguished from his *Exempla of the Rabbis*, cited above, which was taken from a different text with a different version of the story), while R. Akiva is initially told by the dead man that the Kaddish can save him and while the narrator concludes as if the story just proved the efficaciousness of the Kaddish, in the story itself, the son ultimately recites the *barkhu* rather than the Kaddish in the synagogue, saving his father thereby (Moses Gaster, *Ma'aseh Book: Book of Jewish Tales and Legends Translated from the Judeo-German* [Philadelphia: Jewish Publication Society, 1934], 286–89).

66. Sipre Deut. §306 reads:

כי שם ה' אקרא, רבי יוסי אומר מנין לעומדים בבית הכנסת ואומרים ברכו את ה' המבורך שעונים אחרים ברוך ה' המבורך לעולם ועד שנאמר כי שם ה' אקרא הבו גדל לאלהינו

67. A chart of these details may be helpful:

Kallah Rabbati 2:9	MS Parma and Maḥzor Vitry	b. Shabbat 119b
In this version of the story of R. Akiva and the dead man, R. Akiva circumcises the child and takes him to synagogue "to bless in the congregation [*le-varokhei be-qahala*]."	In this version of the story of R. Akiva and the dead man, we are (1) initially told that the congregation should answer *yehei shemeih rabba* to the child's *barkhu*, but then (2) when the child says *barkhu*, the congregation responds *barukh adonay ha-mevorakh*, with no mention that this does not conform to the original prescription.	This is a separate claim (not connected to the story of R. Akiva and the dead man) that one who says *yehei shemeih rabba* with all his strength will have his judgment changed from bad to good.

That is, Kallah Rab. 2:9 states that R. Akiva had the child "bless in the congregation [*le-varokhei be-qehala*]." This seems to have been understood already in some early medieval versions as the saying of the *barkhu* prayer. Separate from this tradition, we find a statement in the Bavli (b. Šabb. 119b) that the proclamation of the *yehei shemeih rabba* can absolve a person from all their sins. Probably as a result of this tradition regarding the power of the *yehei shemeih rabba*, we find that the *yehei shemeih rabba* replaces the *barkhu* as the efficacious prayer. Significantly, MS Parma and Maḥzor Vitry's versions of our story seem to preserve an intermediary version of the story in which they initially state that the child should say the *barkhu*

Of course, in the Bavli, there is nothing magical about the *yehei shemeih rabba*. The declaration of God's greatness (through this act of "blessing" the Lord, as b. Šabb. 119b calls it) acts as supreme atonement annulling whatever ill-fate may have been decreed upon his soul. Whether the attribution to the Palestinian Amora R. Yehoshua b. Levi is correct or not, the theology is completely consistent with both Palestinian and Babylonian rabbinic culture and is even found attributed to God in the admittedly late Palestinian source, Midrash Proverbs.[68] What is new in these later versions of the story is the application to the child rather than the sinner himself, but even here, it is the prayer as emblematic of repentance that would seem to be efficacious. In fact, according to Seder Rav Amram Gaon, a Babylonian Geonic work, even the dead in hell will be able to change their own fate by responding amen to the *yehei shemeih rabba*:

> After they eat, drink, and bless, the Holy One Blessed Be He will bring the Torah and rest it on his bosom and engage in it—in purity and impu-

---

and then have the congregation respond *yehei shemeih rabba,* when the child actually says the *barkhu* in the congregation, however, the congregation's response is not the *yehei shemeih rabba* as was initially claimed, but the usual response to the *barkhu* ("*barukh adonai ha-mevorakh le-'olam va'ed*"). MS Parma and Maḥzor Vitry, therefore, seem to preserve an early hybrid stage when the story was initially shifting from the *barkhu* to the *yehei shemeih rabba,* before it had fully shifted to the latter and to the Kaddish, with which it is most associated.

Of course, one could suggest that the change occurred in the other direction, from the *yehei shemeih rabba* to *barukh adonai ha-mevorakh,* but, given the primacy of Kallah Rab. 1–2 as a text, we should privilege its version, making the shift most likely from *le-varokhei* to the *barkhu* and from there to the *yehei shemeih rabba.* The reverse order would be less likely since Kallah Rab. 1–2 is dated earlier than the other texts in which the story is found. Ta-Shma has shown that the *barkhu* and the Kaddish used to be said together and he has suggested that the *yehei shemeih rabba* may have been said in response to the *barkhu* (Ta-Shma, "Qetzat 'inyanei qaddish yatom," 299–301). See also Kushelevsky, "Ha-'omnam 'aggadah," 52–53 n.21.

68. Midr. Prov. 10:3 (ed. Buber, 33b):

אמר ר׳ ישמעאל בוא וראה כמה קשה יום הדין שעתיד הקדוש ברוך הוא לדון את כל העולם כולו בעמק יהושפט בזמן שתלמידי חכמים באים לפניו אומר לכל אחד מהם כלום עסקת בתורה, אמר לו הן, אומר לו הקדוש ברוך הוא הואיל והודית אמור לפני מה שקרית, ומה ששנית בישיבה, ומה ששמעת בישיבה... בא לפניו מי שיש בידו חמשה חומשי תורה, אומר לו בני למה לא למדת הגדה ולא שנית, שבשעה שחכם יושב ודורש אני מוחל ומכפר עונותיהם של ישראל, ולא עוד אלא בשעה שעונין אמן יהא שמיה רבא מברך, אפילו נחתם גזר דינם אני מוחל ומכפר להם עונותיהם.

R. Yishmael said: Come and see how difficult Judgment Day will be. For, the Holy One Blessed Be He will judge the entire world in the Valley of Jehosaphat. When the *talmidei ḥakhamim* come before him, he will say to each of them, "Did you busy yourself with Torah?" He will say, "Yes." The Holy One Blessed Be He will say to him, "Since you acknowledged it, tell me what [Bible] you studied and what [Mishna] you learned in yeshivah, and what [teachings] you heard in yeshivah."... One who has studied the Pentateuch will come before him. He will say to him, "My son, why did you not study aggada and learn Mishna? For, when a sage sits and expounds I forgive and atone the sins of Israel. And not only that, but when they respond 'Amen, may his name be great and blessed' even if their sentence has been sealed, I forgive and atone their sins."

> rity, prohibitions and permitted things, laws and stories. And David will say a poem before the Holy One Blessed Be He, and the righteous will answer after him, "Amen, may his name be great and blessed forever after! May he be blessed!" from within the Garden of Eden, and the sinners of Israel will answer "Amen!" from Hell. Immediately, the Holy One Blessed Be He will say to the angels, "Who are these who answer 'Amen!' from Hell?" He will say to him, "Master of the Universe, these are the sinners of Israel. For, even though they suffer greatly, they gird themselves and say 'Amen' before you." Immediately, the Holy One Blessed Be He will say to the angels, "Open the gates of the Garden of Eden for them and let them enter and sing before me!" as it is said, "Open the gates that a righteous nation who keeps faith [*shomer 'emunim*] may enter" (Is. 26:2). Do not read "who keeps faith [*shomer 'emunim*]," but rather "who says 'Amens' [*she-'omer 'amenim*]."[69]

In Seder Rav Amram Gaon, we find our first source showing the *yehei shemeih rabba* changing the fate of the dead *even after they have died*. That is, Midrash Proverbs and b. Šabb. 119b have the saying of the *yehei shemeih rabba* during one's lifetime ameliorate one's situation in the afterlife, but not until Seder Rav Amram Gaon can this recital be made after the person's death and still have an impact on her/his fate. On the other hand, Seder Rav Amram Gaon still preserves the righteous act (saying *amen* to the *yehei shemeih rabba*) as conducted by the sinners themselves. It took the combination of the theology found in this Geonic work with Kallah Rab. 2:9's conception of the son changing the fate of his father to produce a reworked version of that story that ultimately engendered the ritual of the Mourner's Kaddish.[70]

---

69. *Seder Rav Amram Gaon, Qaddish shel yaḥid*:

לאחר שאוכלין ושותין ומברכין, מביא הקדוש ברוך הוא את התורה ומניחה בחיקו ועוסק בה בטומאה ובטהרה, באיסור ובהיתר בהלכות ובאגדות, ואומר דוד שירה לפני הקדוש ברוך הוא. ועונין אחריו הצדיקים אמן יהא שמיה רבא מברך לעלם ולעלמי עלמיא יתברך מתוך גן עדן, ופושעי ישראל עונין אמן מתוך גיהנם. מיד אומר הקדוש ברוך הוא למלאכים מי הם אלו שעונין אמן מתוך גיהנם. אומר לפניו רבונו של עולם הללו פושעי ישראל, שאעפ"י שהם בצרה גדולה מתחזקים ואומרים לפניך אמן, מיד אומר הקדוש ברוך הוא למלאכים פתחו להן שערי גן עדן ויבואו ויזמרו לפני שנאמר פתחו שערים ויבא גוי צדיק שומר אמונים +ישעיה כ"ו, ב'+ אל תקרא שומר אמונים אלא שאומר אמנים.

See also Eisenstein, *Otzar ha-midrashim*, 90. Similarly, according to another passage in Seder Rav Amram Gaon (*qeri'at shema' u-berkhoteiha*), the response *yehei shemeih rabba* has the power to ward off this-worldly punishments decreed upon Israel as well. Indeed, in a lengthy passage about dream interpretation, the Bavli states that one who answered *amen yehei shemeih rabba* in a dream is guaranteed life in the World to Come (b. Ber. 57a).

70. Kushelevsky correctly notes the christological elements of some of these Medieval Ashkenazi versions, such as the crown of thorns that the dead man is made to wear in the Parma manuscript (Kushelevsky, *Sigufim*, 262–68; Shyovitz, "You Have Saved Me from the Judgment of Gehenna," 61–62). These elements are not found, however, in Kallah Rab. 2:9, and she is incorrect, therefore, to the extent that she considers them seminal to the earlier production (as opposed to the evolution) of the story. Nevertheless, Kushelevsky is correct

The Zoroastrian Context

While these Babylonian rabbinic notions of dead persons' offspring and of the dead themselves being able to repent after death and thereby effect a change in their fate are by and large contrary to the Palestinian rabbinic theology, they are wholly consistent with a Sassanian Babylonian worldview. Like rabbinic Judaism, Zoroastrian literature advocates repentance before death.[71] Unlike Palestinian rabbinic literature, however, Zoroastrianism does allow certain posthumous acts to help the soul reach a better destination in the afterlife. Indeed, it is incumbent upon the heirs of the deceased to labor for the soul of the deceased. Thus, Question 7 in the *Dādestān ī dēnīg* assumes from the start that the living can help the dead, asking, "After his passing away, how do the good deeds which another does for him go to him and help him?" The answer, however, is not quite as simple as the question might imply. Manūščihr, the author, answers:

> When anyone does a good deed for one who has passed away, after his death, if he who has died did not order that good deed and did not put it in his will and did not bequeath it in his lifetime, and also if it was not (done) by means of his property, then it does not go into the balance and does not reach him.[72]

While Manūščihr allows for posthumous help, he only allows for that help if the deceased designated it as such from his own property during his lifetime. This, of course, makes basic sense. Why should one person be able to get credit for another person's deeds unless those deeds were effectively commissioned and paid for by the person himself? In this way, though the act itself was posthumous, the dedication—the originating act—was designated during the person's lifetime. This is a way to cheat the system a bit and permit heirs to aid the deceased, but it is not in itself a perspective that allows the independent actions and prayers of the deceased's loved ones to aid him in the afterlife. Nevertheless, Manūščihr hedges this answer a bit, qualifying that:

> If he who has passed away did not order that good deed, and did not also give instructions for it, but it (i.e. the good deed) was (done) by means of

---

insofar as she is looking for the wider cultural context(s) of which this Jewish story is a part. In the case of Kallah Rab. 2:9 (and therefore the earlier production of the story), however, that context is Sassanian Babylonia, to which we shall now turn.

71. See, e.g., *Dādestān ī dēnīg* 40:7–8.

72. passox ēd kū ka kas ōy ī bē widardag rāy pas az bē-widerišnīh kirbag kunēd agar ōy ī bē widardag andar zīndagīh ān kirbag nē framūd u-š nē handarzēnīd ud nē bun kard u-š nē-iz pad jād būd ēg-iš bē ō tarāzūg nē šawēd ud nē rasēd. *Dādestān ī dēnīg* 7.2 (transcription and trans. by M. Jaafari-Dehaghi [Paris: Association pour l'avancement des études iraniennes, 1998], 54–57).

his property and (it was) in conformity with what may have been done (by him) in his lifetime, (then it) reaches (him) ... to improve his position.[73]

This still allows for succor to come only from charity from his own property that is in keeping with his nature while alive, so far leaving unparalleled the idea in our story that R. Akiva helps to improve the situation of the completely wicked dead man he encountered in hell. We should notice, however, that our story did not imply that anyone could help the deceased, but specifically that his son could do so. This, in fact, seems precisely in keeping with Zoroastrian notions as expressed in the *Šāyist nē šāyist* (10.22):

"Make a big effort to produce children only in order to accumulate more good deeds!" For, in the *Niyādom nask*,[74] the *dastwars*[75] have taught that work and good deeds performed by a son will become just as if one had performed them with one's own hands. And, in the *Dāmdād (nask)*,[76] it is manifest that it is both the same good deeds and the same amount that becomes the father's own.[77]

As an extension of the father, the deeds of the son go on the father's account. Interestingly, *Šāyist nē šāyist* claims that the *dastwars*, the Zoroastrian sages, are the ones who taught this fact, and in Kallah Rab. 2:9, R. Akiva, the rabbinic sage par excellence, is the one who knows what to do and, through his example, teaches the audience how to save their dead parents from punishment. Kallah Rabbati 2:9 is the only version of this story to preserve the rabbinic sage as having and teaching this knowledge. The other versions record the dead man as imparting this information to the sage as knowledge the dead man overheard from the angels themselves. In Zoroastrianism, however, this is not angelic information, but the domain and teaching of the sage. Once again, Kallah Rabbati's version proves to be most in keeping with this Zoroastrian context.

---

73. agar ān kerbag ōy widardag nē framūd ud u-š nē-iz handarzēnīd bē-š pad jād hamdādestān būd ān ī andar zīndagīh kunīhād ēg-iš pad sedōš bē ō abzōn ī gāh rasēd. (*Dādestān ī dēnīg* 7.4, transcription and trans. by M. Jaafari-Dehaghi, 54–57). See also Rivāyat ī Ēmēd ī Ašwahištān 39.14–16.

74. Part of the Avesta, the sacred corpus of the Zoroastrians, dating at least as far back as the first millennium BCE.

75. Zoroastrian priests/sages.

76. Another part of the Avesta, which has since been lost.

77. abēr tuxšēd pad frazend-zāyišnīh ēwāz frāy kerbag-handōzīh rāy
čē pad nask Niyādom dastwarān čāšt kū kār ud kerbag ī pus kunēd pid ēdōn bawēd čiyōn ka-š pad dast ī xwēš kerd hē. ud pad Dāmdād paydāg kū ham-iz kerbag ham handāzag ī pid ō xwēšīh rasēd. Transcribed and translated by Prods Oktor Skjærvø (I would like to thank him for providing me with this unpublished copy). See also *Šāyast-nē-šāyast. A Pahlavi Text on Religious Customs*, ed. Jehangir C. Tavadia (Hamburg: Friederichsen, de Gruyter, 1930), 138.

Another aspect of Kallah Rabbati's story that requires contextualization is the age of the child. Why does the story spend so much time showing that the child is a minor, emphasizing that he was not yet even born at the time that the dead man and R. Akiva initially were conversing? This point, too, is in keeping with a Zoroastrian worldview, as explained by the Pahlavi Rivāyat accompanying the Dādestān ī dēnīg (29.1), which states:

> Indeed according to this saying: "Until a son is 15 years old his nurture (comes) from his father," then also so long as he [i.e. the father] (is) alive the (son's) earnings belong to the father, and all the good deeds which the son does will thus belong to the father as if he had done them with his own hands.[78]

While the child is still a minor (under fifteen in Zoroastrianism), the deeds of the child go on the ledger of the father. Granted, Pahlavi Rivāyat accompanying the Dādestān ī dēnīg seems to believe that this works only while the father is alive, but other Zoroastrian sources argue that this works even after death, as we find, for example, in the Rivāyat of Ādur Farnbāg 141.2:

> And in every chapter which is regarding atoning for one's father's sins and the good deeds also for the father's soul, when one expiates for one's father's sins, guilt, and debts, it is better to perform services for the father's soul, (offer up) *myazd*[79] and do other good deeds.
>
> For expiating for sins is the most dutiful good deed and one's *warz*[80] and *xwarrah*[81] is increased (thereby).[82]

Thus, if the man failed to repent during his lifetime, and if he failed also to designate that acts of charity be donated from his estate, then the one failsafe left is his son himself—as long as he left one behind.

This is the context in which we ought to understand both Kallah Rab. 2:9 and b. Qidd. 31b. Both specify the son as acting as atonement for the deceased father. The great R. Akiva is unable to help this man by means of

78. az-iz ēn wāzag kū pus tā 15-sālag parwarišn az pid ā-iz windišn pid xwēš tā zīndag hamāg kār ud kerbag ī pus kunēd pid ēdōn čiyōn ka-š pad dast ī xwēš kerd hē. *Pahlavi Rivāyat Accompanying the Dādestān ī Dēnīg*, ed. A. V. Williams (Copenhagen: Royal Danish Academy of Sciences and Letters, 1990), 1:133 and 2:55.

79. A votive offering.

80. Miraculous Power.

81. Glorious Power, fortune. *Warz* and *xwarrah* often come together.

82. u-š pad hamāg dar čē az tōzišn kerdan ī wināh ī pidar ud kerbag ī ruwān-iz pidar rāy ka wināh ud ērang ud abām ī pidar bē wizārēd weh kū pad ruwān ī pidar yazišn ud myazd ud anīy kerbag kunēd čē wināh-wizārišnīh frēzwānīgtom kerbag ud warz ud xwarrah abzāyīhēd

Transcription and translation by Prods Oktor Skjærvø and Yishai Kiel (I would like to thank them for sharing with me this pre-published copy).

any of his righteous deeds. R. Akiva's only recourse is to find his unborn child and help the man through the acts of the child. This point is so obvious in the story that even long after the Kaddish was incorporated into the story and accepted as the salvific element, medieval and early modern rabbis still often insisted that the prayer had this effect only when uttered by the son (a point often lost on the current practice, with people frequently paying a rabbi or a yeshivah student to say Kaddish for them). Thus, after retelling the story in his *Or Zaru'a*, R. Yitsḥaq b. Moshe quotes a saying purportedly from the Tanna de-Vei Eliyahu corpus that it is specifically a son who is a minor who says Kaddish who is able to save his father from punishment.[83] Scholars have struggled to understand how the custom developed of having a minor pray from the pulpit so that he could say the Mourner's Kaddish when this flew in the face of general rabbinic law regarding minors praying for the congregation.[84] The Sassanian context of this story may finally explain how and why this custom might have developed: *because* the child is a minor, the merit goes to the dead father.

Furthermore, as we saw from Seder Rav Amram Gaon, we find evidence of the belief among Babylonian rabbis of the Geonic period that the soul itself can effect its own change in station by repenting in hell and responding amen to the *yehei shemeih rabba*. This too has parallels in Zoroastrian literature. Thus, in the Pahlavi Rivāyat, we learn that Jam effected his own change in status in the afterlife through his posthumous repentance, and in the Dēnkard (3:350), we are taught that those who properly repent in hell can bring themselves to purgatory, and from there even to heaven.[85]

In these ways, we see that the story of R. Akiva and the dead man is deeply steeped in its Sassanian context and only fully understood thereby. While the story did not itself originally advocate the practice of the Mourn-

83. *Or Zaru'a, ḥeleq bet, hilkhot shabbat, siman* 50:

וכן מצא מורי ה״ר אלעזר מוורמשא דתנא דבי אליהו רבא דקטן האומר יתגדל מציל אביו מן הפורענות:

And thus my teacher, R. Eleazar of Worms, found that it was taught in the school of Elijah the Great that a minor who says *yitgadal* saves his father from punishment.

84. Ta-Shma, for example, suggests that the custom developed in the wake of the Crusades because so many minors were suddenly orphaned ("Qetzat 'inyanei qaddish yatom," 306–7).

85. The Pahlavi Rivāyat 31c8 (ed. A.V. Williams, 1:139 and 2:58–59) reads:

ka Jam pad ēn ēwēnag guft būd ā-š petītīgīh ud abaxšīh bē ō mar āmad
Ohrmazd ud amahrspandān ud abārīg yazdān bē āmurzīd
ud az abāxtar nēmag bē ō hamēstagānīh ud xwadāyīh ī hamēstagān mad

When Jam had spoken in this manner, then confession and contrition came into his account, and he was forgiven by Ohrmazd and the *amahraspands* and the other *yazads*, and he went from the northern direction [i.e. Hell] to the state of Limbo and to the lordship of Limbo.

er's Kaddish, the latter could not have developed without the theological impetus of this Sassanian context.

To be clear, I am not trying to overstate the case here. Manūščihr is ambivalent about whether one can do anything to help a deceased person, preferring that the help ultimately have some origination in the deeds of the deceased themselves. The *Šāyist nē šāyist* articulates a notion that the good deeds of children are counted on the parent's account, though it discusses this solely in context of a living parent. The Pahlavi Rivāyat accompanying the Dādestān ī dēnīg clarifies that the son's merits accrue to the father so long as (1) the son is still a minor, and (2) the father is still alive, with the former nicely fitting the context of Kallah Rab. 2:9 and the later development of the Mourner's Kaddish while the latter decisively does not. Finally, the Rivāyat of Ādur Farnbāg articulates a belief system that fully fits Kallah Rab. 2:9, in which the deeds of the son atone for his deceased father's sins. My point, then, is not that the Zoroastrian literature is univocal and that Kallah Rab. 2:9 is merely derivative of that dogma, but that Kallah Rab. 2:9 is part of the discussion and debate being waged in the same place and at the same general time as it was composed, and that we must see it in that context if we wish to understand it properly. That is, Kallah Rab. 2:9 is a product of the Amoraic and post-Amoraic Babylonian/Persian context in which it was composed and not the Tannaitic Palestinian context in which it is set. This Babylonian Jewish and non-Jewish context is essential for understanding the elements at play in Kallah Rab. 2:9 that ultimately gave rise to the ritual of the Mourner's Kaddish as the story left that cultural context and was no longer read with that cultural understanding.

Conclusions

On this most basic of points, whether there is anything that can be done to help a dead loved one's position in the afterlife, the Babylonian rabbinic sources reveal themselves to be thoroughly Babylonian (in the larger sense of that term). In spite of the fact that these Babylonian rabbinic sources present themselves as thoroughly rabbinic, and even as of Palestinian provenance, we see that they are in direct conflict with a Palestinian rabbinic worldview but consistent with a non-Jewish Babylonian (i.e., Zoroastrian) perspective.

The Mourner's Kaddish, then, is the product of ideas prevalent in Sassanian Babylonia that underwent several changes as these Babylonian rabbinic beliefs spread away from that very context. Had the story remained preserved solely in its Babylonian cultural context, it likely would not have been able to morph into the medieval form it took on of the Mourner's Kaddish. In the Zoroastrian context, there is no magical expiatory prayer that can be uttered to save someone's soul from hell. The notion of an expiatory prayer fits much more with the Palestinian sources once they are reread through a Babylonian lens, much as we saw the editors of Maḥzor Vitry do to Sipre Deut. §210. In its original context, then, the blessing in the congregation in Kallah Rabbati's version of the story of R. Akiva and the dead man would likely have remained understood as it was originally intended: as just one of many aspects of proper, righteous behavior, which work together to give merit to the dead father. Granted, the *le-varokhei* could have been misread by almost anyone as the saying of the *barkhu*, especially if the letter *yodh* at the end of *le-varokhei* was accidentally elongated into a *vav* (if the error occurred in a written format at some point—it could also have occurred as an error in oral transmission). But may there have been other factors as well that came together to increase the likelihood of such a misreading or misunderstanding? Here, the medieval European context becomes important. While I agree with the author of the passage in Maḥzor Vitry that the custom of saying Mourner's Kaddish is a direct product of the story of R. Akiva and the dead man,[86] that does not necessarily mean that the story was the only factor that contributed to the development of the custom. Not only were Palestinian and Babylonian sources being read anew in light of one another in Medieval Ashkenaz, as we saw above, but popular contemporary ideas were also playing a role. Shyovitz, for example, has pointed out developing twelfth-century Christian attitudes toward hell and purgatory and their relevance for certain changing details in the transmission of the story of the rabbi and the dead man.[87] While the rabbinic Jewish notion of hell was already much more like the Christian purgatory than the Christian hell, the fact that purgatory was a current topic in twelfth-century Christian Europe might have been one of many factors that contributed to the changing transmission of the story and the development of the ritual of the Mourner's Kaddish.

As Kallah Rabbati was being read in twelfth- and thirteenth-century Spain and Provence (e.g., R. Baḥya b. Asher of Spain and R. Avraham b. Natan ha-Yarḥi) and the story of R. Akiva and the dead man was being brought from there in various versions to Medieval Ashkenaz, perhaps even by one of the editors of Maḥzor Vitry (e.g., ha-Yarḥi), who wrote the earliest extant commentary on Kallah Rabbati, this story seems to have given birth to the practice in Medieval Ashkenaz. Through this story, this fundamentally Babylonian/Zoroastrian worldview was imported into Medieval Ashkenaz. Of course, this is not to claim that the Mourner's Kaddish is a Zoroastrian ritual. Rather, it is *founded upon* a Babylonian/Zoroastrian understanding of the afterlife: that the merits and demerits of a son who is a minor are attributed to the father even after death, and that

86. Maḥzor Vitry §144 (ed. Hurwitz, 1:113). See n. 3 above.
87. Shyowitz, "You Have Saved Me from the Judgment of Gehenna."

this therefore can change the fate of the dead father. On the other hand, in the hands of the rabbis, this practice becomes a uniquely Jewish one, combining with the notion of the salvific properties of the *yehei shemeih rabba*. Indeed, the practice began specifically as a ritual for Saturday night after the Sabbath departed because of the uniquely Jewish theology that the dead are not punished in hell during the Sabbath but that they return to their punishment when the Sabbath ends.[88] This ritual, then, began as a way to help one's parents as they returned to their suffering. In this way, we must see the Mourner's Kaddish as the product of several cultures—Jewish and Zoroastrian, Palestinian and Babylonian, late antique and High Middle Ages—all coming together to produce this unique custom. In this sense, the Mourner's Kaddish is quintessentially Jewish—as much a hybrid of the peregrinations of the Jewish people as the people themselves.[89]

---

88. That the custom of saying Mourner's Kaddish was originally specifically for Saturday night, see Maḥzor Vitry §144 (ed. Hurwitz, 1:113); and *Or Zarua, hilkhot shabbat* §50. That the dead get a reprieve from hell on the Sabbath, see b. Sanh. 65b; this latter point was quite popular in Medieval Ashkenaz and is quoted, for example, in the Peirushei siddur ha-tefilah la-roqeaḥ (18, s.v. *le-David be-shenoto* [89]); Sefer Kolbo §41, s.v. *be-motzei shabbat*.

89. Peter Brown has recently documented relatively similar changes in the notion of the afterlife in Western Christianity across the same general span of time (second through seventh centuries CE), also noting how earlier sources were reread through the eyes of later theologians. See Peter Brown, *The Ransom of the Soul: Afterlife and Wealth in Early Western Christianity* (Cambridge: Harvard University Press, 2015). Here, we can find a similar development from Paul's notion in 2 Cor 5:10 that each person will receive their due upon death to Augustine's *On the Care of the Dead* with his developing notion that the living can affect the fate of the dead through prayer and almsgiving though only if this is in keeping with the actions of the dead during their lifetime to the overt petitions on seventh-century tombstones for the living to pray on behalf of the dead (for discussion of these tombstones, see Brown, *Ransom of the Soul*, 210–11). On the one hand, Western Christianity was a long way geographically, linguistically, and culturally from Amoraic Babylonia and even from Tannaitic Palestine. On the other hand, such parallel phenomena may point to a larger changing zeitgeist that could be worth exploring, although we should also note that the story of Kallah Rab. 2:9 still seems to fit particularly with Babylonian (Zoroastrian) notions of the ways in which the good deeds of young children can benefit their fathers. In any case, these changes in Western Christianity would undoubtedly have impacted the later Jews of Medieval Europe where the practice of the Mourner's Kaddish ultimately coalesced. Such a larger comparison ultimately must be left for a future study.

Notes on Contributors

Michal Bar-Asher Siegal is the Rosen Family Career Development Chair in Judaic Studies at The Goldstein-Goren Department of Jewish Thought, Ben-Gurion University of the Negev. A scholar of Rabbinic Judaism, her work focuses on aspects of Jewish–Christian interactions in the ancient world. She is an elected member of the Israeli Young Academy of Sciences. Her book *Early Christian Monastic Literature and the Babylonian Talmud* (Cambridge: Cambridge University Press, 2013; winner of the 2014 Manfred Lautenschlaeger Award) compared Christian monastic literature to rabbinic sources. She has also published on topics such as the Syriac version of Ben Sira, the Mishnah, and Tannaitic Midrashim. Her forthcoming book will focus on stories found in the Babylonian Talmud relating to heretics.

David Brodsky is an Assistant Professor in the Department of Judaic Studies at Brooklyn College, City University of New York. He received his PhD from New York University in the Skirball Department of Hebrew and Judaic Studies, and is the author of *A Bride without a Blessing: A Study in the Redaction and Content of Massekhet Kallah and Its Gemara*, Texts and Studies in Ancient Judaism 118 (Tübingen: Mohr Siebeck, 2006). He specializes in the study of the Babylonian Talmud in its surrounding cultural contexts.

Yaakov Elman is Professor of Talmud at Yeshiva University's Bernard Revel Graduate School of Jewish Studies, where he holds the Herbert S. and Naomi Denenberg Chair in Talmudic Studies. He has published widely in the field of Talmud, and his research interests include rabbinic theology, unfolding systems of rabbinic legal exegesis, and the cultural context of classical rabbinic texts. However, of particular pertinence to this volume is his ardent engagement in Talmudo-Iranica, which seeks to understand the Babylonian Talmud in its Middle-Persian context.

Simcha Gross is an Assistant Professor in the Department of History at the University of California, Irvine. He specializes in ancient Jewish and Christian history, currently concentrating on Jews and Syriac Christians living under Sasanian Persian and early Arab-Muslim rule. His recent publications include "When the Jews Greeted Ali: Sherira Gaon's *Epistle* in Light of Arabic and Syriac Historiography," *Jewish Studies Quarterly* 24 (2017): 122–44, and (with Aaron Michael Butts) *The 'History of the Slave of Christ': From Jewish Child to Christian Martyr*, Persian Martyr Acts in Syriac: Texts and Translation 6 (Piscataway, NJ: Gorgias Press, 2017).

Geoffrey Herman is a member of the School of Historical Studies at the Institute for Advanced Study in Princeton. His research focuses on Babylonian Jewish history in the Sasanian era and its neighboring religious and cultural world. His recent authored or edited volumes include *A Prince without a Kingdom: The Exilarch in the Sasanian Era*, Texts and Studies in Ancient Judaism 150 (Tübingen: Mohr Siebeck, 2012); *Persian Martyr Acts under King Yazdgird I*, Persian Martyr Acts in Syriac: Text and Translation 5 (Piscataway, NJ: Gorgias Press, 2016); *Jews, Christians, and Zoroastrians: Religious Dynamics in a Sasanian Context*, Judaism in Context 17 (Piscataway, NJ: Gorgias Press, 2014); and *Between Babylonia and the Land of Israel: Studies in Honor of Isaiah M. Gafni*, edited together with Meir Ben Shahar and Aharon Oppenheimer (Jerusalem: Zalman Shazar, 2016).

Yishai Kiel is a research fellow at the Hebrew University of Jerusalem Law School. His scholarship focuses on the legal, historical, and religious dimensions of the intersection of Judaism with Christian, Islamic, Zoroastrian, and Manichaean traditions in the Sasanian and early Islamicate Near East. He also works on the Iranian and Persian context of the Hebrew Bible. Kiel is the author of *Sexuality in the Babylonian Talmud: Christian and Sasanian Contexts in Late Antiquity* (Cambridge: Cambridge University Press, 2016), and his articles have appeared in journals such as *The Journal of Religion, Harvard Theological Review, Journal of Biblical Literature, Vetus Testamentum, Journal of the American Oriental Society, Journal of Jewish Studies, AJS Review, Jewish Studies Quarterly, Journal for the Study of Judaism*, and *The Jewish Law Annual*.

Reuven Kiperwasser is an Alexander von Humboldt Fellow at the Institute of Judaic Studies, Free University of Berlin. He specializes in rabbinic literature, and his research interests include the interactions between Iranian mythology, Syriac-Christian storytelling, rabbinic narrative, and transcultural relationships between cultures of late antiquity. His critical edition of Kohelet Rabbah (7–12) is in press, and he is currently completing a volume that deals with the Babylonian immigrants in the Land of Israel and the acceptance of the Other in rabbinic culture. Among his recent articles are the following: "A Bizarre Invitation to the King's Banquet: The Metamorphosis of a Parable Tradition and the Transformation of an Eschatological Idea," *Prooftexts* 33 (2014): 147–81; "The Bitter Fate of Elihoref and Ahiya: The Metamorphosis of a Story from The Land of Israel That Went to Babylonia" [Hebrew], *Jerusalem Studies in Jewish Literature* 28 (2016): 3–26; and "Wives of Commoners and the Masculinity of the Rabbis: Jokes, Serious Matters and Migrating Traditions," *Journal for the Study of Judaism* 48 (2017): 1–28.

Jason Mokhtarian is an Assistant Professor of Religious Studies and Jewish Studies at Indiana University. His research focuses on the Jews of ancient Persia with a particular focus on the Babylonian Talmud in its Persian context. He is the author of *Rabbis, Sorcerers, Kings, and Priests: The Culture of the Talmud in Ancient Iran*, S. Mark Taper Foundation Imprint in Jewish Studies (Oakland: University of California Press, 2015), as well as articles and essays in the study of late antique religions.

Yakir Paz is a researcher at the Martin Buber Society of Fellows in the Humanities and Social Sciences at the Hebrew University of Jerusalem. His research focuses on Homeric and biblical commentaries, the impact of Roman law on rabbinic halakah; Jews and Christians in the Sasanian Empire; and religious polemics in late antiquity.

Sara Ronis is an Assistant Professor of Theology at St. Mary's University, Texas. Her research focuses on the Talmud in its Sasanian context, constructions of identity and authority in ancient Judaism, and demons, magic, and non-normative rituals. Her recently published articles include "Space, Place, and the Race for Power: Rabbis, Demons, and the Construction of Babylonia," *Harvard Theological Review* (2018): 588–603. She is currently completing a book project on demonic discourse in the Babylonian Talmud in its legal, narrative, and sociocultural contexts.

Jeffrey L. Rubenstein is the Skirball Professor of Talmud and Rabbinic Literature in the Department of Hebrew and Judaic Studies of New York University. His research focuses on the festival of Sukkot, talmudic stories, the development of Jewish law, and topics in Jewish liturgy and ethics. His books include *The History of Sukkot in the Second Temple and Rabbinic Periods*, Brown Judaic Studies 302 (Atlanta: Scholars Press, 1995); *Talmudic Stories: Narrative Art, Composition, and Culture* (Baltimore: Johns Hopkins University Press, 1999); *Rabbinic Stories*, Classics of Western Spirituality (New York: Paulist Press, 2002); *The Culture of the Babylonian Talmud* (Baltimore: Johns Hopkins University Press, 2003); and *Stories of the Babylonian Talmud* (Baltimore: Johns Hopkins University Press, 2010).

Shai Secunda is Jacob Neusner Professor of the History and Theology of Judaism at Bard College, where he teaches in the Religion Department. His research focuses on the Babylonian Talmud and its Iranian context. He is the author of *The Iranian Talmud: Reading the Bavli in Its Sasanian Context*, Divinations: Rereading Late Ancient Religion (Philadelphia: University of Pennsylvania Press, 2014), and co-editor of two volumes: *Shoshannat Yaakov: Jewish and Iranian Studies in Honor of Yaakov Elman*, Brill Reference Library of Judaism 35 (Leiden: Brill, 2012); and *Encounters by the Rivers of Babylon: Scholarly Conversations between Jews, Iranians, and Babylonians in Antiquity*, Texts and Studies of Ancient Judaism 160 (Tübingen: Mohr Siebeck, 2015).

Ancient Source Index

General Index